Diversity and Inclusion in Sport Organizations

Diversity and Inclusion in Sport Organizations: A Multilevel Perspective is a comprehensive introduction to the ways in which people differ—including race, gender, age, mental and physical ability, appearance, religion, sexual orientation, and social class—and the importance of these differences for sport organizations.

It offers strategies for managing diversity in work and sport environments and provides an overview of diversity training that can be implemented in the workplace. Grounded in research and theory and outlining the best practice, this fully updated and revised edition includes more international examples and expanded coverage of topics, such as critical disability studies, women of color, and lesbian, gay, bisexual, transgender, queer, intersex issues, as well as useful teaching and learning features in every chapter and additional online resources.

This is an important reading for students working in the fields of sport business, sport management, sport development or sport coaching, HR management in sport, sport in society, sport participation, ethical leadership in sport, or introductory sport management courses.

George B. Cunningham is Professor of Sport Management and Senior Assistant Provost for Graduate and Professional Studies at Texas A&M University, College Station, Texas. He is Director of the Center for Sport Management Research and Education, as well as the Laboratory for Diversity in Sport, and holds a faculty affiliate appointment in the Women's and Gender Studies Program. He has served as editor-in-chief of *Journal of Intercollegiate Sport* and of *Sport Management Review*, and is a member of the National Academy of Kinesiology.

D1451964

DIVERSITY AND INCLUSION IN sport ORGANIZATIONS

A MULTILEVEL PERSPECTIVE

FOURTH EDITION

George B. Cunningham

Routledge
Taylor & Francis Group

NEW YORK AND LONDON

Fourth edition published 2019
by Routledge
52 Vanderbilt Avenue, New York, NY 10017

and by Routledge
2 Park Square, Milton Park, Abingdon, Oxon, OX14 4RN

Routledge is an imprint of the Taylor & Francis Group, an informa business

First edition published by Holcomb Hathaway 2007
Third edition published by Routledge 2015

British Library Cataloguing-in-Publication Data
A catalogue record for this book is available from the British Library

Library of Congress Cataloging-in-Publication Data
Names: Cunningham, George B., author.
Title: Diversity and inclusion in sport organizations:
a multilevel perspective / George B. Cunningham.
Description: Fourth edition. |
Abingdon, Oxon; New York, NY: Routledge, 2019. |
Includes bibliographical references and index.
Identifiers: LCCN 2018046790 | ISBN 9781138586949 (hbk) |
ISBN 9781138586956 (pbk) | ISBN 9780429504310 (ebk)
Subjects: LCSH: Sports administration—United States. |
Discrimination in sports—United States. |
Diversity in the workplace—United States.
Classification: LCC GV713 .C86 2019 | DDC 796.06/9—dc23
LC record available at https://lccn.loc.gov/2018046790

ISBN: 978-1-138-58694-9 (hbk)
ISBN: 978-1-138-58695-6 (pbk)
ISBN: 978-0-429-50431-0 (ebk)

Typeset in Sabon
by codeMantra

Visit the eResources: www.routledge.com/9781138586956

For Melissa, Harper, and Maggie

Contents

List of Exhibits

List of Boxes

Preface

A Diversity and inclusion are, and will continue to be, among the most important issues managers encounter, particularly in the sport industry. Countries around the world are growing more diverse, in terms of both demographics and attitudes, and today's sport organizations reflect this diversity. Organizational strategies to promote, create, and sustain inclusiveness can influence employees' attitudes, group processes, and the organization's overall effectiveness. Following diversity-related legal requirements, or failing to do so, can also have meaningful implications for an organization. Consequently, it is of paramount importance that managers understand the effects of diversity and inclusion and the strategies to manage differences effectively. The purpose of the fourth edition of *Diversity and Inclusion in Sport Organizations: A Multilevel Perspective* is to provide students with such an understanding.

As the book's new title suggests, in the fourth edition, I draw from multilevel theory to overview diversity and inclusion in sport. Doing so allows for a comprehensive treatment of the topic.

I have divided the book into three parts. Part I provides an overview of diversity and inclusion. Chapter 1 defines diversity and inclusion, and then analyzes why diversity warrants attention by students and managers. Chapter 2 deals with the theoretical tenets of diversity and inclusion, with a focus on the three primary theoretical approaches—managerial, sociological, and social psychological—as well as the practical implications associated with each. Chapter 3 addresses stereotypes, prejudice, and discrimination; the theoretical tenets undergirding those constructs; and their associated outcomes.

Part II is devoted to the various forms of diversity and inclusion. I first develop a multilevel model to guide the discussion of diversity (Chapter 4). Using this model as a foundation, I then focus on race (Chapter 5); gender (Chapter 6); age (Chapter 7); disability (Chapter 8); weight (Chapter 9); religion (Chapter 10); sexual orientation, gender identity, and gender expression (Chapter 11); and social class (Chapter 12).

Part III focuses on creating and sustaining inclusive sport organizations. In Chapter 13, I draw from multilevel theory to highlight several strategies that can be used to effectively manage diverse work environments and promote inclusion. Chapter 14 is devoted to diversity training. Here, I underscore the importance of this training and provide the steps to design, implement, and evaluate effective diversity training programs. Finally, I discuss change and inclusion through sport (Chapter 15). In this chapter, I offer an overview of sport for development and peace programs, potential outcomes, and guiding principles for those who are using sport to promote social change.

The book is intended for upper-level undergraduate and graduate students. Teachers, coaches, managers, marketers, and administrators also will benefit from the text's information. Because the sport industry is composed of many segments, examples are drawn from a bevy of sources—professional sports, university athletics, fitness organizations, physical education, recreation and leisure settings, and nonprofit entities.

THE BOOK'S SPECIAL FEATURES

- **Diversity Challenge.** Each chapter opens with a diversity challenge, a real-life scenario introducing the chapter's topic. It is followed by a series of questions to prompt readers to think about the issues raised.
- **Diversity in the Field.** These sidebars present real-life examples to help readers comprehend chapter concepts.
- **Professional Perspectives.** These recurring boxes reflect interviews of leading professionals with responsibilities in sport (e.g., a sport industry employment recruiter, professors, an athletic director, a high school coach) and provide students with practical, informed opinions on the chapter content.
- **Alternative Perspectives.** Because many topics and issues stimulate a wide range of opinions, I have included Alternative Perspectives boxes to provide readers with additional sides of a discussion.
- **Questions for Discussion, Learning Activities, Reading Resources, and Web Resources.** Each chapter concludes with discussion questions, student activities, and sources of additional information. Many of the Learning Activities are designed for students to explore in small groups. The annotated Web Resources augment chapter material by providing links to online resources such as professional associations, electronic methods of testing prejudicial attitudes, resources for diversity training, and others. Finally, the annotated Reading Resources recommend additional informative books related to the chapter's discussions.
- **Ancillaries.** An Instructor's Manual, a PowerPoint presentation, and a test bank are available for instructors who adopt this text for course use.

I am excited about diversity and inclusion and what they mean for sport, sport organizations, and people associated with the sport industry. I hope I have reflected my enthusiasm in the text and that it will be passed on to instructors and readers. I welcome your comments and look forward to any and all feedback.

Acknowledgments

I would like to thank the wonderful colleagues and students with whom I have worked. In particular, I enjoyed my collaborative efforts with Michael Sagas, Janet Fink, and John Singer. A large debt of gratitude is owed to all of my students, past and present, especially Melanie L. Sartore-Baldwin, Jacqueline McDowell, Claudia Benavides-Espinoza, Woojun Lee, Andrew Pickett, and E. Nicole Melton. They were a joy to work with, and they also reviewed the book and provided helpful and constructive feedback along the way. I am grateful to my doctoral advisor, Packianathan Chelladurai, for his guidance in my professional preparation and for encouraging me to write this book.

I offer my sincere thanks to the reviewers of this and past editions, at various stages of completion. I also thank Simon Whitmore, Rebecca Connor, and the staff at Routledge. I enjoyed working with them and am indebted to them for the opportunity they have provided. Finally, I am also thankful for my family: my wife, Melissa, and our two girls, Harper and Maggie. They are my everything.

PART I

FOUNDATIONS OF DIVERSITY AND INCLUSION

Overview of Diversity and Inclusion

LEARNING OBJECTIVES

After studying this chapter, you should be able to:

- Define diversity and inclusion.
- List and explain the various forms of diversity.
- Summarize the factors that have contributed to an increased interest in diversity and inclusion.

DIVERSITY CHALLENGE

Sport offers people many potential benefits. According to Sport England, people who regularly engage in sport and physical activity enjoy improved physical and psychological well-being, social connections, and individual development. Sport can also positively influence communities, including their overall development and economic growth.

Despite the advantages, researchers have found that many people are excluded from regular sport participation, and others do not have the chance to be active throughout their lives. In other cases, people who differ from the typical majority member—including women, the poor, racial minorities, people with disabilities, and sexual minorities, among others—have access to sport but are frequently treated poorly. Sport participants are not alone, as there are similar trends among volunteers, coaches, and administrators.

As a result, entities like Sport England have developed plans to make sport more diverse and inclusive. The organization recognizes that such transformations require systemic change, noting, "… it's not just about participants and volunteers on the ground. Every part of the sporting landscape needs to change. And that includes us, our partners, and those we invest in." Sport England embedded diversity principles in the 2017–2021 strategic plan, as the organization seeks to increase the diversity of its leadership and ensure their sport volunteers represent the demographic character of the country.

Source: https://www.sportengland.org/media/10629/sport-england-towards-an-active-nation.pdf.

CHALLENGE REFLECTION

 uppose the Sport England organizers asked you to contribute to the initiative. How would you respond to the following questions?

1. What are the major diversity issues facing sport participants today?
2. Beyond what was briefly presented here, how do people's characteristics, such as age, race, income, physical and mental ability, and gender, affect their opportunities to be physically active?
3. What are the steps you would take to make sport inclusive for all people, irrespective of their individual differences?

INTRODUCTION

oday, diversity and inclusion are the critical components of sport and physical activity. As illustrated in the Diversity Challenge, differences do make a difference. People's demographics, psychological characteristics, values, and attitudes can all influence the opportunities they have to participate in sport and physical activity, as well as their experiences while doing so. Substantial evidence also suggests that diversity and inclusion can influence groups, organizations, and communities. Potential outcomes include creativity, breadth of decision-making, community capacity, and overall effectiveness. Furthermore, a confluence of trends and events—including changes in societal and workplace demographics, different attitudes toward work and the nature of work itself, legal and social pressures for change, and the potential for diversity and inclusion to influence subsequent processes and outcomes—has brought these points to the forefront for managers. Effective sport management, marketing, and governance means working with stakeholders from a variety of backgrounds, ensuring sport is a space that is inclusive, and understanding the various laws and social pressures pertaining to the sport environment. The primacy of diversity and inclusion means that coaches, volunteers, and managers understand the effects of diversity and inclusion in the workplace and on the field, as well as the underlying dynamics. Such an understanding will go a long way toward ensuring teams and sport organizations are spaces where all people have access and can thrive, irrespective of their individual differences.

The purpose of this chapter is to provide the foundational components of diversity and inclusion in sport. In the first section, I draw from various scholars' work to develop definitions of diversity and inclusion, and then follow this with a discussion of the various diversity forms. The third section includes a summary of the six factors contributing to the interest in and the importance of diversity and inclusion. In the final section, I provide an overview of the remainder of the text.

DEFINITIONS

 n this section, I offer the definitions of diversity and inclusion used throughout the text.

Diversity

A number of authors have developed their own definitions of diversity. Consider the following examples:

Diversity is a "team-level construct that represents differences among members of an interdependent work group with respect to specific social or cultural attributes" (Joshi & Neely, 2018, p. 362).

Diversity represents "differences between employees on any attribute that may evoke the perception that a coworker is different from oneself" (Guillaume et al., 2014, p. 785).

Diversity refers to "the composition of work units (work group, organization, occupation, establishment, or firm) in terms of the cultural or demographic characteristics that are salient and symbolically meaningful in the relationships among group members" (DiTomaso, Post, & Parks-Yancy, 2007, p. 474).

Diversity reflects "the distributional differences among members of a team with respect to a common attribute" (Bell, Villado, Lukasik, Belau, & Briggs, 2011, p. 711).

Diversity refers to "the variations of traits, both visible and not, of groups of two or more people" (Lambert & Bell, 2013, p. 13).

We can draw several key points from these definitions. First, diversity is a construct that is greater than a single individual. It is concerned with dyads and groups. The former refers to two-person units, such as teammates, a supervisor and an employee, or a customer and a staff member. The latter refers to any collection of three or more people. People must be able to compare their characteristics to those of relevant others. Without such evaluations, people do not know if they are similar to or different from others.

Second, diversity is concerned with differences among people. How, for example, do members of a grounds crew of a professional baseball team differ from one another, and how are they similar? Suppose, for example, that the grounds crew consists of five women. The composition of the group would be unique when it comes to other grounds crews around the league; however, when focusing on the specific group in question, it would be homogenous along the lines of gender. On the other hand, the group would be diverse if it included three women and two men. Thus, it is the characteristics within the dyad or group under consideration that make it diverse or not.

Third, diversity is concerned with both objective and subjective differences. Objective differences are those that we can see or that we can quantify. Examples include demographic or attitudinal characteristics, such as age or political attitudes, respectively. In both cases, we can objectively note group member characteristics, as well as the diversity of the group. Subjective differences refer to people's perceptions of being different. In many ways, subjective evaluations are as relevant as objective differences. Two studies that I have conducted—one with physical activity participants (Cunningham, 2006) and the other with coaches (Cunningham, 2007)—illustrate this point. I observed that people's perceptions of being different from others, more so than their objective differences, reliably predicted subsequent outcomes, including their satisfaction and intentions to leave the unit. In addition, even though we consider them separately, subjective and objective diversities are frequently related to one another. An employee who is the only Latina in a group is likely to perceive her dissimilarity from others based on her race. There are other factors, however, that can influence this relationship, such as how important that particular diversity dimension is to the perceiver, organizational culture, and the manner in which that diversity form affects individual experiences or group functioning, just to name a few.

Finally, diversity is concerned with socially relevant differences. DiTomaso et al. (2007) wrote, "Diversity matters because individuals give social significance to the categories or groups they associate with various people. And they do so because diversity has a context: Meaningful group differences exist because they have structural or institutional bases" (p. 475; see also Apfelbaum, Stephens, & Reagans, 2016). Bunderson and Van der Vegt (2018) arrived at similar conclusions in their review of diversity and inequality in top management teams. They suggested that "to fully understand how diversity and inequality might affect team decisions and outcomes, therefore, we need to consider both dimensions in our theories, models, and measures" (p. 65). From this perspective, some diversity forms have greater social meaning than do others—differences that emanate from cultural arrangements, history, politics, and institutional forces. Socially meaningful differences have the capacity to influence opportunities, work experiences, and group functioning. To illustrate, consider a group of event volunteers that differ in two ways: their religious traditions and the flavor of ice cream they prefer. As we will discuss in Chapter 10, religion can be a source of prejudice and discrimination (Chuah, Gächter, Hoffmann, & Tan, 2016), and the bias is present in teams, among fans, and within organizations. On the other hand, one's favorite ice cream is unlikely to affect her opportunities or experiences at work or the way in which she interacts with the other volunteers. (For the record, mint chocolate chip is the best flavor.) As this example illustrates, it is important to consider diversity forms that can influence subsequent outcomes. As Konrad (2003) notes, the other option—considering all differences as a source of diversity—is so broad that it renders the construct as inconsequential.

Drawing from this discussion, we can define diversity as *the presence of socially meaningful differences among members of a dyad or group*. This definition highlights several important elements: (a) the presence of objective and subjective differences, (b) that are socially relevant, and (c) for members of a particular social unit.

Inclusion

We next examine previous definitions of inclusion:

Inclusion is "the degree to which employees feel part of essential organizational processes including influence over decision-making process, involvement in critical work groups, and access to information and resources" (Downey, Werff, Thomas, & Plaut, 2015, p. 37).

Inclusion is "the degree to which an employee perceives that he or she is an esteemed member of the work group through experiencing treatment that satisfies his or her needs for belongingness and uniqueness" (Shore et al., 2011, p. 1265).

> Inclusion "process in which individuals, groups, organizations, and societies—rather than seeking to foster homogeneity—view and approach diversity as a valued resource. In an inclusive system, we value ourselves and others because of and not despite our differences"
>
> (Ferdman, 2017, p. 238)

An organization is inclusive "to the extent that its policies, practices, and leadership demonstrate that all individuals in the organization have valuable experiences, skills, and ideas to contribute and can integrate their uniqueness without pressure to assimilate in order to be accepted" (Nishii & Rich, 2014, p. 331).

We can take several key points from the definitions. First, individuals experience inclusion but the construct takes on a shared property. Players, for example, will evaluate their own experiences on the team to form beliefs about how inclusive that entity is. The collective, shared evaluations among the team members then reflect the overall inclusiveness of that team.

The second and third points relate to one another. Inclusion satisfies two needs that people have: (a) to be able to express identities important to them (b) while still feeling a sense of connectedness and belonging to the larger group (Brewer, 1991). Let's consider the first point. Everybody has identities that are important to her or him. On my Twitter bio, for example, I list that I am a "partner, dad, diversity scholar, yogi, and Episcopalian." These are all characteristics that are important to me and in some ways are what make unique from others. The identities are salient in many aspects of my life, including my personal life and work life. People do not necessarily check these identities at the door when they arrive at work, practice, or the gym. Thus, inclusive organizations allow people to express identities—that is, what makes them unique—at work and recognize their uniqueness. At the same time, inclusive organizations create cultures where these unique individuals, all with their different identities, feel part of a larger entity. They have a sense of connectedness and belonging. Psychologists have long recognized the need to feel loved, connected, accepted, and part of something larger. Teams spend considerable time to create this sense of connection among their fans, just as universities do for their incoming students.

Inclusive organizations recognize and embrace these dual, potentially countervailing tensions. In these organizations, inclusion means respecting, celebrating, and embracing the various ways in which people differ; establishing structures and processes that allow people to express their multiple identities at work; and, because differences are valued and seen as a source of learning and enrichment, engaging people such that they have a sense of belonging and connection with the workplace. Thus, from the organizational level of analysis, inclusion represents *the degree to which employees are free to express their individuated self and have a sense of workplace connectedness and belonging* (Box 1.1).

Box 1.1 Diversity in the Field: #BeInclusive EU Sport Awards

Governments have increasingly seen sport as a space for creating social change. To do so, sport managers must ensure that sport is inclusive and thereby able to attract people from all walks of life. The European Commission, in seeking to recognize those sport organizations excelling in this area, created the #BeInclusive EU Sport Awards. The awards "recognize organizations using the power of sport to increase social inclusion for disadvantaged groups."

In 2017, three entities won the award: Mitternachts Sport in Germany, De Rode Antraciet in Belgium, and Asociacion danza integrada—MeetShareDance in Spain. Mitternachts Sport focuses on moving disadvantaged youth from the streets to the gym. Focusing on people aged 8–25, the organization opens gyms in social hotbeds around Berlin and Wuppertal. They have done so for 450 weekends, reaching more than 100,000 young people. The second organization, De Rode Antraciet, focuses on prisoners, getting them to be physically active, working together, and focusing on life after prison. The end result is increased mindfulness and peace, at least while engaging in the activities. Finally, MeetShareDance focuses on people with disabilities and increases their physical activity through dance. They do so by connecting people with disabilities with able-bodied partners, and they show that hard work, passion, and being active can help alter stereotypes about people with disabilities.

Source: https://ec.europa.eu/sport/be-inclusive#winners

There are many reasons for sport managers to create and sustain diverse and inclusive workplaces. Business leaders increasingly see the value of inclusion and point to enhanced performance as the impetus for their efforts (Roberson, 2006). For example, Caroline Turner, an author, group facilitator, and consultant, noted that "diversity and inclusion generally are good for business," and they have been "linked with productivity, profitability, employee commitment and retention" (Turner, 2017). Though there are hosts of benefits associated with diverse and inclusive sport organizations, I suggest the primary rationale is a moral one: sport organizations have a moral imperative to develop and maintain inclusive environments. Sport is concerned with people, whether they are volunteers, clients, athletes, coaches, or administrators. As such, it is incumbent upon the sport manager to ensure that all people can be their authentic selves while still feeling a sense of connectedness and belonging. When this happens, people will have a chance to be physically active, to pursue excellence in their sport, and to engage fully in their work. The performance gains that accompany this inclusive environment are the added benefit.

FORMS OF DIVERSITY

Discussions related to diversity frequently focus on gender, race, and age, but, of course, there are a multitude of ways in which people differ. Indeed, as diversity science has matured, so too has the breadth of examination and understanding of differences. Researchers now examine a number of characteristics beyond age, race, and gender, including culture, language, physical and mental ability, education, and attitudes. Following this line of thought, one approach to the study of diversity would be to list all socially meaningful ways in which people differ (e.g., see Box 1.2). Another, more parsimonious, tactic is to consider ways in which differences might relate to one another and create a corresponding typology. Drawing from previous researchers (Harrison, Price, & Bell, 1998), I offer one such framework (see Exhibit 1.1).

Box 1.2 Alternative Perspectives: Comprehensive Listing of Diversity Forms

In this chapter, I offer a classification scheme for parsimoniously classifying the various ways in which people differ. However, sport organizations will eschew this approach and instead list specific diversity dimensions on which they focus. As examples:

Adidas notes "We believe in equal opportunity for all, regardless of race, age, abilities, gender, gender identity, sexual orientation, ethnicity or religion"

Conference USA, an organizing body for various intercollegiate athletics teams in the US, holds that, "In accordance with the generally accepted policies of affirmative action and equal opportunity, Conference USA and its member institutions will not discriminate on the basis of sex, race, religion, sexual orientation, gender identity, age, disability, ancestry or national origin in the conduct of their intercollegiate athletics programs and will promote an inclusive environment for all participants and fans."

In many respects, listing the various diversity dimensions has value, as the sport organization specifically articulates those forms of difference that are meaningful within that context. A potential problem occurs, however, when leaders do not include a specific diversity dimension in the statement. For example, social class is not included in either of the aforementioned statements. Thus, people who are poor might feel that these organizations do not pay particular attention to issues regarding class, income inequality, and the like.

Source: https://careers.adidas-group.com/life-here/diversity?locale=en

exhibit **1.1** Forms of Diversity

Surface-level diversity: differences among individuals based on readily observable characteristics such as age, gender, race, and physical ability.

Deep-level diversity: differences among individuals based on psychological characteristics.

- **Information diversity**: those differences based on knowledge and information, oftentimes resulting from variations in education, functional background, training, and organizational tenure.
- **Value diversity**: those differences in values, attitudes, and beliefs.

Sources: Adapted from Harrison et al. (1998) and Jehn, Northcraft, and Neale (1999).

Surface-Level Diversity

Surface-level diversity refers to those differences that people can readily observe. Examples include race, age, gender, appearance, and physical ability, among others. Researchers have shown that people can recognize and differentiate others almost instantaneously (Miller, Maner, & Becker, 2010), and they use surface-level characteristics to make these distinctions (Rhodes & Gelman, 2009). As we will discuss in Chapter 2, the process can result in biases and negative evaluations of the target. They can also influence how members of underrepresented groups react. An exerciser who is elderly, for example, knows quickly how similar she is to others in the exercise class, and, as a result, forms estimates as to how she might interact with others in the class.

Deep-Level Diversity

Deep-level diversity represents those individual characteristics that people cannot see. Examples include religious tradition, sexual orientation, gender identity, gender expression, social class, values, and beliefs, among others. These attributes only become apparent if the individual or someone else shares the identifying information, or if one learns the information because of social interactions. Over the life of a group, the salience of the different diversity dimensions is likely to vary (Harrison et al., 1998; Harrison, Price, Gavin, & Florey, 2002). To illustrate, consider the exerciser from our previous example. She might initially determine that she is older than her fellow exercisers and, thus, believe she is different. After attending several classes, however, she may come to find that she shares deep-level characteristics with others, such as her religious beliefs and political affiliation. As the example shows, the same two people can be both different and similar to one another, depending on the diversity characteristic.

We can further differentiate between different types of deep-level diversity, including information diversity and value diversity (Huettermann, DeWit, Diewald, Boerner, & Jehn, 2015). Information diversity refers to the knowledge, skills, and expertise that members bring to the group. Examples might include their functional area of expertise, education, tenure in the organization or occupation, and amount of training they have received. Such diversity is common in a number of groups, including executive boards. For example, at the national level of the Y in the US (an organization that focuses on youth development, healthy living, and social responsibility), board members included a president of a university, the development officer of another university, three presidents of local Y's, the president of a diversity-focused nonprofit sector, the chair of an international accounting firm, and the president of a large newspaper. The individuals each brought unique experiences, expertise, and perspectives to the board, thereby allowing the board conceivably to have a greater breadth of decision-making and strong connections with various industries.

Value diversity represents the second level of deep-level diversity. A group has high value diversity when members vary in their attitudes, beliefs, preferences, and values. Value diversity is frequently associated with strongly held beliefs, such as people's political attitudes or the religious traditions they follow. Because they are salient to the individuals, disagreements along these diversity dimensions can be a source of strife. Recognizing this potential, some sport organizations have taken steps to be more inclusive. The Premier League, for example, used to award the Man of the Match with a bottle of champagne; however, as alcohol is prohibited in many religious traditions, the recipient now receives a small trophy (Shergold, 2016).

Relationship between Surface- and Deep-Level Diversity

Though I have presented them separately, surface- and deep-level differences frequently relate to one another. For example, when group members vary in age, they also frequently differ in their life experiences, ideologies, and perspectives. In this case, the surface-level diversity might correspond with deep-level differences. For example, in a study of job applicants, Ng, Kulik, and Bordia (2016) found that perceived organizational surface-level differences were strongly and positively linked with perceptions that the organization also had deep-level diversity. I have observed similar associations in the sport context. In one study of collegiate athletic coaches (Cunningham, 2007), I found that perceived age diversity on the coaching staff was positively correlated with perceived deep-level diversity, which, in turn, was associated with both coworker satisfaction and organizational turnover intentions. Similarly, in a study of group exercisers, I found that people are aware of their dissimilarity from others (Cunningham, 2006). Actual age, race, and gender dissimilarity strongly corresponded with perceptions of such differences. As perceived surface-level dissimilarity increased, so too did exercisers' beliefs that they differed from others along deep-level characteristics.

Surface- and deep-level diversity forms might also work together to form *fault lines* (Thatcher, 2013). Fault lines represent dividing lines that split groups into two or more subgroups based on a combination of various diversity dimensions. A minor league baseball team's grounds crew would have a fault line, for example, if half of the crew consisted of three women who were young and had a college education, whereas the other three persons were older men with only a high school education. In this case, we are considering two surface-level attributes—gender and age—and one deep-level attribute—educational attainment. The dimensions cross such that, within this particular group, individuals who possess one characteristic (i.e., being a woman) have the other distinguishing characteristics, too (i.e., being young and college educated). As I mentioned previously, people use various cues to classify themselves and others into social groups, and this categorization process can result in bias and stereotyping. The theory of fault lines suggests that this process is made easier when multiple categories align, as age, gender, and education did in the example. When this occurs, people will engage in behaviors that promulgate similarities in their own subgroup and distinguish it from other subgroups. As a result, effective group functioning becomes difficult (Kerwin, Walker, & Bopp, 2017).

UNDERSTANDING THE EMPHASIS ON DIVERSITY AND INCLUSION

In this section, we consider the various reasons for an emphasis on diversity and inclusion. As seen in Exhibit 1.2, I offer six primary reasons: changing demographics, changes in organizational structures, legal mandates, social pressures, the negative effects of exclusion, and the benefits of diversity and inclusion.

exhibit   **1.2**   Factors Contributing to the Interest in and Importance of Diversity and Inclusion

- **Changing demographics:** shifts in population demographics—including those based on age, race, gender, disability status, social class, gender identity and expression, and religious tradition—that correspond with changes in the workforce.
- **Changes in the nature of work:** Increases in the number of organizations that structure work around teams, the impact of globalization, and the frequency of mergers and acquisitions.
- **Legal mandates:** Federal and state laws that require equal employment opportunities for all persons, irrespective of demographic characteristics or background.
- **Social pressures:** The notion that organizations have a moral and ethical obligation to have a diverse, inclusive workplace.
- **Negative effects of exclusion:** Exclusive organizational practices and cultures can lead to negative outcomes such as low satisfaction, conflict, and poor team performance.
- **Value of diversity and inclusion:** Diversity and inclusion are associated with process and performance gains for teams and organizations.

Changing Demographics

One of the primary reasons for an emphasis on diversity and inclusion comes to simple numbers: countries around the world are witnessing dramatic shifts in their population demographics. When such changes occur, they correspond with increased diversity in the workplace.

In subsequent chapters, I offer a detailed overview of how various demographic and personal characteristics influence people's opportunities and experiences. For the purposes of this chapter, I draw from the Pew Research Center (Cilluffo & Cohn, 2017), which is a nonpartisan organization that collects and issues reports about topics influencing the world. The organization highlighted a number of demographic trends that would influence the world in 2017 and beyond. Cilluffo and Cohn (2017), the authors of the report, note "demographic forces are driving population change and reshaping the lives of people around the world."

First, Baby Boomers (people born between 1946 and 1964) have long been the largest generation cohort in the US. By 2019, however, demographers expect Millennials (people born between 1981 and 1996) to assume this position (Cilluffo & Cohn, 2017). The shift is important for a host of reasons, including that, relative to previous generations, Millennials are more likely to live with their parents, less geographically mobile, and less likely to be married. Second, and related to the first point, people's home lives are changing. The presence of multigenerational households has risen over the past several decades, and people are now more likely to cohabitate with a romantic partner than in previous decades (Cilluffo & Cohn, 2017).

Third, the proportion of women in the US workforce increased from 29.6 percent in 1950 to 46.8 percent in 2015 (Cilluffo & Cohn, 2017). In the European Union, the figure is 46.5 percent (see Exhibit 1.3 for an illustration of

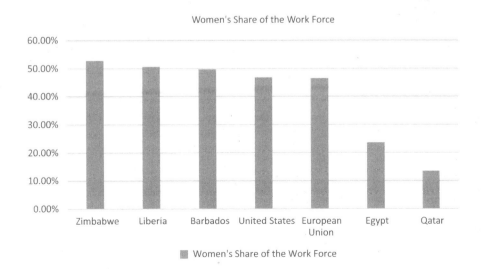

Women's Share of the Workforce around the World | *exhibit* **1.3**

Women's Share of the Work Force

Source: Letterolf (2017).

how women's share of the workforce differs around the world). Despite the increases, the US Bureau of Labor Statistics estimates that the proportion of women comprising the US workforce will rise to 47.1 percent in 2025 and then decrease. Further, women in the US continue to earn less than men do—just 83 cents to the dollar—and the disparities are observed across demographics. Finally, women are underrepresented in leadership positions, including those in government, private industry, and sport.

Fourth, as the Baby Boomers have aged out of full-time employment, the US workforce has largely grown due to the immigrant population. The Pew Research Center (Cilluffo & Cohn, 2017) estimates that, without new immigrants or US-born children of immigrants, the labor force in the US would drop between 2015 and 2035. Thus, immigrants represent a key driver of the US economy. Given that many countries around the world are also experiencing an aging workforce, similar trends are likely to take place globally. In addition, the Pew Research Center (Cilluffo & Cohn, 2017) reports that the number of unauthorized immigrants in the US slightly dipped in 2015. Most of these individuals were working or looking for work, constituting about 5 percent of the labor force in the country.

Birth rates are also likely to influence demographic trends in the future (Cilluffo & Cohn, 2017). Births outside marriage declined for immigrant women, but they are still likely to have more overall children than their US-born counterparts. In fact, the overall increase in the number of births in the US has increased from 3.74 million to 4.00 million since 1970, and these increases are largely due to births by immigrant mothers. In addition, birth rates vary by the religious tradition one follows. Worldwide, children born to Christian mothers (223 million) outnumber those born to Muslim mothers (213 million). By 2035, however, this pattern is expected to change, largely due to the aging Christian population and the high fertility rates of Muslim women.

Social class also affects diversity and inclusion around the world. According to the Pew Research Center (Cilluffo & Cohn, 2017), between 1991 and 2010, the proportion of people living in middle-class households fell. The trend occurred around the world, including Norway (82 percent to 80 percent), Germany (78 percent to 72 percent), and the US (62 percent to 59 percent). There were exceptions to this trend, as the Netherlands (76 percent to 79 percent), France (72 percent to 74 percent), Ireland (60 percent to 69 percent), and the UK (61 percent to 67 percent) all saw an increase in the proportion of people living in middle-class households.

Finally, refugee status is likely to affect countries and sport organizations (Cilluffo & Cohn, 2017). European countries received 1.2 million first time asylum seekers in 2016. The figure is the second highest on record, trailing only the 1.3 refugees from 2015. Germany received 45 percent of the applicants—the most among European countries. Europe was not alone, however, as the US admitted nearly 85,000 refugees in 2016. California, Texas, and New York were the states to receive the most. Researchers have shown that refugees understandably face a number of physical and psychological health problems (Garkisch, Heidingsfelder, & Beckmann, 2017), and sport and physical activity can serve as a mechanism for reducing these concerns (Woodhouse & Conricode, in press).

Changes in the Nature of Work

Changes in the nature have also influenced an increased emphasis on diversity and inclusion. Three changes particularly relevant to the sport industry include the focus on service provision, the organization of work around teams, and increased globalization.

Service-Based Organizations

Much of the sport industry is involved with the delivery of services, and sport managers are concerned with ensuring high service quality for consumers (Funk, 2017; Yoshida, 2017). A key element of service provision is the interaction between the employee and the customer. Examples include an usher helping a fan to her seat, a personal trainer interacting with an exerciser, and so on. The personal interactions among employees and consumers mean that individual differences might influence the perceived quality of the consumer experience. For example, Sagas and I found that when fans at a tennis tournament believed they differed from the service provider, their satisfaction with the exchange decreased (Cunningham & Sagas, 2006). The more time the customer and service provider spent in their interaction, the stronger the effects. Other researchers have shown that service providers commonly face harassment from customers, including sexual harassment (Good & Cooper, 2016). Harassment and uncivil behaviors from consumers can negatively affect the employee's well-being, enhance the desire to leave the organization, and hurt performance (Han, Bonn, & Cho, 2016; Walker, van Jaarsveld, & Skarlicki, 2017).

Team-Based Work

The prevalence of team-based work can also influence diversity and inclusion in the workplace. To illustrate this point, let us compare your hypothetical experience as an employee at a minor league Hockey Club B to the experience of your friend who works at Hockey Club A. In Hockey Club A, people work in silos, completing their tasks by themselves and coming together only to discuss what they have accomplished (or, potentially, to collaborate, though the latter rarely occurs). In Hockey Club B, employees from various functional areas work in teams to complete their tasks. In this way, they can draw on expertise, perspectives, and experiences from a broad array of people, increasing decision-making capacity. Clearly, the number and nature of interactions differ in the two workplaces, as employees in the latter accomplish work together, in a reciprocal fashion. Differences among employees are also more likely to manifest in Hockey Club B. At Club B, you interact with group members on a regular basis and depend on them to accomplish your work. The differences between you and your coworkers are likely to influence your ability to accomplish your tasks. On the other hand, your friend at Club A rarely interacts with others in the workplace, and dissimilarities among coworkers are unlikely to affect the outcomes of your friend's work one way or the other. Thus, task interdependence serves to influence the relationship between group differences and work outcomes (Welbourne & Sariol, 2017).

Globalization

Finally, globalization can influence work in sport organizations and the emphasis on diversity and inclusion. Sport is truly a global phenomenon (Woratschek, Schafmeister, & Ströbel, 2018), as sport organizations routinely seek to reach consumer markets worldwide. Some professional leagues in North America will schedule games outside the US or Canada as a way to further their base. The National Football League (NFL), for example, started playing games in London in 2007. Interest grew such that, by 2017, the league played four games in London and another in Mexico City (Seifert, 2017). The NFL sees the games and expansions as unique ways to grow revenues. NFL executive Mark Waller commented, "You take a step back, we sold over 400,000 tickets for five games, and that's something to be proud of…. Five huge games in large stadiums, capacity crowds, that shows the appeal of the live game experience" (as cited in Breer, 2017).

In addition to reaching new markets, sport organizations are increasingly seeking to attract and retain talented employees and athletes, irrespective of where they were born. An analysis from the *New York Times* (Aisch, Quealy, & Smith, 2017) showed that soccer clubs are likely to be most diverse when it comes to international talent. The Premier League is tops among the professional leagues, with over 60 percent of the players coming from outside England and Wales. International players are a mainstay in men's soccer across Europe and the US. Though not as diverse as the men's side, about one of four players in the National Women's Soccer League is foreign born. Among men's professional leagues in North America, Major League Baseball has the most international players, with the largest number coming from the Dominican Republic. Adopting a global view allows sport managers to draw from a larger pool of talented athletes. Though access to talent is greater, the international diversity can impede performance when communication among the players is key—such as the back line of defenders on soccer teams (Nüesch, 2009; see also Waltemyer & Cunningham, 2009).

Legal Mandates

Legal issues, particularly personnel matters, also affect diversity and inclusion in sport organizations. Who is hired, the benefits they are offered, how they are treated on the job, and their termination are all affected by laws and regulations at local, state, and federal levels. Within the US, these matters are governed primarily by civil rights legislation passed in the 1960s and later in the 1990s.

Legal matters are culturally and time bound. Consider, for example, rights for lesbian, gay, bisexual, and transgender (LGBT) individuals. In Iran, Saudi Arabia, Yemen, Sudan, Somalia, Nigeria, and Iraq, being LGBT is outlawed and punishable by death (Carroll & Mendos, 2017). Other countries (Afghanistan, Mauritania, Pakistan, Qatar, and the UAE) have such prohibitions codified into law but do not apply for same-sex behaviors specifically. These laws offer a vast contrast from other countries, such as Bolivia, Mexico, or Sweden, among others, where there are Constitutional prohibitions against discrimination against people based on their sexual orientation (Carroll & Mendos, 2017). Religious beliefs, traditions, customs, and norms all influence the differences.

Constitutional and employment laws certainly affect sport organizations, but other laws do, as well. Title IX is one example. Passed in the US in 1972, the law holds that all people, irrespective of their sex, should be afforded equal opportunities to participate in federally funded educational activities. Given that many youth sports in the US are connected with public schools, and the schools receive governmental monies, the law has had a substantial, positive influence on opportunities for girls and women in sport (Staurowsky, Zonder, & Riemer, 2017).

Social Pressures

Social pressures represent another reason for the heightened interest in diversity and inclusion. Sport managers adopting this perspective hold that sport organizations have a moral and ethical obligation for diversity and inclusion. For example, Saul Klein, of the Gustavson School of Business at the University of Victoria, argued that organizations have a moral imperative to promote and sustain diversity and inclusion (Klein, 2017). He further suggested that "the future of our planet and our society are bleak if we sit back and do nothing." I have advanced similar sentiments, writing "all persons have an obligation to ensure sport is inclusive and socially just" (Cunningham, 2014, p. 1).

Importantly, it is not just academics who advance such arguments but practicing sport managers, too. John Singer and I interviewed campus officials, coaches, and athletes in National Collegiate Athletic Association (NCAA) athletic departments that were known for their diverse and inclusive practices (Cunningham & Singer, 2009). We asked them about their motivations, organizational processes, and the outcomes of such activities. We also analyzed internal documents, newspaper articles about the departments, and other reports. We found that in these exemplary departments, employee valuing of diversity served as the foundation. They sensed a moral obligation to treat people fairly, they believed diversity represented a key source of learning, and they worked to develop a strong culture of inclusion within the workplace.

Increasingly, consumers demand that organizations engage in a fair and responsible manner, and having a diverse and inclusive workplace is one way to signal such a commitment. But how does this happen? One way is through signaling. Some organizational characteristics are publicly available, such as the mission statement, statements of inclusion, who sits on the executive board, and the like. A quick Internet search of your favorite sport team or the club with which you are associated will demonstrate as much. People are likely to use this information to form opinions about the organization, including how committed it is to diversity or the inclusiveness of its policies. These perspectives then influence subsequent behaviors and consumer decisions (Miller & del Carmen Triana, 2009). For example, companies that are rewarded or penalized for their diversity performance (a signal) see their valuation change (the outcome; Johnston & Malina, 2008; Wang & Schwarz, 2010). Diversity and inclusion signals can also influence purchase decisions (Tuten, 2005), the decision to join a fitness club (Cunningham & Melton, 2014), and organizational attractiveness among job seekers (Lee & Cunningham, 2015). Together, the research evidence suggests that people have an expectation for sport organizations to be inclusive, rewarding them when the expectations are met and penalizing when they are not.

Box 1.3 Professional Perspectives: Consumer Expectations of Socially Responsible Sport Organizations

Ryan Rudominer is the principal and founder of R2 Strategic Consulting. He also serves as the chair of the Midwest division of the Sports Fan Coalition, an organization that engages in public policy discussions to advocate for sports fans.

Rudominer is an expert on organization-consumer interactions. He suggested that corporate social responsibility is important among consumers, especially younger ones. "By almost any measure, Millennials place a premium on corporate social responsibility," Rudominer wrote.

Beyond simply noting a commitment to engaging in ethical and responsible business practices, Millennials expect organizations to demonstrate such assurances through their actions and the ways in which they engage consumers. Rudominer notes that "Millennials want to know what companies are doing to make the world a better place." Indeed, more than 80 percent of young consumers believe companies should be actively involved in societal issues. Rudominer also notes that companies failing to engage in ethical, socially just activities do so at their own peril, as Millennials will "punish companies on social media not deemed to be fully transparent as well as those that pay lip service to [corporate social responsibility} and causes important to them."

Sources: http://www.sportsfans.org/press_release_sports_fans_coalition_names_ryan_rudominer_chairman_of_the_mid_atlantic_region; https://www.huffingtonpost.com/ryan-rudominer/corporate-social-responsi_9_b_9155670.html.

Consumers also expect sport organizations to be actively involved in other socially responsible matters. Box 1.3 offers more information on the topic.

Negative Effects of Exclusion

Another reason to focus on diversity and inclusion is the negative effects that could result from not doing so. For example, researchers have shown that nationality diversity among defenders on German soccer teams was linked with decreased performance (Brandes, Franck, & Theiler, 2009). The findings could be due to the need for close communications among these soccer players and the language differences frequently present among players from different countries (Haas & Nüesch, 2012). Or consider a study I conducted of NCAA college coaching staff members (Cunningham, 2009). I found that as perceived surface-level diversity increased, value congruence on the staffs decreased. I also found that value congruence was linked with life satisfaction among the coaching staff members.

Some might take these research findings to suggest that diversity can result in negative outcomes. A more accurate assessment, however, is that the aforementioned research findings are likely a reflection of poor team or workplace cultures. Sport organizations with poor workplace environments are likely to link differences with deficits, and people different from the majority are unlikely to have the sense of belonging that is critical among inclusive units. On the other hand, in inclusive workplaces, people's differences are appreciated, valued, and seen as a source of learning. In such organizations, differences represent a source of competitive advantage (Roberson, 2006). Thus, it is the culture of the work environment, not the differences themselves, that is important in influencing subsequent outcomes. As Fredette, Bradshaw, and Krause (2016) noted after their multistage study, "the impact of increasing diversity on board performance and viability is largely contingent on the board's commitment to diversity" (p. 455).

Values of Diversity and Inclusion

The final reason for an increased interest in diversity and inclusion rests in the possibility for enhanced team or organizational performance. Sport managers, marketers, and coaches are always keen on improving the effectiveness of their units. If they learn of evidence that diverse, inclusive workplaces contribute to this desired end, they are likely to take it. A review of the scholarship in the area suggests that diversity and inclusion are associated with a number of positive individual, group, and organizational outcomes, and I offer a summary in Exhibit 1.4.

The benefits that accompany diversity and inclusion are appealing to coaches and managers. However, a primary focus on improved business processes and outcomes is likely misguided. Rather, as a number of sport management scholars have argued (Cunningham, 2014; Spaaij et al., 2018; Zeigler, 2007), sport management is primarily a people-oriented sector, and in many cases, the provision

---

Positive Outcomes Associated with Diversity and Inclusion   *exhibit* **1.4**

- **Individual level:** participation in decision-making, authenticity, sense of belonging to the workplace, job satisfaction, organizational commitment, and sense of autonomy.
- **Group:** breadth of decision-making, innovation, creativity, learning from others, idea generation, and task performance.
- **Organization:** appreciation of difference, attraction and retention of diverse workforce, attraction of new club members, reflection of community or state, role modeling, revenue generation, and workplace productivity.

of sport and opportunities to be active represents a public good, a right. What's more, establishing exclusionary policies and actively limiting people's ability to engage in sport can negatively affect their psychological and physical well-being (Cunningham & Buzuvis, 2017). These factors represent primary reasons to have a diverse and inclusive sport organization; the positive outcomes that accompany such work environments represent an added bonus.

PUTTING IT ALL TOGETHER

As the preceding discussions illustrate, diversity and inclusion are the important topics for coaches and sport administrators. Because sport organizations have become more diverse over time—along both surface-level and deep-level dimensions—the emphasis on these topics is in some respects reactionary in nature. That just tells part of the story, though. As discussed throughout the chapter, real benefits can be associated with having inclusive workplaces in which people of various backgrounds and beliefs can thrive.

The purpose of this text is to provide readers with an overview, understanding, and analysis of diversity and inclusion in sport organizations. In Part I, I offer an overview of the theories undergirding these topics (Chapter 2) and of stereotypes, prejudice, and discrimination (Chapter 3). I provide definitions and key points, introduce and explain relevant theories, and outline the effects of prejudice and discrimination on persons in the workplace.

Part II is devoted to various forms of diversity. I examine the ways in which people differ and how these differences influence people's lives and experiences, as well as organizational initiatives and functioning. In doing so, I offer an overview how these theories can be incorporated into a single, multilevel model (Chapter 4). We use the model to understand how various diversity forms influence people's experiences, opportunities, attitudes, and behaviors. Drawing from the model, I focus on race (Chapter 5), gender (Chapter 6), age (Chapter 7), mental and physical ability (Chapter 8), weight (Chapter 9), religious beliefs (Chapter 10), sexual orientation and gender identity (Chapter 11), and social class (Chapter 12).

Part III focuses on strategies sport managers and coaches can use to make sport inclusive. I examine strategies for developing inclusive organizations (Chapter 13) and for engaging in diversity-focused education and training (Chapter 14). Finally, in Chapter 15, I offer an analysis of how people can use sport and physical activity to create social change in communities around the world. Here, I shift the focus to allow for a better understanding of how sport organization can positively affect inclusion and social justice in its communities.

CHAPTER SUMMARY

The purpose of this chapter was to provide an opening glimpse of diversity and inclusion in sport organizations. As the Diversity Challenge illustrated, these topics are the important issues for persons involved in sport and physical activity, and they will be for years to come. Having read the chapter, you should now be able to:

1. Define diversity and inclusion.

    Diversity is the presence of socially meaningful differences among members of a dyad or group. Inclusion represents the degree to which employees are free to express their individuated self and have a sense of workplace connectedness and belonging.

2. List and explain the various forms of diversity.

    I overviewed two forms of diversity: surface-level, which is related to observable characteristics, and deep-level, which is related to differences in psychological characteristics. Information diversity, or those differences based on the knowledge and information that members bring to the group, and value diversity, which is related to differences in the values, attitudes, and beliefs of group members, are both subsumed under the broader category of deep-level diversity.

3. Summarize the factors that have contributed to an increased interest in diversity and inclusion.

    Changing demographics; changes in the nature of work, legal mandates, social pressures, and the negative effects of exclusion; and the value of diversity and inclusion have all spurred an interest in diversity and inclusion among sport managers and coaches.

Questions FOR DISCUSSION

1. Why is it important to understand diversity and inclusion?
2. Do you differentiate between diversity and inclusion? Why or why not?
3. Based on your experiences, how much emphasis do coaches and sport managers place on diversity and inclusion? Why is this the case?
4. Consider the ways in which people differ. Are some differences more meaningful than others within sport organizational settings? Why is this the case?
5. What is the most compelling reason to focus on diversity and inclusion? Provide the rationale for your response.

LEARNING Activities

1. Demographic trends can influence the emphasis on diversity and inclusion. Visit the United Nations Population Fund (https://www.unfpa.org/world-population-trends) and gather data concerning other demographic and population trends. How do countries differ in the major trends facing each?

2. Some people oppose an emphasis on diversity and inclusion within the workplace or educational settings. Why do you think this is the case, and are there counterarguments? Divide into small groups, with each adopting a particular position. Be prepared to present your position to the class.

Web RESOURCES

Laboratory for Diversity in Sport, www.diversityinsport.com
Research center focusing on diversity and inclusion in sport and physical activity; includes various resources.
Sportsocs: Sociologists airing sport's dirty laundry, https://sportsocs.wixsite.com/sdscgroup
Official page for the Sport, Diversity and Social Change group, whose mission focuses on social justice, equity, and inclusion in sport and physical activity.
Diversity, Inc., www.diversityinc.com
Site devoted to diversity in the general organizational context.

READING Resources

Bell, M. P. (2012). *Diversity in organizations* (2nd ed.). Mason, OH: Thomson South-Western.
   A diversity textbook with a business management focus; the author devotes considerable attention to race and ethnicity, as well as addressing other topics.
Equality, Diversity and Inclusion: An International Journal, https://www.emeraldinsight.com/journal/edi.
   An academic journal whose mission is to publish research related to diversity, inclusion, and inequality in society, organizations, and work.
Roberson, Q. M. (Ed.). (2013). *The Oxford handbook of diversity and work*. New York, NY: Oxford University Press.
   A collection of chapters from many of the leading diversity and inclusion scholars around the world.

REFERENCES

Aisch, G., Quealy, K., & Smith, R. (2017, December). Where athletes in the Premier League, the NBA, and other leagues come from, in 15 charts. *New York Times*. Retrieved from https://www.nytimes.com/interactive/2017/12/29/upshot/internationalization-of-pro-sports-leagues-premier-league.html

Apfelbaum, E. P., Stephens, N. M., & Reagans, R. E. (2016). Beyond one-size-fits-all: Tailoring diversity approaches to the representation of social groups. *Journal of Personality and Social Psychology, 111*(4), 547–566.

Bell, S. T., Villado, A. J., Lukasik, M. A., Belau, L., & Briggs, A. L. (2011). Getting specific about demographic diversity variable and team performance relationships: A meta-analysis. *Journal of Management, 37*(3), 709–743.

Brandes, L., Franck, E., & Theiler, P. (2009). The effect from national diversity on team production. *Schmalenbach Business Review, 61*(2), 225–246.

Breer, A. (2017, November). Less of the week: NFL International Series poised to take big step forward in London in 2018. *SI.com*. Retrieved from https://www.si.com/nfl/2017/11/23/nfl-international-series-london-stadium-mexico-city

Brewer, M. B. (1991). The social self: On being the same and different at the same time. *Personality and Social Psychology Bulletin, 17,* 475–482.

Bunderson, J. S., & Van der Vegt, G. S. (2018). Diversity and inequality in management teams: A review and integration of research on vertical and horizontal member differences. *Annual Review of Organizational Psychology and Organizational Behavior, 5*(1), 47–73.

Carroll, A., & Mendos, L. R. (2017). *State-sponsored homophobia: A world survey of sexual orientation laws: Criminalization, protection and recognition.* Geneva, Switzerland: International Lesbian, Gay, Bisexual, Trans and Intersex Association.

Chuah, S. H., Gächter, S., Hoffmann, R., & Tan, J. H. (2016). Religion, discrimination and trust across three cultures. *European Economic Review, 90,* 280–301.

Cillutfo, A., & Cohn, D. (2017, April). 10 demographic trends shaping the U.S. and the world in 2017. *Pew Research Center.* Retrieved from http://www.pewresearch.org/fact-tank/2017/04/27/10-demographic-trends-shaping-the-u-s-and-the-world-in-2017/

Cunningham, G. B. (2006). The influence of demographic dissimilarity on affective reactions to physical activity classes. *Journal of Sport and Exercise Psychology, 28,* 127–142.

Cunningham, G. B. (2007). Perceptions as reality: The influence of actual and perceived demographic dissimilarity. *Journal of Business and Psychology, 22,* 79–89.

Cunningham, G. B. (2009). Examining the relationship among coaching staff diversity, perceptions of diversity, value congruence, and life satisfaction. *Research Quarterly for Exercise and Sport, 80,* 326–335.

Cunningham, G. B. (2014). Interdependence, mutuality, and collective action in sport. *Journal of Sport Management, 28*(1), 1–7.

Cunningham, G. B., & Buzuvis, E. E. (2017, March). Better locker rooms: It's not just a transgender thing. *The Conversation.* Retrieved from https://theconversation.com/better-locker-rooms-its-not-just-a-transgender-thing-74023

Cunningham, G. B., & Melton, E. N. (2014). Signals and cues: LGBT inclusive advertising and consumer attraction. *Sport Marketing Quarterly, 23*(1), 37–46.

Cunningham, G. B., & Sagas, M. (2006). The role of perceived demographic dissimilarity and interaction in customer service satisfaction. *Journal of Applied Social Psychology, 36,* 1654–1673.

Cunningham, G. B., & Singer, J. N. (2009). *Diversity in athletics: An assessment of exemplars and institutional best practices.* Indianapolis, IN: National Collegiate Athletic Association.

DiTomaso, N., Post, C., & Parks-Yancy, R. (2007). Workforce diversity and inequality: Power, status, and numbers. *Annual Review of Sociology, 33,* 473–501.

Downey, S. N., Werff, L., Thomas, K. M., & Plaut, V. C. (2015). The role of diversity practices and inclusion in promoting trust and employee engagement. *Journal of Applied Social Psychology, 45*(1), 35–44.

Ferdman, B. M. (2017). Paradoxes of inclusion: Understanding and managing the tensions of diversity and multiculturalism. *The Journal of Applied Behavioral Science, 53*(2), 235–263.

Fredette, C., Bradshaw, P., & Krause, H. (2016). From diversity to inclusion: A multimethod study of diverse governing groups. *Nonprofit and Voluntary Sector Quarterly, 45*(1_suppl), 28S–51S.

Funk, D. C. (2017). Introducing a Sport Experience Design (SX) framework for sport consumer behaviour research. *Sport Management Review, 20*(2), 145–158.

Garkisch, M., Heidingsfelder, J., & Beckmann, M. (2017). Third sector organizations and migration: A systematic literature review on the contribution of third sector organizations in view of flight, migration and refugee crisis. *Voluntas, 28,* 1839–1880.

Good, L., & Cooper, R. (2016). 'But it's your job to be friendly': Employees coping with and contesting sexual harassment from customers in the service sector. *Gender, Work & Organization, 23*(5), 447–469.

Guillaume, Y. R., Dawson, J. F., Priola, V., Sacramento, C. A., Woods, S. A., Higson, H. E., … West, M. A. (2014). Managing diversity in organizations: An integrative model and agenda for future research. *European Journal of Work and Organizational Psychology, 23*(5), 783–802.

Haas, H., & Nüesch, S. (2012). Are multinational teams more successful? *The International Journal of Human Resource Management, 23*(15), 3105–3113.

Han, S. J., Bonn, M. A., & Cho, M. (2016). The relationship between customer incivility, restaurant frontline service employee burnout and turnover intention. *International Journal of Hospitality Management, 52,* 97–106.

Harrison, D. A., Price, K. H., & Bell, M. P. (1998). Beyond relational demography: Time and the effects of surface-and deep-level diversity on work group cohesion. *Academy of Management Journal, 41*(1), 96–107.

Harrison, D. A., Price, K. H., Gavin, J. H., & Florey, A. T. (2002). Time, teams, and task performance: Changing effects of surface-and deep-level diversity on group functioning. *Academy of Management Journal, 45*(5), 1029–1045.

Huettermann, H., DeWit, F., Diewald, J., Boerner, S., & Jehn, K. A. (2015). Diversity and conflict in teams: A meta-analysis. *Academy of Management Proceedings, 2015,* 14259–14259.

Jehn, K. A., Northcraft, G. B., & Neale, M. A. (1999). Why differences make a difference: A field study of diversity, conflict, and performance in workgroups. *Administrative Science Quarterly, 44,* 741–763.

Johnston, D., & Malina, M. A. (2008). Managing sexual orientation diversity: The impact on firm value. *Group and Organization Management, 33,* 602–625.

Joshi, A., & Neely, B. H. (2018). A structural-emergence model of diversity in teams. *Annual Review of Organizational Psychology and Organizational Behavior, 5,* 361–385.

Kerwin, S., Walker, M. B., & Bopp, T. (2017). When faultlines are created: Exploring the conflict triggering process in sport. *Sport Management Review, 20*(3), 252–260.

Klein, S. (2017, November). Diversity and inclusion are moral imperatives. *Times Colonist.* Retrieved online: http://www.timescolonist.com/ opinion/columnists/opinion-diversity-and-inclusion-are-moral-imperatives-1.23104447.

Konrad, A. M. (2003). Defining the domain of workplace diversity scholarship. *Group & Organization Management, 28,* 4–17.

Lambert, J. R., & Bell, M. P. (2013). Diverse forms of difference. In Q. M. Roberson (Ed.), *The Oxford handbook of diversity at work* (pp. 13–31). New York, NY: Oxford University Press.

Lee, W., & Cunningham, G. B. (2015). A picture is worth a thousand words: The influence of signaling, organizational reputation, and applicant race on attraction to sport organizations.

International Journal of Sport Management, 16, 492–506.

Letterolf, J. (2017, March). In many countries, at least four-in-ten in the labor force are women. *Pew Research Center*. Retrieved from http://www.pewresearch.org/fact-tank/2017/03/07/in-many-countries-at-least-four-in-ten-in-the-labor-force-are-women/

Miller, S. L., Maner, J. K., & Becker, D. V. (2010). Self-protective biases in group categorization: Threat cues shape the psychological boundary between "us" and "them." *Journal of Personality and Social Psychology, 99*, 62–77.

Miller, T., & del Carmen Triana, M. (2009). Demographic diversity in the boardroom: Mediators of the board diversity–firm performance relationship. *Journal of Management Studies, 46*(5), 755–786.

Ng, Y. L., Kulik, C. T., & Bordia, P. (2016). The moderating role of intergroup contact in race composition, perceived similarity, and applicant attraction relationships. *Journal of Business and Psychology, 31*(3), 415–431.

Nishii, L. H., & Rich, R. E. (2014). Creating inclusive climates in diverse organizations. In B. M. Ferdman & B. R. Deane (Eds.), *Diversity at work: The practice of inclusion* (pp. 330–363). San Francisco, CA: Jossey-Bass.

Nüesch, S. (2009). Are demographic diversity effects spurious? *Economic Analysis & Policy, 39*(3), 379–388.

Rhodes, M., & Gelman, S. A. (2009). A developmental examination of the conceptual structure of animal, artifact, and human social categories across two cultural contexts. *Cognitive Psychology, 59*(3), 244–274.

Roberson, Q. M. (2006). Disentangling the meanings of diversity and inclusion in organizations. *Group & Organization Management, 31*, 212–236.

Seifert, K. (2017, April). Ranking the NFL's five international games in 2017. *ESPN*. Retrieved from http://www.espn.com/nfl/story/_/id/19203296/ranking-five-international-games-nfl-2017-schedule-london-mexico-city

Shergold, A. (2016, August). Premier League's new man-of-the-match award is a gold colored brick (and some people are poking fun at the new design). *Daily Mail*. Retrieved from http://www.dailymail.co.uk/sport/football/article-3742900/Premier-League-s-new-man-match-award-yellow-brick-poking-fun-new-design.html

Shore, L. M., Randel, A. E., Chung, B. G., Dean, M. A., Ehrhart, K. H., & Singh, G. (2011). Inclusion and diversity in work groups: A review and model for future research. *Journal of Management, 37*, 1262–1289.

Spaaij, R., Farquharson, K., Gorman, S., Jeanes, R., Lusher, D., Guerra, C., ... Ablett, E. (2018). *Participation versus performance: Managing (dis)ability, gender and cultural diversity in junior sport. Summary report*. Melbourne, VIC: Centre for Multicultural Youth.

Staurowsky, E. J., Zonder, E. J., & Riemer, B. A. (2017). So, what is Title IX? Assessing college athletes' knowledge of the law. *Women in Sport and Physical Activity Journal, 25*(1), 30–42.

Thatcher, S. M. B. (2013). Moving beyond a categorical approach to diversity: The role of demographic faultiness. In Q. M. Roberson (Ed.), *The Oxford handbook of diversity at work* (pp. 52–70). New York, NY: Oxford University Press.

Turner, C. (2017, December). The business case for gender diversity. *Huffington Post*. Retrieved from https://www.huffingtonpost.com/caroline-turner/the-business-case-for-gen_b_7963006.html

Tuten, T. L. (2005). The effect of gay-friendly and nongay-friendly cues on brand attitudes: A comparison of heterosexual and gay/lesbian reactions. *Journal of Marketing Management, 21*, 441–461.

Walker, D. D., van Jaarsveld, D. D., & Skarlicki, D. P. (2017). Sticks and stones can break my bones but words can also hurt me: The relationship between customer verbal aggression and employee incivility. *The Journal of Applied Psychology, 102*(2), 163–179.

Waltemyer, D. S., & Cunningham, G. B. (2009). The influence of team diversity on assists and team performance among National Hockey League Teams. *International Journal of Sport Management, 10,* 391–409.

Wang, P., & Schwarz, J. L. (2010). Stock price reactions to GLBT nondiscrimination policies. *Human Resource Management, 49,* 195–216.

Welbourne, J. L., & Sariol, A. M. (2017). When does incivility lead to counterproductive work behavior? Roles of job involvement, task interdependence, and gender. *Journal of Occupational Health Psychology, 22*(2), 194–206.

Woodhouse, D., & Conricode, D. (in press). In-ger-land, In-ger-land, In-ger-land! Exploring the impact of soccer on the sense of belonging of those seeking asylum in the UK. *International Review for the Sociology of Sport.*

Woratschek, H., Schafmeister, G., & Ströbel, T. (2018). Export of national sport leagues. In M. Dodds, K. Heisey, & A. Ahonen (Eds.), *Routledge handbook of international sport business* (pp. 3–14). New York, NY: Routledge.

Yoshida, M. (2017). Consumer experience quality: A review and extension of the sport management literature. *Sport Management Review, 20*(5), 427–442.

Zeigler, E. F. (2007). Sport management must show social concern as it develops tenable theory. *Journal of Sport Management, 21*(3), 297–318.

Theoretical Tenets of Diversity and Inclusion

LEARNING OBJECTIVES

After studying this chapter, you should be able to:

- Summarize what theory is and why theory is important in understanding diversity and inclusion.

- List and describe the different theories used to understand diversity and inclusion.

- Paraphrase how sport managers can apply the different theories to diversity and inclusion issues within organizations for sport and physical activity.

DIVERSITY CHALLENGE

Theory sometimes has a negative connotation. People might consider it abstract, esoteric, or lacking practical relevance—all descriptions of theory I have heard. In reality, though, people theorize all the time, both formally and informally. They develop explanations for why different phenomena occur. They seek explanations for how and why various activities take place. They might even discuss when and where the events will likely occur. All of these are examples of theorizing.

Theory helps people to effectively engage in their practice. Kurt Lewin (1952) famously remarked that "there is nothing more practical than a good theory" (p. 169). Though managers frequently seek a quick answer or for experts to tell them the supposed best practice, theory helps move beyond these one-time solutions to better understand their organizations, consumers, employees, and their environment.

To illustrate, consider a recent practice relevant to discussions of diversity and inclusion: universities' efforts to diversify the student body. A common narrative is that states, administrators, and faculty see the ethical obligation and value of ensuring *all* people have access to higher education.

Though university administrators' narratives are often welcomed by key constituents, interest convergence theory offers another point of view. The late Derrick Bell, a Harvard law professor, first advanced this position. He suggested that racial minorities' opportunities will only improve when their interests converge with those of Whites. Put another way, diversity gains are most likely to materialize when they are in the best interest of those who have traditionally held power. Critical theorists have used perspective to examine several major diversity moments in history, such as the *Brown v. Board of Education* Supreme Court Decision that barred racial segregation of children in schools or the Brooklyn Dodgers' signing of Jackie Robinson, which served to racially integrate professional baseball.

Recently, David Shih, an English professor at the University of Wisconsin-Eau Claire, examined college diversity programs through an interest convergence lens. He suggested universities likely pursue diversity programs because it helps them. National rankings and the ability to attract top scholars are frequently associated with having diverse campuses. Further, students learn more when they are around people who are different from them. Given that most college students are White, their interests—that is, more learning—are enhanced when universities are more diverse.

Shih concedes that interest convergence is not without its critics. Further, there are multiple ways one can examine diversity-related phenomena. He correctly notes, however, that "so much depends on our capacity to be open to the idea." It is in that openness that growth can occur.

Source: Lewin, K. (1952). *Field theory in social science: Selected theoretical papers by Kurt Lewin.* London: Tavistock. https://www.npr.org/sections/codeswitch/2017/04/19/523563345/a-theory-to-better-understand-diversity-and-who-really-benefits

Challenge Reflection

1. What were your impressions toward theory and its usefulness prior to reading the chapter?
2. What steps can be taken to make people more aware of how they can increase understanding of diversity and inclusion?
3. Do you think university diversity programs would exist of the interests of the powerful or majority were not served? Why or why not?

As the Diversity Challenge illustrates, people are sometimes hesitant to learn about theory or engage in the theory process. Despite this reticence, theory has considerable value, helping people to understand the world around them. Theory can help coaches and sport managers engage in better decision-making and to be proactive in managing their teams and organizations. Indeed, the best theories are the ones that inform the research process but also do more, helping to guide practice and teaching (Cunningham, Fink, & Doherty, 2016; Shaw, 2016; Zhang, Kim, & Pifer, 2016).

Guided by this perspective, the purpose of this chapter is to provide an overview of the theories undergirding the discussion of diversity and inclusion. To do so, I begin by defining theory and elaborating on why it is important in the study of diversity and inclusion. I then discuss the major categories of theory related to these topics, briefly outlining the specific theories in each category and their major tenets. I also describe the application of theories to the management of sport organizations.

DEFINING THEORY

Theory is a "statement of constructs and their relationships to one another that explain[s] how, when, why, and under what conditions phenomena take place" (Cunningham, 2013, p. 1). Constructs are approximated units (Bacharach, 1989) representing psychological, economic, or social phenomena that cannot otherwise be easily observed. Propositions represent the statements of how constructs relate to one another. In articulating these associations, theorists explain what is occurring and, of equal importance, why, when, where, and under what conditions they take place. The latter elements of theory are the "real meat of the theory" (Cunningham et al., 2016, p. 1) and serve to separate theory from description. Through theory, people come to understand the rationale underlying relationships, they are able to predict what might occur in subsequent interactions, and therefore, they better understand how their actions might affect the team or workplace.

To illustrate, let's consider a project Drew Pickett and I conducted focusing on people's attitudes toward lesbian, gay, bisexual, and transgender (LGBT) individuals (Cunningham & Pickett, 2018). We focused prejudice toward LGBT individuals and thought that over time, people's prejudice toward LGBT individuals would decrease. Indeed, we observed as much. This relationship is consistent with a proposition or, when empirically tested, a hypothesis (Kerlinger & Lee, 2000).

Importantly, theory also explains when and under what conditions various phenomena take place. These conditional effects represent boundaries conditions (Bacharach, 1989) or moderators (Barron & Kenny, 1986). In our study, we found that the type of prejudice moderated the relationship. The reduction in prejudice expressed toward LGB individuals was significantly greater than that expressed toward transgender persons. Exhibit 2.1 provides an illustrative summary.

Finally, theory offers an explanation of why various relationships occur. Description, or understanding what is occurring, has value, but theory offers so much more. Theory helps explain why these relationships might occur. Pickett and I suggested that the decrease in prejudice over time was due to more inclusive attitudes toward LGBT individuals in general, including their rights and the ability to live free from bias and persecution (see also Anderson, Magrath, & Bullingham, 2016; McCormack & Anderson, 2014). The moderating effects of prejudice type, we argued, resulted from transgender individual challenging the notion sex assigned at birth should align with people's gender identities and expression—that is, they disrupt people's idea of a gender binary (Norton & Herek, 2012). Transgender individuals might also evoke fear about the destabilization of cultural ideas around gender (Cahn, 2011; Sykes, 2006).

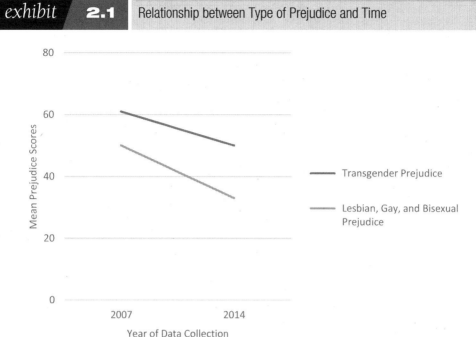

exhibit **2.1**   Relationship between Type of Prejudice and Time

The best theories have practicality and utility. This is illustrated most frequently in the research process. Various authors have described theory as everything from the cornerstone of good scholarship (Cunningham, 2013) to the foundation for new knowledge generation (Doherty, 2013), and the primary aim of science (Kerlinger & Lee, 2000). Thus, theory is clearly important in scholarly endeavors and in research related to diversity and inclusion.

In addition to guiding research, theory is an important element in learning, teaching, engagement, and practice (Doherty, 2013; Fink, 2013; Irwin & Ryan, 2013). Admittedly, these connections are not always made. Irwin and Ryan illustrated as much by pointing to a famous quote from former MLB player Yogi Berra: "In theory, there is no difference between theory and practice. In practice, there is" (as cited in Irwin & Ryan, 2013, p. 12). However, the presence of a theory–teaching or theory–practice gap does not render theory useless; instead, it points to the need to strengthen such ties. For learning, teaching, engagement, and practice, theory helps people to move beyond "quick fix" solutions to a deeper understanding of the issue at hand. Theory allows students and sport managers to explain phenomena and ultimately make educated predictions of future occurrences.

Janet Fink, an expert in the field of diversity and theory, has recognized such linkages, too. See her comments in Box 2.1.

Box 2.1 Professional Perspectives. The Importance of Theory in Understanding Diversity and Inclusion

Janet Fink is a Professor and Department Chair in the Mark H. McCormack Department of Sport Management at the University of Massachusetts. She has an extensive experience in studying diversity and inclusion, including issues related to gender and diversity management.

When asked how she defines theory, Fink responded, "I agree with Mintzberg (2005) that theory is about explaining things. Such explanations can range from lists to fully explanatory models, but a theory is any set of ideas that help us understand *how* and *why* things happen."

Fink also noted that

Theory is important to diversity and inclusion research because it helps us predict things that will happen and why they occur. Without any theoretical guidance, researchers and practitioners

would be 'shooting in the dark,' or perhaps worse, relying on 'common sense' notions that perpetuate ineffective and detrimental practices. However, by using diversity and inclusion research grounded in theory, sport practitioners can confidently address any number of issues that arise in sport from developing interventions to break down stereotypes and prejudice in the workplace, to creating more effective marketing campaigns for women's sport, to ensuring persons with disabilities have the opportunity to participate in sport. Indeed, guided by theory, diversity and inclusion researchers have amassed a variety of discoveries that practitioners can utilize to ensure sport organizations are more diverse and inclusive.

THEORIES USED TO UNDERSTAND DIVERSITY

Theory is useful for academics, students, and practitioners who seek to understand diversity and inclusion. As such, I offer an overview of the relevant theories and return to the theories throughout the book. There are many theories relevant to the discussion, and rather than offer a listing, it is useful to classify them into broader categories: managerial, sociological, and social psychological (see Exhibit 2.2).

Before continuing, I highlight three points. First, my classification represents one of many ways to think about diversity-related theories, and other approaches to the topic are plausible (e.g., Cunningham, 2016; Gearity, Mills, & Callary, 2016). Second, I highlight the *main* theories used in diversity research

exhibit **2.2**   Theories Used to Understand Diversity

Managerial

- Focus: the impact of diversity on group and organizational processes and outcomes.
- Theories: information/decision-making, resource-based view of the firm, pro-diversity beliefs, and creative capital theory.

Sociological

- Focus: structural determinants, power, and conflict, and how they influence diversity and persons who are different from the majority.
- Theories: functionalism, conflict, cultural, and interactionist.

Social psychological

- Focus: interpersonal relationships and the ways in which social identities influence people's experiences.
- Theories: social categorization framework, optimal distinctiveness theory, and stigma theory.

and education; thus, there will necessarily be some that are excluded. Finally, you will likely notice that the theories interrelate in some ways. This is increasingly common, as scholars are likely to draw from multiple disciplines to develop their frameworks (Chelladurai, 2013; Fink, 2013).

Managerial Theories

Managerial theories focus on the relationship among diversity forms, inclusion, and outcomes for employees, work groups, and organizations. A theoretician might explore, for instance, how different diversity forms are associated with group functioning, including outcomes such as time to decision, decision-making effectiveness, and creativity of solutions. For example, Kerwin, Walker, and Bopp (2017) suggested that prolonged task conflict could influence the formation of faultiness (see Chapter 1) and ultimately enhance the presence of emotional conflict in teams.

Information/Decision-Making Theory

In information/decision-making theory, Gruenfeld, Mannix, Williams, and Neale (1996) suggested that some forms of diversity, such as informational diversity discussed in Chapter 1, should give rise to better decision-making and group outcomes. When people differ based on their functional background, education, or tenure, they bring different ideas to the table and have contacts that other group members might not possess. The additional information and varied perspectives should allow for better group processes and, ultimately, improved group functioning.

Suppose, for example, that a working group at a local korfball club is tasked with generating more revenues for the club. The group may be more successful in accomplishing this task if members come from various backgrounds, such as banking, development, marketing, coaching, and so on. In this way, not only do group members bring wide-ranging expertise, but they also have dissimilar professional networks from which they can draw. The group members can consult with their professional networks for advice and fund-raising leads, and then bring the information back to the working group.

The underlying premise that varied backgrounds, education, tenure, and expertise adds value to the group is an appealing one. That noted, some iterations of the theory suggest that specific diversity forms are more likely to add value to the group than others. Pelled (1996), for example, suggested that visible diversity forms, such as gender, race, and age, might elicit biases and negative group outcomes. An extension of such a position is that sport managers should eschew supposed diversity forms that are not job related in favor of other, potentially more task-relevant ways in which people differ.

There are multiple problems, however, with such a position. First, it is socially and legally irresponsible to seek surface-level similarity in the workforce. Second, as we will discuss in later sections, empirical research does not support this theory; instead, researchers have shown that multiple diversity forms are linked with group and organizational effectiveness (Lee & Cunningham, in press). Finally, other managerial theoretical perspectives show the fallacy of such beliefs. Let's take a look at three examples.

Resource-Based View

Barney (1991) developed the resource-based view of the firm. Drawing from this perspective, sport organizations can hold an advantage over their competitors when possessing resources that are valuable, rare, and difficult to imitate. Though many resources potentially have these characteristics, several scholars have noted that unique human resources (Wright, Dunford, & Snell, 2001), and in particular, a diverse workforce, are likely to provide such advantages. As Richard, Murthi, and Ismail (2007) note, "The most valuable natural resource in the world is not oil, diamonds, or even gold; it is the diverse knowledge, abilities, and skills immediately available from cultural diversity" (p. 1213). Central to this argument is the idea that diversity is related to more perspectives, new information, and novel ideas, all of which have the potential to enhance productivity (Andrevski, Richard, Shaw, & Ferrier, 2014). We have drawn from these ideas to show that racial diversity in coaching staffs (a diversity dimension that is not considered "job related" in intervening process theory) is associated with greater success of college athletic teams (Cunningham & Sagas, 2004).

Pro-Diversity Theory

Another theory that points to the value of diversity to organizations is pro-diversity theory. van Knippenberg and colleagues have suggested that the views people hold toward diversity are likely to influence its relationship with subsequent outcomes (van Knippenberg, Haslam, & Platow, 2007; van Knippenberg & Schippers, 2007). Specifically, when people adopt pro-diversity attitudes, they believe that differences among people are a source of competitive advantage and learning. When these mindsets couple with a diverse workforce, the group or organization is likely to thrive. On the other hand, absent such pro-diversity viewpoints, the positive association between employee diversity and subsequent outcomes will likely be muted or even be negative (Guillaume, Dawson, Otaye-Ebede, Woods, & West, 2017). The pro-diversity mindsets are particularly effective when people understand the nature of diversity in their group, how the differences might influence processes and outcomes, and how then to engage diversity (van Knippenberg, van Ginkel, & Homan, 2013).

A number of scholars have supported this perspective. Guimond et al. (2013) collected data from thousands of students across four counties: Canada, the US, the UK, and Germany. They found that the countries differed in their pro-diversity attitudes, as did the individuals within the countries. These attitudes were important predictors of prejudice expressed toward Muslims. In the sport context, pro-diversity beliefs interact with group diversity to predict a number of important outcomes, including improved group processes, creativity, and organizational effectiveness (Cunningham, 2008, 2009, 2011a, 2011b).

Creative Capital Theory

Creative capital theory represents the final managerial theory (Florida, 2002, 2003, 2012). Richard Florida, a geographer, developed the theory to explain how certain regions enjoyed greater economic prosperity and growth than others. He suggested that creative people were the key, and that these individuals were attracted to areas marked by a high concentration of educated people, technological advances, and inclusion. Of particular importance to our discussion is Florida's emphasis on inclusion. According to his theory, people consider inclusion of LGBT individuals as a signal of inclusive attitudes toward most other differences, too.

We applied Florida's ideas in an experimental study of people's attitudes toward inclusive fitness clubs (Cunningham & Melton, 2014). Study participants reviewed a flyer for a new club, and the flyer included the name, price per month, amenities, and so on. Some of the flyers also included a rainbow flag on the bottom and a statement about the club's commitment to inclusion of sexual orientation and gender identity diversity. The other flyers did not have this information. Participants who saw the inclusive flyer were more likely to believe the club valued diversity along a host of dimensions, including race, gender, and age—findings consistent with creative capital theory. Importantly, when they believed the club valued diversity, they were also more likely to express interest in joining.

Together, these theories offer a meaningful departure from the traditional managerial theory approach to diversity. Rather than seeing some diversity forms as helpful and others as not, recent theoretical advancements suggest that *all* diversity forms can be sources of learning, improved decision-making, creativity, and overall effectiveness. The key to realizing these benefits is ensuring that the workplace culture is inclusive—one where people can freely express their various differences, allowing those around them to benefit from their perspectives. We will discuss strategies to create and sustain an inclusive work environment in Part III.

Sociological Theories

In the previous section, we focused on the ways in which diversity and inclusion might be associated with group and organizational processes and outcomes. It is also important to consider the role of diversity and inclusion in people's lives, the opportunities they have to be active or to pursue various lines of work, and their experiences doing so. Therein lies the importance of sociological theories, which focus on macro issues, such as societal norms, institutional practices, and organizational polices. Although there are a number of theories under the broad sociological umbrella, Sage and Eitzen (2016) have grouped them into four categories: functionalism, conflict theory, cultural theories, and interactionist theory. I follow their classification scheme in this chapter.

Functionalism

From a functionalist perspective, just as bodies are comprised of cells, tissues, and organs, all of which help the body to work, various institutions in society work in concert to maintain the social system as a whole. Examples of institutions include the economy, educational systems, religious institutions, and so on. The institutions work with one another, exhibiting unity, collaboration, and perseverance. Sage and Eitzen (2016) suggest "the high degree of social system cooperation— and societal integration—is accomplished because there is a high degree of consensus on societal goals and on cultural values" (p. 12).

Researchers following a functionalist perspective focus on how the parts of the system work with one another to ensure the stability of society. Sport, as an institution, plays a role in this harmony. Functionalists hold that sport embodies key societal values, such as competition, fair play, and success. Youth are socialized through sport, and in doing so, learn desirable values, knowledge, and understanding of society. Thus, functionalist theorists note the importance of youth sports, interscholastic sport, and other sport experiences in athletes maintaining their grades, learning importance values, and enhancing their self-esteem. In short, from a functionalist perspective, sport serves an important good in society, helping to inform people of proper behaviors to follow, uniting fans, and inspiring citizens.

In some respects, work related to sport for development and peace (SDP; see Chapter 15) offers an illustrative example. SDP refers to the purposeful "use of sport to exert a positive influence on public health, the socialization of children, youths and adults, the social inclusion of the disadvantaged, the economic development of regions and states, and on fostering intercultural exchange and conflict resolution" (Lyras & Welty Peachey, 2011, p. 311; see also Schulenkorf, 2017). For example, the leaders at Street Soccer USA use sport as a way of reaching and improving the lives of people who experience homelessness. Street soccer serves to attract people, and sport managers then embed educational and vocational training in the practices and games as a way to enhance participants' skills and networks. Svensson and Woods (2017) have shown that SDP organizations operate over the world, with most focusing on education, improving people's livelihoods, or enhancing health.

Conflict Theory

Drawing from the works of Karl Marx and related theorists, conflict theory offers a stark contrast to functionalist theory. From this perspective, conflict is ever-present in capitalist societies, largely because of the differences in social classes. Power, prestige, and privilege reside in the hands of the wealthy elite, and people in this social class use their resources to maintain these advantages, all the while subjugating others, particularly those in the working class.

Conflict theorists suggest the elite maintain their standing through multiple mechanisms. Sometimes, they subjugate others through force and coercion. In other cases, they use more subtle means, working through societal institutions, such as the church, educational system, the media, and other social institutions. As Sage and Eitzen (2016) explain, the techniques represent effective approaches to maintaining elites' status and privilege, largely due to "popular compliance, resulting in the underclass of individual defining conditions that are actually hostile to their interests as being legitimate—a condition that Karl Marx called *false consciousness*" (p. 13, emphasis original).

As one example, consider people's ongoing support for using public monies to support professional stadiums and arenas (Kellison & Kim, 2017). Despite the substantial influx of public funds, attendance at professional sporting events are activities largely reserved for the wealthy. Let's examine Team Marketing Report's (see Interactive, n.d.) Fan Cost Index—a measure that includes the costs of attending a professional sports game, including four tickets, four soft drinks, two beers, four hot dogs, two programs, two caps, and parking. In the 2015–2016 season, it cost a family of four $339.02 to attend an NBA game and $502.84 to attend a National Football League (NFL) game. These costs must be juxtaposed against household incomes in the US. According to the US Census Bureau (Semega, Fontenot, & Kollar, 2017), the median household income in 2016 was $59,039, and earners in the top 5 percent had household incomes of $225,252 or more. As illustrated in Exhibit 2.3, purchasing season tickets is a much more feasible option for high-income individuals than it is for others. In fact, the average American household would have to spend 7 percent of its annual income to have NFL season tickets and 24 percent of its income for NBA season tickets.

Household Income and the Costs of Attending All Home Games
for Selected North American Professional Sports

exhibit   **2.3**

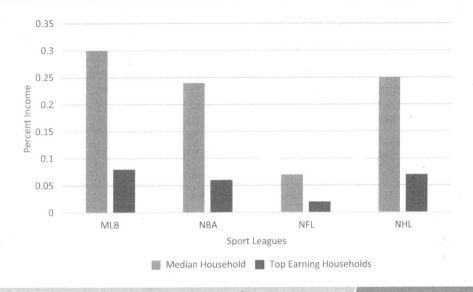

Sources: Data from Semega, Fontenot, & Kollar (2017), Interactive (no date). Data for 2016 MLB
season, 2015–2016 NBA season, 2016 NFL season, and 2014–2015 NHL season.

The ticket price data show that, even with a large influx of public funds used
to finance stadiums, not all members of the public have access to professional
sport. Conflict theorists suggest cases such as this show the power of the elite over
other members of society. Importantly, though, people are not passive recipients
of their environment and can resist. Saito (in press), for example, showed how the
poor and underserved effectively mobilized to resist efforts of the NFL to build a
stadium in a particular neighborhood. We will return to conflict theory in other
portions of the book, including the discussion of social class (Chapter 12).

Cultural Theories

The third category of theories in Sage and Eitzen's classification is cultural theories. Subsumed under this broad class includes three theories particularly relevant
to the discussion of diversity: hegemony theory, feminist theory, and critical race
theory.

Hegemony theorists focus on the political, economic, and cultural arrangements of privilege and dominance within society. Sage (1998) explained, "Hegemony theory sensitizes us to the role dominant groups play in American
government, economic systems, mass media, education, and sport in maintaining
and promoting their interests" (p. 10). Their cultural and social privilege offers

opportunities and power to some groups at the expense of others, such as heterosexuals over LGBT individuals, men over women, rich over poor, and Whites over racial minorities. Researchers applying this perspective focus on how issues related to race, gender, sexual orientation, and class, as some examples, operate within sport and reproduce social norms and patterns. For instance, Sveinson and Hoeber (2016) examined the experiences of highly identified sport fans who were women. They found that women sometimes faced marginalization—something that largely stemmed from hegemonic forms of masculinity that pervade much of sport. One fan noted, "… because I am a female, I feel inferior sometimes to other people because they're like, 'oh, you're just a girl watching football'" (p. 17).

Next, feminist theory holds that "inequalities faced by women are related to differential access, different treatment and exploitation, patriarchy, and male dominance" (Sage & Eitzen, 2016, p. 14). Feminist theorists focus on a number of topics, including equality in the workplace, political representation, educational opportunities, legal rights, and health care, including abortion. Central to feminist theory are two propositions: all experiences are gendered in nature, and women are routinely oppressed through patriarchy and must fight for change. For example, Thorpe (2018) examined action sports, such as surfing, skateboarding, or snowboarding. She noted that, despite the alternative sport form and the corresponding possibility of greater inclusiveness, White men have traditionally dominated the sports. That noted, a growing number of women have contested their marginalization, thereby creating new space for themselves in sport and in broader society.

Importantly, a growing critique of feminist theory is that it captures the sentiments of White, wealthy women, but not those of racial minorities, the poor, and other women who do not otherwise have privileged identities (hooks, 2000). Box 2.2 offers a detailed discussion of these points.

Critical race theory represents the third cultural theory (Sage & Eitzen, 2016). Theorists adopting this perspective hold that societal arrangements are structured in such a way to privilege Whites and subjugate racial minorities. The theory holds that racism is embedded deeply into society and its institutions, including religion, education, criminal justice, and so on. As a result, racial minorities continually encounter racism in their everyday lives. A key objective of critical race theorists, then, is to analyze critically, deconstruct, and challenge racist system, advocating for change and empowerment.

As an example, Bimper (2017) used critical race theory as a lens to examine a mentoring program for student athletes in US colleges and universities. He found that the mentors challenged the athletes to consider their race in a context that included mostly White peers. The athletes were also encouraged to develop social capital as a way to become advocates. In another study, Coram and Hallinan (2017) examined the hostility expressed toward and booing of Australian Indigenous athlete Adam Goodes. Though others offered counter narratives, Coram and Hallnina used critical race theory to illustrate the historical racism and antagonism Indigenous athletes faced. They argued, therefore, that the booing represented a way in which fans denigrated and vilified Goodes.

Box 2.2 Alternative Perspectives: Intersectionality

In many cases, people think about diversity along singular diversity dimensions. For example, we might consider how race, gender, or sexual orientation affects people's opportunities to be physically active. Although such an approach might be appropriate in some settings, people do not have just a single identity that influences their opportunities and experiences. Instead, they have multiple identities (i.e., multiple diversity dimensions) that operate simultaneously.

The idea that multiple identities influence people's experiences, and specifically those of women, is consistent with hooks' (2000) ideas of *intersectionality*. Intersectionality brings to light the multiple forms of exclusion women of color experience due to various structural and systemic pressures. More recent iterations of the theory also bring to the forefront issues related to gender expression, sexual orientation, social class, and ability. Importantly, intersectionality scholars do not adhere to additive effects of various identities, but instead focus on the qualitative effects of multiple differences. As Watson and Scraton (2013)

explain, "It moves beyond an additive approach that deals with fixed, static concepts of gender, race, class and looks at inequalities at the intersections and at how they are routed through each other with no single cause" (p. 37).

Pavlidis and Fullagar (2013) adopted an intersectionality perspective in their study of roller derby. This is a full-contact sport in which women roller skate around a circular track, with the aim of having a particular player on each team lap the opposing players. The other players on the team seek to hinder the opposing players' progress. Pavlidis and Fullagar observed that women were able to express various identities important to them while participating in the sport. This served to empower them in some instances, but, because of social pressures, it also resulted in negative affect. The authors concluded, "Roller derby exists as a fluid leisure space where passion and frustration, pride and shame, disgust and pleasure, anger and love, play out amidst everyday negotiations about women's sameness or difference" (p. 433).

Interactionist Theory

Whereas the previous sociological theories had a structural focus, with an emphasis on societal and institutional influences on the individual, interactionist theory focuses on how people engage in, make sense of, and interpret their social worlds. Sage and Eitzen (2016) note, "the important sociological insight here is that the meaning is not inherent in an object; instead, people learn how to define reality from other people in interaction and by learning the culture" (p. 16). Sociologists refer to the learning process as social construction.

As a research example, Barker, Quennerstedt, and Annerstedt (2015) examined how learning takes place through interaction in physical activity classes. They found that, among other factors, the students' shared perceptions of the world influenced how they learned and moved together. As another example, Skey and colleagues (2018) examined the relationship between media and young people's engagement with association football (soccer) in England. They found that people followed football through a number of media platforms, and their understanding of the game was shaped by those engagements.

Social Psychological Theories

Social psychological theories, forming the final class of theories, focus on the individual in relation to others. From a diversity perspective, the theories in this grouping are ideal when considering dyads or groups. In some cases, researchers examine how being different from or similar to others in a particular context affects an individual's well-being. In other cases, scholars might attend to ways that individuals can express identities important to them in the workplace. Still others involve a focus on how different characteristics are devalued in society and, as a result, have a stigma attached to them. Each of these subjects falls under the broad umbrella of social psychology, and the underlying theoretical rationales for each are discussed here.

Social Categorization

Many researchers who examine groups or how people engage with others draw from the social categorization framework. Two theories—social identity theory (Tajfel & Turner, 1979) and self-categorization theory (Turner, Hogg, Oakes, et al., 1987)—contribute to the framework. From these perspectives, people classify themselves and others into social groups. Doing so helps people make sense of a complex social world. The groupings can be based on a myriad of factors, such as fandom (e.g., Sydney Swans or West Coast Eagles), social class (poor or rich), political beliefs (conservative or progressive), and the like. People use the process to define themselves in terms of a social identity. Once they make the categorizations, people engage in social comparisons, and they do so automatically. They create "us" and "them" distinctions, with the "us" representing people who are similar to them and the "them" representing people who are different.

Social categorization and social comparison result in intergroup bias (Fergusun & Porter, 2013). People generally think positively toward in-group members and afford them more liking, help, and trust than they do to out-group members. The end result is a more positive evaluation of in-group members than out-group members, resulting in bias (we will discuss this process more in Chapter 3). Importantly, categorization is not negative, in and of itself. It is a natural process that helps people navigate their social worlds. But when the categorization results in bias, the negative effects of being different manifest (Hogg, Abrams, & Brewer, 2017).

The social categorization framework has been instrumental in helping to understand how people operate in groups, as well as how groups function as a whole. Hogg (2014), for example, used social categorization to explain why people join extreme groups and how extremism emerges in various contexts, such as leadership, politics, religion, and gangs. He suggested that, especially when people feel uncertain about themselves and their identities, they will seek to affiliate with entities that offer clearly defined identities, prescribed behaviors, and prescriptive beliefs. As a result, people might seek out leaders who engage in extreme behaviors or groups that adhere to ethnocentric belief systems. These processes clearly have implications for sport managers and others interested in understanding membership in extreme groups, including some fan groups.

Optimal Distinctiveness Theory

Brewer (1991) and Leonardelli, Pickett, and Brewer (2010) expanded on the original social categorization framework to develop her optimal distinctiveness theory. As discussed in Chapter 1, this theory holds that people have two potentially contradictory needs: (a) to express their individuated self and have their identities recognized by others and (b) to feel a sense of belonging in a larger group. When both of these needs are met, optimal distinctiveness is achieved. As Leonardelli et al. (2010) explain, "people will resist being identified with social categorizations that are either too inclusive or too differentiating but will define themselves in terms of social identities that are optimally distinctive" (p. 68).

This theory has two primary implications for our understanding of diversity and inclusion. The first comes in our discussions of intergroup bias and stereotyping. From an optimal distinctiveness perspective, if the needs are not met at desired levels, then intergroup bias is likely to occur (Brewer, 2007). For example, when people perceive a threat to their distinctiveness, they are likely to engage in activities that highlight the differences between in-groups and out-groups.

The second implication comes in the area of inclusion. Recall from Chapter 1 that inclusion refers to the degree to which employees are free to express their individuated self and have a sense of workplace connectedness and belonging. Clearly, optimal distinctiveness informed this perspective, as it highlights the two needs people have. From a managerial standpoint, this means that teams and organizations should be designed in ways that allow for personal expression while also engendering a sense of attachment. Sport managers should also remain mindful that culture, individual characteristics, and context can influence people's need for distinctiveness and belonging (Leonardelli et al., 2010). Further, there is likely an equilibrium point at which people's needs are satisfied (Ormiston, 2016).

Stigma

Stigma theory represents the final social psychological theory (Goffman, 1963). People who are stigmatized "have (or are believed to have) an attribute that marks them as different and leads them to be devalued in the eyes of others" (Major & O'Brien, 2005, p. 395). Stigmatizing characteristics can take several forms, including being visible or invisible, controllable or not, and associated with appearance, behavior, or membership in a group (Major & O'Brien, 2005). Importantly, stigmas are time and culturally bound, meaning that what is stigmatizing in one setting at a particular time may vary greatly from a stigmatizing mark at a different time or in another context.

Hatzenbuehler (2017) noted that stigma can manifest at different levels, including the individual, interpersonal, and structural. Individual stigma represents cognitive, affective, and behavioral ways in which people respond to stigma. For example, people might express self-stigma when they internalize negative evaluations of themselves or people who are like them (e.g., Lillis, Thomas, Levin, & Wing, in press). In other cases, people might be self-conscious of their stigmatized status, something referred to as stigma consciousness (Brown & Pinel, 2003). Interpersonal stigma refers to the prejudice and discrimination that people express toward members of stigmatized groups. As we will discuss in the following chapter, interpersonal stigma can be overt, such as when people commit hate crimes, or covert, such as when people engage in subtle slights and incivility. Note both forms negatively affect people who are stigmatized (Jones, Peddie, Gilrane, King, & Gray, 2016). Finally, structural stigma represents the societal factors that subjugate and disadvantage stigmatized people. Examples include cultural norms, policies, and institutionalized practices. Structural stigma limits people's opportunities, the quality of their experiences, and their overall well-being (Hatzenbuehler & Link, 2014).

From a different perspective, Summers et al. (2018) developed a typology to understand when an attribute would be stigmatizing, and they focused on the degree to which it is visible, controllable, and legally protected at work. They considered visibility to describe characteristics that were discernable by another. Some characteristics, such as race, might be easily visible, whereas others, such as one's smoking behavior, might be discernable through other senses. Controllable refers to the degree to which the stigmatized individual is responsible for the stigmatizing characteristic. In general, stigmatizing characteristics elicit a stronger negative reaction when people believe the target is responsible for that attribute. Finally, legalization is important because of the associated permissible actions taken on

exhibit 2.4 Framework for Understanding Stigma

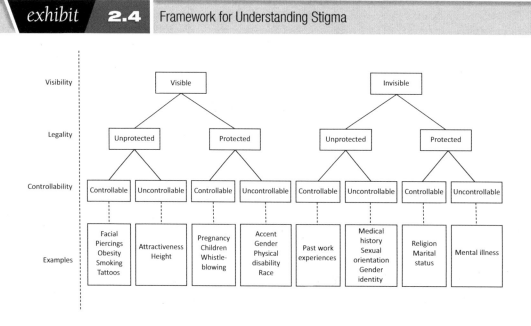

Source: Adapted from Summers et al. (2018).

behalf of the organization. A sport organization can refuse to hire someone, for example, if the individual has facial tattoos but not because of the person's race. An overview of Summers et al. framework is presented in Exhibit 2.4.

People who possess a stigmatized characteristic frequently have poor work experiences (Hebl & King, 2013). They are likely to underperform on tests when they are mindful of their stigmatizing condition. They also experience discrimination: relative to their peers, people with a stigmatized characteristic are likely to have poorer letters of recommendation written for them, experience more bias in the selection process, lack opportunities for training and development, and receive less pay. They also face subtle forms of discrimination, as people smile at them less, use fewer words when conversing, and are generally less friendly. As we will discuss throughout the text, these patterns are observed across a number of diversity dimensions, including race, ability, weight, sexual orientation, gender identity, and religious beliefs, among others. Box 2.3 offers a broader discussion of the potential stigma associated with being LGBT.

Box 2.3 Diversity in the Field: Stigma in Sport

In July 2014, Ian Thorpe announced he was gay. The news was noteworthy on several fronts. First, Thorpe is a highly decorated Australian swimming star, having won five Olympic gold medals. He had denied that he was gay for over a decade. Doing so, he said, resulted in depression, alcoholism, and attempted suicide. Over time, he came to see the benefits of disclosing his true sexual orientation. In an interview with Sir Michael Parkinson, Thorpe noted, "The lie became so big that I didn't want people to question my integrity."

Thorpe's longstanding denial of his sexual orientation caused some observers, such as Matt Peacock, to question whether identifying as LGBT was a stigmatizing characteristic within the sport context. For instance, Thorpe indicated that, by denying his gay identity, he "was trying to be what I thought was the right athlete by other people's standards. . . . Part of me didn't know if Australia wanted its champion to be gay." Recent data support Thorpe's hesitation. In a 2014 study sponsored by the Australian Sports Commission, 84 percent of LGBT Australian athletes surveyed indicated they had heard anti-LGBT language, 28 percent had witnessed bullying, 28 percent had observed social exclusion, and 13 percent had seen physical abuse toward LGBT individuals.

These data, when coupled with Thorpe's commentary, suggest LGBT status might be a stigmatizing condition in the Australian sport context. Work from Eric Anderson and others shows that attitudes toward LGBT individuals have improved considerably over time, but there is still much work to be done.

Sources: Anderson (2011), Buzinski (2014, July 13), Buzinski (2014, July 15), and Peacock (2014, July 14).

CHAPTER SUMMARY

I n this chapter, we focused on various theories and how they can be used to understand diversity and inclusion in sport organizations. As the Diversity Challenge illustrated, knowledge of the basic theories that undergird diversity is crucial in fully understanding this complex topic. The theories we use to study diversity influence the questions we ask, the focus of our examination, and the way we see the world in general.

After reading the chapter, you should be able to do the following:

1. Explain what a theory is and why theory is important in understanding diversity and inclusion.

   Theory provides "a statement of constructs and their relationships to one another that explain[s] how, when, why, and under what conditions phenomena take place" (Cunningham, 2013, p. 1). Theory is important because of its practicality and its utility in helping managers understand their complex social surroundings.

2. Discuss the different classes of theory used to understand diversity and inclusion.

   Three classes of theory are used to study diversity: managerial, sociological, and social psychological. Managerial theories focus on the impact of diversity on organizational outcomes. Sociological theories focus on structural issues, power, and conflict, and how these factors influence diversity and persons who differ from the majority. Finally, social psychological theories focus on how being dissimilar from others in social settings influences an individual's affect and behavior.

3. Discuss how the different theories can be applied to diversity issues within organizations for sport and physical activity.

   Managerial theories illustrate the need to recognize how the various types of diversity influence work- and team-related outcomes. The sociological theories require managers to ask questions about how organizational factors, such as power structure, influence the experiences of persons who differ from the majority. Finally, social psychological theories suggest that managers should pay attention to the composition of work groups and employee-customer relationships, as surface- and deep-level differences within these relationships can lead to negative outcomes.

Questions FOR DISCUSSION

1. Some readers may express an aversion to a discussion of theory. Prior to studying this chapter, what were your attitudes toward theory? Identify several benefits of studying theory that you learned from the chapter.

2. The chapter includes one definition of theory, but there are many ways to think about it. How would you define theory in your own words?

3. How do issues of power in organizations influence people who differ from the majority?
4. Social psychological theories suggest that being different from others in a dyad or group will negatively influence subsequent affective reactions and behaviors. How might a manager reduce these negative effects?
5. Four approaches to the study of diversity were identified. Which approach makes the most sense to you? Why?

LEARNING Activities

1. Some people believe that students should not be taught theory because it has limited applicability to workplace settings. Divide into groups and argue the pros and cons of understanding theory and theoretical principles as they apply to diversity in sport organizations.
2. Visit a local sport organization and ask the manager, employees, and athletes how diversity and inclusion impact the workplace, group dynamics, and overall outcomes for the organization. Then, compare their responses with the theoretical tenets outlined in this chapter.
3. Visit your school's athletic department and ask administrators and student-athletes how diversity and inclusion impact the department, group dynamics, and outcomes. Compare their responses with the theoretical tenets outlined in this chapter.

Web RESOURCES

- Gender and Diversity in Organizations, http://division.aomonline.org/gdo/
  A division of the Academy of Management; provides diversity resources related to research and teaching.
- Laboratory for Diversity in Sport, www.diversityinsport.com
  Provides overviews of research initiatives, as well as other diversity-related online sources.
- North American Society for the Sociology of Sport, www.nasss.com
  Provides a resource center and directory of experts in several diversity-related areas.

READING Resources

Cunningham, G. B., Fink, J. S., & Doherty, A. J. (Eds.). (2016). *Routledge handbook of theory in sport management*. New York, NY: Routledge.

Offers an overview of theory and why it is important in sport management; includes chapters focusing on the development and application of sport management theory.

Giulianotti, R. (Ed.) (2015). *Routledge handbook of the sociology of sport*. New York, NY: Routledge.

Offers an overview of the sociology of sport, including the contributions of major social theorists.

Van Lange, P. A., Krulanski, A. W., & Higgins, E. T. (Eds.) (2011). *The handbook of theories of social psychology* (Vol. 2). Thousand Oaks, CA: Sage.

Contains chapters of direct relevance to diversity and inclusion, including chapters focusing on implicit theories, social identity theory, optimal distinctiveness theory, and others.

REFERENCES

Anderson, E. (2011). *Inclusive masculinity: The changing nature of masculinities*. London, UK: Routledge.

Anderson, E., Magrath, R., & Bullingham, R. (2016). *Out in sport: The experiences of openly gay and lesbian athletes in competitive sport*. New York, NY: Routledge.

Andrevski, G., Richard, O. C., Shaw, J. D., & Ferrier, W. J. (2014). Racial diversity and firm performance: The mediating role of competitive intensity. *Journal of Management, 40*(3), 820–844.

Bacharach, S. B. (1989). Organizational theories: Some criteria for evaluation. *Academy of Management Review, 14,* 496–515.

Barker, D., Quennerstedt, M., & Annerstedt, C. (2015). Learning through group work in physical education: A symbolic interactionist approach. *Sport, Education and Society, 20*(5), 604–623.

Barney, J. (1991). Firm resources and sustained competitive advantage. *Journal of Management, 17,* 99–120.

Barron, R. M., & Kenny, D. A. (1986). The moderator-mediator variable distinction in social psychological research: Conceptual, strategic, and statistical considerations. *Journal of Personality and Social Psychology, 51,* 1173–1182.

Bimper Jr, A. Y. (2017). Mentorship of Black student-athletes at a predominately White American university: Critical race theory perspective on student-athlete development. *Sport, Education and Society, 22*(2), 175–193.

Brewer, M. B. (1991). The social self: On being the same and different at the same time. *Personality and Social Psychology Bulletin, 17,* 475–482.

Brewer, M. B. (2007). The importance of being *we*: Human nature and intergroup relations. *American Psychologist, 62,* 728–738.

Brown, R. P., & Pinel, E. C. (2003). Stigma on my mind: Individual differences in the experience of stereotype threat. *Journal of Experimental Social Psychology, 39,* 626–633.

Buzinski, J. (2014, July 13). Ian Thorpe: "I'm comfortable saying I'm a gay man." *Outsports.com*. Retrieved from www.outsports.com/2014/7/13/5895025/ian-thorpe-im-comfortable-saying-im-a-gay-man

Buzinski, J. (2014, July 15). Gay Australian athletes report widespread homophobia. *Outsports.com*. Retrieved from www.outsports.com/2014/7/15/5902705/gay-australia-athletesreport-widespread-homophobia-bingham-cup

Cahn, S. (2011). Testing sex, attributing gender: What caster Semenya means to women's sports. *Journal of Intercollegiate Sport, 4,* 38–48.

Coram, S., & Hallinan, C. (2017). Critical race theory and the orthodoxy of race neutrality: Examining the denigration of Adam Goodes. *Australian Aboriginal Studies, 2017*(1), 99–111.

Chelladurai, P. (2013). A personal journey in theorizing in sport management. *Sport Management Review, 16,* 22–28.

Cunningham, G. B. (2008). Commitment to diversity and its influence on athletic department outcomes. *Journal of Intercollegiate Sport, 1*, 176–201.

Cunningham, G. B. (2009). The moderating effect of diversity strategy on the relationship between racial diversity and organizational performance. *Journal of Applied Social Psychology, 36,* 1445–1460.

Cunningham, G. B. (2011a). Creative work environments in sport organizations: The influence of sexual orientation diversity and commitment to diversity. *Journal of Homosexuality, 58,* 1041–1045.

Cunningham, G. B. (2011b). The LGBT advantage: Examining the relationship among sexual orientation diversity, diversity strategy, and performance. *Sport Management Review, 14,* 453–461.

Cunningham, G. B. (2013). Theory and theory development in sport management. *Sport Management Review, 16,* 1–4.

Cunningham, G. B. (2016). Women in coaching: Theoretical underpinnings among quantitative analyses. In N. M. Lavoi (Ed.), Women in sports coaching (pp. 223–233). New York, NY: Routledge.

Cunningham, G. B., & Melton, E. N. (2014). Signals and cues: LGBT inclusive advertising and consumer attraction. *Sport Marketing Quarterly, 23,* 37–46.

Cunningham, G. B., & Pickett, A. C. (2018). Trans prejudice in sport: Differences from LGB prejudice, the influence of gender, and changes over time. *Sex Roles, 78,* 220–227.

Cunningham, G. B., & Sagas, M. (2004). People make the difference: The influence of human capital and diversity on team performance. *European Sport Management Quarterly, 4,* 3–22.

Cunningham, G. B., Fink, J. S., & Doherty, A. (2016). Developing theory in sport management. In G. B. Cunningham, J. S., Fink, & A. Doherty (Eds.), *Routledge handbook of theory in sport management* (pp. 1–8). New York, NY: Routledge.

Doherty, A. (2013). Investing in sport management: The value of good theory. *Sport Management Review, 16,* 5–11.

Ferguson, M., & Porter, S. C. (2013). An examination of categorization processes in organizations: The root of intergroup bias and a route to prejudice reduction. In Q. M. Roberson (Ed.), *The Oxford handbook of diversity and work* (pp. 98–114). New York: Oxford.

Fink, J. S. (2013). Theory development in sport management: My experience and other considerations. *Sport Management Review, 16,* 17–21.

Florida, R. (2002). The economic geography of talent. *Annals of the Association of American Geographers, 92,* 743–755.

Florida, R. (2003). Cities and the creative class. City & *Community, 2,* 3–19.

Florida, R. (2012). *The rise of the creative class, revisited.* New York: Basic Books.

Gearity, B. T., Mills, J. P., & Callary, B. (2016). Women in coaching: Theoretical underpinnings among qualitative research. In N. M. Lavoi (Ed.), *Women in sports coaching* (pp. 234–254). New York, NY: Routledge.

Goffman, E. (1963). *Stigma: Notes on the management of spoiled identity.* New York, NY: Simon & Schuster.

Gruenfeld, D. H., Mannix, E. A., Williams, K. Y., & Neale, M. A. (1996). Group composition and decision making: How member familiarity and information distribution affect process and performance. *Organizational Behavior and Human Decision Processes, 67,* 1–15.

Guillaume, Y. R., Dawson, J. F., Otaye-Ebede, L., Woods, S. A., & West, M. A. (2017). Harnessing demographic differences in organizations: What moderates the effects of workplace diversity? *Journal of Organizational Behavior, 38*(2), 276–303.

Guimond, S., Crisp, R. J., De Oliveira, P., Kamiejski, R., Kteily, N., Kuepper,

B., ... Sidanius, J. (2013). Diversity policy, social dominance, and intergroup relations: Predicting prejudice in changing social and political contexts. *Journal of Personality and Social Psychology, 104*(6), 941–958.

Hatzenbuehler, M. L. (2017). Structural stigma and health. In B. Major, J. F. Dovidio, & B. G. Link (Eds.), *The Oxford handbook of stigma, discrimination, and health* (pp. 105–121). New York, NY: Oxford University Press.

Hatzenbuehler, M. L., & Link, B. G. (2014). Introduction to the special issue on structural stigma and health. *Social Science and Medicine, 103*, 1–6.

Hebl, M. R., & King, E. B. (2013). The social and psychological experience of stigma. In Q. M. Roberson (Ed.), *The Oxford handbook of diversity and work* (pp. 115–131). New York, NY: Oxford University Press.

Hogg, M. A. (2014). From uncertainty to extremism: Social categorization and identity processes. *Current Directions in Psychological Science, 23*(5), 338–342.

Hogg, M. A., Abrams, D., & Brewer, M. B. (2017). Social identity: The role of self in group processes and intergroup relations. *Group Processes & Intergroup Relations, 20*(5), 570–581.

hooks, b. (2000). *Feminist theory: From margin to center* (2nd ed.). London, UK: Pluto Press.

Interactive analysis of fan cost index (no date). The Business of Sports. Retrieved from http://www. thebusinessofsports.com/2017/02/14/ interactive-analysis-of-fan-cost-index/

Irwin, R. L., & Ryan, T. D. (2013). Get real: Using engagement with practice to advance theory transfer and production. *Sport Management Review, 16*, 12–16.

Jones, K. P., Peddie, C. I., Gilrane, V. L., King, E. B., & Gray, A. L. (2016). Not so subtle: A meta-analytic investigation of the correlates of subtle and overt discrimination. *Journal of Management, 42*(6), 1588–1613.

Kellison, T. B., & Kim, Y. (2017). Public attitudes towards no-vote stadium subsidies: The development and validation of an ex post proxy referendum. *International Journal of Sport Policy and Politics, 9*(3), 469–489.

Kerlinger, F. N., & Lee, H. B. (2000). *Foundations of behavioral research* (4th ed.). Fort Worth, TX: Harcourt College Publishers.

Kerwin, S., Walker, M. B., & Bopp, T. (2017). When faultlines are created: Exploring the conflict triggering process in sport. *Sport Management Review, 20*(3), 252–260.

Lee, W., & Cunningham, G. B. (in press). Group diversity's effects on sport teams and organizations: A meta-analysis. *European Sport Management Quarterly.*

Leonardelli, G. J., Pickett, C. L., & Brewer, M. B. (2010). Optimal distinctiveness theory: A framework for social identity, social cognition, and intergroup relations. *Advances in Experimental Social Psychology, 43*, 63–113.

Lewin, K. (1952). *Field theory in social science: Selected theoretical papers by Kurt Lewin* (p. 169). London: Tavistock.

Lillis, J., Thomas, J. G., Levin, M. E., & Wing, R. R. (in press). Self-stigma and weight loss: The impact of fear of being stigmatized. *Journal of Health Psychology.*

Lyras, A., & Welty Peachey, J. (2011). Integrating sport-for-development theory and praxis. *Sport Management Review, 14*, 311–326.

Major, B., & O'Brien, L. T. (2005). The social psychology of stigma. *Annual Review of Psychology, 56*, 393–421.

McCormack, M., & Anderson, E. (2014). The influence of declining homophobia on men's gender in the United

States: An argument for the study of homohysteria. *Sex Roles, 71*(3–4), 109–120.

Norton, A. T., & Herek, G. M. (2012). Heterosexuals' attitudes toward transgender people: Findings from a national probability sample of U.S. adults. *Sex Roles, 68,* 738–753.

Ormiston, M. E. (2016). Explaining the link between objective and perceived differences in groups: The role of the belonging and distinctiveness motives. *Journal of Applied Psychology, 101*(2), 222–236.

Pavlidis, A., & Fullagar, S. (2013). Narrating the multiplicity of 'Derby Grrrl': Exploring intersectionality and the dynamics of affect in Roller Derby. *Leisure Sciences, 35,* 422–437.

Peacock, M. (2014, July 14). Ian Thorpe's coming out raises questions about homosexuality and stigma in sport. *ABC.* Retrieved from www.abc.net. au/news/2014-07-14/thorpes-coming-out-sheds-light-on-gay-stigma-in-sport/5596482

Pelled, L. H. (1996). Demographic diversity, conflict, and work group outcomes: An intervening process theory. *Organization Science, 7,* 615–631.

Richard, O. C., Murthi, B. P. S., & Ismail, K. (2007). The impact of racial diversity on intermediate and long-term performance: The moderating role of environmental context. *Strategic Management Journal, 28,* 1213–1233.

Sage, G. H. (1998). *Power and ideology in American sport: A critical perspective* (2nd ed.). Champaign, IL: Human Kinetics.

Sage, G. H., & Eitzen, D. S. (2016). *Sociology of North American sport* (10th ed.). New York, NY: Oxford University Press.

Saito, L. (in press). Urban development and the growth with equity framework: The National Football League stadium in downtown Los Angeles. *Urban Affairs Review.*

Schulenkorf, N. (2017). Managing sport-for-development: Reflections and outlook. *Sport Management Review, 20*(3), 243–251.

Semega, J. L., Fontenot, K. R., & Kollar, M. A. (2017). *US Census Bureau, Current Population Reports, P60–259, Income and poverty in the United States: 2016.* Washington, DC: US Government Printing Office.

Shaw, S. (2016). Importance of theory in qualitative enquiry. In G. B. Cunningham, J. S., Fink, & A. Doherty (Eds.), *Routledge handbook of theory in sport management* (pp. 21–29). New York, NY: Routledge.

Skey, M., Stone, C., Jenzen, O., & Mangan, A. (2018). Mediatization and sport: A bottom-up perspective. *Communication & Sport, 6*(5), 588–604.

Summers, J. K., Howe, M., McElroy, J. C., Ronald Buckley, M., Pahng, P., & Cortes-Mejia, S. (2018). A typology of stigma within organizations: Access and treatment effects. *Journal of Organizational Behavior, 39,* 853–868.

Sveinson, K., & Hoeber, L. (2016). Female sport fans' experiences of marginalization and empowerment. *Journal of Sport Management, 30*(1), 8–21.

Svensson, P. G., & Woods, H. (2017). A systematic overview of sport for development and peace organizations. *Journal of Sport for Development, 5*(9), 36–48.

Sykes, H. (2006). Transsexual and transgender policies in sport. *Women in Sport and Physical Activity Journal, 15*(1), 3–13.

Tajfel, H., & Turner, J. C. (1979). An integrative theory of intergroup conflict. In W. G. Austin & S. Worchel (Eds.), *The social psychology of intergroup relations* (pp. 33–47). Monterey, CA: Brooks/Cole.

Thorpe, H. (2018). Feminist views of action sports. In L. Mansfield, J. Cauldwell,

B. Wheaton, & B. Watson (Eds.), *The Palgrave handbook of feminism and sport, leisure, and physical education* (pp. 669–719). London, UK: Palgrave Macmillan.

Turner, J., Hogg, M. A., Oakes, P. J., Reicher, S. D., & Wetherell, M. S. (1987). *Rediscovering the social group: A self-categorization theory.* Oxford, UK: B. Blackwell.

van Knippenberg, D., & Schippers, M. (2007). Work group diversity. *Annual Review of Psychology, 58,* 515–541.

van Knippenberg, D., Haslam, S. A., & Platow, M. J. (2007). Unity through diversity: Value-in-diversity beliefs, work group diversity, and group identification. *Group Dynamics: Theory, Research, and Practice, 11,* 207–222.

van Knippenberg, D., van Ginkel, W. P., & Homan, A. C. (2013). Diversity mindsets and the performance of diverse teams. *Organizational Behavior and Human Decision Processes, 121*(2), 183–193.

Watson, B., & Scraton, S. J. (2013). Leisure studies and intersectionality. *Leisure Studies, 32*(1), 35–47.

Wright, P. M., Dunford, B. B., & Snell, S. A. (2001). Human resources and the resource based view of the firm. *Journal of Management, 27*(6), 701–721.

Zhang, J. J., Kim, M., & Pifer, N. D. (2016). Importance of theory in quantitative enquiry. In G. B. Cunningham, J. S., Fink, & A. Doherty (Eds.), *Routledge handbook of theory in sport management* (pp. 9–20). New York, NY: Routledge.

Bias

3

LEARNING OBJECTIVES

After studying this chapter, you should be able to:

- List and define the different forms of bias, including stereotypes, prejudice, and discrimination.
- Summarize the theoretical underpinnings used to understand bias in sport.
- Paraphrase the outcomes of bias for individuals, groups, and organizations.

DIVERSITY CHALLENGE

Have you ever heard the saying that someone "throws like a girl?" The sentiments are usually meant as an insult, suggesting that one is not an athlete. An online search of "throws like a girl" reveals articles from *Popular Science*, a test from the US-based television show "Myth Busters," and various popular press articles where the authors discuss all sides of the topic. There is also a website titled "Throw Like a Girl" that sells athletic apparel for female athletes.

The stereotype of girls' inferior athletic performance relative to boys has a number of implications. First, it promotes the notion of consistent, inherent athletic differences between girls and boys. Second, and related to the first point, sport managers routinely organize athletic leagues in a sex-segregated fashion, even when the children are as young as five years.

How true is the notion that girls and boys throw differently or perform differently in athletic contests? According to Marnee McKay and Joshua Burns, both from the University of Sydney, not very. They tested hundreds of study participants, taking over 100 measurements of physical ability and performance. The authors found, "Across all measures of physical performance, there was one consistent finding. There was no statistical difference in the capabilities of girls and boys until high-school age (commonly age 12)."

Given their findings, McKay and Burns suggest boys and girls should play on mixed teams until age 12. After this change, hormonal differences resulting from puberty mean that the average boy is stronger and faster than the average girl. Making such changes would likely reduce scheduling conflicts, necessitate fewer teams and leagues to share private and public funds, and a merging of coaching and manager expertise. Finally, the changes would potentially influence boys' perceptions of girls' athletic prowess.

McKay and Burns suggest that gender stereotypes likely emerge at birth and are perpetuated and reproduced thereafter. They note, however, that "whatever the origin of the idea young boys are physically more capable than young girls, the evidence is clear. Boys 'play like a girl', and that's certainly no insult."

Sources: Fink, J. S., LaVoi, N. M., & Newhall, K. E. (2016). Challenging the gender binary? Male basketball practice players' views of female athletes and women's sports. *Sport in Society, 19*(8–9), 1316–1331. McKay, M., & Burns, J. (2017, August). When it comes to sport, boys 'play like a girl.' *The Conversation*. Retrieved from https://theconversation.com/when-it-comes-to-sport-boys-play-like-a-girl-80328.

Reflection

1. Have you heard these or other stereotypes concerning sports performance? What are some of the prevailing stereotypes in sport?
2. Why do stereotypes about girls' and boys' athletic performance persist, even though there is evidence to the contrary?
3. Given that the gender stereotypes related to athletic performance are not accurate, what changes, if any, would you make to sport leagues for children?

As the Diversity Challenge illustrates, a number of people experience stereotypes in sport. Other forms of bias persist as well, including prejudice and discrimination. The end result is that people who differ from the typical majority member have fewer opportunities to be active or pursue meaningful work in sport. When they do participate, their experiences are often poorer than those of their majority member counterparts. Bias does not just influence the target, though, as researchers have shown that people who express bias have shorter lives than those who do not. Teams, work groups, and organizations also suffer.

The purpose of this chapter is to explore bias—stereotypes, prejudice, and discrimination (Cuddy, Fiske, & Glick, 2008)—its theoretical underpinnings, and its impact on individuals, groups, and sport organizations. Stereotypes exist in the cognitive domain, prejudice is an affective reaction, and discrimination is behavioral in nature. Exhibit 3.1 offers an overview of the three components of bias.

Components of Bias	*exhibit* **3.1**

Stereotypes: Within the cognitive domain; represent the beliefs about the attributes, skills, and attitudes members of a certain group possess.

Prejudice: Within the affective domain; the differential evaluation of a group or an individual based on her or his group membership.

Discrimination: Within the behavioral domain; negative treatment of individuals due to their group membership.

STEREOTYPES

As Stangor (2009) explains, stereotypes represent "traits that we view as characteristics of social groups, or of individual members of those groups, and particularly those that differentiate groups from each other" (p. 2). The traits could be beliefs we have about people, attributes we assign to them, and skills common among them. Importantly, even people who are thought to belong to a specific group but who, in actuality, are not, also face stereotypes (Allport, 1954). Stereotypes are socially constructed and time bound, meaning that they are relevant to a specific setting or culture and can change over time.

Finally, similar to prejudice, stereotypes can take on implicit or explicit forms (Devine, 1989). Explicit stereotypes are those beliefs that people consciously maintain. For example, a hiring manager might believe that people who are overweight are lazy and unkempt (Grant & Mizzi, 2014). The manager might explicitly maintain these beliefs, irrespective of the specific overweight individual with whom she interacts. On the other hand, another sport manager might articulate positive views toward people who are overweight and their work—and thus, express low explicit stereotypes—but also hold implicit stereotypes. These represent beliefs that are not consciously maintained but are nevertheless expressed in subtle ways, and they are frequently better predictors of people's behaviors, such as hiring, than are self-report explicit beliefs (Agerström & Rooth, 2011). Researchers have shown, for example, that many leaders in the health and physical activity sector harbor implicit stereotypes toward people who are overweight or obese (Zestcott, Blair, & Stone, 2016).

Scholars most commonly draw from social psychological theories to explain stereotypes, and the stereotype content model (Cuddy et al., 2008; Fiske & Tablante, 2015) represents one example. According to this model, stereotypes exist along two domains: warmth and competence. People considered warm are thought to be trustworthy, fair, likeable, and friendly. Competence judgments capture perspectives related to people's confidence, intelligence, ability to execute tasks, and creativity. People then form opinions of groups based on these domains, as the targets can be high or low in each. The dual domains allow for what Cuddy et al. refer to as ambivalent stereotypes; for instance, one might consider group members as very warm but not competent, as is common among people who have mental disabilities (Fiske, 2015). Finally, though both are important, the warmth dimension is more prominent in shaping people's reactions to other individuals or groups (Fiske & Tablante, 2015).

Cuddy and colleagues (2009) conducted a large-scale study to examine the applicability of their model across cultures. They collected data from over a thousand participants in European and East Asian countries. The researchers found that people across cultures used warmth and competence to differentiate people in various groups. Across cultures, many people held the previously mentioned ambivalent stereotypes. In addition, people consider those with high status in a society as highly competent, but those with whom they are in competition are generally regarded as low in warmth. Finally, the authors un-covered an interesting pattern among individualistic countries and those that adopt collectivistic norms: in the former, people who are similar to the self generally have positive stereotypes (high warmth, high competence), but the pattern is not evident among people in the latter countries.

Some researchers have applied these ideas to understand the experiences of sport and exercise participants. Chalabaev and colleagues (2013), for example, suggested that many of the negative behaviors directed toward women in sport could stem from ambiguous stereotypes about them. They suggested that people might consider women as warm or likeable but not competent in sport, especially relative to men. By way of empirical support, researchers have shown that phys-ical educators associate masculinity with sport competence and femininity with warmth (Clément-Guillotin et al., 2013). As another example, Tiffany Wright and I examined the stereotypes toward people with disabilities and how they influ-enced their job prospects (Wright & Cunningham, 2017). Participants rated job applicants with disabilities as warmer than their able-bodied counterparts, but competence ratings did not vary. We also found that raters considered applicants to be a good fit for the workplace when they were considered both warm and competent.

Collectively, this research shows that stereotypes have a meaningful impact in sport. They can be explicit or implicit, and they shape beliefs about others, including perceptions of how suitable they are for various sport roles. Thus, ideas about who should be a point guard, coach, or marketing director can be shaped, at least in part, on stereotypes. Finally, whereas the focus of this dis-cussion has been on the stereotypes people have as others, researchers have also shown that the degree to which people feel or internalize stereotypes can shape their performance. Box 3.1 offers more information about this process, known as stereotype threat.

Box 3.1 Alternative Perspectives. Stereotype Threat

Social psychologist Claude Steele coined the term stereotype threat, which "arises when one is in a situation or doing something for which a negative stereotype about one group applies. The predicament threatens one with being negatively stereotyped, with being judged or treated stereotypically, or with the prospect of conforming to the stereotype" (Steele, 1997, p. 614). With a focus on educational attainment, Steele showed how negative stereotypes about women and racial minorities could serve as a threat to those individuals, negatively affecting their emotions and performance. If perpetuated over time, stereotype threat can result in people disengaging from a particular domain of interest. Thus, even among exceptionally talented individuals, stereotype threat can serve to impede performance and limit the desirability of certain academic tracks or professional fields.

Researchers have shown that stereotype threat is applicable in sport, too. For example, negative stereotypes exist about African Americans' intelligence and Whites' athletic performance. Stone and colleagues showed that stereotype threats in these areas can impede performance (Stone, Lynch, Sjomeling, & Darley, 1999). They found that African American study participants performed poorly when an athletic task was framed as a measure of sports intelligence. Whites, on the other hand, performed poorly when they understood the task to assess their natural athletic ability. Subsequent researchers have shown that stereotype threat can impede women's performance on difficult tasks, but not routine ones (Hively & El-Alayli, 2014), women's belief they can complete tasks (Heidrich & Chiviacowsky, 2015), and motor skill development among overweight exercisers (Cardozo & Chiviacowsky, 2015), among others. Importantly, researchers have also shown that reducing stereotype threat can offset the negative performance and mental effects (Huber, Brown, & Sternad, 2016).

PREJUDICE

Prejudice represents the second dimension of bias. Historically, scholars have considered prejudice as a negative attitude toward a group of people (Allport, 1954), and that position likely is consistent with how student think about the construct. More recently, though, researchers have shown the utility in considering prejudice as a differential evaluation of one group relative to another (Brewer, 2007). From this perspective, which Brewer termed relative positivity, it is possible to view a group favorably but still not as favorable as people who are similar to the self.

Let us consider a point to illustrate. Researchers have shown that some people harbor negative attitudes toward asylum seekers (Anderson, 2018). The topic is of relevance to sport managers because refugees commonly have physical and psychological health concerns (Hebebrand et al., 2016; Marquardt, Krämer,

exhibit   **3.2**   Traditional Prejudice and Relative Positivity

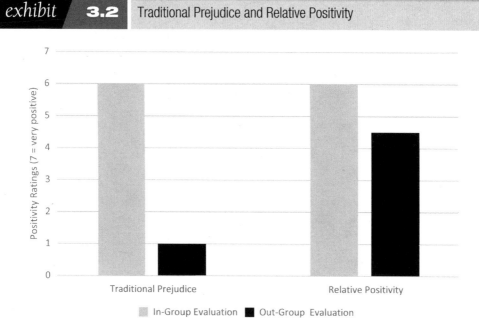

Fischer, & Prüfer-Kämper, 2016), and sport can play a role in helping to alleviate these conditions (Downward, Hallmann, & Rasciute, 2018; Woodhouse & Conricode, 2017). Adopting the traditional perspective, people express prejudice by having positive attitudes toward the in-group (citizens in our current example) and negative attitudes toward the out-group (asylum seekers in our current example). The left part of Exhibit 3.2 shows this pattern. On the other hand, from a relative positivity perspective, people might have positive attitudes toward citizens and asylum seekers. Ratings of citizens are simply more positive than those of asylum seekers. The right side Exhibit 3.2 shows this pattern.

Explicit and Implicit Prejudice

In addition, like stereotypes, prejudice can take implicit or explicit forms. Explicit prejudice represents attitudes that people consciously and deliberately maintain (Dovidio, Kawakami, & Beach, 2001). In this domain, people can articulate their attitudes toward different groups, whether positive or negative. Polling agencies, such as Pew Research Center, routinely ask Americans their attitudes about various topics and groups of people. As one example, the research agency asked participants about Americans living in poverty and how easy their lives were (Krogstad & Parker, 2014). They found that people were generally split when asked if poor people had hard lives or easy lives, and the household income of the respondent largely influenced the pattern of findings.

Explicit forms of prejudice represent a social construction. People's backgrounds, their cultural context, and the time in which they lived largely shape their attitudes. When a given society deems it permissible to express negative attitudes toward a group, people are likely to do so. In the American context, for example, the confluence of various values and norms makes it socially acceptable to express prejudice against some groups, such as child molesters and rapists, but not others, such as people with a disability (Crandall, Eshleman, & O'Brien, 2002). As we will discuss in the following section, prejudice is likely then to give rise to behaviors. Thus, housing options, voting rights, the ability to wed, employment opportunities, and access to sport all vary depending on the socially constructed acceptability of prejudice.

Experimental work I conducted with Ferreira and Fink offers a sport example (Cunningham, Ferreira, & Fink, 2009). Consistent with the material in the Diversity Challenge, we thought that sexism would be more commonly accepted in sport contexts than other forms of prejudice, such as racism; as a result, sexist comments (e.g., "Of course we lost. We played like a bunch of girls") might be viewed as more palatable than racist ones (e.g., "Of course we lost. The other team had more Black players than we do"). We conducted an experiment where college students responded to these comments, and we found support for our expectations. We also found that the demographics of the commenter influenced the reactions: racist comments made by a White person and sexist comments made by a man elicited the strongest aversion. We also asked people to write an explanation of why they responded as they did. Indicative of the deeply engrained belittlement of women in American culture, one participant wrote, "I think that saying that playing like a bunch of girls is not very offensive because girls' basketball is not even close to the level that men's basketball is, even though it is sexist I do not find it offensive" (p. 68).

In addition to explicit prejudice, people can express implicit prejudice. Implicit attitudes are elicited when there is a match between an external stimulus and the individual's association set that links the stimulus with various attributions (Blair, Dasgupta, & Glaser, 2015; Dovidio, Kawakami, & Gaertner, 2002). These reactions are automatic and do not require deliberate thought on the part of the actor. Implicit attitudes also operate independently of what Blair and colleagues call "perceived truth value" (p. 666); that is, the associations can be triggered even when the individual does not believe them to be accurate. People hold implicit attitudes toward a variety of stimuli, such as different sodas or political candidates, but for our purposes we focus on attitudes toward social groups. In this case, we refer to the attitudes as *implicit prejudice*.

A number of factors influence people's implicit attitudes, including societal factors and lived experiences. In fact, Devine, Forscher, Austin, and Cox (2012) suggested that implicit attitudes are similar to a learned habit, and thus, interventions aimed at decreasing bias are similar to those used to break bad habits. Although environmental factors do play a role, there is also evidence that infants demonstrate an automatic preference for others who are similar to themselves (Wolf, Maio, Karremans, & Leygue, 2017).

Though they both focus on prejudice, implicit and explicit attitudes are not always related (Dovidio et al., 2002). This disconnect helps explain why some people think of themselves as fair-minded and holding egalitarian attitudes, yet still express implicit prejudice. The automated responses germane to implicit prejudice are most likely to manifest when social forces are weak, such as when individuals are presented with ambiguous information (Son Hing, Chung-Yan, Hamilton, & Zanna, 2008). Note that these are the very situations in which sport managers find themselves on a routine basis. Leading involves making decisions when the information is messy, complex, ambiguous, and oftentimes equivocal (Bolman & Deal, 2017). Understanding the nature of bias and leadership helps managers plan and develop checks that might alleviate the effects of implicit biases.

As an example, Ottoboni and colleagues (2017) examined people's implicit attitudes toward persons with a disability. They were also interested in understanding if being around people with a disability helped reduce implicit prejudice. They collected data from 161 Italian school children aged 10–12. The research team collected data at the beginning of the year (October) and then again at the end (May). Consistent with the patterns previously discussed, there was no association between implicit and explicit forms of prejudice toward people with disabilities. The researchers found that being around people with disabilities throughout the school year helped reduce implicit bias (but not explicit bias). The pattern was especially strong when the interactions occurred in a sport context, as opposed to in the classroom. Ottoboni et al. (2017) attributed the changes to the nature of sport, the interdependence among the players, and the necessity of collaboration in order to be successful.

DISCRIMINATION

Discrimination represents the final element of bias. Allport (1954) considered discrimination as a behavior that "comes about only when we deny to individuals or groups of people equality of treatment" (p. 51). More recently, scholars have defined the construct as "unfair treatment of different categories of people" (Assari, Moazen-Zadeh, Caldwell, & Zimmerman, 2017, p. 1), or "the desire to treat two groups differently based on social identity or the harm caused by doing so" (Simon, Moss, & O'Brien, in press). These definitions highlight several key points. First, whereas stereotypes focus on cognitions and prejudice reflects an attitude, discrimination is behavioral in nature. Second, discrimination is concerned with the unfair treatment of people based on their group membership, whether that membership is actual or perceived.

Theoretically, both sociological and social psychological theories help to explain discrimination. From a social psychological perspective, people are likely to classify themselves and others into groups. People who are similar to the self are in-group members, and those who are different are out-group members. All else equal, people are likely to treat in-group members more favorably than they do out-group members (Dovidio, Gaertner, & Pearson, 2017). From this perspective, discrimination is an interpersonal phenomenon. Sociological theories, however, point to societal explanations for discrimination. Major institutions, including religion, housing, education, and the justice system, among others, are situated in ways that privilege those with power and resources, and subjugate others. Thus, from a sociological perspective, even absent individual bias, discrimination would persist because it deeply engrained into society's fabric. It is the institutional form of discrimination, for example, that makes evictions common in American, especially among those most vulnerable (Desmond, 2016).

My experiences and research suggest that, theoretically, a discussion of either-or misses the point; instead, both-and is more applicable. That is, discrimination is a function of *both* interpersonal relations *and* systems that perpetuate inequalities.

Access and Treatment Discrimination

Researchers have differentiated between two types of discrimination: access and treatment (Greenhaus, Parasuraman, & Wormley, 1990). People who face access discrimination are denied the opportunity to pursue a course of action relevant to them. That action might include an educational path, sport choice, or a particular career interest. For example, in 2017 in the US, Latinos represented about 18 percent of the total population (https://www.census.gov/quickfacts/fact/table/US/RHI725217) but only 5 percent of all athletes participating in National Collegiate Athletic Association sports (National Collegiate Athletic Association, 2017). These figures exist despite Nielson data showing that 94 percent of Latino men consider themselves sport fans, and over half consider themselves diehard fans (Huddle Up, 2013). There could be a number of reasons for this disconnect, including limited access to participate in sport (Vidal, 2016). We can see similar patterns elsewhere. In Germany, for example, women constitute 51 percent of the population but only 12 percent of executive board members (Sullivan, 2018). The figures are better, albeit marginally, for women in the sport context, where they routinely represent fewer than 20 percent of all board members of German sport clubs (Pfister & Radtke, 2009). As a final example, Australian adults living in rural communities face some of the same barriers as persons living in urban areas (e.g., family commitments); however, they also experience constraints unique to the rural setting, such as geographic climate and systemic norms that do not value exercise (Eley, Bush, & Brown, 2014).

Box 3.2 offers another example of how some groups have limited access to sport.

Whereas access discrimination denies people the opportunity to join a sport organization or be physically active, treatment discrimination occurs within an organization or in the course of an activity. In this case, individuals or members of a particular group have differential access to resources, experience negative behaviors directed toward them, or are afforded fewer chances for growth than they deserve (Greenhaus et al., 1990). Researchers have shown that treatment discrimination in the workplace has decreased over time but still persists (McCord, Joseph, Dhanani, & Beus, 2018). The types of mistreatment also vary based on diversity form. For example, women are more likely to experience sex-based discrimination than are men, and racial minorities more likely than Whites to

Box 3.2 Diversity in the Field. First-Generation College Students and Sport Participation

Sport is commonly seen as the great equalizer. Many have heard stories of players who came from poverty only to achieve fame and fortune through their sports participation. In other cases, college athletics are cast as activities that offer athletes the chance to earn a college degree and climb the social ladder.

For its part, the National Collegiate Athletic Association promotes this storyline. During basketball tournaments each spring, the organization runs commercials highlighting athletes who come from disadvantaged backgrounds.

Despite these narratives, the facts paint a different picture. Tom Farrey and Paul Schreiber showed that fewer than one in five college basketball players are the first in their family to go to college. When looking at all college sports, the figures drop to one in seven.

Further analysis of the data shows the number is dropping. The biggest declines are observed in sports that have traditionally had a number of first-generation students. These include men's and women's basketball and football.

How do these figures compare with college students, overall? Interestingly, college athletes are less likely than their peers on campus to be first-generation students. Put another way, college athletes are more likely than the average college student to come from an advantaged background.

Farrey and Schreiber point to several potential causes for this trend. They include rising academic standards, the increased cost of youth sport activities, and a growing Black middle class that can afford the high costs of youth sport.

In all, Farrey and Schreiber's analysis shows that, increasingly, sports are for people who have means and come from educated households. What was once an activity for all is increasingly one that excludes certain people, including those from first-generation households.

Source: Farrey and Schreiber (2017).

encounter race-based mistreatment. When it comes to more generalized forms of poor treatment, though, the between-group differences are reduced.

Researchers have also identified treatment discrimination among sport organization employees and among sport participants. Norman (2010) interviewed women who coached men's and women's teams in the UK. Many of the participants noted they felt their accomplishments were trivialized and devalued, and they also reported fewer development opportunities, relative to men in the profession. The coaches also noted that structures and norms related to heterosexuality contributed to their feelings of marginalization. In the sport and physical activity context, Edwards and I examined the physical activity among older racial minority adults living in the US (Edwards & Cunningham, 2013). We found that when

Box 3.3 Professional Perspectives. Adidas and the Promotion of Inclusive Sport

Discrimination is common across many areas of sport. There are examples, however, of cases where sport organizations took a stand against such practices. Adidas offers one such case.

In 2015, Adidas America joined the Human Rights Campaign and other corporate partners to oppose discrimination against lesbian, gay, bisexual, and transgender (LGBT) individuals. A statement from the company read:

> Sports are a platform for fairness and mutual respect.... adidas has a firm stance and commitment to fostering an inclusive, diverse workplace in America and around the world. We condemn laws

that could lead to discrimination toward our employees, business partners, athletes and anybody in the adidas LGBTQ family. We'll continue our dedicated work with the Human Rights Campaign and our business partners to promote an accepting and diverse world.

The statement was not the first time Adidas promoted equality. In 2013, the global sport organization endorsed same-sex marriage in Oregon.

This example is one of many where sport organizations and sport leaders use sport as a platform to oppose bias and champion more inclusive communities for all persons.

Source: Miller (2015, April).

community racism was low, they found ways to be active, even if there were few opportunities available. On the other hand, when community racism was high, the lack of opportunities significantly impeded how active they were. The activity levels were important, as they were a key contributor to the adults' subjective health (see also Richman, Pascoe, & Lattanner, 2018).

Recognizing the harmful effects of discrimination, sport organizations executives frequently speak out against such mistreatment. Box 3.3 offers one such example.

OUTCOMES OF BIAS

People who experience bias are likely to have corresponding decreases in their physical and psychological health, and undesirable behaviors. Although the discussions center around the specific targets of bias, it is important to remember that observing mistreatment of others negatively affects the individual (Benavides-Espinoza & Cunningham, 2010) and groups as a whole (Miner-Rubino & Cortina, 2007). Thus, bias has the potential to influence all who experience it, whether directly or indirectly.

Physical Health

Researchers have consistently shown that members of underrepresented groups experience more physical health problems than do their peers. According to Healt-hyPeople.gov, a number of diversity dimensions are associated with physical health and well-being, including race, gender, sexual orientation, gender identity and expression, social class, and geographic location. The differences in health are due to a number of factors, including stereotypes, prejudice, and discrimination (Bourgois, Holmes, Sue, & Quesada, 2017). Researchers commonly refer to these patterns as health disparities, or "systematic, plausibly avoidable health differences adversely affecting socially disadvantaged groups" (Braveman et al., 2011, p. S149).

To illustrate, O'Keefe, Meltzer, and Bethea (2015) analyzed cancer-related disease in the US data between 2000 and 2010. Across the timespan, there was a significant decrease in cancer mortality rates by gender and race. A number of factors contributed to the improved rates, such as fewer people smoking, better cancer screening, and effective cancer treatments. Further analyses, however, show that the decreases in cancer mortality were not uniform. The authors found that, when adjusting for age, Black women and men have higher cancer mortality rates and shorter survivals than do their White counterparts. In discussing their results, the authors noted that health-care coverage can certainly help reduce these differences; however, even with better coverage, economic, educational, and social biases will continue to adversely affect marginalized groups.

Importantly, the negative effects of bias on physical health are not limited to one's race. People who face discrimination based on their age, weight, physical ability, appearance, HIV status, and sexual orientation, among other diversity forms, are all likely to experience negative physical health outcomes (Logie et al., 2018; Sutin, Stephan, Carretta, & Terracciano, 2015).

Finally, much of the attention on bias and physical health focuses on those who experience stereotypes, prejudice, and discrimination, and rightly so. There is also evidence, though, that bias negatively affects those who express it. Hatzenbuehler, Bellatorre, and Muennig (2014) collected data from various large-scale, national surveys so that they were able to link the responses to the survey with mortality data by cause of death. For example, if a person completed the questionnaire in 1980, the researchers examined the person's responses and linked them with other data that showed whether the person was alive or dead by 2008. They also collected other data that could account for death rates, such as age, race, marital status, nationality, gender, income, education, and self-reported health. The researchers found that, even after statistically controlling for the other variables, LGBT prejudice impacted all-cause mortality (i.e., whether a person died or not). People who expressed high levels of prejudice lived 2.5 years less than those who expressed low levels of prejudice. These findings are consistent with earlier research showing that Whites with high levels of racial prejudice died sooner than their less prejudiced counterparts (Lee, Mueening, & Kawachi, 2012). The authors concluded, "The deleterious health consequences of prejudice are not merely confined to minority group members, but may also result in increased mortality risk for majority group members" (p. 335).

Psychological Health

Bias is also likely to negatively influence one's psychological health. These effects arise from what researchers call minority stress (Meyer, 2003). From this perspective, all people have general stressors in their lives, but minorities have stressors in addition to those that others experience. These stressors are continuous in nature because they are recurrent in the systems within a given society. Finally, the stressors are not caused by the individual—that is, there is not something wrong with the individual; instead, the stressors result from the social systems and structures that produce and reproduce the biases minorities experience.

A number of researchers have conducted large-scale analyses including thousands of participants (Lewis, Cogburn, & Williams, 2015; Paradies et al., 2015; Schmitt, Branscombe, Postmes, & Garcia, 2014). The results consistently demonstrate that experiences with mistreatment are negatively associated with one's psychological well-being. Mistreatment increases the prevalence of negative psychological outcomes, such as anxiety and depression, and reduces positive outcomes, such as positive self-concept and satisfaction. In some cases, the effects remain over a number of years such that experiences with discrimination predict anxiety and depression a decade later (Assari et al., 2017).

A number of scholars have documented these very patterns in sport. Symons, O'Sullivan, and Polman (2017) examined sexist and homophobic language in Australian sports, analyzing data from hundreds of survey respondents. Participants reported various experiences with mistreatment: women encountered sexism and homophobia, and men told of more homophobic episodes. The participants also noted negative psychological effects of bias, including sadness, shame, anger, withdrawal, and a dislike of sport. As another example, Gearity and Metzger (2017) used short stories to illustrate the negative effects of biases on coaches and players. They showed how subtle slights and rude behaviors could result in distress and frustration for sport coaches, as well as anger, anxiety, depression, and a lack of autonomy for players.

Behavioral Outcomes

Finally, bias can have a negative impact on people's behaviors. At the extreme end, there is consistent evidence that people who face continual interpersonal and institutional discrimination have higher rates of suicidality than do their peers (Seelman, 2016). On the other hand, when states and municipalities shift to more inclusive policies and laws, suicide rates decrease. Thus, the environment of diversity and inclusion can have life and death consequences.

Bias can also influence sport participation in sport and access to sport organizations. For example, Hargie, Mitchell, and Somerville (2017) collected data from transgender athletes. The participants noted that, due to their experiences with bias and abuse, they experienced fear in sport and sometimes avoided physical activity. From an employment standpoint, people who face access discrimination have limited access to positions. The end result is fewer people from underrepresented groups in higher levels of the organization, including management and key coaching positions (Burton & Leberman, 2017). Over time, the culture of exclusion becomes reinforced such that those who face bias may not seek leadership roles (Machida-Kosuga, Schaubroeck, Gould, Ewing, & Feltz, 2017). Importantly, differences in career advancement aspirations are a function of the continued stereotypes, prejudice, and discrimination people experience—not something inherent in the individual (Sartore & Cunningham, 2007).

Finally, bias can negatively affect people's performance. Facing bias at work can increase work stressors, which consequently, reduce attention to work and overall productivity (O'Brien, McAbee, Hebl, & Rodgers, 2016; Schat & Frone, 2011). As an example, I conducted interviews with leaders of US sport organizations concerning diversity and inclusion (Cunningham, 2015). The experts noted that, absent an inclusive environment, employees are concerned about managing their identities in the workplace, and this process necessarily takes away from their work. However, when people from underrepresented groups work in inclusive spaces, they can bring their authentic, whole selves to work. The complete focus on work allows for creativity and enhanced productivity.

CHAPTER SUMMARY

The focus of this chapter was on bias and its three components: stereotypes, prejudice, and discrimination. As illustrated in the Diversity Challenge, bias is still prevalent in the context of sport and physical activity. It influences the opportunities people have, how others think about them, their experiences in sport and physical activity, and the choices they make about their future. Having read this chapter, you should be able to:

1. List and define the different forms of bias, including stereotypes, prejudice, and discrimination.

   Bias is reflected in cognitive, affective, and behavioral forms. Stereotypes represent beliefs about the attributes, skills, and attitudes members of a particular group possess. Prejudice is an affective component of bias and represents the differential evaluation of a group or an individual based on group membership. Finally, discrimination exists in the behavioral domain and represents the negative treatment of individuals because of their group membership.

2. Summarize the theoretical underpinnings used to understand bias in sport.

   Scholars have used various theories to explain bias. The stereotype content model holds that stereotypes exist along two domains: warmth and competence. Social psychological theories help to explain prejudice, in terms of both the content (whether based on negative evaluations or relative positivity) and the nature (explicit or implicit). Finally, sociological theories and social psychological theories help explain why people are denied access to sport and sport organizations, as well as why they are treated differently in those contexts.

3. Paraphrase the outcomes of bias for individuals, groups, and organizations.

Bias is associated with three types of outcomes. The first is physiological, including physical health and well-being. The second is psychological, including depression, anxiety, and life satisfaction. Finally, behavioral outcomes of bias include behavioral health outcomes, access to sport and career choices, and performance at work.

Questions FOR DISCUSSION

1. How do stereotypes affect people's participation in sport and physical activity?
2. Think about different groups and how they might map on the stereotype content model. How would you go about deflecting or rebutting some of these stereotypical perceptions?
3. What are the major differences between explicit and implicit forms of bias? What are the examples of each?
4. Which form of prejudicial attitude is most prevalent in sport today? Are some sectors of sport and physical activity more likely to see certain types of prejudice than others? Why do you think this is the case?
5. Using a sociological and a social psychological lens, identify the factors that contribute to discrimination in sport.
6. What are the major distinctions between access and treatment discrimination?

LEARNING Activities

1. Visit the Project Implicit website (https://implicit.harvard.edu/implicit/) and test your implicit attitudes toward various targets (e.g., age, race, disability).
2. Look online for recent examples of discrimination and prejudice in the context of sport and physical activity. Based on your discoveries, which group or groups are most likely to face discrimination?

Web RESOURCES

Play by the Rules
    An Australian-based organization that focuses on race-based inclusion and ways to promote it.

Institute for Diversity and Ethics in Sport, www.tidesport.org
    Provides reports concerning diversity and discrimination in university athletics and professional sport settings.

Project Implicit, https://implicit.harvard.edu/implicit/
    Provides an electronic demonstration of how to test for implicit attitudes.

READING Resources

Dovidio, J. F., Glick, P., & Budman, L. A. (Eds.). (2005). *On the nature of prejudice: Fifty years after Allport.* Malden, MA: Blackwell.

An edited collection of essays from the leading social psychologists in the field; focuses on the contributions of Allport's original work related to prejudice; provides updates to the theory and directions for future inquiry.

Kite, M. E., & Whitley, B. E., Jr. (2016). *Psychology of prejudice and discrimination* (3rd ed). New York, NY: Routledge.

The third edition of a text that focuses on the social psychology of prejudice and discrimination.

Healy, J. F., Stepnick, A., & O'Brien, E. (2018). *Race, ethnicity, gender, and class: The sociology of group conflict and change.* Los Angeles, CA: Sage.

The eighth edition of a text in which the authors use sociological theory to examine race, gender, and class in society.

REFERENCES

Agerström, J., & Rooth, D. O. (2011). The role of automatic obesity stereotypes in real hiring discrimination. *Journal of Applied Psychology, 96*(4), 790–805.

Allport, G. W. (1954). *The nature of prejudice.* Cambridge, MA: Addison-Wesley.

Anderson, J. R. (2018). The prejudice against asylum seekers scale: Presenting the psychometric properties of a new measure of classical and conditional attitudes. *The Journal of Social Psychology, 58*(6), 694–710.

Assari, S., Moazen-Zadeh, E., Caldwell, C. H., & Zimmerman, M. A. (2017). Racial discrimination during adolescence predicts mental health deterioration in adulthood: Gender differences among Blacks. *Frontiers in Public Health, 5* (104), 1–10.

Benavides-Espinoza, C., & Cunningham, G. B. (2010). Bystanders' reactions to sexual harassment. *Sex Roles, 63*(3–4), 201–213.

Blair, I. V., Dasgupta, N., & Glaser, J. (2015). Implicit attitudes. In M. Mikulincer & P. R. Shaver (Eds.), *APA handbook of personality and social psychology* (vol. 1, pp. 665–691). Washington, DC: American Psychological Association.

Bolman, L. G., & Deal, T. E. (2017). *Reframing organizations: Artistry, choice, and leadership* (6th ed.). San Francisco, CA: Jossey-Bass.

Bourgois, P., Holmes, S. M., Sue, K., & Quesada, J. (2017). Structural vulnerability: Operationalizing the concept to address health disparities in clinical care. *Academic Medicine, 92*(3), 299–307.

Braveman, P. A., Kumanyika, S., Fielding, J., LaVeist, T., Borrell, L. N., Manderscheid, R., & Troutman, A. (2011). Health disparities and health equity: The issue is justice. *American Journal of Public Health, 101*(S1), S149–S155.

Brewer, M. B. (2007). The importance of being we: Human nature and intergroup relations. *The American Psychologist, 62*(8), 726–738.

Burton, L. J., & Leberman, S. (Eds.) (2017). *Women in sport leadership: Research and practice for change.* New York, NY: Routledge.

Cardozo, P. L., & Chiviacowsky, S. (2015). Overweight stereotype threat negatively impacts the learning of a balance task. *Journal of Motor Learning and Development, 3*(2), 140–150.

Chalabaev, A., Sarrazin, P., Fontayne, P., Boiché, J., & Clément-Guillotin, C. (2013). The influence of sex stereotypes and gender roles on participation and performance in sport and exercise: Review and future directions. *Psychology of Sport and Exercise, 14*(2), 136–144.

Clément-Guillotin, C., Cambon, L., Chalabaev, A., Radel, R., Michel, S., & Fontayne, P. (2013). Social value and asymmetry of gender and sex categories in physical education. *Revue Européenne de Psychologie Appliquée/European Review of Applied Psychology, 63*(2), 75–85.

Crandall, C. S., Eshleman, A., & O'Brien, L. (2002). Social norms and the expression and suppression of prejudice: The struggle for internalization. *Journal of Personality and Social Psychology, 82,* 359–378.

Cuddy, A. J., Fiske, S. T., & Glick, P. (2008). Warmth and competence as universal dimensions of social perception: The stereotype content model and the BIAS map. *Advances in Experimental Social Psychology, 40,* 61–149.

Cuddy, A. J., Fiske, S. T., Kwan, V. S., Glick, P., Demoulin, S., Leyens, J. P., … Htun, T. T. (2009). Stereotype content model across cultures: Towards universal similarities and some differences. *British Journal of Social Psychology, 48*(1), 1–33.

Cunningham, G. B. (2015). Creating and sustaining workplace cultures supportive of LGBT employees in college athletics. *Journal of Sport Management, 29*(4), 426–442.

Cunningham, G. B., Ferreira, M., & Fink, J. S. (2009). Reactions to prejudicial statements: The influence of statement content and characteristics of the commenter. *Group Dynamics: Theory, Research, & Practice, 13,* 59–73.

Desmond, M. (2016). *Evicted: Poverty and profit in the American city.* New York, NY: Broadway Books.

Devine, P. G. (1989). Stereotypes and prejudice: Their automatic and controlled components. *Journal of Personality and Social Psychology, 56,* 680–690.

Devine, P. G., Forscher, P. S., Austin, A. J., & Cox, W. T. (2012). Long-term reduction in implicit race bias: A prejudice habit-breaking intervention. *Journal of Experimental Social Psychology, 48*(6), 1267–1278.

Dovidio, J. F., Gaertner, S. L., & Pearson, A. R. (2017). Aversive racism and contemporary bias. In C. G. Sibley & F. K. Barlow (Eds.), *The Cambridge handbook of the psychology of prejudice* (pp. 267–294). Cambridge, UK: Cambridge University Press.

Dovidio, J. F., Kawakami, K., & Beach, K. (2001). Implicit and explicit attitudes: Examination of the relationship between measures of inter-group bias. In R. Brown & S. L. Gaertner (Eds.), *Blackwell handbook of social psychology: Intergroup processes* (pp. 175–197). Oxford, UK: Blackwell.

Dovidio, J. F., Kawakami, K., & Gaertner, S. L. (2002). Implicit and explicit prejudice and interracial interaction. *Journal of Personality and Social Psychology, 82*(1), 62–68.

Downward, P., Hallmann, K., & Rasciute, S. (2018). Exploring the interrelationship between sport, health and social outcomes in the UK: Implications for health policy. *European Journal of Public Health, 28*(1), 99–104. doi:10.1093/eurpub/ckx063

Edwards, M. B., & Cunningham, G. (2013). Examining the associations of perceived community racism with self-reported physical activity levels and health among older racial minority adults. *Journal of Physical Activity and Health, 10*(7), 932–939.

Eley, R., Bush, R., & Brown, W. (2014). Opportunities, barriers, and constraints to physical activity in rural Queensland, Australia. *Journal of Physical Activity and Health, 11,* 68–75.

Farrey, T., & Schreiber, P. (2017). The gentrification of college hoops. *The Undefeated.* Retrieved from https://theundefeated.com/features/gentrification-of-ncaa-division-1-college-basketball/

Fiske, S. T. (2015). Intergroup biases: A focus on stereotype content. *Current Opinion in Behavioral Sciences, 3,* 45–50.

Fiske, S., & Tablante, C. (2015). Stereotyping: Processes and content. In M. Mikulincer, P. Shaver, E. Borgida & J. Bargh (Eds.), *APA handbook of personality and social psychology, Vol. 1: Attitudes and social cognition* (pp. 457–507). Washington, DC: American Psychological Association.

Gearity, B. T., & Metzger, L. H. (2017). Intersectionality, microaggressions, and microaffirmations: Toward a cultural praxis of sport coaching. *Sociology of Sport Journal, 34*(2), 160–175.

Grant, S., & Mizzi, T. (2014). Body weight bias in hiring decisions: Identifying explanatory mechanisms. *Social Behavior and Personality: An International Journal, 42*(3), 353–370.

Greenhaus, J. H., Parasuraman, S., & Wormley, W. M. (1990). Effects of race on organizational experiences, job performance, evaluations, and career outcomes. *Academy of Management Journal, 33,* 64–86.

Hargie, O. D., Mitchell, D. H., & Somerville, I. J. (2017). 'People have a knack of making you feel excluded if they catch on to your difference': Transgender experiences of exclusion in sport. *International Review for the Sociology of Sport, 52*(2), 223–239.

Hatzenbuehler, M. L., Bellatorre, A., & Muennig, P. (2014). Anti-gay prejudice and all-cause mortality among heterosexuals in the United States. *American Journal of Public Health, 104,* 332–337.

Hebebrand, J., Anagnostopoulos, D., Eliez, S., Linse, H., Pejovic-Milovanevic, M., & Klasen, H. (2016). A first assessment of the needs of young refugees arriving in Europe: What mental health professionals need to know. *European Child & Adolescent Psychiatry, 25,* 1–6.

Heidrich, C., & Chiviacowsky, S. (2015). Stereotype threat affects the learning of sport motor skills. *Psychology of Sport and Exercise, 18,* 42–46.

Hively, K., & El-Alayli, A. (2014). "You throw like a girl:" The effect of stereotype threat on women's athletic performance and gender stereotypes. *Psychology of Sport and Exercise, 15*(1), 48–55.

Huber, M. E., Brown, A. J., & Sternad, D. (2016). Girls can play ball: Stereotype threat reduces variability in a motor skill. *Acta Psychologica, 169,* 79–87.

Huddle Up: US Hispanics could be a boon for nets, leagues, and advertisers. (2013, October). *Nielson.* Retrieved from http://www.nielson.com/us/en/insights/news/2013/huddle-up-u-s-hispanics-could-be-a-boon-for-nets-leagues-and.html?wgu=12765_54264_15297040848838_d0b62f4f57&wgexpiry=1537480084&afflt=ntrt15340001&afflt_uid=tGBCg2AtNhE.8wEmWzldm_2HbEWwTz-0YupIvgCkfjMO&afflt_uid_2=AFFLT_ID_2

Krogstad, J. M., & Parker, K. (2014, February). Public is sharply divided in views of Americans in poverty. *Pew Research Center.* Retrieved from http://www.pewresearch.org/fact-tank/2014/09/16/public-is-sharply-divided-in-views-of-americans-in-poverty/

Lee, Y. J., Mueening, P., & Kawachi, I. (2012, May). *Do racist attitudes harm community health including both Blacks and Whites?* Paper presented at the annual meeting of the Population Association of America, San Francisco, CA.

Lewis, T. T., Cogburn, C. D., & Williams, D. R. (2015). Self-reported experiences of discrimination and health: Scientific advances, ongoing controversies, and emerging issues. *Annual Review of Clinical Psychology, 11*, 407–440.

Logie, C. H., Wang, Y., Lacombe-Duncan, A., Wagner, A. C., Kaida, A., Conway, T., ... Loutfy, M. R. (2018). HIV-related stigma, racial discrimination, and gender discrimination: Pathways to physical and mental health-related quality of life among a national cohort of women living with HIV. *Preventive Medicine, 107*, 36–44.

Machida-Kosuga, M., Schaubroeck, J. M., Gould, D., Ewing, M., & Feltz, D. L. (2017). What Influences collegiate coaches' intentions to advance their leadership careers? The roles of leader self-efficacy and outcome expectancies. *International Sport Coaching Journal, 4*(3), 265–278.

Marquardt, L., Krämer, A., Fischer, F., & Prüfer-Krämer, L. (2016). Health status and disease burden of unaccompanied asylum-seeking adolescents in Bielefeld, Germany: Cross-sectional pilot study. *Tropical Medicine and International Health, 21*(2), 210–218.

McCord, M. A., Joseph, D. L., Dhanani, L. Y., & Beus, J. M. (2018). A meta-analysis of sex and race differences in perceived workplace mistreatment. *Journal of Applied Psychology, 103*, 137–163.

Meyer, I. H. (2003). Prejudice, social stress, and mental health in lesbian, gay, and bisexual populations: Conceptual issues and research evidence. *Psychological Bulletin, 129*, 674–697.

Miller, H. (2015, April). Exclusive: Adidas America take stand against discrimination; speaks up for inclusive workplace. *Human Rights Campaign.* Retrieved from https://www.hrc.org/blog/exclusive-adidas-america-takes-stand-against-discriminationspeaks-up-for-i

Miner-Rubino, K., & Cortina, L. M. (2007). Beyond targets: Consequences of vicarious exposure to misogyny at work. *Journal of Applied Psychology, 92*(5), 1254–1269.

National Collegiate Athletic Association. (2017). Sport sponsorship, participation and demographics Search [Data file]. Retrieved from http://web1.ncaa.org/rgdSearch/exec/main

Norman, L. (2010). Feeling second best: Elite women coaches' experiences. *Sociology of Sport Journal, 27*(1), 89–104.

O'Brien, K. R., McAbee, S. T., Hebl, M. R., & Rodgers, J. R. (2016). The impact of interpersonal discrimination and stress on health and performance for early career STEM academicians. *Frontiers in Psychology, 7*, 615.

O'Keefe, E. B., Meltzer, J. P., & Bethea, T. N. (2015). Health disparities and cancer: Racial disparities in cancer mortality in the United States, 2000–2010. *Frontiers in Public Health, 3*(51).

Ottoboni, G., Milani, M., Setti, A., Ceciliani, A., Chattat, R., & Tessari, A. (2017). An observational study on sport-induced modulation of negative attitude towards disability. *PloS one, 12*(11), e0187043.

Paradies, Y., Ben, J., Denson, N., Elias, A., Priest, N., Pieterse, A., ... Gee, G. (2015). Racism as a determinant of health: A systematic review and meta-analysis. *PloS One, 10*(9), e0138511.

Pfister, G., & Radtke, S. (2009). Sport, women, and leadership: Results of a project on executives in German sports organizations. *European Journal of Sport Science, 9*(4), 229–243.

Richman, L. S., Pascoe, E. A., & Lattanner, M. (2018). Interpersonal discrimination and physical health. In B. Major, J. F. Dovido, & B. G. Link (Eds.), *Handbook of stigma, discrimination, and health* (pp. 203–218). New York, NY: Oxford University Press.

Sartore, M. L., & Cunningham, G. B. (2007). Explaining the under-representation of women in leadership positions of sport organizations: A symbolic interactionist perspective. *Quest, 59*(2), 244–265.

Schat, A. C. H., & Frone, M. R. (2011). Exposure to psychological aggression at work and job performance: The mediating role of job attitudes and personal health. *Work Stress, 25*, 23–40.

Schmitt, M. T., Branscombe, N. R., Postmes, T., & Garcia, A. (2014). The consequences of perceived discrimination for psychological well-being: A meta-analytic review. *Psychological Bulletin, 140*(4), 921–948.

Seelman, K. L. (2016). Transgender adults' access to college bathrooms and housing and the relationship to suicidality. *Journal of Homosexuality, 63*(10), 1378–1399.

Simon, S., Moss, A. J., & O'Brien, L. T. (in press). Pick your perspective: Racial group membership and judgments of intent, harm, and discrimination. *Group Processes & Intergroup Relations*.

Son Hing, L. S., Chung-Yan, G. A., Hamilton, L. K., & Zanna, M. P. (2008). A two-dimensional model that employs explicit and implicit attitudes to characterize prejudice. *Journal of Personality and Social Psychology, 94*, 971–987.

Stangor, C. (2009). The study of stereotyping, prejudice, and discrimination within social psychology: A quick history of theory and research. In T. D. Nelson (Ed.), *Handbook of prejudice, stereotyping, and discrimination* (pp. 1–23). New York, NY: Psychology Press.

Steele, C. M. (1997). A threat in the air: How stereotypes shape intellectual identity and performance. *American Psychologist, 52*(6), 613–629.

Stone, J., Sjomeling, M., Lynch, C. I., & Darley, J. M. (1999). Stereotype threat effects on black and white athletic performance. *Journal of Personality and Social Psychology, 77*(6), 1213–1227.

Sullivan, A. (2018, April). Report highlights the lack of female leaders in German business. DW.com. Retrieved online from: http://www.dw.com/en/report-highlights-lack-of-female-leaders-in-german-business/a-43747520

Sutin, A. R., Stephan, Y., Carretta, H., & Terracciano, A. (2015). Perceived discrimination and physical, cognitive, and emotional health in older adulthood. *The American Journal of Geriatric Psychiatry, 23*(2), 171–179.

Symons, C. M., O'Sullivan, G. A., & Polman, R. (2017). The impacts of discriminatory experiences on lesbian, gay and bisexual people in sport. *Annals of Leisure Research, 20*(4), 467–489.

Vidal, J. (2016, September). Why does American sports have a Latino problem? The latent is there, but it's not being showcased or encouraged on a broader scale. *Rolling Stone*. Retrieved from https://www.rollingstone.com/sports/news/why-does-american-sports-have-a-latino-problem-w440069

Wolf, L. J., Maio, G. R., Karremans, J. C., & Leygue, C. (2017). On implicit racial prejudice against infants. *Group Processes & Intergroup Relations, 20*(6), 789–800.

Woodhouse, D., & Conricode, D. (2017). In-ger-land, In-ger-land, In-ger-land! Exploring the impact of soccer on the sense of belonging of those seeking asylum in the UK. *International Review for the Sociology of Sport, 52*(8), 940–954.

Wright, T., & Cunningham, G. (2017). Disability status, stereotype content, and employment opportunities in sport and fitness organizations. *Sport, Business and Management: An International Journal, 7*(4), 393–403.

Zestcott, C. A., Blair, I. V., & Stone, J. (2016). Examining the presence, consequences, and reduction of implicit bias in health care: A narrative review. *Group Processes & Intergroup Relations, 19*(4), 528–542.

PART II

FORMS OF DIVERSITY

chapter 11

chapter 12

A Framework to Understand Diversity Forms

LEARNING OBJECTIVES

After studying this chapter, you should be able to:

- Summarize the importance of multilevel models for understanding diversity.

- List and describe factors at various levels of analysis that influence diversity.

DIVERSITY CHALLENGE

Sportscotland is the primary national agency promoting sport in Scotland. The organization seeks to make sport a way of life in the country, positively influencing people and communities. To achieve this end, **sport**scotland has several core beliefs, including the following:

- Sport should be an inclusive activity that promotes equality and respect for others.
- Fair play should be central such that success results from honesty, training, and preparation.
- Athletes should comply with international doping standards.
- Athletes, coaches, and managers should put the best interests of sport ahead of their own.
- The ethics and values of sport should guide sponsorship decisions.

The national sport organization has a number of initiatives that help it to achieve its objectives. They work with individuals to ensure they have access to sport and the ability to thrive. Beyond the focus on individuals, **sport**scotland interacts with a number of partners external to the organization, including work in schools, clubs, and local communities. Within schools, **sport**scotland (a) engages leaders to ensure there are ample opportunities for sport; (b) collaborates with physical education professionals to enhance physical literacy among children; and (c) seeks to integrate sport into the larger landscape of play, dance, and other forms of physical activity. In their work with clubs and communities,

sportscotland looks to effectively integrate sport into the community landscape, ensuring a more active Scotland. They do so by ensuring quality and quantity of sport experiences. They facilitate leadership development to increase the capacity within the sport clubs.

As the example illustrates, sport organizations frequently seek to ensure people from a variety of backgrounds have access to sport and can perform at their highest levels. To do so, they must focus their efforts across the sport landscape, working with individuals, teams, schools, communities, and other partners.

Source: Information adapted from https://sportscotland.org.uk/.

Reflection

1. Why is it important for sport managers to understand the multiple factors that can influence diversity and inclusion?
2. Think about diversity and inclusion efforts with which you are familiar. How does the organization include individual, groups, and communities to promote diversity and inclusion?

As the Diversity Challenge illustrates, a number of factors have the potential to influence diversity and inclusion in sport. **sport**scotland engaged with individuals participating in sport and with external stakeholders, such as communities, clubs, and schools. Other scholars and agencies also acknowledge the importance of considering factors at multiple levels of analysis. For example, the Centers for Disease Control and Prevention in the US have adopted a multilevel approach to cancer

exhibit **4.1** Multilevel Factors That Influence Diversity and Inclusion

Macro-level factors. Factors at the societal level that have the potential to influence people's opportunities and experiences in sport. Examples include institutionalized forms of discrimination, the political climate, and stakeholder expectations, among others.

Meso-level factors. Factors at the group and organizational levels that have the potential to influence people's opportunities and experiences in sport. Examples include leaders' biases, organizational policies, and organizational culture, among others.

Micro-level factors. Factors at the individual level that have the potential to influence people's opportunities and experiences in sport. Examples include previous experiences, personal identity, and self-limiting behaviors, among others.

prevention (https://www.cdc.gov/cancer/crccp/sem.htm). Here, the agency focuses on individual, interpersonal, organizational, community, and policy factors—all of which have the potential to influence the incidence of cancer.

I follow a similar approach in this chapter, where I provide a framework for understanding how various diversity forms influence people, their opportunities, and their experiences. We use this framework for each of the other chapters in this section, allowing for a unified overview of race, gender, age, disability, appearance, religious beliefs, sexual orientation, gender identity and expression, and social class. Consistent with the approach of major sport and health agencies, I have developed a multilevel model such that I focus on factors at the micro-level (individuals), meso-level (groups and organizations), and macro-level (societal influences). Exhibit 4.1 offers an overview of these approaches.

A FOCUS ON MULTILEVEL MODELS

In the previous section, I noted that several organizations adopt a multilevel focus when seeking to advance sport and health initiatives. Why, though, do they pursue such an approach, and why is it important for you, as a future sport manager, to understand multilevel factors affecting diversity and inclusion? I point to two reasons, with a focus on theories and the nature of sport organizations.

Diversity Theories

The first reason to learn about multilevel factors influencing diversity is because, as theoreticians have shown, diversity and inclusion are influenced by factors across multiple levels of analysis. In Chapter 2, we reviewed three classes of diversity theories: managerial, sociological, and social psychological. As you will recall, managerial theories largely focus on how diversity and inclusion influence groups and organizations. For example, when people in a sport organization have a pro-diversity mindset, they are likely to see differences as a source of learning and enrichment (Guillaume, Dawson, Otaye-Ebede, Woods, & West, 2017; van Knippenberg & Schippers, 2007). This perspective examines individuals' attitudes—a micro-level factor—and how they collectively influence group or organizational level thinking about differences—a meso-level factor.

Sociological theories, on the other hand, largely focus on societal factors and how they influence organizations, groups, and individuals. For example, critical race theory holds that racism is endemic in society, deeply enmeshed into prominent institutions, such as education, the justice system, religion, and sport, among others (Hylton, 2009). Singer (2005) drew from this theory to examine the experiences of intercollegiate athletes in the US. The athletes articulated that racism served to curtail their access to leadership and decision-making opportunities, and it also resulted in their differential treatment, relative to Whites. As this example, and others like it (Bradbury, 2011, 2013) show, societal factors like racism (a macro-level factor) can influence the opportunities and experiences of individuals (a micro-level factor).

Finally, social psychological theories focused on the individual in relation to others. For example, in stigma theory, Goffman (1963) focused on the attributes people have that make them different or devalued from others. As Hatzenbuehler (2017) noted, stigma can manifest at different levels, including the individual, interpersonal, and structural. Thus, stigma theory is, by its nature, multilevel in nature. As an example, Wareham, Burkett, Innes, and Lovell (2017) noted that societal stigmas devaluing people with disabilities contributed to coaches being unwilling to train athletes with disabilities.

As these examples illustrate, scholars have developed theories that focus on multiple levels of analysis. As theory helps guide practice (Cunningham, Fink, & Doherty, 2016), future sport managers need to understand multilevel frameworks so they can better lead their sport organizations.

Nature of Sport Organizations

Beyond specific diversity theories, another reason to embrace multilevel thinking is because organizations are multilevel entities. Such a perspective is consistent with systems thinking, where systems represent "a set of interrelated and interdependent parts arranged in a manner that produces a unified whole" (Robbins & Coulter, 2017, p. 67). Open systems interact with and are influenced by their external environment.

The human body represents an example of an open system. It is comprised of cells, tissues, organs, and systems that all work together in concert to ensure you live. The body also interacts with the external environment to regulate and adapt. Consider, for example, how the body reacts when watching a cricket contest at Edens Garden, India, where the temperatures can soar past 100 degrees Fahrenheit versus watching an American football game in sub-zero temperatures in Green Bay, Wisconsin.

Just as the body is an open system that interacts with its environment, so too are sport organizations (Chelladurai, 2014). They are comprised of individuals, dyads, groups, and larger units. All must work together to ensure the organization achieves its primary goals. Importantly, sport organizations also interact with their external environments. New products or services might drive consumer demand. In other cases, factors in the environment, such as labor laws, might affect organizational operations. The key takeaway is that there are factors at the micro-, meso-, and macro-levels, all interacting with one another, and all of which influence sport organizations, employees, and athletes.

Box 4.1 offers additional information for why adopting a multilevel perspective is so important for sport managers.

Box 4.1 Professional Perspectives. Adopting a Multilevel Perspective of Diversity

Laura Burton is a Professor of Sport Management at the University of Connecticut. She began her career in the sport industry as an athletic trainer, working several years in intercollegiate athletics in the US. In her own research, she has used a multilevel framework to examine women's experiences in sport leadership. She has a particular interest in understanding the influence of stereotypes in general, and gender stereotypes in particular, and how those stereotypes impact perceptions of leadership and women's experiences in leadership positions. She has found that stereotypes are derived from societal norms (macro), which influence organizational policies, procedures, and subsequent decision-making (meso) and have an impact (positive or negative) on an individual's experience in a particular role (micro).

Beyond a research perspective, Burton points to several reasons why sport managers should focus on multilevel models. She noted,

Sport managers must understand multilevel factors do influence people's opportunities and experiences. As an example, based on research that has examined women's experiences in leadership in sport organizations, at the macro level, sport has historically (and currently) been considered the domain of men and sport has been used to celebrate stereotypical masculinity (i.e., strength, dominance, power, aggression). Within this societal perspective, women (and girls) are considered outsiders to sport. Further, this societal perspective of sport as a masculine domain influences our perspective of

who should be leading sport organizations (meso level). The majority of all sport organizations from youth serving to professional sport leagues are led and managed primarily by men. This influences how policies are developed, decisions are made, who is hired for positions (e.g., coaches), and how the organization is operated (e.g., hours worked, expectations for family commitments). Finally, at the individual level or micro level, individuals make decisions based on stereotypes that sport is a masculine domain. This can impact how young men perceive themselves as a good 'fit' to work in a sport organization and therefore seek out opportunities (e.g., college majors and internship experiences) that align with goals to work in sport organizations. Young women also recognize the stereotype that sport is a masculine domain and may decide to pursue another career path instead of sport management. At the individual level we also apply stereotypes regarding who we perceive to be better or more competent in a particular role. We perceive men to be more competent or better suited for leadership roles in sport organizations and will therefore evaluate their performance in those roles more positively than we would women in those roles as we do not perceive women to be a 'fit' for sport leadership.

As Professor Burton illustrates, adopting a multilevel model helps sport managers to better understand diversity in sport and the decisions people make.

MULTILEVEL FACTORS AFFECTING OPPORTUNITIES AND EXPERIENCES

I have previously written about the efficacy of multilevel modeling (Dixon & Cunningham, 2006) and developed similar models in the past, with a focus on gender (Cunningham & Sagas, 2008), race (Cunningham, 2010, 2012b), sexual orientation (Cunningham, 2012a), and interpersonal mistreatment at work (Cunningham, Bergman, & Miner, 2014). Other scholars have developed similar models to explain work-family conflict (Dixon & Bruening, 2005) and women in leadership positions (Burton, 2015). Drawing from this collective work, I developed a multilevel model to help understand factors that shape people's opportunities. We will use the model as a framework to organize the information in Chapters 5–12.

I offer illustrative summary in Exhibit 4.2. The figure includes the three primary levels of analysis—micro, meso, and macro—as well as examples of factors found at each level. The factors relevant to the conversation are likely to vary by diversity form. Note that I have included the dual arrows among the different levels, thereby suggesting that factors at one level have the potential to influence those at another. For example, macro-level factors might influence one's self-limiting behaviors. Or, leadership prototypes, when widely shared in an industry, might take on the form of institutionalized practices. This position is consistent with Kozlowski and Klein's (2000) notion of homologous multilevel models. It also highlights that any differences in aspirations or behaviors among members of different groups are likely due to a bevy of meso- and macro-level factors, not something inherent in the individual.

exhibit   **4.2**   A Multilevel Model to Explain People's Opportunities and Experiences in Sport

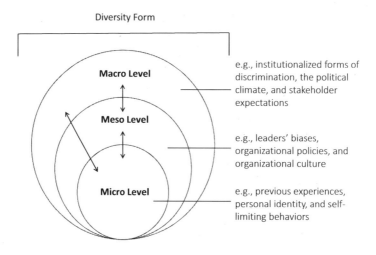

Macro-Level Factors

Macro-level factors operate at the societal level and have the potential to influence people's opportunities and experiences in sport. Salient macro-level factors include institutional forms of discrimination, the political climate, and stakeholder expectations, among others.

As noted in Chapter 3, discrimination is the behavioral form of bias. Whereas interpersonal relationships can potentially explain discrimination, so too can institutionalized forms. This form of discrimination results from unjust systems and processes that are deeply engrained in a society's institutions. Though there are conceptual differences among them, systemic racism (Feagin, 2006), institutional distancing (Lott & Bullock, 2007), heterosexism (Herek, 2007), patriarchy (Broch, 2016), and structural stigma (Hatzenbuehler, 2017) are all constructs that point to the institutionalized nature of discrimination. For example, drawing from a stigma perspective, Samari (2016) outlined how institutionalized forms of Islamophobia can serve to substantially increase health risks among Muslims. As another example, Inderstrodt-Stephens and Acharya (2018) suggested that structural stigma around weight and running serves to continuously remind overweight endurance athletes that they are different and do not fit the mold.

The political climate represents another macro-level factor that can influence people's opportunities and experiences in sport. The political ideology of the ruling party in a government is frequently associated with a number of outcomes, such as a focus (or lack thereof) on human rights and social justice, ideology about the role of government or industry in promoting well-being, immigration policies, and perspectives toward war and peace, among many others. For instance, Brown et al. (2018) collected data from participants in Australia, Malaysia, and Puerto Rico, with the intention of understanding what predicted their attitudes toward diversity. Results indicate that Puerto Ricans reported the most positive attitudes toward diversity, followed by Australians and Malaysians. Brown et al. also found that blind patriotism, which they defined as an unwavering, uncritical commitment to one's country, held a strong, negative association with favorable views toward diversity among Puerto Ricans. The association was less strong among Australians and was positive among Malaysians. The study illustrates how diversity attitudes vary across countries and are influenced by nationalistic views. As another example, Collins and Haudenhuyse (2015) showed how austerity measures implemented in the UK—extreme budget cuts to government services and programming—served to further marginalize and restrict sport access for the poor and people from underrepresented groups.

Finally, stakeholder expectations serve as the third macro-level factor influencing people's experiences and opportunities. Stakeholders are people who have a stake or interest in the sport organization (Clarkson, 1995). They can be internal to the organization, such as coaches or athletes, or external to it, including competitors, governments, and funders, among others. Researchers have shown that key stakeholders frequently have a large role in the operations and decision-making of a sport organization. In intercollegiate athletics in the US, donors play a key role in the financial operations of the unit, and as such, they can also influence key hires, such as the athletic director (Kihl, Leberman, & Schull, 2010). Frequently, however, donors' ideas about who can and should lead sport organizations favor those who have traditionally held power—in this case, men. As a result, their expectations and preferences can limit the opportunities for women to assume leadership roles (Schull, Shaw, & Kihl, 2013). Opportunities for potential leaders from other underrepresented groups are similarly limited because of key stakeholder preferences.

Meso-Level Factors

Meso-level factors are those operating at the group and organizational levels that have the potential to influence people's opportunities and experiences in sport. Examples include leaders' biases, organizational policies, and organizational culture, among others.

As noted in Chapter 3, biases include stereotypes, prejudice, and discrimination (Cuddy, Fiske, & Glick, 2008). Biases expressed by leaders and key decision-makers have the potential to limit opportunities for and worsen the experiences of people from underrepresented groups. Consider, for instance, the stereotype that taller people are stronger and better leaders than their shorter counterparts. Agerström (2014) examined whether the stereotype held among Swedish job recruiters. Results indicate that they did, as recruiters believed tall applicants were more competent, employable, and healthy than were shorter applicants. As another example of bias, Barrett, Pike, and Mazerolle (2018) interviewed women working as athletic trainers and found that, though the relationships with coaches and players were often amicable, the trainers did experience sexism and discrimination. The negative experiences occurred while they were students and throughout their professional careers.

Organizational policies represent another macro-level factor that can influence people's experiences and opportunities in sport. The policies might dictate, for example, who can compete against whom. In many states in the US, for example, interscholastic sport-governing bodies have policies that athletes can play in sports based on their gender identity and expression (Cunningham, Buzuvis, & Mosier, 2018). Such policies mean, therefore, that an interscholastic athlete assigned male at birth and who identifies as a girl can compete on girls' teams. Such policies result in increased participation opportunities for and better mental health of transgender athletes.

Relatedly, organizational culture can influence opportunities and experiences. Culture reflects "a pattern of shared basic assumptions . . . that has worked well enough to be considered valid and, therefore, to be taught to new members as the correct ways to perceive, think, and feel in relation to those problems" (Schein, 2004, p. 17). A number of scholars have shown that members from underrepresented groups have more leadership opportunities and better work experiences when the sport organization's culture is one that values diversity and inclusion (Doherty & Chelladurai, 1999; Fink & Pastore, 1999; Singer & Cunningham, 2012). Illustrative of these relationships, Gündemir, Dovidio, Homan, and De Dreu (2017) conducted a series of studies to understand how a culture that emphasized diversity was associated with racial minorities' self-perceptions and goals. In organizations that recognized and valued differences among groups (i.e., multicultural organizations), racial minorities expressed the highest levels of self-efficacy and willingness to apply for upper-level positions. Other researchers have found that a pro-diversity culture has a meaningful, positive effect on refugee employees. Specifically, Newman, Nielsen, Smyth, Hirst, and Kennedy (2018) found that perceptions of a diversity culture were positively related to hope, optimism, and resilience, which, in turn, were associated with organizational commitment.

Micro-Level Factors

Finally, micro-level factors are those operating at the individual level and that have the potential to influence people's opportunities and experiences in sport. Examples include previous experiences and attitudes, personal identity, and self-limiting behaviors, among others. Importantly, individual characteristics frequently interact with factors at other levels to predict experiences and opportunities.

People's previous experiences can influence their opportunities and experiences in a number of ways. Past encounters with discrimination can influence sensitivity to future mistreatment (Feinstein, Goldfried, & Davila, 2012). Previous experiences and attitudes might also influence whether people seek out or avoid interactions with others who are different (Pettigrew, 1998). For example, Pettigrew outlined examples of how wartime experiences, the dynamics of the neighborhood in which one was raised, and school experiences all shaped how people view others.

Personal identities can influence people's experiences and opportunities, and they do so in two ways. The first relates to the identity people hold for themselves. One's personal identity refers to the identity that is critical to her or his self-concept. It constitutes a critical part of the person's self-image and how the individual feels about the self (Brewer, 1991; Randel & Jaussi, 2003). To illustrate the effects of personal identity, consider two people over age 65—Ramón and José. Suppose age identity is important part of Ramón's personal identity but is less consequential for José. In this case, the effects of age stereotypes, being the minority in terms of age, or facing age-based discrimination are likely to be more harmful for Ramón than for José.

Personal identities can also influence people's experiences and opportunities by way of how others perceive that identity. That is, people use cues to estimate how important various personal identities are to an individual—that is, they make estimates of others' identities. Researchers have shown that Whites in the US will frequently penalize racial minorities who Whites believe hold a strong racial identity (Kaiser & Pratt-Hyatt, 2009). For instance, in a series of experimental studies, colleagues and I have found that raters penalize racial minority job applicants who they believe hold a strong racial identity. On the other hand, racial minorities who are not thought to hold a strong racial identity are rated more convivially. Job-related penalties include negative job fit ratings and low salary offers, and we have observed as much among student samples and among professionals working in the field (Steward & Cunningham, 2015; Vick & Cunningham, 2018).

Finally, self-limiting behaviors might influence people's experiences and opportunities. Members of underrepresented groups are likely to experience various forms of bias, and as a result, have missed opportunities, negative work feedback, and limited chances for advancement (Ilgen & Youtz, 1986; Sartore, 2006). Over time, people start to internalize the negative feedback they receive, and this can affect their attitudes and behaviors. For example, coaches who are routinely passed over for a job because of their race might quit applying. Administrators who continually face harassment at work because of their gender might choose to leave the sport profession. Fitness instructors who routinely receive negative performance feedback because of their sexual orientation might internalize the feedback and actually perform poorer over time. These are examples of self-limiting behaviors. They result from negative, unfair treatment—not because of deficiencies within the individual (see also Knoppers, 1987).

Model Summary

In all, the integrated model shows how factors at various levels of analysis can influence the experiences of and opportunities for people from underrepresented groups. In considering the model, there are several key takeaways. First, factors at macro-, meso-, and micro-levels can influence individuals and one another. Second, I have offered illustrative examples for each level, but the specific factors are likely to vary based on the diversity dimension. For example, salient macro-level factors affecting racial minorities might be different than those impacting religious minorities. Finally, we can use the general model as a guide to understand the experiences people have and opportunities afforded them.

CHAPTER SUMMARY

The purpose of this chapter is to provide a multilevel model for understanding diversity and inclusion in sport organizations. As the Diversity Challenge illustrated, these topics are important issues for persons involved in sport and physical activity, and they will be for years to come. Having read the chapter, you should now be able to:

1. Summarize the importance of multilevel models for understanding diversity.
   Sport managers should understand multilevel models for two primary reasons. First, theories about diversity are largely multilevel in nature. As theory helps guide good practice, understanding multilevel models helps students become better sport managers. Second, sport organizations are, by their nature, multilevel, open systems. As such, understanding sport organizations necessitates an understanding of multilevel models.

2. List and describe the various levels of analysis that influence diversity.
   Three levels influence diversity. First, macro-level factors are those operating at the societal level, and examples include institutionalized forms

of discrimination, the political climate, and stakeholder expectations, among others. Second, meso-level factors function at the group and organizational levels, such as leaders' biases, organizational policies, and organizational culture, among others. Finally, micro-level factors are at the individual level and include previous experiences, personal identity, and self-limiting behaviors, among others.

Questions FOR DISCUSSION

1. Sport organizations represent open systems. What are some external entities with whom sport organizations interact? What is their influence?
2. Are there any levels of analysis you think are more important than others? What is the basis for your answer?
3. The chapter included examples of factors at each level of analysis. What are some relevant factors not included?
4. The multilevel model might apply differently to specific diversity forms such that factors at one level of analysis might be relevant for one diversity form but not another. What are some examples of where this would occur?

LEARNING Activities

1. **sport**scotland and the Centers for Disease Control and Prevention were cited in the chapter as two organizations that specifically attend to factors at multiple levels of analysis. Search the Internet for examples among other sport organizations, and report your findings back to the class.
2. Interview sport managers and ask them about the degree to which they believe micro-, meso-, and macro-level factors influence people's opportunities to participate in sport. What strategies do they employ to combat any barriers?

Web RESOURCES

Centers for Disease Control and Prevention, https://www.cdc.gov/violenceprevention/overview/social-ecologicalmodel.html
 Offers an overview of the social ecological model used in preventative health.

British Athletes Commission, Stakeholders, https://www.britishathletes.org/stakeholders
 An independent association for elite athletes across 40 sports; the page lists key stakeholders of the organization.

READING **Resources**

Klein, K. J., & Kozlowski, S. W. J. (Eds.). (2000). *Multilevel theory, research, and methods in organizations: Foundations, extensions, and new directions.* San Francisco, CA: Jossey-Bass.

    An edited volume devoted to understand multilevel theory.

Chelladurai, P. (2014). *Managing organizations for sport and physical activity: A systems perspective* (4th ed.). New York, NY: Routledge. (Chapter3)

    Offers an overview of systems organizing for sport organizations.

Dixon, M. A., & Cunningham, G. B. (2006). Multi-level analysis in sport management: Conceptual issues and review of aggregation techniques. *Measurement in Physical Education and Exercise Science, 10*(2), 85–107.

    Offer an overview of conceptual, methodological, and analytical considerations for multilevel research in sport.

REFERENCES

Agerström, J. (2014). Why does height matter in hiring? *Journal of Behavioral and Experimental Economics, 52,* 35–38.

Barrett, J., Pike, A., & Mazerolle, S. (2018). A phenomenological approach: Understanding the experiences of female athletic trainers providing medical care to male sports teams. *International Journal of Athletic Therapy and Training, 23*(3), 113–120.

Bradbury, S. (2011). From racial exclusions to new inclusions: Black and minority ethnic participation in football clubs in the East Midlands of England. *International Review for the Sociology of Sport, 46*(1), 23–44.

Bradbury, S. (2013). Institutional racism, whiteness and the under-representation of minorities in leadership positions in football in Europe. *Soccer & Society, 14*(3), 296–314.

Brewer, M. B. (1991). The social self: On being the same and different at the same time. *Personality and Social Psychology Bulletin, 17*(5), 475–482.

Broch, T. B. (2016). Intersections of gender and national identity in sport: A cultural sociological overview. *Sociology Compass, 10*(7), 567–579.

Brown, J., Jiménez, A. L., Sabanathan, D., Sekamanya, S., Hough, M., Sutton, J., ... García Coll, C. (2018). Factors related to attitudes toward diversity in Australia, Malaysia, and Puerto Rico. *Journal of Human Behavior in the Social Environment, 28*(4), 475–493.

Burton, L. J. (2015). Underrepresentation of women in sport leadership: A review of research. *Sport Management Review, 18*(2), 155–165.

Chelladurai, P. (2014). *Managing organizations for sport and physical activity: A systems perspective* (4th ed.). New York, NY: Routledge.

Clarkson, M. E. (1995). A stakeholder framework for analyzing and evaluating corporate social performance. *Academy of Management Review, 20*(1), 92–117.

Collins, M., & Haudenhuyse, R. (2015). Social exclusion and austerity policies in England: The role of sports in a new area of social polarisation and inequality? *Social Inclusion, 3*(3), 5–18.

Cuddy, A. J., Fiske, S. T., & Glick, P. (2008). Warmth and competence as universal dimensions of social perception: The stereotype content model and the BIAS map. *Advances in Experimental Social Psychology, 40,* 61–149.

Cunningham, G. B. (2010). Understanding the under-representation of African American coaches: A multilevel perspective. *Sport Management Review, 13*, 395–406.

Cunningham, G. B. (2012a). A multilevel model for understanding the experiences of LGBT sport participants. *Journal for the Study of Sports and Athletes in Education, 6*, 5–20.

Cunningham, G. B. (2012b). Occupational segregation of African Americans in athletic administration. *Wake Forest Journal of Law & Policy, 2*, 165–178.

Cunningham, G. B., & Sagas, M. (2008). Gender and sex diversity in sport organizations: Introduction to a special issue. *Sex Roles, 58*, 3–9.

Cunningham, G. B., Bergman, M. E., & Miner, K. N. (2014). Interpersonal mistreatment of women in the workplace. *Sex Roles, 71*, 1–6.

Cunningham, G. B., Buzuvis, E., & Mosier, C. (2018). Inclusive spaces and locker rooms for transgender athletes. *Kinesiology Review, 7*, 365–374.

Cunningham, G. B., Fink, J. S., & Doherty, A. (2016). Developing theory in sport management. In G. B. Cunningham, J. S., Fink, & A. Doherty (Eds.), *Routledge handbook of theory in sport management* (pp. 1–8). New York, NY: Routledge.

Dixon, M. A., & Bruening, J. E. (2005). Perspectives on work-family conflict in sport: an integrated approach. *Sport Management Review, 8*(3), 227–253.

Dixon, M. A., & Cunningham, G. B. (2006). Multi-level analysis in sport management: Conceptual issues and review of aggregation techniques. *Measurement in Physical Education and Exercise Science, 10*(2), 85–107.

Doherty, A. J., & Chelladurai, P. (1999). Managing cultural diversity in sport organizations: A theoretical perspective. *Journal of Sport Management, 13*(4), 280–297.

Feagin, J. R. (2006). *Systemic racism: A theory of oppression.* New York, NY: Routledge.

Feinstein, B. A., Goldfried, M. R., & Davila, J. (2012). The relationship between experiences of discrimination and mental health among lesbians and gay men: An examination of internalized homonegativity and rejection sensitivity as potential mechanisms. *Journal of Consulting and Clinical Psychology, 80*(5), 917–927.

Fink, J. S., & Pastore, D. L. (1999). Diversity in sport? Utilizing the business literature to devise a comprehensive framework of diversity initiatives. *Quest, 51*(4), 310–327.

Goffman, E. (1963). *Stigma: Notes on the management of spoiled identity.* New York, NY: Simon & Schuster.

Guillaume, Y. R., Dawson, J. F., Otaye-Ebede, L., Woods, S. A., & West, M. A. (2017). Harnessing demographic differences in organizations: What moderates the effects of workplace diversity? *Journal of Organizational Behavior, 38*(2), 276–303.

Gündemir, S., Dovidio, J. F., Homan, A. C., & De Dreu, C. K. (2017). The impact of organizational diversity policies on minority employees' leadership self-perceptions and goals. *Journal of Leadership & Organizational Studies, 24*(2), 172–188.

Hatzenbuehler, M. L. (2017). Structural stigma and health. In B. Major, J. F. Dovidio, & B. G. Link (Eds.), *The Oxford handbook of stigma, discrimination, and health* (pp. 105–121). New York, NY: Oxford University Press.

Herek, G. M. (2007). Confronting sexual stigma and prejudice: Theory and practice. *Journal of Social Issues, 63*(4), 905–925.

Hylton, K. (2009). *'Race" and sport: Critical race theory.* New York, NY: Routledge.

Ilgen, D. R., & Youtz, M. A. (1986). Factors affecting the evaluation and development of minorities in organizations. In K. Bowland & G. Ferris (Eds.), *Research in personnel and human resource management:*

A research annual (pp. 307–337). Greenwich, CT: JAI Press.

Inderstrodt-Stephens, J., & Acharya, L. (2018). "Fat" chicks who run: Stigma experienced by "overweight" endurance athletes. *Journal of Sport and Social Issues, 42*(1), 49–67.

Kaiser, C. R., & Pratt-Hyatt, J. S. (2009). Distributing prejudice unequally: Do Whites direct their prejudice toward strongly identified minorities? *Journal of Personality and Social Psychology, 96*(2), 432–445.

Kihl, L. A., Leberman, S., & Schull, V. (2010). Stakeholder constructions of leadership in intercollegiate athletics. *European Sport Management Quarterly, 10*(2), 241–275.

Knoppers, A. (1987). Gender and the coaching profession. *Quest, 39*(1), 9–22.

Kozlowski, S. W. J., & Klein, K. J. (2000). A multilevel approach to theory and research in organizations: Contextual, temporal, and emergent processes. In K. J. Klein and S. W. J. Kozlowski (Eds.), *Multilevel theory, research, and methods in organizations: Foundations, extensions, and new directions* (pp. 3–90). San Francisco, CA: Jossey-Bass.

Lott, B., & Bullock, H. E. (2007). *Psychology and economic injustice: Personal, professional, and political intersections.* Washington, DC: American Psychological Association.

Newman, A., Nielsen, I., Smyth, R., Hirst, G., & Kennedy, S. (2018). The effects of diversity climate on the work attitudes of refugee employees: The mediating role of psychological capital and moderating role of ethnic identity. *Journal of Vocational Behavior, 105*, 147–158.

Pettigrew, T. F. (1998). Intergroup contact theory. *Annual Review of Psychology, 49*(1), 65–85.

Randel, A. E., & Jaussi, K. S. (2003). Functional background identity, diversity, and individual performance in cross-functional teams. *Academy of Management Journal, 46*(6), 763–774.

Robbins, S. P., & Coulter, M. (2016). *Management* (13th ed., Global ed.). New York, NY: Pearson.

Samari, G. (2016). Islamophobia and public health in the United States. *American Journal of Public Health, 106*(11), 1920–1925.

Sartore, M. L. (2006). Categorization, performance appraisals, and self-limiting behavior: The impact on current and future performance. *Journal of Sport Management, 20*(4), 535–553.

Schein, E. H. (2004). *Organizational culture and leadership* (3rd ed.). San Francisco, CA: Jossey-Bass.

Schull, V., Shaw, S., & Kihl, L. A. (2013). "If a woman came in... she would have been eaten up alive:" Analyzing gendered political processes in the search for an athletic director. *Gender & Society, 27*(1), 56–81.

Singer, J. N. (2005). Understanding racism through the eyes of African American male student-athletes. *Race Ethnicity and Education, 8*(4), 365–386.

Singer, J. N., & Cunningham, G. B. (2012). A case study of the diversity culture of an American university athletic department: Perceptions of senior level administrators. *Sport, Education and Society, 17*(5), 647–669.

Steward, A. D., & Cunningham, G. B. (2015). Racial identity and its impact on job applicants. *Journal of Sport Management, 29*, 245–256.

van Knippenberg, D., & Schippers, M. (2007). Work group diversity. *Annual Review of Psychology, 58*, 515–541.

Vick, A., & Cunningham, G. B. (in press). Bias against Latina and African American women job applicants: A field experiment. *Sport, Business, Management: An International Journal, 8*(4), 410–430.

Wareham, Y., Burkett, B., Innes, P., & Lovell, G. P. (2017). Coaching athletes with disability: Preconceptions and reality. *Sport in Society, 20*(9), 1185–1202.

Race

5

LEARNING OBJECTIVES

After studying this chapter, you should be able to:

- Define race, ethnicity, and minority.

- Describe the representation of racial minorities in leadership positions in sport.

- Summarize the reasons for the underrepresentation of racial minorities in leadership positions in sport.

- Paraphrase the manner in which race influences opportunities and experiences of sport and physical activity participants.

DIVERSITY CHALLENGE

Racial minorities have long played a key role in sport. As some examples, Jack Johnson won the heavyweight championship of the world in 1908. Althea Gibson became the first African American to win a Grand Slam title (French Open) in tennis in 1956. Ichiro Suzuki broke the Major League Baseball record for hits in a season (256) in 2004. As a final example, American Jesse Owen broke three world records and won four gold medals in the 1936 Olympics Games held in Berlin.

Racial minorities' strength and influence is not limited to the court or gridiron, however. Recently, contributors at *Forbes* conducted an analysis to determine the most influential racial minorities in sports today. To do so, they collected multiple rounds of data from a panel of influential thought-leaders in the field, including women and men in academia, journalism, sports and entertainment, and law. The panelists first submitted a list of 25 names. After the list was culled, the experts then ranked the individuals from 1 to 25. In providing the assessments, they considered quantitative measures (e.g., sales figure and revenues generated), sphere of influence (i.e., whether the individual impacted others outside their specific role), and impact (i.e., the power they have in their work and on the global stage). As seen in the following space, the final list included 17 African Americans, 5 Asian Americans, and 3 Latinos.

In commenting on the influencers, Jason Belzer noted the individuals "deserve to be celebrated for their willingness to overcome countless obstacles and break barriers, paving the way for millions of sports fans everywhere who aspire to follow in their footsteps."

List of Most Influential Minorities in Sport (Forbes)

1.   Michael Jordan, Owner of Charlotte Bobcats and Jordan Brand
2.   Magic Johnson, Owner, Los Angeles Dodgers
3.   DeMaurice Smith, Executive Director, NFL Players Association
4.   Michele Roberts, President, NBA Players Association
5.   Trevor Edwards, President, Nike Brand
6.   Indra Nooyi, Chair and Chief Executive Officer, PepsiCo
7.   Lebron James, Los Angeles Lakers
8.   Mark Tatum, Deputy Commissioner and COO, NBA
9.   Serena Williams, Professional Tennis Player
10. Tony Clark, Executive Director, MLB Players Association
11. Shahid Khan, Owner, Jacksonville Jaguars and Fulham FC
12. Arturo Morena, Owner, Los Angeles Angles
13. Kim Ng, Sr. Vice President for Baseball Operations, Major League Baseball
14. Troy Vincent, Executive Vice President of Football Operations, NFL
15. Larry Miller, President, Jordan Brand
16. Gene Smith, Vice President and Director of Athletics, The Ohio State University
17. Juan Carlos Rodriguez, President, Univision Deportes
18. Doc Rivers, Head Coach, Los Angeles Clippers
19. Sheila Johnson, Co-Owner, Washington Mystics, Wizards, Capitals
20. Rob King, Sr. Vice President, SportsCenter and News at ESPN
21. Ray Anderson, Vice President for University Athletics, Arizona State University
22. Pamela El, Executive Vice President and CMO, NBA
23. Farhan Zaidi, General Manager, Los Angeles Dodgers
24. Carlos Sanchez, Executive Vice President and GM, Fox Deportes
25. Kim Fields, Chief Strategy Officer

Sources: Belzer, J. (2016, February 24). The most influential minorities in sports. *Forbes.* Retrieved from https://www.forbes.com/sites/jasonbelzer/2016/02/24/the-most-influential-minorities-in-sports/#4dd226342e7b; Lomonico, D. (no date). The 15: Racial barriers broken in sports. *Pressbox.* Retrieved from https://www.pressboxonline.com/story/10231/the-15-racial-barriers-broken-in-sports.

CHALLENGE REFLECTION

1. Look at the list of the 25 most influential minorities in sport. Are there patterns you observe?
2. Given your understanding of sport, are there others you would include on the list?
3. Two athletes were included on the list. Do you think well-known racial minorities in sport are more likely to be an administrator or an athlete? Is this the same for White athletes, too?

The Diversity Challenge illustrates the influence racial minorities can have on sport and the sport industry. Race has the potential to influence people's opportunities and experiences as elite athletes, casual exercisers, administrators, and others working in sport. People's explicit racist attitudes have improved over time. Nevertheless, implicit biases persist, as do systemic forms of racism and discrimination—a pattern observed worldwide (Adair, 2011). Consequently, racial minorities are overrepresented in some areas of sport, including as athletes in some women's and men's sport, but underrepresented elsewhere. There are similar patterns for exercise and physical activity participants.

The purpose of this chapter is to examine the influence of race in greater detail. Two points are worth noting. First, I largely compare the experiences of racial minorities to those of Whites and do so for several reasons. Feagin (2006) and Zinn (2003) have outlined how the US and other Western countries have a history of racial subjugation and oppression. Over time, racism was built into laws, health care provision, educational opportunities, religious institutions, and other major institutions. Many of these overt laws have changed, but as outlined in critical race theory, the vestiges of institutionalized racism remain. As a result, many opportunities and experiences of racial minorities are qualitatively different than those of Whites. Second, though I draw from examples from around the world, much of the text focuses on African Americans. The decision is based on the available research and data in the field. I offer this rationale in hopes that readers recognize the focus is a reflection of historical context and available research, and not intended to diminish the experiences among other racial minorities.

I organize the chapter as follows. First, I define and overview *race, ethnicity,* and *minority.* I then offer an overview of how race influences the work environment, including the representation of racial minorities. Drawing from the multilevel model developed in Chapter 4, I then offer explanations for the underrepresentation of racial minorities in leadership positions. Finally, I summarize the opportunities and experiences of athletes engaged in formal sport and those participating in more casual forms of physical activity.

RACE, ETHNICITY, AND MINORITY

Though people sometimes use the terms interchangeably, *race, ethnicity,* and *minority* have different meanings (Sage & Eitzen, 2016). Race refers to a classification of people based on supposed genetic differences and similarities.

Box 5.1 Diversity in the Field: Race, Sport, and Protest

Athletes (and to a lesser degree, coaches) have engaged in protest to voice their discontent with social injustices. Many have engaged in activism aimed at disrupting structures that oppress, challenging norms, and giving voice to those disadvantaged groups (Cooper, Macauly, & Rodriguez, in press). Many times, the protests center on race and racism, both in sport and broader society.

Harry Edwards is a sociologist who has helped facilitate resistance movements and studied them. He developed a typology of athlete activism, suggesting athlete protest takes place in waves (Edwards, 2016). The first wave occurred between 1900 and 1945 and included athletes, such as Paul Roberson and Fritz Pollard, seeking legitimacy through their participation and excellence. The second wave occurred from 1946 to the early 1960s. During this time, athletes such as Althea Gibson (professional tennis) and Jackie Robinson (Major League Baseball) sought political access and positional diversity. In the third wave, which took place from the mid-1960s the 1970s, athletes engaged in activism and protest to demand dignity and respect. A well-known example includes Tommie Smith and John Carlos, who during the 1969 Olympics medal ceremony, raised their gloved fists and bowed their heads as a form of protest against human rights abuses in the US (Edwards, 1969). According to Edwards,

the fourth wave of athlete activism started in 2005. Examples include members of the Women's National Basketball Association's (WNBA) Minnesota Lynx, LeBron James (National Basketball Association), and Colin Kaepernick (National Football League, NFL), all of whom protested racism and police brutality in the US. In addition, members of Northwestern Missouri's football team refused to practice or play in protest of racialized practices on their campus (see also Yan, Pegoraro, & Watanabe, 2018).

In many respects, protests against racism have resulted in change. At the University of Missouri, for example, the chancellor and president both stepped down, and the institution initiated large-scale changes designed to end racialized practices (Yan et al., 2018). Protests among professional athletes and coaches (e.g., Greg Popovich and Steve Kerr; Schoenfeld, 2017) generated dialog and similar action worldwide. The president of the US at the time even commented on the protests, albeit to chide them. He suggested, NFL owners should respond to athlete protest by saying, "Get that son of a bitch off the field right now, out. He's fired! He's fired!" (as quoted in Serwear, 2017).

Collectively, the evidence suggests athletes have and will continue to engage in protest against a variety of social injustices, including racism and racial discrimination.

Ethnicity, on the other hand, refers cultural patterns among groups of people, with a focus on cultural heritage, language customs, and so on. People from a given ethnicity might also share common norms, beliefs, and values.

Because of the lack of scientific validity in the supposed genetic differences, several scholars argue for the disuse of the term race and instead advocate for the use of ethnicity (Abercrombie, Hill, & Turner, 2000). To their point, there are many more similarities than differences between people who are supposedly of different races. Other scholars combine the terms, seeking to capture important concepts from both terms (e.g., Carrim, in press).

Recognizing these critiques, I suggest there are many good reasons to continue to use the term *race*. First, though there might be few genetic differences among people from different races, the word *race* does have historically engrained social meanings associated with it. Race and racism are social constructions—the manifestation of social thoughts and relations (Delgado & Stefancic, 2017). As such, whether people are conscious of the effect or not, race can impact people's experiences, opportunities, and interactions with others. Second, race is also at the fore of a number of societal issues, including those pertaining to education, religion, politics, and criminal justice. As Box 5.1 illustrates, race and its impact influence those in sport, too. Consequently, it is important to consider race, the meanings people attach to their own race and the race of others, and the theories that can assist the understanding of how race affects people in sport and physical activity.

In addition, *minority* refers to a collection of individuals who share a common characteristic and face discrimination in society because of their membership in that group (Coakley, 2015). Minorities face systemic forms of discrimination and will sometimes have a sense of social togetherness because of their shared lived experiences (Bone, Christensen, & Williams, 2014). Conceptualizing minority in this way de-emphasizes numbers, as a numerical minority can still be the social majority. Within the context of sport and physical activity, we can consider all persons who are not White, including African Americans, Asians, Hispanics, and so forth, as racial minorities.

RACE IN THE WORK ENVIRONMENT

As discussed in Chapter 1, across many Western countries, racial minorities represent a sizeable portion of the population and workforce, and demography experts expect that figure to increase (Cilluffo & Cohn, 2017). For example, according to US Census Bureau Statistics (Vespa, Armstrong, & Medina, 2018), the US had a population of roughly 323 million people in 2016, and of which, 60.1 percent (or 198 million) were White. By 2030, the Census Bureau predicts that the proportion of Whites will drop to 55.8 percent, and by 2060, to 44.3 percent. Similar trends are apparent around the world. In New Zealand, for example, people of European descent constituted 74.6 percent of the population in 2013. Experts expect that figure to decrease to 65.5 percent by 2038. On the other hand, the Māori, Asian, Pacific, and Middle Eastern populations are all expected to increase (National Ethnic Population Projections, 2017). These figures are important for sport managers, as changes to the population will correspond with shifts in the race of customers, athletes, clients, and employees.

Though the racial diversity of the workforce has increased, racial minorities are largely underrepresented in key leadership roles. How, though, do scholars make such determinations? Context plays a big role.

Let's first consider coaches. Though there are some exceptions, collegiate and professional coaches usually have experience playing the sport at that level. If this is the case, then the proportion of players from a particular race should generally correspond with the proportion of assistant and head coaches (Cunningham & Sagas, 2005; see also Everhart & Chelladurai, 1998). In Exhibit 5.1, I offer a statistical overview of the percent of racial minority players, assistant coaches, and head coaches across the major professional leagues and collegiate sports in the US. You will undoubtedly notice that, with the exception of Major League Baseball, there is a downward trend in each league or sport such that the proportion of racial minorities outpaces the corresponding proportion of assistant coaches and head coaches. The differences are starkest in women's collegiate basketball, where racial minorities are 3.76 times more likely to be a player than they are to be a head coach. Even in baseball, where the percentage of racial minority assistant coaches (45.9 percent) is greater than the corresponding figure for players (42.5 percent), only 13.3 percent of the head coaches are racial minority.

Note, this is not just a US problem. In Australia, Aboriginal and Torres Strait Islander peoples represent less than 1 percent of all coaches despite constituting roughly 10 percent of athletes in elite-level competitions (Apoifis, Marlin, & Bennie, in press). In the UK, only 8 of the 92 (8.7 percent) Premier and Football League clubs have a manager who is from a Black, Asian, or Minority Ethnic (BAME) background (Sky Sports News, 2018). The figure is substantially lower than the percentage of BAME players (33 percent; Dibble, 2017). The founder of the anti-racism organization Kick It Out, Lord Ousley, commented that although there are opportunities on the pitch—and these have increased over the years—there are still barriers for BAME individuals to remain in soccer following their playing days. The chair of the Football Association's board for inclusion, Paul Elliott, noted, "what we want to do now is make that next step, so that BAME players can move into coaching, into management and into boardrooms with the sample equal opportunities as they enjoy on the field of play" (as cited in Dibble, 2017).

These data show that racial minorities are largely underrepresented as assistant and head coaches. What about administrators? In this work role, previous playing experience is less crucial. Thus, it is helpful to use a different standard—the proportion of racial minorities in the population. In Exhibit 5.2, I offer an overview of the percentage of racial minorities serving as general managers (in professional sports) or athletic directors (in intercollegiate athletics) in the US. These data tell a similar story. Though racial minorities make up 39.1 percent of the US population, their proportion in key leadership roles in sport organizations is considerably less. Note that the league that comes closest to having proportional representation is the WNBA (27.3 percent). Over 85 percent of WNBA players, 53.8 percent of the assistant coaches, and 41.7 percent of the head coaches are racial minority. Thus, although there is room for improvement, the WNBA is the league that has the most racial diversity and comes closest to reaching appropriate points of comparison.

As discussed in Chapter 3, the differences represent a form of access discrimination (Greenhaus, Parasuraman, & Wormley, 1990). Recall that access discrimination occurs when people are denied the opportunity to participate in a particular activity, such as coaching or being a top-level administrator. There are a number

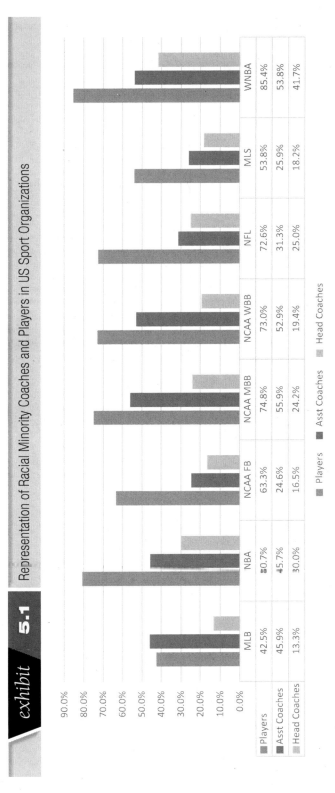

exhibit **5.1**   Representation of Racial Minority Coaches and Players in US Sport Organizations

	MLB	NBA	NCAA FB	NCAA MBB	NCAA WBB	NFL	MLS	WNBA
Players	42.5%	80.7%	63.3%	74.8%	73.0%	72.6%	53.8%	85.4%
Asst Coaches	45.9%	45.7%	24.6%	55.9%	52.9%	31.3%	25.9%	53.8%
Head Coaches	13.3%	30.0%	16.5%	24.2%	19.4%	25.0%	18.2%	41.7%

■ Players   ■ Asst Coaches   ■ Head Coaches

Sources: Data for professional leagues from 2017 season. Data from NCAA for 2016–2017 season. Data gathered from The Institute for Diversity and Ethics in Sport (www.tidesport.org) and NCAA Sport Sponsorship, Participation, and Demographics Research (http://web1.ncaa.org/rgdSearch/exec/main).

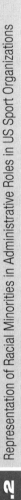

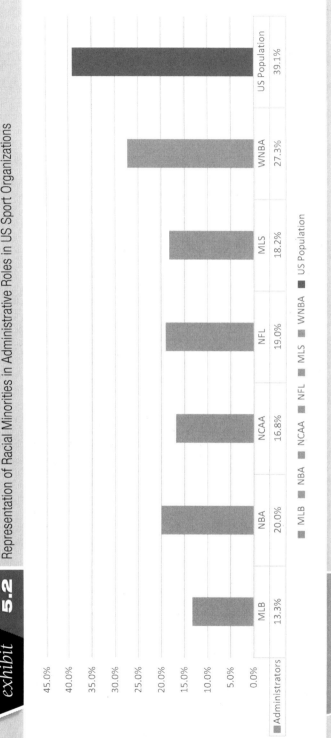

exhibit 5.2   Representation of Racial Minorities in Administrative Roles in US Sport Organizations

	MLB	NBA	NCAA	NFL	MLS	WNBA	US Population
Administrators	13.3%	20.0%	16.8%	19.0%	18.2%	27.3%	39.1%

■ MLB ■ NBA ■ NCAA ■ NFL ■ MLS ■ WNBA ■ US Population

Sources: Data for professional leagues from 2017 season. Data from NCAA for 2016–2017 season. Data gathered from The Institute for Diversity and Ethics in Sport (www.tidesport.org) and NCAA Sport Sponsorship, Participation, and Demographics Research (http://web1.ncaa.org/rgdSearch/exec/main).

Box 5.2 Alternative Perspectives: Other Discrimination Forms

Greenhaus et al. (1990) suggested there are two forms of discrimination: access, where people are denied the opportunity to pursue a particular career or sport path; and treatment, where people receive poorer treatment than they would otherwise deserve based on their work performance.

In addition to these discrimination forms, other scholars have examined occupational segregation (Bergmann, 1974). This process refers to the clustering of people into specific roles based on their personal demographics. Thus, racial minorities might have access to be an assistant coach, as one example, but only in particular roles. That is, they might be clustered into peripheral roles—ones that have limited influence and authority.

Examination of data from the National Collegiate Athletic Association (NCAA)—the primary collegiate sport body in the US—offers evidence of occupational segregation in the American football coaching ranks. In American football, the top assistant coach positions are the coordinators—the people who oversee the offense and defense. In these roles, Whites represent 83 percent and 72.4 percent of the coaches, respectively. There are other coaching roles, too, such as position coach or recruiting coordinator. Among the other assistant coaches, Whites represent 55.9 percent of the coaches. These trends, which has persisted for years (Anderson, 1993; Cunningham & Bopp, 2010; Turick & Bopp, 2016), show that, when considering evidence of discrimination, it is important to consider the type of role one occupies.

Sources: Data from NCAA for 2016–2017 season. Data gathered from NCAA Sport Sponsorship, Participation, and Demographics Research (http://web1.ncaa.org/rgdSearch/exec/main).

of reasons for the prevalence of access discrimination, which we cover later in the chapter. See Box 5.2 for other forms of discrimination.

In addition to access discrimination, there is evidence of treatment discrimination in sport and physical activity. According to Greenhaus et al. (1990), treatment discrimination occurs when people are treated more poorly than they deserve. The differences can manifest through differences in pay, work experiences, advancement opportunities, chances to take part in professional development, and the like. In the US, for example, the Bureau of Labor Statistics provides data related to race and people's weekly earnings. Data are included in Exhibit 5.3. Results show that Asians and Whites earn the most in the US, and African Americans and Hispanics earn the least. The differences, which have persisted over time, are stark, with Hispanics earning 62 percent of what Asians do on a weekly basis.

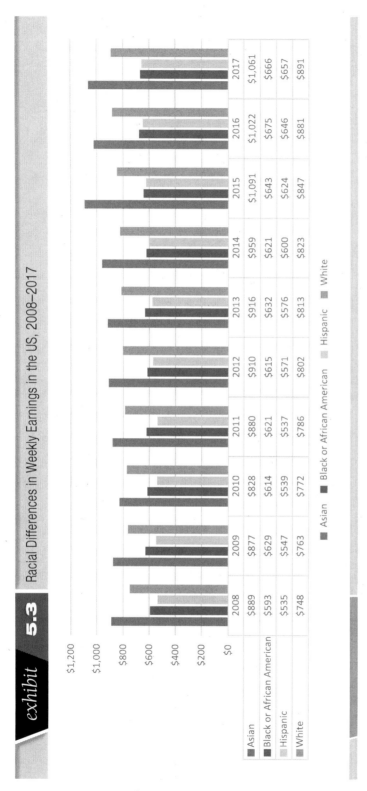

exhibit 5.3   Racial Differences in Weekly Earnings in the US, 2008–2017

	2008	2009	2010	2011	2012	2013	2014	2015	2016	2017
Asian	$889	$877	$828	$880	$910	$916	$959	$1,091	$1,022	$1,061
Black or African American	$593	$629	$614	$621	$615	$632	$621	$643	$675	$666
Hispanic	$535	$547	$539	$537	$571	$576	$600	$624	$646	$657
White	$748	$763	$772	$786	$802	$813	$823	$847	$881	$891

■ Asian   ■ Black or African American   ■ Hispanic   ■ White

Source: Bureau of Labor Statistics. Data retrieval: Labor force statistics (CPS). https://www.bls.gov/webapps/legacy/cpswktab3.htm.

Though Asians earn the most, as an entire group, they also experience the most within-race income inequality (Kochhar & Cilluffo, 2018). An analysis of government data by the Pew Research Center showed that, among Asians, those earning the most had incomes over 10 times greater than those earning the least. This disparity was greater than that observed among African Americans (9.8), Whites (7.8), or Latinos (7.8). Further analysis showed that income inequality among Asians has nearly doubled since 1970—again, the most among any racial group considered. Kochhar and Cilluffo pointed to differences in immigration patterns, educational attainment, and historical legacies of discrimination as sources for the variance.

Other forms of treatment discrimination are present, as well. For example, Bradbury, Van Sterkenburg, and Mignon (2018) interviewed 40 racial minority soccer coaches from England, France, and the Netherlands. The coaches told of poor experiences in high-level coaching education, the need to combat racism and discrimination in the coaching context, and being excluded from informal networks that are important in the selection of future coaches. Other researchers have shown that African American coaches are held to a higher standard of excellence than are Whites, and as a result, their race factors into dismissal decisions (Madden, 2004; Madden & Ruther, 2009). These patterns, and others like them, influence people who are considering the coaching profession as a line of work. Kamphoff and Gill (2008) observed that, among collegiate athletes in the US, racial minorities expected they would face differential treatment if they became coaches.

MULTILEVEL EXPLANATIONS

In Chapter 4, I offered a multilevel framework for understanding the experiences of and opportunities for people from underrepresented groups. In this section, I draw from that framework to focus on the macro-, meso-, and micro-level factors that influence racial minorities working in sport. Exhibit 5.4 provides an overview of the factors.

Multilevel Factors Affecting Racial Minorities in Sport   *exhibit* **5.4**

Macro-level factors: Those operating at the societal level, including employment laws, institutional racism, political climate, and stakeholder expectations.

Meso-level factors: Those operating at the team and organizational levels, including bias in decision-making, organizational culture, and diversity policies.

Micro-level factors: Those operating at the individual level, including capital investments, self-limiting behaviors, and personal identity.

Macro-Level Factors

As you will recall, macro-level factors operate at the societal level. A number of macro-level factors might influence racial minorities working in sport, including employment laws, institutional forms of racism, the political climate, and stakeholder expectations, among others.

Employment Laws

Employment laws can shape the opportunities for and experiences of members of different groups, including racial minorities (Chelladurai & Kerwin, 2017). Laws are shaped by culture and values within a given society. As such, what is acceptable at one time can and frequently does shift over time. As an example, in the US, the Supreme Court ruled in 1896 that racial segregation was permissible in public spaces, so long as the provisions were equal (*Plessy v Ferguson*, 1896). Almost 60 years after *Plessy*, the Supreme Court ruled that separate but equal was not equal and instead represented a form of racial discrimination (*Brown v. Board of Education*, 1954).

   In the US, a number of laws forbid employment decisions based on the race of the applicant or employee. At the federal level, most of these prohibitions exist as part of Title VII of the Civil Rights Act of 1964. This law applies to (a) all organizations with at least 15 employees, including state and local governments, (b) labor unions, (c) employment agencies, and (d) the federal government. Exhibit 5.5 provides an overview of Title VII's key provisions.

   Even though federal laws prohibit employment discrimination, such mistreatment persists. According to the Equal Employment Opportunity Commission (EEOC), employees reported 28,528 complaints of racial discrimination in 2017. In that same year, the Commission recovered $75.9 million in damages for the charging parties and other aggrieved persons. This figure does not include additional monies obtained through litigation. In addition to race discrimination, color discrimination—another diversity form covered in Title VII—is also prevalent at work. Exhibit 5.6 offers an overview of how color discrimination operates in sport.

Institutional Racism

Recall from Chapter 2 that some scholars focus on the interpersonal nature of prejudice, whereas others concentrate on the societal manifestations. It is the latter form that serves as the basis of discussion here. From a critical race theory perspective, racism is endemic in society, deeply engrained in society's systems and institutions (Hylton, 2009). Critical race theorists argue that racism is enmeshed in the cultural fabric and value systems. For example, researchers have used critical race theory to analyze performance among students (Cobb & Russell, 2015). They criticized the notion of meritocracy, or the idea that hard work is directly related to success. Such assumptions assume that all people have equal access to the resources needed to be successful, a position which is clearly fallible. Focusing

Title VII protects people from discrimination based on their race or skin color in hiring and firing decisions, promotions, compensation, and training opportunities. This law also prohibits employment decisions based on the stereotypes associated with people from a particular race—assumptions about people's work ethic, personal traits, or their overall abilities. The law also forbids employers from making employment decisions based on membership in or affiliation with race- or ethnic-based organizations (e.g., the Black Coaches and Administrators), attendance at schools or places of worship that might be associated with a particular racial group (e.g., having attended a historically Black college or university, such as Grambling State University), or a spouse's race.

Title VII prohibitions also include the following:

- **Race-related characteristics and conditions.** Discrimination based on a characteristic often associated with a particular race (e.g., specific hair texture, skin color) is unlawful. Organizations cannot make employment decisions based on conditions that predominantly affect members of one race more than they do members of other races unless it can be conclusively demonstrated that such practices are job related and are a business necessity. For example, a fitness club that has a policy of not hiring people with sickle cell anemia discriminates against African Americans because that condition is predominantly found among members of that race and is not job related.

- **Harassment.** Harassment takes many forms, including racial slurs, racial jokes, comments that could be deemed offensive, and other verbal or physical contact that is based on one's race.

- **Segregation or classification of employees.** An organization may not physically isolate members of a racial minority group from other employees or from customers. This prohibition also applies to the assignments people receive. It is unlawful, for example, to assign Hispanics to a mostly Hispanic division or geographic region. Finally, it is also illegal to group people from a protected class into certain positions. Suppose an athletic department always assigns African American employees to life skills coordinator or academic advisor positions, as opposed to positions dealing with development or finances, based on the assumption that people in the coordinator and advisor positions have the most contact with the athletes, many of whom are also African American. Classifying employees in this manner is unlawful. Based on NCAA data (2014; www.ncaa.org), this practice actually does occur frequently.

- **Pre-employment inquiries.** With a few exceptions, it is unlawful to ask job applicants what their race is. Employers that use affirmative action in the hiring process or track applicant flow may ask for information on race. Under these circumstances, it is best that the employer use a separate form to keep this information separate from the application. This ensures that the information will not be used in the remainder of the selection process.

exhibit   **5.6**   Color Discrimination in Sport

Commonly, when researchers examine race, they focus on groups as a whole. How, for example, do the experiences of Latinos differ from those of Whites? Are there different opportunities for meaningful work or to hold leadership positions? Lost in these analyses are within-group differences. Members of a given race are not all alike. They have different life experiences, education, and social networks. They also frequently have different skin tone.

It is this difference that served as the focus of a study McGovern (2017) conducted. She collected decades of data from baseball records, examining who held leadership positions as a player, manager, or broadcaster. She also collected data on the players' place of birth, their ethnicity, and their skin tone. McGovern found that, in the baseball context, skin tone was a better predictor of having a leadership role than ethnicity was. Regardless of their ethnicity, lighter skinned individuals were more likely to be in prominent leadership positions, both on and off the field. Light-skinned individuals were the smallest proportion of Latino players, but they were most likely among Latinos to work as managers, coaches, and broadcasters. They were also most likely to play catcher—one of the key positions on the team.

But why do these findings occur? McGovern suggests that deeply embedded cultural norms and understanding might be to blame. Since colonial times, having light skin has been linked with intelligence, capability, and beauty. On the other hand, darker skin was associated with danger and inferiority. Though some of these stereotypes have decreased, they are still prevalent, influencing people's behaviors and attitudes. Overall, the findings show that a number of factors influence the relationship between race and leadership opportunities, including one's skin color.

on meritocracy also suggests racial differences in outcomes are due to individual differences, ignoring the systems in place that perpetuate disparities.

Racism is also embedded in the business sector (Feagin, 2006), including individuals working in sport and physical activity (Hylton, 2012). Prevailing values, systems, and cultural understandings are situated in a way that privilege Whites. As an example, Feagin critiqued capitalism in the US, arguing that it "has been, from the beginning, a white-crafted and white oriented economic system imbedded in white-made business laws" (p. 198). Thus, even absent individual biases, systemic forms of racism are established in ways to limit the opportunities for racial minorities to be successful.

People certainly challenge racism and engage in activities to diminish its presence and impact. However, when certain practices persist over time, they become taken-for-granted and accepted as the way activities and processes take—that is, they become institutionalized. As the institutionalized practices continue, year after year, they become embedded, solidified, and highly resistant to change. New members of sport organizations or the sport industry in general learn that these practices are legitimate, further perpetuating them (see also Washington & Patterson, 2011). Thus, in the case of institutionalized forms of racism, the oppressive systems and structures remain, ultimately hurting racial minorities' opportunities and experiences in sport (Cunningham, 2012).

Political Climate

The political climate is another macro-level factor influencing racial minorities in sport. Prevailing political attitudes and the related policies can influence a number of sport and health outcomes, such as funding for sport activities (Harris & Adams, 2016; Nassif & Amara, 2015) and monies devoted to address health disparities (Bourgois, Holmes, Sue, & Quesada, 2017). Political attitudes are also associated with a host of diversity-related attitudes and behaviors, including attitudes toward affirmative action (Sidanius, Pratto, & Bobo, 1996), social justice activities (Leath & Chavous, 2017), and educational opportunities (Hess & McAvoy, 2014), among others.

The political climate also influences employment protections for racial minorities. Title VII of the Civil Rights Act of 1964 (see Exhibit 5.5) guaranteed that racial and ethnic minorities could not be subjected to discrimination while searching for a job or while employed. The law, and other laws protecting the rights of racial minorities (e.g., Voting Rights Act of 1965), was signed by President Lyndon Johnson, a progressive American president. The passage of diversity-focused laws are influenced by the political party in office, as is the enforcement of the laws. Researchers have shown that enforcement of diversity-related laws and fair labor practices is more stringent when the political climate is progressive than when it is more conservative (Marshall, 2005). This research suggests that opportunities for and the experiences of racial minorities in sport might be dependent upon the political climate in the region or country.

Finally, many scholars focus on explicit measures of racism when considering the link between politics and racial prejudice. However, as shown in Box 5.3, economist Seth Stephens-Davidowitz (2014) has identified other, more powerful ways to examine such linkages, and the patter of his findings calls into question previous assumptions about liberal-leaning areas of the US.

Stakeholder Expectations

Stakeholder expectations represent the final macro-level factor influencing racial minorities in sport. Recall from Chapter 4 that stakeholders are people who have a stake or interest in the sport organization (Clarkson, 1995). Examples include players, coaches, trainers, parents, financial supporters, community members, and fans, among others. Depending on the perspective of the sport organization leader, stakeholder input has the potential to impact decision-making.

In many countries, the government provides financial support for sport at the elite and community levels, and as such, the government serves as a stakeholder

Box 5.3 Professional Perspectives: A New Way to Think about Measuring Racism

Many times, scholars and pollsters will collect data on explicit measures of racism. They might ask people about their attitudes toward members of different groups, their behaviors, and rights. The analysts will then link these responses with other measures to identify how racism influences various outcomes. For example, do people in liberal states (based on voting records) express less racism than people living in more conservative states? Do ideas about race influence how people respond to race-related activities in sport, such as athlete protests? These are just two of many options.

One potential problem with this approach is that people are generally unwilling to admit they are racist. As far back as the 1940s, expressing racist ideas has been socially taboo (Campbell, 1947). Looking to address this problem, Seth Stephens-Davidowitz reasoned that people's Internet searches are likely a better indicator of their biases and beliefs than are paper-and-pencil questionnaires. Consider, for example, that most people use their computer in isolation. They also type in search queries that they might not ask others. Thus, people's searches might reveal biases, attitudes, or behaviors that they would be otherwise unwilling to share with others.

With this in mind, Stephens-Davidowitz examined search trends across the US using Google trends (Chae et al., 2015; Stephens-Davidowtiz, 2014). He examined how many times people searched for the N-word, the derogatory term expressed toward African Americans. Through a series of studies, he then examined how these search patterns were associated with other events.

The findings were striking. First, as expected, people in the Deep South were likely to Google things using the N-word, such as jokes. But, others were, too, including people in West Virginia, parts of Pennsylvania, and parts of New York, among other places.

He also found that the search patterns were predictive of a number of social events. For example, in communities where people Googled something with the N-word, they were less likely to vote for President Obama. In another study, he drew from research showing that community racism negatively affected racial minorities' health. Stephens-Davidowitz found that N-word searches in communities were predictive of mortality rates among African Americans.

Collectively, Stephens-Davidowitz's findings suggest that what we search for on the Internet, including diversity-related material, is often a good predictor of our other behaviors.

of sport programs. For example, many governments provide financial support to sport organizations as a way to offset the costs for the users. Thus, the governments serve as one stakeholder. In some cases, government agencies might make their financial support contingent upon the sport organizations engaging in diversity strategies aimed at increasing participation rates among racial minorities. In other cases, the funding might be linked with personnel selection processes aimed at increasing racial diversity. In either case, the stakeholder (i.e., the government entity) provides feedback (i.e., pursue a race-related diversity initiative), and sport organizations can adhere to such requests or forego the funding.

Meso-Level Factors

As outlined in Chapter 4, meso-level factors operate at the group and organizational levels. A number of meso-level factors might influence racial minorities working in sport, including bias in decision-making, organizational culture, diversity policies, and glass cliffs, among others.

Bias in Decision-Making

Recall from Chapter 3 that bias refers to stereotypes, prejudice, and discrimination (Cuddy, Fiske, & Glick, 2008). Bias among decision-makers can limit the opportunities racial minorities have for development opportunities, career advancement, and meaningful work.

In terms of stereotypes, decision-makers will frequently develop stereotypes about typical leaders, and then draw from these ideas when thinking about who should or could fill particular roles (Lord & Maher, 1991). The cognitive process informs who decision-makers consider a good fit and who lacks those qualities. Frequently, the idea of who embodies leadership qualities are racialized (Rosette, Leonardelli, & Phillips, 2008). In many Western countries, people consider—perhaps implicitly—Whites as more suitable for leadership roles than racial minorities. Consider, for example, that people consistently see Whites in leadership positions within business and the public sector. This pattern has been constant throughout US history, where political (presidents, senators, and governors) and business leaders (e.g., John D. Rockefeller, Steve Jobs, Warren Buffett) have predominantly been White. This historical conditioning shapes how people perceive potential leaders and who they think should hold leadership roles. Indeed, Rosette and colleagues (2008) found that Whiteness was seen as a prototype for business leaders—though not necessarily for everyday employees—and White leaders were considered to be more effective than leaders of color, especially when an organization's success was attributed to the leader.

These effects are evident in sport, too. Borland and Bruening (2010), for instance, interviewed African American women who coached at the collegiate level. They pointed to racial stereotypes—others saw African Americans as best suited for recruiting roles—as limiting their career advancement. Welty Peachey and colleagues (2015) conducted an extensive review of the leadership research in sport management. Their analysis revealed that "as a result of the dominant influence of White, able-bodied, heterosexual men in sport leadership, women and other minority groups are negatively affected by stereotypes of what is deemed acceptable sport leadership at all levels of the leadership process" (p. 581). The statistics in Exhibits 5.1 and 5.2 offer strong support for these dynamics.

Prejudice represents the second component of bias. As noted in Chapter 3, people can express explicit or implicit prejudice, both of which are likely to negatively influence racial minorities' experiences and opportunities. Jones and colleagues (2017) conducted a large-scale study to examine the influence of racism on people's work. They found that racism was associated with felt discrimination at work, discriminatory selection, bias performance evaluations, and opposition to diversity policies. Researchers have also shown that aversive racism might influence the help people receive (Pearson, Dovidio, & Gaertner, 2009). Other diversity factors might also influence employee behavior, including the race of the chief executive. McDonald, Keeves, and Westphal (2018) examined the behaviors of White male managers and found that, after the appointment of a female or racial minority chief executive officer, the managers expressed a weaker connection to the organization and offered less help to colleagues. The reduction was especially pronounced among help give to minority colleagues.

Researchers have observed similar dynamics in sport. Bruening, Straub, and I examined the experiences and career expectations of men's basketball and football coaches of collegiate teams (Cunningham, Bruening, & Straub, 2006). Racial minorities expressed that their race served as a barrier for their advancement in the field. The effects were especially pronounced among football coaches—a context where Whites hold a majority of the powerful positions (see Exhibit 5.1).

Organizational Culture

Schein (2004) defined culture as "a pattern of shared basic assumptions ... that has worked well enough to be considered valid and, therefore, to be taught to new members as the correct ways to perceive, think, and feel in relation to those problems" (p. 17). Organizational culture signals what is important in the workplace, who has power, and who can thrive. When an organizational culture is one that values diversity and inclusion, all organizational members are likely to thrive. This is because inclusive workplaces are ones where people can express identities important to them, such as their race, and also feel a sense of connectedness and belonging in the workplace (see Chapter 1).

To illustrate, McKay et al. (2007) collected data from thousands of managers in the US, asking them about the diversity culture in the organization and their attitudes toward the workplace. They found that, especially among African Americans, a pro-diversity culture helped spur a stronger commitment to the organization and lower turnover intentions. The pattern was the same, albeit with weaker relationships, among Whites and Hispanics. These data show that a diversity-focused culture can improve work attitudes and behaviors for all employees, racial minorities, and Whites, alike. In another study, McKay, Avery, and Morris (2008) found that sales performance of both Whites and Africans Americans improved when the culture was pro-diversity, and the increase was particularly pronounced among African Americans.

The benefits of an organizational culture marked by diversity and inclusion are also apparent in sport. Rosselli and Singer (2015) focused on golf—a sport that, with a few notable exceptions (e.g., Tiger Woods), is stereotypically White. They argued that the cultures of similarity within the golf industry helped perpetuate these trends. Their position is consistent with Bradbury's (2013). He analyzed the underrepresentation of racial minorities as soccer coaches among professional squads in Europe and pointed to "the 'invisible centrality of whiteness' embedded within the senior organizational tiers of the game" (p. 299; see also Rankin-Wright, Hylton, & Norman, 2016). The centrality of Whiteness meant that Whiteness was linked with insider status, power, and being included. Importantly, the effects of a culture of exclusion can reach outside the organization, as potential job applicants (Lee & Cunningham, 2015) and consumers who are racial minority are likely to shy away (Santucci, Floyd, Bocarro, & Henderson, 2014). From a different perspective, research I have conducted with athletic departments in the US (Cunningham, 2009) has shown that racial diversity is associated with objective measures of performance, especially when the department culture is inclusive. Absent such culture, the benefits of racial diversity disappeared. Thus, while racial diversity in sport organizations is linked with improved performance (Lee & Cunningham, in press), the association is strengthened when set within an organization that has an inclusive culture.

Organizational Policies

Organizational policies can contribute to the overall culture of the workplace but they also have their own unique effects. Sport organizations might institute policies related to hiring, promotions, or performance evaluations that affect the opportunities and experiences of racial minorities. One example is the NFL's Rooney Rule.

The NFL has historically experienced poor diversity figures when it comes to racial minorities in leadership positions. As a result, in 2003, the league implemented the Rooney Rule, which requires teams to interview at least one racial minority during the search for a new head coach. The league recently expanded the rule to also include senior-level administrators.

DuBois (2015) analyzed the effects of the Rooney Rule to determine whether the mandate resulted in increased diversity. Importantly, she also compared diversity in the NFL head coaching ranks to other groups, such as diversity among the top assistant coaches or diversity in the college ranks. In doing so, she could rule out the possibility of societal or industry changes.

She found that the Rooney Rule did, indeed, affect the hiring of minority NFL coaches. Specifically, relative to the two comparison groups, a racial minority was 19–21 percent more likely to fill an NFL head coaching vacancy in the post-Rooney era.

DuBois' findings show the value of the Rooney Rule. Importantly, NFL teams are not required to hire a certain number of minority coaches, but simply to interview one during the process. The findings raise the question of whether these strategies could be effective in other contexts, too, including the selection of college coaches, faculty members, or even CEO's. If the NFL data are applicable across settings, requiring companies to interview at least one racial minority would go a long way toward improving the diversity in leadership positions. Recognizing this potential, in 2018, the English Football Association implemented the Rooney Rule for national team coaching and administrative positions (English Soccer, 2018).

Micro-Level Factors

Finally, we examine micro-level factors, which operate at the individual level. They include capital investments, self-limiting behaviors, and personal identity.

Capital Investments

People make various personal investments in their career, and scholars have generally classified them into two categories: human and social (Becker, 1993; Coleman, 1986). Human capital investments include education, training, roles held, experience, and so on. Social capital, on the other hand, refers to the social networks and connections one has. Researchers usually consider the breadth of the network, such as the overall number of contacts, characteristics of network members (i.e., similar level or higher in the organizational hierarchy), and the strength of the connections. For many, as human and social capital investments increase, so too does career success.

From a capital perspective, racial differences in the career success are likely due to (a) differences in human and capital investments or (b) different returns for similar investments. The notion of different returns is consistent with the notion of treatment discrimination, previously discussed (Ibarra, 1995; Sagas & Cunningham, 2005). Researchers have provided more evidence for the latter explanation (Day, 2015, 2018; Day & McDonald, 2010). Specifically, Whites and racial minorities are differentially rewarded for similar human capital investments. That is, given similar human capital investments, Whites are more likely to enjoy various measures of career success than are African Americans (Sagas & Cunningham, 2005). Further, Whites and racial minorities need different kinds of social networks to be successful. Same-race networks benefit Whites' promotion rates, but mixed-race social contacts benefit racial minority members' promotion rates. This finding might be explained by the overrepresentation of Whites in hiring positions; thus, if racial minorities want to advance in their career, having social networks that include Whites might be beneficial. In addition, strong professional relationships with network members benefit Whites, whereas more informal relationships benefit racial minorities. Finally, African Americans benefit from having a large number of high-status contacts, but this effect is not observed among Whites.

Personal Identity

One's personal identity can also influence experiences and opportunities. For people with a strong racial identity, their race is an important part of who they are, how they see themselves, and their overall self-concept. From one perspective, racial identity can influence how we see the world. Sellers and Shelton

(2003), for example, found that even after considering other factors, racial identity was positively associated with perceived racial discrimination. Thus, as one increased, so too did the other. Although racial identity might be linked with perceived discrimination, it is also associated with well-being. Smith and Silva (2011) aggregated the findings from previous studies and found that, overall, racial identity is positively correlated with various measures of well-being, such as self-esteem. The patterns are stronger for younger individuals than for people over age 40.

In the work context, others' perceptions of racial minorities' racial identity can affect hiring decisions. Colleagues and I have conducted experiments across contexts (fitness organizations and intercollegiate athletics) and samples (students and working professionals). Across the studies, we found that when White raters believe a racial minority applicant strongly identifies with her race, they view the applicant less favorably. Relative to applicants believed to be weakly identified, job applicants perceived to strongly identify with their race are considered a poorer fit for the job, and raters recommend lower salary offers (Steward & Cunningham, 2015; Vick & Cunningham, 2018). The salary differences are nontrivial and amount to a difference of $39,000 over 15 years at the organization. The findings, and other like them (Kaiser & Pratt-Hyatt, 2009), lend credibility to the reported increased incidence of prejudice and discrimination among highly racially identified racial minorities (Major, Quinton, & McCoy, 2002).

Self-Limiting Behaviors

Recall from Chapter 4 that, because of the biases and barriers racial minorities face on a continual basis, they might choose to disengage from their particular career path. Examples include decreased performance, not seeking promotions, leaving a particular role, or leaving sport all together. All of these actions refer to self-limiting behaviors.

Researchers have shown that racial minorities will sometimes engage in self-limiting behaviors, and importantly, the behaviors are associated with barriers they encounter. As one example, Wells and Kerwin (2017) collected data from sport administrators working in intercollegiate athletics in the US. They found that women and racial minorities had the same belief in their abilities as did White men, and they also believed they had similar levels of supports in their careers. There were differences between the two groups, though. Relative to White men, women and racial minorities encountered more barriers to their career progression and had fewer intentions to ultimately become an athletic director.

Within the coaching context, researchers have shown that racial minorities anticipate and experience more barriers to their career progression than do Whites (Cunningham & Singer, 2010; Cunningham et al., 2006; Kamphoff & Gill, 2008). Unlike the aforementioned study related to administrators, though, there is limited evidence that such barriers influence their career aspirations, relative to Whites. Thus, commonly held sentiments among some administrators, such as "we would love to hire more racial minorities, but they are simply not applying," ring false.

Commenting on why he keeps applying for jobs despite the racial discrimination he has experienced in his career, one coach noted,

> After a while, it makes you think, "Why go through with it?" because you've seen the track record. But at the same time, you have to make yourself go through with it because you don't want to allow the excuse, "Well, they're not applying."
>
> (as cited in Wixon, 2006)

Occupational turnover, or the decision to leave one's career field, represents another self-limiting behavior. In this area, racial differences are more reliable. Across a number of studies in different contexts, we have observed that racial minorities plan on leaving coaching earlier than Whites (see Cunningham, Dixon, Ahn, & Anderson, 2017). A number of factors contribute to this trend, including health concerns, a lack of time with family, a lack of advancement opportunities, low career satisfaction, and treatment discrimination.

RACE AND SPORT PARTICIPATION

In addition to influencing employment opportunities and experiences, race can affect people's access to and experiences in sport. Consider, for example, results from the National Health Interview Survey, conducted by the Centers for Disease Control and Prevention in the US (www.healthypeople.gov). In one question, the researchers examined the proportion of adults who engage in recommended levels of aerobic activity each week: 150 minutes of moderate activity, 75 minutes of vigorous activity, or some combination thereof. As shown in Exhibit 5.7, Whites are more likely than other groups to achieve the recommended physical activity levels. In fact, their rate of participation is above the population figures, and they are the only group to have over 50 percent of participants reach the threshold in each of the six years considered.

These patterns are not specific to the US. In Australia, for instance, persons from Indigenous populations report lower physical activity levels and overall health and well-being, relative to White populations (Stronach, Maxwell, & Pearce, in press). That noted, sport participation can help to improve health outcomes among Indigenous persons (Stronach Maxwell, & Pearce, in press). In the UK, results from the Active Lives Survey (https://www.sportengland.org/research/active-lives-survey) demonstrated that British Whites were more active than were Asians, Chinese, and Black individuals. Interestingly, people of mixed ethnicity were most active among the different groups.

Several factors contribute to these trends. Historically, various forms of oppression, racism, and segregation limited the participation of racial minorities in physical activity, and in many respects, vestiges of these practices continue today. McNeill, Kreuter, and Subramanian (2006) pointed to the primacy of the social environment, including support networks, income, discrimination, neighborhood factors, and social cohesion. Several of these factors, including discrimination and neighborhood factors, are likely to differentially impact Whites and racial minorities. Edwards and I focused on these very factors in a study of physical activity

| Race and Physical Activity Rates among US Adults | *exhibit* | **5.7** |

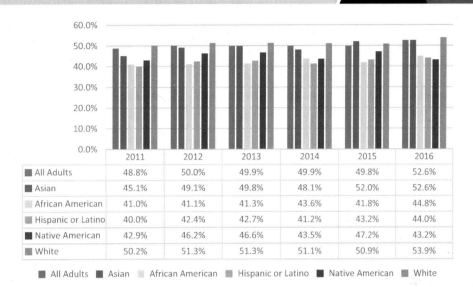

	2011	2012	2013	2014	2015	2016
■ All Adults	48.8%	50.0%	49.9%	49.9%	49.8%	52.6%
■ Asian	45.1%	49.1%	49.8%	48.1%	52.0%	52.6%
▨ African American	41.0%	41.1%	41.3%	43.6%	41.8%	44.8%
■ Hispanic or Latino	40.0%	42.4%	42.7%	41.2%	43.2%	44.0%
■ Native American	42.9%	46.2%	46.6%	43.5%	47.2%	43.2%
▨ White	50.2%	51.3%	51.3%	51.1%	50.9%	53.9%

■ All Adults   ▨ Asian   ▨ African American   ■ Hispanic or Latino   ■ Native American   ▨ White

Source: www.healthypeople.gov

among older racial minorities (Edwards & Cunningham, 2013). We found that community characteristics made a difference. Specifically, among people who lived in communities marked by high levels of racism, the more the community offered opportunities to be active, the more days a week the older adults engaged in physical activity. However, people were unlikely to be active when community racism was high and when the community did not offer recreational activities for its members.

Race can also influence sport and physical activity participation through cultural norms and social class. Prevailing cultural norms influence sport participation by sending signals about what is popular and appropriate (Sage & Eitzen, 2016). These norms explain why some activities (e.g., snow skiing) are more popular among some groups (i.e., Whites) than others. Social class also influences the amount of time people spend working or engaged in other activities, including sport and exercise (Wiltshire, Lee, & Williams, in press). As previously noted, many racial minorities have less discretionary income than Whites, on average, and this difference corresponds to the differing participation levels among the groups.

Race can also influence access and quality of experience in formal sport. Relative to their population, racial minorities are less likely to participate in formal sport than are Whites (Coakley, 2015). There are exceptions: African Americans are highly represented in basketball and football, whereas Latinos are well represented in soccer, softball, and baseball. There are also some sports, though, where few if any racial minorities participate; these include skiing, yachting, and hiking.

A number of factors affect racial minorities' participation in sport, such as support from others, the threat of deportation, and the number of generations the family has resided in the country (Coakley, 2015). Evidence also shows that the delivery of sport can influence participation. Kanters, Bocarro, Edwards, and colleagues (2013) conducted a study of how the delivery of sport in junior high schools (grades 6 through 8) affected students' participation. Half of the schools had interscholastic sport programs, whereas the other half had only intramural sports programs, the latter of which are generally considered more inclusive. They found that African Americans and children from low-income families had substantially greater sport involvement when the school had intramural sports. This pattern held true not only across sports in which African Americans usually participate, such as basketball (30.3 percent vs. 8.1 percent) and football (25.9 percent vs. 4.7 percent), but also in those sports in which their involvement has traditionally been low, such as soccer (14.7 percent vs. 0.8 percent), volleyball (12.4 percent vs. 1.1 percent), and softball (4.4 percent vs. 0.3 percent). Thus, the inclusiveness of the sport program affects racial minorities' participation.

Finally, there is some evidence that racial minorities have poor experiences while participating in sport. This comes in the form of bias. Just as racial stereotypes influence attitudes about who should and should not be a leader, race also affects perceptions about athletes' physical and mental abilities. Prevailing stereotypes cast African Americans, for example, as superior athletes but lacking in intellectual capabilities. Thus, people associate African Americans' athletic accomplishments with natural abilities rather than hard work (Moskowitz & Carter, 2018). These stereotypes exist for both women and men participating in sport (Withycombe, 2011) and are frequently gendered in nature (Galinsky, Hall, & Cuddy, 2013).

CHAPTER SUMMARY

In this chapter, I examine the effects of race in sport and physical activity. As illustrated in the Diversity Challenge, race and sport frequently intersect, influencing the access, experiences, and performance of athletes and sport managers. Having read this chapter, you should now be able to:

1. Define race, ethnicity, and minority.
   Though people sometimes use the terms interchangeably, race and ethnicity have distinct meanings. Race refers to a socially constructed construct used to differentiate people based on supposed genetic differences. Ethnicity, on the other hand, refers to the cultural heritage of a particular group of people, with an emphasis on the common culture certain groups of people share. Finally, a minority group is a collection of persons who share common characteristics and face discrimination in society because of their membership in that group.

2. Describe the representation of racial minorities in leadership positions in sport.
   Racial minorities are underrepresented as both coaches and administrators. Many racial minorities also experience treatment discrimination via differential pay, though in the US, Asians earn the highest wages.

3. Summarize the reasons for the underrepresentation of racial minorities in leadership positions in sport.

     Macro-, meso-, and micro-level factors all influence the underrepresentation of racial minorities in sport. Macro-level factors include employment laws, institutional racism, political climate, and stakeholder expectations. Meso-level factors include bias in decision-making, organizational culture, and diversity policies. Finally, micro-level factors include capital investments, self-limiting behaviors, and personal identity.

4. Paraphrase the manner in which race influences opportunities and experiences of sport and physical activity participants.

     Race is associated with participation in both physical activity and formal sports, with racial minorities having fewer opportunities than Whites. Race is also associated with negative experiences in sport and exercise, resulting from racial stereotypes, prejudice, and discrimination.

Questions FOR DISCUSSION

1. What are the primary distinctions between race and ethnicity? Do you think that the distinction between the two terms is meaningful? Why or why not?
2. Though the proportion of racial minorities in various countries is increasing, they continue to be disadvantaged in several areas. What are some of the reasons for this differential treatment?
3. Which of the multilevel factors do you think has the biggest impact on the access to and experiences of racial minorities in sport? Why?
4. Discuss the various ways that race influences sport and physical activity participation.
5. Race influences the treatment of sport participants in several ways. Which of the factors identified in the chapter has the largest impact on sport participants? Why?

LEARNING Activities

1. In this chapter, I used different standards when examining the representation of coaches and administrators. What are the pros and cons of the different benchmarks discussed in the chapter (e.g., the composition of the general population versus the composition of the pool of former athletes)? Divide into two groups, with each group adopting one perspective, and discuss.
2. What is the role of sport organizations or sport-governing bodies in creating racial equality in sport and physical activity? Using online sources, identify examples of where such efforts have taken place.

Web RESOURCES

Sport and Ethnicity, https://www.sportengland.org/research/
    understanding-audiences/sport-and-ethnicity/
        A site from Sport England that examines the role of ethnicity in sport
    participation.
USC Race and Ethnicity Center, http://race.usc.edu
        A research center at the University of Southern California, with a focus on
    race, ethnicity, and education, including sports and athletics.
NCAA Race and Ethnicity
        Part of the National Collegiate Athletic Association's Inclusion page, with
    resources focusing on race and ethnicity.

READING Resources

Delgado, R., & Stefancic, J. (2017). *Critical race theory: An introduction* (3rd ed.). New York, NY: New York University Press.
    Offers an overview of critical race theory and its application to various contexts.

Hylton, K. (2009). *"Race" and sport: Critical race theory*. New York, NY: Routledge.

Focuses on race and racism in sport, with an emphasis on critical race theory.

Long, J., & Spracklen, K. (Eds.). (2011). *Sport and challenges to racism.* Hampshire, UK: Palgrave Macmillan.
    Provides essays about racism, racial discrimination, and ways to end these practices in sport.

REFERENCES

Abercrombie, N., Hill, S., & Turner, B. S. (2000). *The Penguin dictionary of sociology* (4th ed.). New York, NY: Penguin Books.

Adair, D. (2011). *Sport, race, and ethnicity: Narratives of differences and diversity*. Morgantown, WV: Fitness Information Technology.

Anderson, D. (1993). Cultural diversity on campus: A look at intercollegiate football coaches. *Journal of Sport and Social Issues, 17*(1), 61–66.

Apoifis, N., Marlin, D., & Bennie, A. (in press). Noble athlete, savage coach: How racialised representations of Aboriginal athletes impede professional sport coaching opportunities for Aboriginal Australians. *International Review for the Sociology of Sport.*

Becker, G. S. (1993). *Human capital.* Chicago, IL: University of Chicago Press.

Bergmann, B. R. (1974). Occupational segregation, wages and profits when employers discriminate by race or sex. *Eastern Economic Journal, 1*(2), 103–110.

Bone, S. A., Christensen, G. L., & Williams, J. D. (2014). Rejected, shackled, and alone: The impact of systemic restricted choice on minority consumers' construction of self. *Journal of Consumer Research, 41*(2), 451–474.

Borland, J. F., & Bruening, J. E. (2010). Navigating barriers: A qualitative examination of the under-representation of Black females as head coaches in collegiate basketball. *Sport Management Review*, 13(4), 407–420.

Bourgois, P., Holmes, S. M., Sue, K., & Quesada, J. (2017). Structural vulnerability: Operationalizing the concept to address health disparities in clinical care. *Academic Medicine: Journal of the Association of American Medical Colleges*, 92(3), 299–307.

Bradbury, S. (2013). Institutional racism, whiteness and the under-representation of minorities in leadership positions in football in Europe. *Soccer & Society*, 14(3), 296–314.

Bradbury, S., Van Sterkenburg, J., & Mignon, P. (2018). The under-representation and experiences of elite level minority coaches in professional football in England, France and the Netherlands. *International Review for the Sociology of Sport, 53*(3), 313–334.

Campbell, A. A. (1947). Factors associated with attitudes toward Jews: In T. Newcomb & E. Hartley (Eds.), *Readings in social psychology* (pp. 518–527). New York, NY: Holt.

Carrim, N. M. (in press). The in-betweeners: Racio-ethnic and masculine identity work of Indian male managers in the South African private sector. *The Journal of Men's Studies*.

Chae, D. H., Clouston, S., Hatzenbuehler, M. L., Kramer, M. R., Cooper, H. L., Wilson, S. M., ... Link, B. G. (2015). Association between an internet-based measure of area racism and black mortality. *PloS One, 10*(4), e0122963.

Chelladurai, P., & Kerwin, S. (2017). *Human resource management in sport and recreation* (3rd ed.). Champaign, IL: Human Kinetics.

Cilluffo, A., & Cohn, D. (2017, April). 10 demographic trends shaping the U.S. and the world in 2017. *Pew Research Center*. Retrieved from http://www.pewresearch.org/fact-tank/2017/04/27/10-demographic-trends-shaping-the-u-s-and-the-world-in-2017/

Clarkson, M. E. (1995). A stakeholder framework for analyzing and evaluating corporate social performance. *Academy of Management Review*, 20(1), 92–117.

Coakley, J. (2015). *Sports in society: Issues and controversies* (11th ed.). New York, NY: McGraw-Hill.

Cobb, F., & Russell, N. M. (2015). Meritocracy or complexity: Problematizing racial disparities in mathematics assessment within the context of curricular structures, practices, and discourse. *Journal of Education Policy, 30*(5), 631–649.

Coleman, J. S. (1986). Social theory, social research, and a theory of action. *American Journal of Sociology, 91*, 1309–1335.

Cooper, J. N., Macauly, C., & Rodriguez, S. H. (in press). Race and resistance: A typology of African American sport activism. *International Review for the Sociology of Sport*.

Cuddy, A. J., Fiske, S. T., & Glick, P. (2008). Warmth and competence as universal dimensions of social perception: The stereotype content model and the BIAS map. *Advances in Experimental Social Psychology, 40*, 61–149.

Cunningham, G. B. (2009). The moderating effect of diversity strategy on the relationship between racial diversity and organizational performance. *Journal of Applied Social Psychology, 36*, 1445–1460.

Cunningham, G. B. (2012). Occupational segregation of African Americans in intercollegiate athletics administration. *Wake Forest Journal of Law & Policy, 2*, 165–178.

Cunningham, G. B., & Bopp, T. D. (2010). Race ideology perpetuated: Media representations of newly hired football coaches. *Journal of Sports Media, 5*(1), 1–19.

Cunningham, G. B., & Sagas, M. (2005). Access discrimination in intercollegiate athletics. *Journal of Sport and Social Issues, 29*, 148–163.

Cunningham, G. B., & Singer, J. N. (2010). "You'll Face Discrimination Wherever You Go": Student athletes' intentions to enter the coaching profession. *Journal of Applied Social Psychology, 40*(7), 1708–1727.

Cunningham, G. B., Bruening, J. E., & Straub, T. (2006). The underrepresentation of African Americans in NCAA Division IA head coaching positions. *Journal of Sport Management, 20*(3), 387–413.

Cunningham, G. B., Dixon, M. A., Ahn, N. Y., & Anderson, A. J. (2017, September). *Leaving sport: A meta-analysis of racial differences in occupational turnover.* Paper presented at the annual conference for the European Sport Management Association, Bern, Switzerland.

Day, J. C. (2015). Transitions to the top: Race, segregation, and promotions to executive positions in the college football coaching profession. *Work and Occupations, 42*(4), 408–446.

Day, J. C. (2018). Climbing the ladder or getting stuck: An optimal matching analysis of racial differences in college football coaches' job-level career patterns. *Research in Social Stratification and Mobility, 53,* 1–15.

Day, J. C., & McDonald, S. (2010). Not so fast, my friend: Social capital and the race disparity in promotions among college football coaches. *Sociological Spectrum, 30,* 138–158.

Delgado, R., & Stefancic, J. (2017). *Critical race theory: An introduction* (3rd ed.). New York, NY: New York University Press.

Dibble, A. (2017, August). Proportion of British BAME players has doubled since the Premier League began— talkSPORT special report. *TalkSPORT.* Retrieved from https://talksport.com/football/269320/proportion-british-bame-players-has-doubled-premier-league-began-talksport-special-report/

DuBois, C. (2015). The impact of "soft" affirmative action policies on minority hiring in executive leadership: The case of the NFL's Rooney rule. *American Law and Economics Review, 18*(1), 208–233.

Edwards, H. (1969). *The revolt of the Black athlete.* New York, NY: Free Press.

Edwards, H. (2016, November). *The fourth wave: Black athlete protests in the second decade of the 21st century.* Keynote address at the North American Society for the Sociology of Sport conference.

Edwards, M. B., & Cunningham, G. (2013). Examining the associations of perceived community racism with self-reported physical activity levels and health among older racial minority adults. *Journal of Physical Activity and Health, 10*(7), 932–939.

English soccer adopts 'Rooney Rule' for national team jobs. (2018, January). *USA Today.* Retrieved from https://www.usatoday.com/story/sports/soccer/2018/01/09/english-soccer-adopts-rooney-rule-for-national-team-jobs/109290066/

Everhart, B. C., & Chelladurai, P. (1998). Gender differences in preferences for coaching as an occupation: The role of self-efficacy, valence, and perceived barriers. *Research Quarterly for Exercise and Sport, 68,* 188–200.

Feagin, J. R. (2006). *Systemic racism: A theory of oppression.* New York, NY: Routledge.

Galinsky, A. D., Hall, E. V., & Cuddy, A. J. C. (2013). Gendered races: Implications for interracial marriage, leadership selection, and athletic participation. *Psychological Science, 24,* 498–506.

Greenhaus, J. H., Parasuraman, S., & Wormley, W. M. (1990). Effects of race on organizational experiences, job performance, evaluations, and career outcomes. *Academy of Management Journal, 33,* 64–86.

Harris, K., & Adams, A. (2016). Power and discourse in the politics of evidence in sport for development. *Sport Management Review, 19*(2), 97–106.

Hess, D. E., & McAvoy, P. (2014). *The political classroom: Evidence and ethics in democratic education*. New York, NY: Routledge.

Hylton, K. (2009). *"Race" and sport: Critical race theory*. New York, NY: Routledge.

Hylton, K. (2012). Talk the talk, walk the walk: Defining critical race theory in research. *Race Ethnicity and Education, 15*(1), 23–41.

Ibarra, H. (1995). Race, opportunity, and diversity of social circles in managerial networks. *Academy of Management Journal, 38*(3), 673–703.

Jones, K. P., Sabat, I. E., King, E. B., Ahmad, A., McCausland, T. C., & Chen, T. (2017). Isms and schisms: A meta-analysis of the prejudice-discrimination relationship across racism, sexism, and ageism. *Journal of Organizational Behavior, 38*(7), 1076–1110.

Kaiser, C. R., & Pratt-Hyatt, J. S. (2009). Distributing prejudice unequally: Do Whites direct their prejudice toward strongly identified minorities? *Journal of Personality and Social Psychology, 96*(2), 432–445.

Kamphoff, C., & Gill, D. (2008). Collegiate athletes' perceptions of the coaching profession. *International Journal of Sports Science & Coaching, 3*(1), 55–72.

Kanters, M. A., Bocarro, J. N., Edwards, M. B., Casper, J. M., & Floyd, M. F. (2013). School sport participation under two sport policies: Comparisons by race/ethnicity, gender, and socioeconomic status. *Annals of Behavioral Medicine, 45*(Suppl 1), S113–S121.

Kochhar, R., & Cilluffo, A. (2018, July). Key findings on the rise in income inequality within America's racial and ethnic groups. *Pew Research Center*. Retrieved from http://www.pewresearch.org/fact-tank/2018/07/12/key-findings-on-the-rise-in-income-inequality-within-americas-racial-and-ethnic-groups/

Leath, S., & Chavous, T. (2017). "We really protested": The influence of sociopolitical beliefs, political self-efficacy, and campus racial climate on civic engagement among Black college students attending Predominantly White Institutions. *The Journal of Negro Education, 86*(3), 220–237.

Lee, W., & Cunningham, G. B. (2015). A picture is worth a thousand words: The influence of signaling, organizational reputation, and applicant race on attraction to sport organizations. *International Journal of Sport Management, 16*, 492–506.

Lee, W., & Cunningham, G. B. (in press). Group diversity's influence on sport teams and organizations: A meta-analytic examination and identification of key moderators. *European Sport Management Quarterly*.

Lord, R., & Maher, K. (1991). *Leadership and information processing*. New York, NY: Unwin Hyman.

Madden, J. F. (2004). Differences in the success of NFL coaches by race, 1990–2002. *Journal of Sports Economics, 5*, 6–19.

Madden, J. F., & Ruther, M. (2009). Reply to: Differences in the success of NFL coaches by race: A different perspective. *Journal of Sports Economics, 10*(5), 543–550.

Major, B., Quinton, W. J., & McCoy, S. K. (2002). Antecedents and consequences of attributions to discrimination: Theoretical and empirical advances. *Advances in Experimental Social Psychology, 34*, 251–330.

Marshall, A. M. (2005). *Confronting sexual harassment: The law and politics of everyday life*. Burlington, VT: Ashgate.

McDonald, M. L., Keeves, G. D., & Westphal, J. D. (2018). One step forward, one step back: White male top manager organizational identification and helping behavior toward other executives following the appointment of a female or racial minority CEO. *Academy of Management Journal, 61*(2), 405–439.

McGovern, J. (2017). The boundaries of Latino sport leadership: How skin tone, ethnicity, and nationality construct baseball's color line. *Sociological Inquiry, 87*(1), 49–74.

McKay, P. F., Avery, D. R., & Morris, M. A. (2008). Mean racial-ethnic differences in employee sales performance: The moderating role of diversity climate. *Personnel Psychology, 61*(2), 349–374.

McKay, P. F., Avery, D. R., Tonidandel, S., Morris, M. A., Hernandez, M., & Hebl, M. R. (2007). Racial differences in employee retention: Are diversity climate perceptions the key? *Personnel Psychology, 60*(1), 35–62.

McNeill, L. H., Kreuter, M. W., & Subramanian, S. V. (2006). Social environment and physical activity: A review of concepts and evidence. *Social Science & Medicine, 63*(4), 1011–1022.

Moskowitz, G. B., & Carter, D. (2018). Confirmation bias and the stereotype of the Black athlete. *Psychology of Sport and Exercise, 36*, 139–146.

Nassif, N., & Amara, M. (2015). Sport, policy and politics in Lebanon. *International Journal of Sport Policy and Politics, 7*(3), 443–455.

National Ethnic Population Projections: 2013 (base) – 2038 (update) (2017, May). *Stats NZ*. Retrieved from http:// archive.stats.govt.nz/browse_for_stats/ population/estimates_and_projections/ NationalEthnicPopulationProjections_ HOTP2013-2038.aspx

Pearson, A. R., Dovidio, J. F., & Gaertner, S. L. (2009). The nature of contemporary racism: Insights from aversive racism. *Social and Personality Psychology Compass, 3*, 314–338.

Rankin-Wright, A. J., Hylton, K., & Norman, L. (2016). Off-colour landscape: Framing race equality in sport coaching. *Sociology of Sport Journal, 33*(4), 357–368.

Rosette, A. S., Leonardelli, G. J., & Phillips, K. W. (2008). The White standard: Racial bias in leader categorization. *Journal of Applied Psychology, 93*, 758–777.

Rosselli, A., & Singer, J. N. (2015). Toward a multilevel framework to examine the underrepresentation of racial minorities in golf within the United States. *Quest, 67*(1), 44–55.

Sagas, M., & Cunningham, G. B. (2005). Racial differences in the career success of assistant football coaches: The role of discrimination, human capital, and social capital. *Journal of Applied Social Psychology, 35*(4), 773–797.

Sage, G. H., & Eitzen, D. S. (2016). *Sociology of North American sport* (10th ed.). New York, NY: Oxford University Press.

Santucci, D. C., Floyd, M. F., Bocarro, J. N., & Henderson, K. A. (2014). Visitor services staff perceptions of strategies to encourage diversity at two urban national parks. *Journal of Park and Recreation Administration, 32*(3), 15–28.

Schein, E. H. (2004). *Organizational culture and leadership* (3rd ed.). San Francisco, CA: Jossey-Bass.

Schoenfeld, B. (2017, September). The justice league. *Esquire*. Retrieved from https:// www.esquire.com/sports/a12461360/ nba-activism/

Sellers, R. M., & Shelton, J. N. (2003). The role of racial identity in perceived racial discrimination. *Journal of Personality and Social Psychology, 84*(5), 1079–1092.

Serwear, A. (2017, September). Trump's war of words with Black athletes. *The Atlantic*. Retrieved from https://www. theatlantic.com/politics/archive/2017/09/ trump-urges-nfl-owners-to-fire-players-who-protest/540897/

Sidanius, J., Pratto, F., & Bobo, L. (1996). Racism, conservatism, affirmative action, and intellectual sophistication: A matter of principled conservatism or group dominance? *Journal of Personality and Social Psychology, 70*(3), 476–490.

Sky Sports News. (2018, March). England teams to introduce BAME coaches to staff. *Sky Sports*. Retrieved from http://www.skysports.com/football/ news/12016/11297762/england-teams-to-introduce-bame-coaches-to-staff

Smith, T. B., & Silva, L. (2011). Ethnic identity and personal well-being of people of color: A meta-analysis. *Journal of Counseling Psychology, 58*(1), 42–60.

Stephens-Davidowitz, S. (2014). The cost of racial animus on a black candidate: Evidence using Google search data. *Journal of Public Economics, 118,* 26–40.

Steward, A. D., & Cunningham, G. B. (2015). Racial identity and its impact on job applicants. *Journal of Sport Management, 29,* 245–256.

Stronach, M., Maxwell, H., & Pearce, S. (in press). Indigenous Australian women promoting health through sport. *Sport Management Review.*

Turick, R., & Bopp, T. (2016). A current analysis of black head football coaches and offensive coordinators at the NCAA DI-FBS level. *Journal of Intercollegiate Sport, 9*(2), 282–302.

Vespa, J., Armstrong, D. M., & Medina, L. (2018). Demographic turning points for the United States: Population projections for 2020 to 2060. *Current Population Reports,* P25–1144. Washington, DC: US Census Bureau.

Vick, A., & Cunningham, G. B. (2018). Bias against Latina and African American women job applicants: A field experiment. *Sport, Business, Management: An International Journal, 8*(4), 410–430.

Washington, M., & Patterson, K. D. W. (2011). Hostile takeover or joint venture: Connections between institutional theory and sport management research. *Sport Management Review, 14,* 1–12.

Wells, J. E., & Kerwin, S. (2017). Intentions to be an athletic director: Racial and gender perspectives. *Journal of Career Development, 44*(2), 127–143.

Welty Peachey, J., Zhou, Y., Damon, Z. J., & Burton, L. J. (2015). Forty years of leadership research in sport management: A review, synthesis, and conceptual framework. *Journal of Sport Management, 29*(5), 570–587.

Wiltshire, G., Lee, J., & Williams, O. (in press). Understanding the reproduction of health inequalities: Physical activity, social class and Bourdieu's habitus. *Sport, Education and Society.*

Withycombe, J. L. (2011). Intersecting selves: African American female athletes' experiences in sport. *Sociology of Sport Journal, 28,* 478–493.

Wixon, M. (2006, May 17). Black coaches see dearth of opportunity in suburbs: High schools diverse, but few land top football jobs. *Dallas Morning News.* Retrieved May 17, 2006, from www.dallasnews.com

Yan, G., Pegoraro, A., & Watanabe, N. M. (2018). Student-athletes' organization of activism at the University of Missouri: Resource mobilization on Twitter. *Journal of Sport Management, 32*(1), 24–37.

Zinn, H. (2003). *A people's history of the United States: 1492–present.* New York, NY: HarperCollins.

Gender

6

LEARNING OUTCOMES

After studying this chapter, you should be able to:

- Define sex and gender, and differentiate between the two.
- Describe the representation of women in leadership positions in sport.
- Summarize the reasons for the underrepresentation of women in leadership positions in sport.
- Paraphrase the manner in which gender influences opportunities and experiences of sport and physical activity participants.

DIVERSITY CHALLENGE

In 1973, Billie Jean King and Bobby Riggs competed in a tennis match known as the Battle of the Sexes. King was one of the top tennis players at the time, a 29-year-old champion of Wimbledon, and the first woman to earn over $100,000 in one year. Riggs, though 55 years old, had held the world's #1 ranking for years and had won several major championships. What's more, he had earlier beaten Margaret Court, a top ranked women's player at the time. King, who was competing in the name of equality—of both respect and prize money—handily beat Riggs, the self-declared chauvinist.

The event had a lasting impact. The public was captivated, with over 90 million watching on television. King wore blue suede shoes, and her outfit is on display at the Smithsonian Museum in Washington, DC. In 2017, Emma Stone and Steve Carrell starred in a movie about the event.

The film's release prompted sports journalists and scholars to reflect on the state of gender equality in sport. Some pointed to strides women have made in sport in terms of participation, access, and prestige. For example, women participate in World Cup events in cricket, soccer, and rugby. Paul Hayward noted that "many of the most admired stars in British sport are female, especially at the Olympic and Paralympic level, and their stories are being told." Hayward also noted that attitudes toward the quality of women's sports have dramatically improved.

Despite the gains, gender equality is still not a reality. Women remain under-represented as board members of sport organizations. What's more, stereotypical and sexist language persists. As Vicki Hodges argued, "For every milestone achieved, some sporting organisations remain littered with archaic views, draconian rulings and stereotypical behaviour towards women in sport." Despite the argument that older individuals perpetuate sexism in sport, Hodges points to examples of younger individuals propagating stereotypes, largely through social media posts.

Collectively, the evidence suggests that although improvements have occurred, gender equality is still not a reality in sport.

Sources: Dockterman, E. (2017, September). The true story behind the *Battle of the Sexes* movie. *Time*. Retrieved from http://time.com/4952004/battle-of-the-sexes-movie-true-story/. Hodges, V., & Hayward, P. (2017, November). Sexism in sport: Has anything really changed since *Battle of the Sexes*? *Telegraph*. Retrieved from https://www.telegraph.co.uk/films/battle-of-the-sexes/sexism-in-sport/. Thomas, J. (2017, September). What's fact and what's fiction in *Battle of the Sexes*? *Slate*. Retrieved from http://www.slate.com/blogs/browbeat/2017/09/25/fact_vs_fiction_in_the_movie_battle_of_the_sexes.html.

CHALLENGE REFLECTION

1. Do you think the culture for girls and women participating in sport has improved since the 1970s? What is the basis for your answer?
2. Sport journalists report that, still today, players, sport managers, and fans continue to make derogatory comments about women athletes and women's sports. Why do you think this is the case? How prevalent do you think such comments are?

The Diversity Challenge illustrates that although there is progress toward gender equality, women and men are still treated differently in sport. Evidence suggests that fans, coaches, athletes, and sport managers treat women and women's sports differently and frequently poorer than they do men's. As a result, girls and women routinely encounter barriers to meaningful participation in sport and physical activity.

In this chapter, I continue to examine the effects of different diversity forms, this time with an emphasis on sex and gender. In the first section, I define key terms, illustrate ways in which people perform gender, and overview sources of gender socialization. I then focus on the work environment, exploring issues of access and treatment discrimination, and drawing from the multilevel model from Chapter 4, suggest various factors that influence the underrepresentation of women in leadership positions. Finally, I summarize the data related to gender and participation in sport and physical activity, as well as the quality of experiences in those pursuits.

Before proceeding, it is important to note that some of the topics I discuss in this chapter intersect with those in Chapter 11, where the focus is on sexual orientation, gender identity, and gender expression. For instance, considerable evidence indicates that women face discrimination in the workplace and that this limits their career progression—a topic discussed in subsequent sections. Evidence also indicates that women face discrimination when others perceive them to be lesbian. For instance, rival coaches will try to use a coach's lesbian status against her when recruiting potential athletes. So as not to create redundancy, I limit the latter discussion and related topics to Chapter 11.

SEX AND GENDER

For decades, scholars have noted differences between sex and gender (Muehlenhard & Peterson, 2011). Many scholars consider sex in terms of biology and the physical and chromosomal differences between females and males. Gender, on the other hand, refers to the traits that are culturally appropriate for women and men (Unger, 1979). In some respects, making such distinctions has value. Being precise with one's language is an important skill for sport managers, and if the terms are distinct, then specifying the correct term is important. Similar precision is needed among researchers as they theorize and conduct research related to sex and gender.

Though some have argued for distinguishing between the constructs—I have done the same in previous versions of this text—scholars increasingly recognize the lack of utility in that exercise. Lips (2017) summarized this position well, writing,

> We cannot cleanly and clearly separate "sex" and "gender," however. Cultural expectations for women and men (gender) are not separable from observations about women's and men's physical bodies (sex). Thus, cultural constructions of gender include sex, in some sense. Conversely, history illustrates that even the most obvious biological "facts" about sex are susceptible to misperception and misinterpretation when they violate investigators' assumptions about gender (p. 6).

Richardson (2013) offered additional evidence about the cultural influences on people's biology (sex). Given these points, Lips (2017) suggested attempts to conceptually distinguish sex and gender are not profitable. Consistent with her position, in this book, I use gender when discussing differences between women and men that are caused by environmental factors or a combination of the environment and biology. On the other hand, I use sex to refer to biological differences among people assigned male at birth, people assigned female at birth, and people with an intersex condition.

Performing Gender

Bem (1974, 1977) provided some of the foundational work on the ways in which people perform gender. She suggested that masculinity and femininity are distinct: a person could conceivably rank high on both attributes, low on both, or somewhere in between. Thus, a person could be: masculine (high masculinity, low femininity), feminine (high femininity, low masculinity), androgynous (high femininity, high masculinity), or undifferentiated (low femininity, low masculinity). Bem's notion of androgyny—a word that comes from the Greek *andr* (meaning "man") and *gyne* (meaning "woman")—is unique to the gender identity literature. People with androgynous characteristics are thought to possess more desirable outcomes, such as high self-esteem and greater confidence, than people in other categories.

Woodhill and Samuels (2003) expanded on Bem's (1974, 1977) work, suggesting that gender roles can be both positive and negative. Consider an elite korfball coach with high levels of independence, ambition, compassion, and tolerance. These characteristics fit desirable masculine (the first two characteristics) and feminine (the latter two characteristics) gender roles and are *positively* androgynous. Another korfball coach might have high levels of both selfishness and submissiveness, characteristics that are negative attributes of masculinity and femininity, respectively. The latter coach represent *negative* androgynous characteristics. The same distinctions apply for people with only feminine, or only masculine, characteristics. The demarcation of gender roles in this manner is useful when we examine various outcomes, such as overall well-being. Woodhill and Samuels, for example, found that positively androgynous people scored higher on indicators of mental health and well-being than persons who were negatively androgynous, negatively masculine, negatively feminine, or undifferentiated androgynous. Thus, the gender roles that one adopts can have a meaningful impact on a variety of outcomes and overall well-being.

Gender Socialization

If gender is based on environment and biology, then a portion of it is learned behavior. The communities in which we live, music to which we listen, movies we watch, friends with whom we interact, and many other factors all socialize us. They teach us what is appropriate or not within a given time or setting.

Martin and Ruble (2009) focused on the developmental aspect of gender socialization—that is, how people learn about gender from birth through adolescence. They observed that children develop ideas about gender at a very young age. Consider, for instance, that children begin using gender labels in their speech at around 18 months. They begin to stereotype about behaviors and relational capacities among other boys and girls by age four. Children as young as 6 years are able to differentiate among the status associated with various jobs, and by the time they reach 11 years, they are able to attach the gender associations with those positions. For example, children at this age view "jobs for men" as more prestigious than "jobs for women." Finally, there is evidence that preschoolers react negatively to their peers who violate gender norms.

Given that these are all learned behaviors, it is useful to consider the various gender socialization agents. Drawing from a number of sources (Kane, 1995; Martin & Ruble, 2009; Powell, 2011; Valian, 1999), I highlight the influences of parents, peers, schools, the media, and sport.

Parents play an influential role in a child's gender role identity. They transfer ideas about what is appropriate and what is not. They signal appropriate and inappropriate behaviors through their attitudes, beliefs, and behaviors. Halpern and Perry-Jenkins (2016) conducted a longitudinal study of families, examining the influence of parents on their children's gender attitudes. They found that parents' gendered behaviors were a stronger predictor of children's gender role attitudes than were their gendered ideological beliefs. Thus, the parents' actions spoke louder than their words.

Peers also play a role, largely through the ways in which the children respond to one another. Interestingly, girls respond favorably to other girls, irrespective of whether the peer behaviors are feminine, masculine, or neutral. Boys, on the other hand, play favorably with other boys who display masculine behaviors, but not necessarily with those who do not. Children as young as age two model this behavior, leading Valian (1999) to conclude, "In this respect, two-year-olds are already like adults" (p. 54). The influence of their peers continues as children mature such that through their interactions, the children learn what gender roles are appropriate, normative, or deviant within a given context.

Schools also influence the development of gender attitudes and roles. Girls generally perform better academically than boys in school—a trend that exists in all academic areas, including math and science, across all ages, and through all levels of education. The differences in grades are not necessarily the result of varying cognitive ability; rather, they are usually the result of the girls' better work habits and study skills. Ironically, though, boys often receive more attention, both positive and negative, in the classroom than do girls. They are called on more often, praised more, criticized more, and express more ideas that are both rejected and accepted. Though girls volunteer to answer questions more often than boys do, they are called on less frequently and are afforded less time to provide answers. The cumulative effects potentially result in lower self-esteem among girls, relative to boys. The decrease in self-esteem, in turn, negatively influences girls' choice of academic course work, the degrees they seek, and the career paths they pursue. As Box 6.1 illustrates, school rules are also gendered and can negatively affect girls.

In addition, media—television, movies, print, radio, and the Internet—have a significant influence on individuals and on the culture, prompting some observers to suggest that the media "have become one of the most powerful institutional forces for shaping values and attitudes in modern culture" (Kane, 1988, pp. 88–89). The media affect how we think, influence our attitudes toward various topics, and shape our perceptions of the roles men and women should play in society. Fink (2015) highlighted as much in her review, noting that the media serve to reinforce gender roles and perpetuate the negative stereotypes of women and women's sport. Not only do women receive less coverage than men, but they also are depicted in qualitatively different ways. Fink showed that women frequently are portrayed in hypersexualized ways, their accomplishments are minimized, and photographs show them in passive poses rather than in athletic ones. The end result is a devaluation of women and their achievements, including in sport (Biscomb & Matheson, in press).

Box 6.1 Diversity in the Field: Dress Codes

Dress codes are common in public and private schools, ostensibly promoting student well-being. For example, in College Station schools, the student handbook reads the district established the dress code "to teaching grooming and hygiene, prevent disruption, and minimize safety hazards." What happens, however, when a seemingly neutral or innocuous dress code actually serves to perpetuate sexist stereotypes? Increasingly, researchers from around the world are examining this very issue.

Siner (2017), for example, questioned why girls are prohibited from wearing shirts that show their shoulders, or wearing shorts that do not reach past the fingertips. Both pieces of clothing would be prohibited in College Station schools. She argued that such restrictions run contrary to the freedom of expression ensured by the 1st and 14th amendments in the US Constitution. Shiner

noted that students do not forego their constitutional rights upon entering the school.

Other scholars, such as Buzuvis and Newhall (2017), have suggested that dress codes might violate Title IX. This is a law prohibiting sex discrimination in educational activities receiving federal funding. When the dress code differentially impacts girls, Title IX is likely violated. As a final example, Keller, Mendes, and Ringrose (2018) examined ways in which students resisted what they considered sexist dress codes. Use of social media was common. Girls in the study also noted the hypocrisy that frequently accompanied the dress codes, as girls were differentially penalized, relative to boys. These examples show that dress codes might have unintended consequences, perpetuating sexist ideals among girls and boys in the school. When this occurs, the districts might also be violating federal laws.

Finally, the structure and delivery of sport serve to socialize people related to gender and gender roles (Kane, 1995). Sport is usually designed in such a way that it magnifies differentiation between women and men. Powerful individuals and institutions perpetuate and rigorously maintain these differences so as to promote the ideas that (a) men are superior athletically to women and (b) the differences are biologically based and, therefore, inherent.

Consider an example to illustrate this point: the structure of sport differs based on the gender of the participant. At early ages, boys and girls are separated and play with similarly gendered others. As they age, the differences between boys and girls are maintained and accentuated. Greater value is placed on skills predominantly observed among men (e.g., dunking a basketball), whereas the importance of skills accentuated in women's games (e.g., passing, team-based offensive schemes) is minimized. There are also different standards, such as the number of sets played in professional tennis (best of three for women, best of five for men) that privilege men and perpetuate the notion that they are physically superior. Kane (1995) suggested that conceptualizing sport performance along a continuum could break down these barriers, a point discussed in Box 6.2.

Box 6.2 Alternative Perspectives: Sport Performance along a Continuum

Sport performance is frequently cast in such a way that it positions men as naturally superior to women—something based in biology. Proponents of such an idea will point to record holders: the fastest man is faster than the fastest woman, the long-jump record is held by a man, the strongest people on earth are men, and so on.

Mary Jo Kane, a sport sociology professor, suggests such thinking masks the accomplishments of women and perpetuates the notion that men are naturally better athletes. As an alternative, she suggests considering sport performance along a continuum. At one end is exceptional performance, and at the other is poor performance. Examination of the data will show that both women and men fall all along the continuum. Thus, some women will outperform some men, just as some men will outperform some women. Note that if men were inherently

better athletes than women, such a dispersion would not occur.

Let's consider the Rock 'n' Roll San Antonio Marathon. In 2017, with 1,551 men running the full marathon, the top performer, San Antonio native Erik (e-Dragon) Burciaga, completed the 26.2-mile race with a time of 2:31:19. That same year, 1,358 women completed the race, with the top performer (Caroline Veltri) doing so in 2:56:08. Alone, these data would support the notion of men's superiority. But what the data do not show is that Kincaid came in eighth place overall and ran her marathon quicker than 1,544 of the men who ran the same race. Thus, the notion that all men are naturally superior to all women—when it comes to completing a marathon or participating in any other sport—is simply not correct. To the organizers' credit, they list the finish times overall and by gender, depending on how the user wants to sort the data.

GENDER IN THE WORK ENVIRONMENT

Given this background, I now turn to an examination of gender in the work environment, including the degree to which women and men experience various forms of discrimination. As you will recall, access discrimination occurs when people are denied the opportunity to participate in a particular activity, such as coaching or being a top-level administrator (Greenhaus, Parasuraman, & Wormley, 1990). The Sydney Scoreboard (http://www.sydneyscoreboard.com/) is an organization that offers information about women in sport leadership, and I draw from this site to examine whether women are underrepresented in leadership positions.

The Sydney Scoreboard offers information about women serving as board of directors, board chairs, and chief executives. Board members come from all walks of life, and previous experience as an elite athlete is not a membership requirement. According to the World Bank, women represent 49.6 percent of all people in the world in 2017 (https://data.worldbank.org/indicator/SP.POP.TOTL.FE.ZS?view=chart). Thus, absent access discrimination, women should represent about 50 of all board members. In 2014, women represented 20.7 percent of all board members in national sport organizations, and they constituted 13.3 percent of the board members in international federations. See Exhibit 6.1 for a country-by-country listing. Analyses of national Olympic committees around the world demonstrate a similar trend, where in 2017, women held 19.7 percent of board positions (Ahn & Cunningham, 2017). The distributions are not uniform, as 5 percent of national Olympic committees around the world have no women on the board, and 18 percent have board comprised of less than 10 percent women.

Coaching represents another leadership opportunity. The National Collegiate Athletic Association (NCAA) in the US provides data on coach demographics across levels of competition (NCAA, 2017). In the 2016–2017 academic year, women represented 40.6 percent of all head coaches of women's teams. In other words, there are more men coaching women's teams than there are women doing so. These data would not be as damning if women had the same chance to coach men's teams. But, that is not the case, as women represent 5 percent of the head coaches of men's teams. Women represent 43.7 percent of all college athletes

exhibit 6.1   Women in Sport Leadership, by Country

Country	Number of National Sport Organizations	Number of Women Board Members	Total Number of Board Members	Women Board Members (%)
American Samoa	14	25	89	28.09
Australia	52	105	366	28.69
Bangladesh	40	55	1,029	5.35
Botswana	35	63	250	25.2
Brazil	23	26	202	12.87
Canada	50	138	495	27.88
Colombia	11	14	57	24.56
The Cook Islands	24	80	187	42.78
Costa Rica	30	66	224	29.46
Croatia	69	66	543	12.15
Cyprus	21	39	286	13.64
Czech Republic	80	72	632	11.39
Denmark	58	89	455	19.56
England	56	128	574	22.3

Country	Number of National Sport Organizations	Number of Women Board Members	Total Number of Board Members	Women Board Members (%)
Estonia	63	54	407	13.27
Finland	65	127	551	23.05
France	82	149	724	20.58
Germany	60	87	524	16.6
Greece	26	41	354	11.58
Haiti	14	20	132	15.15
Iceland	28	41	163	25.15
Iran	28	28	254	11.02
Ireland	59	133	579	22.97
Italy	61	98	925	10.59
Japan	60	112	1,339	8.36
Malta	44	53	322	16.46
The Marshall Islands	10	17	62	27.42
The Netherlands	75	80	475	16.84
Northern Ireland	33	77	327	23.55
Norway	51	173	463	37.37
Poland	37	37	398	9.3
Scotland	57	105	453	23.18
Spain	38	88	590	14.92
Tanzania	14	36	165	21.82
Tunisia	24	47	231	20.35
The United States	39	165	574	28.75
Venezuela	25	48	225	21.33
Wales	53	126	432	29.17
Zambia	32	67	285	23.51

Source: http://www.sydneyscoreboard.com/.

(217,621 out of 497,637), but only 24.1 percent of the head coaches (4,873 of the 20,220).

Collectively, these data show that women are underrepresented in leadership positions, lending support to the notion that women face access discrimination in sport. The discrimination occurs at all levels, from coaching, to board members, to directors of athletics (see Exhibit 6.2). Finally, it is worth noting that gender inequality is not uniformly distributed. Instead, the impact of access discrimination is stronger for racial minority women than it is White women—a principle consistent with intersectionality (hooks, 2000; see Chapter 2). For example, White women constitute a five times larger share of the US population than do African American women. However, they are 11.2 times more likely to be a head coach of an NCAA women's team, 6.5 times more likely to be the head coach of an NCAA men's team, and 90.5 times more likely to be a director of athletics for an NCAA department. Similar trends are apparent when making other comparisons based on race.

Not only do women—and especially racially minority women—face access discrimination, but there is also evidence of treatment discrimination. Recall from Chapter 3 that treatment discrimination occurs when individuals or members of a particular group have differential access to resources, experience negative behaviors directed toward them, or are afforded fewer chances for growth than they

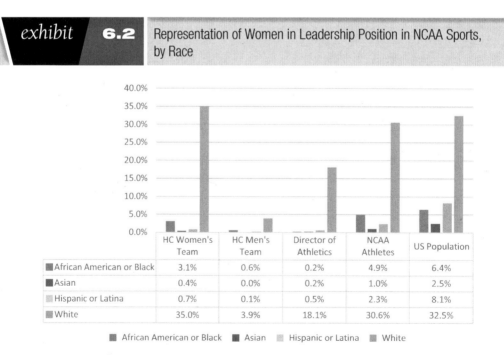

| *exhibit* | **6.2** | Representation of Women in Leadership Position in NCAA Sports, by Race |

	HC Women's Team	HC Men's Team	Director of Athletics	NCAA Athletes	US Population
African American or Black	3.1%	0.6%	0.2%	4.9%	6.4%
Asian	0.4%	0.0%	0.2%	1.0%	2.5%
Hispanic or Latina	0.7%	0.1%	0.5%	2.3%	8.1%
White	35.0%	3.9%	18.1%	30.6%	32.5%

African American or Black   Asian   Hispanic or Latina   White

Sources: Annual Estimates (2018); NCAA (2017).

deserve (Greenhaus et al., 1990). I examine two areas to illustrate this point: treatment in the workplace and pay.

Results from large-scale studies indicate that women experience more gender-based mistreatment in the workplace than do men (McCord, Joseph, Dhanani, & Beus, 2018). The same patterns emerge in sport, where sexism and discrimination dampen the experiences of women in sport and serve as barriers to their career progression (Burton & Leberman, 2017; LaVoi, 2016a). Gender inequalities and the mistreatment of women in sport hurt not only the direct targets but also other women and men in sport. As LaVoi (2016b) has illustrated, gender equality in sport leadership is important because women in leadership roles (a) serve as role models, (b) offer support and mentoring for other women, (c) bring different perspectives to the sport organization, (d) frequently advocate for equality and fairness, and (e) are less likely than men to sexually abuse athletes. Furthermore, policies and practices that create gender equality are good for all employees, irrespective of their gender (LaVoi, 2016b).

As discussed in Chapter 3, not all mistreatment is overt or explicit. Instead, people frequently discriminate in subtle ways, such as behaving uncivilly. According to Andersson and Pearson (1999), workplace incivility refers to "low-intensity deviant behavior with ambiguous intent to harm the target, in violation of workplace norms of mutual respect. Uncivil behaviors are characteristically rude and discourteous, displaying lack of regard for others" (p. 457). Cortina, Kabat-Farr, Leskinen, Huerta, and Magley (2013) referred to incivility as a form of modern discrimination in organizations that negatively affected people's intentions to remain at their workplace. Employees frequently have a hard time leaving the effects of incivility at home; instead, those who experience it at work are likely to have strained relationships with their loved ones at home (Ferguson, 2012). The negative effects of incivility are also apparent in sport teams. Colleagues and I have shown that incivility from a head coach negatively impacts women's commitment to the team (Cunningham, Miner, & McDonald, 2013) and hurts the performance of women's basketball teams (Smittick, Miner, & Cunningham, in press).

Not only are women treated poorer than men but they are also paid less. The Bureau of Labor Statistics (http://bls.gov) offers data related to weekly wages (see Exhibit 6.3). The data show that the median weekly income for men ($946) is higher than that of women ($769). Put another way, in 2017, women in the US earned 81 cents on the dollar relative to men's earnings. The data also illustrate the influence of race, as not all women earn the same. Asian women earn the most, followed by White women, African American women, and Latinas. These patterns illustrate the importance of considering multiple diversity forms when examining experiences and opportunities (hooks, 2000).

Some commentators might suggest that gender gaps in pay are diminishing, and given enough time, they will subside. Blau and Kahn (2017) examined gender wage gaps from 1980 to 2010, and their work addresses such a position. The researchers found that gender differences have declined over time, but they still persist. They also found that, although wage differences have declined at the lower and middle-income brackets, the decline is much slower at the top end of the wage spectrum. Blau and Kahn concluded that a number of factors influence the gender

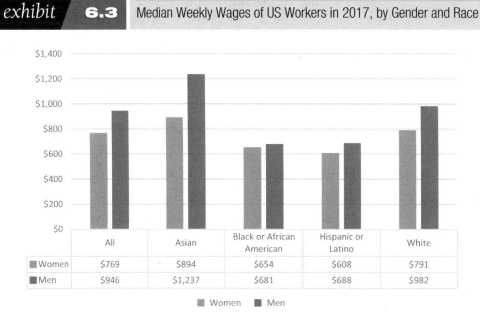

exhibit **6.3** Median Weekly Wages of US Workers in 2017, by Gender and Race

	All	Asian	Black or African American	Hispanic or Latino	White
Women	$769	$894	$654	$608	$791
Men	$946	$1,237	$681	$688	$982

Source: Bureau of Labor Statistics.

wage gap, including work force interruptions, differential access to certain populations and industries, and gender roles, among others.

Gender norms also influence how people report their income, or so indicates research from Murray-Close and Heggeness (2018). They analyzed how mixed-gender married couples reported their earnings in a US Census Bureau survey, with their actual income, as reported in administrative income tax records. When the wife earned more than the husband did, they were likely to inflate the husband's earnings on the survey and underreport the wife's income. The pattern was also influenced by who completed the survey such that the underreporting or overreporting was inflated when the husband was the survey respondent. The authors suggest gendered social norms likely influence the reporting incongruities.

MULTILEVEL EXPLANATIONS

Collectively, the evidence suggests women working in sport face access and treatment discrimination. In Chapter 4, I offered a multilevel framework for understanding the experiences of and opportunities for people from underrepresented groups. In this section, I draw from that framework to focus on the macro-, meso-, and micro-level factors that influence women working in sport. Exhibit 6.4 provides an overview of the factors.

Macro-level factors: Those operating at the societal level, including employment and antidiscrimination laws, institutional sexism, and stakeholder expectations.

Meso-level factors: Those operating at the team and organizational levels, including bias in decision-making, organizational culture, power relations, and diversity policies.

Micro-level factors: Those operating at the individual level, including capital investments and self-limiting behaviors.

Macro-Level Factors

Macro-level factors are those operating at the societal level that can influence women's experiences and opportunities in sport organizations. Examples include employment and antidiscrimination laws, institutional sexism, and stakeholder expectations.

Employment Laws

A number of employment laws are in place to protect employees against gender discrimination. In the US, Title VII of the Civil Rights Act of 1964 and the Equal Pay Act of 1963 are two such laws, and I offer an overview in Exhibit 6.5. Of course, countries around the world have laws prohibiting gender discrimination in society, in general, and work, specifically (for an overview of laws in European countries, see Timmer & Senden, 2016). Collectively, the laws are designed to inform the recruitment, selection, and retention of employees, ensuring that all people, irrespective of their gender, have equal access to employment and the chance to engage in meaningful work.

Even though employment protections are in place, gender discrimination persists. Based on the number of complaints filed with the EEOC (25,605 in 2017), incidents of gender discrimination are common. Companies that discriminate based on gender can receive severe financial punishments. In 2017 alone, over $135.1 million damages were collected for persons who made complaints. (This figure does not include damages recovered through litigation.)

Antidiscrimination Laws

Employment laws protect employees from gender discrimination. Other laws focus on gender discrimination in other contexts, and they have the potential to

exhibit 6.5   Women's Share of the Workforce around the World

Many of the legal protections for women in the workplace are provided by Title VII of the Civil Rights Act of 1964, which was later amended by the Civil Rights Act of 1991. As discussed in Chapter 5, this law protects individuals against employment discrimination based on race, color, religion, sex, or national origin. It applies to employers who are involved in interstate commerce and have 15 or more employees, including federal, state, and local government; educational institutions; labor unions; and players associations.

Title VII prohibits discrimination based on a person's gender. It is unlawful to make employment decisions related to hiring, firing, compensation, the availability or type of training, or any other term, condition, or privilege of employment based on an employee's gender. The law also forbids employment decisions influenced by gender stereotypes concerning traits, abilities, or performance. This law prohibits employers from intentionally or unintentionally creating policies that disproportionately exclude people because of gender for reasons unrelated to the job.

Title VII prohibitions include the following:

- **Sexual harassment.** The term *sexual harassment* covers a variety of behaviors, including requesting sexual favors and creating a hostile work environment. A hostile work environment exists

  when an employee is subjected to repeated unwelcome behaviors that do not constitute sexual bribery but are sufficiently severe and pervasive that they create a work environment so hostile that it substantially interferes with the harassed employee's ability to perform his or her job.

  (Sharp, Moorman, & Claussen, 2014, p. 142)

  People of either sex can be sexually harassed. This prohibition also covers same-sex harassment.
- **Pregnancy-based discrimination.** Title VII was amended by the Pregnancy Discrimination Act of 1978. Pregnancy-related protections include hiring, pregnancy and maternity leave, health insurance, and fringe benefits.

Another issue related to sex discrimination is inequality of compensation for women and men. The Equal Pay Act of 1963 requires that women and men in the same organization receive equal pay for equal work. The jobs do not have to be identical; rather, the jobs have to be substantially equal. For example, if a kinesiology department hires two professors, a woman and a man, who have the same rank, possess roughly the same experience, and perform the same duties, the department must pay both professors the same salary, even though they may teach different courses.

Five factors are considered to determine violations of the Equal Pay Act:

1. **Skill.** The pay may differ between women and men if the two people have dissimilar job-related skills. For example, a coach with 500 career wins is considered to have more skill than a coach with only 42 career wins because the number of games won is a job-related skill. However, two ticket-clerk jobs at a professional sport franchise are considered equal even if one of the clerks has a master's degree because the advanced degree is not required for the job.

2. **Effort.** Compensation can vary if there are differences in the physical or mental efforts needed to complete a certain task or hold a particular job. For example, an employee at a fitness club who is charged with moving the weight machines around the facility exerts considerably more physical effort than the employee who checks the membership status of patrons when they enter the facility. Thus, the former employee may be paid more than the latter, regardless of the employees' sex.

3. **Responsibility.** People who hold more meaningful responsibilities may be paid more than their counterparts. A regional salesperson who also coordinates the efforts and responsibilities of other salespeople earns a greater salary because of the extra responsibilities. It should be noted, however, that the increased responsibilities must be meaningful.

4. **Working conditions.** Two factors are considered with respect to working conditions: the physical surroundings and hazards. People with more challenging or difficult work conditions may be paid more than others.

5. **Establishment (place of employment).** The Equal Pay Act applies only to differences in compensation among employees of the same organization.

---

influence educational and athletic opportunities. Title IX is one such law and states,

> No person in the United States shall, on the basis of sex, be excluded from participation in, be denied the benefits of, or be subjected to discrimination under any educational program or activity receiving Federal financial assistance.
> (Title IX of the Education Amendments of 1972, RL. 92–318, 20 U.S.C. § 1681)

Note that the words *sport, athletics, physical education,* and *recreation* do not appear in the law. Nevertheless, this legislation affects sport perhaps more than any other educational program or activity. In essence, it requires that equal opportunities be provided to women and men participating in activities that receive federal financial assistance. Because almost every high school and institution of higher education in the US receives some federal financial assistance, either directly or indirectly, the law influences almost all aspects of amateur athletics. Indeed, Title IX dramatically changed the landscape of education and sport in the US. I offer an overview of Title IX, including its history and enforcement, in Exhibit 6.6.

exhibit **6.6** History and Enforcement of Title IX

Lawmakers passed Title IX in 1972 as part of the Education Amendments. The law provided little direction to administrators about how to provide equal opportunities for men and women in educational settings. Thus, the Office of Civil Rights (OCR) developed regulations that "would breathe an enforceable life into Title IX" (Carpenter & Acosta, 2005, p. 6). Congress approved these regulations in 1975, giving them the force of law. The courts and sport organizations use the regulations to interpret, measure, and enforce Title IX.

Of particular application to athletics are the following regulations:

- **Section 106.37:** When athletic scholarships are offered, they must be offered to both women and men in proportion to the number of women and men participating in athletics overall.
- **Section 106.41(a):** No person shall, on the basis of sex, be excluded from, denied the benefits of, or be discriminated against in any form of athletics (e.g., interscholastic, intercollegiate, club, or intramural).
- **Section 106.41(b):** Separate athletic teams can be formed for women and men. If a school supports a men's team but does not offer a similar sport for women, then women must be allowed to try out for the men's team. The exceptions to this are contact sports such as rugby, ice hockey, football, and basketball.
- **Section 106.41(c):** Schools that support athletic teams should provide equal opportunities to both women and men. To do so, the athletic director should consider 10 factors:
  - whether the teams are congruent with the interests and abilities of members of both sexes;
  - the provision of equipment and supplies;
  - the manner in which games and practices are scheduled;
  - travel and per diem;
  - coaching and academic counseling;
  - compensation of the coaches and academic tutors;
  - the provision and quality of locker rooms and facilities (both practice and game);
  - the provision of medical and training staff and their facilities;
  - the provision of housing, dining facilities, and dining services; and
  - overall publicity.

Later, policy interpretations identified two additional factors: recruitment and support services. Thus, the financial aid regulations identified in Section 106.37, the 10 regulations in Section 106.41(c), and the two factors identified in the policy interpretations established 13 areas to consider in the enforcement of Title IX.

Institutions had until 1978 to comply with the law, but few met the deadline. In 1984, a meaningful blow was dealt to Title IX by the US Supreme Court's decision in *Grove City College v. Bell*, 465 U.S. 555. The Court addressed two issues: (a) does the word *program* refer to the institution as a whole or to individual programs within that entity and (b) does an institution have to receive direct federal funding in order for it to be subject to Title IX guidelines? With respect to the first issue, the Court found that only those units receiving federal monies were included in the term *program.* Therefore, if an athletic department did not receive federal funds, it was not bound by Title IX regulations. However, with respect to the second issue, the Court ruled that an institution did not have to receive direct federal funds to be subject to the Title IX regulations.

The effects of the *Grove City* decision were severe. Because many (if not most) university athletic departments did not receive federal monies, they were now not subject to Title IX. As a result, many schools immediately cut women's scholarships and selected women's teams to be cut at the end of the academic year. In addition, all complaints that had been filed with the OCR were closed, and many Title IX lawsuits were dismissed.

According to Carpenter and Acosta (2005), Congress considered the Supreme Court's interpretation of *program* to be incorrect. To remedy this situation, the Civil Rights Restoration Act of 1987 was passed over President Reagan's veto in 1988. This Act clarified issues surrounding the word *program.* According to the Civil Rights Restoration Act, the term *program* refers to the entire institution, not just individual programs within that entity. Most physical education departments and athletic departments do not receive federal funds; however, the universities in which they are housed *do* receive such funds. Thus, every entity within a university now fell under Title IX guidelines.

Two other cases of particular relevance to the history of Title IX are *Franklin v. Gwinnett County Public Schools*, 503 US 60 (1992) and *Jackson v. Birmingham Board of Education*, 544 US 167 (2005). The key issue in *Franklin* was whether or not monetary damages could be awarded to persons who successfully sued under Title IX. In this case, a student who had been sexually harassed filed a Title IX lawsuit, but neither the statute nor the regulations contained any language related to monetary damages. The Supreme Court unanimously ruled that monetary damages could be awarded under Title IX. As a result of this ruling, Title IX enforcement changed dramatically. It is now in the best financial interest of institutions to comply with Title IX mandates. Failing to do so means losing potentially large sums of money—money the institutions can ill afford to relinquish. The *Jackson* case is also relevant. Roderick Jackson, a male coach of a girls' high school basketball team, alleged that the girls on the team were discriminated against. He complained to the Board of Education about this discrimination and was subsequently fired. He sued the board, claiming that his termination was in retaliation for complaining about the discrimination. The Supreme Court ruled that Title IX whistle-blowers who were subjected to retaliation for filing a Title IX claim could recover damages.

Title IX Compliance

The 1979 policy interpretations, together with a 2003 letter of clarification, established a three-prong test for evaluating Title IX compliance by universities and colleges (Carpenter & Acosta, 2005). According to this framework, often referred to as *the three-prong test*, a school must select one of the following in order to be compliant with the law:

1. Provide participation opportunities for female and male athletes that are in proportion to their respective enrollments at the university (referred to as substantial proportionality). [Note that the numbers need not be equal; they need only be in proportion. Consider the following examples, which are based on US Department of Education data (n.d.). In 2017, among schools in the Southeastern Conference, 53 percent of the undergraduates were women, but 46 percent of the athletes were women. The differences were particularly large at Mississippi State University, where 51 percent of the undergraduates were women, but only 38 percent of the athletes. On the other hand, at Texas A&M University, women constituted 49 percent of the undergraduate students and athletes. Thus, from the first prong, Mississippi State was out of compliance in 2017, whereas Texas A&M University was in compliance.]

2. Demonstrate a history and continued practice of program expansion for athletes of the underrepresented sex. [Under this condition, the school need not be compliant at the time of its evaluation; rather, it only has to demonstrate that it has continually strived to be more equitable and provide opportunities for persons of the underrepresented sex to develop their skills and compete in athletic events.]

3. Effectively demonstrate that the programs and opportunities offered are congruent with the interests and abilities of the underrepresented sex (referred to as the accommodation of interest and ability test). [Critics from both sides have weighed in on this test. One might ask, if women are the underrepresented sex and do not have an interest in playing varsity sports, why should the athletic department spend the time and money to field a team? On the other hand, interest in sports may wane if opportunities are not provided. How can an athletic department claim in good faith that women are not interested in participating in sports if few women's sports are offered? If sports are offered, perhaps they would attract women to the campus who might not otherwise have come.]

In its 2003 letter of clarification, the OCR notes that, traditionally, schools have viewed substantial proportionality (the first prong) as a "safe harbor" for Title IX compliance. That is, they primarily sought to satisfy this requirement to the neglect of the other prongs. This is a misinterpretation. According to the OCR, each of the three tests is a viable option for determining Title IX compliance, and no single test is preferred over the others.

Some researchers have explored factors that influence university compliance with Title IX. Lee and Won (2016), for example, drew from representative bureaucracy theory to explore the degree to which the presence of women in key administrative positions affected compliance. Contrary to their expectations, administrative gender diversity was not a key factor. On the other hand, as the presence of women as faculty members increased, so too did spending on women's sports. Furthermore, the researchers found that increased gender diversity on state legislatures affected Title IX compliance among public institutions.

Stakeholder Expectations

Recall from Chapter 4 that stakeholders represent key constituents who are either internal or external to a sport organization (Clarkson, 1995). Examples include players, coaches, community members, and financial supporters. Stakeholders wield influence through their voice, money, and power. In many cases, their expectations for the sport organization serve to reinforce gendered norms and stereotypes, as well as gender diversity and inclusion (Staurowsky, Zonder, & Riemer, 2017). These dynamics can help to perpetuate the underrepresentation of women in leadership, especially when the individuals doing the hiring rely on these stakeholders or give preference to their requests.

Hoeber (2007) collected data from Canadian university stakeholders and found that they perpetuated gender inequalities in the athletic department. Some did so by denying inequalities existed, whereas others rationalized the differences (see also Hoeber, 2008). Schull, Shaw, and Kihl (2013) also investigated the influence of stakeholders in their study of a change in leadership at an NCAA member athletic department. One group of stakeholders for this department consisted of men who had given generously to the university and athletic department in the past. These individuals used their collective influence to shape media messages concerning who should (a man) and should not (a woman) be the next athletic director. They used politically savvy techniques to promote men for the position and cast women as ill-suited for the role. In doing so, they helped construct the narrative of an ideal man who would, they felt, best serve the interests of the department. Their influence was effective and helped determine who was hired for the role.

Given the influence of stakeholders on the operations of sport organizations, sport managers would be well served to identify proactive strategies for addressing their potentially conflicting needs and desires. Friedman, Parent, and Mason (2004) offered such a framework. They suggested sport managers first need to identify the various stakeholders, their claims, and their motivations. In doing so, sport managers need to consider the stakeholders' power, legitimacy, and urgency, particularly as the claims pertain to the management of the workplace.

Institutional Sexism

Finally, institutional sexism represents another macro-level factor affecting the opportunities and experiences of women in sport. Through such practices, ideas about gender and appropriate roles and behaviors of women and men become entrenched within a given culture (Duncan, 1993; Fink, 2016). These norms and values become embedded into everyday systems and institutions, influencing the way people think and act, as well as what they take for granted. The relationship between sexist attitudes and religion offers one example, as evidenced by research studies conducted in Poland (Mikołajczak & Pietrzak, 2014), Turkey (Glick, Sakallı-Uğurlu, Akbaş, Orta, & Ceylan, 2016), Belgium (Haggard, Kaelen, Saroglou, Klein, & Rowatt, in press), and the US (Haggard et al., in press). Many Western religious teachings hold that men should lead women—a mindset that has resulted in men serving as the head of the family, women being forbidden to hold certain roles in places of worship, and different role expectations for women and men. As noted, these ideals are largely culturally bound; some Eastern religious traditions, in fact, feature a feminine deity (Simmer-Brown, 2001).

Institutionalized sexism can also privilege men over women in the employment arena. Differential treatment occurs, for example, through occupational segregation, where women are overrepresented in some roles (e.g., nursing, clerical work, elementary school teaching) and underrepresented in others (e.g., manufacturing, truck driving). Similar patterns occur in sport, where men hesitate to fill certain positions because they feel these are "women's work" (Shaw & Slack, 2002, p. 93). Coaching is frequently portrayed as best suited for men, even though many coaching activities, such as nurturing athletes, facilitating their play, and providing them with individualized consideration, are more associated with the feminine nature than the masculine (Knoppers, 1992; Walker & Sartore-Baldwin, 2013). Similarly, Taylor and Hardin (2016) observed that deeply engrained, gendered ideas about who should and can serve as a senior sport administrator serve to limit opportunities for women.

Meso-Level Factors

Meso-level factors, or those operating at the team and organizational levels, also influence women's access to and experience in sport organizations. Factors in these grouping include bias in decision-making, organizational culture, power relations, and diversity policies.

Bias

Recall from Chapter 3 that bias reflects stereotypes, prejudice, and discrimination (Cuddy, Fiske, & Glick, 2008). I first examine stereotypes. In her classic work, Schein (1973, 1975) asked middle managers to rate how well a list of descriptors matched a woman in general, a man in general, and an effective middle manager. She observed that the characteristics believed to embody the successful middle manager were closely aligned with those thought to describe a man in general. This was true for both women and men in her sample. Thus, to think of a successful manager was to think of a man, not a woman. Although her work was conducted 40 years ago, Schein's findings are still applicable today (Koenig, Eagley,

Mitchell, & Ristikari, 2011). The strength of these associations has decreased over time, but they remain salient and are likely to be reinforced among men.

Even when people think about a woman serving in a leadership role, they have different expectations for her than they do of a man (Bierema, 2016; Brescoll, 2016). Common stereotypes of women in leadership roles include them being nurturing, caring, and supportive. Common stereotypes for men in leadership roles include them strong, authoritative, and someone who takes charge. Violations of these stereotypes are met with negativity and dissonance.

These stereotypes persist in sport, as people are likely to associate leadership with men and masculine characteristics (Burton, Barr, Fink, & Bruening, 2009; Hovden, 2010). Furthermore, people are more likely to use masculine, rather than feminine, pronouns when they describe an ideal manager (Knoppers & Anthonissen, 2008). Employees are likely to make different, gender-based attributions for leader behaviors such that "a strong man is direct and a direct woman is a bitch" (Shaw & Hoeber, 2003, p. 347). If organizational decision-makers associate "being a manager" with "being a man," then women are at a distinct disadvantage in the hiring and promotion processes.

Prejudice—the second component of bias—also influences women's access and experiences at work. In some cases, the prejudice is associated with gendered stereotypes of leaders. Women are penalized when they violate leadership expectations—for instance, when a woman acts in ways perceived to be masculine, such as being aggressive or dominant (Rudman & Phelan, 2008). This penalty is manifested through prejudice and lower evaluations of the counter-stereotypical woman relative to her peers and to men. This linkage occurs for several reasons (Rudman, Moss-Racusin, Phelan, & Nauts, 2012). In some cases, people want to take steps to justify and maintain the status quo, whereas in other cases, non-stereotypical women might be viewed as a threat. For still others, they express prejudice as a way of supporting dominant gendered systems and beliefs. Irrespective of the reason, women face prejudice and, as a result, are deemed to be ill-suited for leadership roles.

Context can also influence the degree to which women experience prejudice. Biggs, Hawley, and Biernat (2018) collected data from faculty members, asking them about their experiences at academic conferences. The events are an important part of an academician's professional development and serves as an ideal place for networking. Women in their study were more likely than men to consider the conference climate as sexist. The climate improved, however, as more women attended the conference. A sexist conference climate negatively affected all involved. For women, it prompted them to consider leaving the field, and for men, a sexist climate was associated with their desire to exit the conference.

Sexism in sport organizations negatively affects all involved, both women and men (Fink, 2016). It can result in psychological harm to those who experience it (Taylor, Smith, Welch, & Hardin, 2018). Sexism and other gender-related barriers signal a lack of support from the sport organization, which is subsequently associated with people's desire to leave that workplace (Spoor & Hoye, 2014). Finally, sexism among key decision-makers in sport organizations can influence the utility of subsequent diversity-focused actions. Fielding-Lloyd and Meân (2008) conducted a study of personnel and participants in a Football Association coach education program. They found that modern sexism was prevalent. People viewed diversity policies, such as affirmative action, with suspicion and instead cast such approaches as evidence of favoritism. The participants also worked to maintain the status quo, denying that gender inequality was a problem.

Finally, as previously noted, women are more likely than men to face both access and treatment discrimination in sport. The differential access and treatment is largely a function of stereotypes and prejudice. For example, Eagly and Karau (2002) developed role congruity theory, which holds that the association between men and leadership serves to disadvantage women leaders. As a result, women find it more difficult to obtain a leadership position or to achieve success as a leader. The effects of role congruity are likely to be especially strong in gendered occupations and roles, such as coaching or sport. Consistent with this theory, Koch, D'Mello, and Sackett (2015) aggregated the results from hundreds of studies and found that employment decision-makers preferred men over women when the job field was dominated by men. They also observed that men were especially likely to demonstrate these tendencies in their ratings of job applicants.

Other researchers have observed that women have a better chance of obtaining a leadership position when the unit they will guide has a history of poor performance. This process represents the glass cliff (Ryan & Haslam, 2007). In this case, the organizational decision-makers seek dramatic change and are thus most likely to employ someone who has historically differed from the norm—in this case, women. Fields and colleagues tested this possibility by examining NCAA women's soccer teams over a 10-year span, resulting in 631 observations (Fields, Cunningham, & Wicker (2018). Results showed that women were more likely than men to be fired following poor performance by the team, supporting the existence of gender stereotypes in evaluating performance of female coaches. Moreover, in support of the glass cliff, women were more likely to be hired as new coaches following poor performance of a team. The results suggest women had the most opportunity to coach when placed in a precarious position.

Stereotypes and sexism can also affect performance evaluations. Smith, Rosenstein, Nikolov, and Chaney (in press) analyzed a large dataset from the US military, including over 81,000 evaluations of over 4,000 individuals. Consistent with previous research, they found that women and men did not differ in objective measures of performance. These included grades, fitness scores, and class standing, among others. There were gender differences, though, in the language raters used in their evaluations. In fact, the research team observed differences in 28 descriptions used to describe performance. For example, even though their actual performance did not differ, women were assigned more negative attributes than were men. Further, raters most frequently used "arrogant" as a negative evaluation for men, but they used "inept" to describe women. Even when the description was positive, the type of language differed. The most common term for men was "analytical," whereas women were most frequently described as "compassionate." Describing someone as analytical or task-focused suggests the individual can reason, strategize, and achieve objectives. Someone who is compassionate focuses on relationships and a positive work environment. Clearly, there are differences in who might be considered for a leadership role. The study shows that, even when performance is the same, people tend to use gendered language.

Organizational Culture

Organizational culture is another meso-level factor affecting women and men in the workplace (Burton, 2015). Recall from Chapter 4 that culture is "a pattern of shared basic assumptions ... that has worked well enough to be considered valid and, therefore, to be taught to new members as the correct ways to perceive, think, and feel in relation to those problems" (Schein, 2004, p. 17). Values, processes, organizational artifacts (e.g., banners, trophies), and practices all represent elements of culture. In many respects, organizational cultures in which women are marginalized and subjugated are commonplace in sport (Cunningham, 2008). These cultures have been established and maintained over time such that they now are taken for granted. When this occurs, people do not think about or critically examine structures, values, and processes that privilege men over women. When questioned about it, employees will frequently note that the practices are commonplace and routine. Thus, change becomes challenging.

That many sport organizations have organizational cultures that privilege men is disappointing. Such work environments limit women's contributions to sport and the prospects of inclusive workplaces where all can thrive. Organizational cultures that privilege men also reinforce the notion that men are best suited for leadership positions (Knoppers & McDonald, 2010), thereby ensuring women's underrepresentation in those roles. The specific components that comprise culture also matter. As Shaw (2006) has shown, organizational practices, such as the way women and men dress, humor around the topic of gender, and social processes can all influence the power, opportunities, and experiences women have in sport organizations.

From another perspective, organizational culture can facilitate the career progression of coaches and administrators. Norman, Rankin-Wright, and Allison (in press) explored these possibilities in a study of English Football Association coaches. They found that three elements of culture were especially influential: the presence of a learning culture, inclusive leadership, and relationships with peers and persons higher in the organizational hierarchy. Their findings suggest that coach development is most effective when espied as a journey—especially one in which people can take multiple paths and have starts and stops. Norman et al. also suggested that organizational cultures embrace diversity and inclusion such that these principles are central in the day to day operations. Finally, organizational cultures that emphasize supportive, positive, sustained relationships with multiple entities are key for the development of all employees, including women.

Power

Power also influences women's access to leadership positions and their experiences in sport organizations (Burton & Leberman, 2017). According to Northouse (2019), "power is the capacity or potential to influence. People have power when they have the ability to affect others' beliefs, attitudes, and courses of action" (p. 9). Within sport organizations, individuals' acquisition of power can be a function of their position, expertise, knowledge, networks, or skills. The exercise of power manifests in the way of interactions with others, resource allocations, opportunities, and personnel decisions, among others. See Exhibit 6.7 for a discussion of gender, power, and salutations.

In many sport organizations, power resides with a few individuals who are members of traditional majority groups—White, heterosexual, Protestant, and able-bodied men. Recall from the discussion of the social categorization framework in Chapter 2 that people are likely to classify themselves and others into social groups. Intergroup bias can result such that people afford more positive attitudes and behaviors to people who are similar to them (i.e., in-group members) than to those who are different (i.e., out-group members). Auster and Prasad (2016) have shown how these dynamics, when coupled with other organizational culture characteristics, can influence decision-making regarding personnel decisions. The end result is that people who do not have power, or who differ from those who do, are passed over for leadership roles. A number of researchers have demonstrated similar effects in sport organizations such that opportunities for women vary based on the gender of the person making the personnel decision (Regan & Cunningham, 2012; Sagas, Cunningham, & Teed, 2006; Stangl & Kane, 1991).

---

exhibit 6.7 Power, Gender, and Salutations

Language is a powerful medium. It can be used to brighten someone's day or to hurt them; to encourage an individual or belittle them. At the organizational level, patterns of language reinforce norms, customs, and traditions. One example of language's power is seen when we speak with or introduce others. Referring to a doctor as Ms. or Mr. could be an honest mistake. Or, it could represent a slight to that individual such that the person's credentials are not valued. When people use formal titles for some groups but not others, then the pattern might signal a form of subtle bias.

Files and colleagues (2017) examined these possibilities in hospital settings. The authors examined how speakers at an academic medical center were introduced. All the speakers held an MD, PhD, or in some cases, both an MD and PhD. Of interest to the research team was whether the speaker's formal title was used in the introduction, and whether the gender of the introducer or speaker influenced this outcome. Over 300 cases were included in the analysis.

The authors found that women who offered the introductions were about 50 percent more likely than men to use the speaker's formal title. One could take these findings as evidence that women are just more formal than men. But that is not exactly the case. When women served as the introducer, they were just as likely to use the formal title when introducing a woman as they were when introducing a man. But men used formal titles more frequently when introducing other men. In fact, they used formal titles less than half the time when introducing women. The authors note that "differential formality in speaker introductions may amplify isolation, marginalization, and professional discomfiture expressed by women faculty in academic medicine" (p. 413).

Polices

Finally, policies can influence women's experiences and opportunities in sport leadership. Adriaanse (2017) outlined how gender-focused policies related to hiring can take two forms: targets and quotas. Targets represent aspirational goals for sport organizations, such as the goal to have at women represent at least 40 percent of the board members. Importantly, there are no repercussions for failing to meet the targets. On the other hand, legislation or regulatory requirements drive quotas. They are frequently embedded into the sport organization's bylaws or constitution. They are not negotiable and must be met within a specified timeline. Failure to meet the quotas can result in fines or other sanctions. Given the differences, especially in terms of sanctions, sport managers usually more readily agree to targets than to quotas.

A number of sport organizations and other governing body have recognized the value of targets and quotas (Adriaanse, 2017). For example, in building on other agreements, participants from over 100 nations adopted the Brighton Plus Helsinki Declaration. Among other principles, the declaration held:

> Women remain under-represented in the leadership and decision making of all sport and sport-related organisations. Those responsible for these areas should develop policies and programmes and design structures which increase the number of women coaches, advisers, decision makers, officials, administrators and sports personnel at all levels with special attention given to recruitment, mentoring, empowerment, reward and retention of women leaders.
>
> (International Working Group on Women and Sport, 2016, p. 10)

Adriaanse (2017) suggested that, despite the presence of the Brighton Plus Helsinki Declaration and others like it, the proportion of women in leadership roles has remained stagnant. The lack of change, she argued, is likely due to the voluntary nature of the policies—that is, the policies reflect targets. Thus, she effectively argued that "the limited progress made so far suggests that the use of gender quotas warrants consideration as a strategy to accelerate women's representation in sport governance" (p. 95).

Micro-Level Factors

Finally, micro-level factors, or those factors operating at the individual level, can also influence leadership opportunities and experiences. Salient micro-level factors include capital investments and self-limiting behaviors. It is important to note that micro-level factors do not operate in a vacuum. Men are not, for example, predisposed to remain in coaching any more than women are. Instead, any gender differences in vocational interests, turnover, or social networks are a function of other factors operating at the meso- and macro-levels (Cunningham, Bergman, & Miner, 2014). Failure to recognize these influences results in blaming the victim: women are faulted for their attitudes and behaviors related to sport. Such attributions are false.

Capital Investments

As noted in Chapter 4, capital investments can take the form of human capital or social capital. Human capital includes investments in education, tenure, and training, and conceptually, as human capital increases, so too should opportunities for advancement and career success. We previously found that women had greater human capital than did men, but they received fewer returns for it (Cunningham & Sagas, 2002). More recently, Blau and Kahn (2017), in their study of income discrimination in the US, found that human capital investments were not meaningful predictors of what people earned.

Social capital, on the other hand, refers to people's social networks and includes the number of contacts people have, how close their relationships are with these individuals, and the influence members of the network have in the workplace and sport industry. The social network members provide important information about opportunities, and they also advocate on behalf of the individual (Seibert, Kraimer, & Liden, 2001). The "old boy's network" is alive and well within sport. It serves to privilege men, ensuring their maintenance as the power holders in sport (Kilty, 2006). Social capital differences affect the presence of women across the sport industry, including whether they serve as coaches of men's teams (Walker & Bopp, 2010). Women and men working in sport not only have different amounts of social capital but also enjoy different returns on their social capital investments. Sagas and I observed these effects in a study of collegiate athletics administrators (Sagas & Cunningham, 2004). We examined the role of both human capital investments and social capital investments in the promotions women and men received. Consistent with the idea of differential returns, men's social capital investments resulted in increased promotions, while similar returns were not apparent for women.

Self-Limiting Behaviors

Women routinely receive messages communicating that men are better suited for leadership roles in sport. Over time, this feedback can become internalized, and when it does, women might stop seeking advancement or even decide to leave sport altogether. These actions are referred to as self-limiting behaviors. They are the result of continuous negative feedback—at the macro-, meso-, and micro-levels—pertaining to women's ability and their effectiveness (Norman, 2010; Sartore & Cunningham, 2007).

Self-limiting behaviors take several forms. In some cases, it might be limited attraction to leadership roles and other forms of advancement. We have observed as much in studies of assistant coaches of college sports teams in both the US (Sagas, Cunningham, & Pastore, 2006) and Canada (Cunningham, Doherty, & Gregg, 2007). In these studies, women, relative to men, expressed fewer intentions to become a head coach and were less likely to have applied for a head coaching position in the past. Other researchers have found similar results among coaches in the UK (Norman, 2014) and sport managers in Syria (Megheirkouni, 2014).

To help further explain the patterns, consider a student from Brands and Fernandez-Mateo (2017). They examined how people respond to rejection after applying for a job and whether people were willing to apply for leadership roles at the same company multiple times? They collected data across three studies, with the focus on people applying for leadership roles in various industries. The researchers found that if people applied for and got rejected for a leadership position, they were unlikely to apply for the same job if it opened again. But, there were a number of factors also involved. Women were less likely than men to apply for the position a second or third time. These differences emerged not because the women were rejected, *per se*, but because they believed they were treated unfairly in the process. The result of said treatment, Brands and Fernandez-Mateo argued, is a confirmation effect, where women's suspicions that they will experience bias in the job hunt process is reinforced. The findings have meaningful implications. As the authors of the research note, women can only be hired for senior roles if they are in the applicant pool. But, the fairness of the search, or lack thereof, actually deters their participation. Played out over time, the end result is what sociologists call cumulative advantage. That is, small differences at the early stage of a process are amplified over time.

In other cases, self-limiting behaviors mean that women leave sport sooner than men. In a study I conducted with Sagas and Ashley, 68 percent of the women in the sample reported that they planned to leave the profession before age 45, whereas only 15 percent of men expressed similar plans (Sagas, Cunningham, & Ashley, 2000). A similar pattern exists among sport officials (Nordstrom, Warner, & Barnes, 2016; Tingle, Warner, & Sartore-Baldwin, 2014). Collectively, the self-limiting behaviors—again, behaviors resulting from the various macro-, meso-, and micro-level factors—limit the number of women in leadership roles.

GENDER AND PARTICIPATION IN PHYSICAL ACTIVITY AND SPORT

Participation

Gender also influences participation in sport and physical activity. In Exhibit 6.8, I draw from the National Health Interview Survey, conducted by the Centers for Disease Control and Prevention in the US (www.healthypeople.gov). As discussed in Chapter 5, researchers in this study examined the proportion of adults who engage in recommended levels of aerobic activity each week: 150 minutes of moderate activity, 75 minutes of vigorous activity, or some combination thereof. Results show that men are more likely than women to get the recommended levels of physical activity. In fact, in 2016, men were 13.6 percent more likely to meet guidelines for physical activity than were women.

According to the World Health Organization, women around the world do not meet physical activity goals (Physical Activity and Women, n.d.). The organization lists several reasons for these differences. First, women have lower income than

exhibit   6.8   Gender and Physical Activity Rates among US Adults

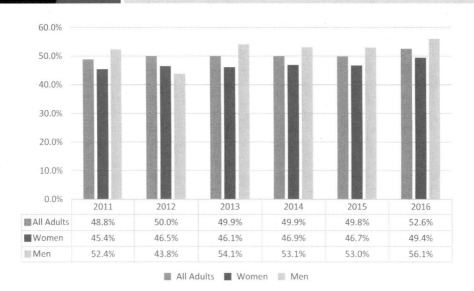

	2011	2012	2013	2014	2015	2016
All Adults	48.8%	50.0%	49.9%	49.9%	49.8%	52.6%
Women	45.4%	46.5%	46.1%	46.9%	46.7%	49.4%
Men	52.4%	43.8%	54.1%	53.1%	53.0%	56.1%

■ All Adults   ■ Women   ■ Men

men, and as such, financial barriers might be salient. Second, in some cultures, the head of the household must permit the woman to be physically active, and absent such consent, she will remain sedentary. Additionally, women may have a high workload at home, including childcare, which limits their participation. Finally, some cultural expectations might restrict the opportunities for women to be physically active, especially in the presence of men.

Many of these factors also affect girls' and women's participation in formal sport. One place this pattern is seen is in high school athletics within the US. Exhibit 6.9 offers a summary of data collected from the 2016–2017 High School Athletic Survey, conducted by the National Federation of State High School Associations. Two points are particularly relevant. First, substantial changes have occurred over time. In the 1971–1972 academic year (the year prior to Title IX's enactment), girls represented just 7 percent of all high school athletes. In the years following Title IX, the participation began to narrow, dropping from 12-fold difference in 1971–1972 to a smaller difference in 2001–2002. That gap has remained relatively constant since 2001–2002. This highlights the second point: girls continue to be underrepresented as high school athletics participants. Girls constituted 42 percent of all participants during the 2013–2014 academic year. This figure is lower than what we would expect based on their proportion of all high school students: 48 percent, according to the US Census Bureau (Davis & Bauman, 2008).

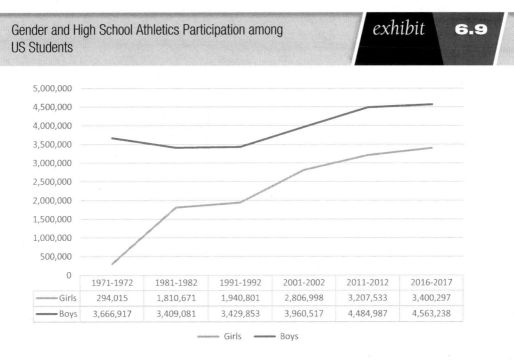

Gender and High School Athletics Participation among US Students

exhibit | 6.9

	1971-1972	1981-1982	1991-1992	2001-2002	2011-2012	2016-2017
Girls	294,015	1,810,671	1,940,801	2,806,998	3,207,533	3,400,297
Boys	3,666,917	3,409,081	3,429,853	3,960,517	4,484,987	4,563,238

Girls   Boys

Experiences in Sport and Physical Activity

Not only are girls and women underrepresented in sport and physical activity, but when they do participate, they frequently encounter negative experiences in the form of marginalization, sexual abuse, and objectification.

Women and women's sport are frequently marginalized. The disparate treatment is evidenced, for example, in the difference in attention paid to men's sports and to women's sports. Sport activities associated with boys and men receive more coverage in newspapers, in online sites, in radio broadcasts, and on television (Fink, 2015, 2016). In fact, so much attention is devoted to men's sports that sport and men are automatically associated with one another. Illustrative of this point, the sports-focused website ESPN does give some attention to women's sports, but most of the site is devoted to men, their sports, and their accomplishments. Why else would ESPN create a separate site, ESPNW—a site devoted to female athletes and women's sports? The absence of the corresponding ESPNM, which might include content focusing on men and their sports, suggests that the primary focus of ESPN is men and men's sports.

The marginalization of women's sports is also seen in the delivery of sport. In many interscholastic athletics events, the girls' teams regularly play prior to the boys' teams, as a sort of opening act, so to speak. At the collegiate level, comparatively less money is devoted to women's sports, to their coaches, and to their operations (Fulks, 2017). Finally, as Coakley (2015) has noted, programs for boys and men are unlikely to be cut when budget cuts occur because they are considered to be more legitimate—again, a phenomenon that illustrates the gendered nature of sport.

Girls and women are also more likely than boys and men to face sexual abuse in sport. It is possible for any athlete to experience sexual abuse from teammates, coaches, or sport administrators; however, evidence suggests that girls and women are at a heightened risk of this behavior. The abuse from Larry Nassar, who was sentenced to up to 175 years in prison for the sexual abuse of over 150 girls and women athletes, serves as one of many examples. It was the biggest sexual abuse case in US sports history and, as Blaschke (2018) noted, was representative of the long history of abuse of women in sport. Fasting and Sand (2015) showed that sexual abuse and harassment of female athletes take place at all age levels, across all levels of competition. These behaviors include sexual jokes, threatening and intimidating language and behavior, and actions that are sexual in nature. Such abuse has a negative effect on the athletes' psychological well-being, their physical health, and their performance. Mistreatment also negatively affects individuals who observe the abuse, as well as the group as a whole (Cunningham et al., 2014).

Rodríguez and Gill (2011) examined this topic in a study of former female athletes from Puerto Rico. Some of the athletes told of feeling "like a piece of meat" (p. 329) when they were harassed. The women reported that verbal abuses, such as crude verbal abuse or sexual remarks, were more common and socially sanctioned than were physical forms of harassment. The mistreatment took a negative psychological and physical toll on the athletes, including feelings of disgust, guilt, shame, and fear. The athletes also reported negative consequences associated with reporting the harassment; not only were their careers hurt, but they were blamed for the occurrences and cast in a disparaging light. Women in the study told of using several coping techniques, including avoidance, seeking social support from others, resistance, confronting the harasser, and seeking advocacy.

Many strong leaders have emerged to fight for sport to be a space free from sexual abuse and harassment. Box 6.3 illustrates this work.

Finally, the media portray women in hypersexualized ways, reinforcing gender stereotypes (Cooky, Messner, & Hextrum, 2013; Kane, 2013). Whereas male athletes are routinely depicted in active poses—such as throwing a pitch during a baseball game—the same is not true for women. Instead, they are frequently shown in supportive poses, such as cheering on a teammate, or outside of the sport context altogether, such as in a dinner gown. The media is likely to focus on a woman's appearance, femininity, and heterosexuality, reinforcing gendered norms. These patterns are observed across media types, including print, radio, major online news sites, and as Geurin-Eagleman and Burch (2016) have shown, on social media platforms, too.

Women's objectification spills over into sport marketing efforts. Women athletes who are hired as product endorsers are frequently depicted in hypersexualized poses—a tendency not observed among men. Some evidence suggests that when people are asked to evaluate the effectiveness of a woman athlete as a product or event endorser, her attractiveness is one of the primary factors they consider

Box 6.3 Professional Perspectives. Combatting Sexual Abuse and Harassment

In 2018, Larry Nassar, a team doctor for USA Gymnastics and employee of the athletic department at Michigan State University, was sentenced to up to 175 years in prison for the sexual abuse of over 150 girls and women. Several women stepped up and told of the abuse, making the conviction and sentence possible. One of them was Aly Raisman, a two-time Olympian and gold medal winner.

Since the Nassar trial, Raisman has been a strong champion for change. She noted, "being a survivor is nothing to be ashamed of, and going through a hard time does not define you." Raisman has partnered with Darkness to Light, a US-based organization that advocates for the end of child abuse and assault. The partnership will allow for support for the gymnasts who Nassar abused and for change efforts to take place, ensuring that gymnastics is a safe space for all athletes.

Raisman commented,

To address this terrible problem, we all need to be willing to confront it head-on…. Sexual abuse is something that needs to be discussed openly—especially now—given the challenges our sport is facing, and all adults should become educated as to how to prevent it. Ignoring the issue, in hopes that it goes away, is unacceptable. Athlete safety must be the highest priority.

Raisman is not the only advocate for change. Former US Olympian and attorney Nancy Hogshead-Maker is another strong advocate for the protection of women in sport. Hogshead-Maker was sexually assaulted herself—an event that nearly led her to retiring from swimming early. She remained in the sport, though, and thrived. Today, as an attorney, Hogshead-Maker works with lawmakers and others to create change. She was instrumental in the passage of Protecting Young Victims from Sexual Abuse and Safe Sport Authorization Act. She commented, "The passage of this statute is just the beginning," she says. "Abuse is in every single sport, but we now have protection for 8 million children."

Sources: Ali Raisman (2018), Loudin (2018).

(Cunningham, Fink, & Kenix, 2008; Fink, Parker, Cunningham, & Cuneen, 2012). It is possible that marketers might use these results to justify a "sex sells" mentality, even though the practice has damaging effects on various sport stakeholders. There is folly in such an approach, however, as despite the prevalence of using sexual images to promote a product, researchers have shown that the practice can negatively affect consumers and their attitudes (Bongiorno, Bain, & Haslam, 2013). The negative effects largely stem from the belief that hypersexualized images dehumanize women.

The objectification of women in sport has several negative outcomes. First, it trivializes sport participants, casting them as sex objects rather than serious athletes.

This is contrary to how elite athletes prefer to be depicted (Kane, LaVoi, & Fink, 2013). Second, as a testament to people's interconnectedness with one another (Cunningham, 2014), the effects reach beyond the specific consumer or athletes involved in the portrayal. In a series of experiments, Daniels (Daniels, 2009, 2012; Daniels & Wartena, 2011) shows that girls and women who view images of hypersexualized athletes have negative body images themselves and express feelings of anger. Boys viewing such images see women as sex objects. However, the effects can be reversed. When they view women in athletic poses, girls and women have positive body images and believe female athletes are role models while boys value women for their accomplishments.

CHAPTER SUMMARY

In this chapter, I focused on the experiences of men and women in regard to their gender in the sport context. The Diversity Challenge demonstrated the substantial influence of sex and gender on who participates in sport, the allocation of resources, and attitudes toward sport. In the workplace, work experiences, compensation, access to managerial and leadership positions, and attitudes toward their careers differ between women and men. Having read this chapter, you should be able to:

1. Define sex and gender, and differentiate between the two.

    Many scholars consider sex in terms of biology and the physical and chromosomal differences between females and males. Gender, on the other hand, refers to traits that are culturally appropriate for women and men. Though many scholars differentiate between the two concepts, there is considerable overlap. Thus, I used gender when discussing differences between women and men that are caused by environmental factors or a combination of biology and environment.

2. Describe the representation of women in leadership positions in sport.

    Across a variety of contexts, research suggests that, relative to men, women are less likely to be members of the workforce, they receive less compensation for their work, and they are less likely to hold upper-echelon management positions. These trends are present in the sport and physical activity context.

3. Summarize the reasons for the underrepresentation of women in leadership positions in sport.

    Macro-, meso-, and micro-level factors all affect the opportunities for and experiences of women in sport. Macro-level factors include employment and antidiscrimination laws, institutional sexism, and stakeholder expectations. Bias in decision-making, organizational culture, power relations, and diversity policies are all meso-level factors. Finally, micro-level factors include capital investments and self-limiting behaviors.

4. Paraphrase the manner in which gender influences opportunities and experiences of sport and physical activity participants.

Girls and women, relative to boys and men, are more likely to be sedentary and less likely to engage in physical activity or in formal sport. They are also likely to have poorer experiences than boys and men while participating in those activities. These differences are manifested through marginalization, sexual abuse, and objectification.

Questions FOR DISCUSSION

1. What are the primary gender stereotypes associated with women and men? Are those stereotypes observable today?
2. What are the primary factors that influence the formation of gender stereotypes? Which is likely to have the strongest impact?
3. What is the influence of gender stereotypes on participation in sport and physical activity?
4. Why are gender differences in earnings still present today? How do intersecting identities influence earnings?
5. What are the basic tenets of Title IX, and what are the steps an athletic department can take to comply with the law?
6. Several potential explanations for the underrepresentation of women in management and leadership positions were discussed in the chapter. Which is the most important in explaining this phenomenon? Why?
7. Why does the participation of women in sport and physical activity lag behind that of men? What steps can sport managers take to reverse this trend?

LEARNING Activities

1. Suppose you are involved in searching for a coach for a women's team at your university. What emphasis would you put on the gender of the coach in the hiring process? What about the assistant coaches? Divide into two groups and discuss.
2. Search online for the presence of women administrators in national sport organizations such as USA Basketball.

Web RESOURCES

■ National Association of Collegiate Women Athletic Administrators, www. nacwaa.org
   Provides information for administrators who are women.

- Title IX, www.titleix.info
  Provides an overview of Title IX across various domains of higher education, including sport.
- Women's Sports Foundation, www.womenssportsfoundation.org
  Provides a wide range of resources related to girls' and women's participation in sport.

READING Resources

Burton, L. J., & Leberman, S. (Eds.) (2017). *Women in sport leadership: Research and practice for change.* New York, NY: Routledge.

Edited book that examines women in sport leadership, with examples and research from around the world.

Powell, G. N. (2011). *Women and men in management* (4th ed.). Thousand Oaks, CA: Sage.

Comprehensive overview of the issues surrounding women in the workplace; examines historical aspects, sex and gender, and the influence of sex and gender on employment decisions, leadership, and career aspirations.

Roper, E. A. (Ed.) (2013). *Gender relations in sport.* Boston, MA: Sense Publishers.

An edited volume for introductory students; focuses on several key issues, including Title IX, sexual harassment, gender and media, and intersectionality, among others.

REFERENCES

Adriaanse, J. A. (2017). Quotas to accelerate gender equity in sport leadership: Do they work? In L. J. Burton & S. Leberman (Eds.), *Women in sport leadership: Research and practice for change* (pp. 83–97). New York, NY: Routledge.

Ahn, N. Y., & Cunningham, G. B. (2017). Cultural values and gender equity on National Olympic Committee boards. *International Journal of Exercise Science, 10*(6), 857–874.

Ali Raisman is ready to #FliptheSwitch on abuse in youth sports. (2018, March). *Sport Illustrated.* Retrieved from https://www.si.com/swim-daily/2018/03/08/aly-raisman-stop-abuse-youth-sports-flip-the-switch

Andersson, L. M., & Pearson, C. M. (1999). Tit for tat? The spiraling effect of incivility in the workplace. *Academy of Management Review, 24*(3), 452–471.

Annual Estimates of the Resident Population by Sex, Race, and Hispanic Origin for the United States: April 1, 2010 to July 1, 2017 (2018, June). *US Census Bureau.* Retrieved from https://factfinder.census.gov/faces/tableservices/jsf/pages/productview.xhtml?src=CF

Auster, E. R., & Prasad, A. (2016). Why do women still not make it to the top? Dominant organizational ideologies and biases by promotion committees limit opportunities to destination positions. *Sex Roles, 75*(5–6), 177–196.

Bem, S. L. (1974). The measurement of psychological androgyny. *Journal of Consulting and Clinical Psychology, 42,* 155–162.

Bem, S. L. (1977). On the utility of alternative procedures for assessing psychological androgyny. *Journal of Consulting and Clinical Psychology, 45,* 196–205.

Bierema, L. L. (2016). Women's leadership: Troubling notions of the "ideal" (male) leader. *Advances in Developing Human Resources, 18*(2), 119–136.

Biggs, J., Hawley, P. H., & Biernat, M. (2018). The academic conference as a chilly climate for women: Effects of gender representation on experiences of sexism, coping responses, and career intentions. *Sex Roles, 78*(5–6), 394–408.

Biscomb, K., & Matheson, H. (in press). Are the times changing enough? Print media trends across four decades. *International Review for the Sociology of Sport.*

Blaschke, A. (2018, January). Nassar's abuse reflects more than 50 years of men's power over females. *The Conversation.* Retrieved from https://theconversation. com/nassars-abuse-reflects-more-than-50-years-of-mens-power-over-female-athletes-90722

Blau, F. D., & Kahn, L. M. (2017). The gender wage gap: Extent, trends, and explanations. *Journal of Economic Literature, 55*(3), 789–865.

Bongiorno, R., Bain, P. G., & Haslam, N. (2013). When sex doesn't sell: Using sexualized images of women reduces support for ethical campaigns. *PLoS One, 8*(12), e83311.

Brands, R. A., & Fernandez-Mateo, I. (2017). Leaning out: How negative recruitment experiences shape women's decisions to compete for executive roles. *Administrative Science Quarterly, 62*(3), 405–442.

Brescoll, V. L. (2016). Leading with their hearts? How gender stereotypes of emotion lead to biased evaluations of female leaders. *The Leadership Quarterly, 27*(3), 415–428.

Burton, L. J. (2015). Underrepresentation of women in sport leadership: A review of research. *Sport Management Review, 18*(2), 155–165.

Burton, L. J., & Leberman, S. (2017). An evaluation of current scholarship in sport leadership: Multilevel perspective. In L. J. Burton & S. Leberman (Eds.), *Women in sport leadership: Research and practice for change* (pp. 16–32). New York, NY: Routledge.

Burton, L. J., Barr, C. A., Fink, J. S., & Bruening, J. E. (2009). "Think athletic director, think masculine?": Examination of the gender typing of managerial sub-roles within athletic administration positions. *Sex Roles, 61,* 416–426.

Buzuvis, E., & Newhall, K. (2017, April). Title IX dress code case survives motion to dismiss. *Title IX Blog.* Retrieved from http://title-ix.blogspot.com/2017/04/title-ix-dress-code-case-survives.html

Carpenter, L. J., & Acosta, R. V. (2005). *Title IX.* Champaign, IL: Human Kinetics.

Clarkson, M. E. (1995). A stakeholder framework for analyzing and evaluating corporate social performance. *Academy of Management Review, 20*(1), 92–117.

Coakley, J. (2015). *Sports in society: Issues and controversies* (11th ed.). New York, NY: McGraw-Hill.

Cooky, C., Messner, M. A., & Hextrum, R. H. (2013). Women play sport, but not on TV: A longitudinal study of televised news media. *Communication & Sport, 1,* 203–230.

Cortina, L. M., Kabat-Farr, D., Leskinen, E. A., Huerta, M., & Magley, V. J. (2013). Selective incivility as modern discrimination in organizations: Evidence and impact. *Journal of Management, 39*(6), 1579–1605.

Cuddy, A. J., Fiske, S. T., & Glick, P. (2008). Warmth and competence as universal dimensions of social perception: The stereotype content model and the BIAS map. *Advances in Experimental Social Psychology, 40,* 61–149.

Cunningham, G. B. (2008). Creating and sustaining gender diversity in sport organizations. *Sex Roles, 58,* 136–145.

Cunningham, G. B. (2014). Interdependence, mutuality, and collective action in sport. *Journal of Sport Management, 28,* 1–7.

Cunningham, G. B., & Sagas, M. (2002). The differential effects of human capital for male and female Division I basketball coaches. *Research Quarterly for Exercise and Sport, 73*(4), 489–495.

Cunningham, G. B., Bergman, M. E., & Miner, K. N. (2014). Interpersonal mistreatment of women in the workplace. *Sex Roles, 71*, 1–6.

Cunningham, G. B., Doherty, A. J., & Gregg, M. J. (2007). Using social cognitive career theory to understand head coaching intentions among assistant coaches of women's teams. *Sex Roles, 56*, 365–372.

Cunningham, G. B., Fink, J. S., & Kenix, L. J. (2008). Choosing an endorser for a women's sporting event: The interaction of attractiveness and expertise. *Sex Roles, 58*, 371–378.

Cunningham, G. B., Miner, K., & McDonald, J. (2013). Being different and suffering the consequences: The influence of head coach–player racial dissimilarity on experienced incivility. *International Review for the Sociology of Sport, 48*(6), 689–705.

Daniels, E. A. (2009). Sex objects, athletes, and sexy athletes: How media representations of women athletes can impact adolescent girls and college women. *Journal of Adolescent Research, 24*, 399–422.

Daniels, E. A. (2012). Sexy versus strong: What girls and women think of female athletes. *Journal of Applied Developmental Psychology, 33*(2), 79–90.

Daniels, E. A., & Wartena, H. (2011). Athlete or sex symbol: What boys think of media representations of female athletes. *Sex Roles, 65*, 566–579.

Davis, J. W., & Bauman, K. J. (2008). *School enrollment in the United States: 2006 (Census Bureau Publication No. P20–559)*. US Census Bureau. Retrieved from http://www.census.gov/prod/ 2008pubs/ p20–559.pdf

Duncan, M. C. (1993). Beyond analyses of sport media texts: An argument for formal analyses of institutional structures. *Sociology of Sport Journal, 10*(4), 353–372.

Eagly, A. H., & Karau, S. J. (2002). Role congruity theory of prejudice toward female leaders. *Psychological Review, 109*(3), 573–598.

Fasting, K., & Sand, T. S. (2015). Narratives of sexual harassment experiences in sport. *Qualitative Research in Sport, Exercise and Health, 7*(5), 573–588.

Ferguson, M. (2012). You cannot leave it at the office: Spillover and crossover of coworker incivility. *Journal of Organizational Behavior, 33*(4), 571–588.

Fielding-Lloyd, B., & Meân, L. J. (2008). Standards and separatism: The discursive construction of gender in English soccer coach education. *Sex Roles, 58*(1–2), 24–39.

Fields, D., Cunningham. G. B., & Wicker, P. (2018, June). *The glass cliff as an explanation for the under-representation of women in coaching*. Paper presented at the annual conference of the North American Society for Sport Management, Halifax, Nova Scotia, Canada.

Files, J. A., Mayer, A. P., Ko, M. G., Friedrich, P., Jenkins, M., Bryan, M. J., … Duston, T. (2017). Speaker introductions at internal medicine grand rounds: Forms of address reveal gender bias. *Journal of Women's Health, 26*(5), 413–419.

Fink, J. S. (2015). Female athletes, women's sport, and the sport media commercial complex: Have we really "come a long way, baby"? *Sport Management Review, 18*(3), 331–342.

Fink, J. S. (2016). Hiding in plain sight: The embedded nature of sexism in sport. *Journal of Sport Management, 30*(1), 1–7.

Fink, J. S., Parker, H. M., Cunningham, G. B., & Cuneen, J. (2012). Female athlete endorsers: Determinants of effectiveness. *Sport Management Review, 15*, 13–22.

Friedman, M. T., Parent, M. M., & Mason, D. S. (2004). Building a framework for issues management in sport through stakeholder theory. *European Sport Management Quarterly, 4*(3), 170–190.

Fulks, D. L. (2017). *Revenues & expenses: 2004–2016 NCAA Division I intercollegiate athletics programs report.* Indianapolis, IN: National Collegiate Athletic Association.

Geurin-Eagleman, A. N., & Burch, L. M. (2016). Communicating via photographs: A gendered analysis of Olympic athletes' visual self-presentation on Instagram. *Sport Management Review, 19*(2), 133–145.

Glick, P., Sakallı-Uğurlu, N., Akbaş, G., Orta, İ. M., & Ceylan, S. (2016). Why do women endorse honor beliefs? Ambivalent sexism and religiosity as predictors. *Sex Roles, 75*(11–12), 543–554.

Greenhaus, J. H., Parasuraman, S., & Wormley, W. M. (1990). Effects of race on organizational experiences, job performance, evaluations, and career outcomes. *Academy of Management Journal, 33,* 64–86.

Haggard, M. C., Kaelen, R., Saroglou, V., Klein, O., & Rowatt, W. C. (in press). Religion's role in the illusion of gender equality: Supraliminal and subliminal religious priming increases benevolent sexism. *Psychology of Religion and Spirituality.*

Halpern, H. P., & Perry-Jenkins, M. (2016). Parents' gender ideology and gendered behavior as predictors of children's gender role-attitudes: A longitudinal exploration. *Sex Roles, 74*(11–12), 527–452.

Hoeber, L. (2007). Exploring the gaps between meanings and practices of gender equity in a sport organization. *Gender, Work & Organization, 14*(3), 259–280.

Hoeber, L. (2008). Gender equity for athletes: Multiple understandings of an organizational value. *Sex Roles, 58*(1–2), 58–71.

hooks, b. (2000). *Feminist theory: From margin to center* (2nd ed.). London, UK: Pluto Press.

Hovden, J. (2010). Female top leaders—prisoners of gender? The gendering of leadership discourses in Norwegian sports organizations. *International Journal of Sport Policy, 2,* 189–203.

International Working Group on Women and Sport (2016). Past IWG World Conference and their legacies. Retrieved from http://iwg-gti.org/index.php/iwg-content/cid/110/past-iwg-world-conferences-and-their-legacies/

Kane, M. J. (1988). Media coverage of the female athlete before, during, and after Title IX: *Sports Illustrated* revisited. *Journal of Sport Management, 2,* 87–99.

Kane, M. J. (1995). Resistance/transformation of the oppositional binary: Exposing sport as a continuum. *Journal of Sport & Social Issues, 19,* 191–218.

Kane, M. J. (2013). The better sportswomen get, the more the media ignore them. *Communication & Sport, 1,* 231–236.

Kane, M. J., LaVoi, N. M., & Fink, J. S. (2013). Exploring elite female athletes' interpretations of sport media images: A window into the construction of social identity and "selling sex" in women's sports. *Communication & Sport, 1*(3), 269–298.

Keller, J., Mendes, K., & Ringrose, J. (2018). Speaking 'unspeakable things': Documenting digital feminist responses to rape culture. *Journal of Gender Studies, 27*(1), 22–36.

Kilty, K. (2006). Women in coaching. *The Sport Psychologist, 20,* 222–234.

Knoppers, A. (1992). Explaining male dominance and sex segregation in coaching: Three approaches. *Quest, 44,* 210–227.

Knoppers, A., & Anthonissen, A. (2008). Gendered managerial discourses in sport organizations: Multiplicity and complexity. *Sex Roles, 58,* 93–103.

Knoppers, A., & McDonald, M. (2010). Scholarship on gender and sport in *Sex Roles* and beyond. *Sex Roles, 63,* 311–323.

Koch, A. J., D'mello, S. D., & Sackett, P. R. (2015). A meta-analysis of gender stereotypes and bias in experimental simulations of employment decision making. *Journal of Applied Psychology, 100*(1), 128–161.

Koenig, A. M., Eagley, A. H., Mitchell, A. A., & Ristikari, T. (2011). Are leadership stereotypes masculine? A meta-analysis of three research paradigms. *Psychological Bulletin, 137,* 616–642.

LaVoi, N. M. (2016a). A framework to understand experiences of women coaches around the globe: The ecological-intersectional model. In N. M. LaVoi (Ed.), *Women in sport coaching* (pp. 13–34). New York, NY: Routledge.

LaVoi, N. M. (2016b). Introduction. In N. M. LaVoi (Ed.), *Women in sport coaching* (pp. 1–9). New York, NY: Routledge.

Lee, Y. J., & Won, D. (2016). Applying representative bureaucracy theory to academia: Representation of women in faculty and administration and Title IX compliance in intercollegiate athletics. *Journal of Diversity in Higher Education, 9*(4), 323–338.

Lips, H. M. (2017). *Sex and gender: An introduction* (6th ed.). Long Grove, IL: Waveland Press.

Loudin, A. (2018, April). The crusader protecting kid athletes from sex abuse. *Outside.* Retrieved from https://www.outsideonline.com/2277976/fighting-sexual-abuse-behalf-young-athletes

Martin, C. L., & Ruble, D. N. (2009). Patterns of gender development. *Annual Review of Psychology, 61,* 353–381.

McCord, M. A., Joseph, D. L., Dhanani, L. Y., & Beus, J. M. (2018). A meta-analysis of sex and race differences in perceived workplace mistreatment. *Journal of Applied Psychology, 103*(2), 137–163.

Megheirkouni, M. (2014). Women-only leadership positions in the Middle East: Exploring cultural attitudes towards Syrian women for sport career development. *Advancing Women in Leadership, 34,* 64–78.

Mikołajczak, M., & Pietrzak, J. (2014). Ambivalent sexism and religion: Connected through values. *Sex Roles, 70*(9–10), 387–399.

Muehlenhard, C. L., & Peterson, Z. D. (2011). Distinguishing between sex and gender: History, current conceptualizations, and implications. *Sex Roles, 64*(11–12), 791–803.

Murray-Close, M., & Heggeness, M. L. (2018). Manning up and womaning down: How husbands and wives report their earnings when she earns more. SESHD Working Paper # 2018–20. Retrieved from https://www.census.gov/content/dam/Census/library/working-papers/2018/demo/SEHSD-WP2018-20.pdf

National Collegiate Athletic Association. (2017). Sport Sponsorship, Participation and Demographics Search [Data file]. Retrieved from http://web1.ncaa.org/rgdSearch/exec/main

Nordstrom, H., Warner, S., & Barnes, J. C. (2016). Behind the stripes: Female football officials' experiences. *International Journal of Sport Management and Marketing, 16*(3–6), 259–279.

Norman, L. (2010). Bearing the burden of doubt: Female coaches' experiences of gender relations. *Research Quarterly for Exercise and Sport, 81,* 506–517.

Norman, L. (2014). A crisis of confidence: Women coaches' responses to their engagement in resistance. *Sport, Education and Society, 19*(5), 532–551.

Norman, L., Rankin-Wright, A. J., & Allison, W. (in press). "It's a concrete ceiling; it's not even glass": Understanding tenets of organizational culture that supports the progression of women as coaches and coach developers. *Journal of Sport and Social Issues.*

Northouse, P. G. (2019). *Leadership: Theory and practice* (8th ed.). Los Angeles, CA: Sage.

Physical activity and women. (n.d.). *World Health Organization.* Retrieved from http://www.who.int/dietphysicalactivity/factsheet_women/en/

Powell, G. N. (2011). *Women & men in management* (4th ed.). Thousand Oaks, CA: Sage.

Regan, M., & Cunningham, G. (2012). Analysis of homologous reproduction in community college athletics. *Journal for the Study of Sports and Athletes in Education, 6*(2), 161–172.

Richardson, S. S. (2013). *Sex itself: The search for male and female in the human genome.* Chicago, IL: University of Chicago Press.

Rodríguez, E. A., & Gill, D. L. (2011). Sexual harassment perceptions among Puerto Rican female former athletes. *International Journal of Sport and Exercise Psychology, 9*, 323–337.

Rudman, L. A., & Phelan, J. E. (2008). Backlash effects for disconfirming gender stereotypes in organizations. In P. A. Brief & B. M. Staw (Eds.), *Research in organization behavior* (vol. 4, pp. 61–79). New York, NY: Elsevier.

Rudman, L. A., Moss-Racusin, C. A., Phelan, J. E., & Nauts, S. (2012). Status incongruity and backlash effects: Defending the gender hierarchy motivates prejudice against female leaders. *Journal of Experimental Social Psychology, 48*, 165–179.

Ryan, M. K., & Haslam, S. A. (2007). The glass cliff: Exploring the dynamics surrounding the appointment of women to precarious leadership positions. *Academy of Management Review, 32*(2), 549–572.

Sagas, M., & Cunningham, G. B. (2004). Does having the "right stuff" matter? Gender differences in the determinants of career success among intercollegiate athletic administrators. *Sex Roles, 50*, 411–421.

Sagas, M., Cunningham, G. B., & Ashley, F. B. (2000). Examining the women's coaching deficit through the perspective of assistant coaches. *International Journal of Sport Management, 1*, 267–282.

Sagas, M., Cunningham, G. B., & Pastore, D. (2006). Predicting head coaching intentions of male and female assistant coaches: An application of the theory of planned behavior. *Sex Roles, 54*, 695–705.

Sagas, M., Cunningham, G. B., & Teed, K. (2006). An examination of homologous reproduction in the representation of assistant coaches of women's teams. *Sex Roles, 55*(7–8), 503–510.

Sartore, M. L., & Cunningham, G. B. (2007). Ideological gender beliefs, identity control and self-limiting behavior within sport organizations. *Quest, 59*, 244–265.

Schein, E. H. (2004). *Organizational culture and leadership* (3rd ed.). San Francisco, CA: Jossey-Bass.

Schein, V. E. (1973). The relationship between sex role stereotypes and requisite management characteristics. *Journal of Applied Psychology, 57*, 95–100.

Schein, V. E. (1975). Relationships between sex role stereotypes and requisite management characteristics among female managers. *Journal of Applied Psychology, 60*, 340–344.

Schull, V., Shaw, S., & Kihl, L. A. (2013). "If a woman came in... she would have been eaten alive": Analyzing gendered political processes in the search for an athletic director. *Gender & Society, 27*, 56–81.

Seibert, S. E., Kraimer, M. L., & Liden, R. C. (2001). A social capital theory of career success. *Academy of Management Journal, 44*, 219–237.

Sharp, L. A., Moorman, A. M., & Claussen, C. L. (2014). *Sport law: A managerial approach* (3rd ed.). Scottsdale, AZ: Holcomb Hathaway.

Shaw, S. (2006). Scratching the back of "Mr X": Analyzing gendered social processes in sport organizations. *Journal of Sport Management, 20*(4), 510–534.

Shaw, S., & Hoeber, L. (2003). "A strong man is direct and a direct woman is a bitch": Gendered discourses and their influence on employment roles in sport organizations. *Journal of Sport Management, 17*, 347–375.

Shaw, S., & Slack, T. (2002). "It's been like that for donkey's years": The construction of gender relations and the cultures of sports organizations. *Culture, Sport, Society, 5*, 86–106.

Simmer-Brown, J. (2001). *Dakini's warm breath: The feminine principle in Tibetan Buddhism.* Boston, MA: Shambhala Publications.

Siner, A. G. (2017). Dressing to impress? Examination of dress codes in public schools. *Santa Clara Law Review, 57*, 259–284.

Smith, D. G., Rosenstein, J. E., Nikolov, M. C., & Chaney, D. A. (in press). The power of language: Gender, status, and agency in performance evaluations. *Sex Roles.*

Smittick, A. L., Miner, K. N., & Cunningham, G. B. (in press). The "I" in team: Coach incivility, coach gender, and team performance in women's basketball teams. *Sport Management Review.*

Spoor, J. R., & Hoye, R. (2014). Perceived support and women's intentions to stay at a sport organization. *British Journal of Management, 25*(3), 407–424.

Stangl, J. M., & Kane, M. J. (1991). Structural variables that offer explanatory power for the underrepresentation of women coaches since Title IX: The case of homologous reproduction. *Sociology of Sport Journal, 8*(1), 47–60.

Staurowsky, E. J., Zonder, E. J., & Riemer, B. A. (2017). So, what is Title IX? Assessing college athletes knowledge of the law. *Women in Sport and Physical Activity Journal, 25*(1), 30–42.

Taylor, E. A., & Hardin, R. (2016). Female NCAA Division I athletic directors: Experiences and challenges. *Women in Sport and Physical Activity Journal, 24*(1), 14–25.

Taylor, E. A., Smith, A. B., Welch, N. M., & Hardin, R. (2018). "You should be flattered!": Female sport management faculty experiences of sexual harassment and sexism. *Women in Sport and Physical Activity Journal, 26*(1), 43–53.

Timmer, A. S. H., & Senden, L. A. J. (2016). *A comparative analysis of gender equality law in Europe 2016: A comparative analysis of the implementation of EU gender equality law in the EU Member States, the former Yugoslav Republic of Macedonia, Iceland, Liechtenstein, Montenegro, Norway, Serbia and Turkey.* Brussels, Belgium: European Union.

Tingle, J. K., Warner, S., & Sartore-Baldwin, M. L. (2014). The experience of former women officials and the impact on the sporting community. *Sex Roles, 71*, 7–20.

Unger, R. K. (1979). Toward a redefinition of sex and gender. *American Psychologist, 34*(11), 1085–1094.

United States Department of Education (n.d.). The equity in athletics data analysis cutting tool. Retrieved from http://ope.ed.gov/athletics/

Valian, V. (1999). Why *so slow? The advancement of women.* Cambridge, MA: MIT Press.

Walker, N. A., & Bopp. T. (2010). The under-representation of women in the male-dominated workplace: Perspectives of female coaches. *Journal of Workplace Rights, 15*, 47–64.

Walker, N. A., & Sartore-Baldwin, M. L. (2013). Hegemonic masculinity and the institutionalized bias toward women in men's collegiate basketball: What do men think? *Journal of Sport Management, 27*, 303–315.

Woodhill, B. M., & Samuels, C. A. (2003). Positive and negative androgyny and their relationship with psychological health and well-being. *Sex Roles, 48*, 555–565.

Age

LEARNING OUTCOMES

After studying this chapter, you should be able to:

- Define age and age diversity.
- Describe the manner in which age influences access and treatment discrimination.
- Summarize the multilevel factors that influence age effects in the work environment.
- Paraphrase the manner in which age influences opportunities and experiences of sport and physical activity participants.

DIVERSITY CHALLENGE

Physical inactivity rates in the US have steadily risen over time, to the detriment of the country and its citizens. In fact, the World Health Organization estimates that over 60 percent of the population does not achieve the minimum recommendations for daily physical activity. According to the American Heart Association, a lack of physical activity is associated with a host of health problems, including heart disease, high blood pressure, diabetes, obesity, and low levels of good cholesterol. Conversely, participating in regular physical activity provides multiple benefits. According to the American Heart Association, it can help prevent bone loss (reducing the risk of fractures) and reduce the risk of many diseases associated with aging; increase muscle strength and improve balance and coordination, which can reduce the likelihood of falling and help maintain functionality and independence; and reduce the incidence of coronary heart disease, hypertension, non-insulin-dependent (Type 2) diabetes, colon cancer, depression, and anxiety.

Most people do not engage in the recommended levels of physical activity, and participation levels continually decrease with age. The effects are particularly noteworthy in Western countries, where the average age continues to increase. Thus, if trends continue, the current physical activity patterns will only be exacerbated over time.

Of course, physical inactivity is not characteristic of all persons, even all seniors. Rather, many persons aged 50 and over are very active. The Senior Games prove that it is possible to remain active later in life, and that many people do. This is an event, held every two years, that affords persons aged 50 to 100+ the opportunity to participate competitively in 19 medal sport events (e.g., archery, race walking) and seven exhibitions (e.g., fencing, sailing). The 2017 Games were held in Birmingham, Alabama. The Games are a major undertaking: the 2017 event saw 10,500 athletes competing at various sites, with thousands more in attendance. The Senior Games also offer the potential for economic benefits. Rick Davis, senior vice president for economic development at the Birmingham Business Alliance, commented,

> Birmingham's hospitality sector is the immediate economic beneficiary of the Senior Games, but indirectly, we all benefit by having the opportunity to showcase our community to a diverse national audience. . . . Thousands of athletes and fans will be at sporting events all over the region in the next two weeks, traveling our roads, eating at our restaurants and enjoying all Birmingham has to offer.

Sources: Slay, M. W. (2017, June). 30th anniversary National Senior Games convene in Birmingham. Alabama Newsletter. Retrieved from http://alabama newscenter.com/2017/06/07/94577/. American Heart Association (2014, April). The price of inactivity. Retrieved from www.americanheart.org. American Heart Association (2015, January). Physical activity in older Americans. Retrieved from www.americanheart.org

CHALLENGE REFLECTION

1. Despite the many benefits of regular physical activity, participation rates decrease with age. Why is this the case?
2. Organizations such as the Senior Games not only address the problem of physical inactivity but also have the potential to affect other outcomes. What are some of these outcomes, and why are these effects observed?
3. What can sport managers do to increase the physical activity levels of seniors?

As the Diversity Challenge illustrates, one's age plays a meaningful role in sport and physical activity participation. Age also affects a person's experience within sport organizations: it influences the opportunities people have, their interactions with their coworkers and supervisors, and how they relate to others in groups. Interestingly, despite these factors, scholars and sport managers have devoted comparatively little attention to age-based opportunities and experiences at work. To illustrate, I conducted a search on the academic database PsycINFO from 1990 to 2017, with a focus on three keywords: ageism, sexism, and racism. Results indicate that sexism appears 2.5 times as frequently as ageism, and racism appears 8.2 times as often. This disparity is all the more curious when considering that old age is a category into which virtually all people are likely to enter.

The purpose of this chapter, therefore, is to attempt to remedy this situation. To do so, I first provide an overview of key terms and statistics related to age. The discussion then moves to an analysis of the intersection of age and employment. Drawing from the model presented in Chapter 4, I then offer an overview of multilevel factors influencing age effects in sport organizations. In the final section, I examine how age influences sport, physical activity, and leisure participation.

BACKGROUND AND KEY TERMS

I start the discussion of age and age diversity with an overview of key terms, including what constitutes old and young. Dong, Milholland, and Vijg (2016) examined the maximum age at which humans could live. Some scientists have suggested that technological innovations and a better understanding of the human body mean that age limits are flexible. Dong et al. countered such claims. Using data from several sources, they observed that the maximum age people lived increased until 1995 but not thereafter. They approximated the maximum reported age of death for humans is 115 years (see Lenart & Vaupel, 2017, for a counter to this limit). There can be outliers, but these will be rare. Dong et al. found that the chance of the maximum reported age of death in any given year exceeding 125 years is less than 1 in 10,000.

Life expectancy serves as another indicator of relative age. According to the World Health Organization (Life Expectancy, n.d.), life expectancy "reflects the overall mortality level of a population. It summarizes the mortality pattern that prevails across all age groups in a given year—children and adolescents, adults and the elderly." Infant mortality and early life hazards can influence life expectancy rates, so another measure to consider is the adult mortality rate. According to the World Bank, this

> is the probability of dying between the ages of 15 and 60—that is, the probability of a 15 year old. . . dying before reaching age 60, if subject to age-specific mortality rates on the specified year between those ages.
>
> (Mortality rate, n.d.)

Drawing from data provided by the World Bank, I summarize life expectancy and mortality rates over time for the US, Brazil, Egypt, South Korea, and the Netherlands, using data from 1960 to 2016. As seen in Exhibit 7.1, the life expectancy for the world and for the specific countries under consideration have all increased since 1960. Around the world, life expectancy has increased 42 percent over that timeframe, from 50.57 to 72.04 years. Of the countries in the analysis, China had the biggest increase: 80 percent (43.73–78.69 years). As life expectancy rates have increased, mortality rates have decreased. I show the data for adult women in Exhibit 7.2, and the pattern is the same for adult men. Worldwide in 1960, 298 women out of 1,000 died between ages 15 and 60. By 2016, that figure dropped to 123. The biggest drop occurred for China, whose figures decreased almost sixfold. The Netherlands data remained relatively flat, which was a good thing, considering the country had the lowest mortality rates in 1960, and the trend continued through 2014 (the last year data for the country was available).

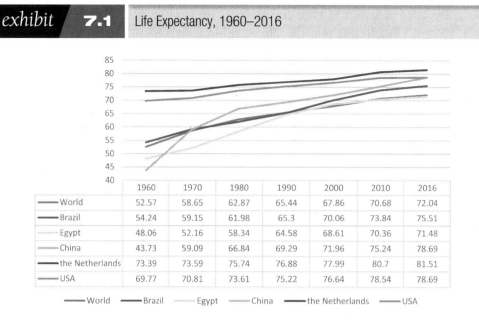

exhibit 7.1	Life Expectancy, 1960–2016						
	1960	1970	1980	1990	2000	2010	2016
World	52.57	58.65	62.87	65.44	67.86	70.68	72.04
Brazil	54.24	59.15	61.98	65.3	70.06	73.84	75.51
Egypt	48.06	52.16	58.34	64.58	68.61	70.36	71.48
China	43.73	59.09	66.84	69.29	71.96	75.24	78.69
the Netherlands	73.39	73.59	75.74	76.88	77.99	80.7	81.51
USA	69.77	70.81	73.61	75.22	76.64	78.54	78.69

Source: Life Expectancy at Birth (no date).

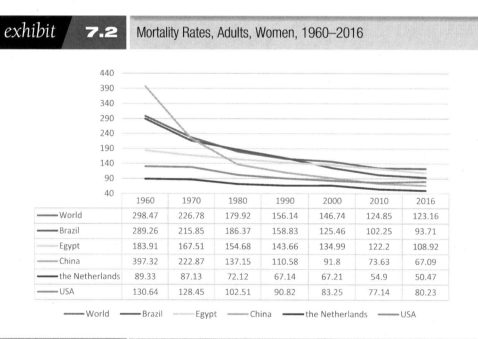

exhibit 7.2	Mortality Rates, Adults, Women, 1960–2016						
	1960	1970	1980	1990	2000	2010	2016
World	298.47	226.78	179.92	156.14	146.74	124.85	123.16
Brazil	289.26	215.85	186.37	158.83	125.46	102.25	93.71
Egypt	183.91	167.51	154.68	143.66	134.99	122.2	108.92
China	397.32	222.87	137.15	110.58	91.8	73.63	67.09
the Netherlands	89.33	87.13	72.12	67.14	67.21	54.9	50.47
USA	130.64	128.45	102.51	90.82	83.25	77.14	80.23

Source: Life Expectancy at Birth (no date).
Notes: Figures per 1,000 adult women. The Netherlands data is through 2014. USA data available through 2015.

Increased life expectancy and adult mortality can result in an increased median age for a country, particularly when birth rates are stagnant or on the decline (see also Cilluffo & Cohn, 2017). In the US, for example, 15 percent of the population was aged 65 or older in 2014. By 2060, experts predict this figure will increase to 24 percent (Colby & Ortman, 2015). These data vary based on a number of personal demographic characteristics, including whether one was born in the US. In 2014, people born in the US represented 86.8 percent of people aged 65 or older. By 2060, that figure is expected to drop to 63.0 percent. Examination of the same data from another lens shows that the share of foreign-born individuals in the US aged 65 or older will increase 314.7 percent from 2014 to 2060 (6,098,000–19,190,000).

According to the Pew Research Center, the population trends in the US are evident worldwide (Attitudes about Aging, 2014). From 1950 to 2010, the world's population nearly tripled, but from 2010 to 2050, the growth rate should abate. During the latter timeframe, Pew researchers expected the percentage of people aged 65 and older to increase considerably. In 2010, people aged 65 or older represented 7.7 percent of the world's population—a figure that should increase to 15.6 percent in 2050. As shown in Exhibit 7.3, these figures vary by country. In Nigeria, only 3.8 of the population will be aged 65 or older by 2060. Experts expect this figure to be considerably higher in Germany (32.7 percent) and Japan (36.5 percent).

Proportion of People Aged 65 or Older, Estimates for 2010 and 2050, by Country

exhibit **7.3**

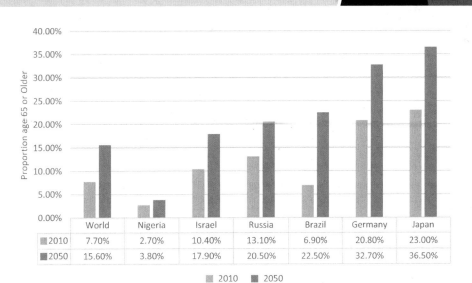

	World	Nigeria	Israel	Russia	Brazil	Germany	Japan
2010	7.70%	2.70%	10.40%	13.10%	6.90%	20.80%	23.00%
2050	15.60%	3.80%	17.90%	20.50%	22.50%	32.70%	36.50%

■ 2010   ■ 2050

Box 7.1 Diversity in the Field: Relative Age Effects

Youth sports are structured such that athletes of particular ages compete against one another. Leagues frequently achieve this by establishing cutoff dates such that children born between, for example, September 1, 2005, and August 31, 2006, all play against one another. Such classification schemes are logical, but they create an advantage for children born early in the age band, something referred to as the relative age effect (Smith, Weir, Till, Romann, & Cobley, in press). This effect—which can last into adulthood—occurs in a variety of settings within sport, such as hockey, track, and soccer, as well as outside of it, such as in the classroom (see Wattie, Schorer, & Baker, 2015). Although physiological explanations might be significant early on, the enduring nature of relative age effects suggests that sociocultural factors might be at play, too (Hancock, Adler, & Côté, 2013). Performance differences between younger and older players might correspond with feelings of confidence and interest in the sport among the players. Coaches and parents are likely to reinforce these sentiments. For their part, coaches might be more likely to select and nurture the athletic advancement of the more physically mature older players. Parental expectations and reinforcement are also influential, as they might encourage the older-grouped children to pursue the tasks in which they excel relative to their peers. Thus, children born earlier in the age band, relative to their younger counterparts, may develop greater confidence and more positive attitudes toward sport, enjoy initial performance advantages, and receive greater reinforcement from parents and coaches. Over time, these forces advantage older children and adolescents, creating relative age effects.

These figures correspond with the degree to which people in the country consider aging a problem (Attitudes about Aging, 2014). Pew Research Center experts asked, "How much of a problem, if at all, is the growing number of older people in (survey country)" (p. 13). In Nigeria, only 28 percent believed aging was a major problem. In Germany and Japan, however, that figure rose to 55 percent and 87 percent, respectively.

These figures offer an overview of aging worldwide. The changes in a country's median age are likely reflected in the workforce, as well. What, though, constitutes young or old in sport organizations? For years, I coached a girls' soccer team, and the players considered me old although I was in my late 30s and early 40s when I coached. Whereas an eight-year-old soccer player might consider 40 as old, this was not the case for a colleague of mine, who, upon turning 40, commented that he looked forward to the next two-thirds of his life. Thus, in some respects, what qualifies as old is in the eye of the beholder.

In the sport context, age affects when people can participate in different sport events. In youth soccer, leagues will frequently separate athletes based on two-year increments, such as U6, U8, and so on. In U6, players younger than age six compete against one another, whereas in U8 soccer, players aged six and seven participate. (Box 7.1 includes information about how relative age effects can influence performance in youth sport and beyond.) The Champions Golf Tour is a professional golf association for players who are at least age 50. Another example is the National Basketball Association (NBA): as of 2018, a player had to be at least 19 years to participate in the league. Concepts of older and younger frequently have different connotations in sport organizations. In US organizations, 40 years is a meaningful age, as that is when employees receive employment protections, per the Age Discrimination in Employment Act (ADEA). The age designation varies, though. In New Zealand, for example, anyone aged 16 or older and suitably qualified for a job is protected against age discrimination (Age discrimination at work, n.d.).

AGE IN THE WORK ENVIRONMENT

Most of the scholarship on age and discrimination in the workplace centers on the experiences of older individuals (Finkelstein, Ryan, & King, 2013). The emphasis likely stems from social norms and societal trends. For example, the Age Discrimination in Employment Act in the US sets legal employment protections for workers aged 40 and older; thus, the law reifies the idea that older individuals are likely to face employment discrimination. In addition, as the proportion of people aged 65 and older increases around the world (see Exhibit 7.3), so too does the proportion of older workers. As such, the emphasis on older workers is understandable. That noted, younger individuals may also face access and treatment discrimination at work. Increasingly, scholars have considered experiences of age discrimination among employees of all ages (Bratt, Abrams, Swift, Vauclair, & Marques, 2018; Marchiondo, Gonzales, & Ran, 2016; Potter et al., in press). The broader emphasis is consistent with New Zealand age discrimination laws, whereby the government recognizes that all people who can legally work might face differential treatment.

Bratt et al. (2018) analyzed data from the European Social Survey. Over 56,000 participants from 29 different countries responded to three questions that were designed to measure their experiences with age discrimination in general. They found that younger people reported more experiences with age discrimination than did older individuals. In fact, in half of the countries, older individuals reported low levels of age discrimination. In other countries, experiences with age discrimination were U-shaped such that older and younger individuals experienced discrimination, but middle-aged individuals did not.

The U-shaped pattern for experiences with age discrimination is consistent with Marchiondo et al.'s (2016) research focusing on workplace age discrimination. They developed a research instrument in which participants responded to how frequently they experienced covert forms of age discrimination. Examples include "my contributions are not valued as much due to my age," "I have been treated as though I am less capable because of my age," and "I have been treated with less respect due to my age" (p. 499). Contrary to the assumption that only older workers experienced age discrimination, the researchers found that younger workers also experienced age-based mistreatment and sometimes at higher frequency levels. Middle-aged workers, on the other hand, were unlikely to experience age-based discrimination. Marchiondo et al. suggested this may be due to the lack of age-based stereotypes about middle-aged individuals—a point to which I return later in the chapter.

MULTILEVEL EXPLANATIONS

Collectively, the evidence suggests that age can influence people's experiences in the work environment, particularly among younger and older employees. In Chapter 4, I offered a multilevel framework for understanding the experiences of and opportunities for people from underrepresented groups. In this section, I draw from that framework to focus on the macro-, meso-, and micro-level factors that influence age-based work discrimination. Exhibit 7.4 provides an overview of the factors.

Macro-Level Factors

Macro-level factors are those operating at the societal level. A number of macro-level factors can influence the prevalence of age discrimination in sport organizations, including changing demographics and work patterns, employment laws, and institutional ageism.

Changing Demographics and Work Patterns

I previously noted changes in demographic trends, with countries around the world aging. This trend coincides with an increasing proportion of employees who choose to work past the traditional retirement age (i.e., 65 years). In fact, in 2018, over 250,000 Americans aged 85 or older were working. That figure represents 4.4 percent of the population of that age and is the highest number recorded (Van Dam, 2018). They work in a variety of occupations, with the most popular including crossing guard, models, funeral directors, and farmers.

exhibit   **7.4**   Multilevel Factors Affecting Age-Based Discrimination

Macro-level factors: Those operating at the societal level, including changing demographics and work patterns, employment laws, and institutional ageism.

Meso-level factors: Those operating at the team and organizational levels, including bias in decision-making and organizational policies.

Micro-level factors: Those operating at the individual level, including personal characteristics and age in context.

Several factors influence this trend (Mehrotra & Wagner, 2009). First, in an effort to encourage longer employment tenures in the US, Social Security was altered so that those who work past the typical retirement age will receive increased monthly Social Security benefits. Second, the fact that most working employees receive health insurance coverage through the workplace means they are incentivized to remain employed until at least age 65, when they become eligible for Medicare. Third, many workers express concerns about having adequate funds after retirement. Only 52 percent of retirees receive some form of pension income; thus, nearly half of the retired workforce lives off personal savings and Social Security benefits. These dynamics make working longer, thereby accruing more Social Security benefits and greater savings, an appealing option. With greater age diversity in the workplace, age-related biases are likely to manifest (Nelson, 2009; North & Fiske, 2012).

Employment Laws

Employment laws influence who is protected from discrimination in selection and treatment in the workplace. In the US, the Age Discrimination in Employment Act is the primary law governing age-based discrimination. I offer an overview in Exhibit 7.5.

Note that under this law, employers cannot compel older employees to retire. Such provisions are not universal, however. Blackham (2018) wrote that, as of 2018, there were still sectors in Australia and the UK where compulsory retirement was in place. Professors at some universities (e.g., Oxford and Cambridge), federal judges, and members of the defense force all must retirement at certain ages. Proponents of the practice suggest that it allows for employees with new ideas and different perspectives to enter the labor force. Blackham noted, however, that mandatory retirement can backfire, especially when the country has a significant increase in median age, as is the case with most Western countries. In these contexts, decreases in labor supply per capita could harm the overall economy. She therefore argued that "one of the key policy measures available to address this looming issue is to increase workforce participation rates for older workers. Eliminating the last vestiges of mandatory retirement is an obvious first step."

In the US, although age-related employment decisions are illegal, there are exceptions. As the US Department of Labor explains,

> under the ADEA, it is unlawful for an agency to discriminate on the basis of age unless the agency can establish that the age limitation is a bona fide occupational qualification necessary to the performance of the duties of the position.
> (What I need to know about, n.d.)

The bona fide occupational qualification (BFOQ) allows organizations to set age limits on who holds a particular job because one must be younger than a certain age to perform the job effectively. For example, according to Federal Aviation Administration guidelines, airline pilots cannot be 65 years or older. It is difficult to envisage a job in sport organizations where a BFOQ would limit participation based on age.

exhibit **7.5** Age and Employment Protections

People aged over 40 are protected from discrimination by the Age Discrimination in Employment Act. This law protects both current employees and job applicants. Employers cannot legally discriminate against people because of their age with respect to any aspect of employment, including hiring, firing, promotion, compensation, benefits, and the quality of job assignments. The Act also protects people from retaliation if they file a complaint. The ADEA applies to all organizations with at least 20 employees, including state and local governments, employment agencies, labor unions, and the federal government. Protections under the law also include the following:

- **Apprenticeship programs.** Under most circumstances, it is unlawful for apprenticeship programs to set age limits.
- **Job notices and advertisements.** When advertising for a position, it is unlawful to include age preferences or limitations. The only exception is when age is a BFOQ.
- **Preemployment inquiries.** Although it is *not* unlawful to ask prospective employees for their age or date of birth, the EEOC has indicated that such requests will be closely scrutinized to ensure that they are made for lawful purposes.
- **Benefits.** Some older employees may need more medical care than their younger counterparts. Because of the cost of such care, this may serve as a disincentive to hire older employees or provide them with benefits. The Older Workers Benefit Protection Act of 1990 amended the ADEA to guarantee benefits to older workers.
- **Waivers of ADEA rights.** Some organizations offer special early retirement packages to their older employees for a variety of cost-saving and human resource reasons. The ADEA and the Older Workers Benefit Protection Act allow for early retirement if the employee willingly chooses to waive his or her rights. A valid waiver must:

  - be written and understandable by all parties;
  - explicitly refer to ADEA rights and claims;
  - not surrender future rights or claims;
  - be in exchange for something that is valuable (e.g., a retirement package worth more than a standard retirement);
  - recommend that the employee seek legal advice before signing; and
  - provide the employee with at least three weeks to consider the agreement and one week to revoke the agreement, even after the document is signed.

Even though employment protections are in place, age-based discrimination persists. Based on the number of complaints filed with the Equal Employment Opportunity Commission (EEOC; 18,376 in 2017), incidents of gender discrimination are common. Companies that discriminate based on gender can receive severe financial punishments. In 2017 alone, over $90.1 million in damages were collected for persons who made complaints. (This figure does not include damages recovered through litigation.)

Institutional Ageism

Bias against people based on their age can take place at the interpersonal level—a dynamic discussed in subsequent sections—but increasingly, scholars have pointed to institutional forms of ageism (Stypińska & Nikander, 2018). Consistent with cultural and critical sociological theories (see Chapter 2), institutional ageism refers to the manner in which society's institutions, such as schools, police, and churches, privilege some people over others based on their age (see also Wilkinson & Ferraro, 2004). From this perspective, the structures, processes, and system in place in a society constrain the opportunities and shape the experiences people have. Even absent individual biases—a hypothetical that does not exist—institutional forms of bias would still shape access and treatment.

Stypińska and Nikander (2018) offered several examples of institutional ageism, including the mandatory retirement age previously discussed. The outcomes, they suggested, are negative for individuals and society. At the individual level, employees experience constrained career paths, and their personal and family well-being are hurt. Institutional ageism's effects move beyond the individual, as they ultimately result in social, economic, and cultural harm. For example, people who experience age discrimination might be isolated from others, and organizations are not as productive as they could be.

Meso-Level Factors

I next move to meso-level factors, or those operating at the team and organizational levels. In this chapter, salient meso-level factors include bias in decision-making and organizational policies.

Bias in Decision-Making

Recall from Chapter 3 that stereotypes, prejudice, and discrimination are all subsumed under the broader umbrella of bias. In their comprehensive review of the literature, Posthuma and Campion (2009) identified several age-related stereotypes, which are outlined in Exhibit 7.6 and in the following space (see also Shore & Goldberg, 2005).

Perhaps the most common stereotype of older employees is that their job performance is expected to lag behind that of their younger counterparts (Posthuma & Campion, 2009). This stereotype might be based on a number of factors, including

exhibit **7.6** Age-Related Stereotypes in Sport Organizations

Age-related stereotypes represent beliefs or expectations about employees based on their age or presumed age. Common stereotypes include the following:

1. **Poor performance:** the belief that older employees perform at lower levels than their counterparts.
2. **Resistance to change:** the belief that older employees are averse to change and set in their ways.
3. **Ability to learn:** the belief that older employees are less able to learn new materials or techniques.
4. **Shorter tenure:** the belief that older employees will remain in the organization for a shorter time than younger employees.
5. **More costly:** the belief that older employees cost more to the organization because of salaries, health care, and retirement costs.
6. **More dependable:** the belief that older employees are more responsible and trustworthy than their younger counterparts.

the belief that older employees have low mental ability, cannot handle stress, or are less competent. Though performance stereotypes do exist, evidence of their actual existence is less concrete; in fact, there are many cases where performance actually improves with age (Ng & Feldman, 2008). The stereotype might appear to be true because of the time needed to complete tasks, as younger employees generally complete work more quickly. However, they do so with more mistakes. When considering both time and quality of the work, older and younger workers are equally productive (Börsch-Supan & Weiss, 2016). For instance, young sales representatives might make more calls, but older representatives might be more thorough when making the calls.

Ng and Feldman (2008) examined this very issue by combining the results across 380 research studies in a meta-analysis. Their study yielded interesting findings. In some cases, older and younger adults did not vary in their performance, such as when they completed their primary job tasks or when performance was measured by the creativity of the product. In other cases, though, age did have an effect. Older employees were found to engage in more helping behaviors at work, be safer on the job, engage in less substance abuse, be absent less frequently, and exhibit less aggression. The one area where they lagged was in training performance. Taken as a whole, Ng and Feldman's research suggests that, if anything, older workers are more productive than younger ones. These findings have led some to suggest that there is greater variability in performance within age groups than between them (Posthuma & Campion, 2009).

People also hold the stereotype that older workers are more resistant to change than are younger ones (Posthuma & Campion, 2009). The idea that older people have an aversion to change could reflect a belief that older people are set in their ways or hesitant to engage in training to learn new skills. In a classic study illustrating this point, Rosen and Jerdee (1976) found that students thought older workers would be unreceptive to changing their negative job behaviors and would lack motivation to adapt to new technologies in the workplace. Not surprisingly, students were likely to favor young employees in promotions, training, and job transfers. A follow-up study (Rosen & Jerdee, 1977) that used a sample of working professionals confirmed this pattern of findings, thereby eliminating concerns that the findings were observed only among college students. These stereotypes persist (Mahon & Millar, 2014). As with many of the other stereotypes, though, there is little empirical evidence to support this belief. In fact, the opposite is actually the case, as younger employees exhibit a stronger aversion to change than their older counterparts (Kunze, Boehm, & Bruch, 2013).

Another stereotype negatively affecting senior employees is the belief that they have low capacities to learn to use new tools, procedures, or materials (Posthuma & Campion, 2009). Ng and Feldman (2012) examined this point in a subsequent meta-analysis. Across all of the studies, there was a small negative association between age and willingness to engage in new learning and development opportunities. That said, the magnitude of the association was small, explaining less than 1 percent of the variance, which suggests that the stereotype tends to exaggerate the truth.

A fourth stereotype negatively affecting older workers is the belief that they will leave the organization sooner than their younger counterparts (Posthuma & Campion, 2009). If this turnover does occur, then the organization will have to recruit, attract, retain, and train a new employee, all of which can cost thousands of dollars. Further, current training efforts, which also require considerable resources, might be a risky investment in older employees because the employer might not reap a return on the investment.

Despite these sentiments, the empirical evidence does not support this stereotype (Hedge, Borman, & Lammlein, 2006). As noted in Chapter 1, the notion that an employee will remain with a sport organization for an entire career has increasingly become outdated. Instead, an employee is likely to move from one organization to another several times throughout a career. Thus, the notion that younger employees will remain with the organization longer than older employees is unfounded. Furthermore, the benefits of training are often realized in the short term, so concerns related to older employees' tenure are misplaced. Some evidence indicates that workplace culture can play a role in the retention of older employees. Specifically, older employees express intentions to remain in an organization when there are practices in place that tend to their needs, when supervisors fairly implement these practices, and when the employees feel their contributions are valued (Armstrong-Stassen & Schlosser, 2011).

Another stereotype negatively affecting the opportunities and experiences of older workers is that they are expensive to the organization (Posthuma & Campion, 2009). Older workers, relative to younger ones, are generally paid higher wages and are closer to retirement. According to the stereotype, older workers also become ill more frequently and, therefore, use more benefits. People might use this evidence to support a belief that older employees are costly, a drain on resources,

Box 7.2 Alternative Perspectives: Age-Based Stereotype Threat

Stereotype threats arise when people (a) feel anxious about confirming group stereotypes and (b) subsequently perform poorly on a task germane to the stereotype (Steele, 1997). For older individuals, negative stereotypes exist concerning their performance on cognitive and physical tasks. Lamont, Swift, and Abrams (2015) examined the degree to which performance in these activities could be explained, at least in part, by age-based stereotype threat. To do so, they collected data from previous studies and aggregated the findings, correcting for various sources of error. The overall sample included over 3,800 participants who had an average age of 69.5 years. Overall, there was a small but statistically significant effect of stereotype threat. The researchers also identified a number of factors that influenced the results. The effects of age-based stereotype threat were larger when performance was tested using cognitive measures and when the researchers assessed the performance close to the stereotype manipulation. Interestingly, the patterns were stronger for studies published in European journals, relative to those published in North America. Gender did not influence the pattern of findings. In discussing their findings, the author suggested that age-based stereotype threat "is a significant problem confronting older people and . . . it will be valuable to explore ways to lift that burden" (p. 191).

and a bad investment for the organization. Despite the prevalence of this stereotype, there is little empirical evidence to support the notion that younger employees are the better economic alternative for an organization. I return to Ng and Feldman's (2012) meta-analysis to examine part of the stereotype: the belief that an older worker's level of health results in higher costs to the organization than a younger employee would require. The researchers found that older employees tended to have higher blood pressure and cholesterol. However, age was not related to a host of other outcomes, such as subjective health and poor physical health symptoms.

The final age-related stereotype, dependability, actually serves to benefit older workers to the detriment of their younger counterparts (Posthuma & Campion, 2009). Specifically, older workers are considered to be loyal, trustworthy, stable, and committed to the workforce (Ng & Feldman, 2010). They are also less likely to steal from their employer or to be absent from work than their younger counterparts (Hedge et al., 2006). Younger employees, on the other hand, are sometimes seen as irresponsible, unreliable, and not loyal to the workplace (Bell, 2007).

In Box 7.2, I consider stereotypes from another perspective—the effects of stereotype threat.

Prejudice represents the second component of bias, and in the context of the current discussion, it manifests in the form of ageism. Ageism refers to negative attitudes people hold toward others who vary from them in age. It goes largely unchecked because it is institutionalized in nature (Nelson, 2009).

There are a number of potential explanations for these negative sentiments about aging. One possibility comes from what is called terror management theory (Becker, 1973). This theory holds that, when confronted with their own mortality, people will engage in a variety of behaviors aimed at distancing themselves from death, thereby lessening their anxiety. One such behavior involves developing negative attitudes toward older individuals and stronger affective ties with younger individuals (see also Popham, Kennison, & Bradley, 2011).

Generational differences and resource scarcity might also help explain prejudice toward older adults (North & Fiske, 2012). From this perspective, ageism is likely to manifest because (a) younger people seek to limit older persons' control over and access to limited resources, such as wealth, prestige, and employment opportunities; (b) older individuals are believed to consume more than their share of limited resources, such as government services or, in the context of work, salary; and (c) younger people are seeking to maintain generational identity boundaries, a desire likely rooted in terror management ideations. Together, these three domains—succession, consumption, and identity—are likely to engender animosity toward older adults.

Age discrimination represents the final form of bias. It is likely influenced by the stereotypes people have developed and the negative attitudes they hold toward older employees. Drawing from Shore and Goldberg's (2005) work, age-based discrimination exists along several domains (see Exhibit 7.7).

Older adults spend considerably more time searching for jobs and remaining unemployed than do their younger counterparts. In 2013, the Department of Labor estimated that older adults remained unemployed for an average of 53 weeks, compared to just 19 weeks for teenagers. These effects are particularly damaging for adults who experience unemployment in their 1950s, even resulting

---

Age-Related Discrimination in the Workplace   *exhibit* **7.7**

A person's age has the potential to influence various opportunities and experiences encountered in the workplace, including the following:

1. Job search and unemployment
2. Selection
3. Training and development
4. Mentoring
5. Performance and promotion potential
6. Exiting the organization

Box 7.3 Professional Perspectives: Training Older Employees

In writing for *Forbes* magazine, Chris Farrell (2017) lamented the lack of training for older employees—something he suggested was "bad for business, bad for workers in their 50s and 60s and bad for the U.S. economy."

He suggests many employers feel they do not need to train older employees because the employees might soon retire. However, such a belief system runs counter to what researchers have shown older employers actually want. In fact, Farrell reports that around 80 percent desire training, and 7 in 10 consider it a key part of their ideal employment.

Even though many organizations fail when it comes to training older employees, there are notable exceptions. In the US, companies such as AT&T and Scripps Health have made major investments and seen positive returns. Farrell points to evidence from the Netherlands to show why the positive returns likely materialize. The country had historically had low rates of employment for people aged 55–64—just 29 percent. The government then introduced new measures, including training and development, and the proportion of older employees rose to 53 percent. Experts have shown that with training, older employees are more motivated and seek to remain working longer.

In short, ensuring training for all employees—irrespective of their age—is likely to benefit the employee, the sport organization, and the broader community.

in decreased life expectancy compared to individuals who do not experience such critical life shifts (Coile, Levine, & McKnight, 2014; Noelke & Beckfield, 2014). Box 7.3 offers more information on training older employees.

Age can also affect the selection process. In some cases, stereotypes about older workers can hurt them in the selection process (Perry & Parlamis, 2007). In other cases, though, the opposite occurs. Raymer, Reed, Spiegel, and Purvanova (2017) conducted a mixed-methods study and found that common stereotypes of younger professionals included the belief that they (a) use language that is too casual, (b) hold a sense of entitlement, (c) have a poor work ethic, and (d) are disrespectful of others and are self-centered. Raymer and colleagues suggested these negative evaluations could negatively affect younger individuals in their job search process. Lee, Pitesa, Thau, and Pillutla (2015) have shown that the nature of the work can influence these processes. When in a cooperative environment, decision-makers prefer older workers for jobs requiring stability and younger workers for tasks calling for creativity. The preferences switch when the workplace is marked by competition.

Training and development represent a third area of age discrimination, with older employees have fewer opportunities than their younger counterparts. With rapidly changing technologies and workplace dynamics, employers must provide effective training and development for employees to ensure workplace competitiveness. The same is true for individual employees, as failing to update one's skills can have serious negative career consequences. Despite the advantages of training, older employees are frequently not afforded opportunities for training and professional development (Van Rooij, 2012). This could be due to stereotypes about their ability to learn and their motivation to adapt to new techniques and strategies, discussed earlier. These stereotypes probably influence sport organizations' willingness to provide development opportunities for older workers. Of course, when people are not afforded training opportunities, their professional skills do not develop. This can result in stagnation in their work and squelching of their intellectual curiosity. Thus, the failure to offer training and development for older employees will end up hurting both the employee and the effectiveness of the organization.

In addition, the age of a person influences the mentoring she or he receives. The perceived career stage of the employee could influence mentoring, as organizations are likely to devote time and energy to develop the skills of younger employees, hoping for a long-term payoff (Kulik, Ryan, Harper, & George, 2014). The same pattern appears in mentoring, where mentors tend to seek out and invest more time with younger employees, perhaps believing that they are in greater need of professional development and career coaching. Such beliefs affect the type of mentoring older employees receive; in particular, there is some evidence that older employees tend to receive informal mentoring, are unlikely to receive guidance about their career progression, and have short relationships with their mentors (Finkelstein, Allen, & Rhoton, 2007).

Another form of discrimination comes in the form of promotion potential. Managers might believe that older workers have little promise or potential for advancement. The effects are especially pronounced when there is a mismatch between the employee and the supervisor. Shore, Cleveland, and Goldberg (2003) reported that "employees who are older than their managers suffer negative consequences when examining data most relevant to their careers—promotability, managerial potential, and development" (p. 535). This mismatch could be a result of supervisor–subordinate dissimilarity or career timetable effects. As an example, a 55-year-old employee of Foot Locker who works for a 35-year-old manager might be seen as lagging behind in her career, and the manager's ratings of her career potential and promotion potential are likely to reflect such a perception.

Finally, employees can exit the organization in one of three ways: voluntary turnover, involuntary turnover (i.e., layoffs, downsizing, firing), or retirement. Interestingly, there is no relationship between age and voluntary turnover, meaning that older and younger employees are equally likely to leave the organization on their own volition (Healy, Lehman, & McDaniel, 1995). There are differences, however, in layoffs because older employees are frequently targeted. The variation is attributable to the fact that older workers are more likely than younger ones to occupy mid-level managerial positions, which are so often the target of corporate layoffs, as well as to negative age-related stereotypes (Perry & Parlamis, 2007).

Organizational Policies

The second meso-level factor, organizational policies, can also impact how age differences manifest in the work environment. Boehm, Kunze, and Bruch's (2014) study illustrates these effects. They collected data from small companies in Germany, with over 14,000 employees participating. They focused on a number of age-inclusive policies, such as age-neutral recruiting, equal access to training for all people, equal access for advancement across ages, age-related training and development for managers, and the promotion of an age-friendly culture. Boehm and colleagues found that age-inclusive policies resulted in a positive workplace culture and the belief among employees that if they worked hard, they would be rewarded. Both of these processes were important, as they gave rise to gains in organizational performance and a decrease in employee turnover. In short, the authors showed that it pays to have age-inclusive policies.

The opposite can also occur. When the workforce is diverse in terms of age and such diversity is not supported by the organization, age-related incidents are likely to occur, such as the violation of age norms and behaviors, stereotype activation, and in-group/out-group distinctions. All of these can affect people's attitudes toward age diversity and their belief that there is a climate of age discrimination in the workplace. When such beliefs take hold, employees' attachment to the workplace is likely to decrease, as is overall organizational performance (Kunze, Boehm, & Bruch, 2011).

Finally, human resource practices might influence the effects of age-related stereotypes on work outcomes. Posthuma and Campion (2009) outlined several approaches that can reduce negative effects of age-related bias. First, using job-specific information in making decisions concerning selection and promotions can help eliminate age bias and stereotyping. Skill is much more important than age in predicting job performance; thus, focusing on applicants' skill sets, rather than their age, should result in fair and effective selection processes. Second, training and development efforts that target ageism help managers avoid stereotyping workers by (a) highlighting the prevalence of stereotyping and the ways in which it is manifested and (b) elucidating the many benefits that workers of all ages bring to the organization. Third, viewing older workers as a source of competitive advantage reduces negative work experiences. Consider, for instance, that older workers bring a wealth of institutional knowledge and expertise to the workplace—an understanding of situations that arises only from experience. Thus, older employees potentially bring benefits to the organization that their younger counterparts cannot. Finally, adding complexity, rather than reducing it, improves employees' cognitive functioning and, as a result, their job performance. Managers should not be tempted to simplify an older employee's job when they are concerned that the person is losing cognitive abilities.

Micro-Level Factors

Micro-level factors can also impact age's influence in the work environment. Personal characteristics and age in context are particularly salient.

Personal Characteristics

Truxillo, Cadiz, and Hammer (2015) conducted a review of the extant research pertaining to age in the workforce. In doing so, they identified five within-person changes that could affect an employee's work. The first is physical changes, including those in the sensory, muscular, cardiovascular, immune response, and homoeostasis domains. These changes can increase the potential for health issues and disabilities as one ages. Next, as people grow older, they potentially encounter cognitive changes, including fluid intelligence (e.g., reduction in processing speed) and crystallized intelligence (e.g., gains in knowledge and wisdom). Affective changes can also occur, including changes to emotional regulation and emotion generation. These changes result in enhanced well-being and the tendency to see events from a positive point of view. Fourth, personality changes can occur, including increased conscientiousness and agreeableness, and decreases in neuroticism. Finally, motivation can change over time. In general, as one ages, intrinsic motivation and helping behaviors increase while external motivation and the desire for mastery experiences declines.

Individual characteristics can also influence how people interpret age discrimination. Potter et al. (in press) examined how race, gender, age, and social class interacted with one another to predict reporting and attributions of discrimination. They collected data from nearly 300 Americans, aged 20–83. As with the Bratt et al.'s (2018) study in Europe, Potter et al. observed that younger people reported more discrimination than did older individuals. Other demographics influenced the pattern, though. Older, highly educated men were likely to attribute the discrimination to their age. For women, however, they were likely to attribute the discrimination to their age when they were in the lower social class.

Age in Context

As illustrated throughout the chapter, a number of factors influence age-related opportunities and experiences in the work environment. One of the more salient is the employee's age in context, including the employee's age relative to career stage and the employee's age relative to others in the unit. For example, older employees might experience more treatment and access discrimination when they are not on the same career or organizational hierarchy as their peers (Shore et al., 2003). In some organizations, the social norms and historical precedents question the appropriateness of a manager who is "too young," creating tensions and unease (Perry, Kulik, & Zhou, 1999). This might occur, for instance, when a head coach is younger than some of the players on her team, or when an athletic director is similar in age to some coaches' children. In such situations, the older employees might engage in withdrawal behaviors, such as being absent from or not fully engaged in their work (Perry et al., 1999).

Dissimilarity from others in a work unit can also negatively influence employee reactions. To illustrate, I collected data from 175 track and field coaches of National Collegiate Athletic Association teams (Cunningham, 2007). I asked them about their perceived dissimilarity from others on the staff and how this impacted their subsequent connectedness with the group. Results showed that as perceived age dissimilarity increased, so too did the coaches' belief that they had different values and attitudes from others on the staff. As deep-level dissimilarity perceptions increased, their coworker satisfaction decreased and intentions to leave the team increased.

AGE AND PARTICIPATION IN SPORT, PHYSICAL ACTIVITY, AND LEISURE

Age is negatively associated with physical activity, meaning that as people age, they become less active. In Exhibit 7.8, I draw from the National Health Interview Survey, conducted by the Centers for Disease Control and Prevention in the US (www.healthypeople.gov). As discussed in previous chapters, researchers in this study examined the proportion of adults who engage in recommended levels of aerobic activity each week: 150 minutes of moderate activity, 75 minutes of vigorous activity, or some combination thereof.

Results show a negative relationship between age and obtaining the recommended levels of physical activity per week. The trends are present for each year in the analysis. In 2011, for example, people aged 18–24 were 42 percent more likely to be active at recommended levels than were people aged 55–64. The figures drop precipitously from there.

A number of factors are associated with decreased sport and physical activity participation across the lifespan. First, there is a positive relationship between age

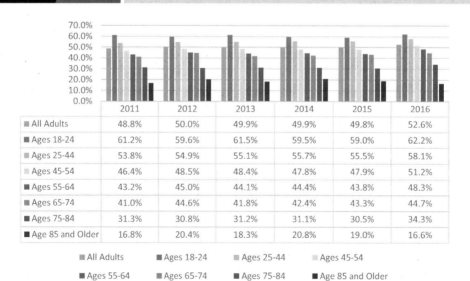

exhibit **7.8** Age and Physical Activity Rates among US Adults

	2011	2012	2013	2014	2015	2016
All Adults	48.8%	50.0%	49.9%	49.9%	49.8%	52.6%
Ages 18-24	61.2%	59.6%	61.5%	59.5%	59.0%	62.2%
Ages 25-44	53.8%	54.9%	55.1%	55.7%	55.5%	58.1%
Ages 45-54	46.4%	48.5%	48.4%	47.8%	47.9%	51.2%
Ages 55-64	43.2%	45.0%	44.1%	44.4%	43.8%	48.3%
Ages 65-74	41.0%	44.6%	41.8%	42.4%	43.3%	44.7%
Ages 75-84	31.3%	30.8%	31.2%	31.1%	30.5%	34.3%
Age 85 and Older	16.8%	20.4%	18.3%	20.8%	19.0%	16.6%

Source: www.healthypeople.gov.

and disability status: as people grow older, they are more likely to experience physical and psychological disabilities. And, although physical activity opportunities for people with disabilities have improved, they are still limited, relatively speaking. Another reason has to do with sport programming. Many sport leagues are geared toward children and adolescents—an important time to encourage physical activity, as behaviors formed during this stage in life typically carry over into adulthood. However, as people age, formal programming and social support for physical activity engagement usually wane. One needs to only observe community soccer fields during soccer season or a list of offerings from a city's parks and recreation department to observe as much. Noting this decline in community support and the benefits of being active, some retirement communities offer organized sport and physical activities for their residents. As Jenkin, Eime, Westerbeek, O'Sullivan, and van Uffelen (2017) noted, sport managers would do well to recognize the heterogeneity of the older population and ensure they provide services for all abilities and interests.

Age also influences participation in leisure-time activities. Leisure is different from sport in that the former refers to:

> an inherently satisfying activity that is characterized by the absence of obligation. Free time alone is not necessarily leisure. Instead, the key variable is how a person defines tasks and situations to create intrinsic meaning. Thus, leisure implies feeling free and satisfied.
>
> (Mehrotra & Wagner, 2009, p. 295)

Retirees engage in a number of leisure activities, including reading or writing, exercising, traveling, listening to music, and participating in religious and spiritual activities (James & Wink, 2007). Thus, contrary to the belief that retirees tend to become disengaged, research indicates that many lead busy, active lives.

Retirees' level and type of volunteerism varies by race. Mehrotra and Wagner (2009) note that "volunteering as a way to help others through informal social networks is common in minority communities" (p. 298). Among African Americans, service to one's church provides a way to incorporate hard work into leisure experiences and service to the community. Asians have been found to volunteer more often in Asian organizations that reinforce their cultural value systems. Native Americans volunteer in ways that provide mutual assistance to others, such as by providing food and shelter to elderly individuals. Finally, Hispanic communities tend to concentrate their volunteer efforts on services that provide neighborhood assistance, care for those who are elderly, and mutual aid.

CHAPTER SUMMARY

Having read this chapter, you should now be able to:

1. Define age and age diversity.

    Age and age diversity can be discussed in many ways. According to antidiscrimination laws in the US, people are protected from various organizational practices at age 40. Sport organizations set different limits for participation, including minimum ages in the NBA (19 years) and the Champions Tour (50 years), among others.

2. Describe the manner in which age influences access and treatment discrimination.

    Many researchers have focused on older individuals when investigating treatment and access discrimination. However, recent research suggests that younger individuals experience age-based discrimination, too. In the workplace, there is a U-shaped pattern of discrimination, with younger and older individuals experiencing differential treatment.

3. Summarize the multilevel factors that influence age effects in the work environment.

    Macro-level factors (i.e., changing demographics and work patterns, employment laws, and institutional ageism), meso-level factors (i.e., bias in decision-making and organizational policies), and micro-level factors (i.e., personal characteristics and age in context) all influence age-related access and experiences in sport organizations.

4. Paraphrase the manner in which age influences opportunities and experiences of sport and physical activity participants.

    Participation in sport and exercise generally decreases with age. Leisure participation, especially volunteering, increases with age, particularly after age 65.

Questions FOR DISCUSSION

1. Researchers have shown that young and older people face age-based discrimination. Was this surprising? Why do middle-aged individuals not report such experiences?

2. What are the common age-related stereotypes, and which of these is most prevalent? Why?

3. Most of the research related to age diversity focuses on older employees. Do younger employees also face age-related stereotypes? If so, what are they?

4. Research suggests that older employees learn differently from their younger counterparts. Knowing this, what are steps managers can take to facilitate older employees' learning in the workplace?

5. How might a sport manager design a volunteer program that would attract older adults of various races?

LEARNING Activities

1. Sport organizations can engage in certain human resource practices that help mitigate incidents of age discrimination. In groups, develop a list of such practices as they relate to selection and promotion.

2. Using the Internet, identify sport organizations and sport events that target senior athletes. Based on your search, how would you characterize the available sport and physical activity opportunities for seniors?

3. Research either local or national sport organizations to determine if they attempt to attract or use the services of older volunteers.

Web RESOURCES

- Administration on Community Living, https:// www.acl.gov/

  Part of the Department of Health and Human Services; provides up-to-date statistics on older Americans across a number of subject areas.

- National Senior Games Association, www.nsga.com

  Offers information about the National Senior Games, competitive sport events for persons aged 50 or older.

- National Alliance for Youth Sports, https://www.nays.org/

  Organization designed to equip youth sport coaches and leaders with skills needed to ensure quality youth sport experiences for all.

READING Resources

Beatty, P. T., & Visser, R. M. S. (Eds.). (2005). *Thriving in an aging workforce: Strategies for organizational and systemic change.* Malabar, FL: Krieger.

This edited text focuses on the way in which age intersects with seven organizational issues: selection, training, career development, employee relations, health, pensions, and retirement.

Field, J., Burke, R. J., & Cooper, C. L. (Eds.) (2013). *The SAGE handbook of aging,* *work, and society.* Thousand Oaks, CA: Sage.

An edited text examining the role of age and age diversity in the workplace.

Mehrotra, C. M., & Wagner, L. S. (2009). *Aging and diversity: An active learning experience* (2nd ed.). New York: Routledge.

Offers a comprehensive overview of how age influences a number of life activities, including work, leisure participation, and retirement.

REFERENCES

Age discrimination at work. (n.d.). New Zealand Government. Retrieved from https://www.govt.nz/browse/work/workers-rights/age-discrimination-at-work/

Armstrong-Stassen, M., & Schlosser, F. (2011). Perceived organizational membership and the retention of older workers. *Journal of Organizational Behavior, 32,* 319–344.

Attitudes about aging: A global Perspective. (2014, January). Pew Research Center. Retrieved from http://pewresearch.org/wp-content/uploads/sites/2/2014/01/Pew-Research-Center-Global-Aging-Report-FINAL-January-30-20141.pdf

Becker, E. (1973). *The denial of death.* New York, NY: Free Press.

Bell, M. P. (2007). *Diversity in organizations.* Mason, OH: Thomson South-Western.

Blackham, A. (2018, April). Why mandatory retirement ages should be a thing of the past. *The Conversation.* Retrieved from https://theconversation.com/why-mandatory-retirement-ages-should-be-a-thing-of-the-past-94484

Boehm, S. A., Kunze, F., & Bruch, H. (2014). Spotlight on age-diversity climate: The impact of age-inclusive HR practices on firm-level outcomes. *Personnel Psychology, 67*(3), 667–704.

Börsch-Supan, A., & Weiss, M. (2016). Productivity and age: Evidence from work teams at the assembly line. *The Journal of the Economics of Ageing, 7,* 30–42.

Bratt, C., Abrams, D., Swift, H. J., Vauclair, C. M., & Marques, S. (2018). Perceived age discrimination across age in Europe: From an ageing society to a society for all ages. *Developmental Psychology, 54*(1), 167–180.

Cilluffo, A., & Cohn, D. (2017, April). 10 demographic trends shaping the U.S. and the world in 2017. Pew Research Center. Retrieved from http://www.pewresearch.org/fact-tank/2017/04/27/10-demographic-trends-shaping-the-u-s-and-the-world-in-2017/

Coile, C. C., Levine, P. B., & McKnight, R. (2014). Recessions, older workers, and longevity: How long are recessions good for your health? *American Economic Journal: Economic Policy, 6*(3), 92–119.

Colby, S. L., & Ortman, J. M. (2015). *Projections of the size and composition of the US population: 2014 to 2060. Current population reports, P25–1143.* Washington, DC: US Census Bureau.

Cunningham, G. B. (2007). Perceptions as reality: The influence of actual and perceived demographic dissimilarity. *Journal of Business and Psychology, 22*(1), 79–89.

Dong, X., Milholland, B., & Vijg, J. (2016). Evidence for a limit to human lifespan. *Nature, 538*(7624), 257–259.

Farrell, C. (2017, October). Employers need to train their older works, too. *Forbes.* Retrieved from https://www.forbes.com/sites/civicnation/2018/07/23/the-politics-of-friendship/#51bb40c882fd

Finkelstein, L. M., Allen, T. D., & Rhoton, L. A. (2007). An examination of the role of age in mentoring relationships. *Group & Organization Management, 28,* 249–281.

Finkelstein, L. M., Ryan, K. M., & King, E. B. (2013). What do the young (old) people think of me? Content and accuracy of age-based metastereotypes. *European Journal of Work and Organizational Psychology, 22*(6), 633–657.

Hancock, D. J., Adler, A. L., & Côté, J. (2013). A proposed theoretical model to explain relative age effects in sport. *European Journal of Sport Science, 13*(6), 630–637.

Healy, M. C., Lehman, M., & McDaniel, M. (1995). Age and voluntary turnover: A quantitative review. *Personnel Psychology, 48,* 335–344.

Hedge, J. W., Borman, W. C., & Lammlein, S. E. (2006). *The aging workforce: Realities, myths, and implications for organizations.* Washington, DC: American Psychological Association.

Jenkin, C. R., Eime, R. M., Westerbeek, H., O'Sullivan, G., & van Uffelen, J. G. (2017). Sport and ageing: A systematic review of the determinants and trends of participation in sport for older adults. *BMC Public Health, 17*(1), 976.

Kulik, C. T., Ryan, S., Harper, S., & George, G. (2014). Aging populations and management. *Academy of Management Journal, 57,* 929–935.

Kunze, F., Boehm, S., & Bruch, H. (2013). Age, resistance to change, and job performance. *Journal of Managerial Psychology, 28*(7/8), 741–760.

Kunze, F., Boehm, S. A., & Bruch, H. (2011). Age diversity, age discrimination climate and performance consequences—A cross organizational study. *Journal of Organizational Behavior, 32,* 264–290.

Lamont, R. A., Swift, H. J., & Abrams, D. (2015). A review and meta-analysis of age-based stereotype threat: Negative stereotypes, not facts, do the damage. *Psychology and Aging, 30*(1), 180.

Lee, S. Y., Pitesa, M., Thau, S., & Pillutla, M. M. (2015). Discrimination in selection decisions: Integrating stereotype fit and interdependence theories. *Academy of Management Journal, 58*(3), 789–812.

Lenart, A., & Vaupel, J. W. (2017). Questionable evidence for a limit to human lifespan. *Nature, 546*(7660), E13–E14.

Life Expectancy. (n.d.). *World Health Organization.* Retrieved from http://www.who.int/gho/mortality_burden_disease/life_tables/situation_trends_text/en/

Life Expectancy at Birth, Total (Years). (n.d.). *World Bank.* Retrieved from https://data.worldbank.org/indicator/SP.DYN.LE00.IN?end=2016&start=1960&view=chart

Mahon, J. F., & CJM Millar, C. (2014). ManAGEment: The challenges of global age diversity for corporations and governments. *Journal of Organizational Change Management, 27*(4), 553–568.

Marchiondo, L. A., Gonzales, E., & Ran, S. (2016). Development and validation of the workplace age discrimination scale. *Journal of Business and Psychology, 31*(4), 493–513.

Mehrotra, C. M., & Wagner, L. S. (2009). *Aging and diversity: An active learning experience* (2nd ed.). New York, NY: Routledge.

Mortality rate, adult, male (per 1,000 male adults). (n.d.). *World Bank.* Retrieved from https://data.worldbank.org/indicator/SP.DYN.AMRT.MA

Nelson, T. D. (2009). Ageism. In T. D. Nelson (Ed.), *Handbook of prejudice, stereotyping, and discrimination* (pp. 431–440). New York, NY: Psychology Press.

Ng, T. W. H., & Feldman, D. C. (2008). The relationship of age to ten dimensions of job performance. *Journal of Applied Psychology, 93,* 392–423.

Ng, T. W. H., & Feldman, D. C. (2010). The relationships of age with job attitudes: A meta-analysis. *Personnel Psychology, 63*(3), 677–718.

Ng, T. W. H., & Feldman, D. C. (2012). Evaluating six common stereotypes about older workers with meta-analytical data. *Personnel Psychology, 65,* 821–858.

Noelke, C., & Beckfield, J. (2014). Recessions, job loss, and mortality among older US adults. *American Journal of Public Health, 104*(11), e126–e134.

North, M. S., & Fiske, S. T. (2012). An inconvenienced youth? Ageism and its potential intergenerational roots. *Psychological Bulletin, 138,* 982–997.

Perry, E. A., & Parlamis, J. D. (2007). Age and ageism in organizations: A review and consideration of national culture. In A. M. Konrad, P. Prasad, & J. K. Pringle (Eds.), *Handbook of workplace diversity* (pp. 345–370). Thousand Oaks, CA: Sage.

Perry, E. L., Kulik, C. T., & Zhou, J. (1999). A closer look at the effects of subordinate–supervisor age differences. *Journal of Organizational Behavior, 20,* 341–357.

Popham, L. E., Kennison, S. M., & Bradley, K. I. (2011). Ageism, sensation-seeking, and risk-taking behavior in young adults. *Current Psychology, 30,* 184–193.

Posthuma, R. A., & Campion, M. A. (2009). Age stereotypes in the workplace: Common stereotypes, moderators, and future research directions. *Journal of Management, 35,* 158–188.

Potter, L., Zawadzki, M. J., Eccleston, C. P., Cook, J. E., Snipes, S. A., ... & Smyth, J. M. (in press). The intersections of race, gender, age, and socioeconomic status: Implications for reporting discrimination and attributions to discrimination. *Stigma & Health.*

Raymer, M., Reed, M., Spiegel, M., & Purvanova, R. K. (2017). An examination of generational stereotypes as a path towards reverse ageism. *The Psychologist-Manager Journal, 20*(3), 148.

Rosen, B., & Jerdee, T. H. (1976). The influence of age stereotypes on managerial decisions. *Journal of Applied Psychology, 61*, 428–432.

Rosen, B., & Jerdee, T. H. (1977). Too old or not too old? *Harvard Business Review, 55*, 97–106.

Shore, L. M., & Goldberg, C. B. (2005). Age discrimination in the workplace. In R. L. Dipboye & A. Collela (Eds.), *Discrimination at work: The psychological and organizational bases* (pp. 203–225). Mahwah, NJ: Lawrence Erlbaum.

Shore, L. M., Cleveland, J. N., & Goldberg, C. B. (2003). Work attitudes and decisions as a function of manager age and employee age. *Journal of Applied Psychology, 88*, 529–537.

Smith, K. L., Weir, P. L., Till, K., Romann, M., & Cobley, S. (in press). Relative age effects across and within female sport contexts: A systematic review and meta-analysis. *Sports Medicine.*

Steele, C. M. (1997). A threat in the air: How stereotypes shape intellectual identity and performance. *American Psychologist, 52*(6), 613.

Stypińska, J. & Nikander, P. (2018). Ageism and age discrimination in the labour market: A macrostructural approach. In L. Ayalon & C. Tesch-Römer (Eds.), *Contemporary perspectives on ageism* (pp. 91–108). Cham, Switzerland: Springer.

Truxillo, D. M., Cadiz, D. M., & Hammer, L. B. (2015). Supporting the aging workforce: A review and recommendations for workplace intervention research. *Annual Review of Organizational Psychology and Organizational Behavior, 2*(1), 351–381.

Van Dam, A. (2018, July). A record number of folks age 85 and older are working: Here's what they are doing. *Washington Post.* Retrieved from https://www.washingtonpost.com/news/wonk/wp/2018/07/05/a-record-number-of-folks-age-85-and-older-are-working-heres-what-theyre-doing/?noredirect=on&utm_term=.2ea7f611cfc9

Van Rooij, S. W. (2012). Training older workers: Lessons learned, unlearned, and relearned from the field of instructional design. *Human Resource Management, 51*, 281–298.

Wattie, N., Schorer, J., & Baker, J. (2015). The relative age effect in sport: A developmental systems model. *Sports Medicine, 45*(1), 83–94.

What do I Need to Know About… Age Discrimination. (n.d.). United States Department of Labor. Retrieved from https://www.dol.gov/oasam/programs/crc/2011-age-discrimination.htm

Wilkinson, J. A., & Ferraro, K. F. (2004). Thirty years of ageism research. In T. D. Nelson (Ed.), *Ageism: Stereotyping and prejudice against older persons* (pp. 339–359). Cambridge, MA: MIT Press.

Disability

8

LEARNING OUTCOMES

After studying this chapter, you should be able to:

- Define disability.
- Describe the manner in which disability status influences access and treatment discrimination.
- Summarize the multilevel factors that influence the effects of disability in the work environment.
- Paraphrase the manner in which disability status influences opportunities and experiences of sport and physical activity participants.

DIVERSITY CHALLENGE

According to the Autism Society, about one percent of the world's population has autism spectrum disorder, and the figure increases to 1 in 68 in the US. To put into context, that comes to about 3.5 million Americans. Despite their prevalence in society, people with autism spectrum disorder sometimes do not have the same opportunities as their peers, and this includes the chance to be physically active. The limited opportunities are disappointing, especially considering the social, psychological, and physical benefits associated with being active on a regular basis.

Recognizing these gaps, a number of communities and sport organizations have started to offer programs and services specifically for people with autism spectrum disorder. For example, Taylor Duncan founded Alternative Baseball. A lifelong baseball fan, Duncan always wanted to play baseball but was unable to because coaches believed his disability served as an injury risk. Dissatisfied with this treatment, Duncan started Alternative Baseball, "a non-profit developmental baseball program for teens and adults with autism and special needs." Cindy Duncan, Taylor's mother, commented, "Everyone deserves a chance to play. Everyone deserves a chance to be accepted for who they are and it thrills me to see him try to do those things for others."

Researchers have explored the efficacy of programs like Alternative Baseball and found they can positively contribute to motor skills and social skills development. The method of program delivery also matters. Individually focused exercise programs, as opposed to group-based activities, result in the best gains. Program participants accrue gains in both motor performance and social interactions. Finally, exercise and sport participation are important across the lifespan, benefitting youth and adults.

Given these findings, a logical question is, what sports are best for people with autism spectrum disorder? Some researchers suggest all types of physical activity prove helpful. Other sources, such as those at the website Very Well Health, advocate for a number of sports, including bowling, swimming, and track and field. Whatever the activity, the key is to move and be active—there are many benefits associated with doing so.

Sources: Alternative Baseball Organization (no date). Retrieved from https://www.alternativebaseball.org/. Robertson, M. (2018, July). "You just cannot give up": Teen with autism starts his own baseball league in Virginia. WUSA. Retrieved from https://www.wusa9.com/article/news/local/virginia/you-just-cannot-give-up-teen-with-autism-starts-his-own-baseball-league-in-virginia/65-578907019. Sowa, M., & Meulenbroek, R. (2012). Effects of physical exercise on autism spectrum disorders: A meta-analysis. *Research in Autism Spectrum Disorders*, 6(1), 46–57.

CHALLENGE REFLECTION

1. Think about your own communities. Are there opportunities for people with a disability to be physically active?
2. Suppose you were a manager of a community sport club interested in offering sports and activities for athletes with disabilities. What are some of the first steps you would take?

As the Diversity Challenge illustrates, despite the many benefits associated with sport and physical activity, people with autism spectrum disorder frequently encounter barriers. The same is true for people with other disabilities, whether mental or physical. As a result, people with disabilities do not have access to sport and are less likely to be active, relative to their peers without a disability. In the case of the Diversity Challenge, an athlete who had long faced discrimination created change. Not everyone has that capacity, though, so it is important for sport managers to do their part in ensuring that everyone has access to sport (Cunningham, 2014; Zeigler, 2007).

The purpose of this chapter is to examine these issues in further depth. Specifically, I first provide a definition of disability and offer a brief historical overview of issues related to mental and physical disabilities. I provide an overview of the access and treatment discrimination people with disabilities face in sport work environments, and then, drawing from the model presented in Chapter 4, discuss the macro-, meso-, and micro-level factors affecting those experiences. In the final section, I summarize the intersection of disability status and sport and exercise participation.

DEFINITIONS, INCIDENCE, AND BACKGROUND

Disability is sometimes difficult to define. For some impairments, such as a complete absence of sight or hearing, the existence of a disability is evident. For others, such as partial hearing loss or some psychological disorders, it may be less evident whether and to what extent the disability impairs an individual's life. The Americans with Disabilities Act of 1990 (ADA) defines what constitutes a disability within the employment context in the US. From a legal perspective, a disability exists when a person has a mental or physical impairment that largely restricts one or more major life activities, when there is a recorded history of such, or when the person is considered to have such impairment.

According to the World Health Organization, approximately 15 percent of the world's population has a disability—over one billion people. The proportion in the US was 12.8 percent in 2016 (disabilitystatistics.org). This figure is about six percent higher than that reported in 2008 (12.1 percent). The US Census Bureau groups disability status into six categories, including difficulties based on hearing, vision, cognitive, ambulatory, self-care, and independent living. People most commonly have an ambulatory disability—that is, they have difficulties walking or climbing stairs—and independent living, such as shopping or visiting a doctor.

The incidence of disability status is not evenly distributed across the population. In Exhibit 8.1, I show the relationship between disability status and age. The differences are striking, as people aged 75 or older are almost nine times as likely

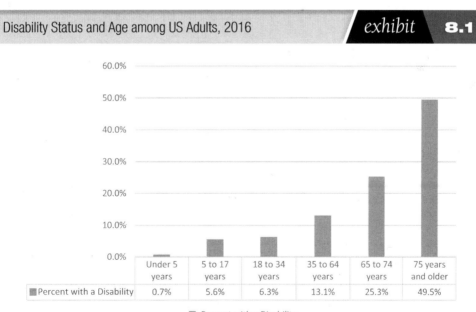

| Disability Status and Age among US Adults, 2016 | | | | | | *exhibit* **8.1** |

	Under 5 years	5 to 17 years	18 to 34 years	35 to 64 years	65 to 74 years	75 years and older
Percent with a Disability	0.7%	5.6%	6.3%	13.1%	25.3%	49.5%

Percent with a Disability

Source: Disability Characteristics (n.d.).

to have a disability as people aged 5–17. This relationship is largely explained by the general deterioration of health as people age, including higher probabilities of heart disease, certain types of cancer, and diabetes. As noted in Chapter 7, most industrialized countries are experiencing an increase in the age of their populations, so the relationship between age and disability status is particularly meaningful.

Other demographics are also associated with disability status (disabilitystatistics.com). In the US, women and men have essentially the same incidence of disability, 12.9 percent and 12.7 percent, respectively. Racial differences are also present. Native Americans are most likely to have a disability (17.0 percent), followed by Whites and African Americans (14.1 percent each), Pacific Islanders (11.1 percent), Latinos (9.1 percent), and Asians (7.1 percent).

These patterns illuminate what Bell, McLaughlin, and Sequeira (2004) refer to as the "permeable boundaries" of disability, or, as Santuzzi and Waltz (2016) suggest, disability is a "unique and variable identity" (p. 1111). Many diversity forms cannot be changed (e.g., race), but in some instances, one's disability status can change: an individual can become ill or have an accident and then be considered a person with a disability. An example of the changeable nature of this type of physical diversity is illustrated by the career of Michael Teuber of Germany. Teuber was an avid windsurfer and snowboarder. After an automobile accident, however, he had limited use of his legs—about 65 percent of their previous capacity. He began mountain biking for rehabilitation and soon became an avid cyclist. This love of cycling led him to compete, and he has done quite well. In fact, Teuber is a Paralympic world champion, a European cycling champion, and a winner of other medals in various forms of cycling, including road racing, trail racing, and pursuit racing (DePauw & Gavron, 2005). It is important to note, however, that while some disabilities are permeable, others are not. For people born with disabilities, those disabilities are likely to be permanent and, thus, socially constructed, much like race and gender.

DISCRIMINATION AGAINST PERSONS WITH DISABILITIES

Persons with disabilities face a number of employment barriers. As Schur et al. (2017) have shown, the access and treatment discrimination (c.f. Greenhaus, Parasuramn, & Wormely, 1990) people with disabilities experience negatively affects their work life. To illustrate further, I draw from Cornell University's Disability Statistics website (www.disabilitystatistics.org), which serves as an online resource for disability statistics in the US. I focus on the year 2016—the most recent data available and offer data from previous years as a point of comparison.

One measure of access discrimination is participation in the workforce. Among non-institutionalized people aged 21–64, 36.2 percent of persons with a disability were employed. This figure is considerably less than the 78.9 percent of people without a disability who were employed that same year. Put another way, disability status means that someone is 2.17 times less likely to be employed. These rates vary based on type of disability, as shown in Exhibit 8.2. Specifically,

| Disability Status and Employment, by Disability Type, 2013–2016 | *exhibit* | 8.2 |

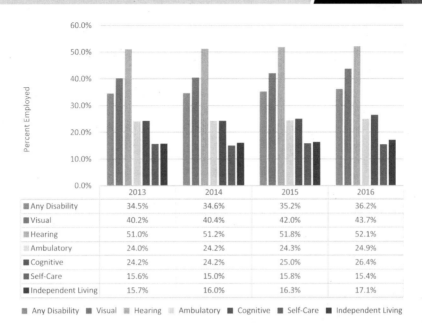

	2013	2014	2015	2016
▨ Any Disability	34.5%	34.6%	35.2%	36.2%
▨ Visual	40.2%	40.4%	42.0%	43.7%
▨ Hearing	51.0%	51.2%	51.8%	52.1%
▨ Ambulatory	24.0%	24.2%	24.3%	24.9%
▪ Cognitive	24.2%	24.2%	25.0%	26.4%
▪ Self-Care	15.6%	15.0%	15.8%	15.4%
▪ Independent Living	15.7%	16.0%	16.3%	17.1%

▪ Any Disability   ▪ Visual   ▨ Hearing   ▪ Ambulatory   ▪ Cognitive   ▪ Self-Care   ▪ Independent Living

persons with vision or hearing disabilities are more likely to be employed than are their counterparts with other disabilities. That noted, their rates of employment still lag behind persons without a disability. These disparities have persisted over time, as evidenced in Exhibit 8.2.

Field experiments from around the world shed light on why these disparate numbers exist. Researchers in France mailed job applications to over 2,000 employers, and the applications varied by the presence of a disability and the qualifications of the applicant (Ravaud, Madiot, & Ville, 1992). Persons without a disability were more likely to receive a favorable response from the employer than were applicants with a disability. The differences were larger when the applicants had moderate qualifications—a finding consistent with the notion of implicit bias discussed in Chapter 3. Baert (2016) observed a similar pattern in Belgium, where persons with a disability were 47 percent less likely to receive a positive response from the employer. Finally, Ameri et al. (2018) found a similar pattern among American employers, where persons with a disability received 26 percent fewer expressions of interest than did their counterparts without a disability. Ameri et al. also found that the discriminatory behaviors were concentrated among small, private companies—those exempt from federal employment laws.

In addition to facing access discrimination, persons with disabilities face treatment discrimination. Among the many examples of this mistreatment, the pay

exhibit   **8.3**   Disability Status and Employment in the US, 2017

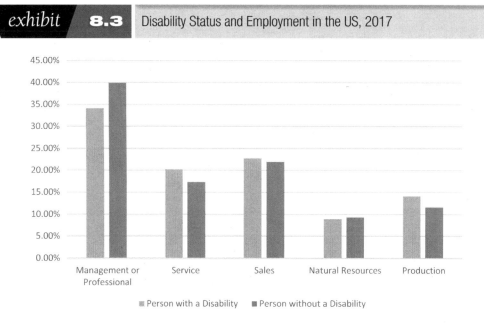

Source: Disability Characteristics (n.d.).

differentials offer one of the clearest examples. In 2016, people with a disability made $40,300 a year, or about 12 percent less than those without a disability ($45,300). Differences in annual household incomes were even more striking: $43,300 versus $68,700.

Differences in salary could be due to a number of reasons, including occupational segregation (Bergmann, 1974). Relative to people without a disability, persons with a disability are less likely to be in managerial or professional positions and more likely to be in service jobs (see Exhibit 8.3). The latter are generally lower paying and afford the worker with less autonomy and discretion.

MULTILEVEL EXPLANATIONS

Drawing from the model I presented in Chapter 4, in this section, I highlight multilevel explanations for the discrimination against persons with disabilities. I focus factors at the macro-, meso-, and micro-levels of analysis and offer a summary in Exhibit 8.4.

Macro-Level Factors

Recall from Chapter 4 that macro-level factors operate at the societal level, including employment laws, structural stigma, and stakeholder expectations.

| Multilevel Factors Affecting Persons with Disabilities in Sport | *exhibit* 8.4 |

Macro-level factors: Those operating at the societal level, including employment laws, structural stigma, and stakeholder expectations.

Meso-level factors: Those operating at the team and organizational levels, including bias in decision-making, policies, champions, and organizational capacity.

Micro-level factors: Those operating at the individual level, including demographics, requests for accommodations, and type of disability.

Employment Laws

Employment laws shape the context and expectations treatment of persons with disabilities. In the US, the Americans with Disabilities Act prohibits private organizations; local, state, and federal government entities; employment agencies; and labor unions from discriminating against persons with disabilities (either mental or physical). From a legal perspective, a person has a disability when she or he possesses an impairment (whether physical or mental) that significantly restricts one or more major life activities. A major life activity, as defined in the ADA, is an activity that is fundamental to human life—"caring for oneself, performing manual tasks, walking, seeing, hearing, speaking, breathing, learning, and working" (Americans with Disabilities Act, 1985). In 2017, the Equal Employment Opportunity Commission received 26,838 claims of disability discrimination and recovered over $135.2 million in damages.

Within sport, as well as other business contexts, a qualified person with a disability is one who can perform the basic elements of a job with reasonable accommodations. Reasonable accommodations are those that the employer can make without undue hardship, and they may include restructuring the nature of the job (e.g., modifying the work schedule), making existing facilities readily accessible by persons with a disability, or modifying equipment. Employers are not required to lower the job standards. If a person with a disability cannot perform the basic job functions with reasonable accommodations, then the person need not be hired. The employer is not required to provide employees with items such as glasses or hearing aids.

The ADA covers medical examinations and inquiries, as well as drug and alcohol abuse. Employers cannot ask job applicants if they have preexisting medical conditions, but they can ask if the applicants are able to perform the basic duties related to the job. Medical examinations are permissible when they are required of all job applicants. The examinations must be job related and consistent with the employer's overall business needs. With respect to drugs and alcohol, the ADA

Box 8.1 Diversity in the Field: Subminimum Wage

In the US, the federal minimum wage in 2018 was $7.25. Recognizing that one could work full time and still not have enough to live, some states and municipalities increased the minimum wage. The District of Columbia, for example, had a minimum wage of $13.25 in 2018—83 percent higher than the national standard.

However, the minimum wage is not in place for all employees. According to a 1938 provision in the Fair Labor Standard Act, employers can pay student learners, full-time students, and persons with a mental or physical disability wages less than the minimum wage. According to the law, the fact that one has a disability is not warrant lower payment. Instead, the exception only applies when "the disability actually impairs the worker's earnings or productive capacity for the work being performed" (Fact Sheet #39, 2008).

Of the persons with disabilities who are employed, about three percent are paid subminimum wages (Dejean, 2017). In fact, sometimes they are paid pennies on the hour. Thus, even when they are employed full time, people with disabilities can make a mere fraction of what others do.

Opponents of the provision point to the segregation it creates. Clyde Terry, or the National Council on Disability, commented, "It creates the perception that somehow people with disabilities can't compete, cannot hold down a job, are not worthy of the same protections all other citizens are" (as quoted in Dejean, 2017). Others suggest that without such provisions in place, persons with disabilities would not have jobs.

does not apply to people who take illegal drugs. Mandatory drug testing is legal, and employers can hold substance abusers who have disabilities to the same performance standards as other employees.

As shown in Box 8.1, employers and sport organizations will sometimes use technicalities or antiquated portions of the law. In doing so, they potentially hurt the welfare of people with disabilities. In other cases, sport organization leaders might seek to get around inclusion-related laws as a way of saving money. I offer an example in Exhibit 8.5.

Structural Stigma

Recall from Chapter 2 that people who have a stigmatized condition "have (or are believed to have) an attribute that marks them as different and leads them to be devalued in the eyes of others" (Major & O'Brien, 2005, p. 395). Stigmatizing characteristics can be visible or invisible, controllable or not, and associated with appearance, behavior, or membership in a group (Major & O'Brien, 2005).

| Trying to Get around ADA Guidelines | *exhibit* **8.5** |

In 2014, the University of Massachusetts completed its three-year renovation of McGuirk Stadium. The university undertook this project, which cost $34.5 million, as part of the move to a higher level of competition. The facelift included a new training facility, locker room, coaching suites, and film rooms. New field turf was also included in the project.

Interestingly, the renovations did not include making the press box compliant with ADA guidelines. In most cases, when an existing structure is renovated, it must be brought up to current standards. If a facility undergoes major renovations, then all elements need to be improved to meet standards; absent such makeovers, older facilities can remain out of compliance for years. The McGuirk Stadium renovation normally would have meant the university would have to bring the 50-year-old facility up to current standards. However, as the press box does not actually touch the stadium, there was no legal requirement to comply with ADA rules for the press box.

University spokesperson Edward Blaguszewski indicated the decision was a financial one, suggesting the university had to make trade-offs during difficult financial times. However, Christine Griffin, executive director of the Disability Law Center, saw things differently, suggesting the university is "responsible for ensuring that people have full access in their communities." Griffin noted that, rather than trying to find loopholes in the law, the university "should be looking at how to make it more accessible" (Redington, 2014).

Stigmas are bound by time and culture; thus, what is stigmatizing in one setting at a particular time may vary greatly from a stigmatizing mark at a different time or in another context.

Hatzenbuehler (2017) noted that stigma can manifest at different levels, including the individual, interpersonal, and structural, the latter of which represents the societal factors that subjugate and disadvantage stigmatized people. Examples include cultural norms, policies, and institutionalized practices. Structural stigma limits people's opportunities, the quality of their experiences, and their overall well-being (Hatzenbuehler & Link, 2014).

Structural stigma influences the access and opportunities people with disabilities have in the US and around the world (Dovidio, Pagotto, & Hebl, 2011). Corrigan, Markowitz, and Watson (2004) identified ways in which governments restricted the lives of people with mental disabilities. They also showed how major institutions created policies that were seemingly neutral but that nevertheless negatively impacted people with disabilities—a process called aversive impact. The media contribute to the structural stigma, as well, rarely showing persons with a disability on television or in print media, or depicting them in stereotypical ways (Beacom, French, & Kendall, 2016). As evidenced in the Diversity Challenge, sport as an institution has also established barriers, thereby casting persons with a disability as the other.

External Stakeholders

Recall from Chapter 4 that stakeholders are constituents who have a stake or interest in the organization (Clarkson, 1995). They might be clients, financial supporters, or even agencies. Kulkarni and Rodrigues (2014) explained that "Organizations conform to expectations set forth by the institutional environment such as from regulatory agencies, industrial associations, leading organizations and other stakeholders such as customers in order to gain legitimacy" (p. 1548). Thus, stakeholder expectations and pressures can shape sport managers actions—whether for good or for ill.

Wooten and James (2005) noted that, conceptually, external stakeholders might mobilize, compelling an organization to offer more inclusive spaces and opportunities for people with disabilities. For example, class action suits related to disability might garner pressures from interest groups. Outside stakeholders might also engage in coercive pressures through, for example, working with state or federal legislators to help pass inclusive legislation. In other cases, mindful of the need to be socially responsible, sport organizations might make intentional efforts to engage in disability-inclusive actions, including those with customers (Garay & Font, 2012).

Kitchin and Howe (2014) demonstrated the manner in which external stakeholders can influence disability sport provision. They examined disability cricket in England and Wales. Government officials promoted inclusion through policy statements. In other cases, sport managers at leading national sport organizations developed management initiatives. Given that many English sport organizations have a substantial amount of their funding from the aforementioned sources, and thus had to follow their directives, the pressures had the potential to increase accountability and create inclusion-related change. Though some change did occur, Kitchin and Howe found that disability cricket remained segregated—something due to individual biases that limited the perceived importance of the sport.

Meso-Level Factors

Meso-level factors are those operating at the interpersonal and organizational levels. In the context of disability, salient meso-level factors include bias in decision-making, policies, champions, and organizational capacity.

Bias

Recall from Chapter 3 that bias includes stereotypes, prejudice, and discrimination (Cuddy, Fiske, & Glick, 2008). People hold a number of negative stereotypes about persons with disabilities, including the belief that they do not have the requisite skills to perform their work effectively; increase the time demands placed on their supervisors; increase health care costs for the rest of the workplace; and have poor emotional adjustment, including being overly bitter, nervous, and depressed (for an overview, see Kulkarni & Lengnick-Hall, 2014; Stone-Romero, Stone, & Lukaszewski, 2007).

Ren, Paetzold, and Colella (2008) examined disability stereotyping by aggregating the results from 51 experimental studies. Consistent with a contention put forward by Stone-Romero and colleagues (2007), they found that people routinely expected poorer performance from persons with disabilities than from able-bodied persons. They concluded,

> These results may stem from perceptions of the individual with a disability as unsuitable for employment because of stigmatized views of the disability itself or because of negative perceptions regarding the ability of a person with a disability to perform a job.
>
> (p. 199)

The stereotype content model discussed in Chapter 3 (Fiske, Cuddy, Glick, & Xu, 2002) allows for a better understanding of the nature of the stereotypes. According to this model, stereotypes exist along two dimensions: warmth and competence. People who have traditionally held privileged status in the US are highly rated along both domains, but this is not the case for people with disabilities. Instead, evidence indicates that people regard persons with mental and physical disabilities as being warm but lacking in competence. This results in people expressing both pity and compassion for persons with disabilities (Colella & Stone, 2005). Compared to compassion, pity is more condescending and is often accompanied by the view that the person with a disability is inferior (Colella & Stone, 2005).

Clearly, pity toward persons with disabilities can have negative effects. Fiske et al. (2002) argued that pity was an inherently mixed emotion because it combined sympathy and superiority. Thus, whereas people who feel pity might express compassion for persons with disabilities (i.e., awareness that they do have a disability and the potential distress that it might cause), they also view such people as inferior and subordinate. In the workplace, such prejudice might result in low leader-member exchange relationships or low performance expectations, both of which were outlined previously.

Wright and I tested these ideas in an experimental study (Wright & Cunningham, 2017). Participants reviewed application files for a personal trainer position at a fitness club. Some of the applicants had a disability and others did not. The qualifications also varied. We randomly assigned the participants to one of four experimental conditions, which varied based on disability status and qualifications of the applicant, and asked the participants to review dossier and respond to questions about the applicant. As expected, participants rated the applicant with a disability as warmer than the applicant without a disability, but competence ratings did not vary. The competence and warmth ratings then predicted person-organization fit: controlling for disability status, applicants rated as warm and competent had the highest assessments of fit with the organization. Our research shows the value of considering the unique context of sport, as we wrote, "stereotypes in sport and physical activity, as a unique context, have the potential to vary from those in other settings" (p. 400).

Prejudice represents the second dimension of bias that negative affects persons with disabilities in the sport environment. From a historical perspective,

exhibit   **8.6**   Language and Disability

As with any discussion of diversity, the language we use is of considerable importance. Some scholars, such as Thomas and Smith (2009), use the term *disabled people*, whereas others, such as Misener and Darcy (2014), prefer the term *persons with disability*. In this book, I opt for the latter—a people-first approach. As DePauw and Gavron (2005) correctly note, doing so recognizes persons as individuals first rather than placing the focus on their disability.

negative perceptions of persons with disabilities have persisted over time. As Bell (2007) explains, these perceptions are manifested in attitudes, distancing, and language (see Exhibit 8.6). In former times, as well as in some cultures today, people considered persons with disabilities as undesirable, defective, and unwanted. These attitudes led to efforts to alienate or remove persons with disabilities. In ancient Greece, babies with club feet were abandoned to die. In the US, in the past, schools would separate children with sensory impairments from their peers, similar to the way people were segregated based on their race. Sometimes, individuals with disabilities found it necessary to hide their disabilities; one famous politician had an agreement with the press that they would not photograph him using a cane. Language, such as use of the terms "cripple," "deaf and dumb," or "crazy," reflects commonly held negative perceptions of persons with disabilities. Another example is the more recent use of the term "retarded" to refer to persons who are perceived as unusual, silly, or out of the ordinary.

Interpersonal stigma (Hatzenbuehler, 2017) serves as another form of prejudice against people with disabilities. Within the work environment, people might consider disability status as stigmatizing because it runs counter to cultural norms and expectations of healthiness (Saal, Martinez, & Smith, 2014). As a result, a person who has visible disabilities might experience uneasy social interactions, heightened anxiety in her or his counterparts, and even behavioral distancing on their part (Dovidio et al., 2011).

The culturally bound and time-bound nature of stigma also helps explain why prejudice varies by context. For instance, a person with a mental disability might be viewed less warmly in the youth sport context, where the disability might impede the person's performance relative to others, than in the Special Olympics setting, where mental disabilities are a normal part of participation. Note here that the mental disability remains constant while the stigma attached to it, as well as subsequent bias and discrimination, varies in each context.

Discrimination represents the third element of bias. One of the most common ways in which people with disabilities face workplace discrimination is in reactions to requests for accommodations. The Americans with Disabilities Act requires that organizations with at least 15 employees make reasonable accommodation for a person with a disability, as long as the accommodation does not place undue hardship on the organization. Such an accommodation for an employee who is hard of hearing might be a requirement that her manager face her and speak loudly when addressing her. A person who uses a wheelchair might need a taller desk (or blocks under the current desk) because her knees hit the current desk.

There is evidence to support the notion that managers do not view all requests the same. For instance, managers respond negatively when they receive a request from a person whom they perceive to be responsible for his or her own disability (Florey & Harrison, 2000). They respond favorably, however, to requests from persons whose previous performance has been high. Stigma also affects managers' reactions. Requests from people who are highly stigmatized (e.g., those with AIDS) are met with negative attitudes and perceived as unfair, particularly when compared with requests from people with less-stigmatized disabilities, such as cerebral palsy (McLaughlin, Bell, & Stringer, 2004). Managers generally view a request positively when they also consider it as legitimate, a necessity for the job, and relatively inexpensive (Telwatte, Anglim, Wynton, & Moulding, 2017). Of course, persons with disabilities are not the only ones who make requests for accommodations, as outlined in Box 8.2.

Box 8.2 Alternative Perspectives. Requests for Accommodations Are Made by All Employees

We frequently think of requests for accommodations as being made by persons with disabilities, but in actuality able-bodied persons make requests, too. Schur and colleagues (2014) demonstrated as much in a study of more than 5,000 employees from multiple companies. The researchers observed that 28.1 percent of able-bodied persons had made requests for accommodations. Some of the requests were made for health reasons, but most were for other purposes. The requests included flexible work schedules, the ability to complete some or all of the work from home, restructuring of job duties, and the like. Most of the participants in the study reported that their requests were fully granted, but the percentage was higher for able-bodied persons (79.3 percent) than it was for persons with disabilities (72.6 percent). The accommodations positively affected the able-bodied employees' work, resulting in greater productivity and satisfaction, as well as an increased likelihood of remaining with the organization (see also Lauzun, Morganson, Major, & Green, 2010).

In addition, Kulkarni and Lengnick-Hall (2014) noted that persons with disabilities face discrimination in their personal development and career advancement opportunities. One area of discrimination is in the leadership positions they are afforded. Few people with disabilities obtain leadership roles in the workplace, and when they do, they are often placed in precarious situations, where the units have a history of failure and there is little opportunity for success. These are referred to as glass cliffs, as the positions are risky (Ryan & Haslam, 2007). When persons with disabilities take on such leadership roles, they have few opportunities to be successful, receive little support from others, and work with limited organizational resources (Wilson-Kovacs, Ryan, Haslam, & Rabinovich, 2008). All of these factors serve to limit their potential effectiveness.

Organizational Policies

The human resource system in the workplace also has the potential to influence whether persons with disabilities face prejudice and discrimination (Bell, 2007; Kulkarni, 2016). This influence can be seen in the selection process, compensation and benefits, training, and performance evaluations.

- **Selection.** Organizations should use the job description in selecting persons who are able to perform the job effectively, with or without reasonable accommodations. Indeed, "having and using a job description can help organizations in selecting appropriately in all situations (not just with applicants with disabilities)" (Bell, 2007, p. 361). Employers should make the selection decision on merit, not stereotypes associated with disability.
- **Compensation.** Persons with disabilities should be paid based on the worth of the job, coupled with their education, experience, and skills. Disability status should not be considered in the compensation process.
- **Training and development.** Persons with disabilities should be provided all of the opportunities other employees are afforded. Not doing so is illegal and thwarts the career advancement opportunities of persons with disabilities.
- **Performance evaluation.** All employees should be evaluated on a regular basis, irrespective of their disability status. Job performance standards should be explicitly outlined and used as the criteria for evaluations. Failure to evaluate performance fairly and accurately not only hurts the employee's development but also is deleterious to the organization.
- **Inclusiveness training.** All persons should have training on a host of diversity forms, including disability. The focus should be on appropriate language and biases, as well as how to overcome the biases.

Champions

Within the work environment, allies are people who strongly advocate for a particular cause, whether a change effort, new product line, or in the case of the current chapter, diversity and inclusion. Champions make extra efforts to tell people about diversity and inclusion; they enthusiastically support it; and they will frequently make personal sacrifices to ensure the success of the diversity initiative. In our previous work, colleagues and I found that champions played a critical role in promoting diversity and inclusion initiatives (Cunningham & Sartore, 2010; Melton & Cunningham, 2014).

Jeanes et al. (2018) also found that champions were important in promoting disability inclusion in sport organizations. They collected data volunteers at community sport clubs in Australia. Results from their study indicated that "policy entrepreneurs and enthusiasts" (p. 46; see also Ball, Maguire, Braun, & Hoskins, 2011), a term that is consistent with champions, were key to ensuring an inclusive sport work environment. In their study, the entrepreneurs were enthusiastic about disability inclusion, promoted policy changes, recruited others to join their efforts, and provided administrative support for the policies.

Having champions or entrepreneurs in the sport organization can make a meaningful difference for members of underrepresented groups, such as persons with a disability. For example, in a related study, Sartore and I found that champions used their power and privilege within the work environment to speak out against exclusionary practices (Sartore & Cunningham, 2010). In doing so, they fought to ensure that all people had a quality work environment.

Capacity

Finally, organizational capacity can influence the opportunities and experiences of persons with disabilities in the work environment. Organizational capacity represents "the overall capacity of a nonprofit and voluntary organization to produce the outcomes and missions it desires" (Hall et al., 2003, p. 4). Capacity exists along five dimensions, including those in the human, financial, infrastructure, planning and development, and networking domains.

Wicker and Breuer (2014) examined organizational capacity among disability sport clubs in Germany. They first compared disability sport clubs to other sport clubs that did not have a disability focus, or what the researchers referred to as their statistical twins. Though the size of the clubs did not differ, there were differences in several capacity measures. Clubs focusing on disability sport had less capacity in term of volunteers and ownership of their facilities. On the other hand, disability sport clubs were more likely than their statistical twins to have formal policies in place and were better equipped to cater to older and poor individuals. They were also better able to leverage relationships with the community. The researches then examined the degree to which capacity was associated with organizational problems. They found that disability sport clubs had a harder time recruiting volunteers and more likely to have ambiguity in terms of the club's future development. Wicker and Breuer found that strategic planning helped to reduce a number of organizational problems, and thus, sport clubs offering services for people with disabilities would do well to enhance this part of their capacity.

Capacity can also influence the long-term success of disability sport programs. Warner and I conducted a case study of a program we called Baseball 4 All (Cunningham & Warner, in press). It was designed to provide opportunities for children and young adults with mental and physical disabilities to participate in baseball on a weekly basis. Program leaders were successful in recruiting players and volunteers, largely because of the joy and inclusiveness associated with the activity. However, a lack of infrastructure capacity, or what we referred to as organizational failure, ultimately resulted in Baseball 4 All's undoing. Despite enthusiasm and participation, the lack of capacity ultimately resulted in a season's cancelation.

Micro-Level Factors

Micro-level factors are those at the individual level. In the context of disability sport, demographics, requests for accommodations, and type of disability are all likely to influence an employee's opportunities and experiences.

Demographics

Demographics can influence the experiences of people with disabilities in a number of ways. Recall from Chapter 2 that the effects of diversity forms are rarely additive. Instead, they manifest in interactive ways such that the effects of being (for example) a racial minority with a disability will be qualitatively different than that of being a racial minority or of being a White person with a disability. The interactive effects represent intersectionality. Watson and Scraton (2013) explain that intersectionality "moves beyond an additive approach that deals with fixed, static concepts of gender, race, class and looks at inequalities at the intersections and at how they are routed through each other with no single cause" (p. 37).

Stone and Colella (1996) addressed the possibility of intersectionality in their theoretical model. With respect to gender, they suggested that stereotypes associated with disability status (e.g., lack of physical strength or endurance) might better align with stereotypes of women than those with men. The mismatch is likely to negatively affect men with a disability more so than women. From this perspective, it is also possible that younger individuals with a disability might be more negatively affected than older persons. With respect to race, Stone and Colella suggested that the negative experiences of racial minorities in the work environment are likely to be augmented when they have a disability.

Requests for Accommodations

The degree to which sport organization employees request accommodations will also influence their experiences and opportunities. As previously discussed, in the US, people with a disability have a legal right to request such accommodations, and organizations must provide them unless doing so presents an undue hardship. The ADA places the responsibility for requesting an accommodation on the employee.

Interestingly, approximately 4 out of 10 employees with disabilities do not make any requests for accommodations (Schur et al., 2014). A number of factors are associated with the decision not to make a request, including social norms that influence such requests. For instance, men are more likely to request accommodations as the severity of their disability increases, though no such relationship exists for women (Baldridge & Swift, 2013). This pattern might result from socially constructed norms related to help-seeking behavior and its interplay with gender norms. People who are older view requesting accommodations less favorably than do their younger counterparts, and the presence of coworkers with a disability influences this pattern (Baldridge & Swift, 2016).

In other cases, not making accommodation requests is linked to the anticipated imposition the accommodation might cause. People with disabilities will withhold accommodation requests when they believe (a) there would be substantial financial costs, (b) doing so would negatively influence others, and (c) negative social consequences could follow the request (Baldridge & Veiga, 2006). Although the anticipation of financial cost inhibits requests, the evidence suggests that, in fact, most accommodations either do not cost anything or have minimal monetary costs (less than $500; Schur et al., 2014).

The social context and previous experiences can also affect the request for accommodations. Kensbock, Boehm, and Bourovoi (2017) conducted interviews with German manufacturing workers and found that the request for accommodation resulted in interpersonal problems and conflicts with others. They also noted a lack of support and poor communications. These findings align with those from Von Schrader, Malzer, and Bruyère (2014). These researchers found that employees' long-term experiences with requesting accommodations were frequently negative. In fact, one in four respondents indicated as much. The participants voiced concerns about being fired, that their employer would focus on the disability more than the work performance, and the potential loss of health benefits, among others.

Type of Disability

Finally, the type of disability is likely to influence the access and opportunities people have in the sport environment (Santuzzi & Waltz, 2016; Stone & Colella, 1996). Exhibit 8.2 demonstrates these effects, as persons with a hearing or vision disability had considerably higher employment rates than did those with other disability forms. Stigma theory offers some explanation for these trends, as Jones et al. (1984) proposed six factors influencing how people react to persons with disabilities:

1. Disruptiveness, or the degree to which the disability influences social interactions or communications among people;
2. Origin, or the degree to which a person is seen as responsible for her or his disability;
3. Aesthetic qualities, or the extent to which the disability negatively influences the person's attractiveness;
4. Course, or the extent to which the disability is transient or permanent;
5. Concealability, or the degree to which the disability can be plainly observed by others; and
6. Peril, or the degree to which a disability is believed to cause others harm.

In drawing from this framework and discussions of how it applies to the work environment (McLaughlin et al., 2004), several points become clear. First, the concept of stigma helps explain why some disabilities are met with greater resistance than others. Consider, for instance, the factors listed above as they pertain to HIV/AIDS status. Persons with HIV/AIDS might be seen as responsible for contracting the illness (high in origin), might have their physical appearance negatively affected by the disease (high in aesthetics), will be affected by the illness for the remainder of their life (high in course), and might be seen as a risk to others (high in peril). These perceptions differ from perceptions of a person who has suffered a stroke: the person did not cause the illness (low in origin), and the person's physical appearance may or may not be affected (moderate level of aesthetics). Negative physical effects might be overcome through rehabilitation, and the person might not be affected for the rest of his or her life (low in course). Finally, others cannot acquire a stroke from the person (low in peril). Thus, a person with HIV/AIDS is likely to be more stigmatized than one who recently suffered a stroke, and the bias and discrimination affecting those two individuals would vary accordingly.

In other cases, one's disability might not be visible, and thus, is concealable. Many cognitive disabilities are concealable. Summers et al. (2018) noted the quandary of concealing such disabilities. On the one hand, people frequently impute negative characteristics on persons with mental disabilities, including being dependent on others, unpredictable, or in some cases, prone to violence. Thus, concealing the disability would allow employees to forego such negative attributions. On the other hand, because mental disabilities are protected under federal employment laws, concealing that identity means not accessing legally permitted accommodations that would potentially improve work experiences and performance.

DISABILITY, PHYSICAL ACTIVITY, AND SPORT PARTICIPATION

In addition to considering the effects of ability in the workplace, it is also instructive to examine persons with disabilities' participation in sport and physical activity. In doing so, I consider participation rates and people's experiences during activity. In Exhibit 8.7, I draw from the National Health Interview Survey, conducted by the Centers for Disease Control and Prevention in the US (www.healthypeople.gov). As discussed in previous chapters, researchers in this study examined the proportion of adults who engage in recommended levels of aerobic activity each week: 150 minutes of moderate activity, 75 minutes of vigorous activity, or some combination thereof.

As shown in Exhibit 8.7, relative to people without a disability, people with disabilities are less likely to engage in the recommended levels of physical activity. The differences remained constant from 2011 through 2016. The low participation rates for individuals with a disability result from a number of factors. Fay (2011) noted that sport is viewed as a luxury for persons with disabilities, not as an inalienable right. This perspective is reinforced through stereotypes, prejudice, and discrimination that have been maintained throughout history, reinforced in public law, and advanced in sport policy. Participation opportunities for youth with disabilities are similarly limited. This is attributable to a lack of resources, coaches,

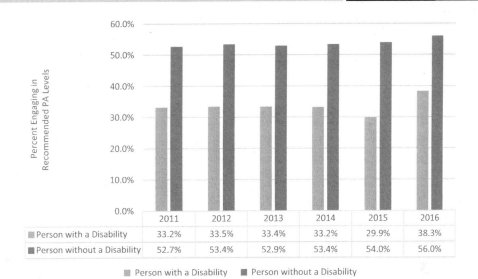

Physical Activity and Disability Status in the US, 2011–2016   *exhibit* **8.7**

	2011	2012	2013	2014	2015	2016
Person with a Disability	33.2%	33.5%	33.4%	33.2%	29.9%	38.3%
Person without a Disability	52.7%	53.4%	52.9%	53.4%	54.0%	56.0%

■ Person with a Disability   ■ Person without a Disability

Source: Healthypeople.gov.

informal sport experiences, and playing space; as a result, the chance for young people with disabilities to develop skills and confidence in the sport domain are thwarted (see also Hodge & Runswick-Cole, 2013). The socially constructed and legitimated bias toward physically active persons with disabilities also gives rise to the potential for internalized ableism (Fay, 2011): persons with disabilities come to accept the prejudices and stereotypes others hold, and in so doing potentially limit what they believe they can accomplish.

Some researchers have drawn from a leisure constraints perspective to examine factors influencing participation among persons with disabilities (Darcy, Lock, & Taylor, 2017; Sotiriadou & Wicker, 2014). From this perspective, individual, interpersonal, and structural factors all have the potential to shape one's leisure activities, including physical activity. Consistent with this view, evidence suggests a number of constraints potentially limit sport and physical activity participation, including community and organizational support, time, equipment, economic considerations, individual factors, interpersonal relationships, and transportation (Darcy et al., 2017). Thus, various factors in people's lives, operating at different levels, affect their opportunities to be active.

Although physical activity levels among persons with disabilities remain low, the popularity and availability of formal sport opportunities have increased over the past decade. *Disability sport* refers to "sport that has been designed for or is specifically practiced by athletes with disabilities" (DePauw & Gavron, 2005, p. 80). This definition includes sports designed specifically for persons with disabilities, such as goal ball for athletes who are blind; sports that able-bodied persons' practice that are altered or modified to include athletes with disabilities, such as wheelchair basketball; and sports that require little or no modification, such as swimming.

Misener and Darcy (2014) offered another lens for classifying disability sport. This organization considers inclusion as the key to delivering sport opportunities and defines those opportunities as follows:

- **Fully integrated**: all athletes participate without adaption or modifications, such as a community fun run and walk.
- **Modified integrated**: athletes with disabilities participate with some modifications to the sport, including the rules, equipment, or sporting area. When bowling, for example, a person in a wheelchair might use a ramp to roll the ball.
- **Parallel activities**: persons with a disability participate in the same activity but do so in their own way. For example, a wheelchair basketball team might train at the same club as other teams without disabilities.
- **Adapted activities**: people without a disability participate in sports designed for persons with a disability; thus, all participants have the same adaptation. An example is when athletes with and without a disability all play wheelchair rugby together.
- **Discrete activities**: people with a disability participate in activities with other athletes who have the same disability. Paralympic sports serve as an example.

The Eastern Collegiate Athletic Conference (ECAC, www.ecacsports.com) provides an example of how sport organizations can embrace these principles. In January 2015, the ECAC became the first National Collegiate Athletic Association (NCAA)-sanctioned conference to offer varsity sport opportunities for athletes with disabilities. The conference developed a multilayered strategy: in some events, reasonable accommodations will be provided, whereas in others, ECAC will add adapted activities. The conference plans to add various sports, such as sled hockey, sitting volleyball, and wheelchair basketball, among others. In speaking of this historic and inclusive decision, ECAC president Kevin McGinniss noted,

> This historic action systemically includes student-athletes with disabilities in intercollegiate sports for the first time in any NCAA division. I believe this action will allow many more athletes, including wounded veterans returning to college, to experience the benefits of competitive intercollegiate sports.
>
> (Eastern Collegiate Athletic Conference, 2015)

Eli Wolff, an Olympian and internationally renowned scholar in the areas of disability, access, and inclusion, offers additional information on disability sport in Box 8.3.

As Legg, Fay, Hums, and Wolff (2009; see also Hums & MacLean, 2013) note, many of the advancements in disability sport can be traced to the efforts of neurosurgeon Sir Ludwig Guttman. During and after World War II, sport and

Box 8.3 Professional Perspectives. Disability Sport Trends

Eli Wolff is a two-time Olympic soccer athlete, a graduate of Brown University, and current director of the Inclusive Sports Initiative at the Institute for Human Centered Design; he also directs the Sport and Development Project at Brown University. According to Wolff, one of the major issues in the area of disability sport today is the inclusion and integration of persons with disabilities within the fabric of mainstream sport. To what degree do mainstream sport organizations at every level of sport actually embrace disability sport opportunities? The answer, according to Wolff, is that full integration and inclusion are still a distant goal.

Wolff points to two primary barriers for persons with disabilities who wish to participate in sport: attitudes toward such participation and the portrayal of disability sport in the media. Wolff notes that there is a misconception about "what it means to be a person with a disability in sport." Too often, people pity disability sport athletes rather than recognizing their efforts as athletes. The same trend occurs in the media, where athletes with disabilities are often portrayed as sources of inspiration for others. This stands in contrast to focusing on the athletes' accomplishments and athletic prowess. Wolff argues that in order to overcome such barriers, awareness of these issues needs to be raised. People in the media, athletes, coaches, and supporters all need to know that the status quo is not how disability sport "has to be."

exercise were used in rehabilitation efforts for wounded soldiers. Guttman recognized the effectiveness of this approach, particularly in reducing boredom during the rehabilitation process. Thus, in 1944, he opened the Spinal Injuries Center at Stoke Mandeville Hospital in England, with a particular emphasis on sport. Within four years, sport as a form of rehabilitation had grown into a competitive venture, with patients in different wards competing against one another. This soon blossomed into an international competition when a team from the Netherlands competed in 1952. The official title of the competition was the Stoke Mandeville Games. The event grew in magnitude, and in 1960 the competition was staged as the Paralympic Games in Rome at the same time as the Olympics. Since that time, the Paralympic Games have been staged in tandem with the Olympic Games every four years. To illustrate the growth of the Paralympic Games, 400 athletes from 23 countries competed in 1960; in 2004, nearly 3,700 athletes representing 136 different countries competed in the Athens Games.

Of course, the Paralympics represent just one of many forms of disability sport (see Exhibit 8.8 for discussion).

Athletes with disabilities report mixed experiences competing in sport. Just as in broader society, athletes with disabilities can face marginalization, stigmatization,

exhibit   **8.8**   Large-Scale Disability Sport Events

Paralympic Games: A showcase of elite athletes with disabilities, including visual impairments, cerebral palsy, amputations, spinal cord injuries, and (on a limited basis) athletes with mental impairments; includes both winter and summer contests.

Deaflympics: Elite competition for athletes who are deaf. The first summer Deaflympics were held in 1924 in Paris, with the winter Deaflympics added in 1949.

Special Olympics: Sport opportunities for persons with cognitive and developmental disabilities; focus on development and social interaction of the athletes and not elite competition.

and exclusion (Dane-Staples, Lieberman, Ratcliff, & Rounds, 2013; Kitchin & Howe, 2014; Purdue & Howe, 2012; Swartz, Bantjes, Knight, Wilmot, & Derman, 2018). This is observed among athletes and reproduced through the media. Persons with disabilities are underrepresented in print and television media. As an example, the BBC broadcast more than 500 hours of the 2,000 Olympic Games but devoted only ten hours to the Paralympic Games that same year (Brittain, 2004). Athletes describe the limited coverage they do receive as fleeting, and the Paralympics and its participants receive no attention after the two or three weeks following the closing ceremonies. The lack of coverage by the BBC is particularly perplexing when we consider that it is a federally funded broadcast; thus, commercial viability (which is sometimes claimed as the reason for a lack of coverage) is not applicable.

Not only do persons with disabilities receive little media attention, but the coverage they do receive is often condescending and trivializing. Thomas and Smith (2009) noted that the media frequently depict persons with disabilities as passive objects of charity. The stereotypical representations serve to evoke fear and pity. The media are also more likely to focus on athletes' disabilities than their athletic prowess. Stories often concentrate on how the athlete overcame obstacles (i.e., disabilities) and demonstrated courage. These patronizing portrayals, which serve to perpetuate stereotypes of these athletes as objects of pity, are notably absent in media coverage of able-bodied athletes, where the focus is instead on their athletic ability and performance on the field.

Despite these negative experiences, many athletes with disabilities report that disability sport serves as a site for them to challenge stereotypes and develop physically, psychologically, and socially. For instance, athletes in adapted (i.e., reverse integration) activities develop a positive athlete identity through their participation, coming to see themselves as athletes, not disabled athletes

(Spencer-Cavaliere & Peers, 2011). Identity formation is important, as it allows people to combat prejudices, develop effective social networks, experience success, and feel fully enmeshed into the sport experience (Lundberg, Taniguchi, McCormick, & Tibbs, 2011). For combat veterans, sport and physical activity allow those with psychological disorders to improve their psychological and social well-being (Caddick & Smith, 2014). Positive outcomes include symptom reduction of post-traumatic stress disorder, active coping, improved self-concept, enhanced sense of achievement, and improved overall social well-being. The benefits are not limited to athletes, as disability sport spectators also report improved attitudes toward the sport and better behavioral tendencies toward athletes with disabilities (de Haan, Faull, & Kohe, 2014).

CHAPTER SUMMARY

The purpose of this chapter was to outline the effects of mental and physical ability in the workplace and sport. As the case in the opening Diversity Challenge illustrates, ability influences people's opportunities and experiences. Having read this chapter, you should be able to:

1. Define disability.

    People have a disability if they have a mental or physical impairment that limits one or more major life activities. Historically, people with disabilities have faced discrimination and been ostracized by others.

2. Describe the manner in which disability status influences access and treatment discrimination.

    People in the work environment face access discrimination, as they are less likely to be employed and more likely to be passed over in the selection process, relative to people without disabilities. Disability status also influences the type of jobs one has and their pay for it.

3. Summarize the multilevel factors that influence the effects of disability in the work environment.

    Factors affecting people with disabilities in the sport working environment include macro-level factors, such as employment laws, structural stigma, and stakeholder expectations; meso-level factors, including bias in decision-making, policies, champions, and organizational capacity; and micro-level factors, such as demographics, requests for accommodations, and type of disability.

4. Paraphrase the manner in which disability status influences opportunities and experiences of sport and physical activity participants.

    People with disabilities are less physically active than are able-bodied individuals. Opportunities to participate in disability sport have grown substantially. Nevertheless, a number of issues affect its delivery, including negative attitudes toward athletes with disabilities, barriers to inclusion, and lack of accessibility.

Questions FOR DISCUSSION

1. The chapter provided a brief historical overview of issues related to mental and physical disabilities. Are some of the ways that persons with disabilities historically faced discrimination still present today? What are the examples?
2. Identify some of the factors that may influence requests for accommodation by persons with disabilities in the workplace. What might be done to overcome some of the potential barriers?
3. Why are the athletic accomplishments of persons with disabilities brought into question by able-bodied athletes?
4. Disabilities are stigmatized in several ways. Which of the dimensions of stigma, as identified by Jones et al. (1984), is most influential?
5. What might be some ways sport managers could market directly to individuals with disabilities?

LEARNING Activities

1. Using the Internet, identify sport organizations and sport events that target athletes with disabilities. Based on your search, how would you characterize the sport and physical activity opportunities available for persons with disabilities?
2. Using the Internet, identify common requests for accommodations within sport organizations and the price incurred to the organization for making such accommodations. Are the prices more or less than you would have anticipated? What impacts would the accommodations have on the organization?

Web RESOURCES

National Disability Leadership Alliance, www.disabilityleadership.org
    A national organization in the US designed to represent the interests of persons with disabilities.
International Paralympic Committee, www.paralympic.org
    Serves as the official website of the Paralympic movement.
Disabled Sports USA, https://www.disabledsportsusa.org/
    Organization that provides national leadership for people with disabilities in sport.

READING **Resources**

DePauw, K. P., & Gavron, S. J. (2005). *Disability sport* (2nd ed.). Champaign, IL: Human Kinetics.

    Provides a historical account of disability sport and athletes with disabilities; also addresses the current challenges and controversies surrounding disability and sport.

Hums, M. A., & MacLean, J. C. (2013). *Governance and policy in sport organizations* (3rd ed.). Scottsdale, AZ: Holcomb Hathaway.

    Provides an overview of governance and policy issues in sport, with one of the most comprehensive treatments of the Paralympics in the literature.

Thomas, N., & Smith, A. (2009). *Disability, sport and society: An introduction.* New York, NY: Routledge.

    Provides an overview of the theories and policies related to disability and sport, with a particular emphasis on sport in the United Kingdom.

REFERENCES

Ameri, M., Schur, L., Adya, M., Bentley, F. S., McKay, P., & Kruse, D. (2018). The disability employment puzzle: A field experiment on employer hiring behavior. *ILR Review, 71*(2), 329–364.

Americans with Disabilities Act, 45 C.F.R. 843(j)(2)(i) (1985).

Baert, S. (2016). Wage subsidies and hiring chances for the disabled: Some causal evidence. *The European Journal of Health Economics, 17*(1), 71–86.

Baldridge, D. C., & Swift, M. L. (2013). Withholding requests for disability accommodation: The role of individual differences and disability attributes. *Journal of Management, 39*(3), 743–762.

Baldridge, D. C., & Swift, M. L. (2016). Age and assessments of disability accommodation request normative appropriateness. *Human Resource Management, 55*(3), 385–400.

Baldridge, D. C., & Veiga, J. F. (2006). The impact of anticipated social consequences on recurring disability accommodation requests. *Journal of Management, 32,* 158–179.

Ball, S. J., Maguire, M., Braun, A., & Hoskins, K. (2011). Policy actors: Doing policy work in schools. *Discourse: Studies in the Cultural Politics of Education, 32*(4), 625–639.

Beacom, A., French, L., & Kendall, S. (2016). Reframing impairment? Continuity and change in media representations of disability through the Paralympic Games. *International Journal of Sport Communication, 9*(1), 42–62.

Bell, M. P. (2007). *Diversity in organizations.* Mason, OH: Thomson South-Western.

Bell, M. P., McLaughlin, M. E., & Sequeira, J. M. (2004). Age, disability, and obesity: Similarities, differences, and common threads. In M. S. Stockdale & F. J. Crosby (Eds.), *The psychology and management of workplace diversity* (pp. 191–205). Malden, MA: Blackwell.

Bergmann, B. R. (1974). Occupational segregation, wages and profits when employers discriminate by race or sex. *Eastern Economic Journal, 1*(2), 103–110.

Brittain, I. (2004). Perceptions of disability and their impact upon involvement in sport for people with disabilities at all levels. *Journal of Sport and Social Issues,* 28, 429–452.

Caddick, N., & Smith, B. (2014). The impact of sport and physical activity on the well-being of combat veterans: A systematic review. *Psychology of Sport and Exercise, 15,* 9–18.

Clarkson, M. E. (1995). A stakeholder framework for analyzing and evaluating corporate social performance. *Academy of Management Review, 20*(1), 92–117.

Colella, A., & Stone, D. L. (2005). Workplace discrimination toward persons with disabilities: A call for some new research directions. In R. L. Dipboye & A. Colella (Eds.), *Discrimination at work: The psychological and organizational bases* (pp. 227–253). Mahwah, NJ: Lawrence Erlbaum.

Corrigan, P. W., Markowitz, F. E., & Watson, A. C. (2004). Structural levels of mental illness stigma and discrimination. *Schizophrenia Bulletin, 30*(3), 481–491.

Cuddy, A. J., Fiske, S. T., & Glick, P. (2008). Warmth and competence as universal dimensions of social perception: The stereotype content model and the BIAS map. *Advances in Experimental Social Psychology, 40,* 61–149.

Cunningham, G. B. (2014). Interdependence, mutuality, and collective action in sport. *Journal of Sport Management, 28*(1), 1–7.

Cunningham, G. B., & Sartore, M. L. (2010). Championing diversity: The influence of personal and organizational antecedents. *Journal of Applied Social Psychology, 40,* 788–810.

Cunningham, G. B., & Warner, S. (in press). Baseball 4 All: Providing inclusive spaces for persons with disabilities. *Journal of Global Sport Management.*

Dane-Staples, E., Lieberman, L., Ratcliff, J., & Rounds, K. (2013). Bullying experiences of individuals with visual impairment: The mitigating role of sport participation. *Journal of Sport Behavior, 36*(4), 365–386.

Darcy, S., Lock, D., & Taylor, T. (2017). Enabling inclusive sport participation: Effects of disability and support needs on constraints to sport participation. *Leisure Sciences, 39*(1), 20–41.

de Haan, D., Faull, A., & Kohe, G. Z. (2014). Celebrating the social in soccer: Spectators' experiences of the forgotten (Blind) Football World Cup. *Soccer & Society, 15,* 578–595.

Dejean, A. (2017, August). Many people with disabilities are bring paid way below the minimum wage, and it's perfectly legal. *Mother Jones.* Retrieved from https://www.motherjones.com/politics/2017/08/many-people-with-disabilities-are-being-paid-way-below-the-minimum-wage-and-its-perfectly-legal/

DePauw, K. P., & Gavron, S. J. (2005). *Disability sport* (2nd ed.). Champaign, IL: Human Kinetics.

Disability characteristics. (n.d.). US Census Bureau. Retrieved from https://factfinder.census.gov/faces/tableservices/jsf/pages/productview.xhtml?pid=ACS_15_1YR_S1810&prodType=table

Dovidio, J. F., Pagotto, L., & Hebl, M. R. (2011). Implicit attitudes and discrimination against people with physical disabilities. In R. L. Wiener, & S. L. Willborn (Eds.), *Disability and aging discrimination* (pp. 157–183). New York, NY: Springer.

Eastern Collegiate Athletic Conference (2015). ECAC board of directors cast historic vote to add varsity sports opportunities for student-athletes with disabilities in ECAC leagues and championships. Retrieved from http://www.ecacsports.com/news/2014-15/sports_opportunities_for_student-athletes_with_disabilities_in_ECAC_leagues_and_championships

Fact Sheet # 39 (2008). The employment of workers with disabilities at subminimum wages. *United State Department of Labor.* Retrieved from https://www.dol.gov/whd/regs/compliance/whdfs39.htm

Fay, T. (2011). Disability in sport—It's our time: From the sidelines to the frontlines

(Title IX—B). *Journal of Intercollegiate Sport, 4*, 63–94.

Fiske, S. T., Cuddy, A. J. C., Glick, P., & Xu, J. (2002). A model of (often mixed) stereotype content: Competence and warmth respectively follow from perceived status and competition. *Journal of Personality and Social Psychology, 82*, 878–902.

Florey, A. T., & Harrison, D. A. (2000). Responses to informal accommodation requests from employees with disabilities: Multistudy evidence on willingness to comply. *Academy of Management Journal, 43*, 224–233.

Garay, L., & Font, X. (2012). Doing good to do well? Corporate social responsibility reasons, practices and impacts in small and medium accommodation enterprises. *International Journal of Hospitality Management, 31*(2), 329–337.

Greenhaus, J. H., Parasuraman, S., & Wormley, W. M. (1990). Effects of race on organizational experiences, job performance, evaluations, and career outcomes. *Academy of Management Journal, 33*, 64–86.

Hall, M. H., Andrukow, A., Barr, C., Brock, K., De Wit, M., Embuldeniya, D., ... & Stowe, S. (2003). *The capacity to serve: A qualitative study of the challenges facing Canada's nonprofit and voluntary organizations.* Toronto, ON: Canadian Centre for Philanthropy.

Hatzenbuehler, M. L. (2017). Structural stigma and health. In B. Major, J. F. Dovidio, & B. G. Link (Eds.), *The Oxford handbook of stigma, discrimination, and health* (pp. 105–121). New York, NY: Oxford University Press.

Hatzenbuehler, M. L., & Link, B. G. (2014). Introduction to the special issue on structural stigma and health. *Social Science and Medicine, 103*, 1–6.

Hodge, N., & Runswick-Cole, K. (2013). "They never pass me the ball": Exposing ableism through the leisure experiences of disabled children, young people and

their families. *Children's Geographies, 11*, 311–325.

Hums, M. A., & MacLean, J. C. (2013). *Governance and policy in sport organizations* (3rd ed.). Scottsdale, AZ: Holcomb Hathaway.

Jeanes, R., Spaaij, R., Magee, J., Farquharson, K., Gorman, S., & Lusher, D. (2018). 'Yes we are inclusive': Examining provision for young people with disabilities in community sport clubs. *Sport Management Review, 21*(1), 38–50.

Jones, E., Farina, A., Hastorf, A., Markus, H., Miller, D., Scott, R., & de Sales-French, R. (1984). *Social stigma: The psychology of marked relationships.* San Francisco, CA: W. H. Freeman.

Kensbock, J. M., Boehm, S. A., & Bourovoi, K. (2017). Is there a downside of job accommodations? An employee perspective on individual change processes. *Frontiers in Psychology, 8*, 1536.

Kitchin, P. J., & Howe, P. D. (2014). The mainstreaming of disability cricket in England and Wales: Integration 'One Game' at a time. *Sport Management Review, 17*(1), 65–77.

Kulkarni, M. (2016). Organizational career development initiatives for employees with a disability. *The International Journal of Human Resource Management, 27*(14), 1662–1679.

Kulkarni, M., & Lengnick-Hall, M. L. (2014). Obstacles to success in the workplace for people with disabilities: A review and research agenda. *Human Resource Development Review, 13*, 158–180.

Kulkarni, M., & Rodrigues, C. (2014). Engagement with disability: Analysis of annual reports of Indian organizations. *The International Journal of Human Resource Management, 25*(11), 1547–1566.

Lauzun, H. M., Morganson, V. J., Major, D. A., & Green, A. P. (2010). Seeking work-life balance: Employees' requests, supervisors' responses, and organizational barriers. *The Psychologist-Manager Journal, 13*(3), 184–205.

Legg, D., Fay, T., Hums, M. A., & Wolff, E. (2009). Examining the inclusion of wheelchair events within the Olympic Games 1984–2004. *European Sport Management Quarterly, 9*, 243–258.

Lundberg, N. R., Taniguchi, S., McCormick, B. P., & Tibbs, C. (2011). Identity negotiating: Redefining stigmatized identities through adaptive sports and recreation participation among individuals with a disability. *Journal of Leisure Research, 43*(2), 205–225.

Major, B., & O'Brien, L. T. (2005). The social psychology of stigma. *Annual Review of Psychology, 56*, 393–421.

McLaughlin, M. E., Bell, M. P., & Stringer, D. Y. (2004). Stigma and acceptance of persons with disabilities. Understanding aspects of workforce diversity. *Group & Organization Management, 29*, 302–333.

Melton, E. N., & Cunningham, G. B. (2014). Who are the champions? Using a multilevel model to examine perceptions of employee support for LGBT inclusion in sport organizations. *Journal of Sport Management, 28*, 189–206.

Misener, L., & Darcy, S. (2014). Managing disability sport: From athletes with disabilities to inclusive organisational perspectives. *Sport Management Review, 17*, 1–7.

Persons with a Disability: Labor Force Characteristics (2018, June). Bureau of Labor Statistics. Retrieved from https://www.bls.gov/news.release/pdf/disabl.pdf

Purdue, D. E. J., & Howe, P. D. (2012). See the sport, not the disability: Exploring the Paralympic paradox. *Qualitative Research in Sport, Exercise and Health, 4*, 189–205.

Ravaud, J. F., Madiot, B., & Ville, I. (1992). Discrimination towards disabled people seeking employment. *Social Science & Medicine, 35*(8), 951–958.

Redington, P. (2014, September). UMass avoids ADA compliance with McGuirk upgrade. *Daily New Hampshire Gazette.* Retrieved from http://www.gazettenet.com/sports/umasssports/13725560-95/umass-avoids-ada-compliance-with-mcguirk-upgrade

Ren, L. R., Paetzold, R. L., & Colella, A. (2008). A meta-analysis of experimental studies on the effects of disability on human resource judgments. *Human Resource Management Review, 18*, 191–203.

Ryan, M. K., & Haslam, S. A. (2007). The glass cliff: Exploring the dynamics surrounding the appointment of women to precarious leadership positions. *Academy of Management Review, 32*(2), 549–572.

Saal, K., Martinez, L. R., & Smith, N. A. (2014). Visible disabilities: Acknowledging the utility of acknowledgment. *Industrial and Organizational Psychology, 7*, 242–248.

Santuzzi, A. M., & Waltz, P. R. (2016). Disability in the workplace: A unique and variable identity. *Journal of Management, 42*(5), 1111–1135.

Sartore, M., & Cunningham, G. (2010). The lesbian label as a component of women's stigmatization in sport organizations: An exploration of two health and kinesiology departments. *Journal of Sport Management, 24*(5), 481–501.

Schur, L., Han, K., Kim, A., Ameri, M., Blanck, P., & Kruse, D. (2017). Disability at work: A look back and forward. *Journal of occupational rehabilitation, 27*(4), 482–497.

Schur, L., Nishii, L., Adya, M., Kruse, D., Bruyére, S. M., & Blank, P. (2014). Accommodating employees with and without disabilities. *Human Resource Management, 53*, 593–621.

Sotiriadou, P., & Wicker, P. (2014). Examining the participation patterns of an ageing population with disabilities in Australia. *Sport Management Review, 17*, 35–48.

Spencer-Cavaliere, N., & Peers, D. (2011). "What's the difference?" Women's wheelchair basketball, reverse integration, and the question (ing) of disability. *Adapted Physical Activity Quarterly, 28*, 291–309.

Stone, D. L., & Colella, A. (1996). A model of factors affecting the treatment of disabled individuals in organizations. *Academy of Management Review, 21*(2), 352–401.

Stone-Romero, E. F., Stone, D. L., & Lukaszewski, K. (2007). The influence of disability on role-taking in organizations. In A. M. Konrad, P. Prasad, & J. K. Pringle (Eds.), *Handbook of workplace diversity* (pp. 401–430). Thousand Oaks, CA: Sage.

Summers, J. K., Howe, M., McElroy, J. C., Ronald Buckley, M., Pahng, P., & Cortes-Mejia, S. (in press). A typology of stigma within organizations: Access and treatment effects. *Journal of Organizational Behavior, 39*(7), 853–868.

Swartz, L., Bantjes, J., Knight, B., Wilmot, G., & Derman, W. (2018). "They don't understand that we also exist": South African participants in competitive disability sport and the politics of identity. *Disability and Rehabilitation, 40*(1), 35–41.

Telwatte, A., Anglim, J., Wynton, S. K., & Moulding, R. (2017). Workplace accommodations for employees with disabilities: A multilevel model of employer decision-making. *Rehabilitation Psychology, 62*(1), 7–19.

Thomas, N., & Smith, A. (2009). *Disability, sport and society: An introduction.* New York, NY: Routledge.

Von Schrader, S., Malzer, V., & Bruyère, S. (2014). Perspectives on disability disclosure: The importance of employer practices and workplace climate. *Employee Responsibilities and Rights Journal, 26*(4), 237–255.

Watson, B., & Scraton, S. J. (2013). Leisure studies and intersectionality. *Leisure Studies, 32*(1), 35–47.

Wicker, P., & Breuer, C. (2014). Exploring the organizational capacity and organizational problems of disability sport clubs in Germany using matched pairs analysis. *Sport Management Review, 17*(1), 23–34.

Wilson-Kovacs, D., Ryan, M. K., Haslam, S. A., & Rabinovich, A. (2008). 'Just because you can get a wheelchair in the building doesn't necessarily mean that you can still participate': Barriers to the career advancement of disabled professionals. *Disability & Society, 23*(7), 705–717.

Wooten, L. P., & James, E. H. (2005). Challenges of organizational learning: Perpetuation of discrimination against employees with disabilities. *Behavioral Sciences & the Law, 23*(1), 123–141.

Wright, T., & Cunningham, G. B. (2017). Disability status, stereotype content threat, and employment opportunities. *Sport, Business and Management, 7*(4), 393–403.

Zeigler, E. F. (2007). Sport management must show social concern as it develops tenable theory. *Journal of Sport Management, 21*(3), 297–318.

Weight

LEARNING OUTCOMES

After studying this chapter, you should be able to:

- Summarize conceptualizations of weight, overweight, and obese.
- Describe the manner in which weight influences access and treatment discrimination.
- Summarize the multilevel factors that influence the effects of weight in the work environment.
- Paraphrase the manner in which weight influences opportunities and experiences of sport and physical activity participants.

DIVERSITY CHALLENGE

In many ways, medical providers and fitness professionals have similar duties: improving their clients' health and well-being. They will both collect data to diagnose a condition, and ultimately prescribe a course of action. For doctors, the process might include lab tests that are used to diagnose hypertension, for which they make a diagnosis, such as taking prescription medicines, meditating, exercising, and the like. For fitness professionals, the data collection might take the form of assessing client needs or assessing their physical fitness. A diagnosis might include the client's desire to improve physical health, and the fitness provider then offers a fitness regimen to follow.

Beyond potential similarities in the decision-making process, medical providers and fitness professionals share other commonalities, too. Increasingly, doctors are prescribing exercise as a way to combat psychological and physical conditions. Evidence points to another similarity: body shaming as a motivational technique.

Joan Chrisler reviewed recent research related to weight discrimination in the medical fields, determining that body shaming and discrimination were rampant. Caroline Praderio made similar arguments about the fitness industry, suggesting clubs use shaming techniques to encourage new members to join. She noted,

> The words and imagery may differ, but the underlying message is the always the same: Excess weight—especially in the form of fat—is something to fear, something to be embarrassed of, and something that must be corrected. How? By joining this gym, of course.

Words matter. In the case of weight bias and mistreatment, they are harmful to the receiver and do not have the intended effects. Instead, researchers have shown that people who experience weight-based prejudices are more likely to gain weight over time than are similarly sized people who do not experience such mistreatment. Furthermore, shaming techniques can actually lead to avoidance behaviors. Chrisler noted, "Disrespectful treatment and medical fat shaming, in an attempt to motivate people to change their behavior, is stressful and can cause patients to delay health care seeking or avoid interacting with providers."

Just as there are similarities among medical providers and fitness professionals in the use of body shaming, the solutions are also the same: stop the practice. Chrisler suggests that, in addition to doctors eschewing body shaming language, universities should change. She argues that professors should address body stigma in the curriculum, and students should understand the harmful effects of such practices.

Sources: American Psychological Association (2017, August). Fat shaming in the doctor's office can be mentally and physically harmful. *Science Daily*. Retrieved from https://www.sciencedaily.com/releases/2017/08/170803092015. htm; Praderio, C. (2017, September). Some gyms are trying to get customers by body shaming them. The Insider. Retrieved from https://www.thisisinsider.com/gyms-marketing-body-shaming-2017-9.

CHALLENGE REFLECTION

1. In your experience, how frequently do fitness clubs focus on appearance rather than health and fitness? What are the examples?
2. Do you know of experiences with body shaming in the past? What were the effects?

Discussions of diversity often focus on race, gender, or age, with some discussions also centering on social class or more deep-level characteristics. Appearance is rarely considered. However, as the Diversity Challenge illustrates, the way people look has the potential to influence a host of outcomes, including their experiences with health professionals. Indeed, one's appearance can affect a constellation of outcomes, including career aspirations, work experiences, interactions with others, and exercise behaviors. The influence of appearance is evident in advertisements and promotions, where marketers choose slim and often athletically built persons to endorse fitness organizations and related products.

The purpose of this chapter is to explore the influence of appearance in greater depth. Appearance has many dimensions, including one's weight, height, and attractiveness, among others. All have the potential to impact access to and experiences in sport organizations. That noted, within the sport and exercise context, weight is particularly salient, and I therefore focus on this diversity form. In doing so, I examine definitions related to weight, the discrimination people experience based on their weight, multilevel factors that influence the discrimination, and the influence of weight on sport and physical activity participation.

DEFINITION AND BACKGROUND

Scholars and practitioners use various terms related to weight, and in some cases the meanings differ. According to the Centers for Disease Control and Prevention (n.d.), people who are overweight or obese have a body weight that exceeds what is considered healthy for their height. The CDC uses the body mass index (BMI) to make such determinations, with the following formula:

$$\text{BMI} = \frac{\text{weight}(\text{kg})}{\text{height}(\text{m})^2} \text{ or } \frac{703 \times \text{weight}(\text{lbs})}{\text{height}(\text{in})^2}$$

To illustrate, let us consider two people who weigh 200 pounds, but who vary in height. A person who is 5′7″ has a BMI of 31.3 and falls into the obese range. On the other hand, a person who is 6′4″ has a BMI of 24.3 and, according to the CDC, is in the normal or healthy weight category.

Some, however, have questioned the validity of the BMI, particularly for persons with high levels of muscle mass. Consider Los Angeles Lakers forward LeBron James. At 6′8″ and 250 pounds, James has a BMI of 27.5, which, according to the Centers for Disease Control and Prevention, means he is overweight. However, anyone who has seen James play would be hard pressed to consider him overweight. Thus, for James and other athletes like him, the BMI does not offer an accurate estimate of healthy weight. See Box 9.1 for further discussion of assessments of healthy weight.

Although scholars and medical professionals frequently use biomedical terms to describe healthy weight, some observers criticize their usage. Activists argue that use of terms such as *obese* and *overweight* belies an assumption that there is such a thing as a normal weight—a point they dispute (Solovay, 2000). Many such standards were based on data obtained from insurance companies, whose measurements came from middle-class Whites (Bell, 2007). Obviously, what is normal or the standard for middle-class Whites might be very different from what is normal for other groups. Furthermore, people who are clinically categorized as overweight might be healthier than persons who are thin as a result of unhealthy practices (e.g., anorexia). Given these concerns, activists and some scholars propose use of terms such as *fat, fatness,* and *corpulent* (Duncan, 2008; Pickett & Cunningham, 2018b).

Box 9.1 Alternative Perspectives. Is BMI the Best Measure of Body Fat?

Scholars and practitioners regularly use the BMI as an indicator of whether a person has a healthy weight (e.g., Kegler, Swan, Alcantara, Feldman, & Glanz, 2014; Zook, Saksvig, Wu, & Young, 2014). For the average adult, this measure corresponds to the level of body fat, but for others, such as athletes and others who are muscular, the BMI is not accurate. In this case, other measures might offer better reflections of body fat. Alternatives include measuring waist circumference or skinfold thickness (e.g., Durnin & Womersley, 1974). For example, men with waists of 40 inches or greater and women with waists of 35 inches or greater are considered unhealthy. More advanced methods include use of ultrasound, computed tomography, and magnetic resonance imaging (MRI; Centers for Disease Control and Prevention, n.d.). The latter techniques might offer more precise body fat estimates, but they are also more expensive and time intensive.

This debate highlights the difficulties and ambiguity surrounding issues related to weight. Nevertheless, there is general consensus among national and international agencies, such as the National Institutes of Health, the World Health Organization, and the Centers for Disease Control and Prevention, that a continuum exists from normal to overweight, obese, and morbidly obese, and that health outcomes grow progressively worse toward the high end of that continuum. Furthermore, determining precisely where a person falls on a medical continuum of fatness misses the larger point that fatness has negative associations. This affects people in their lives, their relationships, and their work (Bell, 2007).

According to the World Health Organization, the incidence of obesity is increasing globally and has doubled since 1980. More than 1.9 billion people worldwide are overweight, and 650 million of them are considered clinically obese (Obesity and Overweight, 2018). Although there is considerable consternation about the obesity rates in Western countries such as the US, obesity is prevalent around the world. The proportion of obese African children under age 5 has increased by 50 percent since 2000. Almost half of the children who are aged 5 or younger and are obese lived in Asia in 2016 (Obesity and Overweight, 2018).

The World Health Organization points to several factors that contribute to obesity, including diet, activity level, and environmental factors (Obesity and Overweight, 2018). People have largely moved away from consuming fresh foods, fruits, and vegetables and, instead, now consume processed foods that lack complex carbohydrates but are high in saturated fats and sugars. Technology and urbanization have also had an impact on physical activity levels. Where people might have performed manual labor in the past, in today's service-and-information economy, jobs require comparatively minimal levels of energy expenditure. City infrastructures often encourage people to take cars or public transportation rather than walk or ride a bicycle. Finally, the lack of supportive policies in education, health, agriculture, food processing, and urban planning, among others, further contributes to the trend.

WEIGHT IN THE WORK ENVIRONMENT

Research evidence suggests persons considered overweight or obese face access and treatment discrimination (Greenhaus, Parasuraman, & Wormley, 1990) in the work environment. Access discrimination is evident in the selection process, where raters routinely express an anti-fat bias in the selection process. Rudolf, Wells, Weller, and Baltes (2009) conducted a study where they statistically aggregated the results of previous work, correcting for various biases and errors. They found strong evidence of weight-based bias in the hiring process, and the pattern held for both managerial and sales jobs. Vanhove and Gordon (2014) later conducted an analysis using the same techniques, but they included even more studies. Their results demonstrated the same pattern such that people considered overweight or obese experience access discrimination.

Colleagues and I have conducted two studies in sport, with results again illustrating the presence of anti-fat bias in selection. In the first study (Sartore & Cunningham, 2007), we conducted three experiments set in the fitness context. We asked study participants to review the application files of persons who were trying to obtain jobs in a fitness company. Across all three studies, we found that raters recommended passing over people considered overweight. In some cases, the raters recommended less qualified but thinner applicants.

In another study, Melton and I collected data from collegiate women's golf coaches in the US (Melton & Cunningham, 2016). They reviewed packets of potential recruits, including a picture of the golfer, her background, golfing accolades, and performance information. The information varied based on golfer's weight and her ability. We asked the coaches to rate the golfers, indicate whether they would offer a scholarship, and to provide personal information. Results showed that the coaches preferred the thinner golfer, and the preference was especially strong among coaches who supported social hierarchies and status differences (i.e., high in social dominance orientation).

For the purposes of this chapter, I calculated the overall effect size of the differences across the four experiments we conducted. I did so by employing the same data aggregation techniques Rudolf et al. (2009) and Vanhove and Gordon (2014) employed—meta-analysis. The overall effect was large ($d = -1.16$), meaning that in the weight-based studies in the sport context, participants had a strong preference for thinner individuals.

People considered overweight or obese also experience treatment discrimination. Judge and Cable's (2011) study of wage differences provides one of the clearest examples. In their first study, they analyzed data from the German Socio-Economic Panel Study, which included over 11,500 people. They found that weight has curvilinear effects and impacted women and men differently. For men, substantial deviation from the mean weight—whether heavier or lighter—resulted in a salary penalty. For women, though, those who were lighter than the average weight earned the most, and heavier women earned the least. Judge and Cable then conducted another analysis using data from the National Longitudinal Surveys of Youth. The dataset represented a longitudinal study of 7,661 Americans. Results showed different effects for women and men. Among women, as weight decreased, earnings increased, but for men, an increase in weight was associated with an increase in salary. Finally, the authors used their findings to predict earnings differences across a 25-year career. American women who are average weight earn $389,300 less than their counterparts who are 25 pounds less than average weight. Among American men, being 25 pounds under the average results in a $210,925 deficit in career earnings.

MULTILEVEL EXPLANATIONS

Drawing from the model presented in Chapter 4, I present multilevel explanations for the influence of weight in the sport work environment. I focus on factors at the societal and community levels (macro-level factors), the organizational and interpersonal levels (meso-level factors), and individual level (micro-level factors). I offer an overview in Exhibit 9.1.

Macro-Level Factors

Macro-level factors are those operating at the societal level, including employment laws, structural stigma, and stakeholder explanations.

Employment Laws

One of the surest indicators that a society deems something unacceptable is that governing officials create laws prohibiting those actions. In the US, for example, lawmakers have developed statues to forbid discrimination in the workplace based on race, gender, age, disability, and religion, among other characteristics.

exhibit **9.1**   Multilevel Explanations for the Influence of Weight in the Sport Work Environment

Macro-level factors: Those operating at the societal level, including employment laws, structural stigma, and stakeholder explanations.

Meso-level factors: Those operating at the team and organizational levels, including bias in decision-making and the culture of inclusion.

Micro-level factors: Those operating at the individual level, including demographics, job type, and qualifications.

These employment protections suggest that enough people believed discrimination behaviors based on these characteristics were intolerable. Such a perspective is consistent with Crandall and Eshleman's (2003) justification-expression model of prejudice, as discussed in Chapter 3. These authors demonstrated that people expressed prejudice against different groups when they believed it was socially acceptable to do so. These dynamics show why people openly express animosity toward child abusers, but not toward members of other groups.

These connections are relevant to the discussion of employment protections—or the lack thereof—based on weight. As of 2018, no federal laws were in place in the US that specifically address the issue of obesity discrimination. This does not mean, however, that people have not successfully sued on the basis of such differential treatment. These suits are usually brought under the Rehabilitation Act of 1973, which prohibits discrimination on the basis of disability alone (Bell, McLaughlin, & Sequeira, 2004). In *Cook v. Rhode Island*, 10 F.3d 17 (1st Cir. 1993), Cook was denied employment at a state facility because it was believed her obesity would limit her job performance, even though Cook had performed at high levels in her previous job. The employer also believed that Cook would miss more time from work compared to other candidates and that the state would face more compensation claims because of her condition. The court, in finding in Cook's favor, ruled that obesity was a disability because it resulted from a metabolic dysfunction.

Because most suits similar to Cook's are not successful, various groups advocate the adoption of laws and ordinances to prohibit weight discrimination (Bell et al., 2004). Local ordinances in San Francisco and Santa Cruz, California, and the District of Columbia prohibit discrimination on the basis of weight. These laws and ordinances can help people fight discrimination and overcome the barriers they encounter because of their weight.

Structural Stigma

Recall from Chapter 2 that people who are stigmatized "have (or are believed to have) an attribute that marks them as different and leads them to be devalued in the eyes of others" (Major & O'Brien, 2005, p. 395). Hatzenbuehler (2017) noted that stigma can manifest at different levels, including the individual, interpersonal, and structural. At the latter level, societal factors, such as norms, laws, customs, and policies, all negatively affect people with the stigmatized characteristics. Individuals who have stigmatized traits have less social capital and power in society than do their counterparts (Link & Phelan, 2001; Lozano, Carless, Pringle, Sparkes, & McKenna, 2016).

A number of authors have suggested that people considered overweight or obese face stigma in society (Bacon, 2010; Flament et al., 2012; Pickett & Cunningham, 2018a). The lack of laws protecting employment discrimination, the presence of an entire industry (i.e., diet) designed to reduce the incidence of obesity, and the perpetuation of fat shaming in popular culture, including songs, social media, books, and film, all perpetuate fatness as a stigmatized characteristic.

As a testament to the quick socialization process with regard to attitudes about weight, children as young as three years reject people considered overweight or obese (Paxton & Damiano, 2017). Large-scale surveys show that overweight adolescents and teens are stigmatized; 20–50 percent indicated they had been teased or bullied about their weight (Crandall, Nierman, & Hebl, 2009). The effects of such abuse are dramatic. Youth who are overweight believe that their weight will negatively affect their lives, limit their opportunities, and thwart their chances to be healthy (Economos et al., 2014). Overweight youth are more likely to engage in risky healthy behaviors, such as purging—behaviors influenced by their depressive symptoms (Armstrong, Westen, & Janicke, 2014). They are also at increased risk of suicidal tendencies (Crandall et al., 2009).

Among adults, weight discrimination negatively affects a person's psychological well-being and overall health (Major, Hunger, Bunyan, & Miller, 2014; Pearl, 2018; Richard, Rohrmann, Lohse, & Eichholzer, 2016). With respect to the latter, Sutin and Terracciano's (2013) work is particularly enlightening. They collected data on more than 6,000 participants age 50 and older. Among those who were overweight, but not obese, participants who experienced weight discrimination were 2.5 times as likely to be obese four years later, compared to those who did not experience such mistreatment. The effects were even more damaging for persons who were already obese, as they were over three times as likely to remain obese as their obese peers who did not experience weight discrimination. The authors reasoned that these patterns were likely attributable to (a) the psychological distress associated with discrimination—which might result in more eating, (b) decreased confidence in physical activity, and (c) avoidance of physical activity.

Stakeholders

Recall from Chapter 4 that stakeholders are internal or external constituents who have a stake or interest in the organization (Clarkson, 1995). External stakeholders can influence many aspects of an organization, including who is hired and the ratings of individuals.

Bento, White, and Zacur (2012) illustrated the potential role of external stakeholders in perpetuating negative experiences for people considered overweight or obese. Many organizations will use 360-degree evaluations to assess performance. In doing so, they gather performance feedback from a variety of individuals, including colleagues, one's supervisor, direct reports, and people external to the unit, which can include individuals outside the organization. Cultural preferences for certain body sizes can negatively influence stakeholders' ratings, even when performance is high.

It is also possible that perceived stakeholder expectations can influence personnel decisions. For example, decision-makers in the fitness industry might presume that clients and potential clients expect employees to have a certain body type. As a result, the hiring director might be unwilling to recruit or hire people considered overweight or obese. Consistent with this rationale, Philips and Drummond (2001) found that US stakeholders expected men fitness leaders to have a lean and defined body. In Japan, body expectations are for exercisers and leaders to be lean, with an emphasis on weight loss (Andreasson & Johansson, 2017). These expectations mean that people considered overweight or obese are likely to face barriers in those settings.

Meso-Level Factors

Meso-level factors operate at the team and organizational levels. Bias in decision-making and the culture of inclusion are likely to influence the opportunities and experiences of people considered overweight or obese in the sport work environment.

Bias

Consistent with the previous chapters, I focus on the three dimensions of bias: stereotypes, prejudice, and discrimination (Cuddy, Fiske, & Glick, 2008). Many negative stereotypes exist about people who are considered overweight or obese, leading Roehling (1999) to conclude that these individuals are considered "fat but not 'jollly'" (p. 983). Common stereotypes of job applicants and employees who are considered overweight or obese include the belief that they lack self-control and self-discipline; are lazy; lack conscientiousness; are incompetent; are sloppy and unkempt, and maintain poor hygiene; are likely to be absent frequently; and are generally unhealthy (Puhl & Heuer, 2009; Roehling, Roehling, & Elluru, 2018). Persons who work in the sport industry also maintain these stereotypes, as evidenced by the series of studies Sartore and I conducted (Sartore & Cunningham, 2007). Across all of the studies, participants ascribed more negative attributions to the job applicants believed to be overweight or obese than they did to the thinner applicants. In some cases, unqualified thin applicants received more favorable ratings than more qualified heavier applicants.

There are many reasons why these stereotypes might exist. Returning to Fiske, Cuddy, Glick, and Xu's (2002) stereotype content model (discussed in Chapter 3), it is likely these stereotypes emanate from notions that those who are overweight or obese are low in both competence and warmth. Individuals who are poor, homeless, or on public assistance—all of whom experience considerable prejudice and discrimination—are also believed to be low in competence and warmth (Fiske, Cuddy, Glick, & Xu's, 2002). From another perspective, Vartanian, Thomas, and Vanman (2013) collected data from community members and college students to understand what predicted their stereotyping of people considered obese. They found that participants felt disgust toward people considered obese, and that feeling predicted stereotypes of the targets as lazy, sloppy, and so on.

Recognizing that some people do actively maintain these weight-based stereotypes, it is useful to consider whether there is any validity to these beliefs. Roehling, Roehling, and Odland (2008) provided a direct analysis of this issue. They collected data from two samples—one from an archival dataset of US residents aged 25–74 and the other of college students in the mid-western US—to examine the relationship between BMI and personality factors associated with stereotypes. These personality factors included extraversion, conscientiousness, agreeableness, and stability. Their results showed there was no empirical evidence to support the stereotypes. If anything, people with a higher BMI were more agreeable than their counterparts.

Prejudice represents the second component of bias. Evidence indicates that persons who are considered overweight or obese are stigmatized and face prejudice (Brochu, Gawronski, & Esses, 2011; Puhl & Heuer, 2009). The prejudice can be explicit or implicit (Elran-Barak & Bar-Anan, 2018; Skinner et al., 2017). In fact, some scholars have described such perspectives as one of the last forms of acceptable prejudice (Brochu et al., 2011). The social acceptability of this form of prejudice is evidenced by the lack of legal protections for persons who are considered overweight or obese, as well as the lack of attention given to weight discrimination among scholars (Ruggs et al., 2013).

In addition, evidence suggests that physical educators hold moderate anti-fat attitudes and tend to consider weight to be largely a function of personal control (Greenleaf & Weiller, 2005; Kenney, Gortmaker, Davison, & Austin, 2015). Students aspiring to work in the sport and fitness industry also endorse anti-fat beliefs (Chambliss, Finley, & Blair, 2004; Duncan, 2008). One student in Duncan's analysis, when asked to respond to the notion that people who are fat are abused by society, wrote,

> In a way it makes me feel bad for people that are fat. But then again I don't feel bad because most of the fat people aren't trying to do anything about it. But honestly, it's hard to hear people actually say that . . . [they] can't help being fat, it runs in their family. They should do something about their body, stop eating so much and exercise three to four times a week.
>
> (p. 2)

As with other forms of prejudice, people can and do maintain implicit prejudices toward persons they believe to be overweight or obese. For instance, some health professionals *who specialize in obesity* express high levels of implicit anti-fat bias and endorse implicit stereotypes of people who are fat as being stupid, indolent, and worthless (Schwartz, Chambliss, Brownell, Blair, & Billington, 2003). In studies, not all health professionals expressed such viewpoints; rather, younger persons, women, fit individuals, and persons with few obese friends all expressed more prejudice than their counterparts. Researchers have uncovered evidence of implicit biases among fitness professionals in multiple countries (Dimmock, Hallett, & Grove, 2009; Robertson & Vohora, 2008).

Weight prejudice has a detrimental effect on people's well-being. As BMI increases, so too do a person's concerns about being stigmatized and about what others think. This stigma concern is negatively associated with psychological well-being (Hunger & Major, 2015). Prejudice also has the potential to affect people's health-related behaviors, as people who experience weight bias are less likely to exercise, particularly when they do not believe the world is a just or fair place (Pearl & Dovidio, 2015).

The stereotypes and prejudice, along with other factors, give rise to discrimination (Summers et al., 2018). In the previous section, I outlined ways in which people considered obese or overweight faced treatment discrimination via differential

Box 9.2 Diversity in the Field. Prejudice against Customers Believed to Be Overweight or Obese

Researchers at Rice University showed that the general treatment of consumers who are obese is substantially poorer than the treatment of those whose weight is normal (King, Shapiro, Hebl, Singletary, & Turner, 2006). They designed a study in which 10 young women donned "fat suits" to make them appear heavier than they really were. The women shopped at various stores in the Houston area and noted the responses they received from the salespersons. In general, salespeople spent little time with the women who were overweight and, in some cases, even wondered aloud why shoppers who are overweight would bother patronizing a particular store. The researchers also found that the treatment the women received was better if they were drinking a diet cola or discussing weight loss. The research shows that when people believe justification for prejudice exists, they will discriminate against overweight people in subtle, covert ways.

salaries. Anti-fat attitudes also have a damaging effect on people's work experiences, particularly in industries where a premium is placed on appearance, as in sport. As a result, persons considered to be overweight suffer discrimination in the selection process, in promotions received, and in performance evaluations (Rudolf et al., 2009). Key organizational actors also negatively evaluate people with larger waistlines, and this is true even when we take into account other factors that might influence their evaluations (King, et al., 2016). In fact, the findings are observed even among top-level executives, suggesting the effects of weight-based discrimination span across hierarchical levels.

Prejudice also negatively affects clients and customers believed to be overweight or obese. Box 9.2 offers one such instance. As another illustrative example, Phelan et al. (2015) examined the influence of obesity stigma on the services health care providers offered. To do so, they analyzed the existing research in the area. They found that many health providers displayed strong anti-fat biases. These attitudes negatively affected their judgments, perceptions of their clients, behaviors directed toward the clients, and their overall decision-making. Given the poor level of care, clients considered overweight or obese may avoid visiting their health care professionals, not trust them, or abandon their treatment plans.

Culture of Inclusion

Whereas stereotypes, prejudice, and discrimination negatively affect people considered overweight or obese in the sport work environment, a culture of inclusion can result in quality, meaningful work experiences. Pickett and I developed a

exhibit **9.2** Dimensions of Inclusive Physical Activity Spaces

> **Cultural commitment to inclusion**: Celebrate body diversity; include people of all body types; and set the expectation of inclusiveness for employees and clients.
>
> **Authentic leadership**: demonstrate sincere, genuine leadership; foster inclusion among all persons; and be more than just a fitness instructor.
>
> **Language**: use inclusive language in instruction and marketing; remove assumptions; and give clients agency in their yoga practice.
>
> **Sense of community**: foster interactions; create inclusive social spaces; build deep relationships; and allow people to be their authentic selves.
>
> **Advocacy**: engage in activism for inclusion; focus on weight inclusiveness and other forms, too, such as social class and feminism.
>
> **Focus on health**: focus on fitness; emphasize body acceptance; and promote the idea of health at every size.

theoretical framework where we identified various dimensions of what we termed body weight inclusive physical activity spaces (Pickett & Cunningham, 2017b). We expected that exercisers in inclusive spaces would develop a strong commitment to the activity, and as a result, experience physical and psychological well-being. We also expected that the various identities and demographic characteristics of the exercisers would influence these patterns.

We then used the theoretical framework to guide a qualitative study (Pickett & Cunningham, 2017a). We asked body-positive yoga instructors how they worked to create inclusive spaces. Their responses helped us to further refine the framework and to identify specific mechanisms for creating an inclusive physical activity space for all persons. I summarize the results in Exhibit 9.2. The framework, developed from existing theory, empirical evidence, and interviews with fitness professionals across North America, gives sport managers concrete steps to create inclusive spaces, welcoming for all employees and clients.

Micro-Level Factors

Finally, several micro-level factors can influence the opportunities and experiences of people with disabilities. These include personal demographics, qualifications, and type of job.

Demographics

Demographics of the discrimination target can influence the incidence of weight discrimination. For example, some evidence suggests that race affects discrimination, in that overweight Whites might be more heavily penalized than their overweight peers of other races (Finkelstein, Frautschy Demuth, & Sweeney, 2007). The differences likely attributable to differences across cultures in the acceptability of larger body types.

Similarly, women are routinely penalized more for being overweight than are men (Bozoyan & Wolbring, 2018; Judge & Cable, 2011). Some evidence suggests that race and gender interact to predict discrimination. Vanhove and Gordon (2014) aggregated data from across field studies (i.e., those not performed in a laboratory setting) and found that gender and race interacted to predict discrimination. Specifically, White women experienced significantly more discrimination than their male peers of any race.

Other researchers have considered how being overweight or obese might actually buffer experiences with prejudice and discrimination. Handron, Kirby, Wang, Matskewich, and Cheryan (2017) examined the manner in which Asian American's weight influenced other's perceptions. Although most Asian countries have low rates of obesity, the US is one of the heaviest countries in the world. Thus, raters might evaluate overweight Asian Americans as prototypically American. The authors conducted 11 studies, whereby people viewed photos of average weight and overweight individuals and then respond to various questions. The photos were of the same target, and the researchers used editing software to make the individual appear bigger or smaller. Consistent with their expectations, Handron and colleagues found that overweight Asians were viewed as more American than their average weight counterparts. For Asian men, being overweight was also associated with the belief that he was in the country legally. Interestingly, similar findings were not observed for Blacks, Latinos, or Whites. Thus, the benefits of being overweight were only observed for Asians. The findings show that although being overweight is usually stigmatizing, it actually helped buffer Asians from negative stereotypes. The research also shows that different diversity forms interact with one another to influence a variety of attitudes and behaviors.

Type of Job

The type of job for which a person is applying might also affect whether the individual faces discrimination. People who are obese are more likely to be hired for jobs that do not require face-to-face interaction, such as inside telephone sales, than jobs that require such interaction (Bellizzi & Hasty, 1998). In sales positions, people considered overweight or obese frequently experience subtle forms of prejudice, largely due to stereotypes (Ruggs, Hebl, & Williams, 2015). These findings are consistent with meta-analysis findings showing that weight bias has more impact in sales positions than in managerial positions (Rudolf et al., 2009). Although the effects appear to be lesser for executives than for managers, it is important to remember that even persons in executive positions face discrimination based on their weight (King et al., 2016).

Though weight bias potentially disadvantages people in service roles, there are exceptions. Smith, Martinez, and Sabat (2016) drew from the stereotype content model (see Chapter 3) to examine the degree to which customer perceptions of the employee's warmth and competence affected weight bias. The researchers found that high levels of warmth (but not competence) offset the negative effects, especially among women.

In addition, a match between the customer and the service provider might offset the effects of weight. Pickett and I conducted an experimental study with a focus on yoga participation (Pickett & Cunningham, 2018b). Participants viewed a video of an instructor leading a yoga practice and then responded to questionnaires items about their attitudes and behavioral intentions. People considered overweight or obese expressed stronger connection to yoga and greater intentions to continue the activity when they viewed a video of a practice led by an instructor considered overweight or obese. Importantly, there were no statistically significant effects among participants who were not overweight or obese. Thus, body size similarity had positive effects for some participants and did not negatively affect the others.

Qualifications

Finally, the qualifications of applicants might influence the occurrence of discrimination, and, conversely, applicants' weight status can affect how their qualifications are viewed. In general, when a job applicant is thin, better qualifications give rise to more favorable ratings, but the same is not the case for applicants who are perceived to be overweight. In the latter case, both highly qualified and unqualified applicants face barriers to employment. This is particularly the case in the sport context, where a premium is placed on appearance (Sartore & Cunningham, 2007). In other settings, the effects are more nuanced, and weight bias is likely to appear only when applicants are marginally qualified for the job (Finkelstein et al., 2007). In such a case, decision-makers can justify their discrimination by pointing to other factors (e.g., the applicant did not have enough experience), whereas such excuses are not available when an applicant is highly qualified.

WEIGHT, PHYSICAL ACTIVITY, AND SPORT

Weight also affects people's physical activity levels. Persons who, based on their BMI, are considered of healthy weight are significantly more likely to meet recommended physical activity levels than are their overweight or obese peers (Hong, Coker-Bolt, Anderson, Lee, & Velozo, 2016; Spees, Scott, & Tucker, 2012; Tucker, Welk, & Beyler, 2011). This is true for both self-reported data and objective measures of physical activity (i.e., use of an accelerometer). Further investigation into the intensity of the activity reveals that those who engage in moderate levels of physical activity do not vary considerably by weight status; instead, the differences become apparent in those participating in vigorous levels of physical activity.

Persons considered overweight or obese may choose not to exercise because they are self-conscious about others seeing them participate, especially when the activities are difficult for them to complete (Carron, Hausenblas, & Estabrooks, 2003). This link is understandable, especially if many of the other participants have lean or muscular body types. Some people experience social physique anxiety, which occurs when they believe others are evaluating their body type (Carron et al., 2003). Those who experience such anxiety are likely to exercise in private (e.g., in their home) or to wear loose-fitting clothes. Social physique anxiety also influences a person's choice of activities. For example, women with social physique anxiety are likely to have a positive attitude toward aerobics classes that emphasize health rather than appearance (Raedeke, Focht, & Scales, 2007). Box 9.3 offers more information on this topic.

Stigma also plays a role in sport and exercise participation. Pickett and I interviewed inclusive yoga professionals about their experiences with weight stigma and the subsequent impact on their lives and physical activity (Pickett & Cunningham, 2018a). Stigma came in many forms, including exclusionary behaviors, cheerleading, and singling out. The participants also alluded to a lack of belonging in the physical activity space and an internalization of the negative feedback. The latter resulted in depressed feelings of self-worth, eating disorders, and a loss of power. Pearl, Pulh, and Dovidio (2015) also found that internalized stigma was harmful for people considered overweight or obese. Among exercisers in that group, internalized weight stigma experienced decreases in their confidence, motivation, and exercise behaviors.

Box 9.3 Professional Perspectives. Promoting Inclusive Physical Activity

People considered overweight or obese sometimes express hesitance about exercising in public, something attributed to stereotypes, prejudices, and discrimination. Samantha Puc, editor-in-chief of Fatventure Mag, recognized the pressures people considered overweight or obese face, noting, "The fact is, as often as people tell us that we should lose weight, they also don't want to see us in their spaces, which includes basically anywhere other than the privacy of our own homes."

Through her publication and advocacy efforts, though, Puc is seeking to create change. The key, she suggests, is to start where you are comfortable:

You don't have to exercise in public if it makes you uncomfortable. Try something at home first, or with friends you trust. Better yet, try taking a class with another fat friend so you can enjoy it together. Having allies and strength in numbers is a significant help in getting past the fear.

What about people who do exercise in public only to encounter ridicule from others. Tuc has advice for those situations, too: "In my own experience, calling people out on their fatphobia or telling them to f— off is the best way to make them leave you alone so you can enjoy your workout in peace."

Source: Chamseddine (2018).

Health and fitness clubs play a potentially key role in this area. The way these clubs position themselves and promote the benefits of physical activity influences people's subsequent exercise intentions. Woods and I conducted an experimental study in which participants viewed an advertisement for a new fitness club and then reported their reactions to the club and their interest in joining (Cunningham & Woods, 2011). The advertisements varied by their focus (appearance: "Look better instantly and get your best body ever," or wellness: "Learn fitness and nutrition strategies; acquire lifelong wellness") and the gender of the model. Results showed that people agreed more with the fitness club's culture when the advertisement focused on wellness rather than appearance, irrespective of the model's gender in the advertisement. Participants' agreement with the club's culture was reliably associated with their interest in joining the club.

These findings suggest that the dominant marketing theme among most fitness clubs—that is, "if you exercise then you will lose weight"—might be misguided. A different, perhaps more effective, approach would be to focus on how membership in a club can result in being healthy, irrespective of one's weight. Use of fit, athletic models—the type who appear predominantly in fitness club advertisements—might be similarly misguided. What is interesting is that clubs' marketing efforts may not effectively reach the primary target audience or the people who need sport and exercise the most—those who are overweight or obese. Recall from Chapter 2 that the social categorization framework for understanding diversity holds that people will have positive attitudes toward and trust those people who are similar to them (in-group members). If that is true, then use of models who are thin and have well-defined muscles will be most effective in attracting people who already embody those characteristics. Persons who are overweight or obese may view those product endorsers as out-group members; hence, the positive attitudes toward, and the trust afforded to, such endorsers are likely to be low. Based on these arguments, for more effective ads, sport and fitness organizations should use models who represent all body types. Of course, drawing from the matchup hypothesis literature, the product endorsers should demonstrate some level of physical fitness.

CHAPTER SUMMARY

The purpose of this chapter was to examine the influence of weight on how people experience work, sport, and physical activity, as well as on sport participation and promotion. As illustrated in the Diversity Challenge, appearance has the potential to shape a person's opportunities. People who do not fit the norm face with a number of challenges in the sport work environment. Having read this chapter, you should be able to:

1. Summarize conceptualizations of weight, overweight, and obese.

    Some organizations classify people as overweight or obese based on the BMI. Others, however, argue that the BMI is a poor measure, not taking into account muscle mass, cultural differences, and the social construction of weight.

2. Describe the manner in which weight influences access and treatment discrimination.

    People considered overweight or obese have less access to jobs and also receive less pay for equal work.

3. Summarize the multilevel factors that influence the effects of weight in the work environment.

    Macro-level factors (e.g., employment laws, structural stigma, and stakeholder explanations), meso-level factors (e.g., bias in decision-making and the culture of inclusion), and micro-level factors (e.g., demographics, job type, and qualifications) all influence access and opportunities for people considered overweight or obese.

4. Paraphrase the manner in which weight influences opportunities and experiences of sport and physical activity participants.

    The available literature suggests that adults who are considered to be overweight are less likely to exercise than their counterparts. Stigma and social physique anxiety contribute to this trend.

Questions FOR DISCUSSION

1. Some consider weight to be a function of individual choices while others point to environmental and genetic influences. What is your position, and why do you hold it?

2. Why are persons who are considered overweight ascribed negative attributes? Do you think similar ascriptions occur for persons who are underweight?

3. Research suggests that people have implicit biases against people considered overweight or obese. Why is this the case? Has this been your experience?

4. Why do you think there are no federal employment protections for people considered overweight or obese?

LEARNING Activities

1. Using online resources, identify job postings for fitness clubs. Does the advertisement include language designed to attract persons who might be considered fit or athletic looking?

2. One could argue that weight *should* be considered in personnel decisions since clients might respond favorably to lean, muscular individuals. An alternative point of view is that such an approach is unreasonable and could be used to justify preferential hiring based on other diversity dimensions (e.g., race). As a class, divide into two teams and debate these positions.

Web RESOURCES

The Obesity Society, www.naaso.org
  National society dedicated to the scientific study of obesity and obesity-related issues, including discrimination.
Rudd Center, www.yaleruddcenter.org
  An academic research center that seeks to improve the world's diet, reduce obesity, and ameliorate weight stigma.
World Health Organization, www.who.int
  An international agency responsible for providing leadership on health matters worldwide, shaping the research agenda, setting health standards, and providing health-related support to countries.

READING Resources

Brownwell, K. D., Schwartz, M. B., Pugh, R. M., & Rudd, L. (2005). *Weight bias: Nature, consequences and remedies.* New York, NY: Guilford Press.

  Edited text from leading scholars in the field; explores the nature and causes of weight discrimination, as well as ways to combat the discrimination.

Rothblum, E., & Solovay, S. (Eds.). (2009). *The fat studies reader.* New York, NY: New York University Press.

  A collection of essays addressing anti-fat bias and weight discrimination; also introduces the field of fat studies.

Health Psychology

  A journal published by the American Psychological Association that regularly includes articles focusing on the psychological effects of anti-fat attitudes.

REFERENCES

Andreasson, J., & Johansson, T. (2017). The new fitness geography: The globalisation of Japanese gym and fitness culture. *Leisure Studies, 36*(3), 383–394.

Armstrong, B., Westen, S. C., & Janicke, D. M. (2014). The role of overweight perception and depressive symptoms in child and adolescent unhealthy weight control behaviors: A mediation model. *Journal of Pediatric Psychology, 39,* 340–348.

Bacon, L. (2010). *Health at every size: The surprising truth about your weight.* Dallas, TX: BenBella Books.

Bell, M. P. (2007). *Diversity in organizations.* Mason, OH: Thomson South-Western.

Bell, M. P., McLaughlin, M. E., & Sequeira, J. M. (2004). Age, disability, and obesity: Similarities, differences, and common threads. In M. S. Stockdale & F. J. Crosby (Eds.), *The psychology and management of workplace diversity* (pp. 191–205). Malden, MA: Blackwell.

Bellizzi, J. A., & Hasty, R. W. (1998). Territory assignment decisions and supervising unethical selling behavior: The effects of obesity and gender as moderated by job-related factors.

Journal of Personal Selling & Sales Management, 18(2), 35–49.

Bento, R. F., White, L. F., & Zacur, S. R. (2012). The stigma of obesity and discrimination in performance appraisal: A theoretical model. *The International Journal of Human Resource Management, 23*(15), 3196–3224.

Bozoyan, C., & Wolbring, T. (2018). The weight wage penalty: A mechanism approach to discrimination. *European Sociological Review, 34*(3), 254–267.

Brochu, P. M., Gawronski, B., & Esses, V. M. (2011). The integrative prejudice framework and different forms of weight prejudice: An analysis and expansion. *Group Processes & Intergroup Relations, 14*(3), 429–444.

Carron, A. V., Hausenblas, H. A., & Estabrooks, P. A. (2003). *The psychology of physical activity*. New York, NY: McGraw-Hill.

Centers for Disease Control and Prevention (n.d.). Defining overweight and obesity. Retrieved from http://www. cdc.gov/ obesity/adult/defining.html

Chambliss, H. O., Finley, C. E., & Blair, S. N. (2004). Attitudes toward obese individuals among exercise science students. *Medicine and Science in Sports and Exercise, 36,* 468–474.

Chamseddine, R. (2018, July). When fat people dare to exercise in public. *The Sydney Morning Herald*. Retrieved from https://www.smh.com.au/lifestyle/health-and-wellness/when-fat-people-dare-to-exercise-in-public-20180709-p4zqd2.html

Clarkson, M. E. (1995). A stakeholder framework for analyzing and evaluating corporate social performance. *Academy of Management Review, 20*(1), 92–117.

Crandall, C. S., & Eshleman, A. (2003). A justification-suppression model of the expression and experience of prejudice. *Psychological Bulletin, 129*(3), 414–446.

Crandall, C. S., Nierman, A., & Hebl, M. (2009). Anti-fat prejudice. In T. D. Nelson (Ed.), *Handbook of prejudice, stereotyping, and discrimination* (pp. 469–487). New York, NY: Psychology Press.

Cuddy, A. J., Fiske, S. T., & Glick, P. (2008). Warmth and competence as universal dimensions of social perception: The stereotype content model and the BIAS map. *Advances in Experimental Social Psychology, 40,* 61–149.

Cunningham, G. B., & Woods, J. (2011). For the health of it: Advertisement message and attraction to fitness clubs. *American Journal of Health Studies, 26,* 4–9.

Dimmock, J. A., Hallett, B. E., & Grove, J. R. (2009). Attitudes toward overweight individuals among fitness center employees: An examination of contextual factors. *Research Quarterly for Exercise and Sport, 80,* 641–647.

Duncan, M. C. (2008). The personal is political. *Sociology of Sport Journal, 25,* 1–6.

Durnin, J. V., & Womersley, J. (1974). Body fat assessed from total body density and its estimation from skinfold thickness: Measurements on 481 men and women aged from 16 to 72 years. *British Journal of Nutrition, 32*(1), 77–97.

Economos, C. D., Bakun, P. J., Herzog, J. B., Dolan, P. R., Lynskey, V. M., Markow, D., … Nelson, M. E. (2014). Children's perceptions of weight, obesity, nutrition, physical activity and related health and socio-behavioural factors. *Public Health Nutrition, 17,* 170–178.

Elran-Barak, R., & Bar-Anan, Y. (2018). Implicit and explicit anti-fat bias: The role of weight-related attitudes and beliefs. *Social Science & Medicine, 204,* 117–124.

Finkelstein, L. M., Frautschy Demuth, R. L., & Sweeney, D. L. (2007). Bias against overweight job applicants: Further explorations of when and why. *Human Resource Management, 46,* 203–222.

Fiske, S. T., Cuddy, A. J. C., Glick, P., & Xu, J. (2002). A model of (often mixed) stereotype content: Competence and warmth respectively follow from perceived status and competition. *Journal of Personality and Social Psychology, 82,* 878–902.

Flament, M. F., Hill, E. M., Buchholz, A., Henderson, K., Tasca, G. A., & Goldfield, G. (2012). Internalization of the thin and muscular body ideal and disordered eating in adolescence: The mediation effects of body esteem. *Body Image*, 9(1), 68–75.

Greenhaus, J. H., Parasuraman, S., & Wormley, W. M. (1990). Effects of race on organizational experiences, job performance, evaluations, and career outcomes. *Academy of Management Journal*, 33, 64–86.

Greenleaf, C., & Weiller, K. (2005). Perceptions of youth obesity among physical educators. *Social Psychology of Education*, 8, 407–423.

Handron, C., Kirby, T. A., Wang, J., Matskewich, H. E., & Cheryan, S. (2017). Unexpected gains: Being overweight buffers Asian Americans from prejudice against foreigners. *Psychological Science*, 28(9), 1214–1227.

Hatzenbuehler, M. L. (2017). Structural stigma and health. In B. Major, J. F. Dovidio & B. G. Link (Eds.), *The Oxford handbook of stigma, discrimination, and health* (pp. 105–121). New York, NY: Oxford University Press.

Hong, I., Coker-Bolt, P., Anderson, K. R., Lee, D., & Velozo, C. A. (2016). Relationship between physical activity and overweight and obesity in children: Findings from the 2012 national health and nutrition examination survey national youth fitness survey. *American Journal of Occupational Therapy*, 70(5), 7005180060p1–7005180060p8.

Hunger, J. M., & Major, B. (2015). Weight stigma mediates the association between BMI and self-reported health. *Health Psychology*, 34(2), 172–175.

Judge, T. A., & Cable, D. M. (2011). When it comes to pay, do the thin win? The effect of weight on pay for men and women. *Journal of Applied Psychology*, 96, 95–112.

Kegler, M. C., Swan, D. W., Alcantara, I., Feldman, L., & Glanz, K. (2014). The influence of rural home and neighborhood environments on healthy eating, physical activity, and weight. *Prevention Science*, 15, 1–11.

Kenney, E. L., Gortmaker, S. L., Davison, K. K., & Austin, S. B. (2015). The academic penalty for gaining weight: A longitudinal, change-in-change analysis of BMI and perceived academic ability in middle school students. *International Journal of Obesity*, 39(9), 1408.

King, E. B., Rogelberg, S. G., Hebl, M. R., Braddy, P. W., Shanock, L. R., Doerer, S. C., & McDowell-Larsen, S. (2016). Waistlines and ratings of executives: Does executive status overcome obesity stigma? *Human Resource Management*, 55(2), 283–300.

King, E. B., Shapiro, J. R., Hebl, M. R., Singletary, S. L., & Turner, S. (2006). The stigma of obesity in customer service: A mechanism for remediation and bottom-line consequences of interpersonal discrimination. *Journal of Applied Psychology*, 91, 579–593.

Link, B. G., & Phelan, J. C. (2001). Conceptualizing stigma. *Annual Review of Sociology*, 27(1), 363–385.

Lozano-Sufrategui, L., Carless, D., Pringle, A., Sparkes, A., & McKenna, J. (2016). "Sorry mate, you're probably a bit too fat to be able to do any of these": Men's experiences of weight stigma. *International Journal of Men's Health*, 15(1), 4–23.

Major, B., Hunger, J. M., Bunyan, D. P., & Miller, C. T. (2014). The ironic effects of weight stigma. *Journal of Experimental Social Psychology*, 51, 74–80.

Major, B., & O'Brien, L. T. (2005). The social psychology of stigma. *Annual Review of Psychology*, 56, 393–421.

Melton, E. N., & Cunningham, G. B. (2016). Weighing the options: Discrimination against fat golfers. *Journal of Intercollegiate Sport*, 9, 268–281.

Obesity and overweight. (2018, February). *World Health Organization*. Retrieved from http://www.who.int/en/news-room/fact-sheets/detail/obesity-and-overweight

Paxton, S. J., & Damiano, S. R. (2017). The development of body image and weight bias in childhood. *Advances in Child Development and Behavior, 52,* 269–298.

Pearl, R. L. (2018). Weight bias and stigma: public health implications and structural solutions. *Social Issues and Policy Review, 12*(1), 146–182.

Pearl, R. L., & Dovidio, J. F. (2015). Experiencing weight bias in an unjust world: Impact on exercise and internalization. *Health Psychology, 34*(7), 741–479.

Pearl, R. L., Puhl, R. M., & Dovidio, J. F. (2015). Differential effects of weight bias experiences and internalization on exercise among women with overweight and obesity. *Journal of Health Psychology, 20*(12), 1626–1632.

Phelan, S. M., Burgess, D. J., Yeazel, M. W., Hellerstedt, W. L., Griffin, J. M., & van Ryn, M. (2015). Impact of weight bias and stigma on quality of care and outcomes for patients with obesity. *Obesity Reviews, 16*(4), 319–326.

Philips, J. M., & Drummond, M. J. (2001). An investigation into the body image perception, body satisfaction and exercise expectations of male fitness leaders: Implications for professional practice. *Leisure Studies, 20*(2), 95–105.

Pickett, A. C., & Cunningham, G. B. (2017a). Creating inclusive physical activity spaces: The case of body positive yoga. *Research Quarterly for Exercise and Sport, 88*(3), 329–338.

Pickett, A. C., & Cunningham, G. B. (2017b). Physical activity for every body: A conceptual model for creating body diverse exercise spaces. *Quest, 69,* 19–36.

Pickett, A. C., & Cunningham, G. B. (2018a). Body weight stigma in physical activity settings. *American Journal of Health Studies, 33*(1), 21–29.

Pickett, A. C., & Cunningham, G. B. (2018b). The fat leading the thin: Relative body size, physical activity identification, and behavioral intentions. *Journal of Applied Sport Management, 10,* 1–12.

Puhl, R. M., & Heuer, C. A. (2009). The stigma of obesity: a review and update. *Obesity, 17*(5), 941–964.

Raedeke, T. D., Focht, B. C., & Scales, D. (2007). Social environmental factors and psychological responses to acute exercise for socially physique anxious females. *Psychology of Sport and Exercise, 8,* 463–476.

Richard, A., Rohrmann, S., Lohse, T., & Eichholzer, M. (2016). Is body weight dissatisfaction a predictor of depression independent of body mass index, sex and age? Results of a cross-sectional study. *BMC Public Health, 16*(1), 863.

Robertson, N., & Vohora, R. (2008). Fitness vs. fatness: Implicit bias towards obesity among fitness professionals and regular exercisers. *Psychology of Sport and Exercise, 9*(4), 547–557.

Roehling, M. V. (1999). Weight-based discrimination in employment: Psychological and legal aspects. *Personnel Psychology, 52,* 969–1016.

Roehling, M. V., Pichler, S., & Bruce, T. A. (2013). Moderators of the effect of weight on job-related outcomes: A meta-analysis of experimental studies. *Journal of Applied Social Psychology, 43*(2), 237–252.

Roehling, M. V., Roehling, P. V., & Odland, L. M. (2008). Investigating the validity of stereotypes about overweight employees: The relationship between body weight and normal personality traits. *Group & Organization Management, 33,* 392–424.

Roehling, P. V., Roehling, M. V., & Elluru, A. (2018). Size does matter: The impact of size on career. In A. M. Broadbridge & S. L. Fielden (Eds.), *Research handbook of diversity and careers* (pp. 105–115). Northampton, MA: Edward Elgar.

Rudolf, C. W., Wells, C. L., Weller, M. D., & Baltes, B. B. (2009). A meta-analysis of empirical studies of weight-based bias in the workplace. *Journal of Vocational Behavior, 74,* 1–10.

Ruggs, E. N., Hebl, M. R., Law, C., Cox, C. B., Roehling, M. V., & Wiener, R. L.

(2013). Gone fishing: I–O psychologists' missed opportunities to understand marginalized employees' experiences with discrimination. *Industrial and organizational psychology, 6*(1), 39–60.

Ruggs, E. N., Hebl, M. R., & Williams, A. (2015). Weight isn't selling: The insidious effects of weight stigmatization in retail settings. *Journal of Applied Psychology, 100*(5), 1483.

Sartore, M. L., & Cunningham, G. B. (2007). Weight discrimination, hiring recommendations, person-job fit and attributions: Implications for the fitness industry. *Journal of Sport Management, 21*, 172–193.

Schwartz, M. B., Chambliss, H. O., Brownell, K. D., Blair, S. N., & Billington, C. (2003). Weight bias among health professionals specializing in obesity. *Obesity Research, 11*, 1033–1039.

Skinner, A. C., Payne, K., Perrin, A. J., Panter, A. T., Howard, J. B., Bardone-Cone, A., … Perrin, E. M. (2017). Implicit weight bias in children age 9 to 11 years. *Pediatrics, 140*(1), e20163936.

Smith, N. A., Martinez, L. R., & Sabat, I. E. (2016). Weight and gender in service jobs: The importance of warmth in predicting customer satisfaction. *Cornell Hospitality Quarterly, 57*(3), 314–328.

Solovay, S. (2000). *Tipping the scales of injustice: Fighting weight-based discrimination.* Amherst, NY: Prometheus Books.

Spees, C. K., Scott, J. M., & Tucker, C. A. (2012). Differences in amounts and types of physical activity by obesity status in US adults. *American Journal of Health Behavior, 36*, 56–65.

Summers, J. K., Howe, M., McElroy, J. C., Ronald Buckley, M., Pahng, P., & Cortes-Mejia, S. (in press). A typology of stigma within organizations: Access and treatment effects. *Journal of Organizational Behavior, 39*(7), 853–868.

Sutin, A. R., & Terracciano, A. (2013). Perceived weight discrimination and obesity. *PLoS One, 8*(7), e70048.

Tucker, J. M., Welk, G. J., & Beyler, N. K. (2011). Physical activity in US adults: Compliance with the physical activity guidelines for Americans. *American Journal of Preventive Medicine, 40*, 454–461.

Vanhove, A., & Gordon, R. A. (2014). Weight discrimination in the workplace: A meta-analytic examination of the relationship between weight and work-related outcomes. *Journal of Applied Social Psychology, 44*, 12–22.

Vartanian, L. R., Thomas, M. A., & Vanman, E. J. (2013). Disgust, contempt, and anger and the stereotypes of obese people. *Eating and Weight Disorders-Studies on Anorexia, Bulimia and Obesity, 18*(4), 377–382.

Zook, K. R., Saksvig, B. I., Wu, T. T., & Young, D. R. (2014). Physical activity trajectories and multilevel factors among adolescent girls. *Journal of Adolescent Health, 54*, 74–80.

Religion

10

LEARNING OUTCOMES

After studying this chapter, you should be able to:

- Define religion and spirituality.
- Describe the manner in which religion influences access and treatment discrimination.
- Summarize the multilevel factors that influence the effects of religion in the work environment.
- Paraphrase the manner in which religion influences opportunities and experiences of sport and physical activity participants.

DIVERSITY CHALLENGE

acrosse is a sport that has grown considerably in the US over the past two decades. In 2001, 253,931 athletes competed in the sport, and by 2016, the number had grown to 826,033—a threefold increase. Twenty-one states offer championship in the sport, there is a 24-hour Internet network devoted to lacrosse, and both women and men have professional leagues.

Lacrosse allows participants to work together on a team toward a common goal. For Josh Snyder, though, the benefits were further reaching. Snyder, a junior at Cherry Creek High School in Colorado, USA, attended a youth leadership conference where the Israeli national lacrosse team was also visiting. He was given the chance to participate with the team in an exhibition match and was later asked to join the Team Israel U19 squad. He competed for the team in 2018 during the Federation of International Lacrosse World Championships, held in Netanya, Israel.

Synder was looking forward to competing at a high level of lacrosse and growing in his religious tradition. He commented,

> Religiously, I'm hoping to gain a deeper understanding for my religion, and see how it's evolved through our ancestors and through time.... It'll mean a lot. I

think it's very special to be representing the Jewish people as a whole, and kind of representing our country and showing the world that Israel can play lacrosse.

Whereas Snyder experienced a positive intersection between lacrosse and religion, participants in a 2018 Connecticut (USA) high school match had vastly different experiences. Fans at Fairfield College Preparatory School recited anti-Semitic chants aimed at Staples High School participants. A third of the Staples team is Jewish. The language was so egregious that Anti-Defamation League officials got involved, meeting with school officials. The school president took responsibility for the actions, apologized, and promised corrective actions.

The two cases illustrate the various ways in which religion and sport can intersect.
Sources: 2016 participation survey. (no date). US Lacrosse. Retrieved from https://www.uslacrosse.org/about-us-lacrosse/participation-survey. Rozner, L. (2018, June). Anti-Defamation League condemns anti-Semitic insults at high school lacrosse game. CBS New York. Retrieved from https://newyork.cbslocal.com/2018/06/05/adl-fairfield-anti-semitic-lacrosse-game-chants/. Temby, T. (2018, July). Lacrosse, religion intersect for local athlete. *9News*. Retrieved from https://www.9news.com/article/sports/high-school/lacrosse-religion-intersect-for-local-athlete-in-israel/73-576224142.

CHALLENGE REFLECTION

1. Can you think of cases where religion and sport intersected? What were they, and were the outcomes positive or negative?
2. The school superintendent in the anti-Semitic chants case questioned why others did not intervene to stop the chants. What is the role of other fans, officials, or coaches in promoting religious inclusion at games or matches?

As the Diversity Challenge demonstrates, sport and religion are often intertwined. For a host of reasons, now more than ever before, people are likely to integrate their religious beliefs into their everyday work activities, athletes are likely to turn to their religious beliefs to make sense of their sport participation, and sport organizations may incorporate religion and faith into their efforts to attract fans to their events. These dynamics are important because people's religious beliefs have the potential to influence their attitudes, the decisions they make at work, and how well they integrate with others in the workplace or on an athletic team. Interestingly, despite the importance of religion to many people, this topic has received little interest in the diversity literature. In fact, Tracey (2012) commented, "Management researchers have stubbornly refused to engage meaningfully with religion and religious forms of organization, or to consider the effects of religious beliefs and practices on secular organizations" (p. 88). Consequently, sport managers must remain cognizant of how this form of deep-level diversity influences the workplace's culture, processes, and outcomes.

The purpose of this chapter is to examine the influence of religion in sport organizations. The chapter begins with a discussion of religion and spirituality and the distinctions between those two constructs. I then highlight the influence of religion in the workplace. In the final section of the chapter, I provide an overview of how athletes incorporate religion into their sport participation.

DEFINITIONS AND BACKGROUND

To understand the effects of religious beliefs in the workplace, it is first necessary to define basic terms. Koenig, King, and Carson (2012) define religion as "beliefs, practices, and rituals related to the *transcendent*, where the transcendent is God, Allah, HaShem, or a Higher Power in Western religious traditions, or to Brahman, manifestations of Brahman, Buddha, Dao, or ultimate truth/reality in Eastern traditions" (p. 45, emphasis original). Religion serves multiple functions (Bruce, 2011; Durkheim, 1965; Koenig et al., 2012). At the individual level, it brings people closer to the divine, provides emotional support, and serves as a source of meaning. Religion is also interpersonal in nature, creating social bonds and shared values among people who have similar beliefs. At the institutional level, religion provides a form of social control by prescribing certain behaviors that are consistent with the values, norms, and beliefs of that faith and of society. Finally, religion provides a form of social integration, uniting people of a common belief system. Religion brings together people of diverse backgrounds, reaffirms the basic customs and values of a society, and unites people in ways that transcend the individual self.

Some authors contrast religion with the concept of spirituality, with the latter term conceptualized as "the basic feeling of being connected with one's complete self, others, and the entire universe" (Mitroff & Denton, 1999, p. 83). Each person is spiritual on account of being human (Del Rio & White, 2012). Terms associated with spirituality include transcendence, meaning, belonging, connection to a higher power, authentic self, and self-actualization (Milliman, Gatling, & Bradley-Geist, 2017). Authors who distinguish between the two concepts often view religion as being structured and organized, as providing external controls, and as being divisive. On the other hand, spirituality is broad and inclusive, providing inner peace, and being the ultimate end in itself (Mitroff & Denton, 1999). For example, one CEO in Mitroff and Denton's study explained, "Not only do you not have to be religious in order to be spiritual, but it probably helps if you are not religious, especially if you want your spirituality to grow and be a basic part of your life" (p. 87).

Whereas some, such as the aforementioned CEO, clearly distinguish between religion and spirituality, others note the connectedness between the two constructs (Koenig et al., 2012), particularly when it comes to the work environment (Chan-Serafin, Brief, & George, 2013). In fact, Bailey (2001) asserted that "a meaningful conversation about spirituality sans religion is dubious" (p. 367). I adopt a similar position here. Consider, for example, that many of the terms associated with spirituality, such as passion, self-actualization, or virtue (Hicks, 2002), are also associated with many people's religious beliefs. Furthermore, Mitroff and Denton (1999) suggested that spirituality is (a) the basic belief that there is a supreme being that governs the universe; (b) the notion that the higher power affects all things; and (c) the ultimate source of meaning in one's life. Christians, Jews, and Muslims would, for the most part, make similar statements about God and their religious beliefs. Given the similarities between and overlap of the two concepts, in the following discussion, I use the terms religion and religious beliefs.

Interest in the interactions among religion, work, and sport has increased over the past several decades, and this is attributable to a number of factors. First, a large majority of the world's population—84 percent, to be exact—follows some religious belief system (Hackett & McClendon, 2017). Exhibit 10.1 offers an overview of the major religious groups and the number of persons affiliated with them. Most people who identify as religious are Christian, followed by Muslims, Hindus, and Buddhists. In interpreting the data, it is important to note that roughly one in six persons expresses no religious affiliation, which makes them the third largest group, more populous than Catholics.

These statistics are important because religion can influence people's values, attitudes, and behaviors—effects observed at the individual, interpersonal, and group levels (Durkheim, 1965; Spilka, Hood, Hunsberger, & Gorsuch, 2018). Religious ceremonies are held for major life events, such as birth, death, marriage, and certain birthdays. Religious tenets influence what is permissible within particular cultures, as well as the laws and policies regulating these practices. Examples include same-sex marriage, divorce, the sale of alcohol on Sundays, holidays observed, and the hours during which some businesses are open. People have used their religious beliefs to justify everything from engaging in violence to pursuing equal rights to engaging in efforts to disassemble social stratification (Edwards, Christerson, & Emerson, 2013; Hinojosa, 2014). Collectively, these factors suggest that (a) people in leadership positions are likely to subscribe to a particular religious belief system, and (b) religion has the potential to influence a person's life meaningful; thus, these leaders' attitudes and behaviors are probably shaped, at least in part, by religious tenets.

The changing nature of work has affected the emphasis on religion in the work environment (Benefiel, Fry, & Geigle, 2014). As noted in Chapter 1, sport organizations have undergone meaningful changes. Corporate scandals have eroded

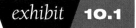

exhibit 10.1   Religious Beliefs around the World, 2015, in Billions

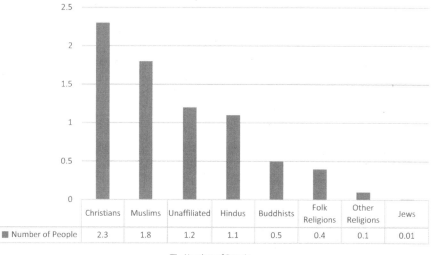

	Christians	Muslims	Unaffiliated	Hindus	Buddhists	Folk Religions	Other Religions	Jews
■ Number of People	2.3	1.8	1.2	1.1	0.5	0.4	0.1	0.01

■ Number of People

Source: Hackett & McClendon (2017).

employees' trust in upper management. Changing technologies and organizational restructuring have resulted in downsizing and variations in the nature of work. The loyalty previously offered by organizations to employees is perceived to be weaker than it once was, making work life uncertain. Despite these negative changes, people are spending more time at work now than they ever have before. Time spent away from home in other activities, such as attending social gatherings, has decreased, while the hours spent at work have increased. This dynamic causes people to seek greater meaning in their lives, a quest that often leads to greater integration of religious and work identities (Osman-Gani, Hashim, & Ismail, 2013). As they seek greater meaning, employees are likely to merge their religious beliefs, values, and identities into their work (Lynn, Naughton, & Vander Veen, 2010). Thus, for many employees, the two identities are no longer separate, and religion is no longer viewed as something to be kept out of the workplace. For example, the Christian Faculty Network is found on many college campuses and serves as a social network for university faculty and staff of the Christian faith.

RELIGION IN THE WORK ENVIRONMENT

Researchers have shown that people can face access and treatment discrimination (Greenhaus, Parasuraman, & Wormley, 1990) based on their religious traditions. As one example, Ghumman and Jackson (2010) collected data from 219 Muslim women in the US. The researchers asked about the women's experiences and expectations of receiving job offers. They found that women who wore a hijab had significantly lower expectations of receiving a job offer, relative to women who did not wear that religious attire. Contact with clients moderated this relationship, as job offer expectations were lowest among women who wore hijabs and would interact regularly with customers.

Whereas Ghumman and Jackson (2010) focused on anticipated access discrimination, Ghumman and Ryan (2013) conducted a study to examine evidence of access discrimination through employer behaviors. They conducted a field experiment where women applied for jobs and did so while wearing a hijab or not. The authors suspected that the presence of a hijab would signal the applicant's Muslim religious tradition and thus activate stigmatized responses. They found that women wearing a hijab, relative to those who were not, were less likely to be given permission to complete a job application and were less likely to get a job call back. Ghumman and Ryan also found evidence of treatment discrimination, as women wearing a hijab experienced more negativity and perceived less interest from the employer.

Ghumman and colleagues are not the only scholars to observe access discrimination. Wallace, Wright, and Hyde (2014) conducted a field experiment in the US and found that applicants who expressed their religious identity were 26 percent less likely than their counterparts to get a call back. Thus, the presence of any religious affiliation in the application process hurt the job applicants. The pattern was strongest among Muslims, pagans, and atheists, less strong among evangelical Christians and Catholics, and Jews did not experience discrimination in the study.

Given the pattern of findings, some readers might conclude that job applicants should take steps to conceal their religious identities. However, as shown in Box 10.1, there is an increasing evidence that such an approach would be misguided.

Researchers have also uncovered evidence of treatment discrimination on the job. Tejeda (2015), for instance, conducted two studies, with a focus on Pagans in the US. He found that Pagans experienced discrimination at work, including victimization, and as a result, also expressed lower levels of job satisfaction than did people from other religious traditions. In another study, King and Ahmad (2010) found that Muslim women in traditional dress experienced subtle forms of bias, such as less smiling, eye contact, and helpfulness from others. As a final example, Scheitle and Ecklund (2017) analyzed data from over 16,000 people who took part in a US-based study. Results showed that although most people did not experience religious discrimination, a sizeable portion did. Muslim, Hindu, Jewish, and atheist respondents were all more likely to report discrimination than were others. In the US, people who follow these religious traditions are religious minorities. The researchers also found that the more religion was a topic of conversation at work, the more likely people were to report experiencing discrimination. This pattern remained even after taking into account other religious-oriented factors.

In Box 10.2, I outline the follies of such discriminatory practices.

Box 10.1 Professional Perspectives: Disclosing Your Religious Identity

Afra Ahmad, Isaac Sabat, and Eden King are experts in the area of identity management. They have conducted a number of studies focusing on if and how job applicants disclose potentially stigmatizing identities, as well as the outcomes of those decisions.

In one of their studies, participants listened to a person seeking a job application at a retail store. During the exchange, the job seeker's religious traditions were disclosed, and they either attempted to openly discuss or conceal their Christian, Jewish, or Muslim identity. The study participants rated the interactions more positively when the religion was openly discussed. They followed this study up with another, and again, they found that participants rated the applicant more positively when religion was openly discussed. In both studies, the positive attitudes were consistent across the specific religious traditions.

In discussing these findings, and those of related studies, Ahmad, Sabat, and King noted,

These results suggest that employees— even those with often-stigmatized identities—can reap benefits by being open and authentic about themselves. When people communicate their true identities, they tend to elicit more positive reactions from others, are more liked and trusted, and have more opportunities for support from their coworkers.

(Ahmad, Sabat, & King, 2018)

Box 10.2 Alternative Perspectives: The Strengths of Religiosity

There are numerous wrongs associated with religious-based discrimination in the sport work environment. Among them is the real possibility that such practices hurt the workplace. As Ghumman and Ryan (2018) noted, being religious is linked with a number of behaviors and attitudes that employers value. The authors observed that religion is linked with well-being and physical health, positive job attitudes, desired work outcomes, and decreased stress. Thus, when employers discriminate against religious people, not only are they breaking the law and violating norms of ethical conduct, but they are also denying opportunities to people who would likely add value to the sport organization.

MULTILEVEL EXPLANATIONS

Drawing from the model I presented in Chapter 4, in this chapter, I outline various factors associated with religious discrimination in the sport work environment. In doing so, I focus on macro-level (i.e., employment laws, structural stigma, and presence of similar others), meso-level (i.e., bias in decision-making and the workplace culture), and micro-level factors (demographics, religious identity, and psychological characteristics; see Exhibit 10.2).

Macro-Level Factors

Macro-level factors are those operating at the societal level. Employment laws, structural stigma, and the presence of similar others all have meaningful effects.

Employment Laws

Countries around the world have laws prohibiting discrimination against employees or job applicants based on their religious beliefs or traditions. In Spain, for example, the *Real Decreto Legislativo 2/2015, de 23 de octubre, Estatuto de los Trabajadores* offers employment protections on the basis of gender, racial and ethnic origin, religion or beliefs, disability, age, and sexual orientation (Cachón, 2017). In the US, employment protections are guided by Title VII of the Civil Rights Act of 1964. I offer an overview of the law's protections in Exhibit 10.3.

These laws are designed to protect people from mistreatment based on their religious beliefs and traditions. However, discrimination still occurs. In the US, the Equal Employment Opportunity Commission reported that in 2017, the agency received 3,436 complaints of religious discrimination. This figure is only a fraction of the number of claims filed in other categories. In 2017, the EEOC recovered $11.2 million in damages for individuals claiming religious discrimination.

exhibit **10.2** Multilevel Explanations for the Influence of Religion in the Sport Work Environment

Macro-level factors: Those operating at the societal level, including employment laws, structural stigma, and presence of similar others.

Meso-level factors: Those operating at the team and organizational levels, including bias in decision-making, organizational culture, and leadership.

Micro-level factors: Those operating at the individual level, including demographics, religious identity, and psychological characteristics.

exhibit **10.3** Religious-Based Employment Protections under Title VII

Discrimination on the basis of religion is prohibited by Title VII of the Civil Rights Act of 1964. Under this law:

- Employers cannot treat people more or less favorably because of their religious affiliation.

- Employers cannot force employees to participate in religious ceremonies or prayers as a condition of employment. This issue often arises in the context of team prayers.

- Employers must accommodate their employees' sincerely held religious beliefs unless doing so would cause undue hardship to the employer. Reasonable accommodations include flexible work hours and the ability to exchange working assignments with other employees. Unreasonable accommodations are those that impose hardships on other employees, jeopardize workplace safety, or decrease efficiency.

- Employers cannot restrict an employee's religious expression any more than other forms of expression that might have a comparable effect. For example, an employer may not restrict personal, silent prayers when they do not negatively impact performance.

- Employers must take all reasonable steps to prevent religious harassment in the workplace.

Structural Stigma

Recall from previous chapters that people who are stigmatized "have (or are believed to have) an attribute that marks them as different and leads them to be devalued in the eyes of others" (Major & O'Brien, 2005, p. 395). Stigmas are culturally and time bound, can be visible or invisible, can be controllable or not, and are associated with appearance, behavior, or membership in a group (Major & O'Brien, 2005). Hatzenbuehler (2017) articulated how stigmas can occur at the societal level by way of policies, norms, and cultural expectations, representing a form of structural stigma.

In the US, structural stigma disadvantages persons from various religious traditions, including Muslims, atheists, and the religiously unaffiliated (Casey, 2018; Cooper & Miltra, 2018). For example, Coopera and Miltra found that African Americans who disengaged from the church faced stigma and backlash from others. As a result, they developed coping strategies as a way of maintaining good relationships with loved ones, engaging in self-care, and protecting themselves from attacks from others. Samari (2016) outlined the health effects of Islamophobia. Samari suggested that stress and identity concealment, negative interpersonal relationships, institutional policies, and media coverage all negatively affected Muslims' health and well-being. The same processes have the potential to negatively affect people who differ from the religious majority and their prospects of quality work in the sport environment.

Presence of Similar Others

People's surroundings are likely to influence the religious traditions they follow and their consumer behaviors. As a testament to the influence of culture and similarly minded others, most people (73 percent) live in a region where their religious group makes up the majority of the population (Pew Research Center, 2012). This association is particularly strong among Hindus, as 97 percent of all Hindus live in the three countries where Hindus are the majority: India, Nepal, and Mauritius. Most Christians (87 percent), Muslims (73 percent), and persons who express no affiliation (71 percent) also live in countries where the majority of residents share their religious beliefs.

With respect to consumer behavior, some customers prefer to patronize organizations that profess to conduct their business practices in line with a specific set of religious principles (Hirschman & Touzani, 2016). This behavior can incentivize business owners not only to develop structures and missions consistent with such belief systems but also to advertise and promote these links. As an example, the goal of the website Christian Owned & Operated (www. christianownedandoperated.com) is to allow businesses in Houston, Texas, and the surrounding area to promote their Christian ties. Organizations listed in the directory agree to the following:

> We are a *Christian Owned and Operated Business* who believes Jesus Christ came into this world as God's one and only son, to forgive us of our sins and give everlasting life to those who accept him as their Lord and Savior. We operate our business under the same guiding principles taught by Jesus Christ.
>
> (emphasis in original)

Several sport organizations are listed, including Trinity Wellness, New Life Fitness, and Texas Spirit Cheer Company, to name a few. Promotional networks are not limited to Christian-based organizations—other websites support or promote organizations following Buddhist principles (such as Buddhist Business Network, www.buddhistbusiness.com) and Jewish businesses (such as the Jewish Business Network of Southern New Jersey, www.jbnsnj.org), among others.

Meso-Level Factors

Meso-level factors are those operating at the interpersonal and organizational levels. In the context of the discussion of religion, bias in decision-making, organizational culture, and leadership are particularly salient.

Bias

Religious dissimilarity can influence the categorization process and ultimately, the prejudice and discrimination decision-makers express. People's religious beliefs can shape how they see themselves and others. Recall from Chapter 2 and the discussion of the social categorization framework that people categorize themselves and others into social groups.

Burris and Jackson (2000), for instance, suggested that "religion has been numbered—along with gender, ethnicity and nationality—among the core social categories around which an individual's social identity is organized" (p. 257). Later, Weeks and Vincent (2007) showed empirically that people spontaneously categorize the self and others with a religious dimension. As these authors noted, "An individual's religious beliefs serve as a dominant schema, acting as a filter and organizer as they view the world" (p. 318).

The categorization process can influence decision-making processes. Van Camp, Sloan, and El Bassiouny (2016) found that about a third of the raters noticed an applicant's religious background when such information was presented on in an application packet. Many of the raters reported using such information to make their decisions, and the proportion who indicated as much was considerably higher than the corresponding number of raters who used the applicant's race. Consistent with the information I have previously presented, participants in Van Camp et al.'s study penalized Muslims and atheists more than they did Christians.

Categorization of the self and others based on religion may have a number of potential outcomes beyond selection. First, consistent with the social categorization perspective outlined in Chapter 2, people who differ religiously from the majority might have poor work experiences. Indeed, I observed as much in a study of NCAA athletic administrators, as people who differed religiously from others in the department perceived that their values differed—that is, they had different ideas about what is right, good, or valuable (Cunningham, 2010). These effects were particularly pronounced when religion was important to the individual (i.e., when the religious personal identity was strong). Persons who perceived that they differed from others based on their religion and values were also less satisfied with their jobs than were their coworkers. These outcomes were present even after accounting for other factors, such as the person's age, gender, and race.

Another outcome of religious categorization is integration into a group. Ragins (2008) recounted the story of a Jewish professor at a Catholic university:

> My mother told me not to take a job at a Catholic university. She told me they'd fire me once they found out I'm Jewish. I thought she was so old school, until my first day on the job. The ex-Dean told me that he moved from a neighborhood because "there were too many Jews there." I decided not to tell anyone I was Jewish. But then my colleagues became my friends, and one day I found myself putting up Christmas ornaments before they came over. I was denying who I was in my very own home. So I decided to come out of the "Jewish closet" at work. I found out later that the Provost kept a list of the Jewish faculty. He added me to the list. (p. 194)

As this story illustrates, people's religious beliefs can influence how others see them, the manner in which they interact with others, and how well they integrate into a social group. Bias also affects how willing people are to work with others who are religiously different, particularly when the perceiver is highly religious (King, McKay, & Stewart, 2014).

Religious categorization can influence fan behavior, as illustrated in Box 10.3.

Box 10.3 Diversity in the Field: Religion and Soccer

Soccer is the most popular sport in the world, and its supporters are the most fanatical. This is especially the case in Ireland with the rivalry between Glasgow's premier soccer clubs, Rangers F.C. and Celtic F.C. *Sports Illustrated* columnist Grant Wahl (1999) described the rivalry as "a purity of hatred that involved politics, class, and above all, religion." Most Rangers supporters are Protestant, whereas Celtic supporters are largely Catholic. For years, the players on the teams reflected these religious divisions, and for years, violence has erupted between the rival teams' fans. In fact, stabbings and bar fights in Glasgow are routinely investigated for Celtic-Rangers links. The players embody disdain for the other team's religious links. Rangers forward Paul Gascoigne once celebrated a goal against Celtic by mimicking a flute player — his way of commemorating William of Orange's victory over the Catholics at the Battle of the Boyne in 1690. Similarly, Celtic players find special meaning in crossing themselves when they score against their rivals. As this case illustrates, religious affiliation and categorization influence the dynamics among soccer fans and players.

Organizational Culture

Schein (2004) defined organizational culture as "a pattern of shared basic assumptions ... that has worked well enough to be considered valid and, therefore, to be taught to new members as the correct ways to perceive, think, and feel in relation to those problems" (p. 17). The culture of a sport organization can influence the access people have to positions and the quality of their work while employed. For example, in a culture of similarity (Doherty & Chelladurai, 1999), organizational decision-makers value those who have similar thoughts and perspectives as they do. Such a mind-set could influence any applicant who differs from the decision-makers in their religious or spiritual beliefs.

Artifacts represent a key component of culture. These refer to, for example, the banner and trophies displayed, pictures on the walls, decorations, and layout of the workspace. Beane, Ponnapalli, and Viswesvaran (2017) examined the influence of religious artifacts displayed during religious holidays. The researchers found that study participants valued the individual's ability to express their religiosity—a component of the individuated self central to inclusiveness, as discussed in Chapter 1—but they were turned off by organizational expressions of religion, such as through Christmas decorations. In fact, organizational attractiveness ratings decreased significantly when the participants learned of organization's displaying holiday artifacts.

In other cases, the culture of the team or unit might conflict with that of the larger organization, creating tensions for all involved. For example, Nite, Singer, and I examined the culture of a university athletic department and how it aligned with the broader, religious-based mission of the university (Nite, Singer, & Cunningham, 2013). We found that athletic administrators and coaches sought to fulfill the university's religious-based mission. They also noted, however, the real pressures to win and lead successful programs. The competing logics and cultures sometimes conflicted with one another. The different priorities resulted in conflicts in scheduling, coaches' time and commitments, and the promotion of both cultures.

Leadership

Leaders frequently draw from their spiritual and religious positions to inform the decisions they make, their influence on followers, and the path on which they lead the organization (Gotsis & Grimani, 2017; Joelle & Coelho, in press; Pawar, 2014). Conceptually, it is reasonable to assume that people's religious beliefs can influence their decisions across life contexts—for example, the partner they seek in life; the social organizations in which they are involved; and, in the workplace, the strategic decision-making in which they engage. A number of factors are likely to influence whether this occurs. Religious identity is one such factor, as the influence of religious beliefs on decision-making is likely to be stronger when religious beliefs are central to the person's identity. Organizational context is another influential factor, as it is possible for a leader to have strong religious beliefs but, because of the organizational culture in place, not be at liberty to express those beliefs at work or turn to them in the decision-making process.

A number of examples from sport illustrate how religion can influence strategic decision-making. Brigham Young University is an institution affiliated with the Church of Jesus Christ of Latter-Day Saints; in fact, it is named after the second president of the church. The university follows Latter-Day Saints principles, which require that university athletic teams not participate in events on Sundays. This requirement certainly impacts the university's athletic scheduling practices and has influenced other entities, as well. When the university's basketball teams play in the NCAA national tournament, they are always placed in those team brackets that play on Thursdays and Saturdays, rather than the men's alternative Friday and Sunday brackets.

As another example, prayer is a common occurrence at high school football games, particularly those held in the southern US. These prayers are unconstitutional when led by coaches and athletic administrators, but they occur nonetheless and are broadcast over the public address system at events (Geier & Blankenship, 2017). There are cultural influences, as the South is generally considered the most religious part of the US; however, there is also evidence that athletic directors' religious beliefs factor into these decisions. Miller, Lee, and Martin (2013) found that nearly all athletic directors (90 percent) indicated that their religious beliefs influenced their decision-making at work, a high proportion indicated that their athletic teams had team-only prayers prior to the games, and few (30 percent) considered the legal ramifications of their actions.

In addition to examining the role of religion and spirituality on leaders' choices, other scholars have examined leadership styles linked with religious and spiritual tenets. Most of this work, however, has adopted a Western approach to religion, focusing on Christian or Jewish principles (Kriger & Seng, 2005; Whittington, Pitts, Kageler, & Goodwin, 2005). Missing from this dialog is attention to Eastern religious beliefs. Eisenbeiss (2012) addressed this shortcoming by drawing from the religious and ethical teachings of the world's major religions to develop an integrative framework. She suggested that ethical leaders have four central orientations: human, justice, responsibility and sustainability, and moderation (see Exhibit 10.4 for definitions of each). Leaders who express these orientations are likely to engender trust among followers and customers, which should, ultimately, result in improved organizational success.

Another leadership style with religious overtones is that of servant leadership (van Dierendonck, 2011). Servant leaders recognize their moral responsibility not only to their organization but also to their followers, customers, and others with a stake in the organization. The moral compass that servant leaders use is what separates them from other leaders. Servant leaders focus on empowering others, are humble, demonstrate authenticity, create an environment where people feel safe, clearly demonstrate to followers what is expected of them, and act as both role models and caretakers (van Dierendonck, 2011). Recognizing the value of such characteristics, Burton, Welty Peachey, and Wells (2017) argued that more servant leaders are needed in sport organizations, as they would have the potential to transform the sport setting. Specifically, servant leaders would develop organizational cultures of trust and helping behaviors; their followers would work collaboratively with one another; and, as a result, the sport organization would

exhibit   **10.4**   Orientations of Ethical Leaders

The four orientations of ethical leaders, as proposed by Eisenbeiss (2012).

- **Human orientation:** refers to the belief that all people should be treated with dignity and respect, rather than as a means to an end. This orientation is expressed in the full recognition of people's rights and concern with their well-being.
- **Justice orientation:** refers to the mind-set of making fair, consistent decisions that do not privilege one group over another. This orientation is expressed through a concern for fairness and diversity, and an opposition to discrimination.
- **Responsibility and sustainability:** refers to the leader's focus on long-term success, as well as the concern for society and the environment. This orientation is expressed in a sense of obligation to the company and community, the long-term viability of the organization, and recognition that her or his actions have the potential to impact the environment and future generations.
- **Moderation orientation:** refers to the leader's humility, restraint, and self-control. This orientation is reflected in the leader's temperance, humbleness, and ability to balance organizational objectives with stakeholder interests.

thrive (see also Parris & Peachey, 2013). The authors also suspected that external pressures for ethical decision-making would result in more leaders adopting a servant leadership mind-set.

Micro-Level Factors

Micro-level factors are those at the individual level. These include demographics, religious identity, and psychological characteristics.

Demographics

One's demographics are linked with a number of religious outcomes, including the religious tradition one follows. The Pew Research Center data (Religious Landscape Study, n.d.) offer an extensive analysis of this topic. In 2014, researchers collected data from over 35,000 people in all 50 states in the US. Drawing from this dataset, I examine how demographics are related to affiliation with Evangelical Protestants, Mormons, Muslims, and atheists. As seen in Exhibit 10.5, there are many demographic differences. Atheists and Muslims, for example, have a larger share of 18- to 29-year olds and a larger share of men than do Evangelical

Demographics and Religious Affiliation in the US, 2014   *exhibit* **10.5**

Item	Atheist (%)	Evangelical Protestant (%)	Mormon (%)	Muslim (%)
Age (years)				
18–29	40	17	22	44
30–49	37	33	40	37
50–64	14	29	22	13
65 and older	9	20	16	5
Gender				
Women	32	55	56	35
Men	68	45	46	65
Race				
African American	3	6	1	28
Asian	7	2	1	28
Latino	10	11	8	4
White	78	76	85	38
Other	2	5	5	3
Immigration Status				
Immigrants	13	9	7	64
Second generation	13	7	7	17
Third generation or higher	74	84	86	18
Household Income				
Less than $30,000	24	35	27	34
$30,000–$49,999	18	22	20	17
$50,000–$99,999	28	28	33	29
$100,000 or more	30	14	20	20
Educational Attainment				
High school or less	26	43	27	36
Some college	31	35	40	25
College	26	14	23	23
Postgraduate degree	16	7	10	17

Source: Religious Landscape Study (n.d.).

Protestants or Muslims. Whites represent at least three out of every four Atheists, Evangelical Protestants, and Mormons, but only 38 percent of Muslims. Immigrants represent a substantially higher share of Muslims (64 percent) than they do the other groups. Fifty-eight percent of atheists and 53 percent of Mormons have a household income of at least $50,000—figures higher than those of Evangelical Protestants or Muslims. Finally, 43 percent of Evangelical Protestants have a high school diploma or less as their highest level of education, and this figure is higher than the other comparison groups.

In addition, demographic characteristics can influence opportunities and experiences. Recall from Chapter 2 and the discussion of intersectionality that people's personal characteristics frequently interact to predict subsequent outcomes (hooks, 2000). Importantly, intersectionality scholars do not adhere to additive effects of various identities, but instead focus on the qualitative effects of multiple differences. As Watson and Scraton (2013) explain, "It moves beyond an additive approach that deals with fixed, static concepts of gender, race, class and looks at inequalities at the intersections and at how they are routed through each other with no single cause" (p. 37). Intersectionality is important in the context of religion and discrimination, as it is possible that members of underrepresented groups are doubly impacted when they also adhere to a religious tradition that is stigmatized. For example, racial minorities who are Muslim are likely to face barriers because of their race, their religious tradition, and the combination of the two. This example might also explain why Westerners commonly conflate Islam with race (Desmond-Harris, 2017).

Religious Identity

People who hold the same religious beliefs might differ in the degree to which they identify with that religion. Religious identity reflects the importance religion plays in people's lives, including their self-concept, self-image, and how they think about themselves (Ladd, 2007; Markus, 1977; see also Brewer, 1991).

Religious identities are important for a number of reasons. First, as discussed in Chapter 1, personal identities, like religious identity, serve as an important part of people's individuated selves. It is what makes them unique, and the ability to express personal identities in the workplace is key to have an inclusive work environment (Shore et al., 2011). Second, the negative effects of being different from others in a sport work environment are amplified when the individual's religious identity is high. I found as much in the previously discussed study of athletic administrators (Cunningham, 2010). Other researchers have found that employees who are religious minorities and whose religious personal identity is high are considerably more likely than their peers to face mistreatment in the workplace (Padela, Adam, Ahmad, Hosseinian, & Curlin, 2016).

Finally, religious and spiritual identities can influence behaviors. For example, Vitell et al. (2016) collected data from well-educated young adults in five countries. They found that as their spiritual identity increased, so too did their ethical dispositions. The relationship was stronger as the internalization of the moral identity increased. In another study, Hertz and Krettenauer (2016) aggregated data from 111 previous studies to investigate the relationship between a moral identity and moral behaviors, such as prosocial behavior and ethical behavior. They found that as moral identity increased, so too did moral behavior, and the effects were stronger in countries with a predominantly individualistic culture.

Psychological Factors

Psychological factors can also influence the role of religion in the sport work environment. One prominent factor is religious fundamentalism, or the steadfast set of beliefs that there is one set of inerrant teaching (truths) about people and their relationship with a deity (Altemeyer & Hunsberger, 1992). Religious fundamentalists believe there is one true path to the deity and one correct set of teachings. They are likely to reject people who deviate from these beliefs. Evidence suggests that it is religious fundamentalism, not religion *per se*, that is associated with categorization and prejudice toward others (Johnson et al., 2011; Schaafsma & Williams, 2012). These patterns remain across religious traditions (Kunst, Thomsen, & Sam, 2014).

Melton and I have observed the effects of religious fundamentalism on bias toward sexual minorities. In our first study, we found that as parents' religious fundamentalism increased, so too did their prejudice toward lesbian, gay, and bisexual coaches (Cunningham & Melton, 2012). These effects were particularly strong for Whites, Asians, and Latinos. In our next study, we observed a strong relationship between fundamentalism and sexual prejudice (Cunningham & Melton, 2013). Importantly, though, we also found that contact with lesbian and gay persons affected this relationship: when the participants had lesbian and gay friends, the relationship between fundamentalism and sexual prejudice was negated. These findings show that, while religious fundamentalism is generally associated with bias, its effects can be offset.

Other researchers have focused on psychological factors that promote an openness to different religious traditions. One such characteristic intellectual humility, or "having an accurate view of one's intellectual strengths and weaknesses, as well as the ability to negotiate different ideas in an interpersonally respectful manner" (Hook et al., 2015, p. 499). Hook et al. (2017) found that, as one's intellectual humility increased, so too did their tolerance of diverse religious views. The relationship was particularly strong when the people had been around others who held different views. Results also show the benefits of being around people who are different—something researchers refer to as intergroup contact. That is, when people are around others with different views or beliefs, learning takes place, and anxiety and prejudice are likely to decrease.

RELIGION, SPORT, AND PHYSICAL ACTIVITY

Religious beliefs affect sport participants in two ways. First, religion influences who participates in sport and their reasons for doing so. Second, some athletes rely on their religious beliefs while participating.

People's religious beliefs can influence their healthy eating habits, physical activity, and sport participation (Kim & Sobal, 2004; Merrill & Thygerson, 2001). Sage and Eitzen (2016) provided a historical account of the issue. According to them, primitive societies used sport and physical activity to defeat their foes, influence supernatural forces, or increase crop and livestock fertility. The ancient Greeks employed sport in a religious context. In fact, the early Olympics were a religious performance intended to please Zeus. In contrast to these cultures' use of sport in various religious capacities, according to Eitzen and Sage, early 17th-century Puritans viewed sport as antithetical to Christian ideals. Eitzen and Sage noted that no Christian group opposed sport and sport participation more than the Puritans. Opposition to sport was largely maintained by Christian churches in North America until the 20th century. Subsequently, however, changes in the US—industrialization, urbanization, and an awareness of the health benefits of sport and physical activity—resulted in a more positive relationship between sport and religion. Consequently, some churches now include sport in their social programs, and attendees are often actively involved in sport and physical activity (Lindsey, Kay, Jeanes, & Banda, 2017).

Other religions also influence decisions about who participates in sport and their reasons for participating. For example, Walseth and Fasting (2003) found that Egyptian women's participation in sport and physical activity was largely shaped by their Islamic beliefs (for further discussion, see Toffoletti & Palmer, 2017). The women in their study believed that Islam called for people to be physically active for various reasons, including to care for their overall health and to be ready in case of war. Because Islam says that women may participate in sport as long as the sport movements are not exciting for men who might watch them, the extent to which the women participated in sport and physical activity depended on whether they adopted a more modern or more traditional view of Islam. Women who adopted a more modern view of Islam considered most activities (not including gymnastics, dancing, and aerobics) appropriate and not likely to excite men. Women with a more traditional view felt that all sport forms were inappropriate unless the sport was conducted in sex-segregated venues. Because such venues were limited in Egypt, so was their sport participation.

From a different perspective, some people use their religious beliefs to give meaning to their sport participation and cope with the related pressures. Though research in this area is generally scarce, Coakley (2015) suggested that there are seven reasons why athletes use religion (see Exhibit 10.6).

Athletes use religion as a way of coping with the anxiety-producing uncertainty that is a fact of life in many sports, whether the uncertainty pertains to the risk of bodily harm, pressure to perform well, or not knowing whether they will be traded or cut from a team. Some athletes use prayer, scriptures, meditation, or other religious rituals to reduce this anxiety. Athletes may also use religion as a way of keeping out of trouble. As previously discussed, individuals who hold strong religious beliefs may behave differently from those who do not. Their beliefs also provide focus in their lives. Thus, even in environments that offer temptations

According to Coakley (2015), athletes use religion for one or more of the following reasons:

- Reduce anxiety
- Keep away from trouble
- Give meaning to sport participation
- Gain perspective
- Increase team unity
- Maintain social control
- Achieve personal success

to behave in ways contrary to their beliefs, some athletes return to their religious traditions for inspiration and guidance.

Athletes also use religion to give personal meaning to their sport participation. Athletes spend countless hours training and practicing. Even in team sports, the focus is primarily on the self and improving individual performance. How do people rationalize spending so much time focusing on the self or, from another perspective, so much time focusing on sport in general? Athletes of faith often consider sport participation an act of worship, bringing glory to God. In addition, some athletes use religion to keep their sport participation in perspective. If an athlete perceives that her participation is part of God's calling, then facing challenges in sport becomes easier. The athlete does not become so consumed by sports that she is overwhelmed by its challenges and the failures that regularly occur in that context.

Religion is also used to increase team unity. Former National Football League coach George Allen commented that religion and prayer united teammates like no other factor he witnessed as a coach (Coakley, 2015). In a related way, some coaches use religion as a way of motivating and controlling their athletes. Given that most religious traditions emphasize following commands and being obedient to those in control, coaches might use religious tenets to persuade athletes to obey team rules.

Finally, some athletes use religious beliefs as a means to improve performance. While this might take the form of praying for specific wins, many athletes will pray that they perform to the best of their ability, and if success comes as a result, then so be it. Other athletes pray as a way of showing their gratitude for their athletic abilities. The latter kind of prayer expresses gratitude for performance rather than petitioning for success.

CHAPTER SUMMARY

T his chapter focused on the intersection of religion and sport. Unlike other, more visible diversity dimensions, an individual's religious beliefs are generally not known to others unless they are disclosed. Nevertheless, as the Diversity Challenge illustrates, religious beliefs have the potential to affect people's actions, preferences, and beliefs substantially. Religious beliefs also influence strategic decision-making, organizational practices, and marketing efforts. Having read this chapter, you should be able to:

1. Define religion and spirituality.

    Religion represents a set of beliefs and practices related to sacred things that unite all those who adhere to them (Durkheim, 1965). The influence of religion is seen at the individual, interpersonal, institutional, and social integration levels. Spirituality is the feeling of connectedness and unity with others and the universe (Mitroff & Denton, 1999).

2. Describe the manner in which religion influences access and treatment discrimination.

    People face access and treatment discrimination based on their religious beliefs. The available research evidence suggests Muslims, atheists, and the religiously unaffiliated are likely to experience mistreatment, especially when visible markers of their religious tradition (e.g., wearing a hijab) are present.

3. Summarize the multilevel factors that influence the effects of religion in the work environment.

    Various factors influence the opportunities and experiences for religious minorities. Macro-level factors include employment laws, structural stigma, and presence of similar others. At the meso-level, bias in decision-making, organizational culture, and leadership are salient. Finally, micro-level factors include demographics, religious identity, and psychological characteristics.

4. Paraphrase the manner in which religion influences opportunities and experiences of sport and physical activity participants.

    Religious beliefs influence how and why people participate in sport. Sport participants use religion to (a) reduce anxiety, (b) avoid trouble, (c) give meaning to sport participation, (d) gain perspective, (e) increase team unity, (f) serve as a source of control, and (g) achieve personal success.

Questions FOR DISCUSSION

1. Some people distinguish between religion and spirituality. Do you? If so, what do you feel are the major differences between religion and spirituality? If not, how are the two concepts similar?

2. Is the influence of religion on organizational practices stronger or weaker in sport than it is in other contexts? Why or why not?

3. How much should a person's religious beliefs influence the decisions one makes on behalf of an organization, such as its strategic path? Why?

4. In your experience, how much do athletes rely on their religious beliefs while participating in sport? What is the primary reason for this reliance?

LEARNING Activities

1. The courts have consistently ruled that public school coaches cannot lead their teams in prayer. Divide the class into two groups and debate the issue. Would the arguments be the same if the person leading the prayer was the instructor of this class?

2. As an outside assignment, interview current and former athletes about the degree to which they incorporated religion into their playing careers. If they did, in what ways was it incorporated, and what were the outcomes of doing so?

Web RESOURCES

Fellowship of Christian Athletes, www.fca.org

> An organization that challenges coaches and players to use sport to spread their Christian faith.

Jewish Community Centers Association of North America, www.jcca.org

> An organization that helps its affiliates offer education, Jewish identity-building, and cultural and recreational programs for persons of all ages and backgrounds.

Athletes in Action, www.athletesinaction.org

> An international organization that uses sport competition as a way for athletes to spread their Christian faith.

READING Resources

Benn, T., Pfister, G., & Jawad, H. (Eds.) (2010). *Muslim women and sport.* London, UK: Routledge.

> An edited book that offers a conceptual framework for understanding the sport and physical activity experiences of Muslim women; contains contributions from women and men, as well as Muslims and non-Muslims.

Spilka, B., Hood, R. W., Jr., Hunsberger, B., & Gorsuch, R. (2018). *The psychology of religion: An empirical approach* (5th ed.). New York, NY: Guilford.

> Provides a comprehensive analysis of the psychology of religion; research-focused text.

Koenig, H., King, D., & Carson, V. B. (2012). *Handbook of religion and health.* Oxford, UK: Oxford University Press.

> A comprehensive collection of chapters offering an overview of religion and spirituality, and their effects on people's health and well-being.

REFERENCES

Ahmad, A., Sabat, I., & King, E. (2018). Research: The upsides of disclosing your religion, sexual orientation, or parental status at work. *Harvard Business Review*. Retrieved from https://hbr.org/2018/03/research-the-upsides-of-disclosing-your-religion-sexual-orientation-or-parental-status-at-work

Altemeyer, B., & Hunsberger, B. E. (1992). Authoritarianism, religious fundamentalism, quest, and prejudice. *International Journal for the Psychology of Religion, 2*, 113–133.

Bailey, J. R. (2001). Book review of J. A. Conger and associates: Spirit at work: Discovering the spirituality in leadership. *The Leadership Quarterly, 12*, 367–368.

Beane, D., Ponnapalli, A., & Viswesvaran, C. (2017). Workplace religious displays and perceptions of organization attractiveness. *Employee Responsibilities and Rights Journal, 29*(2), 73–88.

Benefiel, M., Fry, L. W., & Geigle, D. (2014). Spirituality and religion in the workplace: History, theory, and research. *Psychology of Religion and Spirituality, 6*, 175–187.

Brewer, M. B. (1991). The social self: On being the same and different at the same time. *Personality and Social Psychology Bulletin, 17*, 475–482.

Bruce, S. (2011). Defining religion: A practical response. *International Review of Sociology, 21*, 107–120.

Burris, C. T., & Jackson, L. M. (2000). Social identity and the true believer: Responses to threatened self-stereotypes among the intrinsically religious. *British Journal of Social Psychology, 39*, 257–278.

Burton, L. J., Welty Peachey, J., & Wells, J. E. (2017). The role of servant leadership in developing an ethical climate in sport organizations. *Journal of Sport Management, 31*(3), 229–240.

Cachón, L. (2017). *Country report: Non-discrimination: Spain*. Brussels, Belgium: European Commission.

Casey, P. M. (2018). Stigmatized identities: Too Muslim to be American, too American to be Muslim. *Symbolic Interaction, 41*(1), 100–119.

Chan-Serafin, S., Brief, A. P., & George, J. M. (2013). How does religion matter and why? Religiosity and the organizational sciences. *Organization Science, 24*, 1585–1600.

Coakley, J. (2015). *Sports in society: Issues and controversies* (11th ed.). New York, NY: McGraw-Hill.

Cooper, W. P., & Mitra, R. (2018). Religious disengagement and stigma management by African-American young adults. *Journal of Applied Communication Research, 46*(4), 509-533.

Cunningham, G. B. (2010). The influence of religious personal identity on the relationships among religious dissimilarity, value dissimilarity, and job satisfaction. *Social Justice Research, 23*, 60–76.

Cunningham, G. B., & Melton, N. (2012). Prejudice against lesbian, gay, and bisexual coaches: The influence of race, religious fundamentalism, modern sexism, and contact with sexual minorities. *Sociology of Sport Journal, 29*, 283–305.

Cunningham, G. B., & Melton, E. N. (2013). The moderating effects of contact with lesbian and gay friends on the relationships among religious fundamentalism, sexism, and sexual prejudice. *Journal of Sex Research, 50*, 401–408.

Del Rio, C. M., & White, L. J. (2012). Separating spirituality from religiosity: A hylomorphic attitudinal perspective. *Psychology of Religion and Spirituality, 4*, 123–142.

Desmond-Harris, J. (2017, February). Islam isn't a race. But it still make sense to think of Islamophobias as racism. *Vox*. Retrieved from https://www.vox.com/policy-and-politics/2017/2/2/14452388/

muslim-ban-immigration-order-islamophobia-racism-muslims-hate

Doherty, A. J., & Chelladurai, P. (1999). Managing cultural diversity in sport organizations: A theoretical perspective. *Journal of Sport management, 13*(4), 280–297.

Durkheim, E. (1965). *The elementary forms of religious life*. New York, NY: Free Press.

Edwards, K. L., Christerson, B., & Emerson, M. O. (2013). Race, religious organizations, and integration. *Annual Review of Sociology, 39*, 211–228.

Eisenbeiss, S. A. (2012). Re-thinking ethical leadership: An interdisciplinary integrative approach. *The Leadership Quarterly, 23*(5), 791–808.

Geier, B. A., & Blankenship, A. (2017). Playing for touchdowns: Contemporary law and legislation for prayer in public school athletics. *First Amendment Law Review, 15*, 381–436.

Ghumman, S., & Jackson, L. (2010). The downside of religious attire: The Muslim headscarf and expectations of obtaining employment. *Journal of Organizational Behavior, 31*(1), 4–23.

Ghumman, S., & Ryan, A. M. (2013). Not welcome here: Discrimination towards women who wear the Muslim headscarf. *Human Relations, 66*(5), 671–698.

Ghumman, S., & Ryan, A. M. (2018). Religious group discrimination. In A. J. Colella & E. B. King (Eds.), *The Oxford handbook of workplace discrimination* (pp. 143–158). New York, NY: Oxford University Press.

Gotsis, G., & Grimani, K. (2017). The role of spiritual leadership in fostering inclusive workplaces. *Personnel Review, 46*(5), 908–935.

Greenhaus, J. H., Parasuraman, S., & Wormley, W. M. (1990). Effects of race on organizational experiences, job performance, evaluations, and career outcomes. *Academy of Management Journal, 33*, 64–86.

Hackett, C., & McClendon, D. (2017). Christians remain world's largest religious group, but they are declining in Europe. *Pew Research*. Retrieved from http://www.pewresearch.org/fact-tank/2017/04/05/christians-remain-worlds-largest-religious-group-but-they-are-declining-in-europe/

Hatzenbuehler, M. L. (2017). Structural stigma and health. In B. Major, J. F. Dovidio, & B. G. Link (Eds.), *The Oxford handbook of stigma, discrimination, and health* (pp. 105–121). New York, NY: Oxford University Press.

Hertz, S. G., & Krettenauer, T. (2016). Does moral identity effectively predict moral behavior? A meta-analysis. *Review of General Psychology, 20*(2), 129.

Hicks, D. A. (2002). Spiritual and religious diversity in the workplace: Implications for leadership. *The Leadership Quarterly, 13*, 379–396.

Hinojosa, F. (2014). *Latino Mennonites: Civil rights, faith, and evangelical culture*. Baltimore, MD: Johns Hopkins University Press.

Hirschman, E. C., & Touzani, M. (2016). Contesting religious identity in the marketplace: Consumption ideology and the boycott halal movement. *Journal of Islamic Studies, 4*(1), 19–29.

hooks, b. (2000). *Feminist theory: From margin to center* (2nd ed.). London, UK: Pluto Press.

Hook, J. N., Davis, D. E., Van Tongeren, D. R., Hill, P. C., Worthington, E. L., Jr, Farrell, J. E., & Dieke, P. (2015). Intellectual humility and forgiveness of religious leaders. *The Journal of Positive Psychology, 10*, 499–506.

Hook, J. N., Farrell, J. E., Johnson, K. A., Van Tongeren, D. R., Davis, D. E., & Aten, J. D. (2017). Intellectual humility and religious tolerance. *The Journal of Positive Psychology, 12*(1), 29–35.

Joelle, M., & Coelho, A. M. (in press). The impact of spirituality at work on workers' attitudes and individual performance. *The International Journal of Human Resource Management*.

Johnson, M. K., Rowatt, W. C., Barnard-Brak, L. M., Patock-Peckham, J. A., LaBouff, J. P., & Carlisle, R. D. (2011). A mediational analysis of the role of right-wing authoritarianism and religious fundamentalism in the religiosity–prejudice link. *Personality and Individual Differences, 50,* 851–856.

Kim, K. H. C., & Sobal, J. (2004). Religion, social support, fat intake and physical activity. *Public Health Nutrition, 7*(6), 773–781.

King, E. B., & Ahmad, A. S. (2010). An experimental field study of interpersonal discrimination toward Muslim job applicants. *Personnel Psychology, 63*(4), 881–906.

King, J. E., Jr., McKay, P. F., & Stewart, M. M. (2014). Religious bias and stigma: Attitudes toward working with a Muslim co-worker. *Journal of Management, Spirituality & Religion, 11,* 98–122.

Koenig, H., King, D., & Carson, V. B. (2012). *Handbook of religion and health.* Oxford, UK: Oxford University Press.

Kriger, M., & Seng, Y. (2005). Leadership with inner meaning: A contingency theory of leadership based on the worldviews of five religions. *The Leadership Quarterly, 16,* 771–806.

Kunst, J. R., Thomsen, L., & Sam, D. L. (2014). Late Abrahamic reunion? Religious fundamentalism negatively predicts dual Abrahamic group categorization among Muslims and Christians. *European Journal of Social Psychology, 44,* 337–348.

Ladd, K. L. (2007). Religiosity, the need for structure, death attitudes, and funeral preferences. *Mental Health, Religion, & Culture, 10,* 451–472.

Lindsey, I., Kay, T., Jeanes, R., & Banda, D. (2017). *Localizing global sport for development.* Manchester, UK: Manchester University Press.

Lynn, M. L., Naughton, M. J., & Vander Veen, S. (2010). Connecting religion and work: Patterns and influences of work-faith integration. *Human Relations, 64,* 675–701.

Major, B., & O'Brien, L. T. (2005). The social psychology of stigma. *Annual Review of Psychology, 56,* 393–421.

Markus, H. (1977). Self-schemata and processing information about the self. *Journal of Personality and Social Psychology, 35,* 63–78.

Merrill, R. M., & Thygerson, A. L. (2001). Religious preference, church activity, and physical exercise. *Preventive Medicine, 33*(1), 38–45.

Miller, J. F., Lee, K., & Martin, C. L. L. (2013). An analysis of interscholastic athletic directors' religious values and practices on pregame prayer in Southeastern United States: A case study. *Journal of Legal Aspects of Sport, 23,* 91–106.

Milliman, J., Gatling, A., & Bradley-Geist, J. C. (2017). The implications of workplace spirituality for person–environment fit theory. *Psychology of Religion and Spirituality, 9*(1), 1–12.

Mitroff, I. I., & Denton, E. A. (1999). A study of spirituality in the workplace. *Sloan Management Review, 40,* 83–92.

Nite, C., Singer, J. N., & Cunningham, G. B. (2013). Addressing competing logics between the mission of a religious university and the demands of intercollegiate athletics. *Sport Management Review, 16*(4), 465–476.

Osman-Gani, A. M., Hashim, J., & Ismail, Y. (2013). Establishing linkages between religiosity and spirituality on employee performance. *Employee Relations, 35,* 360–376.

Padela, A. I., Adam, H., Ahmad, M., Hosseinian, Z., & Curlin, F. (2016). Religious identity and workplace discrimination: A national survey of American Muslim physicians. *AJOB Empirical Bioethics, 7*(3), 149–159.

Parris, D. L., & Peachey, J. W. (2013). A systematic literature review of servant leadership theory in organizational contexts. *Journal of Business Ethics, 113*(3), 377–393.

Pawar, B. S. (2014). Leadership spiritual behaviors toward subordinates: An empirical examination of the effects of a leader's individual spirituality and organizational spirituality. *Journal of Business Ethics, 122*(3), 439–452.

PEW Research Center (2012, December). *The global religious landscape.* Retrieved from http://www.pewforum.org/2012/12/18/global-religious-landscape-exec/

Ragins, B. R. (2008). Disclosure disconnects: Antecedents and consequences of disclosing invisible stigmas across life domains. *Academy of Management Review, 33,* 194–215.

Religious Landscape Study (no date). *Pew Research Center.* Retrieved from http://www.pewforum.org/religious-landscape-study/

Sage, G. H., & Eitzen, D. S. (2016). *Sociology of North American sport* (10th ed.). New York, NY: Oxford University Press.

Samari, G. (2016). Islamophobia and public health in the United States. *American Journal of Public Health, 106*(11), 1920–1925.

Schaafsma, J. & Williams, K. D. (2012). Exclusion, intergroup hostility, and religious fundamentalism. *Journal of Experimental Social Psychology, 48,* 829–837.

Schein, E. H. (2004). *Organizational culture and leadership* (3rd ed.). San Francisco, CA: Jossey-Bass.

Scheitle, C. P., & Ecklund, E. H. (2017). Examining the effects of exposure to religion in the workplace on perceptions of religious discrimination. *Review of Religious Research, 59*(1), 1–20.

Shore, L. M., Randel, A. E., Chung, B. G., Dean, M. A., Ehrhart, K. H., & Singh, G. (2011). Inclusion and diversity in work groups: A review and model for future research. *Journal of Management, 37,* 1262–1289.

Spilka, B., Hood, R. W., Jr., Hunsberger, B., & Gorsuch, R. (2018). *The psychology of religion: An empirical approach* (5th ed.). New York, NY: Guilford.

Tejeda, M. J. (2015). Skeletons in the broom closet: Exploring the discrimination of Pagans in the workplace. *Journal of Management, Spirituality & Religion, 12*(2), 88–110.

Toffoletti, K., & Palmer, C. (2017). New approaches for studies of Muslim women and sport. *International Review for the Sociology of Sport, 52*(2), 146–163.

Tracey, P. (2012). Religion and organization: A critical review of current trends and future directions. *Academy of Management Annals, 6*(1), 87–134.

Van Camp, D., Sloan, L. R., & ElBassiouny, A. (2016). People notice and use an applicant's religion in job suitability evaluations. *The Social Science Journal, 53*(4), 459–466.

van Dierendonck, D. (2011). Servant leadership: A review and synthesis. *Journal of Management, 27,* 1228–1261.

Vitell, S. J., King, R. A., Howie, K., Toti, J. F., Albert, L., Hidalgo, E. R., & Yacout, O. (2016). Spirituality, moral identity, and consumer ethics: A multi-cultural study. *Journal of Business Ethics, 139*(1), 147–160.

Wahl, G. (1999, May). Holy war. *Sports Illustrated.* Retrieved from http://www.si.com

Wallace, M., Wright, B. R., & Hyde, A. (2014). Religious affiliation and hiring discrimination in the American South: A field experiment. *Social Currents, 1*(2), 189–207.

Walseth, K., & Fasting, K. (2003). Islam's view on physical activity and sport: Egyptian women interpreting Islam. *International Review for the Sociology of Sport, 38,* 45–60.

Watson, B., & Scraton, S. J. (2013). Leisure studies and intersectionality. *Leisure Studies, 32*(1), 35–47.

Weeks, M., & Vincent, M. A. (2007). Using religious affiliation to spontaneously categorize others. *The International Journal for the Psychology of Religion, 17,* 317–331.

Whittington, J. L., Pitts, T. M., Kageler, W. V., & Goodwin, V. L. (2005). Legacy leadership: The leadership wisdom of the Apostle Paul. *The Leadership Quarterly, 16,* 749–770.

Sexual Orientation, Gender Identity, and Gender Expression

LEARNING OUTCOMES

After studying this chapter, you should be able to:

- Define sexual orientation, gender identity, and gender expression.
- Describe the manner in which sexual orientation, gender identity, and gender expression influence access and treatment discrimination.
- Summarize the multilevel factors that influence the effects of sexual orientation, gender identity, and gender expression in the work environment.
- Paraphrase the manner in which sexual orientation, gender identity, and gender expression influence opportunities and experiences of sport and physical activity participants.

DIVERSITY CHALLENGE

Two events in February 2017 encapsulated the uneven playing field for lesbian, gay, bisexual, and transgender (LGBT) athletes. The first occurred in Cypress, Texas (USA), where Mack Beggs won the 110-pound division Class 6A wrestling championship. In Texas, 6A is the classification with the largest schools and the highest level of competition. Winning a state championship is a tremendous accomplishment. What made the achievement even more noteworthy is that Beggs is a transgender boy, meaning that his sex assigned at birth was female, and his gender identity and expression are that of a boy. Beggs was on testosterone treatment as part of his transition process. The treatment was permitted under state guidelines as students can take steroids as long as they are "dispensed, prescribed, delivered and administered by a medical practitioner for a valid medical purpose." Though Beggs wanted to compete against boys, the athletic governing body's rules called for him to participate in sports based on his sex assigned at birth. As a result, although Beggs identified as a boy, was taking testosterone to transition, and wanted to compete against other boys, he had to compete against girls. He earned the championship while fans jeered and some parents sued. Beggs won the championship again in 2018.

During the same month in 2017, National Hockey League goalie Braden Holtby wore a goalie mask with You Can Play theme. You Can Play is an organization whose purpose is to promote LGBT inclusion in sport, ensuring the space is safe and welcoming for all persons, irrespective of their gender identity, gender expression, or sexual orientation. In 2013, the organization partnered with the National Hockey League to promote inclusiveness in the league and hockey in general. The slogan "Hockey is for Everyone" materialized from the collaboration, and several events ensued. The Washington Capitals, Holtby's team, engaged in several inclusive activities, such as the players using rainbow "Pride Tape" during practice and then auctioning the sticks.

The two examples illustrate how LGBT inclusion is varied in sport.

Sources: Cunningham. G. B. (in press). Understanding the experiences of LGBT athletes in sport: A multilevel model. In M. Anshel (Ed.), *APA handbook of sport and exercise psychology*. Washington, DC: American Psychological Association. Floreck, M. (2017, February 19). Euless Trinity transgender wrestler Mack Beggs wins state championship, is met with both cheers and boos. *Dallas News*. Retrieved from http://sportsday.dallasnews.com/high-school/high-schools/2017/02/25/euless-trinity-transgender-wrestler-mack-beggs-advances-state-finals-meets-boos. Gulitti, T. (2017, February 13). Braden Holtby's mask to support You Can Play Project: Capitals goalie will auction off helmet at Hockey Is For Everyone game on Feb. 24. *NHL.com*. Retrieved from https://www.nhl.com/news/braden-holtbys-mask-to-support-you-can-play-project/c-286724644.

CHALLENGE REFLECTION

1. The Diversity Challenge included two examples of recent LGBT-related issues in sports. What are others with which you are familiar?
2. The Washington Capitals took a number of actions to signal LGBT inclusion. Are you familiar with other sport organizations doing the same? If so, what strategies do they use?

As the Diversity Challenge illustrates, the state of affairs for LGBT individuals in sport is mixed. For some, coaches, administrators, and policymakers seek to restrict their participation. In other cases, sport organizations are working with other entities to create inclusive spaces for all people, irrespective of their sexual orientation, gender identity, or gender expression. In both instances, it is clear that LGBT status can influence opportunities and experiences in sport.

The purpose of this chapter is to examine the influence of sexual orientation, gender identity, and gender expression in greater depth. To do so, I begin with terminology and background material, defining key terms and offering contextual information. I then discuss the experiences and gender minorities and sexual minorities in the sport work environment. Drawing from the model in Chapter 4, I follow with an outline of macro-, meso-, and micro-level factors influencing the opportunities and experiences of LGBT individuals. In the final section, I discuss the intersection of LGBT, physical activity, and sport participation.

DEFINITIONS AND BACKGROUND

Sexual Orientation

Sexual orientation, gender identity, and gender expression are separate constructs, with different meanings. Sexual orientation refers to "an enduring pattern of emotional, romantic, and/or sexual attractions to men, women, or both sexes," as well as "a person's sense of identity based on those attractions, related behaviors, and membership in a community of others who share those attractions" (American Psychological Association, 2008, p. 1). Depending on how sexual orientation is measured, lesbian, gay, and bisexual (LGB) individuals comprise between 1 and 21 percent of the population, with most estimates near 10 percent (Savin-Williams, 2006, 2016). To put this figure in perspective, consider that the US population in 2018 was roughly 326 million people; thus, there were about 3.3 million lesbian, gay, or bisexual individuals living in the country at the time. This is more than the proportion of Asians, but less than the proportion of Latinos. Thus, sexual minorities constitute a sizeable segment of the US population.

Historically, people viewed sexual orientation as a binary construct: a person was either heterosexual or homosexual, and more recently, researchers have categorized people as heterosexual, bisexual, or homosexual (Bailey et al., 2016). Kinsey and his colleagues challenged this assumption decades ago (Kinsey, Pomeroy, & Martin, 1948; Kinsey, Pomeroy, Martin, & Gebhard, 1953). They considered sexual orientation as existing on a continuum from completely heterosexual to completely homosexual, with various gradations between, including bisexuality. In line with this perspective, Savin-Williams and Vrangalova (2013) demonstrated that a small but meaningful proportion of people (between 7.6 and 9.5 percent of women, and 3.6 and 4.1 percent of men) consider themselves mostly heterosexual, expressing a slight amount of same-sex attraction but not enough to consider themselves bisexual. This attraction increases during the teenage years, peaks in a person's early 20s, and then remains stable over time. Follow-up research further supports these findings (Savin-Williams, 2016, 2018; Savin-Williams, Cash, McCormack, & Rieger, 2017).

Sexual orientation is complex, with dimensions beyond simply the sex of a person's sexual partners, and includes self-image, fantasies, attractions, and behaviors (Ragins & Wiethoff, 2005). These elements can interact in seemingly contradictory ways (Savin-Williams, 2014). A person can, for example, be attracted to and have fantasies about both women and men, yet exhibit exclusively heterosexual behavior. Contradictions such as this make it difficult to obtain precise estimates of the number of persons who are LGB. The malleability of one's sexuality also makes it difficult to gauge the number of persons who are LGB. Some people do not recognize their LGB identity until late in their lives. Others form relationships with members of the opposite sex after years of having a same-sex partner.

An interesting study from Korchmaros, Powell, and Stevens (2013) illustrates this complexity. They collected data from members of LGBT groups, asking them about their self-identified sexual orientation, their preference of sex partners, and the type of sexual partners they had recently. They found that for many of the participants (23 percent for men and 41 percent for women), their stated sexual orientation did not match their preference in sexual partners. For example, a woman might identify as bisexual but prefer only women as sexual partners. In other cases, the predominant classification schemes proved to be inadequate: some people identified as other than heterosexual, lesbian, gay, or bisexual (e.g., they preferred the term queer) while some did not have a preference in sexual partners because they did not have sex.

Research from Anderson and colleagues offers another example. In a study of heterosexual-identified men who were cheerleaders, Anderson (2008) found that 40 percent engaged in same-sex relationships. Scoats, Joseph, and Anderson (2018), in another study of collegiate men who identified as heterosexual, found a similar pattern, as many engaged in sexual relationships involving other men (see also Silva, 2017). The authors suggested the findings point to a more inclusive form of masculinity, as well as a form of sexual recreation.

Gender Identity and Gender Expression

Gender identity and gender expression are separate constructs from sexual orientation. Beemyn and Rankin (2011) defined gender identity as "an individual's sense of hir own gender, which may be different from one's birth gender or how others perceive one's gender" (p. 20). The authors used "hir" as a gender-neutral pronoun that can be used in place of "her" or "him." Scholars and advocates also suggest words "ze" and "sie" as gender-neutral replacements for "she" and "he." Another option is to use the grammatically incorrect but inclusive "they" for all people, irrespective if the singular or plural pronoun is needed. Perhaps the easiest approach is to simply ask "what pronouns do you use?" and then follow suit (Cunningham, Buzuvis, & Mosier, 2018).

Gender identity refers to the gender with which an individual identifies. In some cases, a person's gender identity might be congruent with the sex assigned at birth (i.e., the decision that a doctor makes at a baby's birth, based on the external genitalia); in other cases, the gender identity and sex might differ. Related to gender identity is gender expression, a construct Beemyn and Rankin (2011) defined as "how one chooses to indicate one's gender identity to others through behavior and appearance, which includes clothing, hairstyle, makeup, voice, and body characteristics" (p. 21). The way people express their gender can change over time and can vary based on context. For example, a cross-dresser might present as a woman in most situations but not in others.

These terms inform the discussion of transgender, intersex, and cisgender individuals. According to Carroll (2014), transgender "describes an individual whose gender identity (one's psychological identification as a boy/man or girl/woman) does not match the person's sex at birth" (p. 368). As discussed in the Diversity Challenge, Mack Beggs was assigned female at birth but identified as a boy; thus,

Beggs is transgender. Gates (2011) estimated there are about 700,000 transgender persons in the US.

Transgender individuals should not be confused with people who have intersex conditions. People with intersex conditions have "atypical combinations of chromosomes, hormones, genitalia, and other physical features" (Buzuvis, 2011, p. 11). Most people with intersex conditions identify as either male or female and do not experience ambiguity about their gender identity. In fact, most people who have an intersex condition are not aware of it unless they learn about it during a medical procedure (Carroll, 2014).

Cisgender refers to persons "whose gender assigned at birth has always coincided with their identity/expression" (Beemyn & Rankin, 2011, pp. 197–198). The term *cis* has a Latin origin, meaning "the same side as." Thus, a person who is assigned a female sex at birth, who identifies as a woman, and whose gender expression is also that of a woman would be considered cisgender.

Though I will use the terms transgender and cisgender throughout the chapter, it is important to note that this terminology is not universally accepted. In Beemyn and Rankin's (2011) comprehensive study, 1,211 persons identified as transgender. These persons offered 479 unique descriptors they believed better captured their gender identity and expression. Examples include "genderqueer," "cross-dresser," "bigender," and "two-spirited," among others. Despite these variations, the term transgender is commonly used in the popular press, among academic societies, and in academic writing; hence, I follow this practice here.

Demographics of LGBT Community

The Williams Institute at the University of California Los Angeles is an exceptional source for LGBT-related data, trends, and research. I draw from their data repository (Same-Sex Couple Data & Demographics, n.d.) to review demographic differences among LGBT Americans.

According to the Williams Institute, 52 percent of Americans who identify as LGBT are women (compared to 50.5 percent in the total population). In terms of race, 61 percent are White, 15 percent Latino, 11 percent African American, 2 percent Asian or Pacific Islander, 1 percent Native American or Alaska Native, and 10 percent indicate "other" as their race. Recall from Chapter 5 that 60.1 percent of Americans are White—a similar proportion to that of LGBT individuals who are White. The LGBT community is generally younger than the US population: 54 percent are between age 18 and 39, compared to 36 percent of the US population in that age range. Most members of the LGBT community (71.3 percent) are not raising children.

There are also differences in employment, education, and earnings. About 1 in 8 LGBT individuals is unemployed, compared to 1 in 13 heterosexuals. Relative to their heterosexual counterparts, sexual and gender minorities are less likely to have health insurance (79 percent versus 86 percent) and more likely to have an income less than $24,000 (32 percent versus 24 percent).

SEXUAL ORIENTATION, GENDER IDENTITY, AND GENDER EXPRESSION IN THE WORK ENVIRONMENT

Sexual orientation, gender identity, and gender expression are likely to influence both dimensions of discrimination: access and treatment (Greenhaus, Parasuraman, & Wormley, 1990).

A number of researchers have offered evidence of access discrimination based on sexual orientation. Patacchini, Ragusa, and Zenou (2015) conducted a field study in Italian cities, sending fictitious resumes for a variety of job openings. They found that gay men received 20 percent fewer call backs than did heterosexual men, and the call back rate among women did not vary based on sexual orientation. Drydakis (2015) conducted a similar field experiment among hiring organizations in the UK. Similar to aforementioned study, Drydakis observed that lesbian and gay job applicants faced more barriers to getting a call back, even when their qualifications were identical to those of heterosexuals.

The barriers are present in the sport and physical activity context, too. Research, Sartore and I conducted illustrates this point (Sartore & Cunningham, 2009). In our first study, we observed that former and current athletes' level of sexual prejudice was highly predictive of their unwillingness to play on teams coached by gay men or lesbians (Study 1). We also found that parents' willingness to let their children play on teams coached by gay men or lesbians was largely a function of the parents' sexual prejudice (Study 2). Finally, we asked the parents to provide a rationale for their decisions. Overwhelmingly, the resistance was based on distrust of members of sexual minorities, the perceived immorality of persons who are LGBT, and reliance on gay and lesbian stereotypes. All of these attitudes can contribute to LGBT individuals' being denied access to jobs. Getting to know LGBT persons on a personal level might help offset some of these negative attitudes and behaviors (Cunningham & Melton, 2012, 2013).

Although some parents are openly against letting their children play on teams led by LGBT coaches, others express support. Melton and I interviewed parents to understand better the nature of their support (Cunningham & Melton, 2014b). For some parents, the support was unequivocal, and they saw no reason why LGBT persons would not be well suited to lead sport teams. For about half of the parents, though, the positive attitudes were expressed in what we called conditional support. That is, they expressed positive attitudes toward coaches of gender or sexual minorities as long as the coaches did not engage in certain behaviors, such as promoting their sexual orientation. These conditional forms of support promoted outdated stereotypes (e.g., LGBT persons are promiscuous or untrustworthy) and were not expressed toward heterosexual or cisgender coaches. Thus, we argued that although the parents openly expressed support, they actually expressed prejudice in subtle, nuanced ways—something that ultimately negatively affects LGBT coaches' access to positions.

As another example, colleagues and I (Cunningham, Sartore, & McCullough, 2010) conducted an experiment where participants reviewed one of four application packets for a person who was applying for a personal trainer position at a fitness club. The packets varied by the applicant's gender and the person's supposed sexual orientation. In the supposed sexual minority condition, the applicant was a medalist in the Gay Games, whereas in the control (heterosexual) condition, the applicant was a medalist in Amateur Athletic competitions. All applicants were highly qualified, as evidenced by degrees in exercise science, certifications, and previous personal training experience. After reviewing the packet, participants were asked to rate the qualifications of the applicant, provide attribution assessments (i.e., the degree to which the person was ethical, moral, and trustworthy), and submit hiring recommendations. All job applicants were viewed as qualified, irrespective of their gender or sexual orientation. However, male raters provided less positive attributions for members of sexual minorities than they did for heterosexuals. Women did not provide differential ratings. The attribution ratings were important because they were reliably related to hiring recommendations. Thus, even though the applicants who were LGBT were qualified, men raters would deny them access to the position because of more subtle biases.

In addition to facing access discrimination, employees who are LGBT face wage discrimination (Pizer, Sears, Mallory, & Hunter, 2012). This research shows that, in the US, gay men earn between 10 and 32 percent less than their heterosexual male counterparts. Lesbians have earnings on par with other women but earn less than men. Among transgender individuals, many are not employed, and for those who are, they generally earn less than $25,000 annually. In fact, data from a national survey conducted in 2011 show that one in seven transgender individuals earn less than $10,000 annually. This is about two-thirds of the salary a person would earn from full-time employment at minimum wage. Bryson (2017) conducted a similar analysis in the UK and found that bisexual men earned 20 percent less than did heterosexual men. He also found that lesbians got paid 30 percent less than heterosexual women unless they worked in an organization with a non-discrimination policy that specifically referenced sexual orientation.

In addition to the wage discrimination they face, persons who are LGBT also are negatively affected in the area of company benefits. Heterosexuals routinely have the option of including their spouses in a benefits package. As a result, their spouses receive medical coverage, dental coverage, life insurance, and other benefits. Heterosexual men also regularly have the option of taking leave when their spouses give birth. These benefits are often taken for granted among heterosexuals, but they are a rarity among employees who are LGBT. According to a report from the Human Rights Campaign (Fidas, Bailey, & Cooper, 2017), only 60 percent of all Fortune 500 companies offer domestic partner benefits. These figures mean that 4 of every 10 Fortune 500 companies do not offer any partner benefits. Furthermore, only 58 percent of all Fortune 100 companies provide transgender-inclusive health insurance. When benefits are not included, the transgender employees must cover medical costs associated with sex reassignment, hormone therapies, and other related medical treatments.

Discrimination and mistreatment of people based on their sexual orientation, gender identity, and gender expression hurts those individuals, as well as those around them. As shown in Box 11.1, LGBT inclusion is linked with a number of benefits to sport organizations.

Box 11.1 Alternative Perspectives: The Many Benefits of LGBT Inclusion

Although many sport organizations remain characterized by prejudice and discrimination directed toward LGBT individuals, an increasing number seek inclusive work environments. For example, in a study of NCAA athletic departments, I found that although 17 percent of the units reported no sexual orientation diversity among the employees, approximately 10 percent indicated that their department was very heterogeneous along this diversity dimension (Cunningham, 2010). Subsequent research I conducted in that same context showed the benefits of having a diverse workforce. Specifically, athletic departments that coupled an LGBT-diverse workforce with an inclusive work environment had more creative work environments (Cunningham, 2011a) and higher performance on objective measures of success (Cunningham, 2011b) than did their more homogeneous peers. Follow-up work has shown that LGBT-inclusive policies are associated with better objective performance, especially when the organization is a community with a high concentration LGBT individuals (Cunningham & Nite, 2018).

Why do these patterns exist? I suspect Florida's (2003, 2012) creative capital theory (see Chapter 2) holds the answer. This theory suggests that talented, creative people are attracted to certain geographic areas—those marked by high levels of educated people, technological innovation, and diversity. As a result, geographic regions that have these characteristics attract the best and the brightest individuals and then thrive economically. Florida is a geographer, and his work on regional economic development supports these premises. We have adapted this perspective in our own work, with the thinking that people prefer to work in organizations where there are many bright people, where innovation is key, and where diversity and inclusion are the norms. If this is the case, then these organizations should thrive relative to their less attractive peers. And, as the aforementioned examples of NCAA athletic departments show, this is indeed the case.

Building further on this concept, we explored the possibility of whether sport organizations could attract new people (customers and employees) by casting themselves as LGBT-inclusive entities. In our first study, we observed that inclusive organizations were appealing to job searchers, particularly those people who valued justice and equality (Melton & Cunningham, 2012a). In the second study, we found that people believed LGBT-inclusive fitness clubs were also diverse along other diversity dimensions, and these characteristics were appealing to the potential club members. Again, this was especially the case among people who valued social justice and equality (Cunningham & Melton, 2014a). Collectively, this research suggests that sport organizations benefit from LGBT diversity and from advertising their inclusiveness.

MULTILEVEL EXPLANATIONS

Drawing from the model in Chapter 4 and other work I have published (Cunningham, 2012; in press), I offer multilevel explanations to explain the influence of sexual orientation, gender identity, and gender expression in the sport work environment. Exhibit 11.1 provides a summary.

Multilevel Factors Affecting Sexual Orientation, Gender Identity, and Gender Expression in the Sport Work Environment

exhibit **11.1**

Macro-level factors: Those operating at the societal level, including employment laws, structural stigma, and institutional norms.

Meso-level factors: Those operating at the team and organizational levels, including bias in decision-making, organizational culture, and leadership.

Micro-level factors: Those operating at the individual level, including demographics, rater demographics, and personal identity.

Macro-Level Factors

Macro-level factors are those operating at the societal level. In the context of LGBT inclusion, employment laws, structural stigma, and institutional norms are especially salient.

Employment Laws

Employment protections can help curb access and treatment discrimination, and encourage individuals to disclose what might otherwise be stigmatizing characteristics in their work. Across many European countries, it is illegal for employers to discriminate on the grounds of sexual orientation (ILGA Europe, 2017). In the US, however, LGBT individuals do not have federal employment protections. At the state level, in 2017, only 21 states had laws protecting individuals from employment discrimination based on sexual orientation and gender identity and expression, and another 2 offered such protections for sexual orientation only (Non-discriminatory Laws, 2017). These data indicate that in most states in the US, it is legally permissible to not hire someone, fire someone, pay them less, or pass them over for promotion because of their sexual orientation, gender identity, or gender expression. Other laws can also affect sport and sport organizations, as shown in Box 11.2.

Barron and Hebl (2013) conducted a series of studies to examine the effects of such laws on employment discrimination. In their first study, they contacted households, some of which were in areas offering employment protections and some of which were not, and asked about their awareness of the laws. In the second study, they examined employment discrimination against job applicants who were ostensibly LGBT, doing so in cities that offered employment protections and in those that did not. In the third study, they asked participants to interview an applicant who the interviewer believed was lesbian. Prior to interviewing, the participants were led to believe that their city either did or did not have employment

Box 11.2 Diversity in the Field: Limiting Rights of Transgender Individuals Hurts Sport Organizations and the Economy

A number of LGBT-related laws can influence sport organizations, including those seemingly unrelated to sport or physical activity. In the US in 2017, legislators in 16 states proposed laws that would limit the bathrooms transgender individuals could use. They varied in subtle ways, but in general, each bill sought to restrict access to the facility one could use based on that person's sex assigned at birth. Under these laws, a transgender woman—who was assigned male at birth and who now identified as a woman—would need to use a men's bathroom or facility. Ultimately, none of the laws passed, and lawmakers in the one state that did pass such mandate in 2016 (North Carolina) later repealed it.

Researchers have shown that passing or even considering such discriminatory laws negatively affects a number of entities. For example, LGBT-focused suicide hotlines saw their cases double during the time that Texas lawmakers considered the bill (Wright, 2017). These data are consistent with researchers who have shown that transgender individuals facing discrimination are more likely than their peers to attempt suicide (Seelman, 2016). At the community level, discriminatory laws serve to repel business (Cunningham, 2017). North Carolina experienced a $600 million economic loss because of its law. Part of the loss was due to sport leagues moving their events, such as the National Basketball Leagues' All-Star game. In Texas, San Antonio hosted the men's collegiate basketball championship in 2018, generating millions for the economy. However, had the "bathroom bill" passed, the National Collegiate Athletic Association (NCAA) was ready to move the event.

As these examples illustrate, sport organizations and leagues do not want to be associated with laws people deem discriminatory. Thus, the lack of inclusion hurts individuals and the business bottom line.

protections based on sexual orientation, gender identity, and gender expression. The results of the three studies showed that (a) people were more aware of employment laws when their cities had such provisions, (b) the presence of LGBT employment protections decreased discriminatory behaviors, and (c) even when researchers randomly assign employment protections (such as in the third study), discrimination decreases.

Mallory, Brown, Russell, and Sears' (2017) study offers more evidence pointing to the importance of LGBT employment protections. They examined the prevalence of discrimination in Texas—one of the largest states in the US and one that does not have LGBT employment protections at the state level. More than one in four (27 percent) transgender individuals reported being not hired, not promoted, or terminated in the previous year because of their gender identity and expression. Thirteen percent had faced harassment at work. Their experiences are not lost on the public, where 79 percent of Texas residents believe LGBT individuals face discrimination. The prevalence of discrimination and mistreatment—at work, in searching for housing, and in other contexts—results in serious psychological and physical harm. Beyond the increase in suicidality previously discussed, the health effects hurt the economy. The authors estimated that reducing the health disparities could save the state over $600 million annually in health care costs.

Structural Stigma

Prejudice against LGBT individuals is grounded in stigma (Herek 2007, 2009; Herek & McLemore, 2013). As you will recall from previous chapters, people who are stigmatized "have (or are believed to have) an attribute that marks them as different and leads them to be devalued in the eyes of others" (Major & O'Brien, 2005, p. 395). The devalued status is socially constructed, and there is a shared understanding of its presence among people in a given context or culture. The differential status of stigmatized people reflects the power relations in a particular setting, such that, relative to their counterparts, stigmatized people have less access to resources, are not as influential, and exercise less autonomy in their lives (see also Goffman, 1963).

Structural stigma operates at the institutional level, and some authors refer to these dynamics as heterosexism (Herek, 2000). The term refers to the systems, structures, and organizational practices in place that reinforce the stigmatized status of LGBT individuals (Herek, 2007). Structural stigma works through several mechanisms. First, systems, structures, and practices promote heterosexuality and cisgender status as the assumption or the standard, and as a result LGBT individuals and their experiences become invisible. Second, and related to the first point, when LGBT individuals do become visible, they take on the status of "other" and may be seen as problematic. Transgender and LGB individuals "are presumed to be abnormal and unnatural and, therefore, are regarded as inferior, as requiring explanation, and as appropriate targets for hostility, differential treatment and discrimination, and even aggression" (Herek, 2007, pp. 907–908).

Structural stigma is largely created and reinforced through the rules, laws, and customs present in a given society. One excellent example of this within the sport setting is the rules in place governing participation by transgender athletes (Buzuvis, 2012; Carroll, 2014; Krane, Barak, & Mann, 2012; Love, 2014; Travers & Deri, 2011). The policies are designed to regulate who can and cannot participate in different sport settings. For many years, the International Olympic Committee (IOC) had one of the more restrictive policies, as a transgender athlete could compete if (a) they had transitioned via sex reassignment surgery, (b) they had undergone hormone treatment for at least two years, and (c) they had legal papers documenting their transitioned sex. The conditions were onerous, placed an undue hardship on the athletes, and ultimately restricted participation. Cognizant of these shortcomings, IOC officials revamped the policy in November of 2015 (IOC Consensus, 2015). Now, transgender men—those assigned female at birth and how identify as a man—can compete without restriction; transgender women—athletes assigned male at birth and who identify as a woman—can compete if they are on hormone treatment and their testosterone level is below certain thresholds.

The NCAA has a separate policy governing the participation of transgender athletes. This entity allows a transgender athlete who identifies as a woman to participate on women's teams if she has undergone at least one year of hormone treatments designed to nullify any effects of added testosterone in the body. Notably absent from the NCAA's policy is the requirement for sex reassignment surgery or legal documents outlining the transition. The NCAA policy also allows for a transgender athlete who identifies as a man to continue participating on women's teams. He can do so until he starts hormone treatments. The NCAA's policy is restrictive in that it prohibits participation on women's teams by those transgender women who have yet to begin hormone treatments. The presumption is that forbidding such participation levels the playing field. However, even the NCAA acknowledges the logical inconsistencies:

> A male-to-female transgender woman may be small and slight, even if she is not on hormone blockers or taking estrogen. . . . The assumption that all male-bodied people are taller, stronger, and more highly skilled in a sport than all female-bodied people is not accurate.
>
> (National Collegiate Athletic Association, 2011, p. 7)

Finally, some sport organizations adopt what Buzuvis (2012) considers inclusive policies. One example comes from the Washington Interscholastic Athletic Association, which allows high school students to take part in sports in a manner that is consistent with the athletes' gender identity. This policy does not require medical treatment or any legal documents. When questions arise about the legitimacy of the gender identity claim, an eligibility committee can hear the case to make a determination. The focus of this policy, and others like it (e.g., the policy in Massachusetts), is on the athletes' gender identity, which is a reasonable approach considering that the athletes themselves are the best judges of their own gender identity. Note the differences between the policies in Washington and those in Texas, as described in the Diversity Challenge.

As these examples illustrate, policies and guidelines regulating transgender athletes' participation serve to reinforce stigmas. The restrictive nature of some policies reinforces stereotypes and promotes ideas that are unsubstantiated by empirical evidence. Restrictive policies are usually found in contexts promoting high levels of elite competition or in politically conservative regions, and the policies ultimately serve to limit participation. On the other hand, more inclusive policies put participation at the fore, promote the idea that transgender athletes should be fully engaged in the sport enterprise, and are in more progressive regions and among athletic associations that seek to encourage full participation.

Institutional Norms

According to Meyer and Rowan (1977), activities become institutionalized when "social processes, obligations, or actualities come to take on rule-like status in social thought and action" (p. 341). I argue that activities, perspectives, and attitudes around the LGBT community and LGBT individuals in the sport work environment are taken-for-granted in nature, thereby becoming practiced without question (e.g., among youth sport parents, see Trussell, Kovac, & Apgar, 2018). They have become entrenched, repeated over time. As a result, sport managers and others in the sport context have reinforced the practices such that there is legitimacy associated with them (Washington & Patterson, 2011). The institutionalized norms are context specific, such that activities and processes taken-for-granted in one setting might be antithetical to customs in another. Illustrative of these dynamics, LGBT-inclusive practices, such as softball leagues, are common in some portions of the US but not in others (Buzuvis, 2012). I offer another example in Exhibit 11.2.

Institutionalized norms, practices, and activities surrounding LGBT individuals are evident in sport. According to McCormack and Anderson (2014), homohysteria, which they define as men's fear of being thought gay, serves to impinge upon what might otherwise be an inclusive environment. On the other hand, when homohysteria is low, men and boys feel free to practice more inclusive forms of masculinity. As a result, people in sport settings more readily accept gay and bisexual peers, as well as emotional intimacy. They are also likely to reject the "one-time" rule of homosexuality and refute violence against members of the LGBT community. Researchers have conducted a number of studies, much of which takes place in Europe, to support these tenets (Anderson & McCormach, 2015; Cleland, 2018).

Other researchers, however, have observed the other end of the spectrum. That is, if decreased homohysteria relates with more inclusive attitudes, then the maintenance of homohysteria should result in restricted forms of masculinity and antagonism toward the LGBT community. Melton and I have shown that college athletes sometimes hide their sexual orientation for fear others, including their coach, will

The Varied Nature of Pro-LGBT Attitudes in Europe, 2015   *exhibit* **11.2**

Stigma and institutionalized norms are context and time bound. As such, they can vary from one setting to another, even within a seemingly homogeneous setting. Illustrative of these dynamics, TNS Opinion & Social conducted an analysis of discrimination in the EU in 2015. The researchers asked participants a host of questions, including two particularly relevant to the discussion of LGBT individuals: "gay, lesbian, and bisexual people should have the same rights as heterosexual people," and "there is nothing wrong in a sexual relationship between two persons of the same sex." People in the Netherlands had the most positive attitudes toward LGBT rights and relationships, and people in Croatia and Poland fell on the other end of the spectrum.

Source: http://www.equineteurope.org/IMG/pdf/ebs_437_en.pdf

use the information to harm them (Melton & Cunningham, 2012b). Supervisor threats and the fear of retaliation curtails sexual orientation disclosure of many coaches (Griffin, 2012), and many athletics program promote the preference of heterosexual relationships through the information they provide on coaching bios (Bass, Hardin, & Taylor, 2015). As coaches role model expectations for their players—whether the coach is LGBT or not (Cunningham, 2015a)—restrictive forms of identity maintenance harm all involved. Finally, the media routinely promote traditional forms of masculinity and cisgender status as the norm, and consumers react with skepticism to deviations from these norms (Staurowsky, 2012).

Meso-Level Factors

Meso-level factors are those operating at the team and organizational levels, including bias in decision-making, organizational culture, and leadership.

Bias

Stereotypes represent one form of bias, and researchers have shown that stereotypes of people based on their presumed sexual orientation can affect their experiences and opportunities. For example, Rule, Bjornsdottir, Tskhay, and Ambady (2016) found that people often infer men's sexual orientation based on the target's facial features and expressions. These inferences can affect job decisions, as raters indicate men presumed to be gay are more suitable for jobs consistent with stereotypes (e.g., nurse or English teacher as opposed to a surgeon or math teacher). In another study, Drydakis (2015) conducted a field experiment in the UK, and he signaled the applicants' LGBT status by their participation in lesbian and gay university student unions. He found that LGBT applicants were 5 percent less likely to get an invitation for an interview, relative to heterosexual applicants. Important for the discussion of stereotypes, he drew from Bem's work (see Chapter 6) to examine the degree to which the job announcements emphasized masculine or feminine characteristics for the desired job holder. Drydakis found that gay men received fewer interview requests when the position emphasized masculine characteristics, and lesbians received fewer callbacks when the announcement emphasized feminine traits.

Much of the work related to LGBT bias in the workplace has focused on prejudice, as expressed through stigma. Gender and sexual stigma are promoted through three manifestations of stigma toward individuals. The first, enacted stigma (Herek, 2007; Herek & McLemore, 2013), refers to behavioral expressions of stigma. These include the use of derogatory comments, bullying, ostracizing LGBT individuals, and other forms of discrimination. Research evidence suggests that LGBT people are more likely than their peers to face various forms of discrimination and abuse (Morrison, Bishop, & Morrison, in press; West, 2016), and this is true in the sport context (Drury, Stride, Flintoff, & Williams, 2017; McCloughan, Mattey, & Hanrahan, 2015).

Stigma also manifests at the individual level through felt stigma, which reflects LGBT individuals' knowledge that stigma exists and includes the steps they take to avoid it. In some cases, this occurs through the modification of behaviors, such as when female athletes or coaches try to accentuate their femininity (e.g., extra makeup, bows in hair, high heels) as a way of offsetting the assumption that they might be lesbian or bisexual. The fear among male athletes of being thought gay and the subsequent actions they take to mitigate such beliefs comprise what McCormack and Anderson (2014) refer to as homohysteria.

Finally, internalized stigma refers to the acceptance of gender and sexual stigma as part of a person's own value system. For heterosexuals and cisgender individuals, this takes the form of gender and sexual prejudice (see Cunningham & Pickett, 2018; Lee & Cunningham, 2014, 2016; Sartore-Baldwin, 2013). A number of personal characteristics are associated with this form of internalized stigma, and these are listed in Exhibit 11.3. Internalized stigma can also manifest among LGBT individuals, at which point it takes the form of self-stigma. When this occurs, individuals from gender or sexual minorities develop negative feelings about themselves because of their stigmatized status. Internalized stigma has negative health effects for all people. Among LGBT individuals, internalized stigma negatively affects self-esteem, positive affect, and physical health while it increases the occurrence of depressive symptoms and state anxiety (Russell & Fish, 2016). Evidence also suggests that expressing prejudice toward LGBT individuals can be harmful to a person's health—a point explored in Box 11.3.

Decision-makers can also express bias through discriminatory behavior. In previous sections, I highlighted how LGBT individuals face access discrimination,

---

Correlates of Sexual Prejudice   *exhibit* **11.3**

Sexual prejudice is associated with people's personal characteristics. According to Herek (2009), persons who exhibit high levels of sexual prejudice are likely to:

- be male
- be older
- have limited formal education
- reside in the Midwest or southern portions of the US
- hold fundamentalist religious beliefs
- be a Republican
- demonstrate high levels of psychological authoritarianism
- not be sexually permissive
- hold traditional gender role attitudes
- view sexual orientation as a free choice
- have few or no friends who are LGBT

Box 11.3 Alternative Perspective: Prejudice Is Bad for Your Health

Most of the work on the effects of internalized stigma focuses on how it negatively affects LGBT individuals. There is also evidence, though, that people who express gender and sexual prejudice are adversely impacted. Hatzenbuehler, Bellatorre, and Muennig (2014) collected data from more than 20,000 individuals from across the US and analyzed how anti-gay attitudes were associated with mortality risks. They found that people who expressed sexual prejudice had a higher mortality risk than did their counterparts who did not, and this resulted in a 2.5-year difference in life expectancy. Expressing such attitudes was also associated with a higher risk of cardiovascular-related causes of death. These results suggest that reducing prejudice helps all people—minority and majority populations.

are paid less, and have fewer benefits than do heterosexuals in the sport work environment. As might be expected based on the preceding discussion, persons who are LGBT frequently face less positive work experiences and have shorter careers than their heterosexual counterparts. Between 25 and 66 percent of employees who are LGBT experience sexual orientation discrimination at work (Ragins, 2004; see also Pizer et al., 2012). These figures are probably conservative because few people fully disclose this information at work. In fact, Ragins, Singh, and Cornwell (2007) found that only 26.7 percent of the participants in their study reported full disclosure of their sexual orientation to everyone at work. In another analysis, half of the gay men working in professional sports reported having experienced work negatively because of their sexual orientation (Cavalier, 2011). People who experience discrimination based on their sexual orientation or gender identity have low satisfaction and commitment, are likely to seek employment elsewhere, are unlikely to progress in their career, and experience depressive symptoms (Button, 2001; Law, Martinez, Ruggs, Hebl, & Akers, 2011; Smith & Ingram, 2004; Velez & Moradi, 2012).

Organizational Culture

Schein (2004) defined organizational culture as "a pattern of shared basic assumptions ... that has worked well enough to be considered valid and, therefore, to be taught to new members as the correct ways to perceive, think, and feel in relation to those problems" (p. 17). Culture shapes organizational members' behaviors and teaches newcomers of expected behaviors and perspectives. In addition to influencing other diversity forms, organizational culture can affect LGBT individuals working in sport organizations.

As an example, I conducted a case study of inclusive athletic departments in the US, examining internal documents, drawing from popular press articles, and interviewing coaches and administrators (Cunningham, 2015a, 2015b). I found that in these departments employees could bring their "whole selves" to work—a key component of organizational inclusiveness (Chapter 1). They did not have to hide their identity, relationships, or other parts of themselves, and could instead focus completely on their work. In doing so, the coaches, administrators, and athletes could concentrate on excellence in their tasks instead of being pre-occupied with concealing what might otherwise be a stigmatizing characteristic. These qualitative findings are consistent with our empirical work showing that LGBT-inclusive workplaces allow for greater creativity and overall organizational performance (Cunningham, 2011a, 2011b; Cunningham & Nite, 2018).

A number of factors are related to leaders' adoption of an LGBT-inclusive organizational culture. Everly and Schwarz (2014), for instance, examined Fortune 100 companies and found that those companies located in states with progressive laws are also likely to follow inclusive cultures. Furthermore, when some companies show the utility of having an inclusive cultures, others are likely to follow—a sort of mimicking of best practices. As another example, Shaw (in press) examined New Zealand sport organizations' attempts to move to a more inclusive space for LGBT individuals. She found that the organizations recognized the lack of efficacy in their current model and, thus, sought change. In doing so, many followed the lead of New Zealand Rugby, which was seen as an early adopter of an inclusive approach.

Leadership

Leadership plays a critical role in the access LGBT individuals have to sport organizations and to their experiences in the sport work environment. Bandura's (1986) social learning theory offers insights into why leadership is so important. He wrote, "virtually all learning phenomena, resulting from direct experience, can occur vicariously by observing other people's behaviors and the consequences for them" (p. 19). Thus, people learn appropriate behaviors by looking to others, and leaders are frequently those with the most influence. For example, Sartore and I found that leaders' support of diversity initiatives was a strong predictor of whether employees shared similar attitudes (Cunningham & Sartore, 2010).

When LGBT individuals are supported in the workplace, they are likely to have positive work experiences. The benefits of supportive others even override the potential negative effects of experiencing discrimination (Velez & Moradi, 2012). What's more, supportive policies and colleagues send a positive message to various external constituencies, including customers (Cunningham & Melton, 2011; Volpone & Avery, 2010). Coworkers and organizational leaders can offer support in many ways. In some cases, this means offering vocal support for inclusiveness (Sartore & Cunningham, 2010). In other cases, leaders and coworkers show support through advocacy efforts, even while personally sacrificing their own well-being for the advancement of workplace equality (Melton & Cunningham, 2014a, 2014b).

Speaking to the powerful effects of supportive others, an athletic department employee in one of our studies relayed the following:

> I struggled with accepting the fact I was gay. . . . For several years I basically just convinced myself there was no way I was gay . . . and even if I was, I decided I would never act on it. . . . So I was really scared . . . I'd say terrified to tell [Name of Coworker] I was gay. We had worked together for five years . . . he was my best friend and my roommate. I figured he would want to move out immediately and never be seen with me again. . . . But when I finally told him, he just said it was alright [*sic*], nothing was going to change between us, and then he hugged me. That was huge for me (pauses) . . . just to know people would still love me and I wasn't going to lose all of my friends because I was gay. Him being there for me helped me a lot during that time in my life. . . . He was more okay with me being gay than I was.
>
> (Melton & Cunningham, 2014a, p. 29)

Finally, Huffman, Watrous-Rodriguez, and King (2008) offered a number of strategies managers can employ to promote a supportive environment. These are provided in Exhibit 11.4.

---

exhibit **11.4** Managerial Strategies for Promoting LGBT Inclusiveness

Sport managers can adopt a number of strategies to promote inclusiveness in the sport work environment. According to Huffman et al. (2008), these include the following:

1. Provide mentoring opportunities.
2. Offer social networking events.
3. Remain cognizant of one's actions toward all employees.
4. Interact with employees from various backgrounds.
5. Offer diversity training for employees and managers.
6. Relay the LGBT-inclusive standards of the organization to job applicants.
7. Gather employee input concerning practices that are not supportive.
8. Encourage all significant others (e.g., spouses and same-sex partners) to attend social events.
9. Do not assume the sexual orientation of any employee.
10. Schedule meetings with LGBT support group or listserv members and leaders.
11. Become acquainted with LGBT organizations that monitor sexual prejudice and discrimination in the workplace.
12. Allow time off for all persons the employee considers family.
13. Use inclusive language (e.g., partner rather than spouse) and respond quickly and negatively to sexual prejudice.

Micro-Level Factors

Micro-level factors operate at the individual level. They include demographics, rater demographics, and personal identity.

Demographics

Individual demographics, including LGBT status, race, and gender, can all influence experiences and opportunities. Throughout the chapter, I have used the term LGBT, which suggests a common set of experiences among LGBT individuals. That is not the case, however. Researchers and advocates, for example, frequently focus on lesbians and gay men, to the relative exclusion of bisexuals and transgender individuals.

Pickett and I have argued and empirically demonstrated that the experiences of transgender individuals are different than those of lesbians, bisexuals, or gay men (Cunningham & Pickett, 2018). First, one focuses on gender identity and expression (transgender) while the other focuses on sexual orientation (LGB individuals). More fundamentally, differences in prejudice and bias are likely due to gender binaries assumptions. People commonly presume or expect that one's sex assigned at birth aligns with the individual's gender identity and expression. They react negatively when deviations exist, expressing bias and negativity (Cahn, 2011). Destabilization of cultural norms surrounding gender and identity thus serves as a root cause of the fear, anxiety, and bias related to transgender individuals (Sykes, 2006). People routinely seek alignment and uniformity, but such wishes are contrary to how nature operates. Alice Dreger aptly commented, "humans like categories nice and neat...nature is a slob" (as quoted in Clarey, 2009, p. B3).

The structure of sport only reinforces these differences. Sport managers organize most leagues around gender, and they present records and championships accordingly. Even pre-pubescent children commonly compete against same-gender athletes, even though there is no physiological rationale for doing so (see Chapter 6). As people move up to higher levels of sport competition, the differences become magnified. Consequently, people frequently reject athletes, and by extension coaches and administrators, who do not fit into the rigid gendered system. They cite concerns of fairness and advantage as justification (Buzuvis, 2012; Pérez-Samaniego, Fuentes-Miguel, Pereira-García, López-Cañada, & Devís-Devís, in press). Pickett and I offered empirical support for these dynamics in our multiyear study, where prejudice against transgender individuals was higher than that expressed toward LGB persons, and the pattern remained over time (Cunningham & Pickett, 2018).

Beyond LGBT status, other demographics influence opportunities and experiences, though the pattern of findings is equivocal. A number of researchers have shown that gay men experience more negativity in sport (Gill, Morrow, Collins, Lucey, & Schultz, 2006; Sartore & Cunningham, 2009). As previously noted, though, other authors have offered evidence of more inclusive masculinities in the sport and physical activity domains (Anderson, 2011; McCormack & Anderson, 2014). From this perspective, bias toward gay men might be on the decline. Griffin (2012) arrived at a similar conclusion, albeit while approaching the topic from a

different perspective. She suggested that bias was rooted in sexism and privileging of men; as a result, athletes, coaches, and administrators who are lesbian are
silenced in sport. With respect to race, researchers have shown that people commonly associate LGBT status with Whiteness (Herek & Capitanio, 1995; Whitley,
Childs, & Collins, 2011). As a result, racial minorities in the LGBT community
are likely to experience more negativity and prejudice than are their White peers.

Rater Demographics

Rater demographics are also associated with bias expressed toward LGBT individuals. Herek (2009) noted that men, older individuals, people with little formal
education, and conservatives are all more likely to express prejudice than are their
peers (see Exhibit 11.3). These differences can influence access to work, as researchers shown that women decision-makers provide more favorably ratings of LGBT
job applicants than do men (Everly, Unzueta, & Shih, 2016). Race is also associated
with the expression of prejudice. Melton and I found that Asians expressed more
prejudice toward sexual minority youth sport coaches than did members of other
races (Cunningham & Melton, 2012). We also found that correlates of prejudice,
such as knowing sexual minorities, sexism, and religious fundamentalism, varied by
race. On the other hand, Pickett and I found that Whites expressed more transgender prejudice than did racial minorities (Cunningham & Pickett, 2018).

Personal Identity

People of a given group, such as members of the LGBT community, can vary in
the degree to which that membership represents an important part of who they
are. According to social identity theory (Tajfel & Turner, 1979), people's personal identity is that identity they consider important to their self-concept. It helps
differentiate people within a given context (Brewer, 1991), is key to one's self-
image, reflects their personhood, and informs how people feel about themselves
(Luhtanen & Crocker, 1992; Randle & Jaussi, 2003).

In the work environment, LGBT personal identity can influence professional development (Ragins, 2004). If people fail to recognize or appreciate a personal identity, the individual may withdraw psychologically (Pinel & Swann, 2000). On the
one hand, people who feel the need to suppress their personal identities frequently
feel shame and guilt, as well as internalized stigma (Herek, 2009; Pietkiewicz &
Kołodziejczyk-Skrzypek, 2016; Wagner, Kunkel, & Compton, 2016), and they may
alter their behaviors (Melton & Cunningham, 2012b). On the other hand, when in
inclusive, psychologically safe environments, and people feel free to express their
individuated selves (Cunningham, Pickett, Melton, Lee, & Miner, 2014).

SPORT, PHYSICAL ACTIVITY, AND LGBT INDIVIDUALS

A person's sexual orientation and gender identity can influence her or his
participation in sport and physical activity. Consider, for example, a large-
scale study conducted in England in 2016 (Englefield, Cunningham, Mahoney,

Stone, & Torrance, n.d.). The researchers found that LGBT women and men were less likely than their heterosexual peers to be active enough to maintain good health. Results from large-scale studies in the US show that sexual minority youth are less likely to engage in physical activity and some formal sports than are heterosexuals (Calzo et al., 2014; Rosario et al., 2014; Zipp, 2011).

A large-scale, international study entitled *Out on the Fields* helps illustrate why these differences occur (Denison & Kitchen, 2015). The research team collected data from over 9,400 participants in the US, UK, Australia, Canada, Ireland, and New Zealand. The sample included heterosexuals and LGB individuals. The researchers found almost three in four study participants described sport as a space that is unsafe and unwelcoming for LGB people. Many of the respondents did not participate in your sport, citing negative experiences in physical education classes and the fear of rejection because of their sexuality as the main reasons for not doing so. Only 1 in 100 respondents felt LGB individuals were completely accepted in sport. Among the respondents who reported negative personal experiences, gay men and lesbians received homophobic slurs, threats, and physical abuse (see Exhibit 11.5).

The lack of acceptance was not just on the field: 78 percent indicated that sexual minorities would not be welcome as spectators. In fact, 41 percent indicated that homophobia was most common in the stands at sport events (Denison & Kitchen, 2015).

Finally, Denison and Kitchen (2015) asked participants about their LGB disclosure. Most of the participants under age 22 (81 percent of gay men and 74 percent

Prejudice and Discrimination Directed toward Lesbians and Gay Men in Sport

exhibit   **11.5**

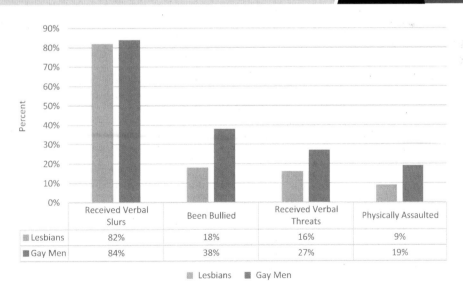

	Received Verbal Slurs	Been Bullied	Received Verbal Threats	Physically Assaulted
Lesbians	82%	18%	16%	9%
Gay Men	84%	38%	27%	19%

Lesbians   Gay Men

Source: Denison & Kitchen (2015).

of lesbians) had not fully disclosed their sexual orientation. They engaged in passing because of their fear of rejection from coaches and teammates. Although LGB athletes were more likely to reveal their sexual orientation when playing on adult teams, many were still closeted. The authors noted that, "Athletes who did 'come out' said the most helpful things were having an ally or supporter on their team and playing for a team that has a culture which is supportive of diversity" (p. 18). King, Mohr, Peddie, Jones, and Kendra (2017) also observed the importance of pro-LGBT cultures in the identity disclosure process.

I offer more information about the coming out process in Exhibit 11.6. Box 11.4 highlights the experiences of one LGBT athlete who disclosed his identity to his teammates.

These findings suggest that LGBT persons might not have welcoming, positive experiences in the sport, and physical activity context. This has traditionally been the case, and in many ways, it still is (Lucas-Carr & Krane, 2012; Melton & Cunningham, 2012b; Worthen, 2014). That said, there is also evidence showing

---

exhibit　**11.6**　Options for Passing or Revealing One's Sexual Orientation

---

Passing: the practice of withholding or failing to reveal a personal identity that is invisible or unrecognizable to others. Passing can take several forms:

- **Fabrication**: a type of passing that occurs when someone deliberately provides incorrect or false information about the self.
- **Concealment**: a type of passing that occurs when people actively try to withhold information or prevent others from acquiring information that would reveal their sexual orientation.
- **Discretion**: a type of passing that occurs when people avoid questions related to their sexual orientation.

Revealing: the practice of disclosing a personal identity that would otherwise be indistinguishable to others. Revealing can take several forms:

- **Signaling**: a type of revealing that occurs when people disclose their sexual orientation by sending messages, providing subtle hints, or giving certain clues.
- **Normalizing**: a type of revealing that occurs when people reveal their sexual orientation to others and then attempt to make their difference from others seem commonplace or ordinary.
- **Differentiating**: a type of revealing that occurs when people disclose their sexual orientation and highlight how it makes them different from others who do not share such identities.

Source: Claire, Beatty, & MacLean (2005).

Box 11.4 Professional Perspectives: The Coming Out Process

In May 2018, Jacob Van Ittersum disclosed to his football teammates at Northwood University that he is bisexual. Prior to doing so, he was apprehensive, concerned that his teammates would reject him. He noted,

> As a kid, you get in your head what a football player is supposed to be like. Anything that deviates from the perceived norm wouldn't seem to be accepted….. Everyone has their own differences. For me, my biggest difference was being bisexual.

His fears allayed, however, after receiving support from his teammates, coaches, and followers on social media. The quarterback on the team was especially supportive. Van Ittersum recalled,

> As I enter my senior season as a starting offensive lineman, a huge weight is lifted off of my shoulders. I can finally be myself without fear of ridicule. Any worries about the locker room were ended by my quarterback's support.

In commenting on the disclosure process, Van Ittersum noted the importance of being true to yourself and the many benefits of having a supportive environment. He recounted,

> It shouldn't be a big thing. We should let people be who they want to be….. From my personal experience, hiding that part of me was really hurtful. It felt like I wasn't being real and was putting on a mask…. People should be allowed to be open with themselves without the thought of ridicule or harassment. Football is an especially hard sport to do so, but times are changing for the better.

Source: Van Ittersum (2018).

that LGBT athletes are experiencing increasingly positive team environments. For instance, most lesbian athletes in the northeastern US who disclose their sexual orientation experience acceptance and support from their teammates, something they largely attribute to the "trailblazers" who came out before them (Fink, Burton, Farrell, & Parker, 2012). Other lesbian athletes report similar experiences, leading Griffin (2012, 2014) to suggest that the sport environment is more accepting for lesbian athletes than it is for lesbian coaches. Similarly, some evidence suggests that men's team sports have more inclusive cultures now than ever before (Anderson & McCormack, 2018). This change in the cultures allows heterosexuals to display more inclusive forms of masculine behaviors (e.g., hugging or kissing a friend) and allows gay men to participate openly, without the need to mask or hide their identity. Pro-gay attitudes are observed among elite soccer players (Magrath, Anderson, & Roberts, 2015), Australian contact sport participants (Murray & White, 2017), and British soccer players (Gaston, Magrath, & Anderson, 2018), among other populations.

Finally, some scholars have investigated the presence of gay and lesbian sport clubs. Elling, De Knop, and Knoppers (2003) report that an increasing number of persons who are LGBT are choosing to participate in gay and lesbian sport clubs or informal gay sport groups (see also Denison & Kitchen, 2015; Jones & McCarthy, 2010). The LGBT sport teams often compete against mainstream teams in various tournaments or leagues, or alternatively may choose to participate in competitions or tournaments specifically for athletes who are LGBT. Elling and colleagues examined why persons who are LGBT chose to participate in those clubs and what their experiences were when they did so. They learned that many club participants found the culture of mainstream sport clubs to be discriminatory toward LGBT athletes, especially men who are gay. The most important reason, however, for joining the club was that the respondents felt more at ease and believed they were better able to socialize with people like them (i.e., other persons who are LGBT) in those clubs.

CHAPTER SUMMARY

T he purpose of this chapter was to explore the influence of sexual orientation, gender identity, and gender expression on people's experiences in the workplace and their sport participation. As evidenced by the Diversity Challenge, attitudes toward these identities can seriously affect a person's well-being. Members of gender and sexual minorities are likely to face prejudice, they have varied work experiences, and they must decide when and whether to disclose their identity to others. From a different perspective, some organizations opt to pursue LGBT consumers and employees actively, with the belief that doing so will better their business. Having read this chapter, you should be able to:

1. Define sexual orientation, gender identity, and gender expression.

      Sexual orientation is a multidimensional construct consisting of a person's self-image, fantasies, attractions, and behaviors. Gender identity refers to people's sense of their own gender, which could be the same as or different from their sex assigned at birth. Gender expression refers to the ways in which people indicate their gender to others through behavior and appearance.

2. Describe the manner in which sexual orientation, gender identity, and gender expression influence access and treatment discrimination.

      People who are LGBT face access discrimination, even when they have the same qualifications as their heterosexual and cisgender peers. They are also paid less and are less likely than heterosexual or cisgender individuals to employment benefits.

3. Summarize the multilevel factors that influence the effects of sexual orientation, gender identity, and gender expression in the work environment.

      Macro-, meso-, and micro-level factors all influence opportunities and access. Employment laws, structural stigma, and institutional norms are salient at the macro-level; bias in decision-making, organizational culture, and leadership are relevant at the meso-level; and demographics, rater demographics, and personal identity are germane at the micro-level.

4. Paraphrase the manner in which sexual orientation, gender identity, and gender expression influence opportunities and experiences of sport and physical activity participants.

    LGBT individuals are less likely to be physically active or to engage in formal sport, relative to their cisgender and heterosexual counterparts. Some evidence indicates that prejudice against LGBT athletes is not as great as it is against LGBT coaches and administrators.

Questions FOR DISCUSSION

1. Various ways of conceptualizing sexual orientation were presented in the chapter. With which approach do you most closely identify and why?
2. Many authors suggest that gender prejudice and sexual prejudice are prevalent in the sport context. Has this been your experience? Provide some examples.
3. Research suggests that attitudes toward men who are gay are more negative than attitudes toward lesbians. Why do you think this is the case?
4. Sexual orientation and gender identity disclosure in the workplace is potentially one of the most anxiety-producing decisions an individual who is LGBT can make. Do you think the same is true for persons who disclose other invisible diversity forms? Why or why not?
5. What are some of the outcomes, both positive and negative, that can be predicted for an organization seeking to target customers who are LGBT?

LEARNING Activities

1. Visit the Outsports site (www.outsports.com) and research the stories told by athletes who have disclosed their sexual orientation; also, research the activities of allies, or persons who offer support and look to create a welcoming environment for LGBT persons.
2. Although some sport organizations see tremendous value in actively recruiting employees and consumers who are LGBT, others are hesitant to adopt such an approach. As a class, divide into two groups and debate the issue.

Web RESOURCES

European Gay and Lesbian Sport Federation, https://www.eglsf.info/
    Organization devoted to supporting LGB sport communities and athletes, as well as fighting discrimination.

OutSports, www.outsports.com
>   Site devoted to providing the most comprehensive information related to the gay sport community.

The Williams Institute, www.law.ucla.edu/williamsinstitute/home.html
>   A center at the UCLA School of Law dedicated to advancing the field of sexual orientation law and public policy.

READING **Resources**

Cunningham, G. B. (Ed.) (2012). *Sexual orientation and gender identity in sport: Essays from activists, coaches, and scholars.* College Station, TX: Center for Sport Management Research and Education.
>   An edited book with contributions from coaches, social activists, and scholars who all focus on gender identity and sexual orientation in sport.

Hargreaves, J., & Anderson, E. (Eds.) (2014). *Routledge handbook of sport, gender and sexuality.* New York, NY: Routledge.

>   A comprehensive handbook with chapters from authors around the world; offers an overview of pertinent issues related to sex, gender, and sexuality.

Sartore-Baldwin, M. L. (Ed.) (2013). *Sexual minorities in sports: Prejudice at play.* Boulder, CO: Lynne Rienner Publishers.
>   Edited book with contributions from some of the leading scholars in the field; focuses on prejudice expressed toward LGBT individuals and ways to reduce those occurrences.

REFERENCES

American Psychological Association (2008). *Answers to your questions: For a better understanding of sexual orientation and homosexuality.* Washington, DC: Author.

Anderson, E. (2008). "Being masculine is not about who you sleep with...." Heterosexual athletes contesting masculinity and the one-time rule of homosexuality. *Sex Roles, 58,* 104–115.

Anderson, E. (2011). Masculinities and sexualities in sport and physical cultures: A three decades of evolving research. *Journal of Homosexuality, 58,* 565–578.

Anderson, E., & McCormack, M. (2015). Cuddling and spooning: Heteromasculinity and homosocial tactility among student-athletes. *Men and Masculinities, 18*(2), 214–230.

Anderson, E., & McCormack, M. (2018). Inclusive masculinity theory: Overview, reflection and refinement. *Journal of Gender Studies, 27*(5), 547–561.

Bailey, J. M., Vasey, P. L., Diamond, L. M., Breedlove, S. M., Vilain, E., & Epprecht, M. (2016). Sexual orientation, controversy, and science. *Psychological Science in the Public Interest, 17*(2), 45–101.

Bandura, A. (1986). *Social foundations for thought and action: A social cognitive theory.* Englewood Cliffs, NJ: Prentice-Hall.

Barron, L. G., & Hebl, M. (2013). The force of law: The effects of sexual orientation antidiscrimination legislation on interpersonal discrimination.

Psychology, Public Policy, and Law, 19(2), 191–205.

Bass, J., Hardin, R., & Taylor, E. A. (2015). The glass closet: Perceptions of homosexuality in intercollegiate sport. *Journal of Applied Sport Management, 7*(4), 1–31.

Beemyn, G., & Rankin, S. (2011). *The lives of transgender people.* New York, NY: Columbia University Press.

Brewer, M. B. (1991). The social self: On being the same and different at the same time. *Personality and Social Psychology Bulletin, 17,* 475–482.

Bryson, A. (2017). Pay equity after the Equality Act 2010: Does sexual orientation still matter? *Work, Employment and Society, 31*(3), 483–500.

Button, S. B. (2001). Organizational efforts to affirm sexual diversity: A cross-level examination. *Journal of Applied Psychology, 86,* 17–28.

Buzuvis, E. E. (2011). Transgender student-athletes and sex segregated sport: Developing policies of inclusion for intercollegiate and interscholastic athletics. *Seton Hall Journal of Sports and Entertainment Law, 21,* 1–59.

Buzuvis, E. E. (2012). Including transgender athletes in sex-segregated sport. In G. B. Cunningham (Ed.), *Sexual orientation and gender identity in sport: Essays from activists, coaches, and scholars* (pp. 23–34). College Station, TX: Center for Sport Management Research and Education.

Cahn, S. (2011). Testing sex, attributing gender: What Caster Semenya means to women's sports. *Journal of Intercollegiate Sport, 4,* 38–48.

Calzo, J. P., Roberts, A. L., Corliss, H. L., Blood, E. A., Kroshus, E., & Austin, S. B. (2014). Physical activity disparities in heterosexual and sexual minority youth ages 12–22 years old: Roles of childhood gender nonconformity and athletic self-esteem. *Annals of Behavioral Medicine, 47,* 17–27.

Carroll, H. J. (2014). Joining the team: The inclusion of transgender students in United States school-based athletics. In J. Hargreaves & E. Anderson (Eds.), *Routledge handbook of sport, gender and sexuality* (pp. 367–375). New York, NY: Routledge.

Cavalier, E. S. (2011). Men at work: Gay men's experiences in the sport workplace. *Journal of Homosexuality, 58,* 626–646.

Clair, J. A., Beatty, J. E., & MacLean, T. L. (2005). Out of sight but not out of mind: Managing invisible social identities in the workplace. *Academy of Management Review, 30,* 78–95.

Clarey, C. (2009, August 20). Gender test after a gold-medal finish. *The New York Times,* B13.

Cleland, J. (2018). Sexuality, masculinity and homophobia in association football: An empirical overview of a changing cultural context. *International Review for the Sociology of Sport, 53*(4), 411–423.

Cunningham, G. B. (2010). Predictors of sexual orientation diversity in intercollegiate athletics. *Journal of Intercollegiate Sport, 3,* 256–269.

Cunningham, G. B. (2011a). Creative work environments in sport organizations: The influence of sexual orientation diversity and commitment to diversity. *Journal of Homosexuality, 58,* 1041–1057.

Cunningham, G. B. (2011b). The LGBT advantage: Examining the relationship among sexual orientation diversity, diversity strategy, and performance. *Sport Management Review, 14,* 453–461.

Cunningham, G. B. (2012). A multilevel model for understanding the experiences of LGBT sport participants. *Journal for the Study of Sports and Athletes in Education, 6,* 5–20.

Cunningham, G. B. (2015a). Creating and sustaining workplace cultures supportive of LGBT employees in college athletics. *Journal of Sport Management, 29,* 426–442.

Cunningham, G. B. (2015b). LGBT inclusive athletic departments as actors of social change. *Journal of Intercollegiate Sport, 8*, 43–56.

Cunningham, G. B. (2017, February). Beware the company you keep: Anti-LGBT laws foster culture of exclusion that harm state economies. *Salon.* Retrieved from http://www.salon.com/2017/02/13/beware-the-company-you-keep-anti-lgbt-laws-foster-culture-of-exclusion-that-harms-state-economies_partner/

Cunningham, G. B. (in press). Understanding the experiences of LGBT athletes in sport: A multilevel model. In M. Anshel (Ed.), *APA handbook of sport and exercise psychology.* Washington, DC: American Psychological Association.

Cunningham, G. B., & Melton, E. N. (2011). The benefits of sexual orientation diversity in sport organizations. *Journal of Homosexuality, 58*(5), 647–663.

Cunningham, G. B., & Melton, E. N. (2013). The moderating effects of contact with lesbian and gay friends on the relationships among religious fundamentalism, sexism, and sexual prejudice. *Journal of Sex Research, 50*, 401–408.

Cunningham, G. B., & Melton, E. N. (2014a). Signals and cues: LGBT inclusive advertising and consumer attraction. *Sport Marketing Quarterly, 23*, 37–46.

Cunningham, G. B., & Melton, E. N. (2014b). Varying degrees of support: Understanding parents' positive attitudes toward LGBT coaches. *Journal of Sport Management, 28*, 387–398.

Cunningham, G. B., & Melton, N. (2012). Prejudice against lesbian, gay, and bisexual coaches: The influence of race, religious fundamentalism, modern sexism, and contact with sexual minorities. *Sociology of Sport Journal, 29*, 283–305.

Cunningham, G. B., & Nite, C. (2018, June). *LGBT inclusion and institutional characteristics predict organizational performance.* Paper presented at the annual conference of the North American Society for Sport Management, Halifax, NS.

Cunningham, G. B., & Pickett, A. C. (2018). Trans prejudice in sport: Differences from LGB prejudice, the influence of gender, and changes over time. *Sex Roles, 78*(3–4), 220–227.

Cunningham, G. B., & Sartore, M. L. (2010). Championing diversity: The influence of personal and organizational antecedents. *Journal of Applied Social Psychology, 40*(4), 788–810.

Cunningham, G. B., Buzuvis, E., & Mosier, C. (2018). Inclusive spaces and locker rooms for transgender athletes. *Kinesiology Review, 7*, 365–374.

Cunningham, G. B., Sartore, M. L., & McCullough, B. P. (2010). The influence of applicant sexual orientation and rater sex on ascribed attributions and hiring recommendations of personal trainers. *Journal of Sport Management, 24*, 400–415.

Cunningham, G. B., Pickett, A., Melton, E. N., Lee, W., & Miner, K. (2014). Free to be me: Psychological safety and the expression of sexual orientation and personal identity. In J. Hargreaves & E. Anderson (Eds.), *Routledge handbook of sport gender and sexualities* (pp. 406–415). London, UK: Routledge.

Denison, E., & Kitchen, A. (2015). *Out on the fields: The first international study on homophobia in sport.* RepuCom. Retrieved from http://www.outonthefields.com/

Drury, S., Stride, A., Flintoff, A., & Williams, S. (2017). Lesbian, gay, bisexual and transgender young people's experiences of PE and the implications for youth sport participation and engagement. In J. Long, T. Fletcher, & B. Watson (Eds.), *Sport, leisure and social justice* (pp. 84–97). New York, NY: Routledge.

Drydakis, N. (2015). Sexual orientation discrimination in the United Kingdom's labour market: A field experiment. *Human Relations, 68*(11), 1769–1796.

Elling, A., De Knop, P., & Knoppers, A. (2003). Gay/lesbian sport clubs and events: Places of homo-social bonding and cultural resistance? *International Review for the Sociology of Sport, 38,* 441–456.

Englefield, L., Cunningham, D., Mahoney, A., Stone, T., & Torrance, H. (no date). *Sport, Physical Activity, and LGBT: A Study by Pride Sports for Sport England.* Retrieved from https://www.sportengland.org/media/11116/pride-sport-sport-physical-activity-and-lgbt-report-2016.pdf

Everly, B. A., & Schwarz, J. L. (2015). Predictors of the adoption of LGBT-friendly HR policies. *Human Resource Management, 54*(2), 367–384.

Everly, B. A., Unzueta, M. M., & Shih, M. J. (2016). Can being gay provide a boost in the hiring process? Maybe if the boss is female. *Journal of Business and Psychology, 31*(2), 293–306.

Fidas, D., Bailey, B., & Cooper, L. (2017). *Corporate equality index 2018: Rating American workplaces on lesbian, gay, bisexual, transgender, and queer equality.* Washington, DC: Human Rights Campaign.

Fink, J. S., Burton, L. J., Farrell, A., & Parker, H. (2012). Playing it out: Female intercollegiate athletes' experiences in revealing their sexual identities. *Journal for the Study of Sport and Athletes in Education, 6,* 83–106.

Florida, R. (2003). Cities and the creative class. *City & Community, 2,* 3–19.

Florida, R. (2012). *The rise of the creative class, revisited.* New York, NY: Basic Books.

Gaston, L., Magrath, R., & Anderson, E. (2018). From hegemonic to inclusive masculinities in English professional football: Marking a cultural shift. *Journal of Gender Studies, 27*(3), 301–312.

Gates, G. J. (2011). *How many people are lesbian, gay, bisexual, and transgender?* Los Angeles, CA: Williams Institute, University of California, Los Angeles School of Law.

Gill, D. L., Morrow, R. G., Collins, K. E., Lucey, A. B., & Schultz, A. M. (2006). Attitudes and sexual prejudice in sport and physical activity. *Journal of Sport Management, 20*(4), 554–564.

Goffman, E. (1963). *Stigma: Notes on the management of spoiled identity.* New York, NY: Simon & Schuster.

Greenhaus, J. H., Parasuraman, S., & Wormley, W. M. (1990). Effects of race on organizational experiences, job performance, evaluations, and career outcomes. *Academy of Management Journal, 33,* 64–86.

Griffin, P. (2012). LGBT equality in sports: Celebrating our successes and facing our challenges. In G. B. (Ed.), *Sexual orientation and gender identity in sport: Essays from activists, coaches, and scholars* (pp. 1–12). College Station, TX: Center for Sport Management Research and Education.

Griffin, P. (2014). Overcoming sexism and homophobia in women's sports: Two steps forward and one step back. In J. Hargreaves & E. Anderson (Eds.), *Routledge handbook of sport, gender and sexuality* (pp. 265–274). New York, NY: Routledge.

Hatzenbuehler, M. L., Bellatorre, A., & Muennig, P. (2014). Anti-gay prejudice and all-cause mortality among heterosexuals in the United States. *American Journal of Public Health, 104,* 332–337.

Herek, G. M. (2000). The psychology of sexual prejudice. *Current Directions in Psychological Science, 9,* 19–22.

Herek, G. M. (2007). Confronting sexual stigma and prejudice: Theory and practice. *Journal of Social Issues, 63,* 905–923.

Herek, G. M. (2009). Sexual stigma and sexual prejudice in the United States: A conceptual framework. In D. A. Hope (Ed.), *Contemporary perspectives on lesbian, gay, and bisexual identities* (pp. 65–111). New York, NY: Springer.

Herek, G. M., & Capitanio, J. P. (1995). Black heterosexuals' attitudes toward lesbians and gay men in the United States. *Journal of Sex Research*, *32*(2), 95–105.

Herek, G. M., & McLemore, K. A. (2013). Sexual prejudice. *Annual Review of Psychology*, *64*, 309–333.

Huffman, A. H., Watrous-Rodriguez, K. M., & King, E. B. (2008). Supporting a diverse workforce: What type of support is most meaningful for lesbian and gay employees? *Human Resource Management*, *47*, 237–253.

ILGA Europe. (2017, May). *Annual review of the human rights situation of lesbian, gay, bisexual, trans, and intersex people in Europe*. Brussels, Belgium: Author.

IOC Consensus Meeting on Sex Reassignment and Hyperandrogenism. (2015, November). *International Olympic Committee*. Retrieved from https://stillmed.olympic.org/Documents/Commissions_PDFfiles/Medical_commission/2015-11_ioc_consensus_meeting_on_sex_reassignment_and_hyperandrogenism-en.pdf

Jones, L., & McCarthy, M. (2010). Mapping the landscape of gay men's football. *Leisure Studies*, *29*(2), 161–173.

King, E. B., Mohr, J. J., Peddie, C. I., Jones, K. P., & Kendra, M. (2017). Predictors of identity management: An exploratory experience-sampling study of lesbian, gay, and bisexual workers. *Journal of Management*, *43*(2), 476–502.

Kinsey, A. C., Pomeroy, W. B., & Martin, C. E. (1948). *Sexual behavior in the human male*. Philadelphia, PA: W. B. Saunders.

Kinsey, A. C., Pomeroy, W. B., Martin, C. E., & Gebhard, P. H. (1953). *Sexual behavior in the human female*. Philadelphia, PA: W. B. Saunders.

Korchmaros, J. D., Powell, C., & Stevens, S. (2013). Chasing sexual orientation: A comparison of commonly used single-indicator measures of sexual orientation. *Journal of Homosexuality*, *60*, 596–614.

Krane, V., Barak, K. S., & Mann, M. E. (2012). Broken binaries and transgender athletes: Challenging sex and gender in sports. In G. B. Cunningham (Ed.), *Sexual orientation and gender identity in sport: Essays from activists, coaches, and scholars* (pp. 13–22). College Station, TX: Center for Sport Management Research and Education.

Law, C. L., Martinez, L. R., Ruggs, E. N., Hebl, M. R., & Akers, E. (2011). Transparency in the workplace: How the experiences of transsexual employees can be improved. *Journal of Vocational Behavior*, *79*, 710–723.

Lee, W., & Cunningham, G. B. (2014). Imagine that: Examining the influence of sport-related imagined contact on intergroup anxiety and sexual prejudice across cultures. *Journal of Applied Social Psychology*, *44*(8), 557–566.

Lee, W., & Cunningham, G. B. (2016). Gender, sexism, sexual prejudice, and identification with US football and men's figure skating. *Sex Roles*, *74*(9–10), 464–471.

Love, A. (2014). Transgender exclusion and inclusion in sport. In J. Hargreaves & E. Anderson (Eds.), *Routledge handbook of sport, gender and sexuality* (pp. 376–383). New York, NY: Routledge.

Lucas-Carr, C. B., & Krane, V. (2012). Troubling sport or troubled by sport: Experiences of transgender athletes. *Journal for the Study of Sports and Athletes in Education*, *6*, 21–44.

Luhtanen, R., & Crocker, J. (1992). A collective self-esteem scale: Self-evaluation of one's social identity. *Personality and Social Psychology Bulletin*, *18*, 302–318.

Magrath, R., Anderson, E., & Roberts, S. (2015). On the door-step of equality: Attitudes toward gay athletes among academy-level footballers. *International Review for the Sociology of Sport*, *50*(7), 804–821.

Major, B., & O'Brien, L. T. (2005). The social psychology of stigma. *Annual Review of Psychology*, *56*, 393–421.

Mallory, C., Brown, T. N., Russell, S. T., & Sears, B. (2017). *The Impact of Stigma and Discrimination against LGBT*

People in Texas. Los Angeles, CA: Williams Institute, UCLA School of Law.

McCloughan, L. J., Mattey, E. L., & Hanrahan, S. J. (2015). Educating coaches on their role in the prevention of homophobic bullying in adolescent sport. *International Sport Coaching Journal, 2*(3), 317–329.

McCormack, M., & Anderson, E. (2014). The influence of declining homophobia on men's gender in the United States: An argument for the study of homohysteria. *Sex Roles, 71*(3–4), 109–120.

Melton, E. N., & Cunningham, G. B. (2012a). The effect of LGBT-inclusive policies on organizational attraction. *International Journal of Sport Management, 13*, 444–462.

Melton, E. N., & Cunningham, G. (2012b). When identities collide: Exploring minority stress and resilience among college athletes with multiple marginalized identities. *Journal for the Study of Sports and Athletes in Education, 6*, 45–66.

Melton, E. N., & Cunningham, G. B. (2014a). Examining the workplace experiences of sport employees who are LGBT: A social categorization theory perspective. *Journal of Sport Management, 28*, 21–33.

Melton, E. N., & Cunningham, G. B. (2014b). Who are the champions? Using a multilevel model to examine perceptions of employee support for LGBT inclusion in sport organizations. *Journal of Sport Management, 28*, 189–206.

Meyer, J. W., & Rowan, B. (1977). Institutionalized organizations: Formal structure as myth and ceremony. *American Journal of Sociology, 83*, 340–363.

Morrison, M. A., Bishop, C. J., & Morrison, T. G. (in press). A systematic review of the psychometric properties of composite LGBT prejudice and discrimination scales. *Journal of Homosexuality*.

Murray, A., & White, A. (2017). Twelve not so angry men: Inclusive masculinities in Australian contact sports. *International*

Review for the Sociology of Sport, 52(5), 536–550.

National Collegiate Athletic Association. (2011). *NCAA inclusion of transgender student-athletes*. Indianapolis, IN: Author.

Non-discrimination Laws. (2017, February 25). Movement advancement project. Retrieved from http://www.lgbtmap.org/equality-maps/non_discrimination_laws

Patacchini, E., Ragusa, G., & Zenou, Y. (2015). Unexplored dimensions of discrimination in Europe: Homosexuality and physical appearance. *Journal of Population Economics, 28*(4), 1045–1073.

Pérez-Samaniego, V., Fuentes-Miguel, J., Pereira-García, S., López-Cañada, E., & Devís-Devís, J. (in press). Experiences of trans persons in physical activity and sport: A qualitative meta-synthesis. *Sport Management Review*.

Pietkiewicz, I. J., & Kołodziejczyk-Skrzypek, M. (2016). Living in sin? How gay Catholics manage their conflicting sexual and religious identities. *Archives of Sexual Behavior, 45*(6), 1573–1585.

Pinel, E. C. & Swann, W. (2000). Finding the self through others: Self-verification and social movement participation. In S. Stryker, T. J. Owens, & R. W. White (Eds.), *Self, Identity, and Social Movements* (pp. 132–152). Minneapolis: University of Minnesota Press.

Pizer, J. C., Sears, B., Mallory, C., & Hunter, N. D. (2012). Evidence of persistent and pervasive workplace discrimination against LGBT people: The need for federal legislation prohibiting discrimination and providing for equal employment benefits. *Loyola of Los Angeles Law Review, 45*, 715–779.

Ragins, B. R. (2004). Sexual orientation in the workplace: The unique work and career experiences of gay, lesbian and bisexual workers. *Research in Personnel and Human Resources Management, 23*, 35–120.

Ragins, B. R., & Wiethoff, C. (2005). Understanding heterosexism at work: The straight problem. In

R. L. Dipboye & A. Colella (Eds.), *Discrimination at work: The psychological and organizational bases* (pp. 177–201). Mahwah, NJ: Lawrence Erlbaum.

Ragins, B. R., Singh, R., & Cornwell, J. M. (2007). Making the invisible visible: Fear and disclosure of sexual orientation at work. *Journal of Applied Psychology, 4,* 1103–1118.

Randle, A. E., & Jaussi, K. S. (2003). Functional background identity, diversity, and individual performance in cross-functional teams. *Academy of Management Journal, 46,* 763–774.

Rosario, M., Corliss, H. L., Everett, B. G., Reisner, S. L., Austin, B., Butching, F. O., & Birkett, M. (2014). Sexual orientation disparities in cancer-related risk behaviors of tobacco, alcohol, sexual behaviors, and diet and physical activity. Pooled youth risk behavior surveys. *American Journal of Public Health, 104,* 245–254.

Rule, N. O., Bjornsdottir, R. T., Tskhay, K. O., & Ambady, N. (2016). Subtle perceptions of male sexual orientation influence occupational opportunities. *Journal of Applied Psychology, 101*(12), 1687–1704.

Russell, S. T., & Fish, J. N. (2016). Mental health in lesbian, gay, bisexual, and transgender (LGBT) youth. *Annual Review of Clinical Psychology, 12,* 465–487.

Same-sex couple data & demographics. (no date). *The Williams Institute.* Retrieved from https://williamsinstitute.law.ucla.edu/visualization/lgbt-stats/?topic=SS#density

Sartore, M. L., & Cunningham, G. B. (2009). Sexual prejudice, participatory decisions, and panoptic control: Implications for sexual minorities in sport. *Sex Roles, 60,* 100–113.

Sartore, M. L., & Cunningham, G. B. (2010). The lesbian label as a component of women's stigmatization in sport organizations: An exploration of two health and kinesiology departments. *Journal of Sport Management, 24,* 481–501.

Sartore-Baldwin, M. L. (2013). Gender, sexuality, and prejudice in sport. In M. L. Sartore-Baldwin (Ed.), *Sexual minorities in sports: Prejudice at play* (pp. 1–10). Boulder, CO: Lynne Rienner Publishers.

Savin-Williams, R. C. (2006). Who's gay? Does it matter? *Current Directions in Psychological Science, 15,* 40–44.

Savin-Williams, R. C. (2014). An exploratory study of the categorical versus spectrum nature of sexual orientation. *Journal of Sex Research, 31,* 446–453.

Savin-Williams, R. C. (2016). Sexual orientation: Categories or continuum? Commentary on Bailey et al. (2016). *Psychological Science in the Public Interest, 17*(2), 37–44.

Savin-Williams, R. C. (2018). An exploratory study of exclusively heterosexual, primarily heterosexual, and mostly heterosexual young men. *Sexualities, 21*(1–2), 16–29.

Savin-Williams, R. C., & Vrangalova, Z. (2013). Mostly heterosexual as a distinct sexual orientation: A systematic review of the empirical evidence. *Developmental Review, 33,* 58–88.

Savin-Williams, R. C., Cash, B. M., McCormack, M., & Rieger, G. (2017). Gay, mostly gay, or bisexual leaning gay? An exploratory study distinguishing gay sexual orientations among young men. *Archives of Sexual Behavior, 46*(1), 265–272.

Schein, E. H. (2004). *Organizational culture and leadership* (3rd ed.). San Francisco, CA: Jossey-Bass.

Scoats, R., Joseph, L. J., & Anderson, E. (2018). 'I don't mind watching him cum': Heterosexual men, threesomes, and the erosion of the one-time rule of homosexuality. *Sexualities, 21*(1–2), 30–48.

Seelman, K. L. (2016). Transgender adults' access to college bathrooms and housing and the relationship to suicidality. *Journal of Homosexuality, 63*(10), 1378–1399.

Shaw, S. (in press). The chaos of inclusion? Examining anti-homophobia policy development in New Zealand sport. *Sport Management Review*.

Silva, T. (2017). Bud-sex: Constructing normative masculinity among rural straight men that have sex with men. *Gender & Society, 31*(1), 51–73.

Smith, N. G., & Ingram, K. M. (2004). Workplace heterosexism and adjustment among lesbian, gay, and bisexual individuals: The role of unsupportive interactions. *Journal of Counseling Psychology, 51*, 57–67.

Staurowsky, E. (2012). Sexual prejudice and sport media coverage. *Journal for the Study of Sports and Athletes in Education, 6*(1), 121–140.

Sykes, H. (2006). Transsexual and transgender policies in sport. *Women in Sport and Physical Activity Journal, 15*(1), 3–13. doi: 10.1123/wspaj.15.1.3

Tajfel, H., & Turner, J. C. (1979). An integrative theory of intergroup conflict. In W.G. Austin & S. Worchel (Eds.), *The social psychology of intergroup relations* (pp. 33–47). Monterey, CA: Brooks/Cole.

Travers, A., & Deri, J. (2011). Transgender inclusion and the changing face of lesbian softball leagues. *International Review for the Sociology of Sport, 46*, 488–507.

Trussell, D. E., Kovac, L., & Apgar, J. (2018). LGBTQ parents' experiences of community youth sport: Change your forms, change your (hetero) norms. *Sport Management Review, 21*(1), 51–62.

Van Ittersum, J. (2018, August). When college football lineman came out, his QB had his back. *Outsports*. Retrieved from https://www.outsports.com/2018/8/7/17659340/jacob-van-ittersum-northwood-football-bi-coming-out

Velez, B. L., & Moradi, B. (2012). Workplace support, discrimination, and person-organization fit: Tests of the theory of work adjustment with LGB individuals. *Journal of Counseling Psychology, 59*, 399–407.

Volpone, S. D., & Avery, D. R. (2010). I'm confused: How failing to value sexual identities at work sends stakeholders mixed messages. *Industrial and Organizational Psychology, 3*, 90–92.

Wagner, P. E., Kunkel, A., & Compton, B. L. (2016). (Trans) lating identity: Exploring discursive strategies for navigating the tensions of identity gaps. *Communication Quarterly, 64*(3), 251–272.

Washington, M., & Patterson, K. D. W. (2011). Hostile takeover or joint venture: Connections between institutional theory and sport management research. *Sport Management Review, 14*, 1–12.

West, K. (2016). Jamaica, three years later: Effects of intensified pro-gay activism on severe prejudice against lesbians and gay men. *The Journal of Sex Research, 53*(9), 1107–1117.

Whitley Jr, B. E., Childs, C. E., & Collins, J. B. (2011). Differences in Black and White American college students' attitudes toward lesbians and gay men. *Sex Roles, 64*(5–6), 299–310.

Worthen, M. G. (2014). The cultural significance of homophobia on heterosexual women's gendered experiences in the United States: A commentary. *Sex Roles, 71*, 141–151.

Wright, J. (2017, August). Bathroom bills fuel spike in calls from trans youth to suicide hotline. *Out Smart: Houston's LGBTQ Magazine*. Retrieved August 18, 2017, from http://www.outsmartmagazine.com/2017/08/texas-bathroom-bills-reportedly-fuel-spike-in-calls-from-trans-youth-to-suicide-hotline/

Zipp, J. F. (2011). Sport and sexuality: Athletic participation by sexual minority and sexual majority adolescents in the U.S. *Sex Roles, 64*, 19–31.

Social Class

LEADING OBJECTIVES

After studying this chapter, you should be able to:

- Define key terms related to social class inclusion and diversity, including socioeconomic status (SES), social class, and classism.

- Describe the manner in which social class influences access and treatment discrimination.

- Summarize the multilevel factors that influence the effects of social class in the work environment.

- Paraphrase the manner in which social class influences opportunities and experiences of sport and physical activity participants.

DIVERSITY CHALLENGE

Participation in high school athletics provides a number of potential benefits, including character development, learning how to work with others, and engaging in cross-cultural experiences. Relative to their less active peers, students who participate in sports perform better academically, have greater confidence, develop more interpersonal connections, exhibit more pro-social behaviors, and develop more desired personality characteristics. These effects are particularly strong among students from disadvantaged backgrounds because their participation in school-sponsored athletics provides them with after-school activities they might not otherwise have.

Despite the many positive outcomes associated with high school athletics, tight state budgets have forced many schools to drop or scale back their sport offerings. Some school districts have cut all extracurricular activities. Others have consolidated all sports programs in the district into one. The end result of these and other activities is the denial of sport opportunities for students in the poorest districts and the advancement of schools in richer areas.

Another approach for which school administrators advocate is that of pay-to-play, in which students pay a fee to participate in a sport. This is a common practice, as 60 percent of parents indicate they have had to pay for their children to participate in high school athletics. In southwest Ohio, 82 percent of the school districts report having a pay-to-play program. Whereas pay-to-play allows the sports to be offered, the policy negatively affects low-income families. Only 6 percent have received a waiver based on their income level, but close to 20 percent of families earning less than $60,000 annually have had to decrease sport participation because of the fees. Thus, along with the potential cost-saving benefits, pay-to-play programs ultimately privilege the wealthy while cutting out the poor from participation in sport.

Sources: Cook, B. (2017, January). It's tough for low-income kids, especially girls, to participate in sports. *Forbes*. Retrieved from https://www.forbes.com/sites/bobcook/2017/01/06/its-tough-for-low-income-kids-especially-girls-to-participate-in-sports/#1854c345622c / Cook, B. (2012, May). Pay-to-play is squeezing kids out of school sports. *Forbes*. Retrieved from http://www.forbes.com/sites/bobcook/2012/05/15/payto-play-is-squeezing-kids-out-of-school-sports. Linver, M. R., Roth, J. L., & Brooks-Gunn, J. (2009). Patterns of adolescents' participation in organized activities: Are sports best when combined with other activities? *Developmental Psychology, 45*, 354–367. Sagas, M., & Cunningham, G. B. (2014). *Sport participation rates among underserved American youth*. Gainesville, FL: University of Florida Sport Policy & Research Collaborative.

CHALLENGE REFLECTION

1. Other than those listed in the Diversity Challenge, what options could school administrators pursue to balance their athletic budgets?
2. Why do opponents of pay-to-play programs argue that the participation fees hurt low-income students more than other students? Do you agree with this perspective?
3. Are you aware of other ways in which school financing plans tend to disadvantage low-income students or students in low-income districts?

As the Diversity Challenge illustrates, economic means and social power play significant roles in determining the opportunities people have for sport and physical activity. The effects of social class are not limited to the hard court or playing field. A person's class affects many of the opportunities available in life; class ultimately may influence physical and educational opportunities, jobs held, and psychological health, including perception of one's self. Clearly, then, class is a meaningful diversity form that demands our attention.

Despite the primacy of class in people's lives, it is often neglected in discussions of diversity. Major academic entities, such as the American Psychological Association (APA), continually overlook class in multicultural and diversity-related conferences and publications (Dunn, 2017). Academic publications and course texts often follow suit. For instance, in a review of the leading management and organizational psychology journals, Côté (2011) found only four articles with a focus on social class issues. This pattern is also evident in sport management. I searched the abstracts from the annual conference for the North American Society for Sport Management from 2007 to 2018. Of the more than 3,000 abstracts, only 58 included the term "social class," "socio-economic," or "socioeconomic status." Even diversity management texts are guilty of this omission, and many of them (e.g., Triana, 2017) do not include even a chapter devoted to the topic. However, large professional organizations and diversity scholars are not alone: the media often either ignore the poor or portray them negatively and as deficient in moral character (McCall, 2014).

I have experienced this trend in my own classes, as well. Early in the semester, I ask students to complete the "Diversity Pie Chart" (see Powell, 2004), in which they identify group affiliations that meaningfully contribute to their self-concept. Invariably, only one or two students list class as a social identity category, and many times, no students in the class will include that diversity form in their pie chart. This pattern has occurred over a number of years, with both undergraduate and graduate students. For many people, then, class has a taken-for-granted nature such that people think about other characteristics—some of which might be closely linked with class (e.g., gender, race)—when considering their identity markers.

Thus, although class plays an important role in the experiences and chances one has in life, people often overlook it in their discussions of diversity. The purpose of this chapter is to provide an overview of the influence of class and class consciousness on people's lives and in the delivery of sport. I begin by providing an overview of key terms, including SES and social class. I then examine the effects of social class in the work environment and, drawing from Chapter 4, offer multilevel explanations for these effects. The discussion then moves to the effects of classism on people's health and well-being, and the chapter concludes with a focus on the influence of sport participation on people's social mobility.

BACKGROUND AND KEY TERMS

Scholars have offered a number of different conceptualizations of social class. In fact, Liu, Ali, Soleck, and their colleagues (2004), in their review of more than 3,900 psychology articles published between 1981 and 2000, found that nearly *500 different words* were used to describe, conceptualize, or discuss social class and classism. Luckily, a review of all of those terms is not necessary for this discussion. Instead, I highlight two primary approaches that researchers, government organizations, and policymakers have employed (see Exhibit 12.1).

Authors who adopt the materialistic approach focus on the material and economic resources that people possess (APA, 2006; Smith, 2010). Persons adopting this approach favor the term *socioeconomic status* (SES), and they take into account three primary factors: income, education, and occupation. Here, the fundamental focus is on people's access to resources.

Income indicators take several forms, ranging from yearly income to complex formulas that involve a number of variables. For instance, in defining the poverty line, US Department of Health and Human Services sets thresholds that take

exhibit **12.1**   Approaches to the Study of Economic Inequality

SES approach: a materialistic focus, with a particular emphasis on income, occupation, and education.

Class approach: a power and privilege focus, with particular emphasis on how power, political action, and socially constructed realities economically and socially advantage some at the expense of others.

Source: American Psychological Association (2006), Smith (2008).

into account family income and characteristics of the family. In 2018, the poverty threshold for a single-person household was $12,140, while the threshold for a four-person household was $25,100 (Poverty Guidelines, 2018). Some observers have argued that wealth, or one's private assets minus debts, is a better indicator of economic status because it reflects intergenerational transfers of resources that can serve as a buffer against potential fluctuations in annual income (APA, 2006).

Education is considered a reliable indicator of desired economic outcomes, good health and well-being, and the reduction of health risk behaviors (Mehta & Preston, 2016; Sasson, 2016). It is important to understand, however, that incremental increases in educational attainment are not necessarily associated with more positive outcomes. Instead, the jumps are discontinuous in nature, and they occur only after a person is conferred an academic degree (Backlund, Sorlie, & Johnson, 1999). Thus, a student who spends four years in college but fails to earn a degree will not reap the same benefits as another student who spends the same time at college and earns a diploma. This distinction is attributable to the prestige associated with earning the credential or with the presumed positive characteristics (e.g., perseverance) that people associate with degree holders.

Finally, a person's occupation serves as a reflection of overall SES. Policymakers have developed various scales that order occupations based on a number of criteria. For instance, according to the Bureau of Labor Statistics (Standard Occupational Classification, n.d.), federal agencies in the US use the 2018 Standard Occupational Classification System to categorize workers by occupation. This process is a complicated one because people are classified into one of more than *867 occupations*. These categorizations can be further broken down into either 459 broad occupations, 98 minor groups, or 23 major groups. For an example of the system, let's look at a category of particular relevance to our discussion: 27-0000—arts, design, entertainment, sports, and media occupations. This major group is broken down into four minor groups:

1. 27-1000 (arts and design workers),
2. 27-2000 (entertainers and performers, sports and related workers),

3. 27-3000 (media and communication workers), and

4. 27-4000 (media and communication equipment workers).

The Bureau further divides major group 27-2000 into five broad occupational categories:

1. 27-2010 (actors, producers, and directors),
2. 27-2020 (athletes, coaches, umpires, and related workers),
3. 27-2030 (dancers and choreographers),
4. 27-2030 (musicians, singers, and related workers), and
5. 27-2030 (miscellaneous entertainers and performers, sports and related workers.

Each of these occupations is associated with different wage rates, prestige, and power—all factors that contribute to an individual's SES. To illustrate, data from California (USA) in 2018 show that the median wage for athletes and sport competitors was $87,147, while the wage for referees was $26,808—a more than threefold difference (Labor Market Information, 2018).

The use of the materialistic approach is widespread, and researchers have linked income, educational attainment, and occupational status to a number of important outcomes, including psychological and physical health, academic performance, and life expectancy, among others (Pinquart & Sörensen, 2000). Nevertheless, this approach has a number of shortcomings. First, conceptualizations of income, education, and occupation often vary. Even within the US government, the US Census Bureau uses one formula for classifying poverty while the Department of Health and Human Services uses another (see Smith, 2008). There are similar ambiguities with the conceptualizations of education and occupation.

A second shortcoming is that there are considerable differences among occupations within classifications. One can certainly envisage differences in opportunities and access to resources between a television producer and a junior high track and field coach, both of whom are included in the same major occupational category (arts, design, entertainment, sports, and media occupations). Third, and most important, discussions of SES fail to recognize the very important issues of power, privilege, control, and subjugation. As Smith (2008) eloquently notes,

> Creating class divisions according to SES sidesteps the issue of relationship to (or distance from) sociocultural power and carries with it the implication that class-related experiences and oppressions are similar for people who fall within the same numerical SES classification.
>
> (p. 902)

Given this criticism, many sociology and social psychology researchers have turned to the concept of social class.

Social Class Approach

According to Loignon and Woehr (2018), a person's social class "reflects the social context he or she occupies, as defined by the resource that he or she holds and his or her subjective interpretation of that context" (p. 62). Social class involves elements of SES, such as income and education, and it includes occupational prestige and subjective rank relative to others (Côté, 2011). This definition highlights the importance of resources but it also points to the very important role of subjectivity and perceptions. Unlike SES, social class is more overtly political in nature, draws attention to differences in power, and focuses on the socially constructed nature of social standing, including the treatment of persons from various classes (Lott & Bullock, 2007). From this perspective, inequality is a function not *only* of differential access to valued resources but also of the social (re)creation of privilege, power, and domination, particularly within capitalist societies (APA, 2006). As some examples, consider that even though a small portion of Americans are millionaires, many Congressional members are (Hawkings, 2018). In fact, in the 115 Congress, the median wealth of Republican Senators was $1.4 million. As another example, coaches of major college football teams routinely earn 100 times the equivalent compensation for players (i.e., their tuition, room, board, and stipend).

The focus on power, politics, and socially constructed realities allows for different methods for grouping classes. Smith (2008, 2010), in combining the frameworks put forth by Leondar-Wright (2005) and Zweig (2000), advanced the following typology:

- **Poverty**: This class includes working-class persons who, because of various circumstances, including unemployment, low wages, or lack of health-care coverage, do not have the income needed to support their basic needs.
- **Working class**: Persons in this class lack power and authority in the workplace, have little discretion in how they complete their work, and are marginalized when it comes to providing feedback concerning their health care, education, and housing. Relative to people in more powerful classes, working-class persons have lower income levels, lower net worth, and less education.
- **Middle class**: Persons in this class are college educated and salaried, and they typically work as professionals, managers, or small business owners. Relative to the working class, middle-class persons have greater job autonomy and economic security; however, they do rely on their earnings to support themselves.
- **Owning class**: Persons in this class have accumulated enough wealth that they do not need to work to support themselves; further, they generally own businesses and resources from which others make their living. Given their power and access to resources, owning-class persons also maintain substantial social, cultural, and political clout, particularly relative to other classes.

The typology brings to bear several key points. First, unlike SES-based distinctions, the social class–based typology overtly brings into the discussion issues of subjugation, autonomy, and politics, thereby recognizing that power and status help us to make sense of the socially constructed notion of class (Lott & Bullock, 2007; Smith, 2008, 2010). Second, poverty, as outlined in this framework, is not bound by specific numerical cutoff values, but instead the social-class perspective recognizes that persons in this class simply do not have the requisite income to provide them consistently with enough monies to cover basic individual and family needs. Finally, the framework recognizes that people living in poverty predominantly are members of the working class. In doing so, it helps to counter the classic, albeit incorrect, stereotype that the poor are an "under class" of people who are either unwilling or unable to work (see also Zweig, 2000).

Other scholars have advanced different classification schemes, and I highlight two in Box 12.1.

Box 12.1 Alternative Perspectives: Conceptualizing Social Class

Social scientists have thought about class in a number of ways, and French sociologist Bourdieu's (1984) perspective is among the more popular. He suggests that people possess different forms of capital, including the following:

- Economic capital, or their wealth and income;

- Cultural capital, which represents people's ability to appreciate cultural goods and their status achieved through educational success; and

- Social capital, or the connections people have with others—that is, their social networks.

Those who adopt this perspective recognize that social class is about more than just people's wealth; it also has to do with their different forms of capital and the status, opportunities, and privilege they enjoy in society.

Drawing from this perspective, Savage, Devine, Cunningham, and their colleagues (2013) worked with the BBC to conduct the Great British Class Survey. This involved an analysis of the different forms of capital through data from more than 161,000 participants, the largest analysis ever conducted in the UK. Their analysis revealed the presence of seven social classes, as follows:

- **Elite**: This is the most advantaged and privileged class in British society. Members have the highest incomes (mean of £89K), own the most expensive houses (mean of £325K), possess considerable savings (mean of £142K), enjoy close to the highest numbers of social contacts, and score the highest on "highbrow cultural capital" (e.g., engagement in classical music; attendance at art exhibits, theatre, and museums; and patronage at high-end restaurants). People in the elite class are likely to be chief executives and are unlikely to be racial minorities.

- **Established middle class**: This social class, which is much larger than the

Elite class, includes people who have an average household income of £47K, houses worth an average of £177K, and some savings (mean £26K). They have high-status social contacts, are culturally engaged, and are well educated. People in this social class are likely to be working professionals, such as engineers or occupational therapists.

- **Technical middle class**: This is a small social class, representing 6 percent of the population, but its members are prosperous: they have a mean household income of £38K, mean home value of £163K, and mean savings of £66K. They have restricted social networks and score low in cultural capital. Typical occupations include pharmacist, higher education professor, and scientist.

- **New affluent workers**: People in this social class score high on emerging social capital (e.g., engagement in video games and social media, sport participation and attendance, and attendance at rap concerts). Typical occupations include sales, retail, and electrician. Individuals in this class have moderate incomes (mean of £29K), small savings (mean of £5K), and relatively high home values (mean of £129K). An individual in this class generally has not obtained a graduate degree but has nonetheless achieved a middle-class position.

- **Traditional working class**: People in this class are relatively poor, with a mean household income of £13K, and their savings and house size reflect as much. They are not well educated, and they work in

occupations that are traditionally considered working class, such as mechanic and secretarial work. They possess moderate levels of emerging cultural capital and low levels of highbrow cultural capital.

- **Emergent service workers**: People in this social class have modest income levels (mean of £21K), are likely to rent, and have little savings. They have a large social network and a moderate level of emerging cultural capital. People in this social class are often young, and they hold a variety of service jobs, such as working at a bar or in a customer service role.

- **Precariat**: This is the poorest social class, as its members have a mean income of £8K and virtually no savings. They are likely to rent. They have a restricted social network and low levels of cultural capital. They form a relatively large social class, though, constituting 15 percent of the population. Although some members of this class are unemployed, many hold jobs as shopkeepers, carpenters, drivers, and the like.

In discussing their findings, Savage and his colleagues noted that their new model "offers a powerful way of comprehending both the persistence, yet also the remaking of social class divisions in contemporary Britain," and that the model "reveals the polarization of social inequality (in the form of an elite and a precariat), and the fragmentation of traditional sociological and working-class divisions into more segmented forms" (p. 246).

SOCIAL CLASS IN THE WORK ENVIRONMENT

Drawing from Greenhaus, Parasuraman, and Wormley's (1990) conceptualization of discrimination, in this section, I examine how social class influences access and treatment discrimination. The research evidence suggests social class has the potential to influence life chances and opportunities across a number of domains, including the jobs to which one has access.

As one example, Rivera and Tilcsik (2016) conducted a study to examine whether an applicant's presumed social class would influence opportunities in the job hunt. Consistent with other field experiments I have described in previous chapters, the authors sent resumes—all of which contained information about a fictitious applicant—to law firms in the US. The resumes varied based on two factors: the social class and gender of the applicant. They varied the presumed social class by altering the names (Clark or Cabot), the type of scholarships the person received in school (need-based or not), the volunteer work in which the applicant engaged (mentoring students who were the first in their family to attend college or mentoring college students in general), and preferred sports (track and field or sailing). The remainder of the resume, including skills and qualifications, were the same. Results showed that applicants believed to be upper class men were most likely to receive an interview, followed by lower-class women, lower-class men, and upper class women. Upper class men were about three times more likely to get an interview request than the other applicants.

Rivera and Tilcsik (2016) then conducted two follow-up studies, one of which was another experiment and the other involved personal interviews, to further understand these effects. These studies showed that raters considered upper class men to be a better fit to the law firm and their clientele, and more committed. On the other hand, evaluators of upper class women considered the women to be less committed to work, and thus, not an ideal worker. In discussing the findings, the authors noted, "despite the myths of a classless society, social class of origin plays an enduring role in shaping individuals' life chances and economic trajectories" (p. 1125).

In addition to evidence of access discrimination, researchers have documented how social class influences treatment discrimination. Lott and Bullock (2007), for instance, illustrated how people who are poor are frequently the first affected by corporate layoffs, and they also have few benefits of incentives at work. In fact, fewer than 40 percent of low-income workers in the US have employer-sponsored health insurance (Cowley, 2015). As a result, they are left with the choice of foregoing medical treatment and preventative care, or facing financial ruin should a major health crisis occur. The US also holds the unenviable position among highly developed countries as having among the poorest records of ensuring safe, quality working conditions for people in low-income jobs (Heymann & Earle, 2010; Lott, 2012).

Experiences with discrimination, when coupled with the factors discussed in the following section, collectively create income inequalities. One way of conceptualizing income inequality is through a measure called the Gini Index. This figure summarizes the dispersion of income over an entire income distribution.

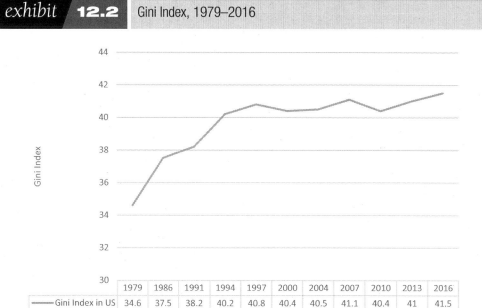

exhibit **12.2** Gini Index, 1979–2016

	1979	1986	1991	1994	1997	2000	2004	2007	2010	2013	2016
Gini Index in US	34.6	37.5	38.2	40.2	40.8	40.4	40.5	41.1	40.4	41	41.5

Source: GINI Index (n.d.).

As the figure increases, income is increasingly received by one group of people. A value of 0 represents perfect income equality, and a value of 100 suggests perfect inequality. The World Bank provides estimates over times (GINI Index, n.d.), and I offer an overview in Exhibit 12.2. Their data show the value in the US in 2016 (41.5) was the highest in the data base. The data also show that since 1979, income inequality has increased by 20 percent.

MULTILEVEL EXPLANATIONS

Drawing from the model I presented in Chapter 4, I present multilevel explanations for the influence of social class in the sport work environment. In doing so, I focus on macro-level factors (i.e., value systems, educational systems, housing, and health care), meso-level factors (i.e., bias among decision-makers, organizational structure, and the delivery of sport), and micro-level factors (i.e., demographics and personality). I offer a summary in Exhibit 12.3.

Macro-Level Factors

Macro-level factors are those operating at the societal level. Particularly germane to the discussion of social class are value systems, educational systems, housing, and sport systems.

Multilevel Explanations for the Influence of Social Class in the Sport Work Environment	*exhibit* **12.3**

Macro-level factors: Those operating at the societal level, including value systems, educational systems, housing, and health care.

Meso-level factors: Those operating at the team and organizational levels, including bias among decision-makers, organizational structure, and the delivery of sport.

Micro-level factors: Those operating at the individual level, including demographics and psychological characteristics.

Value Systems

Prevailing value systems help reinforce class distinctions at the societal level (Bullock, Williams, & Limbert, 2003; Piff, Kraus, & Keltner, 2018). Ideas about merit and meritocracy are especially salient. Meritocracy refers to the worldview that a person's social standing and the rewards each person receives are based on individual effort and merit. This ideal is highly valued and engrained within the US and other Western cultures such that it serves as a dominant ideology (Clycq, Nouwen, & Vandenbroucke, 2013). Key elements in American culture, including children's books (e.g., *The Little Engine That Could*), numerous biographies and autobiographies, and many movies (e.g., *Hoosiers*), promote the notion that with hard work, persistence, and determination anyone can rise from humble beginnings to overcome hurdles placed in front of them and achieve greatness. This belief system is often used, perhaps implicitly, to justify the positions of those in power (e.g., they worked hard to get there) and those in disadvantaged circumstances (e.g., they made poor choices and now must face the consequences; see Jost et al., 2012).

These examples are illustrative of meritocracy's three underlying elements (Daniels, 1978). First, in this view, merit is thought to be a well understood and measurable basis for selecting persons either for positions or for promotion. Second, individuals are thought to have equal opportunities to develop and display their talents, thereby allowing them to advance. Finally, the positions attained by people are thought to vary according to different levels of status, reward, and income.

From a different perspective, observers who adopt a class-based view challenge these underlying premises on a number of fronts (Scully & Blake-Beard, 2007). First, they claim that powerful persons who have access to material and economic resources are those who decide what is meritorious and what is not. Merit is socially constructed so as to privilege elites and ensure that they maintain their power and status, all the while delegitimizing the achievements of persons from disadvantaged groups. As one example, consider the requirements among many sport organizations that employees have an undergraduate, or sometimes even a graduate, degree for even a ticket sales position. As an educator, I certainly value the knowledge, understanding, and experience that people obtain through the formal educational process. I also acknowledge, however, that many times this arbitrarily assigned requisite condition serves to disadvantage persons who are qualified (e.g., with prior sales experience) but whose class background did not direct them to the higher education route.

Second, an individual's family class background is often a better predictor of life success than is individual merit (Scully & Blake-Beard, 2007). Similar to wealth, class is transferred from generation to generation. This is meaningful because if two people differ in class but are otherwise identically meritorious from birth, they are likely to have different experiences and chances in life. Clearly, there are examples of persons, such as Lee Iacocca, Sam Walton, or Barack Obama, who rose from meager backgrounds to do extraordinary things in their lives, thereby supporting the "American Dream" ideal. However, these exceptional cases are just that—exceptions. As Scully and Blake-Beard note, "Any meritocracy needs only just enough permeability of elite ranks to justify the possibility that 'anyone can make it'" (p. 436). Also, this anecdotal evidence does not negate the experiences of millions of others who, despite their meritorious achievements, are overlooked, bypassed, and marginalized because of their class position.

Finally, critics of meritocracy argue that the different values society places on varying jobs, coupled with the status and rewards of those jobs, can be challenged (Scully & Blake-Beard, 2007). From this perspective, wage gaps between the elite and those in the working class or in poverty come into question. These discrepancies are seen as a function of the greed and power of individuals at the top who pay themselves exorbitant salaries that do not reflect true differences in merit or the value that society places on those jobs. This disjunction was aptly observed during the financial crisis that the US experienced in 2008 and 2009, during which period some companies laid off thousands of employees only to pay their executives millions of dollars in bonuses. Note, too, that these "performance bonuses" were paid out even though the companies were in dire financial straits, some surviving only because of governmental assistance.

Elites, of course, seek to justify their incomes, arguing that their salaries are based on market demand and that their unique skills and expertise (i.e., what they have defined as meritorious achievements) call for such compensation. What else should be expected, though? After all, "every highly privileged group develops the myth of its natural superiority" (Weber, 1978, p. 437), and persons in power "use 'autobiographical reasoning' to describe their positions as the outcome of hard work and ability, extrapolating from their own experiences" (Scully & Blake-Beard, 2007, p. 437). The corollary of this argument is that individuals who do not earn such outstanding wages and who have not excelled in the stratified social order are not hard working, do not possess unique skills and attributes, and are not meritorious. The clear problem with such reasoning is the considerable evidence to the contrary: millions of people work extremely hard, completing tasks that require special skills, only to be compensated with wages that do not allow them to provide for their most basic needs and for their families (Abrego, 2014).

Educational Systems

Educational systems also serve to reinforce social class and privilege those with means, power, and status (Putnam, 2015). Specifically, because most schools are funded through property taxes, class inequalities and social injustices are continually reinforced. Eitzen (1996) explains the dynamics in this way:

> Schools receive some federal money, more state money, and typically, about half of their budget from local property taxes. The result is a wide disparity in per-pupil expenditures among the states and within each state. The use of property taxes is discriminatory because rich school districts can spend more money than poor ones on each student, yet *at a lower tax rate*. This last point is important—poor districts have higher mill levies than wealthy districts, yet they raise less money *because they are poor*.
>
> (p. 102; emphasis in original)

To illustrate these disparities, consider differences between school districts in one state in the US: Connecticut. Greenwich school district spends $6,000 more per student than does the Birdgeport school district (Semuels, 2016). Greenwich budgets over $12,000 per year for elementary school libraries, and the figure does not include personnel costs; on the other hand, East Hartford has no money allocated toward libraries. These differences obviously have meaningful ramifications for quality of instruction, sport opportunities, number of teachers and coaches, and quality of facilities and equipment.

The differences in the quality of education between privileged and disadvantaged students have a number of ramifications, including the likelihood of students completing school and their prospects of attending college. Bullock (2004) reported that schoolchildren from the poorest 20 percent of families are six times less likely to finish high school than their wealthier peers. Class inequalities in primary education also affect students' likelihood of pursuing higher education opportunities, as disadvantaged students are unlikely to attend the most elite institutions (Lott & Bullock, 2007; Putnam, 2015) or to earn a degree at all. Courses and extracurricular offerings at poor and rich schools play a role. Putnam (2015) reported that richer schools (fewer than 25 percent of children in poverty) offered three times the number of advanced placement courses as the poorest schools did (75–100 percent of pupils in poverty). The same patterns emerge when considering extracurricular offerings, whether sport-focused or not.

Putnam (2015), in his extensive analysis, noted a number of factors that influence the gap in college graduation rates: family structure, parenting style,

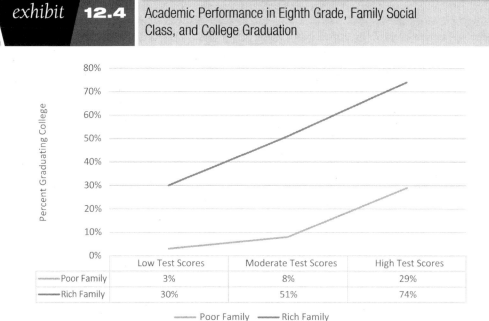

exhibit **12.4**   Academic Performance in Eighth Grade, Family Social Class, and College Graduation

	Low Test Scores	Moderate Test Scores	High Test Scores
Poor Family	3%	8%	29%
Rich Family	30%	51%	74%

Source: Putnam (2015).

development during childhood, peers, and extracurricular activities in which they were involved. A family's social class, however, is the strongest predictor (see Exhibit 12.4). High performing students from wealthy families are *25 times* more likely to graduate from college than are low scoring students from poor families (74 and 3 percent, respectively). Even among average students, those from rich families are six times more likely to graduate college than are those from poor ones (51 and 8 percent, respectively). Perhaps most sobering of all, high scoring students from poor families are less likely to graduate college than are low scoring students from affluent families (29 and 30 percent, respectively). These trends led Putnam to conclude that family social class is a better predictor than test scores in predicting future educational success. Or, as Krugman commented nearly a decade earlier, "the idea that we have anything close to equality of opportunity is clearly a fantasy. It would be closer to the truth, though not the whole truth, to say that in America, class—inherited class—usually trumps talent" (2007, p. 248).

Housing

A third macro-level factor affecting access and opportunities is housing (Desmond, 2016). The ability to provide shelter for one's family—one of the most basic needs people have (Maslow, 1943)—is continuously listed as the most pressing concern for persons in the poverty class (Lott & Bullock, 2007). The high costs of rent and utilities support the reality of this concern. In a comprehensive study, the National Low Income Housing Coalition found that the two-bedroom fair market rent (i.e., the 40th percentile of gross rent across the country) in 2018 was $1,149 per month. To spend no more than 30 percent of income on housing costs, a person would have to earn $17.90 per hour (Out of Reach, 2018). This is considerably more than the federal minimum wage ($7.25 per hour). A person working full time at the federal minimum wage would have to work three full-time jobs to afford the housing (Out of Reach, 2018). These data shed light on why homelessness rates continue to increase and illustrate that even gainfully employed individuals can lose their homes because they are not receiving a living wage.

Cost is not the only way in which institutional distancing occurs in relation to housing. In addition, low-income families are likely to live in communities that are geographically and socially segregated from middle-class and owning-class families (Desmond, 2016). Within large urban areas, the poor are usually segregated while more affluent families live in high-rise apartments. The former housing area is dangerous and poorly maintained, whereas the latter dwellings receive around-the-clock security (Desmond, 2016).

Racial minorities, persons from low-income families, and the unemployed are all more likely than their counterparts to live in neighborhoods with poor air quality (Bell & Ebisu, 2012). Companies that produce environmentally hazardous waste are likely to locate in low-income communities because resistance to such a business move will be less than it would in more affluent neighborhoods. As Pinderhughes (1996) commented, "To save time and money, companies seek to locate environmentally hazardous industries in communities which will put up the least resistance, which are less informed and less powerful, and are more dependent upon local job development efforts" (p. 233). Lott and Bullock (2007) refer to this practice as environmental classism.

Of course, the institutional distancing occurs until an urban location is determined to be an ideal site for a new stadium and urban redevelopment efforts (Kim & Chung, 2018). Once this decision is made, the poverty-class and working-class families who live in the area are displaced, forced to move to other locations. Efforts to clean up, revitalize, and energize the neighborhood are then made—but only after the poor are displaced and the wealthy team owners and fans move into town. This displacement process has a serious negative effect on families. Residents are forced to leave their homes, the local shops they enjoy visiting, and the friends and social networks they have developed. Members of the owner class can reap more profits by placing the new stadium where the poor once lived. Consequent to the urban gentrification process, rent and property values increase. The higher rents force local merchants to move (because they cannot afford the rent) and prohibit them from relocating in a nearby area.

Box 12.2 provides an overview of the displacement process that occurs when communities host the Olympics. Box 12.3 examines arguments and counterarguments about the potential benefits of such urban revitalization efforts.

Box 12.2 Diversity in the Field: Housing and the Olympics

Policymakers and politicians often promote the Olympics as a way for a community to showcase itself and, at the same time, improve the supporting infrastructure. New stadiums and arenas are constructed, roads are built, new jobs are created, and urban centers are revitalized. The Olympics come at a tremendous cost, however. Most often, these costs are discussed in terms of the billions of dollars that local governments and organizations spend to prepare for the Games. This does not tell the whole story, however, because the poor are disproportionately negatively affected by a city's hosting of the Olympics.

The displacement of the poor was highlighted in Vancouver, host of the 2010 Winter Olympics. More than 800 people were displaced in one area of downtown Vancouver after the 2010 Games were announced—the consequence of low-rent hotels being closed and demolished so that high-priced condominiums could be built in their place (Cogman, 2008). No low-rent housing alternatives were to be found in nearby areas. Despite spending over $4.5 billion to support the Games (monies that could have funded the construction of almost 2,800 housing units for the poor), government officials claimed not to have the resources to address the increased number of homeless people on the streets. Such claims seem particularly curious given the fact that "the new RAV [light rail] line is being built to the Vancouver International Airport, a new highway is in the works, and condos are shooting up everywhere" (Cogman, 2008). This kind of displacement of the poor in favor of the Olympics is nothing new. The Sydney Olympics were also accompanied by increased homelessness, an outcome caused by the skyrocketing cost of living in the city. In addressing this trend, Sydney officials literally bused the homeless to different cities (Beadnell, 2000), presumably so that they would not "interfere" with Olympics activities. In response to this disturbing phenomenon, Cogman acutely noted that "if the homeless had an Olympic category, maybe someone would notice."

Health Care

Social class also intersects with health care provision to influence people's access and opportunities. Krugman (2007) noted that the US is unique among wealthy nations in its failure to provide health care to all of its citizens. According to Gallup, 12.2 percent of Americans lacked insurance in 2017, a statistically significant increase from 2016 (Witters, 2018). The lack of insurance coverage is not attributable to a lack of money devoted to health care. According to the World Bank (Current Health Expenditure, n.d.), health care spending represented 16.8 percent of the US' gross domestic product in 2015. This figure is substantially higher in the US than in comparable countries, such as Canada (10.4 percent), France (11.1 percent), Germany (11.2 percent), and the UK (9.9 percent), and it is expected to continue to grow in the future.

Box 12.3 Alternative Perspectives: Are There Benefits to Displacement?

Some observers argue that the potential negative effects associated with displacing families in favor of building a stadium are outweighed by the many benefits associated with the practice. After all, the stadium also brings new restaurants and shops to the neighborhood that people frequent when attending events. Collectively, this new business is thought to provide many benefits to the community, including increased tax revenues. Coakley (2015) notes many fallacies in these arguments. For instance, officials will often give discounted tax rates to the owners of new buildings and their real estate partners as enticement to build in their city. However, considering that property taxes are the primary sources of revenue for public schools, this practice actually serves to *decrease* the potential revenues that schools could receive. Thus, as team owners continue to increase their wealth

through this public subsidization, school systems continue to fail because of poor funding.

Another argument is that the new, publicly financed stadiums and arenas create new jobs; thus, even though people might be displaced, at least they have the work opportunities that otherwise would not have existed. This notion is faulty, as well. First, because the new facilities sit empty for most of the year, the types of jobs that are normally created are seasonal and low paying. Second, the creation of jobs through the public subsidization of sport franchises is remarkably inefficient when compared with government-assisted initiatives. Thus, despite claims of supposed benefits of publicly supported stadiums and the displacement of persons from their homes, the evidence points to the contrary.

Given their high costs, health care and health insurance remain luxury commodities most affordable to persons with power and wealth, while less privileged persons suffer without care. Low-income wage earners in the US are more than three times less likely to have health insurance (Smith & Medalia, 2015)—disparities which result in shorter survival rates when people become seriously ill. This pattern led Lott and Bullock (2007) to conclude that "the resource to which low-income people in this country [the United States] have the least access is health care" (p. 65).

These figures are meaningful on a number of fronts. Though the magnitude of the effects vary based on sample (e.g., all persons or only non-elderly individuals who are healthy) and other measurement, researchers have shown that a sizeable portion of people have to declare bankruptcy because of their medical bills (Dobkin, Finkelstein, Kluender, & Notowidigdo, 2018; Himmelstein, Thorne, Warren, & Woolhandler, 2009). Illness-related expenses are particularly difficult for the poor and insured to recover (Banegas et al., 2016). Lack of adequate health insurance is also associated with people choosing to forgo medical treatments (Tefferi et al., 2015). This means that people in poverty and working-class persons are more likely than members of more affluent classes to contract illnesses and diseases that would otherwise have been prevented, treated, or cured. It is hardly surprising, then, that low-income families are more likely to suffer from a host of health ailments, including obesity, type II diabetes, cancer, and HIV/AIDS. These data support Lott and Bullock's (2007) contention that within the US, social class "is a strong and reliable predictor of health outcomes . . . and all causes of death regardless of ethnicity, gender, and age" (p. 68). See Exhibit 12.5 for further discussion of the health outcomes of classism.

exhibit **12.5** Health Outcomes of Classism

Given the pervasiveness of cognitive, interpersonal, and institutional classism, one should not be surprised to learn that middle- and poverty-class persons face a number of unique life difficulties. Relative to persons in other classes, the poor report higher incidences of anxiety, depression, and hostility; express less optimism and control over their lives; have poor social support; are more likely to be overweight; and are more likely to report physical illnesses, such as type II diabetes, cancer, and heart disease (see Liu et al., 2004, for reviews). It is important to note that these effects are not uniform because class intersects with other diversity dimensions to affect groups differently. Conceptions of social class also vary depending on other diversity dimensions, as illustrated in Box 12.4.

According to the APA (2006), social class influences health through a number of potential pathways. First, as previously outlined, the poor have limited access to health care, and when they do receive health care, it is often of poor quality. Second, poverty- and working-class persons are more likely to encounter hazardous materials in their work settings and in their neighborhoods than are their higher status counterparts. A third pathway is through health behaviors such as smoking, poor diet, and lack of exercise. Finally, social class might be related to health and well-being through differential exposure to stress. Poverty- and working-class persons are likely to experience more acute and chronic stress than their counterparts, and this repeated exposure to stress deleteriously affects the body's ability to fight off illness and disease.

Interestingly, there is evidence that when poor families have a chance to move away from low-income neighborhoods—and thus escape the effects of environmental classism—their health improves (Ludwig et al., 2011). Specifically, when people moved out of neighborhoods with extreme poverty into ones with lower levels of poverty, they experienced a decreased risk of both obesity and diabetes. Given that housing segregation based on income is increasing, the results suggest that "clinical or public health interventions that ameliorate the effects of neighborhood environment on obesity and diabetes could generate substantial social benefit" (p. 1518).

Box 12.4 Professional Perspectives: Alternative Conceptualizations of Social Class

Jacqueline McDowell is a scholar at the George Mason University, where she studies the intersection of race, gender, and social class. According to McDowell, traditional definitions of class focus on issues of income, wealth, power, and standing in society. However, in the African American community, social class takes on a different meaning, and class is "typically defined by someone's attitude that they might have about their life, or their behavior . . . so it is actually independent of the power that they might have in the wider society." She found support for this position in her research with African American women administrators. When asked about their class background, women in her research were reluctant to pigeonhole themselves into a particular class based on their income or occupation; rather, "a lot of them actually felt that their class reflected an attitude about their life." Thus, from McDowell's perspective, ideas people have about class, including where they are situated, are likely to vary with their race.

Meso-Level Factors

Meso-level factors are those operating at the group or organizational level. In the context of social class, bias among decision-makers, organizational structure, and the delivery of sport are all relevant.

Bias

Drawing from Cuddy, Fiske, and Glick (2008), I consider three components of bias: stereotypes, prejudice, and discrimination. Stereotypes, or what Lott (2002) refers to as cognitive distancing of the poor, cast the poor as dishonest, inept, promiscuous, dependent upon others, and uninterested in education (Volpato, Andrighetto, & Baldissarri, 2017). Drawing from the stereotype content model (see Chapter 3), Durante, Tablante, and Fiske (2017) showed how, across countries and cultures, people consider the wealthy as competent but cold, whereas stereotypes of the poor include low competence and higher warmth. The stereotype patterns result in different impression management activities based on social class (Swencionis, Dupree, & Fiske, 2017): the rich attempt to appear more likeable, and the poor seek to increase perceptions of their competence. What's more, some evidence suggests that people associate the poor with savages and animals. Loughnan, Haslam, Sutton, and Spencer (2014) conducted multiple studies across cultures (in the US, the UK, and Australia) and found that, across every setting, the stereotypes of the poor were closely aligned with those associated with apes and dogs. This alignment shows that some people associate the poor with dehumanizing, derogatory stereotypes—linkages not made to individuals who are more affluent and powerful.

A provocative study from Fiske (2007) sheds light on why this takes place. Fiske and her colleagues examined the brain's responses to seeing photos of a homeless man. They made two key observations. First, within moments of viewing the photo, participants' brains set off a sequence of reactions that are linked with disgust and avoidance. The area of the brain that was activated, the insula, is usually triggered when people express disgust toward nonhuman objects, such as garbage or human waste. Also of interest was the part of the brain that was not activated: the dorsomedial prefrontal cortex. This finding is noteworthy because this section of the brain is usually activated when people think about other people or about themselves. Fiske explained, "In the case of the homeless . . . these areas simply failed to light up, as if people had stumbled on a pile of garbage" (p. 157). This research suggests that people are likely to dehumanize the poor—a process that might explain the negative attitudes expressed toward the poor or the shocking nature of certain hate crimes against the homeless. In the UK, for example, while experiencing homeless, one in three people has been hit, kicked, or experienced another form of violence; 9 percent have been urinated on; 7 percent have been sexually assaulted; and over half have been verbally abused or harassed (Foster, 2016).

The negative stereotypes associated with cognitive distancing are also directed toward elements associated with individuals in poverty or the working class, such as speech accents, dress, and manners. Scully and Blake-Beard (2007) noted that, within the organizational context, persons from privileged backgrounds often dress, talk, and act in ways that are associated with style and success. Persons from less privileged backgrounds, however, might dress or talk differently, thereby demonstrating that they lack this form of capital. As a result, the less privileged are either shunned outright or strongly encouraged to alter their behaviors and speech pattern and, in doing so, to leave behind the cultural remnants of their lower-class status (Scully & Blake-Beard, 2007). This process can be disheartening to disadvantaged persons, resulting in anxiety and negative emotional responses (Liu, Soleck, Hopps, Dunston, & Pickett, 2004).

Social class-related prejudice also affects people's experiences in sport and the work environment. Some authors suggest that classism can occur any time some holds negative attitudes toward someone from a different class (Liu, Soleck et al., 2004). Lott (2012) offered a different approach, noting that "classism denotes negative attitudes, beliefs, and behaviors directed toward those with less power, who are socially devalued" (p. 654). The emphasis on power and subjective standing is consistent with the definition of diversity I offered in Chapter 1, as well as the focus on social class instead of SES. Thus, I follow Lott's perspective in this chapter.

Bullock (1995) noted that "poor people commonly experience face-to-face discrimination in their daily lives" (p. 142). Barriers are erected in such a way that the poor cannot enjoy full societal participation. In the workplace, this discrimination is seen in the hiring process and the placement of people into particular jobs. For example, employers are sometimes reluctant to hire people whom they perceive to be from a poor background because the applicants are thought to possess a poor work ethic (Douthat & Leigh, 2017). When they are hired, people from poor backgrounds are likely to be placed in "class appropriate" jobs such as janitorial or parking lot attendant positions (Loignon & Woehr, 2018). Similarly, the elite and poor rarely interact with one another in the workplace: in elite hotels, janitorial staff ride different elevators than do wealthy customers, just as in the workplace janitorial staff clean executives' offices during nonbusiness hours (Gray & Kish-Gephart, 2013). These practices, and others like them, ensure that people from different classes do not interact with one another in a meaningful way within the work environment.

Classism also occurs in the school setting, where teachers have differential expectations for students from a poor social class (Boser, Wilhelm, & Hanna, 2014). Secondary school teachers, for instance, rate students who are living in poverty as 53 percent less likely to earn a college diploma than their peers. These expectations are important because, even after controlling for other factors that could affect the results, students whose teachers set high expectations are three times more likely to graduate from college than those whose teachers set low expectations.

Organizational Structure

The manner in which organizations, including those in sport, are structured reinforces institutional classism. Occupations linked with the middle and owning classes are at the top of the prestige hierarchy, whereas those associated with poverty or the working classes are perceived as low-status positions (Gray & Kish-Gephart, 2013; Loignon & Woehr, 2018). Indeed, when I ask students in my sport management classes to what they aspire upon graduation, many cite the positions of general manager, athletic director, and events coordinator—all high-status positions. Less common are responses related to grounds crew or concessions—positions that are more frequently held by the poor. Note, too, that other characteristics differentiate the two classes of positions. Athletic directors, when compared to concessions workers, are likely to have better benefits, choose their work structure and hours, and travel to exciting destinations. These distinctions are important because the status of a given occupation is partly associated with the benefits it provides, including vacation time, paid leave, health care, salaried work, and retirement.

Class is also reinforced in attitudes held toward high- and low-status employees' behaviors. Let us consider mobilization efforts, for instance. Unions are generally considered to be organizations formed to improve the working conditions of workers and the pay they receive (Huang, Jiang, Lie, & Que, 2017; Wilmers, 2017). Laborers benefit in many ways from unionization and, through their unions, have fought for rights related to fair work practices, just pay, health care benefits, and retirement options, among others. Despite these many benefits, data from the polling agency Gallup (Labor Unions, n.d.) show that in 2009, fewer than half of the Americans surveyed approved of labor unions. Since that time, however, the attitudes have improved, such that, in 2017, 61 percent of Americans approved of labor unions. Even with the improved attitudes, nearly 4 out of 10

Americans still disapprove of the entities (Labor Unions, n.d.). These attitudes are interesting, considering the general positive attitudes that people have toward chambers of commerce and professional associations, both of which are forms of mobilization—albeit by different names—of middle- and owning-class persons (Smith, 2008). This hypocrisy is routinely illustrated in the media coverage of labor strife in the professional sport leagues: relative to the owners (who operate legal cartels), players unions are more likely to be vilified and characterized as greedy when there is a strike or lockout (for other examples, see Zweig, 2000).

Classism within the organizational context is perhaps best illustrated through the wildly disparate pay scales found there. In 2016, the median chief executive pay ratio (the leader's pay relative to the median pay of her employees) was 347-to-1. In 1983, the figure was 41-to-1 (Ritcey & Zhao, 2018). The differences increase as the company becomes larger (Mueller, Ouimet, & Simintzi, 2017). As an example in the sport industry, according to Nike's 2018 Fall/Winter earnings reports, Mark Parker, the chief executive of Nike, earned $9,467,460 in 2018, compared to $24,955 for the average employee salary—a 379-to-1 ratio (Destefano, 2018). As previously noted, these salaries are justified through the promotion of stereotypes and through social reinforcement of belief systems such as meritocracy.

Perhaps not surprising, given these figures, is research suggesting that income inequalities are increasing at substantial rates (Saez, 2016). The top .01 percent of Americans reaped over 5 percent of the total wages in the country, a proportion that is even than that existing immediately before the Great Depression in 1929. Furthermore, as of 2015, the top 10 percent of American earners pulled in over 50 percent of the total wages in the US. Unfortunately, the poor have not made similar gains, and as a result the gap between the "haves" and "have nots" continues to grow. In explaining his findings, Saez wrote,

> The labor market has been creating much more inequality over the last thirty years, with the very top earners capturing a large fraction of macroeconomic productivity gains. A number of factors may help explain this increase in inequality, not only underlying technological changes but also the retreat of institutions developed during the New Deal and World War II—such as progressive tax policies, powerful unions, corporate provision of health and retirement benefits, and changing social norms regarding pay inequality. We need to decide as a society whether this increase in income inequality is efficient and acceptable and, if not, what mix of institutional and tax reforms should be developed to counter it.
>
> (p. 5)

Interestingly, despite the many forms of distancing that reify the current social class system in the US, Americans actually prefer a different distribution of wealth. In a remarkable study, Norton and Ariely (2011) collected data from a nationally representative sample of more than 5,500 people. The researchers asked participants to reflect on the income distributions in three countries (which were not labeled) and decide which one they preferred. They showed pie charts labeled with the percentages of wealth possessed by each quintile of the populations. In the US, the top quintile controls 84 percent of the wealth, while in Sweden, the top quintile controls 18 percent of the wealth. The other quintiles in both countries were also shown. In a third country, all five quintiles controlled equal shares of the wealth. Results showed that 92 percent of the respondents preferred the distribution in Sweden relative to the US, and 77 percent preferred the equal distribution compared to that of the US. This pattern held among women and men, for liberals and conservatives, and across income ranges. In addition, the researchers asked respondents to indicate how much wealth they believed each quintile in the US controlled. The respondents vastly underestimated the wealth controlled by the top quintile (59 percent predicted versus 84 percent actual), and they also desired the top quintile to control just 32 percent of the wealth. These findings highlight interesting points: (a) Americans dramatically underestimate the income inequalities in their own country and (b) they would prefer to live in places where income equality is a reality.

Sport Systems

Within sport, a number of institutionalized activities serve to reinforce classism. Differences in sport participation provide one example. Participation in sport and recreational activities takes time and money, two things that middle- and owning-class persons are likely to have more of than other members of society. People who participate in sport are likely to be highly educated, belong to a high-income bracket, and work in a high-status occupation (Sagas & Cunningham, 2014). This pattern is evident in several segments of the sport industry, including the Olympics, health and fitness, and recreational activities (Sage & Eitzen, 2016). For example, skiing, golf, and tennis can entail substantial costs for club dues and equipment. Therefore, persons from the elite or professional middle class are more likely to participate in these activities than those from the poor or working classes.

The structure and expectations related to corporate wellness centers also contribute to these differences (Sage & Eitzen, 2016). Companies increasingly offer on-site wellness centers and encourage employees to be physically active, but participation varies based on occupational status: powerful, salaried employees generally demonstrate enthusiasm for such programs, while reactions from hourly employees are more tempered. Sage and Eitzen (2016) provided several potential explanations for this dynamic. First, all else equal, members of the middle and owning classes are more likely to engage in healthy behaviors than are persons from the working and poverty classes. Second, the activities offered, such as running or Pilates, have a greater appeal to high-status employees than to their counterparts. In addition, corporate wellness centers might be viewed as something established for those in upper management; thus, hourly workers would be considered outsiders in that context. Finally, hourly workers may resent the monies and time spent on wellness activities, especially considering that these do not address their needs in the workplace (i.e., higher wages, safer conditions, or decreasing the monotony and lack of autonomy in their work).

In addition to participation rates, social class also influences who watches sport events. In part, this is driven by the high costs of attending events, a trend outlined in Chapter 2. And, as more sporting events are handled as paid programming, even watching live broadcasts of sporting events is becoming available only to persons in the professional middle class or the elite. The cost of watching is simply too much for persons from other social classes.

Finally, as evidenced in the opening Diversity Challenge, the increasing use of pay-to-play programs in high school athletics and other school-sponsored activities is privileging to students from families who have the economic resources for such activities and, simultaneously, is disadvantaging to students from poorer families. Such policies guarantee that opportunities to participate in varsity programs will continue to exist for young people born into middle- and owning-class families or who attend wealthy school districts that can afford to finance sport teams. For those students in poor school districts or whose families cannot afford the hundreds of dollars in fees, formal sport participation opportunities are usually eliminated.

As shown in Box 12.5, the effects of the sport systems can influence who can participate in sport activities.

Box 12.5 Diversity in the Field: First-Generation College Athletes

Sport is commonly seen as the great equalizer. Many have heard stories of players who came from poverty only to achieve fame and fortune through their sports participation. In other cases, college athletics are cast as activities that offer athletes the chance to earn a college degree and climb the social ladder. For its part, the National Collegiate Athletic Association (NCAA) promotes this storyline. During basketball tournaments each spring, the organization runs commercials highlighting athletes who come from disadvantaged backgrounds.

Despite these narratives, the facts paint a different picture. Farrey and Schreiber (n.d.) showed that fewer than one in five college basketball players are the first in their family to go to college. When looking at all college sports, the figures drop to one in seven. Further analysis of the data shows the number is dropping. The biggest declines are observed in sports that have traditionally had a number of first-generation students. These include men's and women's basketball and football.

How do these figures on par with college students, overall? Interestingly, college athletes are less likely than their peers on campus to be first-generation students. Put another way, college athletes are more likely than the average college student to come from an advantaged background. Farrey and Schreiver pointed to several potential causes for this trend. They include rising academic standards, the increased cost of youth sport activities, and a growing Black middle class that can afford the high costs of youth sport.

In all, Farrey and Schreiber's analysis shows that, increasingly, sports are for people who have means and come from educated households. What was once an activity for all is increasingly one that excludes certain people, including those from first-generation households.

Micro-Level Factors

Finally, demographics and psychological characteristics, two micro-level factors, can influence opportunities and experiences of the poor.

Demographics

Social class intersects with other diversity dimensions to influence opportunities and access in the sport work environment. Drawing from the APA (2006), salient diversity dimensions include the following:

1. **Race:** The legacy of slavery, prejudice, and discrimination in the US means that racial minorities are disproportionately represented in poverty classes and middle classes. This is particularly true of African Americans, "for whom individual deprivation and poverty are compounded by residential segregation, resulting in a greater proportion of Blacks living in concentrated poverty" (APA, 2006, p. 12).
2. **Gender:** Women are more likely to be in less powerful social classes than men. Women also have lower incomes than men, even when education and experience levels are the same. These differences account, at least in part, for the strikingly high rates of poverty for children living in single-parent households headed by the mother.
3. **(Dis)ability status:** Persons with disabilities are disproportionately represented among the unemployed, underemployed, and those in the poverty class. Fewer than one in five persons with disabilities are employed, and they are twice as likely as their able-bodied counterparts to live in poverty.
5. **Sexual orientation:** Although persons who are lesbian, gay, bisexual, and transgender (LGBT) are perceived to have considerable discretionary income, in reality they are likely to be economically disadvantaged. People who identify as LGBT earn up to 32 percent less than similarly qualified peers. Termination of employees based on their sexual orientation is legal in 29 states. Finally, the incidence of homelessness is higher among individuals who are LGBT than it is among heterosexuals, particularly with youth.
6. **Age:** Poverty is particularly hard on the most vulnerable, including children. Exhibit 12.6 offers an overview of how poverty and extreme poverty affect children around the world. The data show that children represent a meaningful proportion of all people in poverty. Children living in rural settings are even more susceptible to poverty and extreme poverty. Vulnerable populations, including children and the elderly are more likely to experience poverty when governments slash their support programs in the name of austerity (Krugman, 2007).

Psychological Characteristics

Finally, psychological characteristics are also likely to influence people's opportunities and access to the sport work environment. On the one hand, poverty can have negative psychological effects on an individual (Desmond, 2016). Haushofer and Fehr (2014), for example, found that poverty causes one to experience stress and negative affect. As a result, people might adopt a short-term orientation and engage in risk-averse decision-making. The result is a limited focus on favorable goal-directed behaviors and, ultimately, a feedback loop of perpetual poverty.

On the other hand, there are some psychological characteristics that can help buffer poverty's effects. Claro, Paunesku, and Dweck (2016) examined the effects of a growth mindset, which represents the belief that abilities can be nurtured and developed. This perspective differs from a fixed mindset, where people believe personal attributes are stable. They collected data from Chilean students and found that, across every family income decile, students with a growth mindset outperformed their peers with a fixed mindset. These findings were evident for both language and math ability. One may read these findings and interpret them to suggest that psychology is a stronger predictor than social class. The authors, and decades of scholarship, suggest such an interpretation is incorrect. Instead, Claro et al. suggest, "structural inequalities can give rise to psychological inequalities and… those psychological inequalities can reinforce the impact of structural inequalities on achievement and future opportunity" (p. 8867).

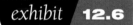

exhibit 12.6 Children in Extreme Poverty around the World, 2016

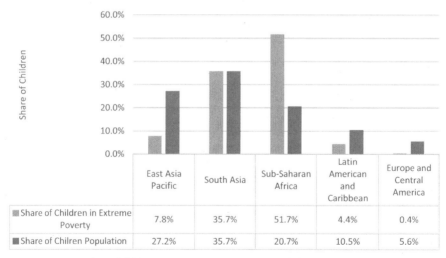

	East Asia Pacific	South Asia	Sub-Saharan Africa	Latin American and Caribbean	Europe and Central America
■ Share of Children in Extreme Poverty	7.8%	35.7%	51.7%	4.4%	0.4%
■ Share of Chilren Population	27.2%	35.7%	20.7%	10.5%	5.6%

■ Share of Children in Extreme Poverty   ■ Share of Chilren Population

Source: Ending extreme poverty (2016).

Psychological characteristics might also influence how decision-makers tend to class inequalities, either on sport teams or in the sport work environment. Social dominance orientation refers to the degree to which people believe that some groups are more worthy or deserving of higher status than others (Sidanius & Pratto, 2001). Rodriguez-Bailon et al. (2017) found that as people's social dominance orientation increased, so too did their opposition to government interventions designed to reduce economic inequalities. These findings are relevant to the sport work environment, as people with a high social dominance orientation might oppose organizational efforts aimed at reducing inequalities. Examples might include reduced insurance premiums for low-income earners, a cost of living increase for all employees (as opposed to increases based solely on work performance), or capping top leader's pay, among others.

SOCIAL CLASS, SPORT, AND PHYSICAL ACTIVITY

In addition to influencing employment opportunities and experiences, social class can affect people's access to and experiences in sport. Consider, for example, results from the National Health Interview Survey, conducted by the Centers for Disease Control and Prevention in the US (www.healthypeople. gov). In one question, the researchers examined the proportion of adults who engage in recommended levels of aerobic activity each week: 150 minutes of moderate activity, 75 minutes of vigorous activity, or some combination thereof. In Exhibit 12.7, I offer the pattern of findings related to family income and physical activity. In doing so, I use the percent of poverty threshold. According to this index, <100 suggests the family falls below the family, poverty threshold, 100–299 percent indicates a family is at or 299 percent above the poverty threshold, and so on. The exhibit illustrates that as family income moves above the poverty threshold, so too does the likelihood one meets recommended physical activity levels. In 2016, people from the richest families were 85 percent more likely to reach the recommended levels than were people from the poorest families. Though the exact figures vary, the patterns have persisted over time.

Though poor individuals are likely to have low physical activity patterns, there are instances where sport participation can improve their life chances. Contrary to popular myths, though, sport involvement does not guarantee one moves up in social standing. Rather, Coakley (2015) suggested that sport participation will be positively related to upward social mobility when it does the following:

- Increases opportunities to be academically successful and effectively compete in the work environment;
- Increases support for growth and development across various domains;
- Offers opportunities to develop strong social networks;
- Provides the material resources needed to create and manage opportunities;
- Expands opportunities, identities, and abilities outside of sport; and
- Minimizes the risks of long-term injury.

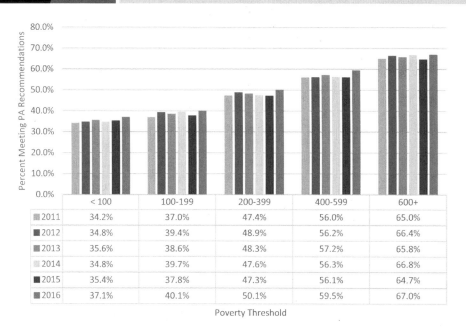

exhibit **12.7** | Family Income and Physical Activity among Americans, 2011–2016

	< 100	100-199	200-399	400-599	600+
2011	34.2%	37.0%	47.4%	56.0%	65.0%
2012	34.8%	39.4%	48.9%	56.2%	66.4%
2013	35.6%	38.6%	48.3%	57.2%	65.8%
2014	34.8%	39.7%	47.6%	56.3%	66.8%
2015	35.4%	37.8%	47.3%	56.1%	64.7%
2016	37.1%	40.1%	50.1%	59.5%	67.0%

Poverty Threshold

■2011 ■2012 ■2013 ■2014 ■2015 ■2016

Source: Healthypeople.gov.

These observations suggest that, under some circumstances, sport will help expand an athlete's opportunities. This is certainly true when sport allows a person to obtain education, skills, and training unrelated to sport. For example, when a volleyball player from a poor family receives a scholarship to a university, she is afforded the chance to obtain an education. To the extent that she takes advantage of this opportunity, develops her skills for the workplace, gains experiences through internships, and cultivates social relationships, her sport participation is likely to be positively related to her upward social mobility and career success.

CHAPTER SUMMARY

The purpose of this chapter was to provide an overview of how class and classism affect people's lives and the delivery of sport. As evidenced in the Diversity Challenge, the decisions sport managers make concerning the structure of sport and how it is financed often serve to hurt those who are already socially and economically disadvantaged. These dynamics are observed in other ways, too, including how people interact with members of classes with less prestige than their own and institutionalized practices that privilege persons from middle and owning classes. Having read this chapter, you should now be able to:

1. Define key terms related to social class inclusion and diversity, including SES, social class, and classism.

    SES refers to a person's economic standing, with a particular emphasis on income, education, and occupation. Social class refers to a person's position within an economic system, with a particular emphasis on how power, politics, and socially constructed realities economically and socially advantage some at the expense of others. Finally, classism refers to the subjugation of the poor through stereotypes, interpersonal discrimination, and institutionalized activities.

2. Describe the manner in which social class influences access and treatment discrimination.

    Social class influences access and treatment discrimination. People from lower social classes are frequently viewed less favorably in the job searching process, and they are relegated to certain jobs over others. High paying jobs with autonomy and discretion are reserved largely for people in higher social classes.

3. Summarize the multilevel factors that influence the effects of social class in the work environment.

    A number of factors influence the opportunities and access people have in the sport environment, including macro-level factors, such as value systems, educational systems, housing, and health care; meso-level factors, such as bias among decision-makers, organizational structure, and the delivery of sport; and micro-level factors, such as demographics and psychological characteristics.

4. Paraphrase the manner in which social class influences opportunities and experiences of sport and physical activity participants.

    The argument that sport involvement is strongly related to social mobility is overstated. Rather, social class standing will improve only when sport participation allows a person to obtain education, social contacts, skills, and training unrelated to sport.

Questions FOR DISCUSSION

1. What are the differences between SES and social class? Which construct do you prefer in discussions of economic inequalities?

2. Some argue that class-related stereotypes can also be directed at persons other than the poor. Is this the case, and if so, do all class-related stereotypes have the same impact on outcomes?

3. Challenging the notion of meritocracy is often a difficult task. Why is this the case, and what arguments could effectively be made to illustrate that the notion of meritocracy promotes classism?

4. Several examples were provided in the chapter illustrating how the structure and delivery of sport reinforce classism. What are other examples of how class and sport interact?

LEARNING Activities

1. Watch the documentary *Inequality for All* and discuss the major points made.
2. Divide into groups and discuss the notion of meritocracy. Is it applicable today?

Web RESOURCES

American Psychological Association Socioeconomic Status Office, http://www.apa.org/pi/ses/
     An entity that focuses on the psychological dynamics of social class and SES.
Socioeconomic Class, Pew Research Center, http://www.pewresearch.org/topics/socioeconomic-class/
     A special section of the Pew research Center that provides articles, reports, and statistical information pertaining to class in America.
Inequality for All, www.inequalityforall.com
     A companion website to the award-winning documentary of the same title.

READING Resources

Krugman, P. (2007). *The conscience of a liberal*. New York, NY: W. W. Norton & Company.
     One of my top five favorite books of all time; a provocative book from the Nobel Prize Laureate, providing an overview of economic inequalities in the US and possible solutions to the problem.
Desmond, M. (2016). *Evicted: Poverty and profit in the American city*. New York, NY: Broadway Books.

A gripping, compelling book emanating from Desmond's three years of ethnographic research in Milwaukee, WI (USA); details poverty in the American city.
Putnam, R. D. (2015). *Our kids: The American dream in crisis*. New York, NY: Simon & Schuster.
     A remarkable book from award-wining researcher and scholar; offers extensive data and analysis related to social class, education, opportunity, and access in America.

REFERENCES

Abrego, L. (2014). *Sacrificing families: Navigating laws, labor, and love across borders*. Stanford, CA: Stanford University Press.

American Psychological Association (2006). *Task force on socioeconomic status (SES)*. Washington, DC: Author.

Backlund, E., Sorlie, P. D., & Johnson, N. J. (1999). A comparison of the relationships of education and income with mortality: The National Longitudinal Mortality Study. *Social Science and Medicine, 49*, 1373–1384.

Banegas, M. P., Guy Jr, G. P., de Moor, J. S., Ekwueme, D. U., Virgo, K. S., Kent, E. E., … Yabroff, K. R. (2016). For working-age cancer survivors, medical debt and bankruptcy create financial hardships. *Health Affairs, 35*(1), 54–61.

Beadnell, M. (2000, February). Sydney's homeless to be removed for Olympics. *World Socialist Web Site*. Retrieved from http://www.wsws.org/articles/2000/feb2000/olymp-f03.shtml

Bell, M. L., & Ebisu, K. (2012). Environmental inequality in exposures to airborne particulate matter components in the United States. *Environmental Health Perspectives, 120*(2), 1699–1704.

Boser, U., Wilhelm, M., & Hanna, R. (2014). *The power of the Pygmalion effect: Teachers' expectations strongly predict college completion*. Washington, DC: Center for American Progress.

Bourdieu, P. (1984). *Distinction: A social critique of the judgement of taste*. Cambridge, MA: Harvard University Press.

Bullock, H. E. (1995). Class acts: Middle-class responses to the poor. In B. Lott & D. Maluso (Eds.), *The social psychology of interpersonal discrimination* (pp. 118–159). New York, NY: Guilford Press.

Bullock, H. E. (2004). Class diversity in the workplace. In M. S. Stockdale & F. J. Crosby (Eds.), *The psychology and management of workplace diversity* (pp. 226–242). Malden, MA: Blackwell.

Bullock, H. E., Williams, W. R., & Limbert, W. M. (2003). Predicting support for welfare policies: The impact of attributions and beliefs about inequality. *Journal of Poverty, 7*(3), 35–56.

Claro, S., Paunesku, D., & Dweck, C. S. (2016). Growth mindset tempers the effects of poverty on academic achievement. *Proceedings of the National Academy of Sciences, 113*(31), 8664–8668.

Clycq, N., Nouwen, W., & Vandenbroucke, A. (2013). Meritocracy, deficit thinking and the invisibility of the system: Discourses on educational success and failure. *British Educational Research Journal, 40*, 796–819.

Coakley, J. (2015). *Sports in society: Issues and controversies* (11th ed.). New York, NY: McGraw-Hill.

Cogman, T. (2008, December). A new Olympic legacy: Homelessness. *The Navigator Newspaper*. Retrieved from http://thenav.ca/2008/12/05/a-new-olympic-legacy-homelessness/

Côté, S. (2011). How social class shapes thoughts and actions in organizations. *Research in Organizational Behavior, 31*, 43–71.

Cowley, S. (2015, October). Many low-income workers say 'no' to health insurance. *New York Times*. Retrieved from https://www.nytimes.com/2015/10/20/business/many-low-income-workers-say-no-to-health-insurance.html

Cuddy, A. J. C., Fiske, S. T., & Glick, P. (2008). Warmth and competence as universal dimensions of social perception: The stereotype content model and the BIAS map. *Advances in Experimental Social Psychology, 40,* 61–149.

Current health expenditure (% of GDP) (no date). *World Bank.* Retrieved from https://data.worldbank.org/indicator/SH.XPD.CHEX.GD.ZS

Daniels, N. (1978). Merit and meritocracy. *Philosophy and Public Affairs, 3,* 206–223.

Desmond, M. (2016). *Evicted: Poverty and profit in the American city.* New York, NY: Broadway Books.

Destefano, M. (2018, July). Here's how much the average Nike employee makes: Revealed in the company's annual Fall/Winter 2018 reports. *Sole Collector.* Retrieved from https://solecollector.com/news/2018/07/how-much-the-average-nike-employee-makes

Dobkin, C., Finkelstein, A., Kluender, R., & Notowidigdo, M. J. (2018). Myth and measurement-The case of medical bankruptcies. *The New England Journal of Medicine, 378*(12), 1076–1078.

Douthat, T. H., & Leigh, N. G. (2017). First source hiring: An essential tool for linking the poor to employment or a "dead letter" progressive policy? *Urban Affairs Review, 53*(6), 1025–1063.

Dunn, D. S. (2017, February). Social class: An overlooked but important aspect of diversity. *Psychology Today.* Retrieved from https://www.psychologytoday.com/us/blog/head-the-class/201702/social-class

Durante, F., Tablante, C. B., & Fiske, S. T. (2017). Poor but warm, rich but cold (and competent): Social classes in the stereotype content model. *Journal of Social Issues, 73*(1), 138–157.

Eitzen, D. S. (1996). Classism in sport: The powerless bear the burden. *Journal of Sport & Social Issues, 20,* 95–105.

Ending extreme poverty: A focus on children. (2016). UNICEF. Retrieved from https://www.unicef.org/publications/files/Ending_Extreme_Poverty_A_Focus_on_Children_Oct_2016.pdf

Farrey, T., & Schreiber, P. (no date). The gentrification of college hoops. The Undefeated. Retrieved from https://theundefeated.com/features/gentrification-of-ncaa-division-1-college-basketball/

Fiske, S. T. (2007). On prejudice and the brain. *Daedalus, 136*(1), 156–159.

Foster, D. (2016, December). Crisis report reveals shocking dangers of being homeless. *The Guardian.* Retrieved from https://www.theguardian.com/housing-network/2016/dec/23/homeless-crisis-report-attack-violence-sleeping-rough

GINI Index (World Bank estimate) (no date). *The World Bank.* Retrieved from https://data.worldbank.org/indicator/SI.POV.GINI?locations=US

Gray, B., & Kish-Gephart, J. J. (2013). Encountering social class differences at work: How "class work" perpetuates inequality. *Academy of Management Review, 38,* 670–699.

Greenhaus, J. H., Parasuraman, S., & Wormley, W. M. (1990). Effects of race on organizational experiences, job performance evaluations, and career outcomes. *Academy of management Journal, 33*(1), 64–86.

Haushofer, J., & Fehr, E. (2014). On the psychology of poverty. *Science, 344*(6186), 862–867.

Hawkings, D. (2018, February). Wealth of Congress: Richer than ever, both mostly at the very top. *Roll Call.* Retrieved from https://www.rollcall.com/news/hawkings/congress-richer-ever-mostly-top

Heymann, J., & Earle, A. (2010). *Raising the global floor: Dismantling the myth that we can't afford good working conditions for everyone.* Stanford, CA: Stanford University Press.

Himmelstein, D. U., Thorne, D., Warren, E., & Woolhandler, S. (2009). Medical bankruptcy in the United States, 2007: Results of a national study. *The American Journal of Medicine, 122*(8), 741–746.

Huang, Q., Jiang, F., Lie, E., & Que, T. (2017). The effect of labor unions on

CEO compensation. *Journal of Financial and Quantitative Analysis, 52*(2), 553–582.

Jost, J. T., Chaikalis-Petritsis, V., Abrams, D., Sidanius, J., Van Der Toorn, J., & Bratt, C. (2012). Why men (and women) do and don't rebel: Effects of system justification on willingness to protest. *Personality and Social Psychology Bulletin, 38,* 197–208.

Kim, K. Y., & Chung, H. (2018). Eco-modernist environmental politics and counter-activism around the 2018 Pyeong Chang Winter Games. *Sociology of Sport Journal, 35*(1), 17–28.

Krugman, P. (2007). *The conscience of a liberal.* New York, NY: W. W. Norton & Company.

Labor Market Information. (2018). State of California Employment Development Department. Retrieved from https://www.labormarketinfo.edd.ca.gov/

Labor Unions. (no date). *Gallup.* Retrieved from https://news.gallup.com/poll/12751/labor-unions.aspx.

Leondar-Wright, B. (2005). *Class matters.* Gabriola Island, BC: New Society Publishers.

Liu, W. M., Ali, S. R., Soleck, G., Hopps, J., Dunston, K., & Pickett, T., Jr. (2004). Using social class in counseling psychology research. *Journal of Counseling Psychology, 51,* 3–18.

Liu, W. M., Soleck, G., Hopps, J., Dunston, K., & Pickett, T., Jr. (2004). A new framework to understand social class in counseling: The social class worldview and modern classism theory. *Multicultural Counseling and Development, 32,* 95–122.

Loignon, A. C., & Woehr, D. J. (2018). Social class in the organizational sciences: A conceptual integration and meta-analytic review. *Journal of Management, 44*(1), 61–88.

Lott, B. (2002). Cognitive and behavioral distancing from the poor. *American Psychologist, 57,* 100–110.

Lott, B. (2012). The social psychology of class and classism. *American Psychologist, 67,* 650–658.

Lott, B., & Bullock, H. E. (2007). *Psychology and economic injustice: Personal, professional, and political intersections.* Washington, DC: American Psychological Association.

Loughnan, S., Haslam, N., Sutton, R. M., & Spencer, B. (2014). Dehumanization and social class: Animality in the stereotypes of "white trash," "chavs," and "bogans." *Social Psychology, 45,* 54–61.

Ludwig, J., Sanbonmatsu, L., Gennetian, L., Adam, E., Duncan, G. J., Katz, L. F., … McDade, T. W. (2011). Neighborhoods, obesity, and diabetes—A randomized social experiment. *New England Journal of Medicine, 365*(16), 1509–1519.

Maslow, A. H. (1943). A theory of human motivation. *Psychological Review, 50,* 370–396.

McCall, L. (2014). The political meanings of social class inequality. *Social Currents, 1*(1), 25–34.

Mehta, N., & Preston, S. (2016). Are major behavioral and sociodemographic risk factors for mortality additive or multiplicative in their effects? *Social Science & Medicine, 154,* 93–99.

Mueller, H. M., Ouimet, P. P., & Simintzi, E. (2017). Wage inequality and firm growth. *American Economic Review, 107*(5), 379–83.

Norton, M. I., & Ariely, D. (2011). Building a better America—One wealth quintile at a time. *Perspectives on Psychological Science, 6,* 9–12.

Out of reach: The high cost of housing. (2018). *National Low Income Housing Coalition.* Retrieved from http://nlihc.org/sites/default/files/oor/OOR_2018.pdf

Piff, P. K., Kraus, M. W., & Keltner, D. (2018). Unpacking the inequality paradox: The psychological roots of inequality and social class. *Advances in Experimental Social Psychology, 57*(1), 53–124.

Pinderhughes, R. (1996). The impact of race on environmental inequality: An empirical and theoretical discussion. *Sociological Perspectives, 39*, 231–248.

Pinquart, M., & Sörensen, S. (2000). Influences of socioeconomic status, social network, and competence on subjective well-being in later life: A meta-analysis. *Psychology and aging, 15*(2), 187–224.

Poverty Guidelines (2018, January). US Department of Health and Human Services. Retrieved from https://aspe.hhs.gov/poverty-guidelines

Powell, G. N. (2004). *Managing a diverse workforce: Learning activities* (2nd ed.). Thousand Oaks, CA: Sage.

Putnam, R. D. (2015). *Our kids: The American dream in crisis*. New York, NY: Simon & Schuster.

Ritcey, A., & Zhao, J. (2018, August). Alphabet CEO Page makes a tiny fraction compared to its median employee. *Bloomberg*. Retrieved from https://www.bloomberg.com/graphics/ceo-pay-ratio/

Rivera, L. A., & Tilcsik, A. (2016). Class advantage, commitment penalty: The gendered effect of social class signals in an elite labor market. *American Sociological Review, 81*(6), 1097–1131.

Rodriguez-Bailon, R., Bratanova, B., Willis, G. B., Lopez-Rodriguez, L., Sturrock, A., & Loughnan, S. (2017). Social class and ideologies of inequality: How they uphold unequal societies. *Journal of Social Issues, 73*(1), 99–116.

Saez, E. (2016). *Striking it richer: The evolution of top incomes in the United States (updated with 2015 preliminary estimates)*. Berkeley, CA: University of California, Department of Economics. Retrieved from https://eml.berkeley.edu/~saez/saez-UStopincomes-2015.pdf

Sagas, M., & Cunningham, G. B. (2014). *Sport participation rates among underserved American youth*. Gainesville, FL: University of Florida Sport Policy & Research Collaborative.

Sage, G. H., & Eitzen, D. S. (2016). *Sociology of North American sport* (10th ed.). New York, NY: Oxford University Press.

Sasson, I. (2016). Trends in life expectancy and lifespan variation by educational attainment: United States, 1990–2010. *Demography, 53*(2), 269–293.

Savage, M., Devine, F., Cunningham, N., Taylor, M., Li, Y., Hjellbrekke, J., … Miles, A. (2013). A new model of social class? Findings from the BBC's Great British Class Survey experiment. *Sociology, 47*, 219–250.

Scully, M. A., & Blake-Beard, S. (2007). Locating class in organizational diversity work: Class as structure, style, and process. In A. M. Konrad, P. Prasad, & J. K. Pringle (Eds.), *Handbook of workplace diversity* (pp. 431–454). Thousand Oaks, CA: Sage.

Semuels, A. (2016, August). Good school, rich school; bad school, poor school. *The Atlantic*. Retrieved from https://www.theatlantic.com/business/archive/2016/08/property-taxes-and-unequal-schools/497333/

Sidanius, J., & Pratto, F. (2001). *Social dominance: An intergroup theory of social hierarchy and oppression*. New York, NY: Cambridge University Press.

Smith, J. C., & Medalia, C. (2015). *U.S. census bureau, current population reports, P60–253, health insurance coverage in the United States: 2014*. Washington, DC: U.S. Government Printing Office.

Smith, L. (2008). Positioning classism within counseling psychology's social justice agenda. *The Counseling Psychologist, 36*, 895–924.

Smith, L. (2010). Psychology, poverty, and the end of social exclusion: Putting our practice to work (Vol. 7). New York, NY: Teachers College Press.

Standard Occupational Classification. (no date). Bureau of Labor Statistics. Retrieved from https://www.bls.gov/soc/2018/#classification.

Swencionis, J. K., Dupree, C. H., & Fiske, S. T. (2017). Warmth-competence tradeoffs in impression management across race and social-class divides. *Journal of Social Issues, 73*(1), 175–191.

Tefferi, A., Kantarjian, H., Rajkumar, S. V., Baker, L. H., Abkowitz, J. L., Adamson, J. W., ... Bennett, J. M. (2015). In support of a patient-driven initiative and petition to lower the high price of cancer drugs. *Mayo Clinic Proceedings, 90*(8), 996–1000.

Triana, M. (2017). *Managing diversity in organizations: A global perspective*. New York, NY: Routledge.

Volpato, C., Andrighetto, L., & Baldissarri, C. (2017). Perceptions of low-status workers and the maintenance of the social class status quo. *Journal of Social Issues, 73*(1), 192–210.

Weber, M. (1978). *Economy and society: An outline of interpretive sociology*. (G. Roth & C. Wittich, Eds.) Berkeley: University of California Press.

Wilmers, N. (2017). Labor unions as activist organizations: A union power approach to estimating union wage effects. *Social Forces, 95*(4), 1451–1478.

Witters, D. (2018). Uninsured rate rises in 17 states in 2017. *Gallup*. Retrieved from https://news.gallup.com/poll/233597/ uninsured-rate-rises-states-2017.aspx

Zweig, M. (2000). *The working class majority*. Ithaca, NY: Cornell University Press.

PART III

CREATING AND SUSTAINING INCLUSIVE SPORT ORGANIZATIONS

Strategies for Inclusion

LEARNING OBJECTIVES

After studying this chapter, you should be able to:

- Identify the benefits of workplace inclusion.
- Summarize strategies for creating an inclusive sport work environment.

DIVERSITY CHALLENGE

Aboriginal, or First Nations, people in Canada are disadvantaged in many ways. Consider the following statistics: the poverty rate is comparable to that in developing nations, 25 percent of all adults are unemployed, the suicide rate among youth is five times that of non-Aboriginals, and the incidence of alcohol and drug abuse is high.

Because of these issues, the Canadian federal government took several steps to improve the quality of life among Aboriginals. Together with economic and social policies, the government is using sport as a way to achieve this goal. Sport is viewed as a tool for economic development and as a mechanism that engages citizens, overcomes social constraints, and contributes to cohesion among people in a community. Sport Canada, the sport governing body in Canada, is on record as being "committed to contributing, through sport, to the health, wellness, cultural identity, and quality of life of Aboriginal Peoples."

Aboriginal persons face many barriers to sport and physical activity participation, including the following:

- A general lack of awareness of sport opportunities,
- Economic difficulties,
- Insensitivity among sport providers to Aboriginal culture and traditions,
- A lack of Aboriginal coaches and/or coaches who are cognizant of the Aboriginal culture,
- The substantial distance of many villages from sport venues,

- Lack of governmental financial support,
- Racism, and
- An inadequate sport infrastructure.

Sport Canada actively works with governmental agencies, Aboriginal communities and leaders, and other entities to achieve the following goals:

- **Enhanced participation**: Sport Canada is increasing the participation of Aboriginal peoples in sport at all levels by providing equitable access, developing programs that meet their unique needs, involving Aboriginal persons in the planning and development of sport, and encouraging youth participation.
- **Enhanced excellence**: Sport Canada creates an environment that welcomes Aboriginal peoples to national teams and encourages high performance levels by increasing the number of qualified Aboriginal athletes, coaches, and officials by providing access to and support for quality facilities, training, and development.
- **Enhanced capacity**: Sport Canada seeks to improve the capacity of individuals, groups, and communities in support of Aboriginal sport in Canada by identifying the needs of Aboriginal people, providing facilities, promoting Aboriginal leaders, and maintaining cultural sensitivity.
- **Enhanced interaction**: Sport Canada increases the levels of communication and interaction among Aboriginal peoples and other sport and governmental entities at the federal, provincial, and local levels.

The Canadian government recognizes that for Canadian sport to be successful, all people must have access to it and be provided an opportunity to achieve excellence. Sport Canada's policies are aimed at driving "the actions necessary to create and maintain an inclusive Canadian sport system that supports Aboriginal participation in sport from playground to podium."

Source: *Sport Canada's Policy on Aboriginal Peoples' Participation in Sport.* Retrieved from www.canadianheritage.gc.ca/progs/sc/pol/aboriginal/2005/1_e.cfm.

CHALLENGE REFLECTION

1. In your opinion, how viable is sport as a vehicle for creating social change? Explain.
2. How effective are the goals outlined by Sport Canada? Are there any you feel might be especially effective? Less effective?
3. What are other sport-related strategies that could be implemented to decrease the disparities Aboriginal peoples face?
4. Are you aware of other instances where sport has been used as a vehicle for promoting change among members of a social group?

As the Diversity Challenge illustrates, organizations or governmental entities will often implement strategic initiatives aimed at diversity and inclusion issues. Here, Sport Canada sought to (a) decrease the negative outcomes associated with prejudice and discrimination in a particular context by improving the quality of life of a certain group of people and (b) capitalize on the unique cultural attributes that Aboriginal peoples and their sports could bring to the overall fabric of Canadian sport. These strategies reflect the sport organization's desire to create diverse, inclusive sporting environments.

The purpose of this chapter is to provide an overview of strategies that can be used to create and sustain diverse and inclusive work environments. I begin with an overview of the success of diversity and inclusion programs, followed by an overview of the multilevel factors affecting diversity and inclusion in the sport work environment.

EFFECTIVENESS OF DIVERSITY AND INCLUSION PROGRAMS

Ideally, sport managers would understand and appreciate the inherent value in having inclusive work environments, recognizing that they allow for all people to participate fully and effectively at work. In many respects, there is a moral imperative for such recognition and actualization (Cunningham, 2017). Whereas some organizational leaders might realize this imperative, others will be more readily persuaded by the linkage between inclusion and subsequent organizational outcomes (Fink & Pastore, 1999). There is considerable evidence for such associations.

Consider first the value to people external to the organization. Diverse and inclusive workplaces are appealing to potential job applicants, and most prefer those work environments over more homogeneous work settings (Lee & Cunningham, 2015; Madera, Dawson, & Neal, 2018; Roberson, Ryan, & Ragins, 2017). The same goes for key stakeholders, such as consumers (Åkestam, Rosengren, & Dahlen, 2017), potential clients (Cunningham & Woods, 2012; Cunningham & Melton, 2014; Pickett & Cunningham, 2018), and investors (Hoobler, Masterson, Nkomo, & Michel, 2018). These benefits explain why many organizations are keen not only to create and sustain inclusive work environments but also to signal this inclusiveness through various external communications to key stakeholders (Connelly, Certo, Ireland, & Reutzel, 2011). In fact, because legal mandates require employment protections for many groups, such as women, racial minorities, and religious minorities, failing to offer inclusive work spaces for all people sends mixed messages to various stakeholder groups. Ultimately, consumers will perceive this as conflicting information and develop negative attitudes toward the organization (Volpone & Avery, 2010).

Inclusiveness benefits athletes, coaches, and administrators, as well as the broader sport organizations. For employees and athletes, inclusion means being able to bring important identities to the workplace and express them without fear of reprisal (Cunningham, 2015a, 2015b; Cunningham, Pickett, Melton, Lee, Miner, 2014). The use of inclusive diversity strategies is associated with increased workplace satisfaction and involvement in decision-making among employees (Bidee et al., 2017; Fink, Pastore, & Riemer, 2003; Hsiao, Ma, & Auld, 2017). In athletic departments, employee diversity serves a role-modeling function for athletes (LaVoi, 2016; Singer & Cunningham, 2012). Finally, in diverse and inclusive work environments, differences are seen as a source of learning and growth (Bruening et al., 2015; Cunningham, 2015a), work group creativity is high (Cunningham, 2008a, 2011), additional financial gains are possible (Cunningham & Singer, 2011), and performance often outpaces that of the organization's competitors (Lee & Cunningham, in press). Collectively, these findings do much to promote the idea that diversity is a source of competitive advantage (Richard & Miller, 2013).

Despite these benefits, many sport organizations are not diverse and inclusion—a point illustrated thus far in the text. The exclusion of persons who differ from the typical majority has been the norm for decades, as illustrated by who serves in leadership positions. Furthermore, members of racial and sexual minorities, women, members of religious minorities, persons with disabilities, and the poor, among others have routinely been marginalized and relegated to "other" status within the sport context.

The lack of a diverse and inclusive environment is further exacerbated by the fact that many efforts to create inclusion are not successful. Dobbin and Kalev (2016) reviewed studies published over several decades to examine the impact of diversity management programs. In many cases, the efforts failed. Strategies put in place to reduce managers' biases have been largely ineffective, and this is true whether the approaches involve training, including bias-reduction criteria in performance evaluations, or creating rules to govern the decision-making process. On the other hand, efforts to promote employee diversity and integration are more successful. Mentoring programs, groups tasked with overseeing the diversity efforts, and full-time managers charged with promoting diversity and inclusion all help facilitate these effects.

Sport organizations have not fared much better than their non-sport peers in implementing diversity efforts. Spaaij, Farquharson, Magee, and their colleagues (2014), for instance, found that the moral imperative for diversity was largely lacking in Australian sport clubs' diversity plans; instead, these clubs focused on the benefits and costs of the programs—a perspective that ultimately limited physical activity participation among members of underrepresented groups. Similarly, I have observed that even when managers of sport organizations seek to undergo diversity change, the efforts are sometimes unsuccessful because of a lack of full integration throughout the organizational system (Cunningham, 2009).

This discussion points to a perplexing quandary: on the one hand, diversity and inclusion can be sources of learning, employee well-being, and overall effectiveness for sport organizations, but on the other hand, many efforts to create and sustain inclusive work environments fail. I believe that these failures stem from a failure to recognize the multilevel nature of successful change efforts. Unless sport managers take into account factor at various levels of analysis, change efforts will be too narrowly focused, and, hence, unsuccessful (Cunningham, 2009). Thus, in the next section, I provide a multilevel model that managers can use to create and sustain diversity and inclusion in their sport organizations.

MULTILEVEL MODEL

C Consistent with the multilevel approach I have adopted in this book, I focus on the macro-, meso-, and micro-level factors that affect inclusiveness in a sport work environment. Exhibit 13.1 offers a summary.

Macro-Level Factors

Community Characteristics

Community characteristics can influence sport organizations in a number of ways. First, when they are located within a diverse, progressive community, sport organizations are more likely to adopt inclusive practices. Inclusive communities comprise people with liberal ideologies, they frequently have laws mandating equality for a number of different groups, and they establish prohibitions against discriminatory behavior. These factors collectively influence inclusiveness in organizations (Barron & Hebl, 2010). It is also important to remember, though, that sport organizations are not simply passive recipients of their environments; instead, some are able to create diverse, inclusive work environments even when embedded in homogeneous communities (see Box 13.1).

In other cases, the demographics of the broader community might influence actions sport managers take. Nite and I examined how the presence of lesbian, gay, and bisexual (LGB) individuals in a state influenced organizational activities and overall effectiveness (Cunningham & Nite, 2018). We collected data from major college athletic programs, including the number of employees, budget, LGB-inclusive policies, and their performance on objective measures of success. We also gathered information about the population density of LGB individuals in each state. Results showed that population density interacted with the strategy used to explain performance. Performance was highest when programs followed in an LGB-inclusive strategy and they were set in a state with high LGB population density. These findings show that the external environment—in this

Multilevel Model for Creating and Sustaining an Inclusive Sport Work Environment	*exhibit* **13.1**

Macro-level factors. Those factors operating at the broader, societal level, including community characteristics and pressures for deinstitutionalization.

Meso-level factors. Those factors operating at the group and organizational level of analysis, including leaders, allies, workplace commitment to diversity, educational activities, and systemic integration of diversity and inclusion.

Micro-level factors. Those factors operating at the individual level, including psychological characteristics, intergroup contact, and difficult dialogues.

Box 13.1 Alternative Perspectives: Inclusion despite the Community

Although local and state regulations and demography can shape organizational practices, evidence suggests that some organizations are able to create diverse, inclusive work environments in homogeneous, conservative geographic regions. This mismatch has a positive effect on external stakeholders, as well as on persons working in the organization. Pugh, Dietz, Brief, and Wiley (2008) examined this very issue and found that employee perceptions of the diversity climate were positive when the organization was racially diverse and set within a homogeneous community. However, as community diversity increased, the linkage between workforce diversity and perceived diversity climate weakened. These findings suggest that sport organizations might be rewarded for exceeding expectations for an inclusive work environment.

case, the proportion of LGB individuals in a state—interacts with organizational factors to influence various outcomes.

Pressures for Deinstitutionalization

In many ways, cultures of similarity and exclusion have become institutionalized, meaning that through habit, history, and tradition, they have become unquestionably accepted as "how things are done" (see also Scott, 2008). Institutionalized practices are highly resistant to change and are maintained over time without objection, as they are seen largely as the legitimate modus operandi. Consequently, despite the documented evidence showing the many benefits of diversity and inclusion, many sport organizations have systems in place that do not allow for these effects to be realized.

If cultures of similarity and exclusion are firmly engrained and legitimated within the sport context, then what factors would spur organizations to change? That is, what prompts sport organizations to seek a culture of diversity and inclusion? The work done in the area of institutional theory (Cunningham, 2008b; Oliver, 1992) points to three primary factors: political pressures, functional pressures, and social pressures.

Political pressures arise when an organization experiences mounting performance deficits, the presence of conflicting interests among stakeholder groups, increasing pressures for innovation, and changing reliance upon external constituents (Oliver, 1992). I have observed the influence of political pressures in my own research on an intercollegiate athletics department undergoing a diversity-related change process (Cunningham, 2009). Specifically, the organization sought to attract diverse fans to the events as a way to generate more revenues. Thus, the pressures for greater revenues from a variety of new, previously unrealized sources drove, at least in part, efforts for diversity and inclusion.

Functional pressures manifest when there are concerns about organizational effectiveness or the utility of a given practice (Oliver, 1992). These pressures are associated with environmental dynamics, such as competition for scarce resources (Dacin, Goodstein, & Scott, 2002). Perhaps the best example of functional pressures comes from what Ladson-Billings (2004) refers to as the "Bear Bryant/Adolph Rupp epiphany" (p. 10). Bryant, the head coach of the University of Alabama football team, watched his all-White squad get soundly beaten by the University of Southern California—a game in which USC's African American tailback, Sam (Bam) Cunningham, ran for 135 yards and two touchdowns on just 12 carries. Similarly, Rupp was the head coach of the University of Kentucky's all-White men's basketball team when his squad was beaten in the championship game by a Texas Western team that started five African Americans. Ladson-Billings suggests that both victories "made clear to big-time college athletics that winning required recruiting players from beyond all-White prep fields" (p. 12). Not surprisingly, both Bryant and Rupp fielded racially integrated teams soon after those defeats.

Finally, social pressures result from differentiation among groups (e.g., increasing employee diversity), disruptions in the organization's historical continuity (e.g., when mergers take place), or changes in laws or social movements that might disrupt the continuation of an institutionalized practice (Scott, 2008). For example, Hebl, Barron, Cox, and Corrington (2016) found that local and state laws can help reduce the incidence of employment discrimination against lesbian, gay, bisexual, and transgender (LGBT) individuals. The laws can also alter the actions of organizational leaders and the policies that put in place. These pressures were also present in my analysis of an athletic department that was seeking greater diversity and inclusion (Cunningham, 2009). Many in the community perceived that the athletic department had a history of excluding racial minority coaches and administrators, and they made their concerns known through various mechanisms; for example, an open letter decrying the abysmal hiring practices was penned by former players and circulated on national websites. In addition, the athletic department's mascot had long been a Native American—a practice that many observers viewed as hostile and offensive (e.g., Whiteside, 2016). Collectively, these issues resulted in mounting concerns voiced by a myriad of external stakeholders, and in response to these concerns the athletic department sought to change its otherwise institutionalized activities.

Meso-Level Factors

Meso-level factors are those operating at the group and organizational levels. In the context of the current discussion, leaders, allies, workplace commitment to diversity, educational activities, and systemic integration of diversity and inclusion are all particularly important.

Leaders

Leaders understandably play a key role in creating and sustaining inclusive environments. My research showed this was manifested through leader advocacy and leader expectations (Cunningham, 2015a, 2015b). People in various leadership roles engaged in advocacy efforts. In some cases, this meant the athletic directors worked for gender equality and LGBT inclusiveness on state, national, and international levels. These efforts were noticed by others in the department and, thus, had an effect on their attitudes, as well. In other cases, coaches took on leadership roles within the department and created activities to promote an inclusive environment. My work with Melton in other settings also supports this pattern, thereby suggesting that advocacy for inclusion comes from many sources (Melton & Cunningham, 2014).

Leaders also set high expectations for others to promote inclusion. One coach, in speaking of the athletic director's expectations, noted, "(Mike) is the leader of that and I don't think he would tolerate anything less . . . (Mike) isn't going to tolerate a lack of inclusiveness and that is true for all types of diversity." These leaders articulate those behaviors and attitudes that are acceptable and those that are not. Leaders can convey as much through formal statements and policies, by modeling the behaviors, or through informal communications. When followers know they are expected to hold inclusive attitudes and demonstrate inclusive behaviors, they are likely to do so.

Allies

Formal leaders play a critical role in ensuring the success of inclusion and diversity initiatives in the workplace. However, they are not the only ones who can make a difference. Instead, all people—athletes, coaches, staff, administrators, and the like—can affect the climate of diversity and inclusion (Trussell, Kovac, & Apgar, 2018). They do so through their attitudes, their words, and their actions. Here, we see the importance of allies, or individuals who offer support for diversity initiatives, social justice causes, and people from underrepresented groups. As members of a majority group, allies can play an important role in offering support for those who are experiencing discrimination. They can also use their power and privilege in the work environment to speak up in support of causes and initiatives (Cunningham, 2014; Ruggs, Martinez, Hebl, & Law, 2015). See Box 13.2 for additional discussion of the power of athletes serving as allies.

I offer two research examples to illustrate ally dynamics. Sartore and I conducted a study of the lesbian stigma present in health and kinesiology departments. Our interviews with lesbians in these academic departments showed that allies played an important role in offering personal support and in vocally advocating for equality (Sartore & Cunningham, 2010). Further, because some of the key allies were full professors and had been married—characteristics that have accompanying power and privilege—encouraging inclusion did not place them in vulnerable positions. Melton and I also observed as much in our study of athletic department members (Melton & Cunningham, 2014). A study participant noted,

Box 13.2 Diversity in the Field: Athlete Ally

Hudson Taylor is a former wrestler at the University of Maryland. When he enrolled at the university, he befriended many LGBT students and became aware of the stress and pain caused by heterosexism and sexual prejudice. This prompted him to become involved in ally activities, and as a way to show support, he even wore a Human Rights Campaign sticker (a blue box with a yellow equals sign in the middle) on his headgear during matches. Following his wrestling career, Taylor founded Athlete Ally (www. athlete ally.org) to promote LGBT equality in sport and beyond.

Athlete Ally works with teams and individual athletes to train athletes on the prevalence of sexual prejudice and ways they can engage in ally behavior. Those who complete the training can sign a pledge, which reads,

I pledge to lead my athletic community to respect and welcome all persons, regardless of their perceived or actual sexual orientation, gender identity, or gender expression. Beginning right now, I will do my part to promote the best of athletics by making all players feel respected on and off the field. (http://donate.athleteally.org/page/s/sign-the-athlete-ally-pledge)

As of September 2018, more than 24,000 persons had signed the pledge. Some notable professional athletes who serve as Athlete Ally ambassadors include Billie Jean King (tennis), Abby Wambach (soccer), Yogi Berra (baseball), D'Qwell Jackson (football), Andy Roddick (tennis), and Sue Bird (basketball), among others.

> A male coach, especially one who is married with three kids, can publically support gay and lesbian issues. People will listen; they might even applaud him for his courage to speak out on a controversial topic. Can a female coach do that? Hell no. She's immediately called a lesbian and all the coaches in her conference are making sure recruits, *and their parents*, know she's lesbian and supports lesbianism on the team.
>
> (p. 202, emphasis in original)

Given the influence allies can have, Sartore and I conducted a study to understand what prompted them to become active advocates for diversity and inclusion; that is, what was it that prompted them to engage in championing behavior (Cunningham & Sartore, 2010)? We drew from previous work (Herscovitch & Meyer, 2002; Holvino, Ferdman, & Merrill-Sands, 2004) to suggest that championing was the highest form of discretionary behavior one could undertake, and it involved employees' making specific sacrifices and exerting considerable effort to support diversity and inclusion. We found that women, members of racial or sexual minorities, people who have an extraverted personality, and people who expressed low levels of racial and sexual prejudice were all likely to champion diversity. In addition to these personal characteristics, people who worked with others who also supported diversity were engaged in championing behaviors. These findings have implications for sport managers who seek to transform their workplace into one of diversity and inclusion.

Commitment to Diversity

The work of leaders and allies should increase overall commitment to diversity among organizational members. Commitment to diversity represents "a force or mindset that binds an individual to support diversity" (Cunningham, 2008a, p. 178). The mindset can be reflected in one of the three ways: affective commitment, a desire to support diversity because of the value of diversity; continuance commitment, the support of diversity because of the costs of not doing so; or normative commitment, the felt obligation to provide support for diversity.

For a sport organization to realize diversity's benefits, commitment to diversity is needed among the employees. I observed as much in a series of studies of NCAA athletic departments (Cunningham, 2008a). Specifically, I found that departments that merged a diverse staff with a strong collective commitment to diversity (i.e., high in all of the above mindsets) outperformed their peers in terms of attracting diverse fans, achieving employee satisfaction, and encouraging employees' creativity. Departments that had high commitment but lacked employee diversity were unable to realize these benefits. These findings suggest that employees should not only recognize the benefits of diversity (have affective commitment) but also adopt a sense of obligation to support it (normative commitment), recognizing that not doing so will adversely affect the workplace (continuance commitment).

Educational Activities

My analyses of various sport organizations show that they routinely engage in various forms of education and programming as a way to enhance diversity and inclusion (Cunningham, 2015a, 2015b). For example, as a way of ensuring their readiness and ability to engage in constructive conflict and difficult dialogues, the staff of one department read the book *Fierce Conversations* (Scott, 2002) and, as a group, discussed its relevance for their everyday interactions. Both departments brought in guest speakers to discuss important topics related to inclusion, watched videos (e.g., the powerful documentary *Training Rules*), and held workshops. In short, they looked to identify areas of need and address those, while also building upon and improving current skill sets. These efforts might also help address some of the concerns that people have about various diversity initiatives, as well as sources of resistance to those initiatives (see Exhibit 13.2). We discuss more educational and training activities in Chapter 14.

| Forms of Resistance to Diversity-Related Change | *exhibit* **13.2** |

Resistance to organizational initiatives, including efforts to enhance diversity can inclusion, can result in various forms of resistance, including individual and organization.

Individual

- **Prejudice**: People may prefer a homogeneous workplace. This preference may come from a strong liking of in-group members or disliking of out-group members.

- **Habit**: People use habits to reduce uncertainty in their lives and to increase efficiencies. The same is true for organizational policies and procedures. When diversity-related strategies are implemented, they might represent a departure from a habit and, therefore, be met with resistance.

- **Security**: People with a high need for security may resist any and all efforts toward change because the changes might impact the power they have, the roles they assume, and so forth—all of which decreases the security people have at work.

- **Economic factors**: Some people resist change that they perceive will negatively affect them monetarily. For example, if a diversity strategy meant (or was perceived to mean) that some people would receive reduced pay increases, then they would probably resist the initiative.

- **Fear of the unknown**: People generally prefer to have an understanding of what the future holds for them, and change alters those perceptions. When diversity management strategies are implemented, people may be unsure of how the strategies will affect their jobs, the relationships they have with others, and their overall standing in the organization. If this is true, they are likely to resist any efforts toward change.

- **Selective information processing**: Once people form perceptions of their world, they are unlikely to change them. This unwillingness to change may result in people selectively interpreting some information while ignoring other input. For example, people may ignore arguments as to how diversity will improve the organization because the arguments are counter to their current perceptions of the organization and how it functions.

Organizational Resistance

- **Limited focus of change**: Because organizations are composed of interrelated systems, changing one part requires changing another if the change is to have a lasting effect. Diversity initiatives often have a narrow focus that is nullified by the larger organizational system.

- **Inertia**: Organizational inertia is the tendency for organizations to resist change and remain in their current state. Even if certain people want the change, the organizational norms and culture may act as constraints.

- **Threat to expertise**: Changes that threaten the expertise of particular groups cause resistance. For example, hiring a diversity officer to oversee the organization's diversity efforts might be resisted by the human resource staff because that threatens their expertise in the area of hiring and employee relations.

- **Threat to established power relationships**: In proactive organizations, the power is held by a multicultural group of people. In other organization types, the power rests primarily with White males. To the extent that diversity is viewed as disrupting established power relationships, it may face resistance.

- **Threat to established resource allocations**: Those groups that control sizable resources may view efforts toward change as threatening. For example, in university athletics, men's teams traditionally have received the lion's share of the budget. Thus, moves to increase the gender equity might be met with resistance by these players or coaches, if they believe it means they will receive fewer resources.

Source: Adapted from Robbins (2011).

Systemic Integration

Efforts to create and sustain inclusive work environments are most effective when inclusive activities are embedded into the organizational system (Cunningham, 2016). The formal policies and procedures, the strategic plan, hiring practices, and facility designs, among others, should include elements of diversity and inclusion. Thus, the principles were embedded into the fabric of the organization. To illustrate, one athletic department in a study I conducted allocated locker room space for transgender individuals as a way of facilitating the sense of inclusion and encouraging physical activity among all persons (Cunningham, 2015b). In the same study, partners were specifically invited to official events and were listed in the department directory (if the employee so desired). The departments were also purposeful in their hiring, specifically seeking to create diverse applicant pools and actively recruiting people from underrepresented backgrounds (for other examples, see also Singer & Cunningham, 2012).

These examples, which represent only a small sampling, show that diversity and inclusion need to be embedded in all the organization does. Too often, sport organizations look to create meaningful change without integrating the principles throughout the organizational system. Without such integration, the diversity efforts will not truly take hold and will undoubtedly fail (Cunningham, 2009).

Micro-Level Factors

Micro-level factors are those at the individual level. In the context of creating and sustaining workplace inclusion, including psychological characteristics, intergroup contact, and difficult dialogues are important.

Psychological Characteristics

People's psychological characteristics can influence their receptivity to inclusive-focused change efforts. Consider, for example, the influence of racial identity. Recall from Chapter 5 that when people have a strong racial identity, their race is an important part of who they are, how they see themselves, and their overall self-concept. Among minorities, racial identity strength is associated with experiences of perceived discrimination (Sellers & Shelton, 2003) and dimensions of overall well-being, such as self-esteem (Smith & Silva, 2011).

Though researchers commonly focus on racial minorities' racial identity, Whites also express racial identity, and it can affect their attitudes toward diversity and inclusion. For Whites with a strong racial identity, increasing diversity can represent a threat to their status and resources (Craig, Rucker, & Richeson, 2018). Researchers have shown that after reading about diversity, Whites express anger toward racial minority groups (Outten, Schmitt, Miller, & Garcia, 2012), demonstrate racial bias (Craig & Richeson, 2014), and are less likely to support diversity initiatives (Outten et al., 2012). Other researchers have shown that not all Whites react the same to increased diversity, though. Instead, reactions vary based on Whites' racial identity. As an example, Major, Blodorn, and Blascovich (2018) found that Whites reacted to increased diversity with a perceived status threat when they also strongly identified with their race. The pattern was not present for Whites with a low racial identity. The status threat also affected their support of different initiatives, such as anti-immigration and opposition to political correctness.

Other psychological characteristics affect people's reactions to inclusion and diversity. For instance, political conservatism (Sibley & Duckitt, 2008), authoritarianism (Van Assche, Roets, Dhont, & Van Hiel, 2016), the support for social hierarchies in society (social dominance orientation; Guimond et al., 2013), and fundamentalist religious beliefs (McDermott, Schwartz, Lindley, & Proietti, 2014) are all linked with opposition to differences and efforts to create inclusive spaces. On the other hand, characteristics such as openness to experience (Gocłowska, Baas, Elliot, & De Dreu, 2017), social justice orientation (Nutter, Russell-Mayhew, Arthur, & Ellard, 2018), and intellectual humility (Hook et al., 2017), among others, are all associated with positive attitudes toward inclusion and differences.

This research suggests that sport managers need to take into account employees' and athletes' psychological characteristics when seeking to create more diverse and inclusive environments. For some, the changes might represent a threat to their standing, position, or access to resources. Thus, efforts to ensure these individuals of their well-being on the team or in the workplace are important. In other cases, sport managers can note the importance of new experiences and learning from others, both of which are likely to be meaningful for people who are open to new experiences and who show intellectual humility.

As shown in Box 13.3, not all of the aforementioned relationships are as straightforward as they might seem.

Box 13.3 Alternative Perspectives: Evidence That Liberals and Conservatives Express Prejudice

Researchers have long shown that political conservatism is linked with lower acceptance of diversity and inclusion, as well as the endorsement prejudice (Sibly & Duckitt, 2008). These patterns could lead one to conclude that the opposites also true: political liberals are accepting of differences and unlikely to express bias. But, is this the case?

Two studies call into question such assumptions. In the first, Stephens-Davidowitz (2014) analyzed Google searches to determine the hidden racial biases of people around the US. He found that many people in the Northeastern portion of the country—an area long considered as more liberal and progressive than the South—expressed racial bias. The content of their Google searches (e.g., searching for racial jokes) was a better predictor of their voting record than were their self-professed racial attitudes.

In another study, Brandt, Reyna, Chambers, Crawford, and Wetherell (2014) examined various measures of intolerance among liberals and conservatives. Outcomes included dislike of the target, political intolerance, and willingness to discriminate. Their results showed that conservatives disliked, were intolerant of, and were willing to discriminate against people who held different political beliefs than they did. Interestingly, the same pattern occurred among liberals. The evaluations manifest from value conflicts, threats to the self and their group, and value violations. Again, the underlying mechanisms held for both groups. Based on these findings, the authors encouraged research in other areas. Conservatives, for example, express bias against atheists, but liberals might express the same level of bias against evangelical Christians. Thus, although the targets might differ, the patterns of prejudice are similar.

Intergroup Contact

Perhaps the most effective way to reduce prejudice and create inclusive spaces is through intergroup contact. Allport's (1954) contact hypothesis is among the earliest and most influential theories related to reducing prejudice. Most of the contemporary theories on bias reduction are grounded in his work (Hodson & Hewstone, 2013), and many scholars and practitioners still incorporate his original piece into their efforts to reduce prejudice (Bruening et al., 2014; Welty Peachey, Cunningham, Bruening, Cohen, Lyras, 2015). The basic premise underlying Allport's contact hypothesis states that prejudice is sustained against others because of unfamiliarity and separation; thus, the key to reducing prejudice is to enable members of various social groups to have contact with one another under the right conditions. Allport suggested intergroup contact is most likely to result in prejudice reduction when there is institutional support; the contact is intimate, resulting in meaningful friendships or associations; people involved in the interaction are of equal status; and the individuals work together in an interdependent, cooperative manner.

Initially, researchers assumed that the aforementioned conditions of contact had a direct effect on prejudice reduction. More recent research suggests that the effects probably occur through a reduction in intergroup anxiety (Pettigrew & Tropp, 2008; Vezzali, Hewstone, Capozza, Giovannini, & Wölfer, 2014). Intergroup anxiety refers to feelings of unease or apprehension that a person experiences when visualizing or having contact with out-group members. This anxiety arises from the misunderstanding and rejection that people anticipate when interacting with people who are different from themselves. As a result of this anxiety, people are likely to harbor negative feelings toward out-group members and, in turn, exhibit prejudice.

The presence of Allport's conditions for contact should reduce intergroup anxiety and, ultimately, prejudice. In an examination illustrative of these effects, Ellers and Abrams (2003) conducted a study of Americans who were studying Spanish in Mexican language institutes. They observed that friendship with out-group members was reliably related to a variety of outcomes, including reduction of anxiety directed toward the out-group and reduction of social distancing. Binder and colleagues' (2009) longitudinal study of minority and majority European schoolchildren yielded similar findings.

Other researchers have shown that contact is particularly effective in the sport and exercise domain (Lee & Cunningham, 2013; Ottoboni et al., 2017). Ottoboni et al., for example, examined ways in which prejudice toward people with disabilities might be reduced. They focused on school-aged children, aged 10–12, and how being around school mates with a disability might shape their attitudes. The research team collected data in October and then again in May. They found a significant reduction in implicit bias among students who were around peers with a disability. Bias did not change among students who did not have such interactions. The type of contact also mattered. Students who participated in team sports with a person with a disability had the biggest decrease in their implicit bias. For those whose contact came in the classrooms, there was a corresponding reduction in bias, but it was not as strong. Ottoboni and colleagues attributed the changes to the nature of sport, the interdependence among the players, and the necessity of collaboration in order to be successful.

Though intergroup contact has many benefits, it does have one primary limitation: the individual must be physically present to interact with one another. However, there might be cases where, for a variety of reasons, intergroup contact should not occur. It might not be responsible, for instance, for persons with a history of violence to meet and interact with one another. In other cases, contact might be advisable, but because of geographic differences, actual contact might be impossible. A number of social psychologists have explored the efficacy of indirect forms of contact.

Extended contact theory is an example of research into indirect contact. From this perspective, simply knowing that a person similar to oneself has out-group friends has the potential to reduce intergroup bias (Dovidio, Eller, & Hewstone,

2011). This transfer is especially likely to occur if the in-group member is held in high regard and the focal individual trusts that person's judgment.

Vezzali, Stathi, Giovannini, and their colleagues (2015) conducted a series of studies to examine whether the effects of extended contact could be realized through reading *Harry Potter* books. In addition to focus on various adventures and magic, all seven books contain themes of inclusion of individuals who differ from the majority (muggles, elves, and goblins, among others). The authors examined whether reading passages that focused on prejudice and its effects would serve to reduce bias, particularly among readers who strongly identified with Harry Potter himself. A study with elementary school students showed that this was the case; further, those students who strongly identified with Voldemort (the evil character in the book, who promotes intergroup distinctions) held negative out-group attitudes. Subsequent work with high school students (Study 2) and college students (Study 3) demonstrated similar findings. This research shows that others' acceptance of out-group members can affect one's own beliefs.

Other elements of the *Harry Potter* books can also improve intergroup relations, as illustrated in Box 13.4.

Box 13.4 Diversity in the Field: Quidditch, Bias, and Inclusion

Many of the characters in the *Harry Potter* books participate in quidditch. This is a sport where the participants fly on broomsticks and try to pass a ball through hoops placed at opposite ends of a playing field while also trying to capture the snitch. (If this is all gibberish to you, I do recommend reading the books; also, the initiated reader can consult the site for the International Quidditch Association, www.iqaquidditch.org.) Interestingly, the sport has caught on across a number of college campuses. The non-fantasy games closely mirror those in the book: team members run instead of fly with broomsticks, attempt to throw balls through hoops at either end of the field, and even attempt to capture a snitch. Importantly (and also consistent with the books), quidditch is played as a coed sport, without special accommodations for women.

Cohen has conducted a number of studies on why people participate in quidditch and what impact it has on them (Cohen, Melton, & Welty Peachey, 2014; Cohen & Welty Peachey, 2015). In one of his studies, Cohen and his colleagues found that the coed nature of the sport allowed for improved attitudes toward participants of the opposite gender. Participation was also linked with an enhanced desire for justice, equality, and inclusion. For example, one player noted, "I never thought my girlfriend could be as good at a sport as me, maybe even better! So yes, this coed sport has changed my thinking" (p. 227). Another noted that the coed structure "makes it a game of inclusion that makes everyone feel welcome" (p. 227). These results provide another example of how sport and intergroup contact can affect people's bias and desire for inclusion.

Imagined intergroup contact represents another form of indirect contact. This approach involves "the mental simulation of a social interaction with a member or members of an outgroup category" (Crisp & Turner, 2009, p. 234). In this case, people imagine they are interacting in an agreeable way with out-group members, and this mental simulation is enough to alter their attitudes toward dissimilar others. Imagined contact can also prepare people to engage in actual contact.

Miles and Crisp (2014) conducted a meta-analysis of experimental studies that examined the effects of imagined contact. Recall that a meta-analysis statistically aggregates the findings from numerous studies to demonstrate the overall effects of the phenomenon under investigation. A common characteristic of the studies in this meta-analysis is that the researchers randomly assigned participants to (a) the experimental group, where they imagined interacting with out-group members in some way, or (b) a control group, where they participated in another activity. Results of the meta-analysis indicate that imagined contact had a significant effect on bias reduction. Outcomes included explicit and implicit measures of prejudice, emotional reactions to the out-group, behaviors, and behavioral intentions.

Lee and I have examined the effects of imagined contact in the sport context (Lee & Cunningham, 2014). We asked people in the experimental group to imagine the following: "You play basketball with a gay man for two hours. Then, you spend about 30 minutes chatting. During the conversation you find out some interesting and unexpected things about him." In the control group, we asked people to imagine that they played basketball with their best friend. We then asked the participants to reflect on the mental simulation and finally respond to a questionnaire. Results indicated that for Koreans the imagined contact served to lessen intergroup anxiety and sexual prejudice; however, the same was not the case for Americans, for whom anxiety actually increased. We reasoned this could be attributable to the participants' previous experiences with LGBT individuals. Few people disclose their sexual orientation in Korea, so Koreans might not have preconceived notions or firmly embedded biases, and, thus, imagined contact would be effective. On the other hand, as Americans might have had more experiences interacting with members of sexual minorities, their attitudes might be more cemented and less malleable. This reasoning is consistent with Miles and Crisp's (2014) findings that imagined contact is more effective among children (i.e., people who are unlikely to have set attitudes toward out-group members) than among adults.

In Exhibit 13.3, I offer an overview of other types of contact that can help reduce bias and create an inclusive work environment.

Difficult Dialogues

Finally, people's willingness to and experience in engaging in difficult dialogues can influence their attitudes toward diversity and inclusion. Difficult dialogues are the discussions people have in the workplace that are sometimes difficult yet nonetheless productive. These conversations are frequently avoided in organizations, but when they are undertaken, they help the parties generate a better understanding of one another. For example, in one of my studies (Cunningham, 2015a), an athletic administrator shared how discussions of gender identity and sexual

exhibit **13.3** Decategorization and Recategorization

Allport's (1954) contact hypothesis is a well-regarded technique for reducing bias, but it is not the only one. Researchers have suggested a number of other techniques, including decategorization and recategorization.

Decategorization

Decategorization is an attempt to reduce intergroup bias by breaking down the categorization boundaries between interacting groups (Brewer & Miller, 1984). This strategy is based on the idea that repeated, individualized interactions among members of different groups will ultimately reduce bias. This is accomplished in two ways. First, recall that through the categorization process, all members of a specific social group are perceived as largely homogeneous (e.g., "all women act *that* way"), and distinctions are not made among members of the group. Decategorization through individualized interactions allows a person to make distinctions among out-group members, a process called *differentiation*. Second, when people interact on a personal level with others, they compare the others to themselves. This results in a process called *personalization*, in which out-group members are viewed "in terms of their uniqueness and in relation to the self" (Hewstone, Rubin, & Willis, 2002, p. 589). Both processes allow one to see oneself and the other person as *individuals*, rather than as members of homogeneous in-groups or out-groups. To the extent that these interactions are repeated over time, this breaking down of categorization boundaries might also be applied in new situations or to hitherto unfamiliar out-group members (Gaertner & Dovidio, 2000).

As a research example, Jones and Foley (2003) focused on the degree to which decategorization reduced bias among schoolchildren. Students were assigned to one of the two conditions: (a) the experimental condition, in which the students heard a presentation emphasizing anthropology (e.g., the origin of humans, the spread of humans across the globe), problems associated with depending on physical biological characteristics to determine differences among people, and the idea that most persons in the US have common ancestry, and (b) the control condition, in which students heard a reading of Dr. Seuss's Oh, *The Places You'll Go!* The researchers found that the students in the experimental condition were more likely to perceive similarities between themselves and others, and as a result their formerly held prejudice toward out-group members was reduced.

Although it may not be referred to as decategorization, this approach is often used in organizational and team settings. For example, many organizations use rope courses or other adventure escapes as methods to build a team. These programs allow people to become acquainted outside the office, build communication skills among team members, and strengthen interpersonal relationships. It is expected that boundaries among team members will be reduced, thereby increasing the team's effectiveness.

Recategorization

According to Gaertner and Dovidio (2000), who developed the Common Ingroup Identity Model, the purpose of *recategorization* is to encourage "members of both groups to regard themselves as belonging to a common superordinate group—*one group* that is inclusive of both memberships" (p. 33, emphasis in original). If members of different groups consider themselves members of a single, common group, then former membership boundaries become less important because all are now members of the same in-group. The common in-group serves to replace the "us" and "them" dynamics with a more inclusive "we." For example, boards of directors are increasingly looking to add demographic diversity to their boards. They are likely to do so when they believe the demographically different new board members share common beliefs, values, or other characteristics. This makes it easier for them to recategorize the new members as common in-group members and helps the board function effectively (Zhu, Shen, & Hillman, 2014).

Experimental work that recategorization is associated with an increase in helpful behaviors directed toward out-group members (Dovidio et al., 1997), satisfaction with the group (Cunningham & Chelladurai, 2004), and preference to work with the group in the future (Cunningham & Chelladurai, 2004). In addition to the aforementioned laboratory work, I have also found evidence of the importance of a common in-group identity among college coaches. In the first study, I observed that coworker satisfaction among people who differ racially from their colleagues was higher when they were on staffs characterized by a common in-group identity than when they were not (Cunningham, 2005). In the next study, I examined the effects of a common in-group identity for the coaching staff as a whole. The results indicated that the stronger the identity, the more effective the team was on multiple measures of success, and the less likely the coaches were to leave the staff (Cunningham, 2007).

Gaertner and Dovidio (2000) propose several methods that a group leader can use to form a common in-group identity. These include the following: spatial arrangement, where members from various groups sit together rather than with members of their own group; common threat, where people focus on a specific target they are seeking to best; common fate, which refers to the idea that if the group does well, then all group members are rewarded; and common goals, where members of a unit collectively identify goals to achieve.

orientation might be uncomfortable for some people in sport; however, there were also benefits, as she noted,

> Don't be afraid to talk about it. Talk about the issues which some people avoid, like sexual orientation. Just being open and saying it is okay to be who you are. I think the relationships and communication and talking to each other creates a good community.

People in both athletic departments echoed these praises, suggesting that engaging in difficult dialogues can help stimulate different ideas, highlight divergent opinions, challenge people to think differently, allow people to take a stand for important issues, and ultimately build a sense of community and trust. For more discussion of the importance of difficult dialogues, see Box 13.5.

Box 13.5 Professional Perspectives: Importance of Difficult Dialogues in the Workplace

Nancy Watson is the founder and president of the Center for Change and Conflict Resolution. She works with a variety of organizations to help them create organizational cultures that are open and inclusive. Part of this process focuses on engaging in constructive conflict and difficult dialogues. Doing so allows people to be engaged and for the culture to be learning-oriented.

Speaking to the importance of these activities, Watson noted,

Open constructive dialogue in the workplace creates an environment for greater trust and productivity among co-workers to occur. Part of open constructive dialogue involves engaging in difficult dialogues as situations and events warrant. By engaging in difficult dialogues people increase their opportunity to learn from one another by suspending judgment, active listening, and learning from others' perspectives.

CHAPTER SUMMARY

In this chapter, I provided an overview of strategies aimed at creating an inclusive work environment. As illustrated in the Diversity Challenge, there is often a need to employ specific strategies to provide equal opportunities to all parties. Without such strategies, dissimilar others may have negative work experiences. Effective inclusion and diversity management strategies generate positive outcomes for the organization as a whole. Having read this chapter, you should now be able to:

1. Identify the benefits of workplace inclusion.

    Organizations benefit from inclusiveness in a number of ways. External stakeholders respond favorably to organizations that are diverse and inclusive. Internally, inclusiveness is associated with improved employee attitudes, better group processes, and higher objective measures of success.

2. Summarize strategies for creating an inclusive sport work environment.

    Creating and sustaining an inclusive work environment necessitates a multilevel focus. Factors at the macro-level of analysis include community characteristics and pressures for deinstitutionalization. At the meso-level, leaders, allies, workplace commitment to diversity, educational activities, and systemic integration of diversity and inclusion are all importance. Finally, at the individual level, psychological characteristics, intergroup contact, and difficult dialogues help shape the success of diversity and inclusion initiatives.

Questions FOR DISCUSSION

1. Why does an organization need an inclusion plan? Isn't the presence of a diverse workforce sufficient for the organization to realize positive outcomes?
2. A multilevel model was presented in this chapter. What are the primary elements of the model? Do you think one particular level of analysis is more important than others?
3. Are there any methods not discussed in this chapter that managers could use to decrease resistance to inclusion programs?
4. If the conditions of contact reduce bias in one situation, will that effect transfer to bias reductions in other situations? Why or why not?
5. For leaders of diverse organizations that are seeking to promote inclusion, of the competencies that they must have, which is likely to be most important and why?

LEARNING Activities

1. Suppose you are hired to manage a recreational sport facility. Identify key stakeholders and external pressures you would want to target and consider in creating an inclusive organizational culture.
2. Interview a coach at your university or a local high school about the strategies she or he uses to manage differences on the team. How do these strategies compare with those outlined in the chapter?
3. Suppose you are implementing a particular strategy to enhance diversity and inclusion in your organization. Develop a written action plan outlining the steps you would take to ensure the success of the program. Address the steps necessary to present the desirability of the program to your employees and to overcome any opposition to it.

Web RESOURCES

Program of Intergroup Relations, www.umich.edu/~igrc
  Program at the University of Michigan aimed at promoting an understanding of intergroup relations.

European Commission: Social Inclusion, http://ec.europa.eu/sport/policy/societal_role/social_inclusion_en.htm
  Outlines the importance of inclusion in sport and ways sport can create social inclusion in the broader society.

Catalyst, www.catalyst.org
  Leading research and advisory organization whose aim is to help organizations build inclusive, diverse work environments.

READING Resources

Gaertner, S. L., & Dovidio, J. F. (2000). *Reducing intergroup bias: The common ingroup identity model*. Philadelphia, PA: Psychology Press.

> Provides an excellent overview of the recategorization process, including research and practical examples.

Paluck, E. L., & Green, D. P. (2009). Prejudice reduction: What works? A review and assessment of research and practice. *Annual Review of Psychology, 60*, 339–367.

Offers a comprehensive review of various strategies to reduce prejudice in group settings.

Roberson, Q. M. (Ed.) (2013). *The Oxford handbook of diversity and work*. New York, NY: Oxford University Press.

> Edited text focusing on diversity and inclusion in the work environment, with specific strategies for change.

REFERENCES

Åkestam, N., Rosengren, S., & Dahlen, M. (2017). Think about it–can portrayals of homosexuality in advertising prime consumer-perceived social connectedness and empathy? *European Journal of Marketing, 51*(1), 82–98.

Allport, G. W. (1954). *The nature of prejudice*. Cambridge, MA: Addison-Wesley.

Barron, L. G., & Hebl, M. R. (2010). Extending lesbian, gay, bisexual, and transgendered supportive organizational policies: Communities matter too. *Industrial and Organizational Psychology, 3*, 79–81.

Bidee, J., Vantilborgh, T., Pepermans, R., Willems, J., Jegers, M., & Hofmans, J. (2017). Daily motivation of volunteers in healthcare organizations: Relating team inclusion and intrinsic motivation using self-determination theory. *European Journal of Work and Organizational Psychology, 26*(3), 325–336.

Binder, J., Zagefka, H., Brown, R., Funke, F., Kessler, T., Mummendey, A., ... Leyens, J. P. (2009). Does contact reduce prejudice or does prejudice reduce contact? A longitudinal test of the contact hypothesis among majority and minority groups in three European countries. *Journal of Personality and Social Psychology, 96*, 843–856.

Brandt, M. J., Reyna, C., Chambers, J. R., Crawford, J. T., & Wetherell, G. (2014). The ideological-conflict hypothesis: Intolerance among both liberals and conservatives. *Current Directions in Psychological Science, 23*(1), 27–34.

Brewer, M. B., & Miller, N. (1984). Beyond the contact hypothesis: Theoretical perspectives on desegregation. In N. Miller & M. B. Brewer (Eds.), *Groups in contact: The psychology of desegregation* (pp. 281–302). New York, NY: Academic Press.

Bruening, J., Fuller, R. D., Cotrufo, R. J., Madsen, R. M., Evanovich, J., & Wilson-Hill, D. E. (2014). Applying intergroup contact theory in the sport management classroom. *Sport Management Education Journal, 8*, 35–45.

Bruening, J. E., Peachey, J. W., Evanovich, J. M., Fuller, R. D., Murty, C. J. C., Percy, V. E., ... Chung, M. (2015). Managing sport for social change: The effects of intentional design and structure in a sport-based service learning initiative. *Sport Management Review, 18*(1), 69–85.

Cohen, A., & Welty Peachey, J. (2015). Quidditch impacting and benefiting participants in a non-fictional manner. *Journal of Sport & Social Issues, 39*(6), 521–544.

Cohen, A., Melton, E. N., & Welty Peachey, J. (2014). Investigating a coed sport's ability to encourage inclusion and equality. *Journal of Sport Management, 28,* 220–235.

Connelly, B. L., Certo, S. T., Ireland, R. D., & Reutzel, C. R. (2011). Signaling theory: A review and assessment. *Journal of Management, 37,* 39–67.

Craig, M. A., & Richeson, J. A. (2014). More diverse yet less tolerant? How the increasingly diverse racial landscape affects white Americans' racial attitudes. *Personality and Social Psychology Bulletin, 40*(6), 750–761.

Craig, M. A., Rucker, J. M., & Richeson, J. A. (2018). The pitfalls and promise of increasing racial diversity: Threat, contact, and race relations in the 21st century. *Current Directions in Psychological Science, 27*(3), 188–193.

Crisp, R. J., & Turner, R. N. (2009). Can imagined interactions produce positive perceptions? Reducing prejudice through simulated social contact. *American Psychologist, 64,* 231–240.

Cunningham, G. B. (2005). The importance of a common in-group identity in ethnically diverse groups. *Group Dynamics: Theory, Research, and Practice, 9,* 251–260.

Cunningham, G. B. (2007). Opening the black box: The influence of perceived diversity and a common in-group identity in diverse groups. *Journal of Sport Management, 21,* 58–78.

Cunningham, G. B. (2008a). Commitment to diversity and its influence on athletic department outcomes. *Journal of Intercollegiate Sport, 1,* 176–201.

Cunningham, G. B. (2008b). Creating and sustaining gender diversity in sport organizations. *Sex Roles, 58*(1–2), 136–145.

Cunningham, G. B. (2009). Understanding the diversity related change process: A field study. *Journal of Sport Management, 23,* 407–428.

Cunningham, G. B. (2011). Creative work environments in sport organizations: The influence of sexual orientation diversity and commitment to diversity. *Journal of Homosexuality, 58,* 1041–1057.

Cunningham, G. B. (2014). Interdependence, mutuality, and collective action in sport. *Journal of Sport Management, 28,* 1–7.

Cunningham, G. B. (2015a). Creating and sustaining workplace cultures supportive of LGBT employees in college athletics. *Journal of Sport Management, 29,* 426–442.

Cunningham, G. B. (2015b). LGBT inclusive athletic departments as actors of social change. *Journal of Intercollegiate Sport, 8,* 43–56.

Cunningham, G. B. (2016). Diversity and inclusion in sport. In R. Hoye & M. M. Parent (Eds.), *SAGE handbook of sport management* (pp. 309–322). Thousand Oaks, CA: Sage.

Cunningham, G. B. (2017, November). *LGBT inclusion as a business advantage.* Paper presented at the annual conference for the Sport Management Association of Australia and New Zealand, Gold Coast, QLD.

Cunningham, G. B., & Chelladurai, P. (2004). Affective reactions to cross-functional teams: The impact of size, relative performance, and common in-group identity. *Group Dynamics: Theory, Research, and Practice, 8,* 83–97.

Cunningham, G. B., & Melton, E. N. (2014). Signals and cues: LGBT inclusive advertising and consumer attraction. *Sport Marketing Quarterly, 23,* 37–46.

Cunningham, G. B., & Nite, C. (2018, June). *LGBT inclusion and institutional characteristics predict organizational performance.* Paper presented at the annual conference of the North American Society for Sport Management, Halifax, NS.

Cunningham, G. B., & Sartore, M. L. (2010). Championing diversity: The influence of personal and organizational antecedents. *Journal of Applied Social Psychology, 40*, 788–810.

Cunningham, G. B., & Singer, J. N. (2011). The primacy of race: Department diversity and its influence on the attraction of a diverse fan base and revenues generated. *International Journal of Sport Management, 12*, 176–190.

Cunningham, G. B., & Woods, J. (2012). The influence of advertisement focus, consumer gender, and model gender on attraction to a fitness club. *International Journal of Sport Management, 13*, 173–185.

Cunningham, G. B., Pickett, A., Melton, E. N., Lee, W., & Miner, K. (2014). Free to be me: Psychological safety and the expression of sexual orientation and personal identity. In J. Hargreaves & E. Anderson (Eds.), *Routledge handbook of sport gender and sexualities* (pp. 406–415). London, UK: Routledge.

Dacin, M. T., Goodstein, J., & Scott, W. R. (2002). Institutional theory and institutional change: Introduction to the special research forum. *Academy of Management Journal, 45*, 45–57.

Dobbin, F., & Kalev, A. (2016). Why diversity programs fail: And what works better. *Harvard Business Review, 97*(7), 52–60.

Dovidio, J. F., Eller, A., & Hewstone, M. (2011). Improving intergroup relations through direct, extended and other forms of indirect contact. *Group Processes & Intergroup Relations, 14*, 147–160.

Dovidio, J. F., Gaertner, S. L., Validzic, A., Matoka, K., Johnson, B., & Frazier, S. (1997). Extending the benefits of recategorization: Evaluations, self-disclosure, and helping. *Journal of Experimental Social Psychology, 33*, 401–420.

Ellers, A., & Abrams, D. (2003). "Gringos" in Mexico: Cross-sectional and longitudinal effects of language school-promoted contact on intergroup bias. *Group Processes & Intergroup Relations, 6*, 55–75.

Fink, J. S., & Pastore, D. L. (1999). Diversity in sport? Utilizing the business literature to devise a comprehensive framework of diversity initiatives. *Quest, 51*(4), 310–327.

Fink, J. S., Pastore, D. L., & Riemer, H. A. (2003). Managing employee diversity: Perceived practices and organizational outcomes in NCAA Division III athletic departments. *Sport Management Review, 6*, 147–168.

Gaertner, S. L., & Dovidio, J. F. (2000). *Reducing intergroup bias: The common ingroup identity model.* Philadelphia, PA: Psychology Press.

Gocłowska, M. A., Baas, M., Elliot, A. J., & De Dreu, C. K. (2017). Why schema-violations are sometimes preferable to schema-consistencies: The role of interest and openness to experience. *Journal of Research in Personality, 66*, 54–69.

Guimond, S., Crisp, R. J., De Oliveira, P., Kamiejski, R., Kteily, N., Kuepper, B., … Sidanius, J. (2013). Diversity policy, social dominance, and intergroup relations: Predicting prejudice in changing social and political contexts. *Journal of Personality and Social Psychology, 104*(6), 941.

Hebl, M., Barron, L., Cox, C. B., & Corrington, A. R. (2016). The efficacy of sexual orientation anti-discrimination legislation. *Equality, Diversity and Inclusion: An International Journal, 35*(7/8), 449–466.

Herscovitch, L., & Meyer, J. P. (2002). Commitment to organizational change: Extension of a three-component model. *Journal of Applied Psychology, 87*, 474–487.

Hewstone, M., Rubin, M., & Willis, H. (2002). Intergroup bias. *Annual Review of Psychology, 53*, 575–604.

Hodson, G., & Hewstone, M. (Eds.) (2013). *Advances in intergroup contact.* New York, NY: Psychology Press.

Holvino, E., Ferdman, B. M., & Merrill-Sands, D. (2004). Creating and sustaining diversity and inclusion in organizations: Strategies and approaches. In M. S. Stockdale & F. J. Crosby (Eds.), *The psychology and management of workplace diversity* (pp. 245–276). Malden, MA: Blackwell.

Hoobler, J. M., Masterson, C. R., Nkomo, S. M., & Michel, E. J. (2018). The business case for women leaders: Meta-analysis, research critique, and path forward. *Journal of Management, 44*(6), 2473–2499.

Hook, J. N., Farrell, J. E., Johnson, K. A., Van Tongeren, D. R., Davis, D. E., & Aten, J. D. (2017). Intellectual humility and religious tolerance. *The Journal of Positive Psychology, 12*(1), 29–35.

Hsiao, A., Ma, E., & Auld, C. (2017). Organizational ethnic diversity and employees' satisfaction with hygiene and motivation factors—A comparative IPA approach. *Journal of Hospitality Marketing & Management, 26*(2), 144–163.

Jones, L. M., & Foley, L. A. (2003). Educating children to decategorize racial groups. *Journal of Applied Social Psychology, 33*, 554–564.

Ladson-Billings, G. (2004). Landing on the wrong note: The price we paid for *Brown. Educational Researcher, 33*(7), 3–13.

LaVoi, N. M. (2016). Introduction. In N. M. LaVoi (Ed.), *Women in sport coaching* (pp. 1–9). New York, NY: Routledge.

Lee, W., & Cunningham, G. B. (2013). The power of sport: Examining the influence of sport-related contact and familiarity on intergroup anxiety and racism. *International Journal of Sport Management, 14*, 462–478.

Lee, W., & Cunningham, G. B. (2014). Imagine that: Examining the influence of sport related imagined contact on intergroup anxiety and sexual prejudice across cultures. *Journal of Applied Social Psychology, 44*, 557–566.

Lee, W., & Cunningham, G. B. (2015). A picture is worth a thousand words: The influence of signaling, organizational reputation, and applicant race on attraction to sport organizations. *International Journal of Sport Management, 16*, 492–506.

Lee, W., & Cunningham, G. B. (in press). Group diversity's effects on sport teams and organizations: A meta-analysis. *European Sport Management Quarterly.*

Madera, J. M., Dawson, M., & Neal, J. A. (2018). Why investing in diversity management matters: Organizational attraction and person–organization fit. *Journal of Hospitality & Tourism Research, 42*(6), 931–959.

Major, B., Blodorn, A., & Major Blascovich, G. (2018). The threat of increasing diversity: Why many White Americans support Trump in the 2016 presidential election. *Group Processes & Intergroup Relations, 21*(6), 931–940.

McDermott, R. C., Schwartz, J. P., Lindley, L. D., & Proietti, J. S. (2014). Exploring men's homophobia: Associations with religious fundamentalism and gender role conflict domains. *Psychology of Men & Masculinity, 15*(2), 191.

Melton, E. N., & Cunningham, G. B. (2014). Who are the champions? Using a multilevel model to examine perceptions of employee support for LGBT inclusion in sport organizations. *Journal of Sport Management, 28*, 189–206.

Miles, E., & Crisp, R. J. (2014). A meta-analytic test of the imagined contact hypothesis. *Group Processes & Intergroup Relations, 17*, 3–26.

Nutter, S., Russell-Mayhew, S., Arthur, N., & Ellard, J. H. (2018). Weight bias and social justice: implications for education and practice. *International Journal for the Advancement of Counselling, 40*(3), 213-226.

Oliver, C. (1992). The antecedents of deinstitutionalization. *Organization Studies, 13*, 563–588.

Ottoboni, G., Milani, M., Setti, A., Ceciliani, A., Chattat, R., & Tessari, A. (2017). An observational study on sport-induced modulation of negative attitude towards disability. *PLoS One, 12*(11), e0187043.

Outten, H. R., Schmitt, M. T., Miller, D. A., & Garcia, A. L. (2012). Feeling threatened about the future: Whites' emotional reactions to anticipated ethnic demographic changes. *Personality and Social Psychology Bulletin, 38*(1), 14–25.

Pettigrew, T. F., Tropp, L. R. (2008). How does intergroup contact reduce prejudice? Meta-analytic tests of three mediators. *European Journal of Social Psychology, 38*, 922–934.

Pickett, A. C., & Cunningham, G. B. (2018). The fat leading the thin: Relative body size, physical activity identification, and behavioral intentions. *Journal of Applied Sport Management, 10*, 1–12.

Pugh, S. D., Dietz, J., Brief, A. P., & Wiley, J. W. (2008). Looking inside and out: The impact of employee and community demographic composition on organizational diversity climate. *The Journal of Applied Psychology, 93*, 1422–1428.

Richard, O. C., & Miller, C. D. (2013). Considering diversity as a source of competitive advantage in organizations. In Q. M. Roberson (Ed.), *The Oxford handbook of diversity and work* (pp. 239–250). New York, NY: Oxford University Press.

Robbins, S. P. (2011). *Essentials of organizational behavior* (11th ed.). New York, NY: Pearson.

Roberson, Q., Ryan, A. M., & Ragins, B. R. (2017). The evolution and future of diversity at work. *Journal of Applied Psychology, 102*(3), 483–499.

Ruggs, E. N., Martinez, L. R., Hebl, M. R., & Law, C. L. (2015). Workplace "trans"-actions: How organizations, coworkers, and individual openness influence perceived gender identity discrimination. *Psychology of Sexual Orientation and Gender Diversity, 2*(4), 404.

Sartore, M., & Cunningham, G. B. (2010). The lesbian label as a component of women's stigmatization in sport organizations: An exploration of two health and kinesiology departments. *Journal of Sport Management, 24*, 481–501.

Scott, S. (2002). *Fierce conversations: Achieving success at work & in life, one conversation at a time.* New York, NY: Berkley Books.

Scott, W. R. (2008). *Institutions and organizations: Ideas and interests* (3rd ed.). Thousand Oaks, CA: Sage.

Sellers, R. M., & Shelton, J. N. (2003). The role of racial identity in perceived racial discrimination. *Journal of Personality and Social Psychology, 84*(5), 1079–1092.

Sibley, C. G., & Duckitt, J. (2008). Personality and prejudice: A meta-analysis and theoretical review. *Personality and Social Psychology Review, 12*, 248–279.

Singer, J. N., & Cunningham, G. B. (2012). A case study of the diversity culture of an American university athletic department: Implications for educational stakeholders. *Sport, Education & Society, 17*, 647–669.

Smith, T. B., & Silva, L. (2011). Ethnic identity and personal well-being of people of color: A meta-analysis. *Journal of Counseling Psychology, 58*(1), 42–60.

Spaaij, R., Farquharson, K., Magee, J., Jeanes, R., Lusher, D., & Gorman, S. (2014). A fair game for all? How community sports clubs in Australia deal with diversity. *Journal of Sport and Social Issues, 38*, 346–365.

Stephens-Davidowitz, S. (2014). The cost of racial animus on a black candidate: Evidence using Google search data. *Journal of Public Economics, 118*, 26–40.

Trussell, D. E., Kovac, L., & Apgar, J. (2018). LGBTQ parents' experiences of community youth sport: Change your forms, change your (hetero) norms. *Sport Management Review, 21*(1), 51–62.

Van Assche, J., Roets, A., Dhont, K., & Van Hiel, A. (2016). The association between actual and perceived ethnic diversity: The moderating role of authoritarianism and implications for outgroup threat, anxiety, and mistrust. *European Journal of Social Psychology, 46*(7), 807–817.

Vezzali, L., Hewstone, M., Capozza, D., Giovannini, D., & Wölfer, R. (2014). Improving intergroup relations with extended and vicarious forms of indirect contact. *European Review of Social Psychology, 25*, 314–389.

Vezzali, L., Stathi, S., Giovannini, D., Capozza, D. & Trifiletti, E. (2015). The greatest magic of *Harry Potter*: Reducing prejudice. *Journal of Applied Social Psychology, 45*, 105–121.

Volpone, S. D., & Avery, D. R. (2010). I'm confused: How failing to value sexual minorities at work sends stakeholders mixed messages. *Industrial and Organizational Psychology, 3*, 90–92.

Welty Peachey, J., Cunningham, G. B., Bruening, J. L., Cohen, A., & Lyras, A. (2015). The influence of a sport-for-peace event on prejudice and change agent self-efficacy. *Journal of Sport Management, 29*, 229–244.

Whiteside, E. (2016). Politics in the toy box: Sports reporters, native American mascots, and the roadblocks preventing change. *International Journal of Sport Communication, 9*(1), 63–78.

Zhu, D. H., Shen, W., & Hillman, A. J. (2014). Recategorization into the in-group: The appointment of demographically different new directors and their subsequent positions on corporate boards. *Administrative Science Quarterly, 59*, 240–270.

Diversity Training

LEARNING OBJECTIVES

After studying this chapter, you should be able to:

- Discuss the positive and negative effects of diversity training.
- Discuss the essential elements of effective diversity training programs.

DIVERSITY CHALLENGE

Canadian hockey coaches receive diversity training as a part of the Respect in Sport Course. In 2018, many also provided training to their players. Specifically, minor league hockey coaches in Ontario, Canada held preseason discussions about diversity, inclusion, and gender identity. Phil McKee, who serves as executive director of the Ontario Hockey Federation, commented, "We want to make the game inclusive and understand that our coaches' responsibility is not to judge individuals on the face of things, but to create an environment where everyone feels respected and comfortable in a hockey arena."

The training was not voluntary, but instead, was part of a larger settlement of a case brought before the Human Rights Tribunal. Jesse Thompson, a transgender teen, brought the case after he was required to use the dressing room that corresponded with his sex assigned at birth instead of his gender identity and expression.

McKee indicated that training and discussions with the players was part of a larger effort to create a more inclusive environment. The league collaborated with Egale Canada, a group focusing on inclusion of lesbian, gay, bisexual, and transgender individuals, to help guide the coaches. As one example, players and coaches will now share their names and pronouns as part of introductory sessions. Egale Canada, in instructions to the coaches, wrote,

> Explain that it is important to ask for and share gender pronouns, just like names, because it is not something you can always tell just by looking at someone. Tell players that it is OK to make mistakes but that it is important to show that they are trying to remember by simply apologizing and correcting themselves if they do slip up.

Reactions to the new mandates were mixed. For some coaches, they likened the training to simply checking a compliance box. For others, they learned from the training and sought to create a more inclusive, welcoming environment for all players.

Source: Strashin, J. (2018, August). Ontario hockey coaches ordered to talk to players about gender diversity. *CBC*. Retrieved from https://www.cbc.ca/sports/hockey/minor-hockey-inclusion-1.4795895.

CHALLENGE REFLECTION

1. Have you attended a diversity training program? If so, what were your impressions of it?
2. The Diversity Challenge suggests that diversity training sessions can have both positive and negative effects. Which do you think are more likely and why?
3. What are some of the reasons that people would oppose diversity training? How would you address their concerns?

Diversity training is the educational process whereby people acquire skills, knowledge, attitudes, and abilities pertaining to diversity-related issues. The training can provide various benefits, both for the organization and for the individuals in it (Bezrukova, Jehn, & Spell, 2012). Writers have suggested that diversity training should be mandatory for aspiring managers (Bell, Connerley, & Cocchiara, 2009) and that there is an ethical obligation to offer it (Jones, King, Nelson, Geller, & Bowes-Sperry, 2013). However, training does not always have its intended benefits, as some of the coaches in the Diversity Challenge suggested. Equivocal results have spurred criticisms of diversity training (e.g., Dobbin & Kalev, 2016). Some diversity training participants question why it is necessary, others feel they are being singled out, whereas still others believe that it does more harm than good. What, then, are the actual effects? Further, how do organizations that seek to conduct such training provide programs that generate the intended benefits? Are there steps managers can take to institute effective diversity management sessions?

The purpose of this chapter is to address these issues. The first section notes the prevalence of diversity training among organizations today. I then discuss the potential positive and negative effects of such programs. The third section outlines the four steps involved in designing effective diversity training programs: conducting a needs analysis, evaluating antecedent training conditions, selecting the training methods, and ensuring effective post-training conditions. The final section addresses general program considerations. This chapter is designed to introduce managers of sport organizations to the tools needed to conduct effective diversity training, with the goal of creating and sustaining a diverse and inclusive work environment.

PREVALENCE OF DIVERSITY TRAINING

 rganizations routinely implement training programs to educate and develop their employees. According to Lipman (2018), companies collectively spend $8 billion a year on diversity training. In organizations that particularly value learning and development, training represents a sizeable percentage of the overall payroll. Google, for example, spent $114 million on diversity programs in 2014 alone. As many as one-in-five US companies offer training on implicit biases, and experts predict the figure will increase to 50 percent in the near future (Lipman, 2018).

Most of the data that are available are for large corporations outside of the sport industry, though there are exceptions. I collected data from 675 National Collegiate Athletic Association (NCAA) athletic departments (239 in Division I, 205 in Division II, and 231 in Division III), asking them about their diversity training practices (Cunningham, 2012). Results indicate that 53 percent of all athletic departments offer training, and larger entities are more likely to provide it than smaller ones (Cunningham, 2012). Kaltenbaugh, Parsons, Brubaker, Bonadio, and Locust (2017) examined the prevalence of diversity training in campus recreation departments at US institutions of higher education. They found that just 43 percent offered such educational activities, and recreations housed in public institutions were substantially more likely to do so than were those situated in private universities (50 and 25 percent, respectively). Finally, Gajjar and Okumus (2018) examined the practices of the top-ranked hospitality and tourism companies. They found that all had cultural awareness programs in place, but only four of the six offered diversity training.

EFFECTS OF DIVERSITY TRAINING

At first glance, instituting a diversity training program would seem beneficial. Providing people with necessary knowledge, skills, attitudes, and abilities with regard to diversity and inclusion is conceivably the first step toward a workplace where the positive effects of diversity are realized. However, these educational programs are sometimes met with resistance and in some instances actually do more harm than good. This section outlines both the positive and negative effects of diversity training in the organizational context.

Positive Effects

Various authors have conducted large-scale meta-analyses to examine the effects of diversity training (Bezrukova, Spell, Perry, & Jehn, 2016; Kalinoski et al., 2013). Recall that meta-analyses involve the statistical aggregation of previous studies, taking into account various artifacts and forms of error. Unlike narrative reviews, where authors describe the patterns they observe in published studies, meta-analyses allow for a statistical estimate, known as an effect size, and the statistical comparison of various factors that might alter the pattern of results (i.e., moderators; see Chapter 2).

This research has shown that diversity training positively influences a number of outcomes, including knowledge acquired, behaviors, and attitudes. The overall effect sizes were positive and small to moderate in size; thus, the impact of diversity training across the studies was beneficial. Furthermore, the meta-analyses show that diversity training improved people's affective states, such as their attitudes toward diversity, motivation, and self-efficacy; cognitive outcomes, including the knowledge they have about diversity and cognitive skills associated with it; and skill-based outcomes, such as their behaviors and the intentions they have to engage in pro-diversity behaviors. Additional analyses showed that diversity training had stronger positive effects on cognitive and behavioral outcomes than on employees' affective states.

In addition to these individual-level outcomes, other investigators have pointed to the potential benefits of diversity training for groups and organizations (Bezrukova et al., 2012; Cunningham, 2012; King, Dawson, Kravitz, & Gulick, 2012; Roberson, Kulik, & Tan, 2013). For instance, diversity training has the potential to improve intergroup relationships, by reducing people's prejudices and facilitating more constructive interactions. In turn, these improved interactions are likely to result in improved employee morale and satisfaction. Finally, by conducting diversity training, organizations might be able to remain in compliance with external mandates and avoid diversity-related lawsuits. These six benefits are captured in Exhibit 14.1.

The benefits also influence leaders' motivation for offering training. In my work with intercollegiate athletic departments, I observed two categories of motivations: *effectiveness*, where leaders sought to increase productivity, improve customer relationships, and enhance workplace dynamics; and *compliance*, where leaders offered training in order to remain in compliance with university or NCAA regulations (Cunningham, 2012). Leaders alluded to both types of stimuli, but the outcomes differed according to the leaders' motivation. Trainees were likely to implement the principles learned in the training into their everyday work when the motivation was effectiveness based, but they were less willing to do so when it was compliance based.

Negative Effects

Although diversity training can positively benefit the organization, there are times when these programs might be detrimental. Programs can have negative effects under certain workplace conditions. For instance, some scholars question the underlying premise of training, noting that a focus on individual actions necessarily ignores that broader macro-level systems in place (Noon, 2018). As noted in Chapter 2, from a sociological perspective, even absent individual biases, institutional forms of bias would still privilege those with power and status. In other cases, employees express resistance to discuss topics that are sensitive or that make them feel uncomfortable. Lindsay (1994) equated diversity training to discuss the "undiscussable" (p. 19). In addition, some trainees note they feel blamed during the training (Holladay, Knight, Paige, & Quiñones, 2003)—reactions more prominent among Whites, men, and heterosexuals than among their counterparts. These negative effects are especially true when the training focuses on topics such as prejudice and discrimination.

Other sources of resistance include the belief among some trainees that they already know the information (Israel et al., 2017). For example, Norman (in press) collected data from professional coaches in the UK, all of whom had recently attended training. Though they identified benefits, the coaches also noted opposition, as they believed they already knew the information. One noted, "I personally don't see the point that I need more equity training because I've already got a view that everybody is the same anyway. I don't really see the point." Finally, some authors suggest the connection between diversity training and organizational performance is tenuous, at best (Dobbins & Kalev, 2016). That is, the training might improve individual-level outcomes, but the relationship between those efforts and improvements for the organization as a whole have not been firmly established. When employees do not see the reason for the training, the effects on the workplace may be negative. Among these negative effects can be the reinforcement of stereotypes and categorization boundaries. This is particularly the case when the training is poorly delivered. The conditions that can result in negative outcomes are listed in Exhibit 14.1.

Making Sense of the Effects

This discussion points to conflicting information about the effects of diversity training. How, then, do people make sense of these varying effects? The answer

---

Potential Outcomes of Diversity Training   *exhibit* **14.1**

Positive Outcomes

- Improved attitudes and motivation
- Enhanced knowledge and understanding
- Improved diversity-related behaviors
- Constructive intergroup relationships
- Improved employee morale and satisfaction
- Compliance with mandates and avoidance of lawsuits

Negative Influences

- Ignores influence of institutional biases
- Resistance to discuss sensitive topics
- Whites, men, and heterosexuals feeling blamed
- Perceived lack of work applicability
- Lack of perceived connection to organizational effectiveness

lies not only in the design and implementation of the diversity training but also in whether or not the lessons can actually be applied in the workplace setting—a process known as transfer of training. When the training sessions are ill-conceived, are held simply for the sake of satisfying external constituents, or do not have support from important organizational decision-makers, they are unlikely to be successful. When the training is designed for the organization's specific needs, is central to the organization's mission, and has top management support, it is likely to benefit the trainees and the organization as a whole. Therefore, consistent with the instrumental design model (Goldstein & Ford, 2002; see also Bell, Tannenbaum, Ford, Noe, & Kraiger, 2017), it is important for sport managers to assess needs and employee characteristics that might affect training, design training to affect change and complement other activities, evaluate the effectiveness of the efforts, and adjust accordingly.

DESIGNING AND DELIVERING EFFECTIVE DIVERSITY TRAINING PROGRAMS

I offer an important lesson before proceeding: no one model is best for all organizations. In spite of this fact, much of the diversity training tends to be standardized. Many consulting organizations offer the same "cookie cutter" diversity training program to every organization they serve. Some administrative bodies require that certain elements are covered in the training held by their institutions. Many university systems offer the same training (usually in an electronic format that takes several minutes to complete) on all of their campuses. There are several reasons why such standardization occurs, including issues related to consistency, reliability, and cost-effectiveness. Nevertheless, most, if not all, of these programs fail to deliver the genuinely positive effects that diversity training can offer.

To realize the full scope of the potential benefits, it is imperative that diversity training be tailored to the needs of the specific organization. For some organizations, issues related to sexual orientation or religious differences may be most salient. For others, harassment of and discrimination against women may be the primary sources of stress and friction. For still other organizations, diversity issues may not be a source of tension; the organization may simply be seeking to reinforce principles and values. The list of diversity issues that could be relevant to a specific organization is virtually endless. For these reasons, it is irresponsible to offer the same training to all organizations. Instead, the training must be tailored to each organization. To design and deliver an effective program, managers must conduct a needs analysis, examine the pre-training conditions, decide on the specific training topics and methods, and consider various post-training factors (e.g., training evaluation, transfer of training).

I discuss each of these issues in the following sections and offer an illustrative summary in Exhibit 14.2. Recognizing that some researchers oppose diversity training efforts, I also overview a different approach in Box 14.1.

Model of Effective Diversity Training Programs   *exhibit* **14.2**

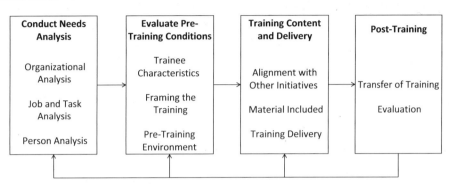

Conduct Needs Analysis	Evaluate Pre-Training Conditions	Training Content and Delivery	Post-Training
Organizational Analysis	Trainee Characteristics	Alignment with Other Initiatives	Transfer of Training
Job and Task Analysis	Framing the Training	Material Included	Evaluation
Person Analysis	Pre-Training Environment	Training Delivery	

Feedback and Change Based on Evaluation

Box 14.1 Alternative Perspectives: A Different Approach to Promote Diversity and Inclusion

Though a number of researchers have demonstrated the utility of diversity training through their meta-analytic studies, others have arrived at different conclusion. Dobbin and Kalev (2016) are two such authors. They note that "most diversity programs aren't increasing diversity" (p. 54). They equate diversity training with efforts to control employees, concluding that "Most diversity programs focus on controlling managers' behaviors, and as studies show, that approach tends to activate bias rather than quash it. People rebel against rules that threaten their autonomy" (p. 55). As an alternative, Dobbins and Kalev suggest three tactics. First, and in line with the information I presented in Chapter 13, increase opportunities for people to be around those who are different. Second, encourage people to work for diversity through various programs, such as mentoring or college recruitment programs. Finally, focus on social accountability. People like to look good in front of others. So, post their unit's diversity metrics, such as the representation of people in leadership roles.

Needs Analysis

Dachner, Saxton, Noe, and Keeton (2013) suggested that "training effectiveness depends on conducting a thorough needs analysis" (p. 239; see also the Diversity in the Field Box 14.2 for related information). Unfortunately, evidence suggests that preliminary analyses are not often conducted (Arthur, Bennett, Edens, & Bell,

2003). This is disappointing because a needs analysis is instrumental in helping managers understand where training is needed, who needs the training, and what material should be included in it (Roberson et al., 2013).

When conducting a needs analysis, sport managers must remember that not all deficiencies are training-related problems. For example, poor customer relations may result from a lack of cultural awareness on the part of the service provider. The cause could also be, however, that the method of providing the services is flawed, that the service provider simply lacks the motivation to provide high-quality services, or that the support necessary to provide the service is lacking. Obviously, these latter issues pertain more to structural or managerial factors than to diversity issues. Thus, once a problem is identified, managers must critically analyze the source of the problem and take appropriate action.

A needs analysis covers three areas: the organization, the job tasks, and the people.

Organizational Analysis

The organizational analysis requires managers to examine all of the elements of the organization that may affect the training's effectiveness (Salas & Cannon-Bowers, 2001). Examination includes the congruence of the training with the organization's overall mission and strategy, the monies available to deliver the training, and the level of support available from top management. The organizational analysis is a critical first step in the overall needs-analysis process because it will identify any constraints or barriers to deliver an effective training program. Salas and Cannon-Bowers noted that too many organizations neglect this step; consequently, training is not as successful for them as it is for those organizations that perform the analysis.

The organizational climate is particularly important to the training process (Bezrukova et al., 2012). Organizations with inclusive organizational cultures are likely to have more supports in place to allow the trainees to apply the information they learn in the training session to the workplace. Because diversity and individual differences are valued in these organizations, the importance attached to the training is likely to be amplified.

Top management support is also key. The Diversity in the Field Box 14.2 offers an example. Without management backing, employees might question how important diversity and the related training really are, and this could undermine the training's overall effectiveness.

Job/Task Analysis

A job/task analysis entails collecting information related to the specific duties of each job; the conditions under which employees complete the job; and the specific knowledge, skills, and abilities necessary to complete the tasks (Salas & Cannon-Bowers, 2001). The job and task requirements are then compared to the existing performance level. If a discrepancy exists, training might be needed (Mathis, Jackson, Valentine, & Meglich, 2017). This analysis is useful because it identifies areas where the employee training can be made more effective.

Box 14.2 Diversity in the Field: How a Needs Analysis Shows the Need for Diversity Training

Brian France heads NASCAR—an entity with a large fan base that is stereotypically homogeneous in race and attitudes. When he was set to take over for his father in 1997, he recognized this problem and noted that his "goal is to make NASCAR look like America." To do so, he reached out to Richard Lapchick, a noted expert in the area of diversity and inclusion. Since that time, Lapchick and his colleagues—who consult with organizations around the world on this topic—have provided more diversity training to NASCAR than any other entity. For many years, every person in the vast organization took part in these educational activities. The training aligns with NASCAR's policies, as the organization has zero tolerance for poor behaviors and language, and has held drivers and others accountable. Lapchick noted,

It's a tribute to their sincerity. . . . I think that the most important thing that an organization can do other than changing the numbers [that is, the diversity of the workforce] is changing the culture, but one can't go without the other.

Source: Diaz (2013).

Person Analysis

The third prong of the needs analysis involves the organization's people (Salas & Cannon-Bowers, 2001). This analysis can be accomplished by examining employees' performance appraisals and focusing on those portions that highlight deficiencies (Mathis et al., 2017). Although some organizations include diversity-related criteria on their performance appraisals (Kochan et al., 2003), most do not. Thus, managers must develop alternative methods to identify the employees' specific diversity training needs. One option is to distribute an organization-wide questionnaire that assesses employee attitudes (and potentially behaviors) toward diversity issues. A sample item might be, "All employees within the organization, irrespective of their differences, are treated fairly (agree or disagree)." Another option is to observe employees and their interactions with others and with clients.

Regardless of how the information is collected, it is imperative that sport managers understand the training needs of each employee. As discussed throughout this book, each person brings different diversity-related experiences, attitudes, preferences, and behavioral tendencies to the workplace. These differences influence the employees' attitudes toward work, the manner in which they interact with their colleagues, and the way they serve customers. Where deficiencies exist, training is needed to achieve the desired behaviors and attitudes.

Pre-training Conditions

Before designing and implementing the training program, it is important to ensure that optimal training conditions are in place. Salas and Cannon-Bowers (2001) argue that "events that occur before training can be as important as (and in some cases more important than) those that occur during and after training" (p. 447). Managers should be particularly mindful of trainee characteristics, framing of the training, and the pre-training environment.

Trainee Characteristics

A number of characteristics influence the trainees' experiences with diversity training and readiness to learn the material, including their ability to learn, their self-efficacy and motivation, and the perceived utility of the training (Bell et al., 2017; Grossman & Salas, 2011; Roberson et al., 2013). First, people bring with them different experiences and attitudes toward diversity, and these might influence how they respond to the training. If people have not had good experiences with past diversity training activities or if they harbor considerable prejudices toward others, their orientation toward the training is likely to be less than ideal.

Second, not all employees have the same ability to learn the training material. Differences might result from a lack of cognitive skills or language acquisition. The key is to provide conditions that ensure employees' ability to learn. For example, if the majority of the workforce is Spanish speaking, then perhaps the training should be presented in Spanish, or at least the option should be available.

Self-efficacy, or "people's judgments of their capabilities to organize and execute courses of action required to attain specific types of performances" (Bandura, 1986, p. 391), also affects learning. If people do not believe they have the ability to learn the material, they are unlikely to be motivated during the training sessions. Managers can take several steps to enhance trainees' self-efficacy (Bandura, 1997). One option is to show that people with characteristics similar to the trainees' have successfully completed the training session. Another is to explain why the training is needed and the possible benefits. Finally, it might be necessary to persuade trainees that they have the skills and capabilities necessary for knowledge acquisition; for example, by beginning with easier activities to ensure initial success.

Trainee motivation, or the vigor and persistence with which the trainees will engage in the training, represents another factor to consider (Grossman & Salas, 2011). People who are motivated to learn will approach the training with a positive attitude, will devote the time and energy needed to ensure they learn the material, and will use the training material in their work environment.

Finally, increasing the perceived utility of the training might also improve trainees' learning (Grossman & Salas, 2011). If people do not believe the diversity training is worth their while or do not see how the training will enhance organizational effectiveness or how they can use it on their jobs, they are unlikely to be fully engaged. For example, people exhibit low motivation for sexual harassment training when they have doubts about the prevalence of the deviant behavior or how effective the training can be in altering it (Walsh, Bauerle, & Magley, 2013).

On the other hand, when people believe in the instrumentality of the training, they are likely to implement what they have learned, particularly when there is organizational support for doing so (Madera, Steele, & Beier, 2011).

Framing the Training

Sport managers must consider how they frame or depict the training, as the manner in which an event is portrayed substantially influences people's behaviors and attitudes. Framing is particularly important when it involves "hot button" issues (Holladay et al., 2003). For example, people's view toward affirmative action often depends on how those policies are framed (Crosby, Iyer, & Sincharoen, 2006). People are more likely to favor affirmative action when it is viewed as a way organizations reach out to traditionally disadvantaged groups than when it is perceived as a quota system. The way a policy is framed or contextualized influences reactions to it.

In the context of diversity training, pre-training attitudes and beliefs influence subsequent motivation and performance. Holladay et al. (2003) explicitly considered the effects of two aspects of framing on trainees' subsequent attitudes: the title of the training ("Diversity Training" versus "Building Human Relations") and the scope of the training (a focus only on racial issues versus a broad focus on race, sex, personality, and lifestyle differences). They found that these two factors interacted to predict backlash to the training and the likelihood of training transfer. Training that had a direct title (e.g., "Diversity Training") and a broad focus received less backlash than the other training formats. The same was true for the likelihood of transfer—trainees in a program that had a direct title and broad focus were the most likely to use the information in their work.

Interestingly, although a broad focus seems to improve people's pre-training attitudes toward diversity training, actual learning does not appear to follow suit. Bezrukova et al. (2016) examined whether training outcomes varied when the training was based on a singular focus (e.g., sexual orientation-based training) or included focus on multiple groups (e.g., emphasis on race, gender, age, sexual orientation, and disability in one session). Their analysis of hundreds of studies showed that the specific or broad focus did not influence training outcomes—that is, trainees learned irrespective of the focus. Instead, the length of the training was more important, as the more time people spent in training, the better their knowledge, attitudinal, and behavioral skills gains.

Pre-training Environment

Finally, managers designing diversity training events must be mindful of the pre-training environment. Several factors contribute to the pre-training environment: support for the training from both managers and coworkers, the training's (in)voluntary nature, and the link between the material and subsequent job-related behaviors.

As previously noted, support is one of the most important factors contributing to the training's success (Cocchiara, Connerley, & Bell, 2010). This support comes from supervisors and coworkers. Although support can positively influence people's training motivation, this effect is likely to be moderated by the extent to which employees are motivated to comply with their supervisors and coworkers (Wiethoff, 2004). Trainees who believe there is support for the training and who are highly motivated to act in accordance with their coworkers and supervisors are more likely than their counterparts to reap the benefits of diversity training.

Further, there is some debate as to whether diversity training should be mandatory or voluntary. Wiethoff (2004) suggests that mandatory training might be counterproductive because it may result in less than positive attitudes among the trainees. On the other hand, others argue that mandatory training conveys the message that the training is important to upper management (Bell et al., 2009; Cocchiara et al., 2010). This is especially true when the team members from top management attend the training session (Cunningham & Singer, 2009). Bezrukova et al. (2016), in their meta-analysis, found that mandatory training was linked with improved behavioral outcomes; however, trainee reactions to the activities are less positive when they are required to attend.

In addition, trainees are likely to be motivated to learn and apply the information from diversity training when doing so is linked to job performance and evaluations (Cunningham, 2012). If people believe that they can use the information in their jobs, that their performance evaluations will be tied to doing so, and that their pay raises to some extent will be linked to applying the information to their everyday work, then the training will likely be successful. If employees do not make such causal links, then their motivation to learn and transfer the information is likely to be low, thereby limiting the training's effectiveness. To help forge a connection between the training and trainees' everyday work, after presenting information related to multicultural competence, a manager might ask the trainees to role-play situations and apply the recently learned knowledge in a scenario they are likely to encounter in their everyday work settings.

Training Content and Delivery

Alignment

Many organizations will conduct diversity training but not link the activities with other organizational initiatives. Sport managers who choose such a tactic run several risks. First, employees are unlikely to associate the training with other organizational activities focused on diversity and continuous improvement (Cunningham, 2009). Second, and related to this point, as a result, the trainees are likely to question to the applicability of the training in their work and the overall quest for organizational improvement (see Exhibit 14.1).

As an alternative, sport managers can opt to strategically align their training with other organizational and employee initiatives focused on diversity and inclusion. Sport managers can also clearly articulate these connections to the trainees and organizational members, demonstrating the integrated, strategic path adopted. Consistent with this perspective, Bezrukova et al. (2016) found that diversity outcomes, including reactions to the training and overall learning, were more positive when the training was integrated into the larger diversity initiatives in the workplace.

Topics

The needs analysis, coupled with the evaluation of pre-training conditions, should offer sport managers with cues on the content to include in the training. Benuto, Casas, and O'Donohue (2018) systematically reviewed the diversity and inclusion training research, seeking to understand the goals and outcomes of the training. They found that training commonly included an emphasis on racism and discrimination, understanding different worldviews, the identities people hold, an overview of culture, understanding biases, and understanding interactions in service encounters.

I examined the diversity training that took place in US athletic departments (Cunningham, 2012). Drawing from previous work, I categorized the training into six categories and asked the respondents to indicate how frequently the topics were covered in their training. Results indicated that the administrators and coaches were most likely to receive training related to sensitivity, followed by understanding different cultures, discrimination, conflict, accommodations for different groups, and reducing backlash of diversity programs.

Increasingly, diversity training focuses on reducing implicit bias. I outline one approach to achieving this goal in Exhibit 14.3.

Reducing Implicit Bias   *exhibit* **14.3**

Implicit bias can negatively affect a number of outcomes, including performance evaluation, personnel selection, and customer interactions. Thus, sport organizations are increasingly seeking ways to reduce this form of bias. Such goals are difficult to achieve, though, as people commonly do not know they express implicit biases.

How, then, do we reduced or eliminate something of which we are not aware and do not intentionally express? Devine and her colleagues examined this very question (Devine, Forscher, Austin, & Cox, 2012; Forscher, Mitamura, Dix, Cox, & Devine, 2017). They approached the problem from the perspective that bias is like a habit that needs to be broken. Thus, they developed an intervention where people learned about bias, the effects it had, and steps they could take to reduce it. Examples of strategies included recognizing stereotypical responses, imagining people who counter popularly held stereotypes, thinking about people as unique individuals instead of members of a homogeneous group, engaging in perspective taking, and being around others who are different than you.

Devine and colleagues found that people who went through the training showed a large decrease in their implicit bias, and the reduction persisted over time. The intervention was most effective for people who showed concern about bias and employed some of the techniques they learned. The effects were also present over an extended period of time, even up to two years later.

Results suggest the focus on habit breaking provides a novel approach to reducing implicit bias. Importantly, training benefits are present immediately following training and for some time thereafter.

Training Delivery

Having completed the aforementioned steps, sport managers now must determine the best way to deliver the training. One consideration is who conducts the training. Some evidence indicates that the characteristics of the trainer influence the trainees' learning and attitudes toward the activity. First, learning is increased when someone internal to the organization leads the training (Kalinoski et al., 2013). Some sport organizations may have human resource personnel on staff who are specifically trained in this area. When there is no staff person available, persons with an expertise in diversity issues or who have had diversity training could lead the sessions. Using in-house personnel reduces the costs associated with training. Because an in-house trainer probably has a working knowledge and understanding of the specific diversity issues facing the organization, the training can be made more individualized.

Trainer demographics might also affect the trainees' learning. Roberson et al. (2013) note that people tend to assume, perhaps implicitly, that women and racial minorities are better suited to lead the training sessions than are White men. This might be attributable to the potential for differences in lived experiences with oppression and subjugation. Whites and men can offset these assumptions by acknowledging the role of privilege and institutionalized discrimination in society. In addition, learning is enhanced when the characteristics of the trainer match those of the trainees. This match might enhance the trainer's credibility and rapport with learners.

Another consideration is the method of delivery. Bell et al. (2017), in their review of training research, concluded the following: (a) learning complex skills is frequently best achieved by engaging in active, self-regulated learning, and (b) the effectiveness of training is determined more by the instructional design and supports provided to the learners than the specific approach used (e.g., online or face-to-face). Bezrukova et al. (2016) arrived at similar conclusions. Training programs that used a variety of instructional techniques produce the same amount of learning as those that rely on a single approach. The one exception is when it comes to reactions to the training: people enjoy the training more when there are multiple ways of delivering it.

Cheryl Kravitz, a diversity training consultant, offers another option for delivering training, as illustrated in Box 14.3.

Post-Training Conditions

Many sport managers consider the delivery of diversity training as the final step, but this represents a misguided belief. Instead, sport managers need to evaluate the training effectiveness, provide supports for people to use the training content in their work, and then amend their future training based on the analyses. They should adopt a continuous improvement approach to their diversity training.

Training Evaluation

When planning for the evaluation of a training's effectiveness, managers must consider what should be evaluated and the method for doing so.

Box 14.3 Professional Perspectives: Diversity behind the Face

Cheryl Kravitz is a diversity training consultant who uses an interesting technique to create empathy and understanding in the programs she delivers. She calls the technique "The Person Behind the Face." In this exercise, participants receive a piece of paper with balloons drawn all over it. They then use as many balloons as they deem necessary to define their personal identities. As the exercise facilitator, Kravitz goes first. She describes herself as "a young mom and an old mom" because she had a child at age 16 and adopted her second child at age 40. She also reveals other bits of information about herself: that she is Jewish, her mother has Alzheimer's, she was once in a coma, and she almost died at the

hands of her abusive ex-husband. Revealing such personal information is beneficial, Kravitz notes, because people will then share information about themselves. Revealing such information has a way of creating empathy among the trainees and sometimes results in bonds being forged among otherwise different people. For example, another woman in the group might reveal that she, too, was a battered wife, or another group member might identify with having an ill parent. Thus, people come to realize that although they differ physically, they might share deep-level characteristics. The exercise "can help unfreeze people's preconceptions of others and help melt prejudice and stereotypes" (Koonce, 2001, p. 30).

Kirkpatrick (1976) developed a framework for assessing training effectiveness that is appropriate for use by sport organizations. He argued that training outcomes can be grouped into four categories.

1. **Reactions**. Sport organizations can evaluate trainees' reactions to the session by interviewing them or asking them to complete post-training questionnaires. The questions might relate to trainees' perceptions about the overall value of the training, how well they liked the instruction style or the trainers, or how useful they believe the training will be in their work. Most often, trainee reactions are gathered immediately after the training; however, data might also be gathered weeks or months after the training takes place so that managers can assess how useful the information has been in the trainees' everyday job duties.

2. **Learning**. Sport organizations can assess how well the trainees learned the material by asking the trainees to complete a simple test on the material covered in the session. This method is particularly useful when the subject matter is primarily factual (e.g., legal issues related to Title IX, sexual harassment, or equal employment opportunity laws).

3. **Behavior**. A third outcome to be evaluated is actual behavior. Suppose a sport organization is subjected to claims of discrimination arising

from differential evaluations of racial minorities and Whites in the hiring and promotion process. Teaching the evaluators how to construct and implement objective evaluations should reduce or eliminate this problem. The trainers can assess the training's effectiveness by tracking the evaluators' behavior prior to the training and again at several points after the training.

4. **Results.** The final issue to be analyzed is how well organizational objectives have been realized. Some desired results of interest are the retention of employees, decreased absenteeism, increased customer satisfaction, increased level of positive employee affect, and increased financial gains. Managers should compare the levels prior to training to the levels after training to determine whether the training was effective.

Which outcome should be assessed? The answer is largely driven by the training content. In general, it is easy to assess trainees' reactions, and the association between diversity training and reactions to the training is strong (Bezrukova et al., 2016). This association likely exists because the reactions are assessed immediately following the training. On the other hand, the impact of training employee outcomes (knowledge, attitudes, or behaviors) or organizational outcomes (diversity of the workplace or performance) is more difficult. The link between diversity training and these outcomes is also weaker, though still statistically significant and moderate in size (Bezrukova et al., 2016). Thus, managers must make trade-offs and weigh the training content against outcomes the organization wishes to achieve.

Having determined what needs to be assessed, sport managers then need to consider how to assess the training effectiveness. In increasing order of the evaluation design's effectiveness, options include a post-training-only design, pre- and post-training design, pre- and post-training design with a control group, and a post-training-only design with a control group (see Exhibit 14.4 for an illustration).

With a post-training-only design, data are collected from the trainees after the training. Trainees can take a test or complete a questionnaire. This approach is easy to design and administer; however, there are no data to which the results can be compared. It is impossible to determine whether the trainees improved over the course of the training or how they compare with people who have received no training.

The pre- and post-training design evaluates the trainees prior to and after the training. If an increase in, for example, knowledge related to diversity laws is observed, then this might indicate that the training was effective. Because there is no control group, it is impossible to determine whether the increase is greater than what would be observed among people who did not receive the training.

The third evaluation design—pre- and post-training with a control group—permits comparisons of the trained people with people who did not receive the training. Managers randomly assign people to one of two groups—the training group or the control group, whose members do not receive the diversity training. Members of both groups are evaluated both prior to and after the

| Evaluating Training Effectiveness | *exhibit* **14.4** |

Post training only

    Training Group -------------- T   E

Pre - and post Training

    Training Group ---- E ---------- T   E

Pre - and post-Training with a control Group

    Training Group ---- E ------ T   E

    Control Group ---- E ----------- E

Post-Training Only with a control Group

    Training Group ------------- T   E

    Control Group   E

T = Training
E = Evaluation

training. Because the members are randomly assigned to the training or control group, differences between the groups are not expected for the pre-training scores. After the training, however, we would expect those people who went through the training to score higher (or have more positive reactions or more desired behaviors) than people who did not complete the training. This design is desirable because it addresses the issues of (a) improvement after the training and (b) improvement relative to a control group. A drawback of the design is that it can be cumbersome and time-consuming to collect data prior to and after the training.

The final design—post-training-only with a control group—is the most desired. Here, managers randomly assign people to one of two groups: a training or a control group. An evaluation is made after the training, and any differences between the groups suggest that the training was effective. The pre-training evaluation is not needed because theoretically the randomly assigned group members should not differ in their scores prior to the training. Of course, this assumption rests on the proper random assignment of employees to the two groups. If this cannot be achieved, then a pretest is required.

In two of the designs, the members of the control group do not receive diversity training. Would we not want those persons to do so, ultimately? One way to address this issue is to evaluate the training's effectiveness with small pilot-test groups before administering it to the entire organization. If the training is effective, then management would require all employees to complete it.

Transfer of Training

One of the most important goals of training is the application of the new knowledge, skills, and abilities to the workplace setting. However, transfer of training often does not occur: the material learned in the training session is not used in the work setting (Roberson et al., 2013). Why provide diversity training if the trainees do not use the information in their work lives? Fortunately, a number of scholars have identified factors that can influence the transfer of training (Bell et al., 2017; Colquitt, LePine, & Noe, 2000; Cunningham, 2012; Lim & Morris, 2006; Roberson, Kulik, & Pepper, 2009; Salas & Cannon-Bowers, 2001). These include the organizational climate, the applicability of the training, and support for transfer.

The organizational climate can have a substantial influence on whether people apply the information from the training to their work. As Salas and Cannon-Bowers (2001) note, the organizational climate can shape "motivations, expectations, and attitudes for transfer" (p. 489). Transfer of training is likely to take place in sport organizations that (a) encourage employees to try new things, (b) promote continuous learning by employees, (c) do not punish people when they are not immediately successful in implementing the information they learned, and (d) reward people for the transfer of training.

In addition, trainees are most likely to use the information that they learn when they believe it is applicable to their work. If they cannot see the connection between what was presented in the training and their job performance, then the information, no matter how valuable managers perceive it to be, is unlikely to be used. Thus, trainers must not only present the information so it can be understood but must also explicitly outline how the information will benefit the trainees in their everyday jobs.

One way of ensuring that trainees observe the applicability of the training is to link the content explicitly with the mission, goals, and strategies of the sport organization. When this occurs, trainees see that the content is important not only to their work but to the organization as a whole. This rationale is consistent with information presented in Chapter 13 indicating that diversity initiatives are most effective when they are embedded in the organizational system rather than occurring as stand-alone events.

Finally, one of the most influential factors involved in the transfer of training is the support trainees receive from their peers and supervisors to make the transfer. The influence of peers is especially important in the transfer process (Colquitt et al., 2000). Much of what people do is influenced by those people who are important to them. If peers and supervisors show support for the training, think it is important, try to transfer the information to their own work, and are supportive of others who are doing the same, then transfer of training among employees is likely to be successful.

Feedback Loop

Finally, as shown in Exhibit 14.2, the model of diversity training includes a feedback loop. Through their training evaluation, sport managers can assess trainee learning, as well as the degree to which they applied the training information in their work. They can then address gaps between the desired and achieved outcomes. Importantly, sport managers will want to include information in the assessment that allows them to target the gaps. That is, they will need to understand where to direct their attention prior to the next training: at the needs analysis, pre-training conditions, or training content and delivery.

CHAPTER SUMMARY

As illustrated in the Diversity Challenge, diversity training can be—and often has been—met with mixed emotions: some managers and employees oppose such programs, whereas others argue that training will result in positive outcomes for employees, work groups, and the organization as a whole. Implementing diversity training can be a complex undertaking because many factors must be considered in the program's design, implementation, and evaluation. The time, resources, and effort associated with designing and delivering a diversity training program are worthwhile because effective programs, when coupled with other diversity initiatives, positively influence a sport organization.

After reading this chapter, you should be able to:

1. Discuss the positive and negative effects of diversity training.

    The positive outcomes include improved attitudes and motivation toward diversity and inclusion, enhanced knowledge and understanding, improved diversity-related behaviors, more constructive intergroup relationships, improved employee morale and satisfaction, and better compliance with mandates and avoidance of lawsuits. Potential contributors to negative effects include the tendency to ignore the institutional biases in place; the discussion of sensitive topics; a feeling of being blamed, especially among Whites and men; and a perception that the training lacks work applicability or connection to organizational effectiveness.

2. Discuss the essential elements of effective diversity training programs.

    Managers must consider several factors when planning and delivering diversity training. The organization must first conduct a needs analysis, which includes an organizational analysis, a job/task analysis, and a person analysis. The antecedent training conditions must be examined, including trainee characteristics, the manner in which the training is framed, and the pre-training environment. Next, the training methods, such as the material included, who should deliver the training, and which delivery method should be used, must be determined. Post-training conditions—conducting a training evaluation and ensuring the transfer of training—must be met. Finally, sport managers need to provide feedback and change based on the evaluations.

Questions FOR DISCUSSION

1. The incidence of diversity training has increased over the past decade, to the point that more companies conduct this type of training than do not. Do you believe there has been a corresponding increase in the number of sport organizations that provide diversity training? Why or why not?

2. Companies that view diversity training as a central part of their strategic plan spend almost three times as much per employee on training as other organizations. Why does such an increase in spending occur, and do you think the organizations receive benefits from the spending?

3. How does one conduct a needs analysis, and why is it important to do so?

4. Several trainee characteristics influence the effectiveness of training. Of those listed in the chapter, which do you think is the most influential and why? What can managers do to improve these characteristics?

5. Several delivery options for training were discussed. What are the advantages and disadvantages associated with each approach? Which is your preferred approach and why?

6. Trainees bring differing needs, attitudes, preferences, and learning styles to the diversity training session. What steps can trainers take to ensure that *all* trainees learn the material?

7. Several factors were identified that could help with the transfer of training. Which of these factors is likely to be most influential and why?

LEARNING Activities

1. Using online resources, identify companies that specialize in diversity training. Which of these companies do you believe would provide the best training and why?

2. Working in small groups, consult the Lambert and Myers book listed in the Reading Resources, and try one of the diversity training activities. Present the activity to the class, and evaluate its effectiveness. Which activities were the most successful and why?

Web RESOURCES

Diversity Builder, www.diversitybuilder.com/diversity_training.php
   Provides diversity training in a variety of areas; provides specialized programs for each client.

Human Resources Discipline of Diversity, https://www.shrm.org/
   resourcesandtools/tools-and-samples/toolkits/pages/introdiversity.aspx

Offers the reader with an overview of diversity and diversity training, from a human resources perspective.

Cultural Competence and Diversity in Athletic Training, https://www.nata.org/sites/default/files/cultural-competence-diversity-athletic-training.pdf

Helps athletic trainers to better understand different cultures, ethnicities, and backgrounds.

READING Resources

Roberson, L., Kulik, C. T., & Tan, R. Y. (2013). Effective diversity training. In Q. M. Roberson (Ed.), *The Oxford handbook of diversity and work* (pp. 341–365). New York, NY: Oxford University Press.

Excellent overview of factors to consider when designing and delivering diversity training.

Bell, B. S., Tannenbaum, S. I., Ford, J. K., Noe, R. A., & Kraiger, K. (2017). 100 years of training and development research: What we know and where we should go. *Journal of Applied Psychology, 102*(3), 305–323.

The authors offer an overview of training research over the past 100 years.

Robbins, S. L. (2008). *What if? Short stories to spark diversity dialogue.* Mountain View, CA: Davies-Black.

Offers short stories as a way of illustrating the prevalence of diversity and inclusion issues in the work environment.

REFERENCES

Arthur, W., Jr., Bennett, W., Jr., Edens, P. S., & Bell, S. T. (2003). Effectiveness of training in organizations: A meta-analysis of design and evaluation features. *Journal of Applied Psychology, 88*, 234–245.

Bandura, A. (1986). *Social foundations of thought and action: A social cognitive theory.* Englewood Cliffs, NJ: Prentice Hall.

Bandura, A. (1997). *Self-efficacy: The exercise of control.* New York, NY: Freeman.

Bell, M. P., Connerley, M. L., & Cocchiara, F. K. (2009). The case for mandatory diversity education. *Academy of Management Learning and Education, 8*, 597–609.

Bell, B. S., Tannenbaum, S. I., Ford, J. K., Noe, R. A., & Kraiger, K. (2017). 100 years of training and development research: What we know and where we should go. *Journal of Applied Psychology, 102*(3), 305–323.

Benuto, L. T., Casas, J., & O'Donohue, W. T. (2018). Training culturally competent psychologists: A systematic review of the training outcome literature. *Training and Education in Professional Psychology, 12*(3), 125–134.

Bezrukova, K., Jehn, K. A., & Spell, C. S. (2012). Reviewing diversity training: Where we have been and where we should go. *Academy of Management Learning & Education, 11*, 207–227.

Bezrukova, K., Spell, C. S., Perry, J. L., & Jehn, K. A. (2016). A meta-analytical integration of over 40 years of research on diversity training evaluation. *Psychological Bulletin, 142*(11), 1227–1274.

Cocchiara, F. K., Connerley, M. L., & Bell, M. P. (2010). "A GEM" for increasing the effectiveness of diversity training. *Human Resource Management, 49*(6), 1089–1106.

Colquitt, J. A., LePine, J. A., & Noe, R. A. (2000). Toward an integrative theory of training motivation: A metaanalytic path analysis of 20 years of research. *Journal of Applied Psychology, 85,* 678–707.

Crosby, F. J., Iyer, A., & Sincharoen, S. (2006). Understanding affirmative action. *Annual Review of Psychology, 57,* 585–611.

Cunningham, G. B. (2009). Understanding the diversity related change process: A field study. *Journal of Sport Management, 23,* 407–428.

Cunningham, G. B. (2012). Diversity training in intercollegiate athletics. *Journal of Sport Management, 26,* 391–403.

Cunningham, G. B., & Singer, J. N. (2009). *Diversity in athletics: An assessment of exemplars and institutional best practices.* Indianapolis, IN: National Collegiate Athletic Association.

Dachner, A. M., Saxton, B. M., Noe, R. A., & Keeton, K. E. (2013). To infinity and beyond: Using a narrative approach to identify training needs for unknown and dynamic situations. *Human Resource Development Quarterly, 24,* 239–267.

Devine, P. G., Forscher, P. S., Austin, A. J., & Cox, W. T. (2012). Long-term reduction in implicit race bias: A prejudice habit-breaking intervention. *Journal of Experimental Social Psychology, 48*(6), 1267–1278.

Diaz, G. (2013, March). Driver suspension for racial slur reflects NASCAR commitment to diversity. *Orlando Sentinel.* Retrieved from http://articles.orlandosentinel. com/2013-03-05/sports/os-george-diaz-nascar-clements-0306-20130305_1_ nascar-commitment-brian-france-jeremy-clements.

Dobbin, F., & Kalev, A. (2016). Why diversity programs fail: And what works better. *Harvard Business Review, 97*(7), 52–60.

Forscher, P. S., Mitamura, C., Dix, E. L., Cox, W. T., & Devine, P. G. (2017). Breaking the prejudice habit: Mechanisms, timecourse, and longevity. *Journal of Experimental Social Psychology, 72,* 133–146.

Gajjar, T., & Okumus, F. (2018). Diversity management: What are the leading hospitality and tourism companies reporting? *Journal of Hospitality Marketing & Management, 27*(8), 905–925.

Goldstein, I. L., & Ford, J. K. (2002). Training in organizations: Needs assessment, development, and evaluation. Belmont, CA: Wadsworth.

Grossman, R., & Salas, E. (2011). The transfer of training: What really matters. *International Journal of Training and Development, 15*(2), 103–120.

Holladay, C. L., Knight, J. L., Paige, D. L., & Quiñones, M. A. (2003). The influence of framing on attitudes toward diversity training. *Human Resource Development Quarterly, 14,* 245–263.

Israel, T., Bettergarcia, J. N., Delucio, K., Avellar, T. R., Harkness, A., & Goodman, J. A. (2017). Reactions of law enforcement to LGBTQ diversity training. *Human Resource Development Quarterly, 28*(2), 197–226.

Jones, K. P., King, E. B., Nelson, J., Geller, D. S., & Bowes-Sperry, L. (2013). Beyond the business case: An ethical perspective of diversity training. *Human Resource Management, 52,* 55–74.

Kalinoski, Z. T., Steele-Johnson, D., Peyton, E. J., Leas, K. A., Steinke, J., & Bowling, N. A. (2013). A meta-analytic evaluation of diversity training outcomes. *Journal of Organizational Behavior, 34,* 1076–1104.

Kaltenbaugh, L. P., Parsons, J., Brubaker, K., Bonadio, W., & Locust, J. (2017). Institutional type and campus recreation department staff as a mediating factor for diversity/multicultural training. *Recreational Sports Journal, 41*(1), 76–86.

King, E. B., Dawson, J. F., Kravitz, D. A., & Gulick, L. M. (2012). A multilevel study of the relationship between diversity training, ethnic discrimination and satisfaction in organizations. *Journal of Organizational Behavior, 33,* 5–20.

Kirkpatrick, D. L. (1976). Evaluation of training. In R. L. Craig (Ed.), *Training and development handbook* (2nd ed., pp. 301–319). New York, NY: McGraw-Hill.

Kochan, T., Bezrukova, K., Ely, R., Jackson, S., Joshi, A., Jehn, K., … Thomas, D. (2003). The effects of diversity on business performance: Report of the Diversity Research Network. *Human Resource Management, 42*(1), 3–21.

Koonce, R. (2001). Redefining diversity. *Training & Development, 55*(12), 22–33.

Lim, D. H., & Morris, M. L. (2006). Influence of trainee characteristics, instructional satisfaction, and organizational climate on perceived learning and training transfer. *Human Resource Development Quarterly, 17,* 85–115.

Lindsay, C. (1994). Things that go wrong in diversity training: Conceptualization and change with ethnic identity models. *Journal of Organizational Change Management, 7*(6), 18–33.

Lipman, J. (2018, January). How diversity training infuriates men and fails women. *Time.* Retrieved from http://time.com/5118035/diversity-training-infuriates-men-fails-women/

Madera, J. M., Steele, S. T., & Beier, M. (2011). The temporal effect of training utility perceptions on adopting a trained method: The role of perceived organizational support. *Human Resource Development Quarterly, 22,* 69–86.

Mathis, R. L., Jackson, J. H., Valentine, S. R., & Meglich, P. A. (2017). *Human resource management* (15th ed.). Mason, OH: Southwestern.

Noon, M. (2018). Pointless diversity training: Unconscious bias, new racism and agency. *Work, Employment and Society, 32*(1), 198–209.

Norman, L. (in press). "It's sport, why does it matter?" Professional coaches' perceptions of equity training. *Sports Coaching Review.*

Roberson, L., Kulik, C. T., & Pepper, M. B. (2009). Individual and environmental factors influencing the use of transfer strategies after diversity training. *Group & Organization Management, 34,* 67–89.

Roberson, L., Kulik, C. T., & Tan, R. Y. (2013). Effective diversity training. In Q. M. Roberson (Ed.), *The Oxford handbook of diversity and work* (pp. 341–365). New York, NY: Oxford University Press.

Salas, E., & Cannon-Bowers, J. A. (2001). The science of training: A decade of progress. *Annual Review of Psychology, 52,* 471–499.

Walsh, B. M., Bauerle, T. J., & Magley, V. J. (2013). Individual and contextual inhibitors of sexual harassment training motivation. *Human Resource Development Quarterly, 24,* 215–237.

Wiethoff, C. (2004). Motivation to learn and diversity training: Application of the theory of planned behavior. *Human Resource Development Quarterly, 15,* 263–278.

Change and Inclusion through Sport

LEARNING OBJECTIVES

After studying this chapter, you should be able to:

- Identify the different ways sport managers use sport and physical activity for social change and inclusion.
- List and describe the positive and negative outcomes associated with using sport-for-development and peace (SDP) activities.
- Highlight the characteristics of effective, inclusive SDP programs.

DIVERSITY CHALLENGE

O n any given night in 2017, about 554,000 people were experiencing homelessness in the US. To put that figure in perspective, one could fill AT&T Stadium, the $1.3 billion, 80,000-seat home of the Dallas Cowboys, almost seven times. Of those who experience homelessness, 35 percent dwell in locations without a shelter; 21 percent are children; 41 percent are Black or African American, even though they represent 12 percent of the US population; and 13.8 percent are veterans. Over half of the homeless population lives in just five states—California, New York, Florida, Texas, and Washington. The National Coalition for the Homeless points to a number of factors that contribute to homelessness, including insufficient employment opportunities, limited public assistance, health care costs, domestic violence, addiction, and psychological disabilities. People who experience homelessness face distress, hunger, stigma, and violence specifically targeted toward them.

Lawrence and Rob Cann know the effects of homelessness. Born and raised in Richmond, Virginia, the brothers were in elementary school when their house burned down—an experience that taught them the importance of community. Their family recovered, and the brothers both went on to play soccer in the National Collegiate Athletic Association. Since then, they have devoted their efforts to helping individuals and communities through Street Soccer USA. This is an organization whose mission is to "improve health, education, and employment outcomes for the most disadvantaged Americans by using sports to transfer the skills necessary so that they can achieve these outcomes for themselves." The organization holds that "sports can be a primary tool in building safe, healthy communities, where everyone has a place to call home."

Street Soccer USA facilitates these positive outcomes in a number of ways. Some programs are directed toward youth aged 8–17. The organization merges regular practices with educational activities designed to facilitate lifelong learning. Coaches design practices such that soccer skills are taught alongside life skills, and they use huddles at the beginning, middle, and end of practice to reinforce lifelong learning. Among adults, practices and life skills training are aimed at improving health and physical fitness, anger management, teamwork, job readiness, and sobriety. Street Soccer offers a number of activities to facilitate these outcomes, including practice twice a week and classes in resume writing, financial literacy, and job counseling, among other topics. As a result, 75 percent of the players who participate in Street Soccer USA no longer experience homelessness after the first year.

Sources: Coleman, S. (2014, April). Final four 2014: Cowboys Stadium is a perfect fit in size, scale. SB Nation. Retrieved from www.sbnation.com/college-basketball/2014/4/1/5563484/final-four-cowboys-stadium-jerrys-world. Henry, M., Watt, R., Rosenthal, L., & Shivji, A. (2017). The 2017 annual homeless assessment report (AHAR) to Congress. Washington, DC: US Department of Housing and Urban Development. National Coalition for the Homeless. Retrieved from www.nationalhomeless.org. Street Soccer USA. Retrieved from www.streetsoccerusa.org.

CHALLENGE REFLECTION

1. What role can sport play in facilitating social change among individuals and communities? How would this take place?
2. What other social issues could sport-focused organizations, such as Street Soccer USA, address?
3. Do you foresee any potential drawbacks in using sport-based activities to facilitate social change?

In my Dr. Earle F. Zeigler Lecture (Cunningham, 2014), I argued that we are all linked to one another. The attitudes I hold, ideas I advance, and behaviors in which I engage certainly affect me, but they also affect others, directly or indirectly. We all share not only a common ancestry but also a common personhood and world; thus, we both affect and are affected by others.

Let's consider a couple of examples to illustrate this point. Sport marketers frequently use hypersexualized images of women to promote sport events or products. The efficacy of such practices in driving sales is debatable, but the deleterious effects are not (Fink, 2016). Among women, the images are often met with anger and feelings of disrespect, whereas boys and men who view the images are influenced to see women as sex objects. On the other hand, when women are represented in powerful, athletic poses, girls' and women's body image improve, as do boys' and men's valuing of women and their accomplishments (Daniels, 2009, 2012; Daniels & Wartena, 2011; Kane, LaVoi, & Fink, 2013). As another example, consider instances of incivility and harassment in the workplace. These behaviors negatively affect the physical and psychological well-being of those directly involved. But incivility's reach is actually further, as it harms bystanders and creates a culture of harassment that negatively affects *all* in the work environment (Cunningham, Miner, & Benavides-Espinoza, 2012; Miner & Costa, in press; Smittick, Miner, & Cunningham, in press). For a third illustration, consider the case of community inclusiveness. Individual and systemic expressions of prejudice toward lesbian, gay, bisexual, and transgender (LGBT) individuals set up a culture of exclusion and hostility toward gender and sexual minorities in a particular community and state. This culture certainly affects LGBT individuals but it also affects their families and friends. Moreover, given that highly skilled and creative people are attracted to LGBT-inclusive communities and subsequently contribute to economic growth (Florida, 2002, 2003, 2012), cultures of exclusion and hostility negatively influence the economic well-being of all persons in that region. The same principles apply in the work environment (Cunningham, 2011a, 2011b, 2015).

Reverend Dr. Martin Luther King, Jr. recognized our interconnectedness with one another. In his "Letter from Birmingham Jail," writing to White clergy in the South, he noted,

> I am cognizant of the interrelatedness of all communities and states. . . . Injustice anywhere is a threat to justice everywhere. We are all caught in an inescapable network of mutuality, tied in a single garment of destiny. Whatever affects one directly affects all indirectly.
>
> (as cited in Gottlieb, 2003, p. 178)

King's words highlight (a) the interconnectedness of one person to another and (b) the impact of injustice and inequality for all people, irrespective of whether we experience it directly.

Drawing from this work, I argued that our connectedness to one another has a profound impact on how we, as members of the sport management discipline, move forward (Cunningham, 2014). I wrote,

> We, as a collective body of sport management scholars, can no longer pretend that the perils of globalization, issues of access, the prevalence of prejudice and discrimination, or the presence of inequality do not impact each and every one of us; because they do. And we can no longer let the few be responsible for ensuring access and equality for all sportspersons; instead, it is the job of the whole—each and every one of us. This understanding of our interdependence and interconnectedness *requires collective action aimed at guaranteeing that sport is characterized by inclusion and social justice.*
>
> (p. 3, emphasis added)

In furthering this position, I noted that failure to act on known injustices would make us complicit in their perpetuation. King also reflected as much. The latter part of his "Letter" was directed toward White moderates—persons who recognized the need for change but were unwilling to engage in such efforts. The clergy urged him to be patient, not cause trouble, and wait for racial equality to come. King countered that no real change has ever come to fruition through placidity or the natural passage of time. Rather, he correctly argued that generations would have to atone "not merely for the vitriolic words and actions of the bad people, but for the appalling silence of the good people. We must come to see that human progress never rolls in on wheels of inevitability. It comes through the tireless efforts and persistent work" of people pursuing change and justice (as cited in Gottlieb, 2003, p. 182).

In advancing this position, I argued that we, as members of a sport management discipline, could engage in collective action through our teaching, research, and service activities. The same is true for people in the sport industry, as they can focus on engaging in inclusive-focused actions in their organization and in their local communities (see Cunningham, Buzuvis, & Mosier, 2018). I further suggested that each effort mattered, no matter how small the task or potentially narrow the reach. Solitary efforts aimed at promoting inclusion might seem insignificant in the grander scheme of things, but it is the collection of these efforts—the synergistic force they create—that ultimately make change. In the words of former United Nations secretary general Dag Hammarskjold, "In our age, the road to holiness necessarily passes through the world of action" (as cited in Cunningham, 2014, p. 23). It is, indeed, action that is required.

I offer this reflection for several reasons. Throughout this book, I have (a) provided evidence of how people from underrepresented or marginalized groups face subjugation, prejudice, and discrimination; (b) discussed the many benefits of a work environment characterized by diversity and inclusion; and (c) offered a number of strategies that can be used to create and sustain these desired organizational cultures. Knowing this information, it is incumbent upon you—whether you currently work in a sport organization or aspire to do so—to act. It is up to you to work for ways to promote access, inclusion, and diversity (see also Lee & Cunningham, in press). Otherwise, no matter how well intentioned you might be, there will, to borrow from Dr. King, be a need to repent for your silence.

Second, our focus thus far has been internal—looking at ways to improve sport organizations. It is also possible, though, for sport organizations to exert a positive impact on their communities. This can take place through corporate social responsibility efforts (Giulianotti, 2015; Rowe, Karg, & Sherry, in press) or, as shown in the Diversity Challenge, through sport-for-development (SFD) initiatives. The focus of this chapter is on the latter and on the manner in which organizations use sport, in some capacity, to address larger social issues, including intergroup relations, public health, crime, and homelessness, among others. These efforts, when strategically organized and managed, have the potential to improve diversity and inclusion in the broader community.

The remainder of this chapter is organized as follows: First, I offer an overview of key terms related to sport and community development, and I also provide a brief historical overview of the initiatives. This is followed by a discussion of the potential benefits and drawbacks of such efforts. In the final section, I draw from recent theoretical advancements to articulate ways that sport managers could effectively leverage sport to effect social change. See Box 15.1 for additional discussion of these topics.

Box 15.1 Professional Perspectives: The Importance of SDP Programs

Jon Welty Peachey teaches at the University of Illinois in the College of Applied Health Sciences, Department of Recreation, Sport, and Tourism. Prior to this appointment, he served as the vice president for international operations and program development at the Institute for International Sport. This is a nonprofit organization that administers SDP events around the world. Its major event is the World Scholar-Athlete Games.

Welty Peachey described SDP as

the use of sport to exert a positive influence on public health, the socialization of children, youth and adults, the social inclusion of the disadvantaged, the economic development of regions and states, and on fostering intercultural exchange and conflict resolution.

He suggests SDP events are important "because they can serve as one engine of development reaching certain population groups and individuals that traditional development efforts have either excluded or for whom these development efforts have not been as efficacious."

Welty Peachey also addressed a number of points to consider when delivering SDP events. First, he noted that sport managers "cannot claim that sport is the most effective development tool, but only one avenue of development and peace building efforts that is important in reaching and effecting change in certain individuals and communities." In addition, it is important to consider context:

While there may be certain components or elements of SDP programs that are common across contexts, as suggested by emerging theory, there also needs to be cultural and contextual sensitivity, and programs should be developed with local stakeholders in order to best address local and specific needs.

Finally, he noted the importance of considering the way the sports are developed. Although sport is inherently a competition, designing the events to be overly competitive can end up resulting in more harm than good. Welty Peachey argued,

A highly competitive sport environment may not evince positive outcomes, or foster social inclusion; it may actually do the opposite. Thus, careful attention should be given to how the sport program is designed and administered, with sensitivity to the needs and background of the population being served.

SPORT AND SOCIAL CHANGE

 n this section, I define key terms and provide a brief historical review of how advocates have used sport to create social change.

Key Terms

Sport Development

It is important to separate sport and social change efforts from *sport development*. The latter term refers to the monies, policies, and competitive cultures leaders use to cultivate elite athletes or encourage mass participation within a particular setting (Berg, Fuller, & Hutchinson, 2018; Rowe, Shilbury, Ferkins, & Hinckson, 2016). For example, Rowe, Sherry, and Osborne (2018) focused on how sport organizations can engage adolescent girls in sport and physical activity. Similar to the approach I adopted in this book, they examined multilevel factors affecting girls' participation in table tennis, noting that multiple barriers negatively affected the growth of the sport. As another example, Warner and I examined a community sport organization's approach to engage children with disabilities (Cunningham & Warner, in press). We found that, although recruitment tactics were effective, a lack of organizational capacity ultimately resulted in the league's failure. Given that sport development is concerned with the improvement of the sport itself, focus on that construct is beyond the scope of this chapter.

SFD and SDP

Scholars use the terms *sport-for-development* (SFD) and *sport-for-development and peace* (SDP) in discussions of sport as a vehicle for social change (Kang & Svensson, in press; Schulenkorf, 2017; Welty Peachey, Cohen, Shin, & Fusaro, 2018). SFD refers to activities that include sport as a way of meeting the goals and tackling concerns related to individual, community, national, and international development. The focus might be social issues, education, public health, inclusion of disadvantaged populations, or improving intergroup relations. When the goals and concerns include fostering peace and reconciliation among traditionally hostile groups, researchers use the term SDP. As SDP is the most encompassing term, inclusive of both SFD and sport for social change, I use it throughout the remainder of this chapter except when specifically referring to more focused efforts.

Street Soccer USA represents one example of SDP, as the organization seeks to address homelessness through sport and other activities. The Magic Bus, another SDP entity, is an organization based in India that uses games and other activities to teach children about education, gender, health, and other factors affecting their well-being (www.magicbus.org). As a third example, Kicking AIDS Out is an international organization that uses sport and physical activity to raise awareness and decrease the incidence of HIV/AIDS (www.kickingaidsout.net). At this writing, the International Platform on Sport for Development and Peace (www.sportanddev.org) provided a list of 563 organizations around the world that have registered as SDP entities. This is a sizeable increase from the 166 entities that Kidd listed in 2008 and the 295 that Hartmann and Kwauk referenced in 2011.

Sport-Only Approach

Researchers generally organize SDP activities into one of three categories (Coalter, 2007). The first is to offer *sport-only* provisions, such as organized leagues or physical activity opportunities without any other educational activities. For instance, in many communities, the parks and recreation department will offer formal (e.g., sport leagues) and informal (e.g., parks, walking trails) opportunities to be physically active. Behind these offerings is the assumption, perhaps implicit, that sport in and of itself has developmental properties. Just through their engagement in the leagues, for instance, community capacity may improve or people might realize greater physical and psychological well-being. Edwards (2015) notes some of the limitations with this approach (see also Coalter, 2013).

Sport-Plus Approach

Another option is to adopt a *sport-plus* model. As Coalter (2007) explained, a sport-plus model includes organizations "whose core activity is sport, which is used and adapted in various ways to achieve certain 'development' objectives, such as HIV and AIDS education or female 'empowerment'" (p. 5). For example, the World Scholar-Athlete Games were designed to bring together youth from around the world to participate in high-level sport competition. Sport represented the main component, but there are also other activities, such as theatre arts events, lectures, and cross-cultural happenings, all of which are designed to bolster the participants' empathy and confidence in creating change in their homeland (see also Lyras & Welty Peachey, 2011). Coalter suggested this is the standard SDP model.

Plus-Sport Approach

Finally, other SDP organizations adopt a *plus-sport* model. Coalter (2007) explained that plus-sport organizations constitute "social development organizations whose core concerns are with issues such as conflict resolution, homelessness and children at risk" (p. 5). Here, the primary focus of the activity is on developing the individuals or community, and leaders might use sport to draw people into the activities. Sport is a secondary component. For example, many programs designed to combat the spread of HIV/AIDS have education and training as their primary components and emphasis. At the same time, program organizers will use sport as a way of attracting people to the program. This practice serves to engage people who otherwise might not have attended the programs, but it still allows for the information and training to be conveyed.

Historical Context

Some people consider SDP programs as a recent phenomenon (Kidd, 2008). Although the interest and growth in the use of sport to create social change has certainly increased over the past decade, it has actually been in place much longer (Coalter, 2013; Darnell, 2012; Giulianotti, 2011). Many observers point to US President Harry Truman's 1949 inaugural address as a key starting point in SDP. Truman called for social, economic, and political improvements in the "underdeveloped areas" of the world (as cited in Darnell, 2012, p. 43). Truman's address represented a key marker for larger development events outside the world of sport and also coincided with important sport-related activities around the world; hence, its identification as a starting point for SDP. As Giulianotti highlighted, sport was increasingly used during this time as a way to break away from existing cultural understandings. Many Caribbean nations' symbolic victories over England in cricket illustrate this nicely. In addition, at this time, major sport governing bodies, such as FIFA, started to include countries long excluded from their membership.

More recently, former Olympic athletes helped initiate concerted efforts in using sport to address social concerns (Giulianotti, Hognestad, & Spaaij, 2016; Kidd, 2008). Four-time Olympic champion Johann Koss of Norway worked with the organizing committee of the Lillehammer 1994 Winter Olympics and other organizations to develop a humanitarian effort called Olympic Aid. Koss and other Olympians, such as Australia's famed swimmer Ian Thorpe, initially helped raise money for various activities. The organization later grew and became known as Right to Play (www.righttoplay.com). It is now a multinational organization dedicated to enhance children's health and community development. Right to Play works in 15 countries across Africa, Asia, and the Middle East, reaching 1.9 million children each week in 2017. The organization engages with girls and boys, works in refugee camps, and partners with international entities, such as UNICEF, to make a meaningful impact on people and communities through sport (Play, 2017). The growth of Right to Play is reflective of the larger SDP landscape. It represents one example, among hundreds, of how SDP entities use sport to effect social change.

The United Nations' Millennium Development Goals (MDGs), established in 2003, further facilitated the growth in SDP events (Coalter, 2013; Darnell, 2012). That year, the UN passed Resolution 58/5, affirming its commitment to education, health, and well-being and the use of sport to help achieve these development goals. Kofi Annan, who served as secretary general at the time, heralded the benefits of sport as a means to development by noting that

> Sport can play a role in improving the lives of individuals, not only individuals, I might add, but whole communities. I am convinced that the time is right to build on that understanding, to encourage governments, development agencies and communities to think how sport can be included more systemically in the plan to help children, particularly those living in the midst of poverty, disease and conflict.
> (As cited in Coalter, 2013, p. 29)

Annan's vocal support helped to drive interest in, financial backing of, and widespread efforts toward using sport and physical activity as tools for effecting change. As a result, leaders and policymakers pursued SDP initiatives with renewed vigor.

SDP OUTCOMES

As Annan's quotation illustrates, many people view sport as a viable tool for development. Analysis of the evidence, however, suggests that the results are not always straightforward. There are cases where SDP initiatives result in various benefits, but there are also instances when the outcomes are null or even negative. In this section, I offer an overview of these findings.

Benefits of SDP

SDP programs can benefit individuals, groups, and communities. As I have done throughout this book, I will examine these benefits from a multilevel perspective. Exhibit 15.1 offers an overview.

Individual-Level Outcomes

SDP programs offer a number of potential benefits to the participants. One of the most direct relationships is that between SDP involvement and physical health (Sherry, Schulenkorf, & Chalip, 2015). Whether the model is sport-only, plus-sport, or sport-plus, SDP programs include physical activity of some sort, providing people the opportunity to enhance their physical fitness and overall physical well-being. Most SDP programs include general physical activity, followed by soccer, and to a lesser degree, basketball, among other sports (Schulenkorf, Sherry, & Rowe, 2016). Inclusion of sport and physical activity has the potential to improve one's health, especially when SDP leaders focus on attracting people who have been historically excluded from sport. In Australia, for instance, some community sport organizations have developed inclusive practices and policies (e.g., accommodating clothing preferences, providing culturally appropriate food) to encourage Muslim women's participation in sport (Maxwell, Foley, Taylor, & Burton, 2013).

Potential Benefits of SDP Programs

exhibit **15.1**

SDP programs have the potential to create positive outcomes at multiple levels of analysis. These include the following:

- **For individuals**: Improvements in health and well-being, sport skills, life skills, and social capital.
- **For groups**: Reduction in intergroup anxiety and prejudice, resulting in improved intergroup relations.
- **For communities**: Facilitation of community capacity.

Some SDP events also assist participants in developing their technical skills. As an example, colleagues and I examined a SDP program in Nicaragua focused on teaching youth how to swim. The program leader, a former collegiate swimmer in the US, taught both basic and advanced skills, allowing the participants to rapidly improve. As part of their participation, children received a scholarship to a private school, thereby dramatically improving their educational and life chances. As another example, in the analysis of a sport-plus event, Welty Peachey and colleagues observed that participants from around the world took part in the event in part because it allowed them to compete against other highly skilled individuals and, thus, cultivate their athletic skills (Welty Peachey, Lyras, Cohen, Bruening, & Cunningham, 2014). Importantly, SDP participants are not the only ones to develop their skills. Wright, Jacobs, Ressler, and Howell (2018) analyzed a program in Belize and found that coaches trained to deliver the program realized marked improvements in their content knowledge and ability to deliver educational programs.

Third, SDP involvement has the potential to foster participants' life skills. Recall from the Diversity Challenge that a major component of Street Soccer USA was the development of non-sport skills, such as managing sobriety, developing financial acumen, and increasing job readiness. Cohen and Welty Peachey (2015) conducted an in-depth study of one of the more successful participants in this SDP program. They observed that the opportunities provided through participation, the supportive people who were involved, and the skills she learned along the way all helped her cultivate her identity as a social entrepreneur—that is, one who seeks to contribute positively to society without expectation of profits or notoriety. Through her experiences, she developed leadership skills, commitment to causes, a yearning to contribute to her community, and fund-raising acumen. Ultimately, these characteristics allowed her to become an effective champion for social inclusion. These findings are consistent with our study of SDP youth participants, as their involvement in the sport and educational components strengthened their belief that they could return to their home countries and effectively promote social change and inclusion (Welty Peachey, Cunningham, Lyras, Cohen, & Bruening, 2015).

In addition, SDP has the potential to enhance participants' social capital. This benefit is similar to, but broader than, the development of life skills. SDP scholars most frequently draw from Putnam's (2000) conceptualization of social capital as the "features of social organization such as networks, norms, and social trust that can facilitate coordination and cooperation for mutual benefit" (p. 66; but see also Adams, Harris, & Lindsey, 2018). As a person's social capital increases, so, too, does the likelihood of career success and life satisfaction. As one example, Spaaij (2012b) conducted research in Brazil to examine the efficacy of the Projecto Vencer, an SDP program for youth employment through sport that sought to improve the lives of youth in disadvantaged communities. The project allowed for participants in football (soccer) to develop social networks with persons outside their regular social networks. These participants were substantially more likely to do so than their peers who did not take part in the Vencer program. This benefit was likely realized through the program's encouragement of volunteerism outside the participants' home communities. Spaaij also considered the role of

Box 15.2 Alternative Perspectives: Effects of SDP Programs on Volunteers and Spectators

SDP participants certainly have the potential to benefit from the programs, but so, too, do program volunteers and event spectators. In fact, Coalter (2013) suggests that coaches and educational leaders might be the people *most likely* to experience benefits from SDP offerings. In our own research, we have observed that SDP volunteers do benefit tremendously from their experiences. They report social capital gains, improvements in their ability to engage in meaningful service to others, enhancement of their career skills, and development of empathy and perspective taking (Welty Peachey et al., 2014). Volunteers from other SDP events report similar outcomes (Welty Peachey, Cohen, Borland, & Lyras, 2011).

Some SDP programs, such as the Homeless World Cup or various marathons, culminate with large-scale events where spectators come to observe the competition. Evidence suggests that simply attending these activities can alter a person's attitude. Spectators report greater awareness of the social concern (e.g., homelessness), improved attitudes toward the participants, and greater empathy (Sherry, Karg, & O'May, 2011). The positive culture and energy that surround SDP events are critical to their success and their ability to "sustain agendas for social and community action" (Chalip, 2006, p. 122).

soccer in the development of social capital (as opposed to the other educational activities), and he made two important observations. First, soccer enhanced the effectiveness of some of the teaching embedded in the SDP program, allowing for "a fluid learning environment for supporting and delivering educational content to young people" (p. 91). Second, soccer fostered the participants' collaboration, social bonding, and commitment, which helped them solidify the benefits they accrued. Other scholars have also observed that sport programs can enhance the participants' social capital (Nols, Haudenhuyse, Spaaij, & Theeboom, in press; Zhou & Kaplanidou, 2018).

Collectively, these data suggest that SDP events can have a meaningful, positive effect on participants' lives. Of course, the participants are not the only ones who can benefit from SDP events, as the volunteers and event spectators might also receive benefits. These possibilities are outlined in Box 15.2.

Group-Level Outcomes

Group-level outcomes of SDP primarily occur in the area of improved intergroup relations, especially among SDP programs that target peace and reconciliation. For instance, Schulenkorf spent three months volunteering at an SDP project in Sri Lanka (Schulenkorf & Edwards, 2012). The project was set in Vavuniya—a city ravaged by the Sri Lankan Civil War—and included a soccer tournament in which thousands of Sinhalese, Tamil, and Muslim persons participated. The authors noted, "Through this experience it was seen that many Sri Lankans—regardless of their social, cultural and ethnic backgrounds—were willing to overcome political rivalries to interact and bridge intergroup divides" (p. 381). The International Run for Peace is another SDP project in Sri Lanka specifically designed to bridge intercultural and ethnic divides.

Where theory is employed in the design of the program or research on programs, SDP organizers and scholars mostly draw from the contact hypothesis (Allport, 1954; Pettigrew, 1998). Recall from Chapter 13 that, according to this theory, people sustain prejudice against others because of unfamiliarity and separation; thus, the key to reducing prejudice is to enable members of various social groups to have contact with one another under the right conditions. Although any contact has the potential to reduce intergroup anxiety and prejudice, this effect is most likely to occur when there is social support for the interactions, there is the possibility for close contact, people have equal status when interacting with one another, they cooperate with one another, and the possibility of developing friendships exists.

Research evidence suggests that SDP programs can facilitate improved intergroup relations (Lyras & Welty Peachey, 2016). Some SDP projects, such as the one in Sri Lanka in which Schulenkorf (2010) was a part, create opportunities for people to develop friendships with dissimilar others. They also afford participants opportunities to express their unique identities within a setting that facilitates common goals and ideals. These factors promote inclusion while also serving, ultimately, to reduce intergroup biases (see also Giulianotti, 2011; Spaaij & Schulenkorf, 2014). As another example, we examined whether participants in World Scholar-Athlete Games experienced decreases in prejudice over the course of the event (Welty Peachey et al., 2015). The project was designed so that participants (a) played on teams with people from other countries; (b) engaged in educational activities that addressed salient issues of worldwide concern (e.g., prejudice, injustice); (c) worked in small groups to develop change strategies (e.g., how to be more effective change agents in their communities); and (d) attended keynote addresses from world leaders who spoke on the importance of the global environment, human rights, and ethics. Participants' prejudices decreased significantly over the course of the project. We also conducted interviews, which allowed participants to reflect on their experience. A basketball player from the US noted,

> It was the activity that really opened you up to find out who people really are . . . you are able to interact with people you don't normally interact with. . . . And this helped me think differently about other people.

In a similar way, a tennis player from Luxembourg noted that her participation in the event allowed her to become more open minded toward diversity and differences: "I feel like it made me more open minded towards other sport, other people, other cultures. I became more open minded about it because you're exposed to it."

Community-Level Outcomes

Although SDP organizers suggest that many community-level benefits are possible, the most realistic is community capacity building, or the collective capital and organizational resources that community members leverage to identify and solve problems and positively affect the well-being of community members (Chaskin, 2001). SDP programs can play an important role in facilitating this process. As Edwards (2015) notes, for SDP projects to be successful, "communities must possess or develop the capability for collective action, the internal resources to support the process, and the necessary skills and knowledge to successfully identify local problems and their solutions" (see also Schulenkorf, 2012).

Drawing from Wendel, Burdine, McLeroy, and their colleagues' work (2009), Edwards (2015) suggested that SDP programs have the potential to affect seven areas of community capacity; these are outlined in Exhibit 15.2. He also suggested that the key to leveraging these community-level impacts was to engage the

SDP Impact on Community Capacity		*exhibit* **15.2**
SDP Components	**Processes**	**Dimensions of Community Capacity**
Available sport resources Volunteer department	Enhanced access to resources in community	Level of skills and resources
Positive interactions among SDP participants, volunteers, and spectators	Sense of community and social capital	Nature of social relations
Interorganizational partnerships Common identity in sport	Improved networks and ways for citizens to offer input	Space and structure for community dialogue
Growing leaders among volunteers Athletes as leaders	Leadership enhancement and sustainability	Leadership
Sport as a basis for community identity and involvement	Power spread among community members who actively engage	Civic engagement
Sport as a right for all Focus on inclusion and diversity	Promotion of egalitarian values and norms Inclusion	Value system
Evaluation of programs Reflection on service delivery	Understanding of community history and critical reflection	Learning culture

Sources: Edwards (2015); Wendel et al. (2009).

community members on issues important to them, such as physical activity, youth engagement, and the like. Based on this information, sport managers can then develop SDP projects specifically tailored to these needs. Addressing the community's needs both through sport and through the educational components ensures relevance, buy-in, and sustainment of these efforts.

When leaders seek to develop community capacity through SDP, it is important to remain mindful of the challenges in doing so. Jones, Edwards, Bocarro, Bunds, and Smith (2018) conducted a study of community sport organizations and found that a number of challenges served to limit the overall effectiveness of the program. These included limited capacity of the sport organizations, including shortcomings in the financial and human resources. The reliance on volunteers further exacerbated these problems, as turnover was high. When volunteers left the organization, core members of the organization—included paid and volunteer staff—had to take on multiple roles and responsibilities. The end result was the decision among leaders to forego important projects that could meaningfully impact broader community capacity. In addition to the limited organizational capacity, community complexity hampered the overall influence of the sport organization. Other obligations among community members, vandalism of the sports facility, and lack of community engagement—when coupled with the challenges in organizational capacity—all limited the potential for community capacity building.

Shortcomings of SDP

Thus far, I have focused on the many potential benefits of SDP programs. However, as with many aspects of sport, there is another side of the coin. Specifically, a number of authors have pointed to shortcomings of SDP, which I outline here (see Exhibit 15.3).

Deficit Model Approach

Coalter (2013) is one of the more outspoken critics of SDP programs. One of his chief concerns is that sport managers operate from a deficit model. In this case,

---

| *exhibit* | **15.3** | Potential Shortcomings of SDP Programs |

- **Deficit model**: SDP organizers operate from a deficit model, viewing SDP participants as persons in need of fixing.
- **Sport evangelism**: A resolute commitment to sport as lever for creating social change and addressing community ills.
- **Overstated benefits**: Promising SDP outcomes on a grander scale than is actually possible.

Coalter says, they engage in "environmental determinism that assumes that deprived communities inevitably produce deficient people who can be perceived, via a deficit model, to be in need of 'development' through sport" (p. 3). When SDP managers operate from this perspective, they believe the targets of the programming are in need of assistance or fixing. Such a mentality has the potential to result in "othering" and stigmatizing of those individuals (see Chapter 2 for discussion of stigma and its effects).

Another problem in operating from a deficit model is that, more times than not, the assumptions are not empirically supported. Coalter (2013) illustrated this point nicely by relaying the story of an SDP event aimed at enhancing the participants' general self-efficacy (i.e., their ability to overcome obstacles to achieve goals). The (perhaps implicit) assumption was that the children who were participating in the event, all of whom came from abject poverty, would have low levels of generalized self-efficacy. This was not the case. When Coalter expressed surprise at the findings, one of the local SDP organizers chastised him, noting that Coalter would not survive three days in the conditions in which the children lived. Given the children's regular struggle, their self-efficacy and resilience would have to be high—it was a matter of survival.

Sport Evangelism

Another potential shortcoming of SDP projects is what Coalter (2013) refers to as sport evangelism: policymakers and SDP organizers herald the utility of sport to create social change and remedy various ills. For instance, the United Nations states that sport

> is about inclusion and citizenship. Sport brings individuals and communities together, highlighting commonalities and bridging cultural and ethnic divides. Sport provides a forum to learn skills such as discipline, confidence, and leadership and teaches core principles such as tolerance, cooperation, and respect.
> (United Nations Inter-Agency Task Force on Sport for Development and Peace, 2003, p. i)

This position is consistent with a functionalist approach (see Chapter 2): sport is believed to provide social goods, develop strong moral fiber, and contribute to people's well-being.

The potential problem with this perspective is that sport is inherently neither good nor bad; instead, it is a context where larger social goods and ills manifest (Cunningham, 2018). As many anecdotes as there are pointing to benefits associated with sport participation, there are others documenting abuse, prejudice, discrimination, and subjugation within that setting. Hence, critical scholars take umbrage with the evangelical statements about sport as an instrument of social change. As Hartmann and Kwauk (2011) articulated,

> Many sport-based development initiatives and proposals have extremely idealized beliefs about sport's positive, prosocial force. In a nutshell, they assume that simply having a sport program or initiative of some kind will automatically

and inevitably serve the development goals of socialization, education, and intervention. Nothing, in our view, could be further from the truth.

(p. 289)

A volunteer in Darnell's (2010) study also recognized as much, noting, "Sport is a great hook, I would say, for social change, but it's not an automatic one" (p. 69). In a similar vein, I offer evidence later in the chapter that it is the design and delivery of sport-plus and plus-sport programs that make sport a viable tool for development and change.

Overstated Benefits

Finally, many critics argue that SDP programs do not deliver benefits or improve communities on the scales purported (Black, 2010; Coalter, 2013; Darnell, 2012; Hartmann & Kwauk, 2011). Consider a couple of examples. As noted in the previous sections, some evidence suggests that SDP participation can increase participants' social capital. However, Spaaij (2012a), in his analysis of a soccer club in Australia, observed that the effects are not uniform. Instead, men, people who were highly educated, and individuals who had social networks consisting of people from different cultural backgrounds were most likely to experience social capital gains. In another case, Richards and Foster (2013) collected data from adolescents who took part in an SDP project in Gulu, Uganda, known as the Gum Marom Kids League. This project has potential importance because of the prevalence of war, poverty, and rape in the area. That noted, the authors did not observe any empirical benefits associated with involvement in the program. This was the case for measures of cardiorespiratory fitness and of mental health.

In other cases, the limited effects of SDP programs are attributable to the short duration of some projects and a lack of community capacity (Edwards, 2015). Some SDP projects represent just one component of an organization's outreach, and many of these are funded through external grants that offer the ability to engage in extra activities. Unless additional capacity has been realized, when the term of the grant ends, so too does the SDP project. These dynamics led Forde, Lee, Mills, and Frisby (2015) to conclude that funding was one of the major obstacles to the success of SDP projects. Another obstacle is the potential for outside violence to disrupt SDP programs. Sugden (2008) encountered this problem in his work with Football 4 Peace, a project aimed at fostering peace and reconciliation among Arabs and Jews. Despite the success of the project, it had to be canceled when armed conflict broke out between Israel and Hezbollah.

EFFECTIVE DELIVERY OF SDP PROGRAMS

The preceding discussion highlights several tensions surrounding SDP projects. While there is evidence that SDP projects can benefit individuals, intergroup relations, and communities, other data point to potential shortcomings of the programs. I argue that these differences reflect the design, implementation,

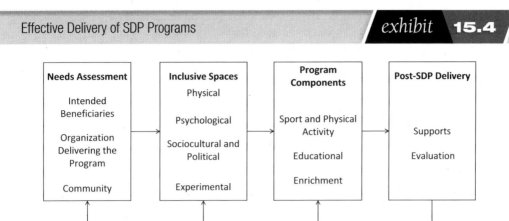

Effective Delivery of SDP Programs — *exhibit* 15.4

Needs Assessment → Inclusive Spaces → Program Components → Post-SDP Delivery

Feedback and Change Based on Evaluation

and leveraging of the SDP projects. This, of course, is a familiar refrain, and we have touched on the importance of intentionality in the design of management and training initiatives to enhance diversity and inclusion (Chapters 13–14). However, because of its importance, the point bears repeating here. Thus, in the final section, I outline several considerations in the design and delivery of SDP programs. See Exhibit 15.4.

Needs Assessment

As in designing a training program for diversity and inclusion, the first step in the SDP process should be a needs assessment. The assessment should cover the intended beneficiaries, the organization delivering the program, and the community.

At the individual level, a deficit model approach will sometimes lead sport managers to make assumptions that are inaccurate. These errors can lead to targeting outcomes that might seem appropriate but that are actually misplaced for the participants (Coalter, 2013). As an alternative, SDP organizers should engage in evidence-based decision-making, drawing from data to inform their decisions. A number of sources of data are available, such as governmental reports, communitywide surveys, and focus-group interviews. See Box 15.3 for one example. Edwards (2015) suggested that community members are frequently the best source of information.

Once the analysis points to the appropriate focus for the SDP program, it is important to consider whether the proposed efforts will actually get to the root of the issue. For instance, many SDP programs are designed to improve race relations. It is plausible that, when appropriately designed, an SDP program can help facilitate reductions in intergroup anxiety and prejudice (Schulenkorf, 2010; Spaaij & Schulenkorf, 2014; Welty Peachey et al., 2015). It is also possible, however, that group relations are not the source of the tensions; instead, the strained race relations might result from systemic issues, such as laws, norms, and institutions that create and recreate a culture that privileges those in power while subjugating racial minorities. It is difficult—but not impossible—for an SDP program, no matter how well delivered, to alter fundamentally how people in a larger community think about race. As Hartmann and Kwauk (2011) observed, "It is not enough to simply do development better by running more responsible, culturally appropriate, sport-based programs. Such intervention must also involve a concomitant attempt to alter the conditions of inequality" (p. 295).

The second component of the needs analysis addresses organizational capacity. Doing so includes examination of policies and practices to ensure that they promote an inclusive environment where SDP participants can thrive (Forde et al., 2015; Maxwell et al., 2013). Another aspect is ensuring that linkages and partnerships with needed external stakeholders are firmly in place (Svensson & Hambrick, in press). For example, local school districts might help in the identification of participants' needs or in ensuring that participants engage in the program (Forde et al., 2015). A third element of the organizational analysis is an examination of the people in place. Change agents and cause champions can make a considerable difference in the success of an SDP program. They understand the important impact the SDP program can have on the participants' lives, and they work to ensure the success of the program (Forde et al., 2015; Schulenkorf, 2012). Finally, it is important to ensure that financial resources are in place to deliver the program for an extended period of time or, if they are not, that plans exist to seek and secure adequate new sources of external funding. Without this critical last component, even highly successful programs might fade away once the life of the original grant runs its course.

Finally, SDP organizers need to examine the community in which the intervention will take place. One element includes examination of the various dimensions of community capacity (refer back to Exhibit 15.2). Furthermore, it is also important to anticipate potential constraints and barriers to the SDP program's success. For instance, Sugden (2008) showed how reconciliation programs such as Football 4 Peace can play an important role in fostering positive intergroup relations. However, he also illustrated how the areas where the SDP initiatives take place are frequently dangerous, presenting a high probability of events that could derail the program altogether. As another example, a number of SDP projects focus on curbing the transmission of HIV/AIDS. Condom use is a frequently discussed strategy that can effectively reduce HIV transmission (Fonner, Kennedy, O'Reilly, & Sweat, 2014). However, some religious traditions prohibit the use of contraception, and in highly religious communities, discussion of condom use, absent cultural sensitivity, could be met with substantial backlash. Thus, it is important that designers of SDP programs consider community norms and customs.

Inclusive Spaces

After conducting the needs analysis and determining the specific focus of the SDP program, the designer should next consider the project's inclusiveness. Doing so

Box 15.3 Diversity in the Field: Evidence-Based Programming

Program design and delivery should be based on data about communities and the people in them. Polling services (such as PEW Research) and government agencies (such as the US Census Bureau or United Nations) are potential sources of data. In other cases, foundations' research on topics relevant to the SDP project might serve as a starting point. The Robert Wood Johnson Foundation, a philanthropic organization that focuses on health, is one entity that conducts such research. Government sponsored research centers and institutes regularly conduct community audits and assessments. This is common practice for research enterprises that focus on public health or rural health, such as the Center for Community Health Development at Texas A&M University. Finally, community members themselves might be the best source of information about specific needs and opportunities. Interviews with community members or focus groups that include persons from around the community can be rich sources of data. We have used some of the latter data sources to increase community capacity in a rural setting (Garney et al., 2017).

can affect the feeling of safety for participants and the overall success of the program (Forde et al., 2015; Spaaij & Schulenkorf, 2014). Drawing from various SDP studies (Maxwell et al., 2013; Spaaij & Schulenkorf, 2014) and our discussion in Chapter 1, we can think of inclusive spaces along four domains:

- **Physical**: the safety of the event, as well as provisions to ensure that people can participate fully while also wearing various kinds of attire.
- **Psychological**: the absence of psychological or emotional hardships to which participants might be exposed and the development of trust, sharing, engagement, and a common in-group identity.
- **Sociocultural and Political**: the acceptance that participants feel, as well as their ability to express openly social identities, beliefs, and attitudes important to them.
- **Experimental**: the participants' ability to take risks and experiment at the event. This domain is likely to have both physical (e.g., learning and experimenting with new technical skills) and psychological (e.g., reaching out and communicating with out-group members) elements.

Given that educational and learning components are critical to an SDP project's success, it is imperative that participants feel psychological safety and inclusion. Thus, the last three elements are of particular relevance.

Sport, Educational, and Enrichment Components

Given the criticisms associated with sport-only models (Coalter, 2013; Darnell, 2012; Hartmann & Kwauk, 2011), I suggest SDP programs should take the form of plus-sport or sport-plus projects. This means that, in addition to considering the sport and physical activity delivery components of the projects, the designer should also consider the educational and enrichment activities (see also Chalip, 2006; Lyras & Welty Peachey, 2011).

Let's first consider the sport components. Lyras and Welty Peachey (2011) strongly advocated for mixed teams that create diversity along gender, ethnic, racial, or nationality lines. With mixed teams, the categorization and intergroup bias processes are less likely to materialize. It is also important to emphasize skill development and improvement over intense competition. Cooperation and a quest to do one's best are principles consistent with a mastery-centered approach that is conducive to improved intergroup relations (see also Hastie, Sinelnikov, Wallhead, & Layne, 2014). Finally, coaches and volunteers should be encouraged to serve as role models while also championing social change.

The educational components should flow from the needs analysis, being both relevant to the specific context and culturally sensitive. Coaches can relay educational principles within the sport context, such as during time-outs or skill demonstrations. Beyond this, effective SDP programs include various learning components that are suited to the learners' needs. These might include group discussions, seminars, keynote addresses, or other pedagogical tools. Throughout the program, coaches and volunteers should seek to display empathy, care, and engagement and to develop these qualities in the participants.

Finally, many SDP programs further enhance the participants' experiences through cultural events (Lyras & Welty Peachey, 2011). Incorporating these elements is consistent with Chalip's (2006) recommendation to create various activities that attract diverse interests. Examples include fine arts involvement, theatre, movie making, and the like. The cultural events might have a standalone entertainment or diversionary purpose, but they are more effective when integrated with the sport and educational components. For instance, persons who make short films might take as their subject social change in their local community or the struggles SDP participants encounter in their everyday lives. These connections help raise awareness and present the SDP components in a cohesive, unified fashion.

Post-SDP Delivery

Finally, just as diversity trainers should focus on training transfer and the evaluation of the training (see Chapter 14), so too should SDP leaders tend to program supports and program evaluation.

Program supports refer to the degree to which leaders, coaches, and volunteers support the SDP participants in effectively employing their new knowledge, skills, and abilities. Drawing from the training literature (Salas & Cannon-Bowers, 2001), SDP leaders and volunteers can encourage the participants to try new things, demonstrate ways in which they can access resources to engage in continuous learning, and reward participants for employing the skills and abilities learned in the program. They can also focus on enhancing the participants' self-efficacy to create change in their own lives and communities (Welty Peachey et al., 2015). Doing so means highlighting the participants' capabilities and showing how others like them have been successful in creating change (see also Bandura, 1997).

SDP leaders should also systematically evaluate the effectiveness of the programs. One option is to engage in empirical analyses and testing, as shown in Exhibit 14.4. Another option is to conduct qualitative assessments. A number of researchers have conducted interviews, focus groups, participant observations, or a combination thereof (Schulenkorf et al., 2016). Shaw and Hoeber (2016; Hoeber & Shaw, 2017) overviewed various options for researchers and analysists interested in conducting qualitative research, including the use of ethnography, auto-ethnography, narrative-based research, and phenomenology, among others. Whatever the approach sport managers choose, the key is to identify the program objectives, pinpoint the ways to determine whether the program was successful in achieving these objectives, and then make changes, accordingly.

Finally, as shown in Exhibit 15.4, the model of SDP includes a feedback loop. Through their SDP evaluation, sport managers can assess SDP program effectiveness. They can then address gaps between the desired and achieved outcomes. Importantly, sport managers will want to include information in the assessment that allows them to target the gaps. That is, they will need to understand where to direct their attention prior to the next training: at the needs assessment, inclusive spaces, and program components.

CHAPTER SUMMARY

I began the chapter with a discussion of our interconnectedness with one another. I argued that when people know about discrimination, prejudice, and suffering, yet do nothing, they become complicit in the perpetuation of these ills. If we accept this premise, then it is incumbent upon us not only to develop diverse and inclusive sport organizations but also to use sport to create positive impacts in our communities. Therein lies the promise of SDP programs. As illustrated in the Diversity Challenge, SDP, when effectively designed and implemented, can create meaningful social change in people's lives.

After reading this chapter, you should be able to:

1. Identify the different ways sport managers use sport and physical activity for social change and inclusion.

    Managers can use SDP programs to promote social change and inclusion. These programs come in the form of sport-only, sport-plus, or plus-sport programs.

2. List and describe the positive and negative outcomes associated with SDP activities.

    SDP programs potentially benefit the health and well-being, sport skills, life skills, and social capital of participants and others involved in the projects. They can improve intergroup relations and facilitate community capacity. SDP programs can have shortcomings, such as when sport managers operate from a deficit model, promote sport evangelism, or overstate the potential benefits of the SDP initiative.

3. Highlight the characteristics of effective SFD and social change programs.

   To develop an effective program, the SDP organizers conduct a needs analysis in order to understand the intended participants, organizational capacity, and community characteristics. They also take steps to ensure the project is inclusive. Finally, based on the data gathered, they focus on tailoring the sport, educational, and enrichment activities to suit the specific needs of the participants.

Questions FOR DISCUSSION

1. I suggested that people have an obligation to work for social justice and inclusion in their work environments. Do you agree? Why or why not?
2. How does sport development differ from SFD and SDP?
3. What are the pros and cons of sport-only, sport-plus, and plus-sport models?
4. Many benefits of SDP programs were listed in the chapter. Do you consider one more important than the others? Why?
5. What are the effects of overstating the benefits of SDP programs?
6. Of the steps identified in creating an effective SDP program, which do you think would be the most difficult to achieve?

LEARNING Activities

1. Using online resources, identify five SDP programs and list the intended audience and benefits of each.
2. Working in small groups, discuss the pros and cons associated with SDP programs and their effects in the community.

Web RESOURCES

International Platform on Sport and Development, www.sportanddev.org
   Offers an overview of SDP initiatives and a list of SDP organizations.

Team UNICEF, www.unicef.org/sports
   Serves as the home site for UNICEF's work ensuring children's right to be active.

Sports and Society Program, www.aspeninstitute.org/policy-work/sports-society
   Home of the Aspen Institute's Sport Initiative, with a focus on ensuring sport and physical activity for all people.

READING Resources

Coalter, F. (2013). *Sport for development: What game are we playing?* New York, NY: Routledge.

　　Offers an overview of SDP activities and a critical analysis of their usefulness.

Darnell, S. (2012). *Sport for development and peace: A critical sociology.* New York, NY: Bloombury.

Offers a sociological perspective on SDP events, highlighting the potential benefits and shortcomings.

Schulenkorf, N. (2017). Managing sport-for-development: Reflections and outlook. *Sport Management Review, 20*(3), 243–251.

　　Reviews the extant literature in the field, with a discussion on paths forward.

REFERENCES

Adams, A., Harris, K., & Lindsey, I. (2018). Examining the capacity of a sport for development programme to create social capital. *Sport in Society, 21*(3), 558–573.

Allport, G. W. (1954). *The nature of prejudice.* Cambridge, MA: Addison-Wesley.

Bandura, A. (1997). *Self-efficacy: The exercise of control.* New York, NY: Freeman.

Berg, B. K., Fuller, R. D., & Hutchinson, M. (2018). "But a champion comes out much, much later": A sport development case study of the 1968 US Olympic team. *Sport Management Review, 21*(4), 430–442.

Black, D. R. (2010). The ambiguities of development: Implications for "development through sport." *Sport in Society, 13,* 121–129.

Chalip, L. (2006). Towards social leverage of sport events. *Journal of Sport and Tourism, 11*(2), 109–127.

Chaskin, R. J. (2001). Building community capacity: A definitional framework and case studies from a comprehensive community initiative. *Urban Affairs Review, 36,* 291–323.

Coalter, F. (2007). *A wider social role for sport: Who's keeping score?* New York, NY: Routledge.

Coalter, F. (2013). *Sport for development: What game are we playing?* New York, NY: Routledge.

Cohen, A., & Welty Peachey, J. (2015). The making of a social entrepreneur: From participant to cause champion within a sport-for-development context. *Sport Management Review, 18,* 111–125.

Cunningham, G. B. (2011a). Creative work environments in sport organizations: The influence of sexual orientation diversity and commitment to diversity. *Journal of Homosexuality, 58,* 1041–1057.

Cunningham, G. B. (2011b). The LGBT advantage: Examining the relationship among sexual orientation diversity, diversity strategy, and performance. *Sport Management Review, 14,* 453–461.

Cunningham, G. B. (2014). Interdependence, mutuality, and collective action in sport. *Journal of Sport Management, 28,* 1–7.

Cunningham, G. B. (2015). Creating and sustaining workplace cultures supportive of LGBT employees in college athletics. *Journal of Sport Management, 29*(4), 426–442.

Cunningham, G. B. (2018, May). *Diversity and inclusion in sport.* Invited paper presented at Loughborough University, Loughborough, UK.

Cunningham, G. B., & Warner, S. (in press). Baseball 4 All: Providing inclusive spaces for persons with disabilities. *Journal of Global Sport Management.*

Cunningham, G. B., Buzuvis, E., & Mosier, C. (2018). Inclusive spaces and locker rooms for transgender athletes. *Kinesiology Review, 7,* 365–374.

Cunningham, G. B., Miner, K., & Benavides-Espinoza, C. (2012). Emotional reactions to observing misogyny: Examining the roles of gender, forecasting, political orientation, and religiosity. *Sex Roles, 67,* 58–68.

Daniels, E. A. (2009). Sex objects, athletes, and sexy athletes: How media representations of women athletes can impact adolescent girls and college women. *Journal of Adolescent Research, 24,* 399–422.

Daniels, E. A. (2012). Sexy versus strong: What girls and women think of female athletes. *Journal of Applied Developmental Psychology, 33,* 79–90.

Daniels, E. A., & Wartena, H. (2011). Athlete or sex symbol: What boys think of media representations of female athletes. *Sex Roles, 65,* 566–579.

Darnell, S. (2012). *Sport for development and peace: A critical sociology.* New York, NY: Bloombury.

Darnell, S. C. (2010). Power, politics, and "sport for development and peace": Investigating the utility of sport for international development. *Sociology of Sport Journal, 27,* 54–75.

Edwards, M. B. (2015). The role of sport in community capacity building: An examination of sport for development and research. *Sport Management Review, 18,* 6–19.

Fink, J. S. (2016). Hiding in plain sight: The embedded nature of sexism in sport. *Journal of Sport Management, 30*(1), 1–7.

Florida, R. (2002). The economic geography of talent. *Annals of the Association of American Geographers, 92,* 743–755.

Florida, R. (2003). Cities and the creative class. *City & Community, 2,* 3–19.

Florida, R. (2012). *The rise of the creative class, revisited.* New York, NY: Basic Books.

Fonner, V. A., Kennedy, C. E., O'Reilly, K. R., & Sweat, M. D. (2014). Systematic assessment of condom use measurement in evaluation of HIV prevention interventions: Need for standardization of measures. *AIDS and Behavior, 18,* 2374–2386.

Forde, S. D., Lee, D. S., Mills, C., & Frisby, W. (2015). Moving towards social inclusion: Manager and staff perspectives on an award winning community sport and recreation program for immigrants. *Sport Management Review, 18,* 126–138.

Garney, W. R., Wendel, M., McLeroy, K., Alaniz, A., Cunningham, G., Castle, B., … Burdine, J. (2017). Using community health development to increase community capacity: A multiple case study. *Family and Community Health, 40,* 18–23.

Giulianotti, R. (2011). Sport, peacemaking and conflict resolution: A contextual analysis and modelling of the sport, development and peace sector. *Ethnic and Racial Studies, 34,* 207–228.

Giulianotti, R. (2015). Corporate social responsibility in sport: Critical issues and future possibilities. *Corporate Governance, 15*(2), 243–248.

Giulianotti, R., Hognestad, H., & Spaaij, R. (2016). Sport for development and peace: Power, politics, and patronage. *Journal of Global Sport Management, 1*(3–4), 129–141.

Gottlieb, R. S. (Ed.) (2003). *Liberating faith: Religious voices for justice, peace, and ecological wisdom.* New York, NY: Rowman & Littlefield.

Hartmann, D., & Kwauk, C. (2011). Sport and development: An overview, critique, and reconstruction. *Journal of Sport and Social Issues, 35,* 284–305.

Hastie, P., Sinelnikov, O., Wallhead, T., & Layne, T. (2014). Perceived and actual motivational climate of a mastery-involving sport education season. *European Physical Education Review, 20,* 215–228.

Hoeber, L., & Shaw, S. (2017). Contemporary qualitative research methods in sport management. *Sport Management Review, 20*(1), 4–7.

Jones, G. J., Edwards, M. B., Bocarro, J. N., Bunds, K. S., & Smith, J. W. (2018). Leveraging community sport organizations to promote community capacity: Strategic outcomes, challenges, and theoretical considerations. *Sport Management Review, 21*(3), 279–292.

Kane, M. J., LaVoi, N. M., & Fink, J. S. (2013). Exploring elite female athletes' interpretations of sport media images: A window into the construction of social identity and "selling sex" in women's sports. *Communication & Sport, 1*(3), 269–298.

Kang, S., & Svensson, P. G. (in press). Shared leadership in sport for development and peace: A conceptual framework of antecedents and outcomes. *Sport Management Review*.

Kidd, B. (2008). A new social movement: Sport for development and peace. *Sport in Society, 11*, 370–380.

Lee, W., & Cunningham, G. B. (in press). Moving toward understanding social justice in sport organizations: A study of engagement in social justice advocacy in sport organizations. *Journal of Sport and Social Issues*.

Lyras, A., & Welty Peachey, J. (2011). Integrating sport-for development theory and praxis. *Sport Management Review, 14*, 311–326.

Lyras, A., & Welty Peachey, J. (2016). The conception, development and application of sport-for-development theory. In G. B. Cunningham, J. S. Fink, & A. Doherty (Eds.), *Routledge handbook of theory in sport management* (pp. 131–142). New York, NY: Routledge.

Maxwell, H., Foley, C., Taylor, T., & Burton, C. (2013). Social inclusion in community sport: A case study of Muslim women in Australia. *Journal of Sport Management, 27*, 467–481.

Miner, K. N., & Costa, P. L. (in press). Ambient workplace heterosexism: Implications for sexual minority and heterosexual employees. *Stress and Health*.

Nols, Z., Haudenhuyse, R., Spaaij, R., & Theeboom, M. (in press). Social change through an urban sport for development initiative? Investigating critical pedagogy through the voices of young people. *Sport, Education and Society*.

Pettigrew, T. F. (1998). Intergroup contact theory. *Annual Review of Psychology, 49*, 65–85.

Play. Protect. Educate. Empower: Right to Play 2017 annual report. (2017). Retrieved from https://issuu.com/righttoplayintl/docs/2017_annualreport_allpages_northame?e=31025504/63670413

Putnam, R. D. (2000). *Bowling alone: The collapse and revival of American community*. New York, NY: Simon & Schuster.

Richards, J., & Foster, C. (2013). Sport-for-development interventions: Whom do they reach and what is their potential for impact on physical and mental health in low-income countries. *Journal of Physical Activity and Health, 10*, 929–931.

Rowe, K., Karg, A., & Sherry, E. (in press). Community-oriented practice: Examining corporate social responsibility and development activities in professional sport. *Sport Management Review*.

Rowe, K., Sherry, E., & Osborne, A. (2018). Recruiting and retaining girls in table tennis: Participant and club perspectives. *Sport Management Review, 21*(5), 504–518.

Rowe, K., Shilbury, D., Ferkins, L., & Hinckson, E. (2016). Challenges for sport development: Women's entry level cycling participation. *Sport Management Review, 19*(4), 417–430.

Salas, E., & Cannon-Bowers, J. A. (2001). The science of training: A decade of progress. *Annual Review of Psychology, 52*, 471–499.

Schulenkorf, N. (2010). Sport events and ethnic reconciliation: Attempting to create social change between Sinhalese, Tamil, and Muslim sportspeople in wartorn Sri Lanka. *International Review for the Sociology of Sport, 45,* 273–294.

Schulenkorf, N. (2012). Sustainable community development through sport and events: A conceptual framework for sport-for-development events. *Sport Management Review, 15,* 1–12.

Schulenkorf, N. (2017). Managing sport-for-development: Reflections and outlook. *Sport Management Review, 20*(3), 243–251.

Schulenkorf, N., & Edwards, D. (2012). Maximizing positive social impacts: Strategies for sustaining and leveraging the benefits of intercommunity sport events in divided societies. *Journal of Sport Management, 26,* 379–390.

Schulenkorf, N., Sherry, E., & Rowe, K. (2016). Sport for development: An integrated literature review. *Journal of Sport Management, 30*(1), 22–39.

Shaw, S., & Hoeber, L. (2016). Unclipping our wings: Ways forward in qualitative research in sport management. *Sport Management Review, 19*(3), 255–265.

Sherry, E., Karg, A., & O'May, F. (2011). Social capital and sport events: Spectator attitudinal change and the Homeless World Cup. *Sport in Culture: Cultures, Commerce, Media, Politics, 14,* 111–125.

Sherry, E., Schulenkorf, N., & Chalip, L. (2015). Managing sport for social change: The state of play. *Sport Management Review, 18,* 1–5.

Smittick, A. L., Miner, K. N., & Cunningham, G. B. (in press). The "I" in team: Coach incivility, coach gender, and team performance in women's basketball teams. *Sport Management Review.*

Spaaij, R. (2012a). Beyond the playing field: Experiences of sport, social capital, and integration among Somalis in Australia. *Ethnic and Racial Studies, 35,* 1519–1538.

Spaaij, R. (2012b). Building social and cultural capital among young people in disadvantaged communities: Lessons from a Brazilian sport-based intervention program. *Sport, Education and Society, 17,* 77–95.

Spaaij, R., & Schulenkorf, N. (2014). Cultivating safe space: Lessons for sport-for-development projects and events. *Journal of Sport Management, 28,* 633–645.

Sugden, J. (2008). Community and the instrumental use of football: Anyone for Football for Peace? The challenges of using sport in the service of co-existence in Israel. *Soccer & Society, 9,* 405–415.

Svensson, P. G., & Hambrick, M. E. (in press). Exploring how external stakeholders shape social innovation in sport for development and peace. *Sport Management Review.*

United Nations Inter-Agency Task Force on Sport for Development and Peace (2003). *Sport for development and peace: Towards achieving the millennium development goals.* New York, NY: Author.

Welty Peachey, J., Cohen, A., Borland, J., & Lyras, A. (2011). Building social capital: Examining the impact of Street Soccer USA on its volunteers. *International Review for the Sociology of Sport, 48,* 20–37.

Welty Peachey, J., Cohen, A., Shin, N., & Fusaro, B. (2018). Challenges and strategies of building and sustaining inter-organizational partnerships in sport for development and peace. *Sport Management Review, 21*(2), 160–175.

Welty Peachey, J., Cunningham, G. B., Lyras, A., Cohen, A., & Bruening, J. (2015). The influence of a sport-for-peace event on prejudice and change agent self-efficacy. *Journal of Sport Management, 29*(3), 229–244.

Welty Peachey, J., Lyras, A., Cohen, A., Bruening, J. E., & Cunningham, G. B. (2014). Exploring the motives and retention factors of sport-for-development volunteers. *Nonprofit and Voluntary Sector Quarterly, 43,* 1052–1069.

Wendel, M. L., Burdine, J. N., McLeroy, K. R., Alaniz, A., Norton, B., & Felix, M. R. (2009). Community capacity: Theory and application. In R. DiClemente, R. Crosby, & M. C. Kegler (Eds.), *Emerging theories in health promotion practice and research* (pp. 277–302). San Francisco, CA: Jossey-Bass.

Wright, P. M., Jacobs, J. M., Ressler, J. D., & Howell, S. (2018). Immediate outcomes and implementation of a sport for development coach education programme in Belize. *Journal of Sport for Development,* 6(10), 51–65.

Zhou, R., & Kaplanidou, K. (2018). Building social capital from sport event participation: An exploration of the social impacts of participatory sport events on the community. *Sport Management Review,* 21(5), 491–503.

Author Index

Subject Index